LIBIDO DOMINANDI

Other Titles of Interest from St. Augustine's Press

E. Michael Jones, *The Slaughter of Cities: Urban Renewal as Ethnic Cleansing*

John F. Harvey, osfs, and Gerard V. Bradley, eds., *Same-Sex Attraction: A Parents' Guide*

Teresa Wagner, ed., *Back to the Drawing Board: The Future of the Pro-Life Movement*

George J. Marlin, *The Amercan Catholic Voter: 200 Years of Political Impact*

George J. Marlin, *Fighting the Good Fight: A History of the New York Conservative Party*

Kenneth D. Whitehead, ed., *The Catholic Citizen: Debating the Issues of Justice*

Kenneth D. Whitehead, ed., *Voices of the New Springtime: The Life and Work of the Catholic Church in the 21st Centutry*

Richard Peddicord, s.j., *The Sacred Monster of Thomism: An Introduction to the Life and Legacy of Reginald Garrigou-Lagrange, o.p.*

Winston S. Churchill, *The River War: An Historical Account of the Reconquest of the Soudan* (in two volumes, slipcased)

Winston S. Churchill, *Savrola*

Bernard J. O'Connor, *Papal Diplomacy: John Paul II and the Culture of Peace*

George A. Kelly, *The Second Spring of the Church in America*

Servais Pinckaers, o.p., *Morality: The Catholic View*

Josef Pieper, *Leisure, the Basis of Culture*

Roger Scruton, *The Meaning of Conservatism* (revised 3rd edition)

Roger Scruton, *An Intelligent Person's Guide to Modern Culture*

Ralph McInerny, *The Defamation of Pius XII*

C.S. Lewis and Don Giovanni Calabria, *The Latin Letters of C.S. Lewis*

John Lukacs, *Confessions of an Original Sinner*

Jacques Maritain, *Natural Law: Reflections on Theory and Practice*

Leszek Kolakowski, *My Correct Views on Everything*

Otto Bird and Katharine Bird, *From Witchery to Sanctity: The Religious Vicissitudes of the Hawthornes*

Friedrich Nietzsche, *On the Future of Our Educational Institutions*

Stanley Rosen, *Nihilism: A Philosophical Essay*

LIBIDO DOMINANDI
Sexual Liberation and Political Control

E. Michael Jones

ST. AUGUSTINE'S PRESS
South Bend, Indiana
2005

Manufactured in the United States of America.

1 2 3 4 5 6   10 09 08 07 06 05

Library of Congress Cataloging in Publication Data
Jones, E. Michael.
    Libido dominandi : sexual liberation and political control /
      E. Michael Jones.
        p.   cm.
    Includes index.
    ISBN 1-890318-37-X
     1. Pornography – United States. 2. Pornography – Political
    aspects – United States. 3. Sex – Political Aspects – United States.
    4. Pornography – History. I. Title
HQ472.U6 J65 2000
363.4'7'0973 – dc21   99-051925

Paperbound edition ISBN 1-58731-465-7

∞ *The paper used in this publication meets the minimum requirements of the
American National Standard for Information Sciences – Permanence of Paper
for Printed Materials, ANSI Z39.48-1984.*

Contents

Introduction

Internet in Gaza
Sexual Liberation as Political Control

Ask for this great Deliverer now, and find him
Eyeless in *Gaza* at the Mill with slaves,
Himself in bonds under *Philistian* yoke;
John Milton, *Samson Agonistes*

London 1996

Since Internet knows no place, it doesn't really matter where it happened, but just for the record I was in England when I started getting e-mail messages from Lisa and Heather. At least, I think that's what their names were. They wanted me to check out their hot web sites. Just as there is no place on the Internet, the names don't mean much either. The important thing was that I was getting unsolicited solicitations for pornography. Spam is, I think, the generic term for this unsolicited material. The pornographic variations are known as blue spam. I was planning to protest to Compuserve and ask them not to make my name available to these agencies when I got some blue spam from Compuserve itself, offering its own pornographic services. *Quis custodiet ipsos custodes?* What sells itself as an e-mail service turns out to be a pimp. The situation I have since learned is even worse with AOL, according to one subscriber to that on-line service, who spends each day clearing his electronic mailbox of hundreds of such solicitations. In the recent court case challenging the constitutionality of the Communications Decency Act, Compuserve signed an *amicus curiae* brief supporting the pornographers. Predictably, given our judicial system, the three-judge panel in Philadelphia handling the case found the CDA unconstitutional. One of the judges opined that "just as the strength of the Internet is chaos, so the strength of our liberty depends upon the chaos and cacophony of unfettered speech."

The word "liberty" coming from one of the regime's mandarins is a dead giveaway that what we're really talking about here is bondage. What I would like to propose here is a paradigm shift of simple but nonetheless revolutionary (or better still counter-revolutionary) proportions by saying what should be obvious to anyone who has visited these web pages and who has had Heather or Lisa ask for his credit card number, namely, that pornography is now and has always been a form of control, financial control. Pornography is a way of getting people to give you money which, because of the compulsive nature of the transaction, is not unlike trafficking in drugs. Unlike prostitution, which is also a transaction benefiting from compulsion, pornogra- phy is closely bound up with technology, specifically the reproduction and transmission of images. Just as the history of pornography is one of progress (technological, not moral progress, of course), so the exploitation of compulsion has been explored in more and more explicit form during the past two hundred years of this revolutionary age. What began as the bondage of sin eventually became financial control and what became accepted as a financial transaction has been forged into a form of political control. Sexual revolution is contemporaneous with political revolution of the sort that began in France in 1789. This means we are not talking about sexual vice when we use the term *sexual revolution*, as much as the rationalization of sexual vice, followed by the financial exploitation of sexual vice, followed by the political mobilization of the same thing as a form of control. Since sexual "liberation" has social chaos as one of its inevitable sequelae, sexual liberation begets almost from the moment of its inception the need for social control. That dynamic is the subject of this book.

It is no secret now that lust is also a form of addiction. My point here is that the current regime knows this and exploits this situation to its own advantage. In other words, sexual "freedom" is really a form of social control. What we are really talking about is a Gnostic system of two truths. The exoteric truth, the one propagated by the regime through advertising, sex education, Hollywood films, and the university system – the truth, in other words for general consumption – is that sexual liberation *is* freedom. The esoteric truth, the one that informs the operations manual of the regime – in other words the people who benefit from "liberty" – is the exact opposite, namely, that sexual liberation is a form of control, a way of maintaining the regime in power by exploiting the passions of the naive, who identify with their passions as if they were their own and identify with the regime which ostensibly enables them to gratify these passions. People who succumb to their disordered passions are then given rationalizations of the sort that clog web pages on the Internet and are thereby molded into a powerful political force by those who are most expert in manipulating the flow of imagery and rationalization.

Like *laissez-faire* economics, the first tentative ideas of how to exploit sex as a form of social control arose during the Enlightenment as well. If the universe was a machine whose prime force was gravity, society was a machine as well whose prime force was self-interest, and man, likewise, no longer sacred, was a machine whose engine ran on passion. From there it was not much of a stretch to understand that the man who controlled passion controlled man.

John Heidenry's history of the sexual revolution, *What Wild Ecstasy*, is one more example of whiggish history – this time, whiggish sexual history.

In fact, all histories of sexual liberation are whiggish. The moral of each piece of this genre is either "People everywhere just wanna be free" or, to give the feminist variant, "Girls just wanna have fun." That Linda Boreman Marchiano, AKA, Linda Lovelace found getting beaten and raped during the filming of *Deep Throat* not much fun is beside the point. The dogma that needs to be promoted here is that sexual license is liberating, and that the quest for liberation is its own justification, so even if a few people get hurt (or killed) in the process, it was generally worth it after all.

Heidenry lays his metaphysical cards on the table at various points during the book. At the very beginning he tells us, for example, that "this . . . is the way we were from about 1965 on, when the particles of revolt and enlightenment coalesced into a sexual Big Bang."[1] We have here, in other words, the classic Enlightenment explanation of everything. Just as the entire physical universe in all its grandeur, beauty and order is really nothing more than the random motion of discrete particles bumping into each other, so every social movement from economics to sexual liberation is essentially the same thing. The same explanation that George Will applies to the economic order, John Heidenry applies to the moral and sexual realm. Instead of atoms, we have atomistic individuals; instead of gravity, we have passion as the great motivating force, and instead of an orderly universe explainable by the laws of physics, we have society reconfigured by social movements like sexual liberation. This is how it is; in other words, the big picture. People everywhere just wanna be free and what gesture could encapsulate this freedom more than, say, masturbating to the dirty pictures in *Hustler*?

As the last example makes clear, we are not talking about freedom here but a form of addiction or moral bondage – certainly for the individual but also for the culture as well. Which brings us back to the dishonesty of Heidenry's book. The sexual revolution was not a grassroots uprising; it was not the coalescing of "particles of revolt and enlightenment"; it was rather a decision on the part of the ruling class in France, Russia, Germany and the United States at various points during the last 200 years to tolerate sexual behavior outside of marriage as a form of insurrection and then as a form of political control. Heidenry's book is part of the general mystification on this subject and so not something that will explain things to the unwary: however, it is worthwhile as a classic expression of how sexual liberation has worked as a form of political control in this country over the past thirty-two years. Bernard Berelson, who worked for the Rockefellers, was a student of the Enlightenment and put those ideas to work in manipulating public opinion for them during the '60s, most specifically in their battle with the Catholic Church over the decriminalization of contraception. Edward Bernays was the nephew of Sigmund Freud and the father of modern advertising. Both were part of the Illuminist tradition of controlling people through their passions, without the knowledge of the person being controlled. And of all the passions – the illuminists make clear – the sexual passions are the most effective when it comes to controlling man.

What Heidenry's book shows is how this control takes place not in theory but in practice. Given the wounded state of human nature after the Fall, flooding a country with pornography means getting a certain number of people hooked on it, just as flooding a country with drugs will result in a certain percentage of addiction. Once people are hooked, the culture's mandarins can use the details of their addictions against anyone who goes against the regime. The subtext of Heidenry's book is that everyone who opposes sexual liberation will be punished. "Several of pornography's most outspoken enemies," he actually says at one point in the book, "had come to an unhappy end."[2] What he fails to tell us is that the unhappy end he describes is just a veiled way of talking about how sexual license is used as a form of political control.

So to give the best known examples cited in Heidenry's book, Preachers Jimmy Swaggart and Jim Bakker were brought down by sexual scandals. Heidenry even admits that Bakker's interlude with Jessica Hahn was a set up but refuses to understand the implications of the facts he brings forth. Nor does he mention the fact that Hahn's seduction of Bakker was portrayed as Bakker's seduction of Hahn in a way calculated to destroy his ministry and the ministries of other televangelists at the time. If Heidenry were a consistent proponent of sexual liberation, he would applaud both Jimmy Swaggart's interlude with a prostitute, a visit clearly motivated by his exposure to pornography, and Bakker's extramarital sex with Jessica Hahn. But that is precisely what he does not do, and the only explanation that makes any sense out of this double standard is that an act of "sexual liberation" is in reality a potential form of political control and only has meaning in light of the politics of the person who commits it. Just why is what Jimmy Swaggart did bad, when Larry Flynt does the same thing and is applauded as a hero when he does it? The answer to that conundrum is political. Jimmy Swaggart was on the wrong side of the political equation, and so could be marginalized by being exposed in *Penthouse* as a hypocrite.

Heidenry's motivation in this is clear enough. He was raised a Catholic, the scion of the family that bought out B. Herder, the American branch of the German Catholic publisher, some time after the outbreak of World War I. Heidenry, after a conservative Catholic upbringing, ended up working for *Penthouse*, and a book like this can be seen as a rationalization of the moral and religious decisions he has made along the way. But the story doesn't stop there. People with Kinsey-like compulsions are put to use by people who can benefit politically from a world in which morals are devalued and money takes the place of morals as the arbiter of social interaction. Those who succumb to sexual addiction but refuse to go along will be outed. Those who refuse to go along but do not have sexual skeletons in their closets will be patronized and ignored. Those who go along with the ideology of sexual liberation, however, can do what they damn well please sexually because in going along they are under the sexual control of the controllers anyway.

The whole system Heidenry praises so dishonestly is based on a double standard which Heidenry exploits but will not acknowledge. Heidenry cites the Jimmy Swaggart expose in *Penthouse* in all of its lurid detail. Conspicuous by its absence from Heidenry's book was the equally lurid *Penthouse* expose of Bill Clinton's affair with Gennifer Flowers. If *Penthouse* is a credible source worth mentioning for the first story, why isn't it mentioned in the second? The answer is obvious. It serves no political purpose to attack President Clinton because he supports sexual liberation, which is to say the vehicle the dominant culture uses to exercise hegemony over its citizens. The regime first promotes sexual addiction in the name of liberation, then exploits it as a form of control. It then uses it to destroy anyone of sufficient prominence who refuses to go along.

As a variation on the same theme, let me propose the following thought experiment. Try to imagine the reaction of the press if Kenneth Starr or Senator Jesse Helms were caught soliciting an undercover agent in a public men's room. Now try to imagine the reaction of the press if Barney Frank were to do the same thing. Why the huge reaction in the first instance, and the non-reaction (when Frank's roommate was actually caught running a homosexual prostitution ring out of his home) in the second? Why is the same act both heinous and liberatory at one and the same time, depending on the politics of who does it? The answer is simple: Sexual liberation is a form of political control. Frank and Clinton are immune because they go along; Swaggart is destroyed for doing the same thing that makes Larry Flynt a cultural hero. The only thing that saves Starr or Helms from a fate similar to that of Swaggart and Bakker is the life each leads.

What follows is the history of an idea. The idea that sexual liberation could be used as a form of control is not a new idea. It lies at the heart of the story of Samson and Delilah. The idea that sin was a form of slavery was central to the writings of St. Paul. St. Augustine in his *magnum opus* in defense of Christianity against the accusations of the pagans that it contributed to the fall of Rome, divided the world into two cities, the City of God, which loves God to the extinction of self, and the City of Man, which loves self to the extinction of God. Augustine describes the City of Man as "lusting to dominate the world" but at the same time "itself dominated by its passion for dominion."[3] *Libido Dominandi*, passion for dominion, then, is a paradoxical project, practiced invariably by people who are themselves in thrall to the same passions they incite in others to dominate them.

The dichotomy Augustine describes is eternal. It will exist at least as long as man exists. The revolutionaries of the Enlightenment created no new world, nor did they create a new man to populate their brave new world.

What they did was adopt the worldview of Augustine and then reverse its values. "The state of the moral man is one of tranquillity and peace, the state of an immoral man is one of perpetual unrest."[4] The author of that statement was not St. Augustine (although he would have wholeheartedly agreed with it); it was the Marquis de Sade. I mention this to show that both Augustine and the Marquis de Sade shared the same anthropology and the same rational psychology, if you will. Where they differed was the values they attributed to the truths of those sciences. For Augustine, motion was bad; for de Sade, the revolutionary, the perpetual motion caused by unruly passions was good because it perpetuates "the necessary insurrection in which the republican must always keep the government of which he is a member."[5]

The same could be said of freedom. What the one called freedom the other called bondage. But the dichotomy of the two cities – one abasing the self because of its love of God, the other abasing God because of its love of the self and its desires – is something that both could agree upon.

What follows is the history of a project born out of the Enlightenment's inversion of Christian truths. "Even those who set themselves up against you," Augustine writes, addressing the Almighty in the *Confessions*, "do but copy you in a perverse way." The same could be said of the Enlightenment, which began as a movement to liberate man and almost overnight turned into a project to control him. This book is the story of that transformation. It can be construed as a history of the sexual revolution or a history of modern psychology or a history of psychological warfare. What all of these histories have in common is a transgenerational project that would come by way of trial and error and with an intention perverted by passion to the same conclusions that Augustine reached at the end of the Roman Empire. A man has as many masters as he has vices. By promoting vice, the regime promotes slavery, which can be fashioned into a form of political control. The only question which remained was whether that slavery can be harnessed for financial and political gain and, if it could, how to do it. The best way to control man is to do so without his awareness that he is being controlled, and the best way to do that is through the systematic manipulation of the passions, because man tends to identify his passions as his own. In defending them he defends his "freedom," which he usually sees as the unfettered ability to fulfill his desires, without, for the most part, understanding how easy it is to manipulate those passions from without. It took the evil genius of this age to perfect a system of financial and political exploitation based on the insight that St. Paul and St. Augustine had into what they termed the "slavery of sin." This book describes the systematic construction of a worldview based on that insight. It explains how sexual liberation became a form of political control.

E. Michael Jones
South Bend, Indiana
February 20, 1999

Part I, Chapter 1

Ingolstadt, 1776

On August 7, 1773, Pope Clement XIV, after four years of stalling, finally acceded to the pressure exerted by the House of Bourbon and its Masonic ministers and suppressed the religious order known as the Society of Jesus throughout the entire world. The Jesuits had already been suppressed civilly in Portugal and France; their suppression by the Church they sought to serve was a move that would have unsuspected consequences for Europe. Scarcely a generation later, not one of the thrones which had collaborated in the suppression of the Jesuits, including the papacy, would be untouched by revolution. The Bourbon king in France would be gone, beheaded by a mob which would soon turn on itself in an orgy of bloodlust that would last well into the nineteenth century and end only with the defeat of Napoleon at the hands of an alliance that would restore monarchy and stability to Europe for 100 years. In spite of that defeat, a new concept had been born, the idea of revolution, and it would haunt the political realm for 200 years thereafter and the cultural realm for even longer than that.

None of this was immediately apparent when the pope acted, of course, and the immediate consequences of the suppression of the Jesuits were more banal. The Masons may have discerned in the suppression their political advantage, but the professors saw advancement of their careers. One of the people who saw his own personal silver lining in the Jesuit cloud was a Bavarian professor by the name of Adam Weishaupt. Weishaupt had been born in Ingolstadt on February 6, 1748, and educated by the Jesuits at the Ingolstadt Gymnasium from the time he was seven until his fifteenth year. Under their tutelage Weishaupt developed a love-hate relationship with the Jesuits that would last him for the rest of his life. It would eventuate in a system of *"Seelenanalyse"* based on Jesuit spirituality, which would have far reaching consequences.

In 1773, Weishaupt was twenty-five years old and already a professor in the law faculty at the University of Ingolstadt. Eleven years later the Bavarian writer Johannes Pezzl would give one of the few character sketches extant of a man who made a career of analyzing the characters of others. Pezzl described Weishaupt as a "pale, seeming hard and stoic man who was so wrapped up in himself that the only people who ever became close to him were a few fellow academics."[1] With the suppression of the Jesuits, Weishaupt was able to enhance his stature at the university by taking over the

Chair of Canon Law and Practical Philosophy, a chair which had been in the hands of the Jesuits at Ingolstadt for over ninety years, and he was able to do this despite the fact that he was not a theologian.

Weishaupt's rapid advance seems to have emboldened him to make plans for a career that would go beyond the usual mundane plotting for university advancement. As a first step in insuring that the Jesuits would not return to power at the University at Ingolstadt, Weishaupt began looking into the prospect of joining either the Masons or the other secret societies that flourished at the end of what has been called the century of secret societies. After a few initial inquiries into lodges in both Munich and Nueremberg, Weishaupt was turned off by the exotic mumbo jumbo of their rituals. The same reaction ensued after he made contact with the Rosicrucians of neighboring Burghausen after being introduced to them by some of his students.

Because of his dissatisfaction with the existing secret societies, Weishaupt decided instead to create a secret society of his own to ensure that the Jesuits would not return to Ingolstadt. Perhaps because of the times or because of his own genius in both personnel management and psychological manipulation, Weishaupt's idea took on a life of its own, one that quickly seemed to demand more room than the confines of the university had to offer. Not that the university was irrelevant to the plan. As a professor, Weishaupt had access to malleable young men into whom he could breathe his anticlerical ideas, and many of his students, intoxicated by the possibilities of the age, were swept into Weishaupt's secret society. On May 1, 1776, Weishaupt created an organization he called the Club of the Perfectible, whose name was later changed to the Order of the Bees, until it was changed again to the name by which it is remembered today, namely, the Order of the Illuminati.

The significance of the Illuminati lay not in its political effectiveness (it existed a little more than eight years), but rather in its method of internal organization. In borrowing freely from both the Jesuits and the Freemasons, Weishaupt created an extremely subtle system of control based on manipulation of the passions. Borrowing the idea of examination of conscience from the Jesuits and sacramental confession from the Catholic Church to which the Jesuits belonged, Weishaupt created a system of "*Seelenspionage*" that would allow him to control his adepts without their knowing that they were being controlled.

The Illuminati might have remained the equivalent of a Bavarian fraternity house were it not for the times and Weishaupt's fortuitous meeting with a northern German aristocrat with extraordinary organizational capabilities. Freemasonry had arrived in the German-speaking world in 1737 when the first German lodge, "Absalom," was opened at the pub known as the "Englischen Taverne" in Hamburg. Then in the same year the lodge "Aux trois aigles blancs," was opened in Berlin, followed by "Aux trois globes" in

1740 and "Aux trois canons" in Vienna in 1742. Weishaupt, who had been fascinated by Freemasonry for some time, finally joined the newly created lodge of the strict observance "Zur Behutsamkeit" in Munich in 1777. In 1780, while attending meetings at the Frankfurt lodge "Zur Einigkeit," Weishaupt met Adolph Freiherr von Knigge, a man four years younger than himself, who immediately fell under Weishaupt's spell. Von Knigge had joined a Masonic lodge of the "strict observance" in Kassel in 1773, but he, like many of his brother Masons, was dissatisfied with the status quo, which involved elaborate rituals and constant bickering and one group splitting off from the other. In Weishaupt's Illuminati, von Knigge saw an instrument to bring order out of chaos, one that would reform the increasingly fractious Masonic groups.

Since the conclusion of the Thirty Years War, Germany had been divided up according to the religion of its princes. Von Knigge, who became a member of the Illuminati on July 5, 1778, gave Weishaupt's essentially Catholic and Bavarian organization access to the Protestant principalities in northern Germany, and as a result of that and von Knigge's zeal and organizing abilities, membership in the Illuminati took off. Shortly after von Knigge's entry into the Illuminati, the membership jumped to 500 men throughout Germany. But the numbers tell only half the story. Perhaps because he was an aristocrat himself, von Knigge added to Weishaupt's following of university students by attracting aristocrats and influential bureaucrats and thinkers from across Germany by clever exploitation of existing Masonic lodges as a pool of recruits.

A crucial event in this regard was the Wilhelmsbad Konvent, a Masonic convention held near Hanau from July 16 to September 1, 1782, which was to have far-reaching consequences not only for lodges of the strict observance but for all of Europe as well. Upon returning from the Wilhelmsbad Congress, Henry de Virieu told a friend who asked him about secret information he might have brought back: "The whole business is more serious than you think. The plot has so carefully been hatched that it's practically impossible for the Church and the Monarchy to escape."[2] Wilhelmsbad may or may not have been the place where plans for the French Revolution were hatched, but it was certainly a windfall for the Order of the Illuminati, which began to siphon off significant numbers of Masons into its own organization. As a result of his efforts at Wilhelmsbad, von Knigge was able to persuade a number of prominent Masons to become Illuminati. That number included Duke Ferdinand of Brunswick and his deputy Prince Karl von Hessen-Kassel, a man who also had connections in Schleswig and Holstein. Someone else who joined the Illuminati after meeting von Knigge in Wilhelmsbad was the publisher Johann Joachim Christoph Bode, who brought Illuminism to Weimar where he founded a lodge which would include Goethe, Karl August, the prince of Weimar, and just about all of the leading lights associated with the German Enlightenment. All in all, it had been an impressive few weeks in Hanau, and now the goal of undermining the lodges of the strict observance and "illuminizing" them, i.e., taking them under secret control, seemed like a plausible idea.

The idea would fail, however, because of strife within the organization. Ironically, it was the Illuminist system of control which led to the break. Von Knigge's success in recruiting new members led Weishaupt to feel that he was being superseded by his subordinate, which led him in turn to increase the control, which led to more strife with von Knigge, who felt that he was being treated badly. Von Knigge would later claim that he hadn't joined to take a subordinate role in which he was "expected to take blind orders from some Jesuit General." According to von Knigge's account, Spartacus, which was Weishaupt's Illuminist code name, abused and tyrannized his subordinates and intended "to subjugate mankind to a more malicious yoke than that conceived by the Jesuits."[3] Eventually the rift became too wide to bridge, and when the Illuminati reached its maximal number of adherents in 1783, it began to unravel.

On July 1, 1784, the Illuminati issued an official expulsion order against von Knigge, which praised, nonetheless, his service in increasing the size of the organization. The expulsion of von Knigge, whose organizational and recruiting abilities had brought the Illuminati to a membership of around 2,000, came at an especially bad time. One week before his official expulsion, on June 22, the Bavaria government issued its first edict forbidding membership in secret societies. Other edicts were to follow on March 2, 1785, and on August 16. On January 2, 1785 the Prince Bishop of Eichstaett demanded that the Prince of Bavaria purge all Illuminati from the University of Ingolstadt. In spite of the secrecy of the Illuminati, Weishaupt was a prime suspect because of the radical Enlightenment books he had ordered for the University library. Weishaupt was removed from his chair of canon law at the University of Ingolstadt on February 11, 1784. Over the next year, the hue and cry against secret societies increased dramatically. Rather than wait for his dismissal to develop into something worse, i.e., criminal prosecution or a hefty fine, Weishaupt fled from Ingolstadt to the neighboring Protestant free city of Regensburg on February 2, 1785. On March 2, when the Prince of Bavaria, Karl Theodore, issued his second edict, the Minerval lodge in Ingolstadt, now without Weishaupt as its head, was dissolved. When the Bavarian government demanded his extradition, and even went so far as to put a reward out for his capture, Weishaupt decided that he had to move again, and in 1787 he fled to the Protestant duchy of Gotha, where he and his family found protection under fellow Illuminatus, Duke Ernst II, who offered him a position on his court council.

If the Bavarian authorities had left it at that, the Illuminati would most probably have been forgotten forever or at best remained a minor footnote in a very small book. But the Bavarian government, after discovering the secret documents associated with the lodge in Munich, made a fateful decision; they decided to publish what they found and in so doing assured Weishaupt and his conspirators an influence they never could have achieved on their own. In June 1785 certain important papers belonging to Jakob Lanz, a secular priest and Illuminatus close to Weishaupt who had been struck dead by a lightning bolt, were found in the course of going through his effects. These papers testified to the Illuminati's intention to subvert the Masonic lodges. Then in October 1786 and May 1787 more papers were discovered when the house of the Illuminatus Franz Xaver Zwack was searched after he had been demoted from his position at the court council and sent to Landshut. These papers, which constituted an internal history of the organization, proved the conspiratorial nature of the secret society beyond a doubt. The first batch of documents was published almost immediately on October 12, 1786, causing a furor that would last for years.

Ever since Voltaire became enamored of Newtonian physics during his visit to England during the third decade of the eighteenth century, the thinkers of the Enlightenment had aspired to create a replacement for the Christian social order based on "scientific" principles. "Mankind," wrote Baron d'Holbach in his influential treatise, *The System of Nature*, "are unhappy, in proportion as they are deluded by imaginary systems of theology."[4] It was out of statements like this that the revolutionary program of the eighteenth century was born, for if man is unhappy because of religion, his happiness would ensue automatically if religion were abolished. But in order to do that, the thrones which protected religion had to be abolished too.

As the initial Illuminist documents began to be published, Weishaupt's revolutionary intent became clear. In his 1782 speech, *"Anrede an die neuaufzunehmenden Illuminatos dirigentes,"* Weishaupt provided his enemies with clear evidence that this secret society was intent on toppling both throne and altar throughout Europe. Rossberg called the "Anrede" "the heart of Illuminism." Professor Leopold Alois Hoffman, one of the leading lights in the counterrevolutionary movement, felt that he could trace the "entire French revolution and its most salient events" back to the maxims of the "Anrede."[5]

But much as the Illuminist papers called for the toppling of throne and altar, the significance of Illuminism did not lie in exhortation. Rather, and this is what the conservative readership found most disturbing, Illuminism seemed to propose an especially effective system which would bring about these ends. Weishaupt had not just issued a manifesto calling for revolution, he had created a system of control that would create disciplined cells which would do the bidding of their revolutionary masters often, it seemed, without the slightest inkling that they were being ordered to do so. Weishaupt's intentions were clearly revolutionary, but the shocking thing about the

Illuminati was the mechanism whereby he put those intentions into effect by controlling the secret society's members' minds. Weishaupt had created an instrument of psychic control which was effective precisely because it did not derive from the mechanistic philosophy of the Enlightenment. "Man," wrote d'Holbach,

> is the work of Nature: he exists in Nature: he is submitted to her laws: he cannot deliver himself from them; nor can he step beyond them even in thought. . . . Man is a being purely physical: the moral man is nothing more than this physical being considered under a certain point of view, that is to say, with relation to some of his modes of action, arising out of his particular organization. . . . His visible actions, as well as the invisible motion interiorly excited by his will or his thoughts, are equally the natural effects, the necessary consequences, of his peculiar mechanism, and the impulse he receives from those beings by whom he is surrounded. . . . His ideas, his will, his actions, are the necessary effects of those qualities infused into him by Nature, and of those circumstances in which she has placed him.[6]

D'Holbach is proposing a crude materialism here which is at least implicitly an instrument of control. The controlling factor is "Nature," man's behavior being a simple expression of Nature's laws:

> The universe, that vast assemblage of every thing that exists, presents only matter and motion: the whole offers to our contemplation nothing but an immense, an uninterrupted succession of causes and effects; some of these causes are known to us, because they strike immediately on our senses; . . . The *moral man*, is he who acts by physical causes, with which our prejudices preclude us from becoming acquainted.[7]

This train of thought would eventually lead to behaviorism and the development of "brain-washing" and psychotropic drugs, none of which would prove effective, but more importantly, none of these instruments were even remotely available to the revolutionaries who populated secret societies during the eighteenth century. The Enlightenment, as a result, was handicapped in terms of political action by the crudity of its own materialistic psychology.

Weishaupt was smart enough to see through this materialism, even if he espoused the same political revolution the materialists desired. His system was a repudiation of the crude materialism of the most well known Enlightenment thinkers. In his treatise "Pythagoras or the consideration of a secret art of ruling both world and government," Weishaupt proposed his system as the only possible way to implement the imperatives of the Enlightenment. "Is there any greater art," he wrote,

> than uniting independently thinking men from the four corners of the earth, from various classes, and religions with no impediment to their freedom of thought, and in spite of their various opinions and passions into one permanently united band of men, to infuse them with ardor and to make them so receptive that the greatest distances mean nothing so that

they are equal in their subordination, so that the many will act as one and from their own initiative, from their own conviction, something that no external compulsion could force them to do?[8]

When his secret society became notoriously public, Weishaupt would describe himself as simply an educator and try to play down his system of control as little more than what any father would try to do in raising his children, but the published documents belied his protestations of innocence. What Weishaupt proposed not only violated the concept of "brotherhood" on which the Masonic lodges were based, his system was based on the organization that was considered the antithesis of Enlightenment. It was based on the Jesuits, or, as Barruel would put it, the Illuminati were a cross between the Jesuits and the Freemasons, in which all of the controls placed on spiritual direction by the Church were lifted and the goal was not to get souls into heaven but to create a paradise on earth. The thing Enlightened thinkers saw in the at-this-point-defunct Jesuits was a machine for control that was superior to any of the mumbo-jumbo that the Masonic lodges had to offer. Illuminism was a machine which stripped the *esprit de corps* of the Jesuit order of all its superstitious accretions and allowed that mechanism to be used to achieve Enlightenment ends. This is precisely what the conservative reaction saw in the Illuminati, and it was precisely this that scared them.

"Anyone who remembers the artificial machine of the former Jesuits," wrote an indignant writer in the conservative-reactionary journal *Eudaemonia* in 1796, "will not find it difficult to rediscover this same machine under another name and with another motive in the Illuminati. The former Jesuits were driven by superstition, and the Illuminati of the present are driven by their unbelief, but the goal of both is the same, the order's universal domination of all of mankind."[9]

It wasn't the goal of world domination, which, in the popular mind at the time the Illuminati shared with the Jesuits that the public found as upsetting; it was the means whereby the Illuminati were going to achieve those goals. Weishaupt took the idea of examination of conscience and sacramental confession from the Jesuits and, after purging them of their religious elements, turned them into a system of intelligence gathering, spying, and informing, in which members were trained to spy on each other and inform their superiors. Weishaupt introduced what he called the *Quibus Licet* notebooks, in which the adept was encouraged to bare his soul for the inspection of his superiors. Weishaupt said of the Quibus Licet books that they were "identical to what the Jesuits call confession," and he told Zwack that he "borrowed the idea from the Jesuit sodalities, where each month you went over your *bona opera* in private."[10] When Utzschneider broke with the Illuminati, he revealed much the same thing:

> The adept sends these monthly reports to the provincial under the title of Quibus Licet, to the provincial under the title Soli and to the general of the

entire order under the title Primo. Only the superiors and the general know the details which are discussed there because all of these letters are transmitted to and fro among the minor superiors. In this way the superiors get to know everything that they want to know.[11]

We can see in the Quibus Licet system the vague outline of the system of spying which would become part and parcel of Communist system of control, both of the underground cells, before they took over a country, and as part of the police state based on spying that was erected after they had taken power. But the Illuminist system of control which Weishaupt created went deeper than that. In addition to creating a system where members spied on each other, Weishaupt created a technique of what came to be called "*Seelenspionage*," or spying on the soul, whereby the superiors in the Illuminati could get access to the adept's soul by close analysis of the seemingly random gestures, expressions, or words that betrayed the adept's true feelings. Von Knigge, who was privy to the system, referred to it as a "*Semiotik der Seele*."

"From the comparisons of all these characteristics," von Knigge wrote, "even those which seem the smallest and least significant, one can draw conclusions which have enormous significance for knowledge of human beings, and gradually draw out of that a reliable semiotics of the soul."[12]

As part of the systemization of this semiotics, Weishaupt, not unlike Alfred Kinsey 150 years later, developed a chart and a code to document the psychic histories of the various members of the Illuminist cells. In his book on the Illuminati, van Duelman reprints the case history of Franz Xaver Zwack of Regensburg. In it we see a combination of the Kinsey sexual history, the Stasi file, and credit rating all rolled up into one document whose purpose is control. In neat columns, the superiors in the Illuminati can learn where the adept was born, his physical characteristics, his aptitudes, his friends, and his reading material, as well as when he was inducted into the order and his code name. Under the heading "Morals, character, religion, conscientiousness," we learn that Zwack had a "soft heart" and that he was "difficult to deal with on days when he was melancholy." Under "Principle Passions," we read that Zwack suffered from "pride, and a craving for honors" but that he was also "honest but choleric with a tendency to be secretive as well as speaking of his own perfection." For those who want to know how to control Zwack, Massenhausen (code name Ajax) says that he got best results by couching all of his communications with Zwack in a mysterious tone.

Once the Illuminist manuscripts were published, the educated public was both appalled and fascinated by what they discovered. They were appalled by the sinister intervention of revolutionaries like Weishaupt into the most intimate recesses of the soul, but they were also fascinated by the horizons of control these discoveries opened before them. Wieland saw in the

Illuminati the basis for pedagogical and political reform. Which was of course, the way Weishaupt saw things too. His goal was the creation of a social order consistent with both Enlightenment science and the notion of a citizen as emancipated from the control of princes who acted *in loco parentis*. "The truly enlightened man," Weishaupt wrote, "has no need of a master." Man will be well governed only when "he is no longer in need of government." In this respect Weishaupt's system had remarkable similarities with nascent American republic, whose Declaration of Independence was proclaimed a little over two months after Weishaupt founded the Illuminati. The American system was the Enlightenment as implemented by English Protestants; the Illuminati, the same philosophy as implemented by Bavarian Catholics. Both felt that man had reached a stage of maturity wherein princes were obsolete. Man, having achieved Enlightenment, could now govern himself.

The fatal flaw of this and other Enlightenment schemes is that it claimed to do away with the morals associated with religion. In America, the principles of the Enlightenment were ameliorated by the refusal to establish a state religion, an idea which eventually came to be known, based on a quote from a letter from Thomas Jefferson, as the separation of Church and state. In the absence of state religion and a centralized Enlightenment government of the sort that would be implemented in France in the not-too-distant future, the various churches were free to form the citizenry according to their various lights, and, as a result, the vacuum at the heart of Enlightenment morals did not lead to social chaos, as it would in France.

But the principle was clear for anyone with eyes to see and a sense of history formed by Plato's judgment in *The Republic* that democracy invariably led to tyranny. The Enlightenment appeal to liberty invariably led to the suppression of religion, which led to the suppression of morals, which led to social chaos. This meant that those who espoused the Enlightenment with any circumspection would also have to be interested in mechanisms of social control, since the erosion of morality which invariably accompanied the proclamation of "freedom" necessitated it. Freedom followed by Draconian control became the dialectic of all revolutions, and, in this regard, the sexual revolution was no exception. In fact, revolution and sexual revolution were, if not synonymous, then certainly contemporaneous, and in fact, the latter was inseparable from the former. Once the passions were liberated from obedience to the traditional moral law as explicated by the Christian religion, they had to be subjected to another more stringent, perhaps "scientific" form of control in order to keep society from falling apart. Social control was a necessary consequence of liberation, something which the French Revolution would make obvious. It was the chaos stemming from the French revolution, in fact, which would inspire Auguste Comte to come up with the "science" of sociology, which was in its way an ersatz religion but most importantly a way of bringing order out of chaos in a world which no longer found the religious foundation of morals plausible.

It was Weishaupt's genius to come up with a system of control that proved effective in the absence of religious sanction. In this regard, Weishaupt's system would become the model of every secular control mechanism of both the left and the right for the next two hundred years. Weishaupt was smart enough to see that "reason" of the sort proposed by the Masonic lodges of the strict observance would never bring about social order. Morals, cut off from their ontological source, became associated as a result with the will of the man who understood the mechanism of control. Since, as the chaos in the lodges of the Strict Observance showed, reason led more often than not to conflicting ideas of which program to take, the Illuminist system had to take the law into its own hands and program behavior as its leaders saw fit. In this Illuminism followed the typical trajectory of every other form of Enlightenment social science which would come into being over the next two hundred years. As in the case of Comte's sociology, the old church was replaced with a new church. The old order, which was based on nature and tradition and revelation, was replaced by a new totalitarian order which was based on the will of those in power. The break-up of the Illuminati and the defection of von Knigge, who found the new order more intolerable than the one he was trying to destroy, showed that this new order was not without its own problems, but faith in ever-more-effective technologies of control, based on newer technologies of communication, would push this disillusionment further and further into the future.

Nosce te ipsum, nosce alios ("know thyself, know others") was the motto which Weishaupt lifted from the oracle at Delphi. The Illuminati were also a concrete manifestation of Bacon's dictum that knowledge was power. In this instance, knowledge of the inner life of the adept was translated into power over him. Extrapolated to the state that functioned according to Illuminist principles, that knowledge translated into political power. What Weishaupt proposed was a technique of noncorporal compulsion, as formerly practiced by the Jesuits, but now in the service of a secular utopia which knew none of the restraints the Church placed on the Society of Jesus. In those controlling these "*Maschinenmenschen,*" both Weishaupt and von Knigge caught first sight of a machine state which created order though its invisible control over its citizens.

Even if Weishaupt and von Knigge failed to implement that vision, the publication of their papers by the Bavarian authorities insured that others would at least have the ultimate fulfillment of that project to entertain. Once released into the intellectual ether, the vision of machine people in a machine state controlled by Jesuit-like scientist controllers would capture the imagination of generations to come, either as utopia in the thinking of people like Auguste Comte or dystopia in the minds of people like Aldous Huxley and

Fritz Lang, whose film *Metropolis* seemed to be Weishaupt's vision come to life. Like Gramsci, Weishaupt proposed a cultural revolution more than a political revolution. Weishaupt wanted to "surround the mighty of this earth" with a legion of men who would run his schools, churches, cathedrals, academies, book stores and governments, in short a cadre of revolutionaries who would influence every instance of political and social power, and so over the long run educate the society to Enlightenment ideas. Van Duelman notices the connection between the cultural revolution which Weishaupt proposed via the Illuminati and the "march through the institutions" which the '68ers brought about less than two hundred years later. The rise of Communism obscured the fact that for the first hundred years or so following the French Revolution, Illuminism was synonymous with revolution both in theory and practice. It was in practice, however, that Illuminsm made its major contribution. In this one small organization we see virtually all of the psychological control mechanisms of both the left and the right *in nuce*. In Illuminism we find in seminal form the system of police state spying on its citizens, the essence of psychoanalysis, the rationale for psychological testing, the therapy of journal keeping, the idea of Kinsey's sex histories, the spontaneous confessions at Communist show trials, Gramsci's march through the institutions, the manipulation of the sexual passion as a form of control that was the basis for advertising, and, via Comte, the rise of the "science" of behaviorism, which attempts, in the words of John B. Watson, to "predict and control behavior." As the last instance makes clear, the one thing which all of these technologies have in common is their desire for control. Weishaupt's system was a system of control, and it was both the dream of the Enlightenment and its only consistent project to expand and refine the technology of social control which Weishaupt envisaged in rudimentary form 200 years ago.

Like so many who would come after him, Weishaupt sought to create a technology of control to take the place of self-control, which he himself lacked. At least part of the outrage which surrounded the publication of the Illuminist manuscripts had to do with the disparity between the morality which Weishaupt preached and the depravity of his actions. Weishaupt became involved in an affair with his sister-in-law, and when she became pregnant, he tried to cover up his involvement by procuring an abortion. It was this behavior which led Prince Karl Theodore of Bavaria to denounce Weishaupt as a "villain, perpetrator of incest, child murderer, seducer of the people, and leader of a conspiracy which endangered both religion and the state." The terminology is extreme, but no more extreme than his actions deserved, and no more extreme than the ideology Weishaupt sought to put into effect. The prince was right in seeing Weishaupt as representing the antithesis of the Christian state, and the essence of this antithesis was the idea of control, the desire to dominate rather than serve which Augustine termed *libido dominandi*. If the Christian faith held as its ideal – no matter how far it strayed from that ideal in praxis – the idea of loving service, then the revolutionary antithesis of that ideal could only be domination. Just what the most effective means to achieve that domination were could and would be worked out in detail over the next two hundred years. Weishaupt, however, made a significant first step in this regard by defining the terms, terms which would be definitive. The battle for liberation would be both a semantic battle and a battle for control of the soul, and control would remain the essence of revolutionary praxis, no matter how much the term *freedom* was used to justify its opposite.

In 1787, the same year that Weishaupt fled to Gotha, Bode, who had now become de facto leader of the Illuminati in exile, traveled to Paris where he met with members of the Paris lodge "Les Amis Reunis," and held long discussions, during which, according to his own account in his travel diary, he tried to interest them in the techniques and doctrines of Illuminism. Whether he succeeded or not is a matter of debate. The fact that the French Revolution broke out two years after his arrival led many to believe that he had succeeded in successfully transplanting Bavarian Illuminism to French soil and that the French was the first of many revolutions that would follow until neither a throne nor an altar would be left standing in once-Christian Europe. "The French," wrote Professor Leopold Alois Hoffmann of Vienna, one of the main counter-revolutionaries of his day, "didn't invent the project of world revolution. This honor belongs to the Germans. To the French belongs only the honor of making a beginning. . . . The *Comites politiques* came into existence following on the heels of Illuminism, which came into being in Germany and became that much more dangerous because it was never extinguished there but merely went underground and then gave birth to the Jacobin clubs."[13]

Bode died in 1793, and by 1795 it seems that all activity associated with the Illuminati as a coherent organization ceased, even though Weishaupt would continue to collect his pension in Gotha and write books until 1830. Bode's trip to Paris, no matter what its immediate effect, gave birth to what has come to be known as the conspiracy theory, according to which one organization promoted revolution from the time of the Illuminati all the way up to the Bolshevik revolution of 1917. Wilson calls that idea "ridiculous." But the transmission of the idea of a science of control, based on the subsequent meditation on ideas proposed in their original form by the Illuminists and transmitted by the very forces which opposed them, is not ridiculous. Far from being that, it is in many ways the intellectual history of the next 200 years.

Part 1, Chapter 2

Paris, 1787

On June 23, 1787, while the Weimar Illuminatus Bode was talking with his Masonic brothers at the Parisian lodge known as "Les Amis Reunis," a French aristocrat by the name of Donatien Alphonse François de Sade began the first draft of what would become one of the most influential novels of the nineteenth century. Sade would eventually call the little book of some 138 pages *Justine ou les Malheurs de la vertu,* and, as if recognizing all the grief it would cause, both to himself and others, he disowned it from the moment of its birth. "They are now printing a novel of mine," Sade wrote to Reinaud, his long-suffering lawyer, when the book's publication was imminent, "but one too immoral to send to a man as pious and as decent as you. . . . Burn it and do not read it if by chance it falls into your hands. I renounce it."[1]

By the time he began writing *Justine*, the Marquis de Sade, as he would be known to posterity, had been in prison for ten years. No charges had ever been filed against him. He never went on trial much less had he been convicted of a crime. He was incarcerated under what was known at the time as a *lettre de cachet*, a sort of warrant for his arrest, which could be, and in Sade's case was, extended indefinitely if the prisoner was considered a threat to decent society. And Sade was certainly considered that, most certainly by his mother-in-law, known, perhaps because of the power she held over him for virtually his entire adult life, as La Presidente. Madame Montreuil considered Sade a monster, and in this judgment she was probably not far off the mark. Raised in an especially decadent aristocratic family, during an especially decadent age in the history of France, Sade embodied all of the vices of his class and then took them all a step further. While in Marseilles on a business trip, Sade gave two prostitutes a candy which was supposed to induce flatulence. Instead it gave the young ladies the impression that they had just been poisoned, which caused them to go to the police and bring charges of sodomy against Sade and his valet, which if proven entailed the death penalty for the perpetrator.

Rather than face the charges, Sade escaped to Italy, where he traveled around with his valet, who played Leporello to Sade's Don Giovanni. Sade would eventually write a book about his travels in Italy, in which he excoriated the Neapolitans for their loose morals. It was a classic instance of the pot calling the kettle black, but by the time the book came out, people had more important things to think about.

Had the Marquis de Sade not been incarcerated at the behest of his mother-in-law, he would probably have followed his sexual fantasies to their logical conclusions and become a latter-day version of Gilles de Rais, one of France's most notorious mass murderers. We know this with some certainty because Sade sketched out the trajectory of sexual vice in exhaustive detail in his never-to-be-finished *magnum opus* of porn, *The 120 Days of Sodom*. In this book, which describes the permutations of perversion in graphic detail, simple passions give way to complex passions, which in turn give way to criminal passions, which in their turn give way to the terminus of the sexual drive when it is diverted from its service to life, namely, the murderous passions of death.

Thanks to the efforts of his mother-in-law, the Marquis de Sade was diverted from a life of increasingly violent, increasingly criminal sexual behavior, and as a result some young French women probably lived longer than they would have otherwise. The downside of La Presidente's efforts is that the Marquis de Sade, as a result of his thirteen-year incarceration at the very end of the *ancien régime*, became a man of letters instead, and by sublimating his murderous sexual passions, turned them into a more potent paradigm for the corruption of future generations. For, if anyone can make the claim that he fired the first shot in the sexual revolution, it is the Marquis de Sade. This is so for a number of reasons. First of all, because sexual revolution is, if not synonymous with revolution in the modern sense of the word, then certainly it is contemporaneous, and to the Marquis de Sade goes the additionally dubious distinction of starting the French Revolution. Sexual revolution is not synonymous, on the other hand, with sexual sin, which has been with us for as long as sexual organs have existed in men whose reason, and not instinct, determined how they were to be governed. Sexual revolution is something slightly different from sexual vice, although it is certainly based on that. Sexual revolution is the political mobilization of sexual vice. In this respect, it differs as well from seduction, which is the manipulation of sexual vice for less than global political ends; it also differs from prostitution, which is the manipulation of sexual vice for financial gain. Sexual revolution makes use of both of these things, but it is more global in scale.

It could be argued that the story of Samson and Delilah is an early example of sex being put to political purposes, but again it is not sexual revolution because it was used on a limited basis aimed at what the Philistines perceived as the Achilles heel of a particularly powerful enemy. It could be argued that the "fertility" regimes of antiquity in the Middle East, based on the cults of Baal and Ashtoreth, were examples of sexual liberation as a form of political control. The Hebrew writers certainly considered them as such, and warned the Hebrew people against their dangers repeatedly, warnings which more often than not went unheeded. But whether those regimes were established as the result of a "sexual revolution" is a question whose answer is lost in the mists of time.

The case of the Marquis de Sade, and by extension the sexual revolution he helped bring into being, is different. Its origins are not lost in some mythic past but have been documented with a clarity which is more apparent because they take place against a background of historical ground that is, if nothing, well trod. The matrix of his writing was the same matrix which brought about the cataclysm which ushered in the modern age, the French Revolution. The same ingredients led to both explosions, and if the two revolutions remain distinct, the one would have been unthinkable without the other. There is no "liberation" without a revolution. Similarly, the concept of "liberation" makes all revolutions possible. Revolution is "liberation" put into praxis. The sexual revolution is no exception in this regard. It happened in France when it did because sexual morals were notoriously low and at a certain point, misery loving company, the masses for whom moral restraint seems an alien imposition, try to clear the air by conforming their morals to their behavior, having failed for so long to achieve the opposite.

The Marquis de Sade, in this regard, was simply someone who acted according to the loose morals of the time and articulated as well the psychological and political consequences of that train of actions. The event which allowed that articulation to happen was prison. "It was in prison," Lever wrote, "(which served as both protection and limitation of his freedom) that Sade liberated his tongue and forged his own style. It was in the depths of solitude, which horrified him (both in itself and for the sanction it represented), that horror, transformed into an object of desire, originated: here, the irresistible need to write, along with a terrifying indomitable power of language, was born. Everything had to be told. The first freedom is the freedom to tell all."[2]

On February 29, 1784, Sade was transferred from Vincennes to the Bastille, to room number three in a tower ironically known as *La Liberté*. Four years later, he would be transferred to number six, a cell which was closer to the battlements on which he was allowed to walk occasionally as well as lighter and airier. It was in the Bastille that Sade did his important writing. The austerity of prison life during the latter days of *the ancien régime* depended on the financial means of the prisoner, who was lodged in a fortified building at his own expense and was allowed to order whatever he wanted to eat or whatever he wanted to read. By the end of the *ancien régime*, the philosophes controlled the culture to such an extent that even prisoners could get the most subversive reading material. "Under Louis XVI," Lever tells us, "it no longer occurred to anyone to deny prisoners the right to read Voltaire."[3] The Marquis de Sade could, and did, order just about any book he had a desire to read, no matter how subversive. The only exception was Rousseau's

Confessions, a prohibition which caused him to rage at his wife, the person who arranged for the delivery of his food and his books.

Sade, however, did get to read all of Voltaire's novellas, which he grew to know by heart, as well as contemporary novels like Laclos's *Les Liaisons dangereueses* and philosophy texts like Baron d'Holbach's *System de la nature*, which was all but ubiquitous in the libraries of revolutionaries of the first sexual revolution from Weishaupt to Shelley. In addition to the usual Enlightenment texts, the Marquis de Sade also read the travel narratives of the time: Abbé de la Porte's *Le Voyageur français*, Cook's *Voyages*, and Diderot's *Voyages de Bougainville*. The latter book was part of the tradition of cultural relativism which Margaret Mead would make famous in the twentieth century with the 1927 publication of *Coming of Age in Samoa*.Common to these travel books was the not-so-veiled attempt to relativize morals geographically. Eventually the cultural relativism that was either the intention of the travel narratives or their effect in the minds of those already depraved and looking for a rationalization would find their way into works like *Justine*. "Virtue," Rodin tells one of his young victims in a moment of detumescence, "is not some kind of mode whose value is incontestable, it is simply a scheme of conduct, a way of getting along, which varies according to accidents of geography and climate and which, consequently, has no reality, the which alone exhibits its futility. . . . there are not upon the entire globe, two races which are virtuous in the same manner; hence, virtue is not in any sense real, nor in any wise intrinsically good and in no sort deserves our reverence."[4]

Sade's appropriation of the travel narratives for sexual purposes in *Justine* illuminates both the topography of sexual liberation and all of Sade's *ouevre* as its first instantiation. It also allows us to give a tentative definition of sexual liberation, based on the historical circumstances of its progenitor – its inventor, so to speak. Sexual liberation is a conflation of Enlightenment thought, which is to say, rationalization based on "science," and masturbation. Masturbation was the logical outcome of Sade's incarceration. A man whose sexual activity was out of control when suddenly cut off from the objects of sexual pleasure will resort to the solitary vice. But there is more to Sade's attachment to masturbation than that, just as there is a more than coincidental connection between sexual liberation and masturbation. Sade's sexual activity had been essentially masturbatory from its inception. "All creatures are born isolated and with no need of one another," he wrote in *Juliette*. In a sexual world like this, where each sexual partner is simply an aid to orgasm, a sexual device, and an instrument for pleasure, masturbation is the theoretical essence of all sexual activity. That theory became practice when the Marquis de Sade was incarcerated in 1777. In the absence of the whores he would hire to stimulate his sexual fantasies, he was forced to create imaginary figures who would serve the same end as masturbation became his actual rather than just theoretical sexual outlet.

That combination of Enlightenment thought and masturbation would not only become the dialectic of Sade's life in prison, where he would read and masturbate and then read and masturbate some more. It would also become the structure of his fiction, and as a result of that it would also become the defining dialectic of sexual liberation. Sexual liberation would become Enlightenment rationalization in the service of masturbation and implemented into later cultural expressions of sexual liberation like *Playboy* magazine, where the photos served as masturbatory aids and Playboy philosophy served as rationalization of that behavior. When the texts which enabled this behavior became widespread enough, pornography would become an instrument of political domination as well as an instrument for financial gain.

Sade's characters spout Enlightenment clichés on morals and physiology as the rationalization of the sexual crimes they have just committed and are about to commit as soon as they can talk themselves back into an erection again. Sade's writing, like most pornography, is an aid to masturbation, both his own and that of the reader. In creating texts like *Justine*, Sade set the pattern for all subsequent versions of sexual liberation and sexual revolution. Science, which is to say the world understood according the *philosophes'* reading of Newton, makes morals and religion unnecessary. Taken in the context of Sade's writings, which is the correct context, Newtonian science becomes a justification for sexual pleasure, in fact, its only real attraction. "When the study of anatomy reaches perfection," Clermont tells Therese after debauching her in *Justine*,

> they will without any trouble be able to demonstrate the relationship of the human constitution to the taste which it affects. Ah, you pedants, hangmen, turnkeys, lawmakers, you shavepate rabble, what do you do when we have arrived there? What is to become of your laws, your ethics, your religion, your gallows, your Gods and your Heavens and your Hell when it shall be proven that such a flow of liquids, this variety of fibers, that degree of pungency in the blood or in the animal spirits are sufficient to make a man the object of your givings and your takings away.[5]

Morality, in other words, is really nothing more than fluid dynamics. Sade felt this would undoubtedly be proven true by some future breakthrough in materialist physiology. In the meantime, his readers can act as if the discovery were a foregone conclusion. Such was the hope of the Marquis de Sade, and it continues to be the hope of those who espouse the Enlightenment's project in the present. Taken in its context, however, the passage betrays the attraction Newtonian physics held for the devotee of the Enlightenment. Newtonian physics made morals unnecessary because it reduced the complexity of life, and all of its moral considerations, to some calculus of matter in motion. What used to be behavior that led to heaven or hell had been reduced by the Enlightenment into a few simple calculations involving fluid dynamics. In the context of both his fiction and the life he led while writing it, the Enlightenment became for the Marquis de Sade an aid to masturbation, and to a great extent as a result of his texts, that is what it would remain for generations of sexual liberationists to come. By the time the Internet arrived as the primary delivery vehicle for pornography two hundred years later, masturbation was still the key to understanding sexual liberation because, as with Sade, the libertine invariably sees his sex partners as instruments, something which makes even sexual activity with other people essentially masturbatory. Perhaps this is why Sallie Tisdale in her book *Talk Dirty to Me* is so insistent on making masturbation synonymous with sex. For her, in fact, all sex is essentially masturbatory. "In this sense," she writes, "all sex is masturbation – the other person's body is an object by which we have intense but wholly internal pleasure, and our orgasm is a self-created and unshared universe. . . . This may be the best explanation for why the orgasms of masturbation can be more powerful and feel more physically whole than those shared. They are simply safer."[6]

The ipsation of liberated sex is intensified by its abhorrence of procreation. "A pretty girl," Madame Sainte-Ange tells Eugenie in *Philosophy in the Bedroom*, "ought simply to concern herself with fucking, and never with engendering. No need to touch at greater length on what pertains to the dull business of population, from now on we shall address ourselves principally, nay, uniquely to those libertine lecheries whose spirit is in no wise reproductive."[7] Here as elsewhere, Sade takes the lead by essentially staking out all of the available ground. His contempt for female genitalia is legendary, something which also explains his choice of sodomy as his preferred form of sexual activity. But sexual preference indicates other truths as well. Sade's misogyny may well be a disguised hatred of the mother whom he felt had abandoned him as a child, or it may have resulted from his undisguised hatred of the mother-in-law who had him imprisoned for thirteen years of his life, but it also bespoke hatred of nature, female nature especially because it was the vehicle for new life, which was, in its way, testimony to the author of life. When he wasn't confined to his cell and limited to masturbation as his only form of sexual expression, Sade invariably tended to engage in both sodomy and sexual blasphemy, typically involving the desecration of communion hosts. In both acts we see defiance of nature, which is to say, defiance of the connection between love and life as ordained by the Creator. Sade's frequent use of the term "Nature" in his pornography is equivocal, and use of the term amounts to what Nietzsche, an avid reader of Sade, would call the transvaluation of values. Nature in its traditional sense meaning purpose is replaced by Nature in its Enlightenment sense which means whatever is, which is to say the absence of purpose. Nature in the latter sense commands all activity, and since this is so, there is no such thing as free will, and as a result terms like *good* and *evil* are chimeras of a bygone age.

As a result, sexual liberation becomes by its very nature a form of domination whereby the strong get to do what they want with the weak. Since strong is synonymous with male and weak with female in Sade's anthropology, "liberation" means the male domination of women. Sexual liberation is, therefore, always a form of control, according to which the idea of nature as rational purpose, implying good and evil as expressions of practical reason, is replaced by the idea of nature as brute force. This also means that any pancultural implementation of sexual liberation will call forth a feminist reaction, as women who are imbued with left-wing fantasies first succumb to unwitting domination and then react with inchoate rage when the outline of their bondage to "liberation" begins to become clear to them.

Sexual liberation, as the foregoing 200-year trajectory indicates, always tends to masturbation by way of rationalization, and in this respect the Enlightenment was the crucial enabling device for sexual revolution, every bit as much as it was the enabling device for the political revolution in France. Sade played a crucial role in both events. Aldous Huxley, who was no stranger to explaining how sexual freedom could be exploited for political ends, traces the tendency back to the Marquis de Sade and his use of Enlightenment "philosophy." In *Justine*, the explication of the true physical nature of morals, as d'Holbach predicted, makes them nonfunctional, hence allowing "liberation" from moral constraint. In reality though, the attraction of Enlightenment physiology lay not so much in its truth as in its satisfaction of desire. Sade's fiction makes clear that materialism of the sort promoted by Baron d'Holbach and de la Mettrie is just another aid to masturbation.

"The real reason why the Marquis could see no meaning or value in the world," Huxley writes in *Ends and Means*, "is to be found in those descriptions of fornications, sodomies and tortures which alternate with the philosophizings of *Justine* and *Juliette*. . . . His philosophical disquisitions, which, like the pornographic day-dreams, were mostly written in prisons and asylums, were the theoretical justification of his erotic practices."[8]

Unlike Huxley, Francine du Plessix Gray accepts Sade's masturbatory fantasies at face value by claiming that science, as expounded in de la Mettrie's tract *Man a Machine*, undermined morals coincidentally by revealing the truth about man. For Gray, who accepts the Enlightenment at face value as well, reason dictates behavior, which is to say that Sade first apprehended the truth of what de la Mettrie had to say and then put it into practice after he realized, like d'Holbach, the true nature of morals as physically derived:

> Sade had also seized on the work of the philosopher La Mettrie, author of *L'Homme Machine*, published in 1748. La Mettrie's views were, in essence, simple and exercised considerable influence on the characters of Sade's fiction, if not directly on their creator. Man, according to La Mettrie, must be defined exclusively by scientific observation and experiment. The conclusion of this method can only be that a human creature is a

machine, as dependent on motion as the machinery and instruments of the new scientific age of the seventeenth and eighteenth centuries had proved to be.[9]

After defending both his masturbatory fantasies and the appropriation of the Enlightenment as masturbatory aid which they entailed, Gray is then forced to defend Sade's treatment of women, turning him into a twentieth-century liberal by claiming that he would not allow this materialist philosophy to be used as an excuse to mistreat people. "In short," she writes, "the materialist, convinced, in spite of the protests of his vanity, that he is but a machine or an animal, will not maltreat his kind, for he will know too well the nature of those actions, whose humanity is always in proportion to the degree of the analogy proved above."[10] One wonders just what edition of Sade Gray had been reading. In *Justine* Sade takes de la Mettrie's idea of man as a machine to its logical sexual conclusion when he writes that "women, who are nothing but machines designed for voluptuousness, who ought to be nothing but the targets of lust, are untrustworthy authorities whenever one has got to construct an authentic doctrine upon this kind of pleasure."[11]

This and other passages indicate that sexual liberation is a system in which behavior dictates reason, and once reason is no longer the light according to which man acts, force takes its place, and force – *pace* Ms. Gray and other feminists – means the sexual exploitation of women. As Sade makes perfectly clear, the inner logic of sexual liberation is always might makes right. The truth is the opinion of the powerful. The good is the desires of the powerful. Sexual liberation is, therefore, of its essence a form of control. In its nascent and crudest form, it is male control of women. Since women according to this view are essentially appliances who get neutered to prevent unwanted offspring from diminishing sexual pleasure, sexual liberation is also essentially masturbatory. In this regard, subsequent generations of sexual liberationists are like moths returning to the same flame, namely, the seminal texts of the Marquis de Sade. They are irrationally attracted to these texts, but they dare not get too close to them lest their attraction be destroyed by the burning logic of domination which lies at their heart.

"The philosopher," Sade writes using the contemporary term for the Enlightenment thinker, "sates his appetites without inquiring to know what his enjoyments may cost others, and without remorse."[12] In that one phrase, Sade gives us the essential definition of sexual liberation. It is the sating of passion without remorse according to the materialist philosophy which the *philosophes* derived from Newtonian physics. By transforming men into machines, de la Mettrie and Sade immediately transform all sex into masturbation, and once that transformation occurs, it is only a matter of time before some social engineer begins to figure out a way to put that newly "liberated" sexual energy to some extrinsic financial and political use. The minute after man gets liberated, he gets controlled.

Gray attempts to domesticate Sade – implicit in the title of her book *At Home with the Marquis de Sade* – but fails to do justice to the word "sadism" which derives from Sade's willingness to inflict pain and cruelty on his victims. Gray also fails to understand the essentially masturbatory nature of Sade's writings. Materialism is not attractive because it is true, it is true because it is attractive. Its appeal is essentially erotic. Huxley, in this regard, is a more sensitive critic than Gray because he is willing to admit just how readily reason succumbs to desire and the role that Enlightenment thought played in this reversal:

> The philosopher who finds no meaning in the world is not concerned exclusively with a problem in pure metaphysics. He is also concerned to prove that there is no valid reason why he personally should not do as he wants to do, or why his friends should not seize political power and govern in the way that they find most advantageous to themselves. The voluntary, as opposed to the intellectual, reasons for holding the doctrines of materialism, for example, may be predominantly erotic, as they were in the case of Lamettrie (see his lyrical account of the pleasures of the bed in *La Volupte* and at the end of *L'Homme Machine*), or predominantly political as they were in the case of Karl Marx.[13]

Taken on the literal level, texts like *Justine* celebrate characters like Dolmance and Rodin, who have liberated themselves from religion and morals and, as a result, engage in any and all sexual activity free from guilt. The libertine is the truly moral man, for, as Baron d'Holbach said, "The *moral man*, is he who acts by physical causes, with which our prejudices preclude us from becoming acquainted."[14] Taken in context, however, the point of these effusions is masturbation. This brings us then to the duality at the heart of the sexual liberationist project, a duality which revolves around the issue of freedom and slavery. The exoteric text of the Enlightenment and sexual liberation is liberation; its esoteric text, however, is control. What appears on the surface to be brave Prometheans liberating themselves from the chains of superstition turns out on closer examination to be a masturbatory fantasy, which sooner or later was going to be exploited as a form of control. The Marquis de Sade pioneered both possibilities; he was simultaneously thrall and manipulator; he proposed sexual liberation as a way of exerting hegemony over the female sex in the interest of sexual pleasure. In this sense, the sexual liberator was also the controller. But he proposed this revolution by writing masturbatory fantasies, and in this sense the sexual liberator was being opened to external control himself, by the exploitation of his own passions to be sure, but also by anyone who knew how to manipulate those passions. By proposing sexual liberation as the overthrow of the moral law, then, the Marquis de Sade simultaneously opened up new vistas for domination for anyone who could manipulate passion. It was a discovery which would have far-reaching consequences. Those who attempted to follow in his footsteps, people like the revolutionaries in France or Shelley and his wife Mary Godwin, soon found that horror, more than pleasure, was the reward for those who sought to become masters of life and the life-force. Sade would learn too. He was both a masturbator and a pornographer who would become aware during the course of the French Revolution of the political implications of his work.

On the morning of July 2, 1789, Donatien Alphonse François de Sade flew into a rage when he was told that he would not be permitted to take his accustomed walk on the battlements of the Bastille that day. Sade had learned from his wife that the disorders in Paris had increased dramatically of late and getting confined to his cell was independent confirmation of what she had told him. Commandante de Launay, who considered Sade an incorrigible criminal and a political revolutionary, could not afford having someone of Sade's temperament coming in contact with the dangerously volatile crowds. In addition to that consideration, de Launay needed the battlements for their original purpose, namely, armament. The battlements were now occupied by canons and barrels of black powder. The Bastille, which had been built as a fortress and then converted into a prison, was in the process of reverting to its original purpose, now to defend not the city but the few remaining inmates – criminals, the insane, and the criminally insane – from the mob which threatened to liberate them.

Sade was in no mood to postpone his walk and so, confined to his cell, he did what he considered the next best thing. He took a white metal funnel normally used to convey the contents of his chamber pot into the Bastille moat and placing it to his lips began to harangue the crowd outside at the top of his lungs, claiming that the prisoner's throats were being cut by the murderous warden and jailers and demanding the crowd's help.

Twelve days later the mob responded to his call, but the Marquis was not there to welcome them. At one in the morning in the night after his funnel outburst, Sade had been dragged out of bed by six armed guards and taken to the insane asylum at Charenton, where he would later achieve fame of sorts as a director of plays. What the mob found instead on the afternoon of July 14 when it burst into Liberty number six, his cell, was a comfortably furnished apartment with a library of 600 books, as well as prints and obscene tapestries, as well as the entire Sadean *oeuvre* to date, all of which got pillaged, which is to say either destroyed or stolen by the mob which he had hoped would liberate him. The fate of Commandant de Launay was less fortunate still. He along with Major de Losme-Salbray and his assistant Miray were dragged out of the Bastille onto the Place de Greve and murdered. A kitchen boy by the name of Desnot then cut off de Launay's head with a pocket knife and, sticking it on the head of a pike, carried it through the streets of Paris as the totem of the city's newfound liberty. It was in that respect an omen of some significance. The head severed from the body, symbolizing the disjunction between reason and the passions, would become the symbol of the revolution. Either that or the instrument of that disjunction, the guillotine.

For the next eight months, Sade would spend his time in the company of "madmen, imbeciles, debauchees and spendthrifts" in "a dark building, buried in dirt up to its roof." If this were liberty it was much more austere than the imprisonment he had endured in his by comparison luxurious apartment at the Bastille. "You will find," he wrote describing his cell in Charenton, "four bare, damp walls covered with insects, with a bed nailed to one wall, a haven for fleas and spiders that have laid undisturbed for a hundred years."[15]

Sade's stay at the madhouse in Charenton was a prelude to being released into a world that was about to go mad or it was an interlude between the private madness of the masturbatory fantasies of his writings and the public madness those writings would at least in part inspire in the public realm. "Without the mad extravagance represented by the name, the life and the truth of Sade," wrote Maurice Blanchot, "the Revolution would have been deprived of a part of its Reason."[16] Or unreason. Whatever the case, Sade walked out of Charenton on Good Friday, which fell in the year 1790 on April 2. His wife, who had served him faithfully during his stay in prison, now refused to take him in. There were no half-way houses in Paris at the time, and so Sade was free to wander the streets with three mattresses, a black coat and one gold louis in his pocket.

Although he still owned the Sade family's ancestral lands in the south of France and the aristocratic title that went with them, Sade saw his newly acquired freedom as the chance to embark upon a new career, one more in keeping with the revolutionary age, namely, man of letters. Sade managed to salvage a few manuscripts from the sacking of the Bastille, and a little over one year after his release from Charenton in June 1791 the most marketable – because it was the most pornographic – was about to be published. That manuscript was *Justine*. *The publisher, Sade wrote to Reinaud, asked for something "quite spicy," and Sade obligingly responded by returning a book "capable of corrupting the devil."*[17] Freedom in 1791 meant *"La Foutromanie,"* which could be translated freely as the freedom to fuck. Given the fact that passions drove the revolution, it was not surprising that the first expression of freedom the revolutionaries chose to exercise was freedom from sexual restraint. Nor was it surprising that sexual passion freed from all restraint would quickly degenerate into passion of another bloodier sort. Sade, after all, had sketched out the trajectory in his now missing manuscript *The 120 Days of Sodom*.

But that was a lesson the French nation would have to learn the hard way in the expensive school of experience, as their idol Ben Franklin had once said. In the meantime, they devoted themselves to gratifying their newly liberated passions, and Sade looked forward to a best seller and the emolument which would accrue therefrom. It seemed like a sure thing because of the *Zeitgeist*. Pornography, as Lever noted, was *à la mode*:

> A veritable wave of licentious fiction had swept across France, mingling titillating visions with the imprecations of revolutionary orators and the *Ca ira!* of patriots. The erotic vein, though apparently so contrary to civic virtue, met with unheard of favor. Sex never sold so well. People went wild for lascivious scenes and lubricious bodies. It was impossible to find debauches outrageous enough, lovemaking furious enough, or perversions new enough to slake the public's lusty appetite. The erotic and the political had never meshed so tightly.[18]

Perhaps no novel since has contributed to the politicization of sex and the sexualization of politics. *Justine* became in effect the hieratic text for sexual liberationists throughout the nineteenth century. Byron owned a copy, as did Swinburne. In the 1920s he became the "Divine Marquis" to the French surrealists, who saw him as the vehicle to revolution. Perhaps because many found the book as appalling as appealing, some felt that interest in it would die out. They were wrong. In 1800 the editor of the *Tribunal d'Appollon* urged the police to seize and destroy the book. "You think that the work is not selling. You are in error."[19]

On June 20, 1791, at around the same time that *Justine* was arriving in the bookstalls, King Louis XVI fled from Paris, where he had been interned a year before after a mob of 30,000 women marched him and his family from Versailles with the heads of his guards on pikes. The king hoped to reach German-speaking lands with his family, where with the help of his brother-in-law, the emperor of Austria, he would return at the head of an avenging army. He got as far as the town of Varennes, where a government official fell on his knees after recognizing the king, betraying him to his revolutionary enemies in this unwitting act of homage. Four days later the royal family was brought back to Paris under armed escort. When the entourage reached the Place de la Revolution, a man burst from the crowd, leaped onto the king's carriage and tossed a letter onto his lap. The man who both wrote and delivered the letter was the Marquis de Sade, and the letter which was soon published under the title "Address of a Citizen of Paris to the King of the French," marked Sade's entry into the field of politics and political propaganda.

"If you wish to reign," Sade informed the doubtlessly grateful Louis XVI, "let it be over a free nation. It is the nation that installs you, that names you its leader. It is the nation that places you on its throne, and not the God of the universe, as people used to have the weakness to believe."[20]

It was one more rant about atheism, a predilection that would eventually get him in trouble when Robespierre decided that the French needed a Supreme Being to keep them in line, one compatible, of course, with his revolutionary program. But all that was in the future. For the moment, Sade eagerly traded in his first love, pornography, and devoted himself to writing political tracts. In his private correspondence, Sade would range from calling Louis XVI his beloved king to proclaiming the most republican of sentiments depending on how the political winds were blowing at the time. Often letters were written to be read by censors, who freely opened the mail of citizens suspected of disloyalty or were left lying around the house for the police when they came to search his lodgings for evidence of antirevolutionary sentiment. Sade was hardly adverse to the idea of revolution. "After dishonoring himself in so many crimes," wrote Michaud, "Sade could hardly fail to support a revolution that in some sense consecrated the principles of those crimes."[21] To say though that Sade had a consistent political point of view during the days of the Revolution would be an exaggeration. It would also be an exaggeration to say that he renounced his sympathy toward his own class, even if he did drop the particle and adopt the ostentatiously republican name of Citizen Louis Sade. When on June 19, 1792, Condorcet ordered that all genealogical documents held in public archives were to be burned, Sade was appalled. Yet not appalled enough to cease calling himself Citizen Sade or to abandon what one would have to call his political opportunism. "As a man of letters," he wrote, "I find myself obliged to work one day for one party, one day for another, and this establishes a certain mobility of opinion that is now without influence on my private thoughts."[22]

Sade took up his residence in the Section de la Place Vendome and quickly became active in the section meetings, which functioned as revolutionary committees whose decisions had the force of law not only in Paris but throughout France. Gradually, over the summer of 1792 the *sans culottes* and other *enrage* operatives took over the meetings at what had once been the Church of the Capuchins and began agitating for more and more radical measures against the monarchy and the now captive king. Before long that agitation would have its effect in what would become known as the September massacres of 1792. For the next six weeks, "Citizen Sade" would write to Ripert, his deputy, ordering him to spirit off his estate books to a safe place so that he could safely prove his aristocratic lineage and his claims on this estates.

In the meantime, while Sade was simultaneously pandering to the mob in Paris and making sure his aristocratic titles were safe, the events of the Revolution had taken on a life of their own. On August 10, 1792, at three in the morning, the insurrectional Commune met at the city hall and then marched to the place du Carousel directly in front of the Tuileries, where the king was being held but guarded by a force of 4,000 men, mainly Swiss guards. The mob which had linked up at six in the morning with delegates from the Left Bank sections was intimidated by the force guarding the king and so decided to wait for reinforcements as word spread throughout Paris and the revolutionary forces began to converge on the palace. Eventually the mob swelled to 10,000, emboldened by the defection of many gendarmes, who now marched with the mob with their hats on their bayonets. Eventually the mob burst through the gates of the palace and swarmed to the grand staircase where a confrontation ensued. When a shot was fired from a second story window, the Swiss took it as their signal and opened fire on the mob leaving 300 dead. At first the mob retreated, then the Swiss retreated; then, in order to avoid further carnage, the King ordered the Swiss to lay down their arms. What followed was even worse carnage as the enraged mob stripped, then castrated, then decapitated the helpless Swiss, then carried their heads through Paris on pikes.

Outrage seemed to fuel outrage in the aftermath of the August 10 assault on the Tuileries, when mobs roamed the street for the next month as rumor provoked reprisal on a massive scale. On August 26 the French forces were defeated at Longwy; on September 2 Verdun fell and the way to Paris was open to English and counter-revolutionary forces, an event which prompted Danton to give his famous speech calling for "*l'audace, encore l'audace, et toujour l'audace*" to rally the revolutionary forces. The immediate effect of the speech was audacious enough. On Sunday September 2, wagons carrying 115 defenseless priests bound for deportation were diverted by an enraged mob to the Abbaye and a Carmelite convent where their throats were slit. One day later on September 3 at the same Abbaye where the priests had been murdered, the mob seized the Princess de Lamballe, stabbed her in the stomach, and then, after cutting off her breasts and decapitating her, they then carried her head through the streets to the Temple where Marie Antoinette was being held. There they displayed the princess's head, whose locks a hairdresser curled after it had been removed from her body, for the queen's inspection, all the while chanting obscene slogans.

Sade recounted the events of September 3 the next day in a letter to Gaufridy, but he gives no indication that the sexual sadism of the outburst might have some connection to his writings. "All of the refractory priests," he wrote, "had their throats cut in the churches where they were being held, among them the archbishop of Arles, the most virtuous and respectable of men."[23] If Sade was moved to pity by the massacre, the movement was short-lived. "There is nothing equal to the horror of the massacres," he wrote on a fold of the same letter, "but they were just."[24] The last line may have been written for the benefit of the censors, who could and did inspect Sade's correspondence in search of counter-revolutionary ideas, but the striking fact remains. Sade had sketched out the trajectory which the revolution was taking as it progressed from sexual "liberation" to sexual sadism to murder. Sexual passion was the fuel which fed the revolutionary blaze and now that blaze would set the revolutionary house itself on fire in an orgy of bloodshed that demanded a totalitarian imposition of order from without in order to save the country from its own destructive passions.

Part I, Chapter 3

London, 1790

On November 4, 1789, the Rev. Richard Price, the noted dissenting divine, gave a sermon on the revolution in France at the meeting house in Old Jewry to the Society for Commemorating the Revolution [of 1688] in Great Britain. "We are met," Price said in a sermon that was republished as a tract in early 1790, "to thank God for that event in this country to which the name of The Revolution has been given; and for which, for more than a century, it has been usual for the friends of freedom, and more especially Protestant Dissenters, to celebrate with expressions of joy and exultation."

The reaction to the sermon was, as one might expect, various. Edmund Burke read the transcription of the talk in early 1790 and wrote his book *Reflections on the Revolution in France* in response, a document which appeared on November 1, 1790, and was to become, according to Russell Kirk, the founding document of conservative political thought. Burke argued that Unitarianism was less a religion than it was a subversive political party and felt that it should be suppressed. As events in France proved Burke's predictions right, the idea of suppression eventually found fruition in the sedition trials of 1792, when Tom Paine fled England to be with his fellow revolutionaries in France.

Unlike Edmund Burke, William Godwin heard Dr. Price's sermon in person. Godwin came from one of the many dissenting families in East Anglia, where he was ordained a minister in 1778. Shortly after that, one of Godwin's colleagues, the Rev. Joseph Fawcett, gave him a strange and disconcerting book entitled *Le Système de la Nature*, published in Holland to escape the censors but written by a Frenchman by the name of Baron d'Holbach. As it would with so many eighteenth century thinkers, *The System of Nature* precipitated a crisis in Godwin's Calvinist faith which would be aggravated by reading Rousseau and Helvétius and would only reach a resolution of sorts when he left the ministry in 1783 and then left the Christian faith behind completely in 1787. Godwin also read Priestley, but unlike Priestley did not settle for the half-way house to atheism known as Unitarianism. Godwin embraced total skepticism and, after another equally unsuccessful stint as a teacher, embarked on a literary career which would last for another fifty years.

In 1790 in the aftermath of Rev. Price's sermon, the world of Grub Street political journalism was alive with fantasies surrounding the revolution in

France, particularly among the tribe of dissenters from East Anglia, many of whom, like Godwin, were drifting out of the ministry and into secular occupations like writer and teacher. Later in life Wordsworth would give expression to the euphoria of the times in his famous couplet from the Preface to the *Excursion*: "Bliss was it that dawn to be alive./But to be young was very heaven! /Oh, Times . . . when reason seemed to most to assert her rights." The events in France focused Godwin's attention in a way that would never happen again. He re-immersed himself in the Enlightenment books which had caused him to lose his faith and began attending meetings of radical societies. Eventually all this intellectual ferment began to bear fruit.

In May 1791, shortly after reading Tom Paine's recently published book *The Rights of Man*, he confided to his diary that he had just conceived of a massive book, in which he would "philosophically place the principles of politics on an immovable basis, which would overbear and annihilate all oppositions."[1] In July of 1791 Godwin sold the idea to the radical publisher Joseph Johnson, and in September of 1791 he set to work on his revolutionary *magnum opus*, a task which would occupy him for the next sixteen months. In Godwin's book we find little more than the English language version of the same project that had motivated the *philosophes* across the channel, namely an application of Newton to the social order. The prime requirement for the project was a particularly vivid imagination as the thinker tried to imagine all of human interaction as the outcome of the random bumping together of insensate atoms. The discovery of "underlying principles" that lay at the center of this project meant the devaluation of everything that man had previously held sacred. In particular family ties and religion were to be eschewed in favor of an objectivity which Godwin at one point compared to an angel looking at the earth from a great height. The erosion of morals followed so naturally from this presupposition that it is difficult not to see it, as Aldous Huxley did in his book *Ends and Means* a century and a half later, as part of the motivation for adopting the Enlightenment worldview from the beginning. This, in many ways is precisely how both the Left and the Right saw Godwin's book. The conservatives criticized it because it eroded morals, and radicals like Percy Shelley, the romantic revolutionary, praised it for the same reason. Except for the values which Shelley attached to sexual liberation, his views are identical with those of the *Anti-Jacobin Review*. "The promiscuous intercourse of the sexes," was, according to the antirevolutionary faction in 1797, when Godwin's star had waned considerably from its zenith two years earlier, "one of the highest improvements to result from *Political Justice*."[2]

Two months into the writing of that book, on November 13, 1791, Godwin went to a dinner party given by his publisher at which he intended to discuss political issues with Tom Paine, the man whose book had inspired Godwin to begin writing seven months before. Also attending the dinner party was a woman by the name of Mary Wollstonecraft, who had recently become famous in London literary circles by writing a response to Burke's *Reflections* called the *Vindication of the Rights of Men*. Godwin considered *Vindication* too polemical and felt that Wollstonecraft, flushed with new-found celebrity, monopolized the conversation. Wollstonecraft, for her part, had reason to be garrulous. Having been raised in the same dissenting culture as Godwin, she was now tasting the fame that he would savor a year later when the publication of *Political Justice* would make him famous – for a while, at least.

Wollstonecraft, like the rest of the dissenting literati, had been moved by the recent events in France. Like Godwin, she was in the process of working out what she felt were the implications of the dissenting faith and found that that meant jettisoning ever more theological baggage as the seas of thought got stormier. And that new-found fame was having an intoxicating effect on Mary Wollstonecraft as well. Theological radicalism was finding its expression in what one would have to term moral radicalism, as the dissenting circle around Wollstonecraft's publisher, Joseph Johnson, began applying the solvent of "reason" to accepted beliefs. Reason in this instance found its highest expression in Newtonian physics, and as a result custom and morals as passed on from one generation to another became suspect.

The suspicion becomes apparent in Wollstonecraft's response to Burke who appeals to tradition as an antidote to what was happening in France at the time. Since Burke's defense of the Glorious Revolution amounts to a justification of a usurpation of the English throne from its rightful hereditary heir, Wollstonecraft is less than impressed with the traditions he purports to defend. If Burke, in other words, were really a supporter of tradition, how could he justify the Reformation? And if he didn't support the Reformation, did he want to return England to the time when, as Wollstonecraft put it, "men worshipped bread as God?" If Burke is not defending tradition or "inbred sentiments" in any straightforward sense, what then is he defending? Wollstonecraft's answer is "security of property," the true "definition of English liberty," upon which "selfish principle every nobler one is sacrificed."

The debate over property and economics would intensify during the nineteenth century. The political debate took on the coloration of the revolutions in France and America, but underpinning it was a psychology that was based on traditional morals. Mary Wollstonecraft may have been a political and theological radical, but her morals and the psychology based on them were as traditional as Burke's. In fact, it was the fact that they shared the same psychology that allowed her to make her moral points in the debate. Instead of custom and "inbred sentiments" as our guide, Wollstonecraft proposes reason, which is the sign that we "are superior to brute creation" and a "guide of passion" as well. "Cultivation of reason," she writes, is "an arduous task, and men of lively fancy, finding it easier to follow the impulse of passion, endeavour to persuade themselves and others that it is most natural." When the passions gain the upper hand over reason that "chaotic state of mind" is known as madness, "when reason is gone, we know not where, the wild elements of passion clash, and all is horror and confusion."[3]

As an encore to her success in attacking Burke, Wollstonecraft wrote the even more polemical *Vindication of the Rights of Women*, a feminist tract, the first of many to come, which earned her the ire of Horace Walpole, who christened her a "hyena in petticoats" for her efforts. The *Rights of Women* also earned Wollstonecraft the reputation of a dangerous radical, a reputation which was in many ways unearned, at least in terms of morals and psychology.

As some indication of her frame of mind at the time, there is the evidence in *Mary, A Fiction*, a novel she submitted to Johnson at around this time in which the heroine leaves a romantic attraction unconsummated as the object of her affection eventually dies. She consoles herself instead with the thought that there is to come "that world where there is neither marrying nor giving in marriage," and by commending to the reader the thought of William Paley, specifically, his *Principles of Moral and Political Philosophy* whose definition of virtue – "the doing good to mankind in obedience to with the *will* of God, and for the sake of *everlasting happiness*." – is congruent with the one found in the Baltimore Catechism. In a letter to her sister Everina, Wollstonecraft, much like the heroine of her eponymous fiction *Mary*, decided that it was better to remain unmarried if one were planning on a life of intellectual work: "I could not now," she wrote, "resign intellectual pursuits for domestic comforts."[4]

This is traditional psychology with a vengeance, but Mary Wollstonecraft was not hanging around with traditional people at the time, and over the course of her years as a polemicist for the French Revolution in England we can see the company she keeps taking a gradual toll on her morals. The fish, according to the French proverb, rots first at the head, and Wollstonecraft seems to perceive the danger that her passions might "pursue objects that the imagination enlarges, till they become only a sublime idea that shrinks from the enquiry of sense, and mocks the experimental philosophers who would confine this spiritual phlogiston in their material crucibles."[5] But perceiving the danger and avoiding it are two different things. Wollstonecraft was neither a moral nor a psychological radical. She proposed a traditional psychology in which reason held sway over unruly passion in the well-governed soul. It was the patrimony of the classical Christian moral tradition, but it was being eroded from within by books from France and from without by the company she chose to keep.

The circle which met in Joseph Johnson's shop and listened to Reverend Price's sermons looked upon the revolution in France as their triumph be-

cause at this point, in 1790, it seemed like the bloodless triumph of their principles, and in many respects it was. It was Voltaire who in many ways
launched the Enlightenment in the third decade of that century by bringing
English ideas back to France. Revolutionary France was the proof that the
radical theories of the dissenters could be put into practice. Dissenters, it
should be remembered, accepted the Calvinist notion of innate and complete
depravity, according to which human nature had been completely eclipsed
by the fall. Man on his own could accomplish nothing good. There was no
such thing as a post-lapsarian human nature, other than the bondage to sin.
The difference between the Calvinist dissenter and the Enlightenment *philosophe* was similar to what Perry Miller had to say about the difference between Jonathan Edwards and Ralph Waldo Emerson. The only thing that
separated them was the idea of original sin. Since original sin had known no
boundary to its sway over human nature according to Calvinist/dissenting
theology, the abandonment of that idea would have the opposite effect on human nature, allowing it to soar from depravity to apotheosis in one quick motion. The one thing that both *philosophe* and dissenter shared was the disdain
for the idea of a perduring human nature. Once the dissenters got rid of the
Calvinist interpretation of original sin, they immediately became Utopians.
Heaven on earth was now possible. This is clearly the message of Price's sermon:

> What an eventful period is this! I am thankful that I have lived to see it;
> and I could almost say, Lord, now lettest thy servant depart in peace for
> mine eyes have seen thy salvation. I have lived to see a diffusion of knowl-
> edge, which has undermined superstition and error. I have lived to see the
> rights of men better understood than ever; and nations panting for liberty,
> which seemed to have lost the idea of it. I have lived to see Thirty Millions
> of people, indignant and resolute, spurning at slavery and demanding lib-
> erty with an irresistible voice; their kind led in triumph, and an arbitrary
> monarch surrendering himself to his subjects. After sharing in the benefits
> of one Revolution, I have been spared to be a witness to two other revolu-
> tions, both glorious. And now, methinks, I see the ardor of liberty catching
> and spreading; a general amendment beginning in human affairs; the do-
> minion of kings changed for the dominion of laws and dominion of priests
> giving way to the dominion of reason and conscience.[6]

Mary Wollstonecraft gradually adopted the euphoric tone of the day.
Talk of renunciation and of reward in heaven where there was neither marrying nor giving in marriage was replaced by the slowly growing conviction
that any number of previously inconceivable arrangements might now be
possible. If France could depose its king, did a man have to remain married to
the same woman if he tired of her? The idea was broached by Thomas
Holcroft, another member of the Johnson circle, in a novel called *Anna St.
Ives*, which Wollstonecraft reviewed when it appeared. The story described a
radical heiress who spends a good deal of her time rationalizing her sexual

appetites in conversations with her lover, who assures her that in the future marriage will cease to exist.

Since sexual revolution is inextricably bound up with political revolution, it is not surprising that the revolution in France should stimulate the revolutionary minded in England to thinking about rearranging their personal lives. Wordsworth got swept away by the same tide, taking a lover in France during the early days of the revolution, then fathering a child, then abandoning both mother and child when the revolution turned in another, more- violent, direction.

It is hard to imagine, then, that the same currents would not affect someone as impressionable as Mary Wollstonecraft. And her letters to Joseph Johnson at the time indicate that no matter how much she believed that reason should still maintain its control over passion in theory, in practice she was having difficulty living up to what she believed. In many ways, Wollstonecraft was proving Burke right, just as the subsequent course of events in France would prove him right as well. Reason, unaided by tradition and social customs, was proving a slim reed upon which lay the burden of human desires, and Wollstonecraft made this clear in her letters as one by one the spiritual practices of her youth fell by the wayside to be replaced by Utopian hopes and schemes which were largely pinned on what was happening in France. Wollstonecraft stopped going to church, and she stopped talking about heaven, and yet in spite of that still longed for some assurance of an afterlife. Yet forced to "live on conjectures," Wollstonecraft found that reason was increasingly incapable to resist the imperious demands of passion.

It was at this point in her life that Wollstonecraft met the Swiss-born painter Henry Fuseli. Fuseli had been born Heinrich Fuessli in Zürich in 1741 and was eighteen years her senior, and already married when she met him as part of the circle of freethinkers that were connected to Joseph Johnson's publishing firm. Fuseli's father had been a court painter, but he had been trained as a Zwinglian minister, and, like Godwin, who had been trained for another branch of the Protestant ministry, he gave up both the faith and the ministry when exposed to the ideas of the Enlightenment. Fuseli was an ardent admirer of things English, and when given the chance by a benefactor whom he met in Berlin, emigrated to England, where he gave up the field of literature – but not before translating Winckelmann – and dedicated himself to painting under the tutorship of Joshua Reynolds. Success came in 1782 with the exhibition of his most famous painting, "The Nightmare," an enigmatic portrait of a sleeping woman with a demon squatting on her chest and a dark horse peering at both through a parted curtain. The painting would provide grist for the mills of political cartoonists in London for the next fifty years, allowing them to satirize political figures like C. J. Fox, the politician with Jacobin sympathies in the election of 1799, as well as William

Pitt, Napoleon, and Lord Nelson, who is portrayed lifting up the woman's dress under the caption "The Source of the Nile."

In his memoir of Mary Wollstonecraft, Godwin claims that she met Fuseli in June or July of 1788, a month or two after Fuseli married Sophia Rawlins. John Knowles, Fuseli's biographer, claims that Mary was swept away by Fuseli's talent for conversation, falling under the spell of his "great power and fluency of words, a poetical imagination and ready wit." Godwin goes out of his way to assure his readers that the relationship was purely platonic. However, the only source we have documenting their relationship is the quotations from her letters to Fuseli which are quoted in the Knowles biography. Mary Shelley, Wollstonecraft's daughter, bought the letters when they went on sale, and either she or her son destroyed them as a way of sanitizing the public memory of her mother in much the same way as she had collaborated in suppressing the truth about her husband's life.

Whether the relationship eventuated in sexual contact or not, it was certainly full of passion, much of which emanated from Miss Wollstonecraft, the passionate defender of revolutionary views who had just turned thirty. Wollstonecraft wrote that "I always catch something from the rich torrent of his conversation, worth storing up in my memory, to exercise my understanding." While conceding that Mrs. Fuseli had the rights to his physical person, Wollstonecraft set about laying claim to his mind. The congeniality of their mutual sentiments, Wollstonecraft claimed, allowed her to hold a place of pre-eminence in Fuseli's heart, allowing her to "unite herself with his mind." Eventually this passion became so imperious, that Wollstonecraft could do little but act as its agent. Eventually she went to Mrs. Fuseli and proposed becoming a member of their household. Wollstonecraft must have known that the proposal was a bit out of the ordinary, even for those revolutionary times and for those frequenting the revolutionary circle surrounding Johnson, but she made it anyway, informing Mrs. Fuseli that "as I am above deceit, it is right to say that this proposal arises from the sincere affection that I have for your husband, for I feel that I cannot live without the satisfaction of seeing and conversing with him daily."[7]

Mrs. Fuseli was undoubtedly convinced of the sincerity of Miss Wollstonecraft's affection toward her husband, but probably not as convinced that that affection would remain on the purely platonic level, and so Mrs. Fuseli not only rejected the offer but immediately banned Wollstonecraft from any further access to the Fuseli household, a move to which Fuseli quietly acquiesced. It's difficult to say at this point what Wollstonecraft found more humiliating, the Fuselis' rejection of her proposal, or the fact that her passions had so gained the upper hand in her life that she was foolish enough to propose the arrangement in the first place. Either way, she felt humiliated. She had been blinded by her own desires, so blinded that she had proposed a *ménage à trois* to the wife of the object of her desires. "I am a mere animal," she wrote to Joseph Johnson after the bubble of passion burst upon contact with reality, "and instinctive emotions too often silence the suggestions of reason."[8] Reason was proving to be less resistant to passion than she had supposed.

Rather than step back and take stock of just where the *Zeitgeist* was leading her, Wollstonecraft, perhaps out of wounded pride, decided to give full rein to the horses of passion and follow the spirit of the age back to its source. She decided to go to Paris to witness the revolution there first-hand. Actually she had planned to travel there earlier with both the Fuselis and Joseph Johnson, but now that traveling with the Fuselis was out of the question, she decided to go alone. Godwin says that "the single purpose she had in view being that of an endeavour to heal her distempered mind."[9] If so, the cure would turn out to be worse than the disease, but as with the imprudent proposal to the Fuselis, she couldn't see this at the time. Wollstonecraft did not terminate the lease on her lodgings in London, and gave every indication that the stay in Paris would be for about six weeks. She would write a book about the Revolution, and being an educator herself, she would advise the French on how to change their system of education and bring it more in line with the practice of the Enlightened English.

What she failed to notice is that over the course of its first three years the revolution in France had become something very different from the way it had started. What began in liberation – and liberated sex in particular – was finding its culmination in violence and death. The English revolutionaries never quite grasped what was happening in France, certainly not as perceptively as conservatives like Burke. They were forever trying to interpret the events there through the lens of English morals, which had not decayed as drastically as they had in France during the course of the seventeenth and eighteenth centuries. Forever out of sync, the English radicals celebrated religious liberty when the French were celebrating sexual liberation, and then when the English radicals turned to sexual liberation, the French were involved in an orgy of sexually induced mayhem, symbolized by the sexual mutilation of the Princess de Lamballe. Citizens of the nascent republic took to expressing their idea of liberty by wrapping the still-warm intestines of decapitated enemies of the state around their heads like a turban. Passions were indeed clouding reason in France, and Mary Wollstonecraft, who still admitted the theoretical possibility of such a thing happening, particularly in her own life, was incapable of seeing it happen to her political heroes. Still acting as if it were the euphoric summer of 1790, Wollstonecraft planned her journey to France in the fall of 1792 when events bespoke another spot on the trajectory the passions inevitably followed from liberated sex to death. When William Roscoe, fellow radical and fellow member of the Johnson circle, brought up the September massacres to Mary, she dismissed them as a momentary aberration in the progress of Progress, comparing the revolutionaries to children who might cut themselves on sharp instruments because they weren't yet adept at handling them effectively:

> let me beg you not to mix with the shallow herd who throw an odium on immutable principles, because some of the mere instrument of the revolution were too sharp. Children of any growth will do mischief when they meddle with edged tools. It is to be lamented that *as yet* the billows of public opinion are only to be moved forward by the strong wind, the squally gusts of passions.[10]

Passion, in other words, was politically necessary to move the inert masses to revolution. Missing from her letter to Roscoe is any sense that these passions, once aroused, might get beyond the ability of reason to call them back. Equally absent was any sense that those out-of-control passions might cause harm. Rather than take her humiliating rejection at the hands of the Fuselis as a warning, Wollstonecraft decided to loosen the reins on her own passions and gallop full tilt into a situation which she was misreading in the light of the English mores of her youth. Wollstonecraft was commissioned by Johnson to write a history of the French Revolution. It would prove to be one of her least satisfactory books. She made the unfortunate choice of beginning at the beginning, and so missed writing about the events which were unfolding before her eyes. But there were other reasons why she would be incapable of reading this text. She never adopted the revolutionary psychology of the Marquis de Sade, and so she couldn't simply become a cheerleader, something that was always easier to do at a distance anyway. She would soon know too much to say that the Revolution, which was now entering its bloody stage, conformed to Rev. Price's expectations and those of his followers. But at the same time she couldn't repudiate her revolutionary ideals either and agree with Burke. The result is an incoherent book that misses the point of what was happening.

There were other more personal reasons for the failure as well. The classical moral tradition had always claimed that lust darkened the mind. In this regard, Wollstonecraft's motivation in going to France was hardly disinterested. Wollstonecraft's book deal with Johnson was done on the rebound from her embarrassing involvement with the Fuselis, but it was also a thinly veiled pretext for sexual tourism. "At Paris, indeed," she wrote, "I might take a husband for the time being, and get divorced when my truant heart longed again to nestle with old friends." It's difficult to imagine a more glaring misreading of the situation in France. At the very moment in which sexual passion was turning into bloody mayhem, Wollstonecraft indicates that she can turn on sexual passion like a light switch, have her fling and then come back unscathed. Experience would prove to be an expensive teacher, but Wollstonecraft seemed at the outset of her trip incapable of learning this lesson any way other than the hard way. Like the Marxists who went on pilgrimage to Moscow during the early 1920s, Wollstonecraft saw the revolution in France as a way to indulge her passions safely concealed from the gaze of English public opinion in the enabling company of other idealists who were there for precisely the same reason.

Part I, Chapter 4

Paris, 1792

On October 28, 1792, at around the same time that Mary Wollstonecraft's infatuation with Henry Fuseli was reaching its climax and rapid denouement, the Marquis de Sade wrote a tract on the hospitals of Paris which so impressed his revolutionary colleagues in the Commune of the Section des Piques that they had it reprinted and sent it to the other forty-seven sections in Paris. Sade followed up on this success by writing another pamphlet "Idea on the Law's Mode of Sanction" a few days later on November 2. In it he argued for a monocameral legislature to replace the now imprisoned king. This position differed from the position he held a year earlier in which he advocated a bicameral legislature much like the one in place in England. France was now at the beginning of its estrangement from things English.

The pamphlet on hospitals signaled the beginning of Sade's rise as a politician. In this he was – at least initially – more successful than in his career as playwright. Seven months earlier on March 5, the sans-culottes had shut down his play *Le Suborneur*. Thrust onto the stage of life by political events, Sade soon learned that his abilities as a dramatist, and even more so, his talent as an actor, would serve him in good stead in the ongoing psychodrama that was the French Revolution.

Mary Wollstonecraft arrived in Paris in December of 1792, under a gray and threatening sky, just in time to see the King of France, now known as Citizen Capet, trundled back and forth to his trial for treason in a vehicle which the French called a *fiacre* and the English a hackney coach. Since Miss Wollstonecraft had arrived in France to write her book on the French Revolution without having first learned the rudiments of the French language, her most striking impressions were visual. At nine o'clock on the morning of December 26, Wollstonecraft watched the King of France pass by her window. She was struck by his dignity, by the silence, made all the more apparent by the occasional strokes on the drum, by the emptiness of the streets, and by the realization that all of Paris was watching the king pass to his trial and eventual death from behind their closed windows as she was. Still the revolutionary, Wollstonecraft was even more impressed with the dignity of the French people, whose language was at this point still incomprehensible – she was "unable to utter a word" and so "stunned by the flying sounds" that she went to bed "each night with a headache."[1] "I bowed to the majesty of the people," she wrote to Johnson, "and respected the propriety of behaviour so perfectly in unison with my own feelings." Then, inexplicably, given her republican sympathies, she bursts into tears at the prospect of the king, "sitting with more dignity than I expected from his character, in a hackney coach going to meet death."

The spiritual daughter of the Puritans who beheaded King Charles was, it turns out, more affected by the prospect of regicide than she expected. Wollstonecraft says that lifting her eye from the letter she was writing, she saw eyes glaring at her "through a glassdoor opposite my chair" and what is more prophetic, "bloody hands shook at me." Since it couldn't have been the servants, whose apartments were in a remote part of the house, Wollstonecraft concludes that it must been phantoms of her troubled imagination – or, perhaps, a vision of things to come. She concluded by wishing that she had her cat or some other living creature by her as an antidote to the pervasive feeling of death all around her. "Death in so many frightful shapes has taken hold of my fancy. I am going to bed, and for the first time in my life, I cannot put out the candle."[2] Revolutionary passion, she would soon discover, had taken on a life of its own.

On January 21, 1793, a little less than a month after Wollstonecraft arrived in Paris, King Louis XVI was decapitated in front of a decapitated statue of his father at the Place de la Revolution which is now known as the Place de la Concorde. Wollstonecraft evidently did not attend the execution, which would have been in keeping with her coverage of the Revolution, because she mentions it in a letter to Ruth Barlow only in passing while discussing her continuing inability to understand the French language. Wollstonecraft had moved out of her original lodgings and was now living with the Christies and circulating largely in the radical anglophone community there, composed of both Americans and Englishmen of equally republican sensibilities.

While in Paris, she renewed her acquaintance with Tom Paine, who had fled to France to avoid a sedition trial in England. While in Paris she also made the acquaintance of Helen Maria Williams, a poetess with revolutionary sympathies, whose writings had inspired the young William Wordsworth. Wordsworth, in fact, set off to Orléans in December of 1791 to be with Miss Williams, but found after he arrived that she had gone to Paris to get a better view of the Revolution. Wordsworth met instead a Captain Beaupuy, who introduced him to the republican cause. While in Orléans, Wordsworth also met a young woman by the name of Annette Vallon, who began their relationship by giving French lessons and ended up getting pregnant by him.

By the late fall of 1792, the baby, christened Caroline, had been born. Wordsworth, who still hadn't got around to marrying the mother of their child, had by now run out of money, and on top of that the political situation had changed drastically as well. The Englishmen who had been feted two summers ago as harbingers of liberty were now considered enemies of the state. Shortly thereafter England declared war on France and would remain at war for the next twenty-two years, until the defeat of Napoleon, preventing Wordsworth from carrying out his plan of bringing Annette and their child to live with him in England. When he returned to England, Wordsworth was supposed to take a position in the ministry, his only prospect for employment at the time. Just how he was to square this with a Roman Catholic wife and a daughter born out of wedlock must have given him pause. Perhaps this is why he didn't go straight back to England after leaving Annette. Perhaps he was just curious about the events in Paris. Whatever the reason he stayed there for months, and as the political situation darkened, his resolve to marry Annette seems to have faded away as well. Wordsworth finally returned to England in late December of 1792. The date corresponds so closely to Wollstonecraft's journey to Paris that we can almost imagine the two English radicals sailing by each other in opposite directions across the channel. The journeys would have been symbolic as well. By the turn of the century, Wordsworth had abandoned his youthful radicalism completely and would go on to become the epitome of cultural and political conservatism. The story of Wordsworth's youthful indiscretion, which would fester like an unhealed wound at the heart of his art, would not come out until the 1920s. The trauma which the first sexual revolution caused was so severe that, in the case of Wordsworth and Shelley in particular, it was blotted completely from the public record. As of 1793, however, Wordsworth was far from over his infatuation with radical politics. In fact, in the early part of that year, his radicalism would reach new heights, propelled there by the publishing event of the year.

On February 13, 1793, Godwin's book, entitled *An Enquiry Concerning the Principles of Political Justice,* went on sale in London. It was, depending on your point of view, the exactly right moment or the exactly wrong moment for a book extolling the Enlightenment. The illusions of the English Jacobins were like an increasingly large balloon that was expanding to ever-closer and ever-more-perilous contact with the actual revolution in France, which had taken a decidedly bloody turn in the late summer and early fall of 1792. On December 19, 1792, a month before Louis XVI's execution, the attorney general in London brought a seditious libel charge against Thomas Paine, who fled to France to join the increasingly bloody revolution still in progress there.

As the Marquis de Sade had noticed in France, so Godwin had noticed in England. Newtonian physics, which was the ultimate basis of Enlightenment thought, had sexual implications. If man is just a machine made up of matter in motion, running on electricity, then marriage as a sacred bond between man and wife made no more sense in England than it did in France. "The institution of marriage," Godwin wrote in a way that scandalized the traditionalists even more than it energized the revolutionaries,

> is a system of fraud; and men who carefully mislead their judgements in the daily affair of their life, must always have a crippled judgment in every other concern. . . . Add to this, that marriage is an affair of property, and the worst of all properties. So long as two human beings are forbidden by positive institutions to follow the dictates of their own mind, prejudice is alive and vigorous. So long as I seek to engross one woman to myself, and to prohibit my neighbor from proving his superior desert and reaping the fruits of it, I am guilty of the most odious of all monopolies.[3]

Godwin was unmarried when he wrote these lines. It is to his credit as a human being that he modified his thought when his state of life changed, but it is not to his credit as a philosopher that he did so. It was statements like this that prompted Leslie Stephen to say that his philosophy was a bubble which burst when it made contact with reality. The views Godwin expressed on the relations between the sexes had their roots in the revolution in France and so it should come as no surprise that they rose and fell in relation to that event, as perceived by the English.

The immediate result of the book was that Godwin became famous overnight. In his diary Godwin noted that "I was nowhere a stranger," after the publication of his book on political justice. "He blazed as a sun in the firmament," wrote William Hazlitt, and like moths drawn to a light, the English Jacobins flew to his door and, more often than not, were singed by the contact with his ideas. "Throw aside your books of chemistry," wrote Wordsworth advising another young student, "and read Godwin on necessity."[4] Two years after the book's publication, the young Jacobins in England were still under its spell. "It was in the spring of this year," wrote radical author Crabb Robinson in 1795, "that I read a book which gave a turn to my mind and in effect directed the whole course of my life – a book which often producing a powerful effect on the youth of that generation, has now sunk into unmerited oblivion. . . . I entered fully into its spirit, it left all others behind in my admiration, and I was willing even to become a martyr for it."[5]

Robinson's quote indicates that Godwin's star was waning on the literary horizon as fast as it rose. Soon it would set altogether as Wordsworth, Southey, and Coleridge changed their minds about both Godwin and their youthful indiscretions and the revolution which enabled both, but this story was far from over at this point. In fact, the younger generation of Romantic writers, especially Shelley, was in many ways to fulfill Robinson's prediction and become a martyr to the cause of unfettered passion.

In the meantime, as if to prove Burke right and Godwin wrong, the revolution in France proceeded headlong into bloody excess. After urging the Parisian mob to sack the city's prisons and murder their inmates, Robespierre consolidated his hold on power throughout the winter of 1792–93. In a political climate in which the rise to power and the subsequent loss of one's head could be measured in a matter of weeks, the Marquis de Sade found that politics took a singularly bizarre turn when the Bastille's most famous prisoner suddenly was made a judge. On April 8, 1793, Sade, along with nineteen other citizens, was appointed to a jury to investigate a case of counterfeit assignats. "You'll never guess . . ." he wrote to Gaufridy, "I am a judge, yes a judge! . . . Member of an investigating jury! Who would have predicted that? . . . As you see, my mind is maturing, and I am beginning to acquire wisdom. . . . But congratulate me, and above all do not fail to send money to *monsieur le juge* or I'll be damned if I don't sentence you to death."[6]

The Marquis de Sade may have been joking about sentencing Gaufridy to death, but during the month of March with the establishment of the Committees of Surveillance and the Revolutionary Tribunal, one didn't need to be a judge to put someone's life in jeopardy. After the years of his married life spent lording his aristocratic heritage over his in-laws, the Montreuils, Citizen Sade was now in a position to exact revenge on them for their unjust treatment of him. Sensing the family's danger, and moved by a sense of desperation that must have been extreme, Sade's aged father-in-law showed up at his apartment in the Section des Piques.

It was also during March of 1793 that the first organized resistance to the Revolution broke out in France. In August of 1792 all priests who refused to take an oath of submission were deported. It was one such group that was massacred in Paris. Those who refused to submit and were not killed went into hiding, and when they did the agitation against the revolution smoldered and then finally broke out into flame in the west of France when the government tried to conscript 300,000 troops to fight foreign invaders. When the draft was announced in the first days of March, rioting followed and the men of draft age fled the towns and regrouped in the forests. Then on March 11, 12, and 13 they counterattacked, taking St. Florent, Chanzeaux, Machecoul, and Challans and ultimately every major town in the region. The republican forces were stunned not only by the ferocity of the attack, but by the vehemence of the antirevolutionary fervor. For the first time since it began, the revolution was in danger, not from foreign troops in the pay of dispossessed aristocrats, but by the very peasants and artisans who were presumed to be revolution's main beneficiaries. The fact that they seemed inspired by the Catholic faith from which they had been so recently liberated only made the uprising more perplexing from the republican point of view.

During the Spring of 1793, at around the same time the Vendée uprisings began and roughly four months after her arrival in Paris, while Godwin's sun was rising in the literary firmament in England and the Marquis de Sade was beginning his judiciary career, Mary Wollstonecraft, in Godwin's words, "entered into that species of connection, for which her heart secretly panted."[7] The man's name was Gilbert Imlay. He was an American adventurer "with no matrimonial ties," an agent of the Scioto Land Development company who had written a well-received book on Kentucky and who would soon follow it up by a novel called *The Emigrants*, which was, in spite of its title, a tract on the advantages of free love and divorce.

The romance may have happened suddenly but it was not a case of love at first sight; in fact, in many respects, it was a case of the exact opposite. Wollstonecraft, who met Imlay at the Barlows (Godwin says it was at the Christies), found him arrogant and self-absorbed but gradually the magic potion of passion turned Bottom's ass's head into something which Wollstonecraft found not only attractive but irresistibly so. On April 12, after the British came to the aid of the counterrevolutionaries at Toulon, all foreigners were prohibited from leaving France, an act which put the English, whose country was now at war with France, in the position of being denounced and arrested. Americans, allies in their revolutionary struggle with France against England, were not liable to arrest, and so to insure Wollstonecraft's safety, Imlay registered her as his wife at the American embassy, although the two never married. This marriage of convenience seemed to fulfill Wollstonecraft's prediction that she would take a husband for a time, although by the time she was fully involved in the relationship brevity was the last thing on her mind. In fact, Wollstonecraft was caught off guard by the passions she so lightheartedly described in her letter proposing to take a husband for a time. Wollstonecraft, who was still a virgin at the time, was talking about sexual passion based mostly on what she had read; she didn't reckon with the ties that sexual intercourse created willy-nilly. No matter what revolutionary dispensation she professed, Wollstonecraft was binding herself to a man she had originally found physically attractive but morally repugnant. By late June, when her first extant letter to Imlay appears, Wollstonecraft had already moved into their secluded bower in Neuilly sur Seine, where they would spend an idyllic summer together mutually gratifying their respective sexual passions, as the French continued unobserved in Paris gratifying passions of a bloodier sort. One year before, during the summer of 1792, Lady Palmerston had noticed an abrupt change in the general mood of the Parisian public from an optimism which verged on euphoria at times to a mood which plummeted just before the September massacres to an "an air of ferocity and self-created consequence in the common people," which made her "very uncomfortable."[8]

In 1793 the mood was back again, but Mary was too busy enjoying, if not connubial bliss, then its counterfeit, while working on what she termed "a great book," *An Historical and Moral View of the Origin and Progress of the French Revolution* . In the end the book would prove to be as great as the relationship. During the summer of 1793, Mary would take evening walks in the woods near Neuilly in spite of the warnings from the gardener, who seems to have developed an attachment to Mary and a desire to serve her by making her bed and bringing her grapes.

The affair ended with the season. In September Mary announced that she was pregnant and shortly after the announcement, Imlay announced that he had to go to Le Havre, then known as Havre Marat, on business. It seems clear with the benefit of hindsight that the pregnancy precipitated the break. Imlay was a libertine and a sexual adventurer whose head was full of the same republican attitudes toward marriage that Godwin was popularizing in England at the time. He had, therefore, no intention of binding himself to a woman, even if that woman was pregnant with his child. He also had no desire to state his intentions openly, thereby precipitating an unpleasant scene or foreclosing future options. So, under the pretext of business, he simply disappeared, and Mary was left to while away the months and weeks of her pregnancy wondering what was taking him so long. She soon began to give vent to her irritation in letters that take on a tone which has endeared them to subsequent generations of feminists. "Amongst the feathered race," she wrote, "whilst the hen keeps the young warm, her mate stays by to cheer her; but it is sufficient for man to condescend to get a child, in order to claim it. A man is a tyrant!"[9]

During the fall of 1793 Wollstonecraft remained in Paris waiting for Imlay's return as Robespierre tightened his grasp on the reins of power and blood began to flow ever more freely in the streets. It's hard to imagine a more ideal position from which to write a history of the French Revolution, but by now, perhaps because of her personal anguish at being abandoned after abandoning herself to her own passions, the revolution was a text which Wollstonecraft simply could not read. If she sensed a connection between sexual passion and its bloody political *sequelae*, she seems to have kept this thought to herself, even if the evidence was all around her.

On October 16, 1793, ten months after the death of her husband, Marie Antoinette was dragged to the scaffold and decapitated as well. In the same month, Mary Wollstonecraft walked from Neuilly to Paris and while crossing the Place de la Revolution slipped and nearly fell. Looking down, she discovered that the entire plaza was slippery with the blood of the recently slain. Unable to contain herself any longer, "the emotions of her soul burst forth in indignant exclamations,"[10] which were imprudent for anyone to utter at the time, but were especially imprudent coming from the mouth of an expatriate Englishwoman. If she hadn't been led away from the scene by a concerned companion, it is entirely possible that her blood might have been mixed in with all the rest. The terror was reaching its full fury, and as it did, Mary Wollstonecraft was no longer able to comprehend what was going on. This was most assuredly not what the Rev. Price had in mind when he compared what was happening in France with their bloodless Glorious Revolution. Wollstonecraft had come to France with a mind formed by the categories established in Price's sermon. Had she not become involved with Imlay, it's possible that some of the thoughts which she had expressed on passion in her attack on Burke might have reasserted themselves and allowed for a more realistic apprehension of what was going on. But as it was, her mind never really gained any purchase on the meaning of the events unfolding around her.

On July 23, 1793, the Marquis de Sade's metamorphosis from aristocrat to republican became complete when he was named president of the Section des Piques. Less than a month later, he was gone, forced out of office because he refused to put what he termed "a horrible, inhumane measure" to a vote. Lever speculates that it might have been the destruction of the Vendée or the transfer of Marie-Antoinette to the Conciergerie, which meant placing her one step closer to a trial before the Revolutionary Tribunal and her death. It turns out that the author of *The 120 Days of Sodom* wasn't bloodthirsty enough for his revolutionary colleagues. As a parting gesture he also spared the lives of the Montreuils by putting them on the "purification list." Lacking resolve as an executioner, Sade returned to the realm of the mind, where he could give his ferocity full rein. On October 9, 1793, he delivered his "Discourse to the Shades of Marat and Le Peletier," at a quasireligious ceremony complete with incense and busts of the slain heroes. Emboldened by his success, Sade launched an all-out attack on religion on November 15, when six sections, including Sade's Section des Piques, renounced all religion except the religion of liberty. Sade may have paled before bloodshed, but he could always warm to atheism, which was in many ways, the core of his belief, or lack thereof: "Reason is replacing Mary in our temples," Sade told the Convention,

> and the incense that used to burn at the knees of an adulterous woman will from now on be kindled only at the feet of the goddess who broke our chains. . . . The philosopher has long laughed in secret at the apish antics of Catholicism, but if he dared to raise his voice, it was in the dungeons of the Bastille, where ministerial despotism soon learned how to compel its silence. How could tyranny fail to bolster superstition? Both were nurtured in the same cradle, both were daughters of fanaticism, both were served by those useless creatures known as the priest of the temple and the monarch of the throne; having a common foundation, they could not but protect each other.[11]

Sade was using his new-found prominence as a political orator to articulate a philosophy of the revolutionary state, which was, by its nature, antithetical to both religion and morals, and, therefore, dedicated to the promotion of passion as a civic virtue. Sade would go on to articulate that idea more fully two years later. For the moment, though, he was too involved in politics to realize that he had committed a serious blunder. Sade's speech announcing that "man is finally enlightened" was an unabashed expression of his atheism, but unfortunately it came less than a week before Robespierre decided to call an end to the anti-Christian campaign on November 21. Sade was *persona non grata* once again, and once again on the 18th of Frimaire in the year II (which is to say on December 8, 1793) he was arrested. This time he was taken to a former convent of the Filles des Madeleine, and interned, since all the cells were full, in the prison's latrine, where Sade would spend the next six weeks. Sade was to learn that revolutionary justice was much more draconian than the sort he endured at the Bastille at the hands of the *ancien régime*. Thrown in with the cream of aristocratic society, Sade discussed literature and politics while awaiting his execution. On January 8, he learned that his publisher Girouard had been guillotined.

A week later, Mary Wollstonecraft, now in the second trimester of her pregnancy and tired of waiting for Imlay to return to Paris, decided to go visit him instead in Le Havre where he was staying while doing business. Mary had spent the fall analyzing their relationship in letters and the verdict was not hopeful. "Of late we are always separating," she wrote in September, "Crack! – crack! – and away you go. This joke wears the sallow cast of thought; for, though I began to write cheerfully, some melancholy tears have found their way into my eyes that linger there whilst a glow of tenderness at my heart whispers that you are one of the best creatures in the world."[12] Wollstonecraft's heart, no matter how tender, was contending with her mind, whose verdict about Imlay, even at this early stage of the game was uniformly negative. "I have found that I have more mind than you in one respect," she wrote in the same letter, "because I can, without any violent effort of reason, find food for love in the same object, much longer than you can. – The way to my senses is through my heart; but, forgive me! I think there is sometimes a shorter cut to yours."[13]

On March 27, 1794, Sade was transferred yet again to another prison, this time Picpus, which again had an aristocratic clientele, including the wife of the Duc d'Orléans, one of the aristocrats who fomented the revolution and who was known as Philippe Egalité until he succumbed to the revolution's excesses as well. On July 26, 1794, Fouquier-Tinville, the notorious executioner during the Terror, issued an indictment against Sade charging him with maintaining "intelligence and correspondence with the enemies of the republic" and being a "vile satellite" of Citizen Capet's conspiracy to overthrow the revolution. The punishment was death, and on the next day the accused were trundled off to the scaffold. By the time they arrived, however, Sade was not with them. The bailiff couldn't find him when he came to his cell to take him to the scaffold. The remaining twenty-seven prisoners were almost saved by the public revulsion at the Terror that would bring it to an end the next day when Robespierre himself lost his head – almost, but not quite. Sade was finally released on October 15, and by then the revulsion at Robespierre known as the Thermidorean reaction was in full swing. Sade was a free man once again, although because he had to pay for the 312 days he spent in prison he was once again deep in debt.

In June 1794, at the height of the Great Terror, Godwin responded to a correspondent who expected him to be critical of the French Revolution now that it had shown its true (and bloody) face, by defending Robespierre as "an eminent benefactor of mankind."[14] In August of 1794 with Robespierre in his grave and the reaction gaining ground, Imlay rushed back to Paris from London to see what was going on. While there he met with Mary who had given birth to their child – alone – on May 14. Mary named the child Frances after a childhood friend, or Fanny for short, and told Ruth Barlow that in spite of her early writings to the contrary, she found "great pleasure in being a mother." She was also grateful for "the constant tenderness of my most affectionate companion," regarding the "fresh tie" as a blessing. Imlay, however, was of another mind when it came to matrimonial ties, fresh or otherwise, and shortly after he arrived in Paris he was on his way back to London again, with the assurance that he would send for Mary and the baby in a few months.

What followed was the bleakest period of Mary's life, a time which corresponded with one of the most brutally cold winters of modern times. Abandoned in Paris in penury and bitter cold, Mary took consolation in analyzing her relationship with Imlay in her letters. They are not letters which we can imagine Imlay rejoiced to receive. At the heart of her letters was the growing realization that Imlay was indifferent to both Mary and her daughter. She had given her heart to him, and he had simply used her as a convenience for the moment. The relationship had lasted during the summer of 1793 and had ended when Mary announced that she was pregnant, which was when it began in earnest for her. Mary's previous claim that no one should be forced to remain in a relationship where mutual affection had ceased now rang hollow and unrealistic in light of the child that had been the fruit of that relationship. Now that Imlay was gone, she was left to carry that burden by herself. Godwin in the meantime was preparing a second edition of *Political Justice*, this time with an expanded section on marriage. Infidelity, he wrote, was loathsome only when it was concealed. It was the sort of thing Imlay would like to hear, but it was no longer plausible to Mary Wollstonecraft, who spent her time writing letters she hoped would awaken Imlay's slumbering conscience.

"Should your sensibility ever awake," she wrote to Imlay, "remorse will find its way to your heart; and, in the midst of business and sensual pleasure, I shall appear to you, the victim of your deviation from rectitude."[15] One biographer claims that Mary playing Banquo's ghost here "sets up a faint irritation in the reader."[16] That irritation probably depends on the reader, but a more apropos literary reference in this regard would be the monster in *Frankenstein*, who announces to his creator, "I will be with you on your wedding night," when he refuses to create for him a mate. Conscience, in other words, is bound to ruin sexual pleasure. The reference is especially apropos because Frankenstein was written by Mary Wollstonecraft's second daughter, the daughter she would never see, who had been re-reading the letters her mother had written to Imlay when she wrote the book.

The monster, in this context, always represents and articulates the insights which the author finds difficult to admit to herself, and at this phase in her life, Mary Wollstonecraft was beginning to understand that the revolutionary philosophy was failing when it came in contact with life. Not only did it not explain anything, it rendered those who espoused it incapable of understanding what was going on around them. It rendered them blind because it was a species of lust, and lust darkened the mind. The new philosophy, Mary Wollstonecraft was learning in the expensive school of experience, was simply a form of rationalization. "I have no criterion for morality," she wrote to Imlay, "and have thought in vain, if the sensation which led you to follow an ancle [sic] or step, be the sacred foundation of principle or affection. Mine has been of a very different nature, or it would not have stood the brunt of your sarcasm. The sentiment in me is still sacred. If there be any part of me that will survive the sense of my misfortunes, it is the purity of my affections. The impetuosity of your senses, may have led you to term mere animal desire, the source of principle."[17]

Morality for Imlay was simply rationalized desire. Those who accepted that belief and acted on it were, as the Enlightenment would say, machines, which is what the Marquis de Sade and de la Mettrie had been saying all along. It is only after she had given birth, that Mary could see sexuality in terms other than the mechanical and expedient. Again she writes to Imlay and tries to articulate a philosophy that is the antithesis of what she claimed to believe as an English sexual revolutionary:

> The impulse of the senses, passions, if you will, and the conclusions of reason, draw men together; but the imagination is the true fire, stolen from heaven, to animate this cold creature of clay, producing all those fine sympathies that lead to rapture, rendering men social by expanding their hearts, instead of leaving them leisure to calculate how many comforts society affords.[18]

Once again we have an image that will reappear in *Frankenstein*, whose subtitle, "The Modern Prometheus," adverts to electricity as the fire stolen from heaven. Unlike Benjamin Franklin and the *philosophes,* who admired his experiments, Wollstonecraft is forever attempting to infuse the images of Enlightenment with the moral patrimony of the West which they were created to replace. Instead of using Newtonian terms like force to rationalize immorality – the Enlightenment project in a nutshell – Wollstonecraft is forever trying to re-humanize desire by connecting it to the heart. Her carping about men in general and Imlay in particular gives her writing the ring of contemporary feminism, yet the thrust of her argument is the opposite. "You know my opinion of men in general," she writes in that vein, "you know that I think them systematic tyrants, and that it is the rarest thing in the world, to meet with a man with sufficient delicacy of feeling to govern desire."[19] Men are tyrants, in other words, because they cannot govern desire. Their desires govern them. The psychology Wollstonecraft applies in her diatribe against men, like her diatribe against Burke, is based on both traditional morality and psychology. Reason is meant to subdue passion, and in subduing it render it useful for human enterprise, in the way that a man would break a horse or tame a dog or confine fire to the hearth. Those who fail to do this are but a galvanized simulacrum of human beings. They are also, as her daughter will bring out in *Frankenstein*, monsters. "Am I always to be tossed about thus?" she asks Imlay, " – shall I never find an asylum to rest contented in? How can you love to fly about continually – dropping down, as it were, in a new world – cold and strange! – every other day? Why do you not attach those tender emotions round the idea of home, which even now dim my eyes? – This alone is affection – every thing else is only humanity, electrified by sympathy."[20]

Again the image of electricity recurs, now half way between its original appearance at the hands of Ben Franklin, the scientist revolutionary, and its final expression as the Monster created by Doctor Frankenstein. The longer she meditates on Imlay and his behavior, the more she sees him as both a typical man and a human failure, a man whose unrestricted passions have coarsened him to a caricature of what he might have been:

> I shall always consider it as one of the most serious misfortunes of my life, that I did not meet you, before satiety had rendered your senses so fastidious, as almost to close up every tender avenue of sentiment and affection that leads to your sympathetic heart. You have a heart, my friend, yet, hurried away by the impetuosity of inferior feelings, you have sought in vulgar excesses, for that gratification which only the heart can bestow.[21]

If there is an alchemy at work here, it is one based on the traditional psychology of the West. Appetite must be tamed by reason before it can be transformed into love:

> The common run of men, I know, with strong healthy and gross appetites, must have variety to banish *ennui*, because the imagination never lends its magic wand, to convert appetite into love, cemented by according reason. Ah! my friend, you know not the ineffable delight, the exquisite pleasure, which arises from a unison of affection and desire, when the whole soul and senses are abandoned to a lively imagination, that renders every emotion delicate and rapturous. Yes; these are emotions over which satiety has no power, and the recollection of which, even disappointment cannot disenchant; but they do not exist without self-denial. These emotions, more or less strong, appear to me to be the distinctive characteristic of genius, the foundation of taste, and of that exquisite relish for the beauties of na-

ture, of which the common herd of eaters and drinkers and *child-beget-ters*, certainly have no idea.[22]

Although she didn't know it at the time – she would still do one more book – Wollstonecraft was at the end of her writing career. This was so because her life would be cut short, but it was so for subtler reasons as well. Wollstonecraft, as the result of being treated so shabbily by Imlay, now came to believe in a psychology that was the antithesis of the one that was needed to produce revolution. The French Revolution had provided the scenario for every progressive psychology which would follow. Those psychologies would become, in effect, parables of revolution, according to which the passions (the peasants) would overthrow the king (reason) on their way to establishing heaven on earth. According to this psychology, the only evil is repression, and any measure which combats repression is legitimate. The same applied to measures taken against the agents of repression, who could be expected to suffer the same fate the Catholic priests suffered at the hands of the revolutionary mob. Wollstonecraft in her letters proposed a psychology that contradicted her politics. Passion was destructive when left untamed by reason. Left unchecked, it destroyed not only the person but the *polis* as well in a maelstrom of conflicting desires, as she watched it do to Paris. But more importantly it destroyed the mind which adopted the gratification of passion as its highest good:

> But it is not possible that *passion* clouds your reason, as much as it does mine? – and ought you not to doubt, whether those principles are so "exalted," as you term them, which only lead to your own gratification? In other words, whether it be just to have no principle of action, but that of following your inclination, trampling on the affection you have fostered, and the expectations you have excited?[23]

The real danger is that reason will extinguish itself in its attempt to rationalize its pleasures. The mind will extinguish reason in its attempt to drown out the guilt which follows inexorably from acting on those desires. "Beware of the deceptions of passion!" she tells Imlay. "It will not always banish from your mind, that you have acted ignobly – and condescended to subterfuge to gloss over the conduct you could not excuse – Do truth and principle require such sacrifices?"[24] Given the conclusions she had to come to as a result of her dealings with Imlay, it is not clear that she could have gone on writing without offending the very people who were her most avid readers. She couldn't tell the story of the revolution favorably without violating her own integrity and what she had learned from Imlay's treatment of her, but she couldn't tell the story unfavorably either without alienating her publisher and the revolutionary readers which supported him. So she began to throw about for more drastic ways to deal with the pain.

In April of 1795 Wollstonecraft returned to London with her daughter.

Imlay not only asked her to return, he sent his servant to accompany her on the journey. If Wollstonecraft had any illusions that her return to London meant a return to Imlay's affection and hearth, those hopes were shattered almost immediately when she discovered that Imlay had moved in with a "young actress," as Godwin put it, "from a strolling company of players." Perhaps remembering her attempted *ménage à trois* with Mr. and Mrs. Fuseli, Wollstonecraft even proposed that both the actress and she would share Imlay, because that at least would give her daughter a father, but when even that daring proposal was rejected by Imlay, she decided that death was the only solution to her suffering.

In October of 1795, unable to accept the suffering which Imlay's selfishness and neglect had inflicted on her any longer, Mary Wollstonecraft resolved to drown herself in the Thames. Feeling that she might be rescued by the crowds near the water in London, she rented a boat and rowed to Putney, where after walking around in the rain until her clothes were thoroughly soaked, she threw herself into the river and, in an agony compounded half of suffocation and half of uncertainty, bobbed around like a cork, buoyed up by the stays and corsets she had criticized in the *Vindication of the Rights of Women*. Finally, a pair of workmen dragged her out of the water and took her to a nearby inn where she revived and decided to recommit herself to living all over again.

At around the same time Mary Wollstonecraft tried to kill herself by drowning in the Thames, insurrection flared up in France once again, this time to be quelled by a young Corsican soldier by the name of Napoleon Bonaparte. The Marquis de Sade knew nothing of the troubles of Mary Wollstonecraft, and probably wouldn't have cared much even if he had, but he was aware that in the Vendée, the revolution beheld its most significant domestic opponent. With this in mind, Sade turned to polemics once again and wrote the classic rationale of all revolutionary governments, a speech entitled "Yet Another Effort, Frenchmen, If You Would Become Republicans," which eventually got inserted, and rightly so, into his pornographic tract, *Philosophy in the Bedroom*. Sade, unlike Wollstonecraft, was learning no lessons in the expensive school of sexual experience. He had fathered children, but the father's experience of birth is abstract compared to that of the mother. The main difference between Wollstonecraft and Sade – and this mirrored the difference between England and France at the time – lay in the realm of morals. Wollstonecraft still had enough of the moral patrimony of the West as part of her lived experience so that traditional psychology still made sense to her. Sade's decadence, on the other hand, propelled him to a political view consonant with his decadent morals.

Neither however could go beyond the psychology which the West had bequeathed them. The best Sade could do was turn the traditional view on its head, which is the essence of all revolution both political and sexual. "The state of a moral man," Sade wrote, "is one of tranquillity and peace; the state of an immoral man is one of perpetual unrest." Thus far the quote could have been taken from St. Augustine's *City of God*, instead of its actual source which is Sade's *Philosophy in the Bedroom*. Sade's point is not to revoke what Augustine had to say, but to stand it on its head, and the gist of the rest of the quote is that perpetual unrest "pushes" the revolutionary "to, and identifies him with, the necessary insurrection in which the republican must always keep the government of which he is a member."

Writing at the time of the collapse of the Roman Empire, St. Augustine both revolutionized and brought to a close antiquity's idea of freedom by connecting it with morals. "Thus," he writes in the *City of God*, "a good man, though a slave, is free; but a wicked man, though a king, is a slave. For he serves, not one man alone, but, what is worse, as many masters as he has vices." Augustine revolutionized the concept of freedom by connecting it to morals: man was not a slave by nature or by law, as Aristotle claimed. His freedom was a function of his moral state. A man had as many masters as he had vices. This insight would provide the basis for the most sophisticated form of social control known to man, and the Marquis de Sade was the first to formulate its basic principles. Like St. Augustine, the Marquis de Sade would agree that freedom was a function of morals. Freedom for the Marquis de Sade, however, meant willingness to reject the moral law. The project of liberating man from the moral law would have far-reaching consequences, all of which were consonant with the use of sex as a form of social and political control which Sade was proposing in "Yet Another Effort, Frenchmen."

The logic is clear enough: Those who wished to liberate man from the moral order needed to impose social controls as soon as they succeeded because liberated libido led inevitably to anarchy, as recent events in France had shown. A revolutionary state must foster immorality among its citizens if it wants to foster the perpetual unrest necessary to foment revolution. Morals meant the advent of tranquillity, and tranquillity meant the end of revolutionary fervor. Therefore, the state must promote immorality. Given man's natural and inordinate inclination to pleasure, the immorality most congenial to manipulation is sexual immorality. Hence the revolutionary state must promote sexual license if it is to remain truly revolutionary and retain its hold on power.

Over the course of two hundred years, those techniques became more and more refined, eventuating in a world where people were controlled, not by military force, but by the skillful management of their passions. It was Aldous Huxley who wrote in his preface to the 1946 edition of *Brave New World* that "As political and economic freedom diminishes, sexual freedom tends compensatingly to increase." Sade's claim is related to Huxley's: The best way to make men unaware of their lack of political freedom is to indulge their sexual passions. Both Augustine and Sade would agree that moral behavior has certain political consequences; both would agree that immoral behavior has certain political consequences as well. What they disagreed on was their vision of the ideal state. Augustine establishes the fundamental options here as well. There is the City of God on the one hand, which espouses the love of God even to the extinction of self, and the City of Man, which espouses the love of self even to the extinction of God. Sade, the apostle of atheism, was clearly a proponent of the latter city. Since the City of God was based on Christianity's exaltation of love and service, as its highest ideal, the City of Man, as its opposite, could only be based on domination, a point which Augustine makes clear at the very beginning of the City of God. "The earthly city," Augustine tells us, "lusts to dominate the world and. . . . though nations bend to its yoke, it itself is dominated by its passion for dominion."

Libido Dominandi, to give the Latin original, is the essence of the revolutionary state. When Lever calls "Yet Another Effort, Frenchmen," "nothing less than a *reductio ad absurdum* of the theory of revolution and a radical mockery of Jacobin philosophy,"[25] he is being far too clever, more clever than the text itself, which evidently embarrasses him because of its frankness. In "Yet Another Effort, Frenchmen," the Marquis de Sade gives the rationale for the revolutionary state, which is indistinguishable from Augustine's City of Man, which is based on the gratification of passion in general and the gratification of *libido dominandi* as its highest expression: "Insurrection," Sade writes, "thought these sage legislators, is not at all a moral condition; however, it has got to be a republic's permanent condition."[26]

The potential for both control and insurrection, however, undergoes a quantum change when sexuality is deregulated and allowed to act as a stimulant for "perpetual unrest." In fact since the revolutionary regime is based on the subversion of morals it can only exist by exploiting sexuality in this fashion. What it proposes to the unruly mob as freedom, however, is really only a form of political control. The Marquis de Sade makes this perfectly clear: "Lycurgus and Solon, fully convinced that immodesty's results are to keep the citizen in the *immoral* [again, his emphasis] state indispensable to the mechanics of republican government, obliged girls to exhibit themselves naked at the theater."[27]

Sade's politics, like Weishaupt's, is the classical tradition turned upside down. The key insight of both the Marquis de Sade and the Christian West is that the moral man is in a state of peace; because he is not in motion, he is, therefore, impossible to direct and control from the outside. The revolutionary's very restlessness, his very rebellion against the moral order, which is the source of his restlessness, holds within it the seeds of control because once in motion the state need only manipulate the revolutionary's desires by controlling his passions, and it succeeds in manipulating and thereby controlling him. Sade is not slow in drawing this very conclusion.

Lust, in other words, is the force which keeps the citizenry of the repub-

lic from succumbing to the inertia of tranquillity which is the fruit of adherence to the moral order. At this point we enter into something like a circular
argument. Both political systems are self-contained. Morals lead to order;
passions lead to revolution. From the revolutionary point of view, lust is
good because it fosters the restlessness of republicanism, but republicanism
is also good because it fosters lust. Either way what we have here is the rationalization of desire as an instrument of simultaneous "liberation" and control; what was hitherto deemed pathological is now to be seen as the social
norm:

> We are persuaded that lust, being a product of those penchants, is not to be
> stifled or legislated against, but that it is, rather, a matter of arranging for
> the means whereby passion may be satisfied in peace. We must hence un-
> dertake to introduce order into this sphere of affairs, and to establish all
> the security necessary so that, when need sends the citizen near the objects
> of lust, he can give himself over to doing with them all that his passions
> demand, without ever being hampered by anything, for there is no mo-
> ment in the life of man when liberty in its whole amplitude is so important
> to him.[28]

We have here in a nutshell the rationale for the pornographic entertain-
ment consumerist culture which would become the dominant culture in the
world by the end of the second millennium. The project at its heart concerns
arrangements whereby passion may be satisfied in peace but with someone
making a profit from its gratification. "Liberty," according to this line of
thought, is not the ability to act according to reason, but rather the ability to
gratify illicit passion, which means that in the very act of attaining his "liberty" man becomes the thrall of the passion he gratifies. Before long, it becomes clear that Sade's politics is in many ways just the physics he says it is.
Man at the beck of passion is in many ways like a particle with no will of its
own, since reason, especially morals, is the sole source of man's ability to
govern himself. Once gratification of passion becomes the definition of "liberty," then "liberty" becomes synonymous with bondage because he who
controls the passion controls the man. Liberty, as defined by Sade, becomes a
prelude to the most insidious form of control known by man precisely because it is based on the stealthy manipulation of his passions. This was the
genius of Enlightenment politics, which is in reality nothing more than a
physics of vice: Incite the passion; control the man. This is the esoteric doctrine of the Enlightenment, one that has been refined for over 200 years
through a trajectory that involves everything from psychoanalysis to advertising to pornography and the role it plays in *Kulturkampf*. Sade clearly understands that sexual liberation leads to social control and sees this liberation
and subsequent control of passion as the basis of the permanent revolution
that life in France would become once Frenchmen "Would Become Republicans."

"No passion has a greater need of the widest horizon of liberty than sexual license," Sade writes:

> here it is that man likes to command, to be obeyed, to surround himself with slaves to satisfy him; well, whenever you withhold from man the secret means whereby he exhales the dose of despotism Nature instilled in the depths of his heart, he will seek other outlets for it, it will be vented upon nearby objects; it will trouble the government. If you would avoid that danger, permit a free flight and rein to those tyrannical desires which, despite himself, torment man ceaselessly: content with having been able to exercise his small dominion in the middle of the harem of sultanas and youths whose submission your good offices and his money procure for him, he will go away appeased and with nothing but fond feelings for a government which so obligingly affords him every means of satisfying his concupiscence.[29]

We see in Sade's articulation of principles the system by which the regime can placate sexual interest groups and thereby maintain its hold on power. There are a number of ironies here – some obvious, some not. One irony is obvious: Once man is freed from the moral order, he is immediately subjected to the despotism of those who know how to manipulate his desires. This is the essence of the Enlightenment regime; not to prohibit, but to enable, to encourage motion or restlessness, and direct the flow of that activity by manipulating desire. This is the political genius behind a regime that is based on advertising and pornography and opinion polls and the other instruments which control "liberated" man.

"People cry out against the *philosophes*," wrote Bernard Berelson, who ran John D. Rockefeller III's Population Council, citing Voltaire; "they are justified in doing so, for if opinion is the Queen of the World, the *philosophes* govern this queen."[30] Berelson was no stranger to the manipulation of sexual desire or public opinion; he ran the opinion polls on contraception during the early '60s that eventually led to the decriminalization of contraception in *Griswold v. Connecticut*. But throughout his career he never forgot his debt to the Enlightenment as his intellectual forebear in the manipulation of opinion and desire. "Opinion, Queen of the World," he writes citing Rousseau, "is not subject to the power of kings; they are themselves its first slaves."[31]

The only problem with this system is that it doesn't really work. Passion seems forever determined to break the system which aspires to nothing more than its orderly gratification. So high school students raised on a diet of sexual laissez faire gun down their fellow students and none of the pundits can fathom why they aren't content to live a life as sexual consumers. Horror, whether in art or in life, is a sign that the Enlightenment isn't working out according to plan. The monster invariably signals the widespread implementation of Enlightenment ideals. Each Enlightenment revolution has its own monster.[32]

Sexual liberation leads to anarchy, chaos, and horror, and chaos invariably leads to forms of social control. The regime which promotes attempts to tame the sexual passion in much the same way it controlled steam, electricity, and the atom can never be sure that the passions they "liberate" won't return to destroy them. Instead of peace based on the tranquillity of order, the revolutionary regime offers "liberation" from the moral order followed by chaos and totalitarian control. We find, then, in Sade a perverse corroboration of the trajectory of horror adumbrated in the epistle of James. Passion leads to sin, and sin, when it reaches its fullness, gives birth to death. The trajectory of horror remains the same in both the classical and Enlightenment traditions. Sade's only dispute with St. James is the values he places on the milestones of the same trajectory. Both admit that sexual passion released from the moral order leads to murder, terror, and death; Sade, however, remains firm in viewing these phenomena through the lens of sexual desire, which is so imperious and all-encompassing that it fails to see them as evil. Vice, it turns out, and not self-interest, is the gravitational force which both moves men and allows the revolutionaries to manipulate them to their own ends. This is the great discovery of the Enlightenment. Those in the grip of sexual passion, as Sade testifies, know how powerful it is. It was the genius of the Enlightenment to make that passion an instrument of political control, and that discovery was so ingenious because vice as a form of control is virtually invisible. Those who in the thrall of their passions see only what they desire and not the bondage those desires inflict on them. Sexual liberation is, as a result, the ideal form of control because it is virtually invisible. The genius here was not Sade's but rather that of Adam Weishaupt, founder of the Illuminati, and prototype for Victor Frankenstein. Weishaupt's genius consists in his use of vice as a vehicle of both subversion and social control. Sade's genius was to bring out the political implications and applications of the personal controls Weishaupt forged.

Three months after her almost fatal immersion in the Thames, on January 8, 1796, Mary Wollstonecraft, now reconciled to life in general and life without Imlay in particular, attended a tea party given by her new friend Mary Hays. Also in attendance was William Godwin, now at the height of his fame as the author of *Political Justice* and a suspense novel titled *Things as They are: or, the Adventures of Caleb Williams*. Both Wollstonecraft and Godwin had attended a dinner party together almost five years earlier, but then the circumstances had been reversed. Then Wollstonecraft was famous and Godwin was obscure. Chastened by five years of pain, Wollstonecraft did not attempt to monopolize the conversation this time. Perhaps her adversity had enhanced her stature in Godwin's eyes; perhaps his newfound fame did something similar to her. Whatever the reason, they began to see more of each other. Wollstonecraft then moved into Somers Town to be near Godwin. Then, on April 14, 1796, she showed up unannounced at Godwin's lodgings on Chalton Street. Thereafter they saw each other daily, and by mid-August their intercourse was as sexual as it was intellectual. Godwin relied at the time on what he called the "chance medley" system of birth control, which was about as effective as his schemes for social betterment, which meant that Wollstonecraft was soon pregnant. As a result, the couple was faced with a dilemma. Should they adhere to their philosophy of sexual Enlightenment and reject the matrimonial bond which Godwin characterized as "the most odious of all monopolies"? Or should they bend the knee to social convention?

In the end, social convention won out and the couple were wed on March 29, 1797, at St. Pancras Church safely before the pregnancy came to term, but not without admitting to friends that they had failed to practice what they preached. It was an admission that would have far-reaching consequences for the next generation. For herself, Mary Wollstonecraft was behaving now less like the angry feminist and more like the docile wife. "I am never so well pleased with myself," she told him, "as when I please you."[33]

On August 25, 1797, Wollstonecraft went into labor, delivering a baby girl, which they named Mary, on August 30. The Godwins brought in a midwife to assist at the birth partly because of Mary's modesty and partly because they felt that nature would run its course without much interference. When Mary's uterus, however, refused to discharge the placenta, Godwin called in an obstetrician, who removed it piece by piece. Or so he claimed. Mary, however, began running a fever, indicating that either the placenta had not been removed completely or that she had contracted postpeural fever during the doctor's ministrations. Godwin, thinking that everything was progressing as it should, went about the normal round of his business, but Mary took a turn for the worse and died on September 10.

Godwin was so distraught that he couldn't attend the funeral on September 15. However, after a few weeks he was hard at work again, this time writing a memoir about his late wife. Mary Wollstonecraft's reputation might have survived the change in intellectual climate that occurred when England turned against the French Revolution and the spirit of '93 that had made *Political Justice* a best seller at the time, but Godwin's memoir insured that this would not happen. Godwin's memoir described the gynecological details of the birth and her subsequent death with a specificity which the age found shocking. In addition to that, Godwin described her affair with Imlay and her subsequent affair with Godwin in terms that were guaranteed to alienate a reading public that was already disposed to blame Godwin and Wollstonecraft for the corruption of English morals. Godwin's statement in the *Memoirs* that "not one word of a religious cast fell from her lips" as she lay dying seems calculated to outrage the sensibilities of the English, and it succeeded in doing just that. *The Anti-Jacobin Review* did an article of the Memoir summarizing everything that was wrong with it and with Godwin's views on sexual relations from the fact that it "inculcates the promiscuous intercourse of the sexes" to the fact that his late wife betook "herself to our enemies" where, according to her amorous constitution, she documented her adventures as a kept mistress.

The Anti-Jacobin Review, founded in July 1798 with the help of a secret government subsidy, announced its aim to expose and destroy the Jacobin conspiracy which it saw at work in the country. Over the course of the next few years, the Anti-Jacobin Review would pretty much succeed at what it set out to do. The cause of revolution was defeated in the war of ideas in England, and with it the idea of sexual revolution went down to defeat as well. Godwin no longer shone like the sun in the literary firmament; in fact, he had become a hated man. His name had become associated with the term "philosophy," which in the common mind was never mentioned without a sneer of contempt and had become synonymous with his name and that of Mary Wollstonecraft as well as atheism, treason, economic redistribution, and sexual immorality. Godwin's *Memoirs*, appearing as it did when the excesses of the Terror were common knowledge, created a reaction that swept the notion of sexual liberation from public discourse, and the names Godwin and Wollstonecraft were linked indissolubly now in the public mind with the theories of revolution that were causing so much carnage and misery in France. The rationalization of sexual vice was just one aspect of the general upheaval in France. In the English mind, it died with the Revolution in France on the same bloody scaffold that had confirmed that passions unfettered by reason inevitably led to death.

Part I, Chapter 5

London, 1797

On May 1, 1797, a little over a month after Mary Wollstonecraft married William Godwin and roughly three months before she died, Edmund Burke, the man who was the occasion of her rise to literary fame, wrote a letter to Abbé Augustin Barruel, a French émigré and priest, upon the publication of the first volume of his *Memoirs Illustrating the History of Jacobinism*. In terms of its breadth and scope, Barruel's *History of Jacobinism* was the book Mary probably hoped she would write; in terms of its politics, it was its antithesis. If there were ever a rout in the battle for the public mind, Barruel's *History of Jacobinism* accomplished it in the utter defeat of revolutionary sympathies in England. Less than ten years after Rev. Price's sermon at Old Jewry, the English radicals were driven from the field in ignominious defeat, and the name of Godwin, their leader, became synonymous with both personal vice and political discord, especially after he wrote the memoir of his deceased wife.

"I have known myself, personally," Burke wrote to Barruel, shortly before he died, "five of your principal conspirators, and I can undertake to say from my own certain knowledge , that so far back as the year 1773, they were busy in the plot you have so well described, and in the manner and on the principle you have so truly represented. To this I can speak as a witness."[1]

The acclaim which followed the publication of Barruel's *History* was almost as passionate as the vehement denunciation which greeted Godwin's Wollstonecraft memoir. Born in 1741, Barruel entered the Society of Jesus in 1756 and was employed as a teacher in Vienna at the court of the Emperor when he received word in 1773 that the Jesuit order had been suppressed. After spending time as a teacher abroad, Barruel returned to France and immediately became embroiled in the *Kulturkampf* that would eventuate in the French Revolution. When Louis XVI ascended to the throne, Barruel wrote an ode in his honor which sold 12,000 copies and endeared his name to Royalist circles as much as it earned him the enmity of the *philosophes*. In 1781, their enmity deepened with the publication of Barruel's book *Les Helviennes*, his attack on Enlightenment thought. Barruel then turned on the clergy who thought some accommodation with the Enlightenment was possible, publishing *La Genese selon M. Soulavie*, which got Abbé Soulavie fired from his teaching post at the Sorbonne, and subsequently led to a lawsuit, which must have been successful since all extant copies of the book were destroyed. During the same period, Barruel became editor of the *Journal écclesiastique*, a post from which he continued his attack on the revolution. By August of 1792, actions had become louder than words. On August 10, Barruel suspended publication of the journal and escaped into hiding in Paris when the September massacres broke out. From there he went to Normandy, whence the Vendee revolt would issue less than a year later, and from there he escaped to England in mid-September 1792.

The parallels with Mary Wollstonecraft's life are striking. Both emigrated in 1792. Wollstonecraft left England and went to Paris to write a book about the revolution which is now pretty much unread by anyone but scholars interested in the psychic details of Wollstonecraft's life. Barruel escaped with his life from the very revolution Wollstonecraft sought to embrace and, emigrating to England, where he was granted patronage by the Clifford family, one of England's most eminent recusant lines, Barruel wrote a book that was to become the classic counter-revolutionary text for the next two hundred years.

In a left-handed tribute to Barruel's book and its subsequent influence, Daniel Pipes dedicates an entire chapter to Barruel in his 1997 book *Conspiracy*, and in an act as audacious as it is dishonest tries to make Barruel responsible for both the Holocaust and the Gulag, failing to mention that the Soviet regime was the logical and historical extension of principles taken from the French Revolution, against which Barruel fought.

Pipes's attempt to link Barruel with the Nazi regime is even more fraught with dishonesty. While admitting at one point that the word *Jew* never appears in the almost 2,000 pages that comprise Barruel's *History of Jacobinism*, Pipes nevertheless accuses Barruel of anti-Semitism based on the alleged fact that he received a letter from an Italian by the name of Simonini who alleged that the Jews were behind the conspiracy which brought about the revolution in France. Pipes claims that Barruel "accepted and endorsed"[2] the notion that the Jews were behind the revolution; he then claims that it became public knowledge, although there is no evidence to support that claim. Pipes cites an obscure French journal as his source, when he got the idea from Nesta Webster's book *World Revolution*, which mentions the Simonini letter, but also claims that Barruel never accepted it. That is not hard to understand, since accepting that thesis would have meant the repudiation of the one he proposed in the *History of Jacobinism*, which attributed the revolution to philosophes, freemasons, and the Illuminati.

Barruel's history earned the ire of the heirs of the Enlightenment because it cut through the pseudo-Newtonian mumbo-jumbo which tried to describe human activity in terms of atoms bumping into each other, and resituated the locus of human responsibility in the human will, where Augustine, his namesake, had placed it 1500 years before. Revolutions were caused by human passions, which, when they got out of control, spread havoc through a culture. "It is undeniable," Barruel wrote

> that virtue ought to be more particularly the principle of democracies than of any other form of government, they being the most turbulent and the most vicious of all, in which virtue is absolutely necessary to control the passions of men, to quell that spirit of cabal, anarchy, and faction inherent to the democratic form, and to chain down that ambition and rage of dominion over the people, which the weakness of the laws can scarcely withstand.[3]

Since the soul, according to the classical tradition, is the microcosm of the state, the French Revolution was the logical consequence of releasing passion on a nation-wide scale:

> The French revolution is in its nature similar to our passions and vices: it is generally known, that misfortunes are the natural consequences of indulging them; and one would willingly avoid such consequences: but a faint-hearted resistance is made; our passions and our vices soon triumph, and man is hurried away by them.[4]

Godwin's rout in the battle of ideas came about primarily because the traditional psychology Barruel espoused as the best explication of political events in France seemed to be born out as true when placed up against the still-unrolling chain of events. Godwin's ideas, like calling Robespierre an "eminent benefactor of mankind," seemed to burst anytime they made contact with events.

The only thing that saved Godwin from total obscurity was the fact that people kept his name in print by attacking him. One of the more significant attacks came in June 1798 when Joseph Johnson published an anonymous book entitled *An Essay on the Principle of Population as it affects the Future Improvement of Society, with remarks on the speculations of Mr. Godwin, M. Condorcet and other writers.* The author was a shy young Anglican pastor with a hare-lip, ten years Godwin's junior, by the name of Thomas Malthus. Malthus took exception to Godwin's idea of human perfectibility, and proposed as a counterexample the idea that man's procreation would always outstrip the available food supply. This was so because food increased in arithmetical progression, whereas human beings procreated in ratios which increased geometrically. Malthus had come by his philosophical credentials by something akin to birth right, in a family which revered philosophical discourse and had as guests in their home David Hume and Jean-Jacques Rousseau. The story of Malthus's intellectual development, however, was the opposite of Godwin. Godwin was raised in a Calvinist home for a career in the ministry, which he threw over after coming in contact with the Enlightenment. Malthus was exposed to Enlightenment thought in the home and became, perhaps as a result, a minister in the Anglican church.

Malthus based his argument against Godwin's notion of moral perfectibility on two axioms: (1) that food is necessary to the existence of man and (2) "that the passion between the sexes is necessary and will remain nearly in its present state." Given these two facts, the only thing that will limit population to the available food supply is war, famine, and disease. Godwin, who subsequently met Malthus at a dinner party given by Johnson on August 14, 1798, suggested that if property were distributed more equitably, that everyone would have enough to live on. Like the earlier dispute between Burke and Wollstonecraft, the Godwin/Malthus dispute set the terms for what one would come to call left and right (in English-speaking lands, at least) for the next two hundred years. The liberal view was that human nature and therefore all human institutions, were completely malleable and therefore perfectible. The conservative view was that man was what he was as the result of immutable "iron" laws of nature, which could not be changed. Hence, according to the latter view, the less man did in terms of tinkering the better off he would be. According to the former view, the notion that man could be whatever he wanted to be – the idea of perfectibility, even to the point of conquering death – almost naturally led to revolution because the only explanation for evil lay in the arbitrary restrictions which the powerful imposed on society for their own benefit. In many ways, the debate was a resurrection in disguised form of the earlier theological debate on original sin. Godwin represented an extreme form of the Pelagian position, according to which nature was sufficient without grace; whereas Malthus represented, in spite of his position as an Anglican minister, the Calvinist position that any effort to ameliorate man's condition was pointless because of man's innate depravity.

Time would show that the crucial issue was "passion between the sexes." Malthus argued from numbers and claimed that sexual activity remained on that level a constant that would eventuate in births in a way that would invariably outstrip food supply. Godwin argued that late marriage and moral restraint would limit family size. Godwin, however, was prevented from making this argument effectively by the evidence from his own life and writings, which seemed to urge promiscuity, divorce, abortion, and anything but moral restraint. The more the two men pursued the argument, the more the argument got cast in terms that would never admit a solution. Malthus, like Burke before him, allowed the terms of the conservative argument to degenerate into the defense of a completely static status quo and an equally vehement defense of economic privilege if not ruthless exploitation of the weak. Godwin, for his part, proposed defenses that were ever more utopian, and the argument has pretty much run in the same ruts ever since.

By 1801 Malthus's theory had already been widely adopted. Two years of poor harvests had led to widespread distress. Prices were up 300 percent from their 1793 level, and although wages had also risen, there had been a drastic fall in the income of the poor. Relieving starvation by public expenditure, many taxpayers now believed, would make the situation worse, and the only answer was to reduce demand even further. In 1800 a law was passed to forbid bakers from selling bread for twenty-four hours after baking – it being well known that since new bread tasted better, the poor ate more if it.

What neither side could anticipate then is how attractive artificial contraception would appear to both sides in the dispute. As of the time of Malthus's book, contraception was technologically unfeasible and morally repugnant, but with the passage of time and the subsequent and simultaneous advance in technology and the erosion of morals, it would soon reassert its utility as a technological solution which allowed both sides to have their cake and eat it too. Birth control allowed the Malthusians to concentrate on fertility reduction to the detriment of higher wages and better working conditions, but it also allowed the Left to indulge its sexual passions and its utopian schemes for social engineering. The rapprochement which contraception enabled would have to wait for a hundred years, but eventually it would be symbolized by the collaboration of Margaret Sanger and John D. Rockefeller Jr. The two poles of the debate – liberation and control, as in sexual liberation and population control – would remain antinomies, but in a way in which the one invariably begat the other in a never ending cycle of more and more liberation eventuating in tighter and tighter social control. The one was always a function of the other, and the contraceptive was the key to both. In providing both liberation of the sexual sort for the Godwinians and control of the population sort for the Malthusians, it allowed the creation of a political system in which "liberation" from sexual restraint could be used as a form of control. The sexual act liberated from procreation was mobilized in ways congenial to those who wanted to make money off its exploitation. By convincing undesirable groups that they should limit their numbers rather than seek higher wages, these groups were deprived of demographic leverage, and political protest was defused by ever more besotting applications of sexual pleasure. All of that was far in the future, but all of it grew out of the dialectic of liberation and control which lay at the heart of the Godwin/Malthus debate.

Godwin at this point had other reasons to think about birth control and moral restraint. At the time of his debate with Malthus he became sexually involved with a certain Mrs. Clairmont, upon whom he was practicing once again the "chance-medley" system of birth control, which predictably led to a pregnancy, which eventuated in the birth in October of 1801 of one more half-sister, Jane or Claire or Clare, being added to the Godwin family ménage.

On March 6, 1801, seven months before the birth of Mary Godwin's half-sister Jane, the Marquis de Sade paid a visit to his publisher Nicholas Masse at his offices on the rue Helvétius. In 1797, the same year that

Barruel's *magnum opus* on the revolution had appeared in London, the Marquis de Sade produced a *magnum opus* of a different sort in Paris. Entitled *La Nouvelle Justine ou les Malheurs de la vertu, suivie de l'Histoire de Juliette sa soeur*, Sade's latest foray into pornography dwarfed anything he had had published up till that time. Its ten volumes of pornographic excess were illustrated with numerous obscene engravings earning it the dubious encomium of being "the most ambitious pornographic enterprise ever assembled."[5] If Sade hoped to get rich from the book, he was once again disappointed. Three years after its publication, Sade was living from hand to mouth in the back room of a farmer's cottage with no residence of his own and not even a set of clothes to wear. Sade was in fact so down and out that the world took him for dead. On August 29, 1799, he read his obituary in the *L'Ami des Lois*, which shed few tears over his reputed passing away, referring to him as an "infamous writer" whose "mere name . . . breathes a cadaverous stench that kills virtue and inspires horror." "Not even the most depraved heart," the report continued, "the most bizarrely obscene imagination could conceive anything so offensive to reason, decency or humanity."[6]

A year and a half after the report appeared, Sade was at Masse, his publisher, hoping for some of the royalties from his latest, most ambitious pornographic work when the police arrived and took him into custody. Masse cut a deal with the police by revealing the location of the warehouse where the copies of *Juliette* were stored and was released within twenty-four hours. Sade was taken to a jail known as the "Mousetrap" and left to stew in his own (and other people's) juices in a holding cell fifteen feet underground. Sade had been drawn into a trap by Masse and the police, who, according to Lever, suspected Sade as the author of *Zoloe*, a satire on Napoleon. Two years after his arrest, after bouncing from one dungeon to another, Sade finally ended up at Charenton, the famous asylum for the insane. It was there, under the direction of the defrocked priest François Simonet de Coulmier, who revitalized the hospital and made it, for a time, the social hub for Paris high society, that Sade finally made a name for himself in the theater as the asylum's new "artistic director." Coulmier not only arranged the performances, he actually joined with the Marquis de Sade and the inmates in performing them. Considering the fact that Sade nearly perished from hunger and exposure during the winter of 1800–1801, things could have been worse, especially since Sade's mistress Constance Quesnet was allowed to move in with him in August of 1804, and occupy the room next to his, where she passed as his illegitimate daughter.

There was of course constant tension with the civil authorities who were authorized to search his room periodically and confiscate any obscene material they found. These same authorities also insisted that Sade be confined to the grounds of the asylum, but Coulmier was lax in the enforcement of this rule, allowing Sade to attend Mass at the parish church of Sainte-Maurice on Easter Sunday 1805, where France's apostle for atheism delivered the communion bread and took up the collection.

Sade did not write the plays which were performed at Charenton, as Peter Weiss would have it in his '60s musical *Marat/Sade*, but he did perform in them, and his presence as director of the theater, although not advertised, was undoubtedly one of the attractions that brought high society from Paris to watch. The performances were also not, as in *Marat/Sade*, performed behind bars, nor did the asylum inmates play the leading roles, which were given to professional actors and actresses from the Parisian stage. One such actress, a Mlle. Flore, described Sade as "a kind of curiosity, like one of those monstrous creatures they display in cages," giving some indication that Sade himself, as much as the therapeutic effects of drama on lunatics, was one of the main draws at Charenton. Sade, at this point in his life retained the obesity he had acquired while a prisoner in the Bastille. His face, according to Flore, "was the emblem of his mind and character," which is another way of saying that it was not handsome. Auguste Delaboueisse-Rochefort, who saw him perform the leading role in *L'Impertinent* by Desmahis, described him as "very big, very fat, very cold, very heavy, a large mass, a vulgar, short man whose head seemed a shameful ruin."[7] Mlle. Flore describes Sade as "the author of several books that cannot be named and whose titles alone are an insult to taste and morality, which is supposed to make you think I haven't read them."[8]

There is a disturbing side, of course, to Mlle. Flore's account. In addition to giving us information on Sade's appearance, she also gives some indication that his influence was spreading through the clandestine circulation of his writings. This influence would continue well into the twentieth century. Sade was the hero of Guillaume Apollinaire and the surrealists of the 1920s, who adopted his sexual practices, particularly sodomy, in his honor. But the evidence indicates that Sade's writings had already, during his lifetime, attracted people who wanted to act out his fantasies. On June 5, 1807, Police Inspector Dubois searched Sade's cell looking for obscene material and discovered "many papers and instruments of the most disgusting libertinage."[9] Evidently the Marquis de Sade still practiced the masturbatory practices he had acquired during his incarceration at the Bastille. After learning that Constance Quesnet was his mistress, Dubois searched her room as well discovering a work entitled *Les Entretiens du chateau de Florbelle*, a work Dubois described as "disgusting to read. It seems that de Sade aimed to surpass the horrors of *Justine* and *Juliette*."[10]

Even more unsettling, however, was the part of Dubois's report that mentioned the letters Sade had been receiving:

    there are several written by a single hand that prove he has disciples as horrifying as their master. The writer describes scenes of libertinage that have recently occurred and boasts of having administered potions that produced an appearance of death lasting several hours in women who were then used in every possible manner, tortured, and forced to drink three enormous bottles of blood. I hope to discover the author of these letters and of these crimes. I have reason to believe that he will not elude the searches I have ordered.[11]

No one knows whether this devotee of Sade was brought to justice. What is known, however, is that the Marquis de Sade's writings became underground classics during the nineteenth century and read by figures as well known as Byron and Swinburne. Once released into the cultural bloodstream, these toxins would circulate with surprising rapidity, creating, as pornography normally does, a sense of possibility where none existed before.

But the immediate reaction at the time, in France as in England, was disgust. Esquirol, now head of the Salpetrière, denounced the theatrical performances at Charenton as "a lie," with no therapeutic benefits. "The lunatics who attended these performances," he continued, "attracted the attention and curiosity of a frivolous, unserious and sometimes mean public. The bizarre attitudes and bearing of these unfortunate individuals drew mocking laughter and insulting pity from the audience. What more did it take to wound the pride and sensitivities of these poor souls, or to disconcert the intelligence and reason of those few who retained the ability to be attentive?"[12]

By January of 1812, when this letter was added to the bulging dossier on Charenton at the ministry of health, Napoleon was on his way to defeat at the hands of the Russians, whose Cossacks would soon be raping and pillaging on French soil. With the defeat of Napoleon, the man who embodied the revolutionary ideals in their terminal phase, the conservative powers in Europe, with England and Austria at their head, brought the age of revolution to a close – for the time being at least. And with the end of revolution came the end of sexual revolution as well – again, for the time being. On May 6, 1813, the ministry of health ordered the suspension of the balls and concerts that were given in Charenton hospital.

On April 14, 1814, Napoleon abdicated at the palace at Fountainebleau, and on May 3 the Bourbon monarchy was restored when King Louis XVIII made his triumphal return to Paris, the city where his grandfather had been executed twenty-one years before. Louis XVIII's government now had no need any longer of a director of Charenton who was both a defrocked priest and a former revolutionary. Nor did they have any need of his dubious experiments in psychodrama. The revolution had provided enough psychodrama to last a lifetime. So Coulmier was dismissed, and before the year had ended Sade was dead. In his will, the Divine Marquis had specified that he wanted no monument, and so he was buried, according to his wishes, in a copse of trees, which promptly obliterated his grave. His monument was his writings, and they, as we have already indicated, would survive the political restoration which saw the revolution and its sexual *sequelae* as a bad dream.

On August 7, 1814, four months before Sade died, Pope Pius VII issued a bull entitled *Sollicitudo Omnium Ecclesiarum*, which restored the Society of Jesus as a religious order in the Catholic Church. On October 18, 1815, Abbé Barruel was readmitted to the Jesuits. Like the works of the Marquis de Sade, Barruel's *Memoirs Illustrating the History of Jacobinism* would go on to have enormous posthumous influence, although of a different kind. Barruel, unlike what his detractors had to say, became convinced that the influence of the Prussian philosopher Immanuel Kant was every bit as pernicious as his more bloodthirsty colleagues in France and dedicated the last five years of his life to writing a book on Kant, a manuscript which he inexplicably burned before it could be published. Barruel died on October 20, 1820, secure in the knowledge that the Jesuits had been restored and the revolution was over. The sexual revolution was over as well, but there would still be one final spectacular act that would gather all of its disparate threads in one hand before it expired of its own wretched excess. Barruel, the implacable foe of revolution, would have been both surprised and disconcerted to know that his *magnum opus* was one of those threads.

Part I, Chapter 6

London, 1812

On January 1, 1812, William Godwin received a letter from a young aristo-crat by the name of Percy Bysshe Shelley. Shelley had been expelled from Cambridge for writing an anonymous pamphlet on atheism, and now he was interested in making an inquiry as to why the French Revolution had failed. Shelley had read *Political Justice* and wanted to discuss it with Godwin. "It is now a period of more than two years since first I saw your inestimable book on *Political Justice*," Shelley wrote, "it opened to my mind fresh and more extensive views; it materially influenced my character, and I rose from its perusal a wiser and better man . . . to you, as the regulator and former of my mind, I must ever look with real respect and veneration."[1]

Godwin was by now all but forgotten. The only time his name was men-tioned was by way of denouncing one or the other deleterious effects of Jaco-binism on the character of England, which was now ready for the final showdown with the Jacobin empire and its emperor Napoleon. Godwin as a result was in permanent financial straits, and so we can imagine him upon re-ception of this letter not only flattered by the attention of the younger genera-tion but also pleased by the prospect of some financial patronage.

Shelley, for his part, had established a sexual trajectory at this point that was similar to that of his master. Reading Godwin as an impressionable teen-ager, Shelley denounced the institution of marriage in a letter to one of his fe-male admirers as "an evil of immense and extensive magnitude."[2] As a teenager Shelley was, however, as libidinous as he was impressionable, and after falling under the spell of the sixteen-year-old friend of his sisters, Har-riet Westbrook, who refused to comply with his free love schemes, Shelley decided, like his mentor Godwin, to chuck principle in favor of sexual grati-fication and get married anyway.

When Shelley finally arrived at Godwin's door, it was as if the Spirit of '93 were made incarnate in the body of this frail and young and even younger looking aristocrat. During the mid-1790s what happened in France seemed a prelude to what was going to happen in England. Following on the heels of the Terror in France, on October 29, 1795, the king's carriage was attacked by a mob at the opening of Parliament resulting in the fatal injury of one of his footmen. The result was a sense of alarm, a sense that the revolution was made to be exported to England as well as throughout Europe, and the deter-mination of the government to suppress sedition of both deed and thought.

Philosophy, so recently resurrected for the English reading public by William Godwin, Mary's father, had now become a term of opprobrium, similar to the way the term *philosophe* was used by Barruel. "Philosophy," as one biographer put it, "meant William Godwin and Mary Wollstonecraft, atheism, treason, economic redistribution, and sexual immorality."[3]

Shelley had read all of the classical revolutionary documents emanating from France. As such he was familiar with the role electricity, especially as introduced by America's ambassador to France, Benjamin Franklin, played in revolutionary politics. It was to take on a new meaning in his wife-to-be's account of Shelley as the monster-begetting Victor Frankenstein. Shelley, like Frankenstein, was a "modern Prometheus" who would free the slaves via scientifically based revolution. As with his poem "Ode to the West Wind," Shelley incorporated the magical *élan vital* into his body as a way of transforming himself into something godlike, superhuman, preternatural, as recounted by his Oxford chum Thomas Jefferson Hogg:

> He then proceeded, with much eagerness and enthusiasm, to show me the various instruments, especially the electrical apparatus; turning round the handle very rapidly, so that the fierce, crackling sparks flew forth; and presently standing upon the stool with glass feet, he begged me to work the machine until he was filled with the fluid, so that his long, wild locks bristled and stood on end. Afterwards he charged a powerful battery of several large jars; labouring with vast energy, and discoursing with increasing vehemence of the marvellous powers of electricity, of thunder and lightning; describing an electrical kite that he had made at home, and projecting another and an enormous one, or rather a combination of many kites, that would draw down from the sky an immense volume of electricity, the whole ammunition of a mighty thunderstorm; and this directed to some point would there produce the most stupendous results.[4]

Shelley's experiments have a touching sort of naiveté to them, a bit like a boy playing with his chemistry set on the way to inventing the cure for some dread disease. But there was a sinister side to what he was doing as well, a willingness to experiment on human beings, himself and his sisters, that bespoke an instrumental attitude toward human life that would reach its fulfillment in matters sexual. "Thou didst sport with life," the monster said to Victor Frankenstein, and as Mary Shelley well knew the charge applied to Shelley as well. Science, from Shelley's point of view, was a way of manipulating nature to get what you wanted from it. The crucial step taken by de la Mettrie and the Marquis de Sade was the transformation of man into a machine as a prelude to manipulating him as the scientist would manipulate inanimate nature. Because Christianity posited a certain sacredness to life, it was also seen as the major obstacle to the fulfillment of forbidden desire. Christianity, as a result, was construed as the enemy by Shelley and his circle. Science was an essential weapon in the arsenal he used to attack Christianity, the family, marriage, property and government. Shelley was not some innocent playing with a chemistry set. He was a magus with a revolutionary agenda. "Oh!" wrote the aspiring young chemist,

> I burn with impatience for the moment of Xtianity's dissolution, it has injured me; I swear on the altar of perjured love to revenge myself on the hated cause of the effect which *even now* I can scarcely help deploring. – Indeed I think it is to the benefit of society to destroy the opinions which *can* annihilate the dearest of its ties . . . – Let us hope that the wound which we inflict tho' the dagger be concealed, will rankle in the heart of our adversary.[5]

He ended his letter with the battle cry of the Enlightenment, "*Écrasez l'infâme; écrasez l'impie.*" The phrase "crush the infamy" comes from Voltaire, who used to end his letters with it, in the manner of Cato the Elder who used to end every speech with a reference to his foes across the Mediterranean: *Carthago delenda est.* But the reference to the concealed dagger was straight from Barruel's account of the Illuminati, which along with Electricity became another of Shelley's obsessions.

Electricity, in this regard, became more than a simple force that can "animate" machinery; it was the force that animated the universe, and since man was nothing more than a complicated machine, he who controlled electricity, controlled man. The revolutionary implications become immediately apparent, especially to one who had read Barruel's *History of Jacobinism,* as Shelley had. In fact, Shelly took Barruel in a perverse way as the Bible for the revolution he planned and forced its reading on all of his protégés, most notably the young Mary Godwin, who read it as part of the revolutionary education Shelley arranged for her. "With Voltaire," Barruel writes, "man is a pure machine."[6] Frederick the Great, Voltaire's protector and fellow *philosophe*, was of the same opinion, but, according to Barruel, took the whole notion a step further to its logical conclusion: "I am well convinced that I am not twofold," Frederick wrote in a direct attack on the idea that man was a body informed by a soul, "hence, I consider myself as a single being. I know that I am an animal organized, and that thinks; hence, I conclude that matter can think, as well as that it has the property of being electric."[7]

Shelley's revolutionary program was simply a series of extrapolations drawn from this rational psychology, which, since there was now no such thing as a soul, was in reality a sort of anthropophysics. Electricity was the force of nature that would break the chains of convention and liberate man. The more Shelley became convinced that he was in possession of the secrets of nature, the more violent became his hatred of "unnatural" conventions like the family, the state and religion, in particular, Christianity: "Yet here I swear, and as I break my oath may Infinite Eternity blast me, here I swear that never will I forgive Christianity! . . . Oh how I wish I *were* the Antichrist, that it were *mine* to crush the Demon, to hurl him to his native Hell never to rise again."[8]

Just as Electricity produced light, which dispelled by its very nature the darkness of superstition, so Electricity as the ultimate force in nature found its political expression in Illuminism, the conspiracy hatched by Adam Weishaupt, professor of law at the University of Ingolstadt, which had thrown the King of France down from his throne and aspired to do the same for every other priest and king throughout Europe.

Shelley finally showed up at the Godwins with his young wife Harriet, and the meeting was a success. By 1814, a complicating factor had arisen in the relationship. Shelley had fallen in love with Godwin's daughter by Mary Wollstonecraft, Mary Godwin. During one of their evening walks in Spa Fields, Shelley explained to Godwin that he had fallen in love with his daughter, who was then sixteen years old, the same age as his first wife when he married her, and that he intended to leave Harriet and live with Mary without the benefit of the sacrament of matrimony in Switzerland. In order to make the arrangement more attractive to the chronically impecunious Godwin, Shelley assured Godwin that the money from one of the many ruinous post-obit bonds Shelley floated would be arriving soon. This money would cover the cost of travel to Switzerland, and there would still be some left over for Godwin, who was once again hoist on his own philosophical petard. As was usually the case in sexual matters, Godwin was forced to choose between his philosophical principles and whatever was left of his innate moral sense as a decent human being and father. Godwin would, to his credit, not give his approval, but this didn't deter Shelley, who had been "educating" young Mary to her father's principles, whether her father believed them anymore or not. On June 26, 1814, Shelley accompanied Mary to her mother's tomb, where they read Wollstonecraft's letters, and where, after sending her sister Jane away, the seduction was consummated either on or near the tomb itself. Shortly thereafter, Mary agreed to elope, which they did, taking her half-sister Jane along as a translator.

Shelley had become Mary Godwin's lover, but he would remain as before her educator as well. During the course of the next few months, Mary would read all of the books which had corrupted Shelley, and among them and of singular importance was Barruel's *History of Jacobinism.* Shelley recommended the book, not because he agreed with the political views of the world's most famous anti-revolutionary Jesuit, but because the book gave the best account of the Illuminist conspiracy then extant, and as part of his political agenda, Shelley wanted to resurrect the Illuminati.

Whether Abbé Barruel described Weishaupt's role in the French Revolution accurately or not is beside the point. It is Barruel's account which became normative for Shelley and Mary Godwin as they pondered it on their honeymoon journey down the Rhine past Schloss Frankenstein. Victor Frankenstein, like Weishaupt, was associated with the University of Ingolstadt but studied medicine, not law, because medicine had a more direct connection with the principle of life Shelley sought to discover in electricity, and control through applied Illuminism, a system which, he confided to Leigh Hunt, "might establish *rational liberty* on as firm a basis as that which would have supported the visionary schemes of a completely-equalized community."[9]

Shelley made the connection between Illuminism and his revolutionary/scientific program explicitly in a letter to Leigh Hunt but suppressed any discussion of it with the older Godwin because it was simply too radical and shocking a proposal to broach. With Godwin, Shelley hinted at his devotion to the Gnostic/Manichean tradition of anti-Christianity more obliquely, using science as his cover, perhaps in deference to the fact that Godwin narrowly escaped being tried for sedition, and many of his friends did not escape at all. The initiate Illuminatus, according Barruel, was urged "*to study the doctrines of the ancient Gnostics and Manichaeans*, which may lead him to many important discoveries of this real Masonry."[10] He was also told that "the great enemies which ,he will have to encounter during this investigation will be ambition and other vices which make humanity *groan under the oppression of Princes and of the Priesthood*."[11] With this in the back of his mind, Shelley writes to Godwin that: "I was haunted with a passion for the wildest and most extravagant romances: ancient books of Chemistry and Magic were perused with an enthusiasm of wonder almost amounting to belief."[12]

Shelley lets the cat out of the bag just enough by linking chemistry and magic, enough to cause Godwin to recoil in horror, as if he understood the full implication of the system Shelley was proposing. Since both the Christian and the anti-Christian systems were internally consistent and mutually antagonistic, it is not surprising that Godwin would react with horror: "You talk of awakening them," he wrote, "they will rise up like Cadmus' seed of dragon's teeth, and their first act will be to destroy each other."[13]

Godwin was smart enough to realize that Shelley was taking Illuminism as his model even if he never mentioned it explicitly – to Godwin at least:

> Shelley secretly turned to the Masonic conception of revolutionary brotherhood as a viable form of reform organization. He was attracted especially by its occultism, its tight communal solidarity, and "seeding" of subversive political ideas. He never wrote of Illuminism to Godwin, who would have been appalled, but to Miss Hitchener in this same letter he recommended the authoritative book on the subject, by the Abbé Barruel, *Memoirs Illustrating the History of Jacobinism*, a translation in four volumes, 1797–98. "To you who know how to distinguish truth, I recommend it."[14]

What began with the discovery of electricity as the revolutionary *élan vital* and culminated in Illuminism as electric politics had as its middle term a series of connecting links which Shelley articulated in his philosophical poem *Queen Mab*, a poem with a long revolutionary pedigree. "Besides reaching American radicals, it is known that the poem was influential in liberal and revolutionary circles on the Continent, and the young Frederick Engels began a translation before the 1848 upheavals."[15] When Mary and her half sister Jane (soon to rename herself Claire) would take walks in the evening, Shelley – as part of his contribution to Mary's education, of course – would unfailingly join them, whereupon Jane would separate from the pair and allow them to pursue their conversations *à deux*. (which Mary characterized as too metaphysical for Jane's untutored mind). As part of his education of Mary, Shelley began plying her with his thoughts as expressed in *Queen Mab*, a compendium in verse of left-wing nostrums concerning everything from free love to vegetarianism. At this point in his life, Shelley was unsure whether he was being called (if that is the right term) to be a philosopher or a poet. After reading *Queen Mab*, Mary suggested poetry as his career path, perhaps because the philosophy was so derivative and derived chiefly from her father, as the poem's notes make clear.

Taking its name from Mercutio's famous speech in Shakespeare's *Romeo and Juliet*, *Queen Mab* is, in addition to being in the tradition of the philosophical poem in the mode of Lucretius' scientific treatises, the first tract on sexual liberation in the English language. Sexual liberation was incorporated into the rest of Shelley's political program, but for all that, it still occupied primacy of place in his Utopian scheme. At the heart of this scheme was Shelley's fervent, extremely fervent, hope that "all judgment cease to wage unnatural war/ With passion's unsubduable array."[16] Reason, in other words, was to become, as Shelley assured Hogg, compatible with "true passion." It was that simple, or so it seemed to Shelley in 1813.

The cause of contention and unhappiness is not the jar of unruly passion against restraining but secretly compliant reason, but rather what Shelley called "Xtianity," which attempts to suppress the passions which are the source of all happiness in the sublunary, which is to say, the only sphere. The villain in this drama is therefore, religion, "the priest's dogmatic roar!/ The weight of his exterminating curse."[17]

Queen Mab is the quintessential Enlightenment poem. All the poet has to do to achieve heaven on earth is defy priestly authority, keep his soul pure from "the polluting woe/ Of tyranny," which involves learning to "prefer/ Hell's freedom to the servitude of heaven."[18] Once the aspiring revolutionary gets that part right, Science will do the rest, which is to say, it will eliminate disease and strife, especially the strife between reason and passion, which is a creation of dogmatic priests anyway. "The consistent Newtonian is necessarily an atheist," Shelley tells us;[19] therefore, science will reconcile reason and passion by abolishing belief in God:

> All things are void of terror: man has lost
> His terrible prerogative, and stands

An equal amidst equals: happiness
And Science dawn though late upon the earth;
Peace cheers the mind, health renovates the frame;
Disease and pleasure cease to mingle here,
Reason and passion cease to combat there;
Whilst each unfettered o'er the earth extend
Their all-subduing energies, and wield
The sceptre of a vast dominion there;
Whilst every shape and mode of matter lends
Its force to the omnipotence of mind,
Which from its dark mine drags the gem of truth
To decorate its paradise of peace.
O happy Earth, reality of Heaven!

She left the moral world without a law,
No longer fettering passion's fearless wing.
Nor searing reason with the brand of God.
Then steadily the happy ferment worked;
Reason was free; and wild though passion went
Through tangled glens and wood-embosomed meads.
Gathering a garland of the strangest flowers,
Yet like the bee returning to her queen,
She bound the sweetest on her sister's brow,
Who meek and sober kissed the sportive child,
No longer trembling at the broken rod.[20]

In order to establish heaven on earth, all the revolutionary need do is, in the words of the song, "act naturally."

Then, that sweet bondage which is freedom's self,
And rivets with sensation's softest tie
The kindred sympathies of human souls,
Needed no fetters of tyrannic law:
Those delicate and timid impulses
In nature's primal modesty arose,
And with undoubting confidence disclosed
The growing longing of its dawning love,
Unchecked by dull and selfish chastity,
That virtue of the cheaply virtuous,
Who pride themselves in senselessness and frost.[21]

The chief safeguard against the dangers of "selfish chastity" is the idea that the world is a machine. He who understands this, Shelley explains in one of the poem's footnotes, is in no danger of seduction from the falsehoods of religious systems, of deifying the principle of the universe.

It is impossible to believe that the Spirit that pervades this infinite machine, begat a son upon the body of a Jewish woman; or is angered at the consequence of that necessity, which is a synonym of itself. All that miserable tale of the Devil, and Eve, and an Intercessor, with the childish mummeries of the God of the Jews, is irreconcilable with the knowledge of the stars. The works of his fingers have borne witness against him.[22]

Since the universe is a machine, and man a machine as well, and woman "a machine for voluptuousness," as the Marquis de Sade put it,[23] then marriage is simply the coupling of atoms in a molecule, and divorce nothing more than their uncoupling and recoupling in a more congenial configuration. The critical issue in the duration of any relationship will based on affection, which is another word for passion, which, given the Enlightenment penchant for rationalization, is surprisingly compatible with "reason":

How long then ought the sexual connection to last? what law ought to specify the extent of the grievance which should limit its duration? A husband and wife ought to continue so long united as they love each other: any law which should bind them to cohabitation for one moment after the decay of their affection, would be a most intolerable tyranny, and the most unworthy of toleration.[24]

Enlightenment morals become, therefore, a matter of calculation in just about every sense of the word. "The connection of the sexes," Shelley tells us, "is so long sacred as it contributes to the comfort of the parties, and is naturally dissolved when its evils are greater than its benefits."[25] Chastity is "a monkish and evangelical superstition, a greater foe to natural temperance even than unintellectual sensuality; it strikes at the root of all domestic happiness, and consigns more than half of the human race to misery, that some few may monopolize according to law. A system could not well have been devised more studiously hostile to human happiness than marriage."[26]

So, the only thing – from the revolutionary point of view, at least – which can bring about "the fit and natural arrangement of sexual connection" is "the abolition of marriage." In the meantime, if passions still prove unruly, Shelley suggests vegetarianism as a palliative. Prometheus, after all, "who represents the human race" was punished for cooking meat by having his entrails "devoured by the vulture of disease."[27] "All vice," Shelley tells us solemnly, including death, "arose from the ruin of healthful innocence,"[28] that came about with the eating of meat.

As anyone who has ever attended graduate school knows, sexual liberation is invariably associated with vegetarianism, especially among the weaker sex. Shelley was no exception to this rule, and in *Queen Mab* he ascribes benefits to the consumption of vegetables that are Godwinian in proportion. "Who will assert," Shelley asks rhetorically, giving what might be termed the vegetarian view of history, "that had the populace of Paris satisfied their hunger at the ever-furnished table of vegetable nature, they would have lent their brutal suffrage to the proscription-list of Robespierre?"[29] Of course, being committed to science, Shelley must admit that "the proselyte to a pure diet must be warned to expect a temporary diminution of muscular strength," but, nonetheless:

> Hopes are entertained that, in April 1814, a statement will be given, that sixty persons, all having lived more than three years on vegetables and pure water, are then *in perfect health*. More than two years have now elapsed; *not one of them has died*; no such example will be found in say sixty persons taken at random.[30]

Of course, all of those people, whether vegetarian or carnivore, all ended up dead, which must have been a blow to Shelley since Godwin was of the opinion that man was so perfectible that he could abolish death.

Mary Godwin and Shelley returned to England after their honeymoon of 1814, but they vowed to leave again, which is what they did in the Spring of 1816, traveling to Lake Geneva to be with Lord Byron. At what has become the most famous house party in English literary history, Byron and Shelley and Mary and Jane and Byron's physician Dr. Polidori, sat around the Villa Diodati, which Byron had rented for the season. Prevented from hiking and sailing by the foul weather, they told ghost stories instead. It was in the aftermath of one of these storytelling sessions that Mary Godwin conceived the idea for *Frankenstein*, which was her meditation on Shelley and Shelley's political project of resurrecting the Illuminati as described by Barruel in his *History of Jacobinism*. Shelley insisted that Mary read Barruel, which St. Clair claims they "read not only as a history of why things had gone wrong but in order to learn the mind of the enemy."[31] Even if we concede this as their intention, it is not clear that intention has hegemony over reality in psychic or literary matters. What matters is that in reading Barruel, Mary Godwin was confronted with the classical tradition of the West in both ethics and politics as it applied to the particulars of the Revolution in France, whose *sequelae* the young trio had just witnessed first-hand on their "honeymoon" in 1814. Given the power of this explication in light of concrete instances that exceeded what both Barruel had described in 1797 and Burke had predicted six years earlier, it is difficult to imagine this lesson having no effect – especially having no effect on Mary Godwin. Barruel was in this regard the antitype of Godwin. By taking human action out of the Enlightenment matrix of pseudo-physics and resituating it in its ethical terms, Barruel achieved the congruity between microcosm and macrocosm which the Godwinian system promised through Newtonian physics and then failed to deliver. In reading Barruel, Mary Godwin got the classical education in ethics and politics that her father had promised but never provided. In reading Barruel, Mary Godwin was confronted with the wisdom of the tradition her husband vowed to overthrow. The French Revolution, according to this reading, was, not random molecules of social interaction, but rather

> similar to our passions and vices: it is generally known, that misfortunes are the natural consequences of indulging them; and one would willingly

avoid such consequences: but a faint-hearted resistance is made; our passions and our vices soon triumph, and man is hurried away by them.[32]

In passages like this, we discern the moral wisdom of the West, which
means the horror tradition which Mary Godwin founded by writing Frankenstein read backwards, so to speak, from the point of view of the moral order
that got suppressed and then returned in disguise. The calamities described in
horror fictions are moral truths in repressed form. Horror is morality written
backwards; it is the moral order viewed through the wrong end of the tele-
scope. Both Mary Shelley's *Frankenstein* and Barruel's *History of Jacobinism* tell the same story, but they tell it in radically different ways. To say that
"the French revolution is in its nature similar to our passions and vices" was,
of course, the antithesis of both the Enlightenment and the Godwin-Woll-
stonecraft family tradition; but then again so was *Frankenstein*, because both
books describe how "misfortunes are the natural consequence of indulging"
the passions. Barruel's history does this directly; *Frankenstein*, like the rest
of the horror tradition, does it by indirection. Barruel's book is a warning;
Frankenstein is an expression of regret; it is full, not of repentance, but remorse. In this, it mirrored the mind of Mary Shelley, especially after the
events of the fall of 1816 had left their indelible mark on her psyche. Mary
Shelley could never repudiate her family's radicalism, nor could she admit
that her participation in that radicalism was wrong, but on the other hand she
also could not deny that people had died because of her actions. Guilt bound
her to Shelley, guilt over what she had done to Harriet Westbrook, but she
had no way of dealing with the guilt because she could not bring herself to repent, or avail herself of the vehicle of repentance, Christianity. Mary Shelley
couldn't go back to the old Godwinian radicalism; nor could she go forward
to the Christian/classical tradition via repentance. So instead of repentance,
she chose respectability as the antidote to the deadly radicalism proposed by
her family. In many ways, the Victorian age was made for her; in many ways,
she created the age by orchestrating Shelley's apotheosis into a Victorian angel from a higher sphere.

Barruel's significance in Mary's education at Shelley's hands lay in the
alternative it provided to Enlightenment philosophy. Barruel's *History of
Jacobinism* was not the only text that refuted the Enlightenment – the
Shelleys reread Shakespeare too – but it was the one which did it most specifically in light of classical morals and classical politics, which was a function
of those same morals. It also did it by using examples from the French Revolution, an event which Shelley wanted to resurrect in England according to
Illuminist principles by creating a network of terrorist Illuminist cells. At the
heart of his project was a revolutionary subversion of the moral order as the
prelude to a similar subversion of the political order. Shelley's *Queen Mab* is
a good example of Helvétius read forward, i.e., taken at face value. *Queen
Mab* articulates the hope that passion can be made compatible with reason:

"And judgment cease to wage unnatural war/ With passion's unsubduable array." With Barruel, Mary Godwin got to read Helvétius backwards, i.e., in light of the tradition he and Shelley hoped to destroy. "Helvétius," according to Barruel,

> will at one time tell us that the only rule by which *virtuous actions* are distinguished from *vicious ones*, is the laws of princes, and public utility. Elsewhere he will say, "that *virtue*, or *honesty*, with regard to individuals, is not more than that the *habit of actions be measured;*" In fine, "that if the virtuous man is not happy in this world, we are justified in exclaiming, *O Virtue! thou are but an idle dream.*"
>
> The same sophister also says, that "*sublime virtue and enlightened wisdom* are only the fruits of those passions *called folly*; or, that stupidity is the necessary consequence of the cessation of passion. That to moderate the passions is to ruin the state. That *conscience* and *remorse* are nothing but the *foresight* of those physical penalties to which crimes expose us. That the man who is above the last can commit, without remorse, the dishonest act that may serve his purpose." That it *little imports* whether *men are vicious*, if they be but enlightened.
>
> The fair sex too will be taught by this author, that "Modesty is only an *invention of refined voluptuousness*: – that *Morality* has nothing to apprehend from *love*, for it is the passion that *creates genius*, and *renders man virtuous*." He will inform children, that "the commandment of loving their father and mother is more the work of education than of nature." He will tell the married couple, that "the law which condemns them to live together becomes *barbarous and cruel* on the day they cease to love each other."[33]

The last sentence, no doubt, made Mary Godwin sit up and take notice. It was a fair description of what had become the Godwin family tradition of denigrating marriage – by the older generation in theory, and by the younger in practice. This was the "scientific" deconstruction of the moral tradition of the West proposed by the Enlightenment, which Barruel "read backwards," i.e., retranslated back into the language of classical ethics and politics. According to that reading, the French Revolution was the result of passion; in fact, it was a crucial stage in the trajectory of passion leading to death. Barruel saw the French Revolution as a calculated effort to unleash passion as the vehicle of subversion, but one that failed to reckon with just how destructive those forces could be when unleashed and attempts to rein them in proved impossible, as during the Terror, the logical outcome of revolutionary principles. Moral decadence led to the Enlightenment, which was the rationalization of passion. The Enlightenment led then to the Revolution, which was the projection of those principles onto the political sphere, and the Revolution in turn led to the Terror, which was the logical outcome of passions unbridled by reason leading to death. Barruel saw in the revolution, therefore, the entire trajectory of horror laid out step by step according to the tenets of Christian philosophy, in writings like the Epistle of James. Mary

Shelley probably did not see things that way; but by the time she was done writing *Frankenstein*, she didn't see things Shelley's way either. *Frankenstein* was her attempt to make sense out of the conflict between the Enlightenment view of a Utopian future and the moral order at the heart of the classical tradition of the West. The difference had to do with Newtonian as opposed to Aristotelian systems of motion, extrapolated to moral systems where stasis/tranquility was good according to the latter system and passion/motion good according to the former. Barruel spends his time both explaining the particulars of the conspiracy that led up to the French Revolution and at the same time explicating these events in the light of the classical tradition of both politics and ethics.

To begin with, the Jacobin conspirators worked to get the Jesuits suppressed so that they could take over education in France. "In many colleges the Jesuits being very ill replaced, the youth, neglected in their education, left a prey to their passions."[34] The same tactic was used to bring princes under the conspirator's control: "they relish them," said Barruel about why princes protected the conspirators, "because they flattered and unbridled their passions. This was the first step toward the revolution."[35]

Subsequent steps follow the same trajectory:

> The French revolution is in its nature similar to our passions and vices: it is generally known, that misfortunes are the natural consequences of indulging them; and one would willingly avoid such consequences: but a faint-hearted resistance is made; our passions and our vices soon triumph, and man is hurried away by them.[36]

Barruel was well aware of the Newtonian dimensions of the revolutionary universe he criticized, but he was careful to re-analyze the quasi-scientific transvaluation of values back into its classical components. Self-interest, according to the Enlightenment, was the human equivalent to gravity, the force which held everything in the universe together in dynamic motion. Just as the planets pursued their own way through the universe and thereby brought about a dynamic harmonious whole, so those who pursued their own self-interest in this life would find their oftentimes selfish actions reconciled to harmony by some "invisible hand" or other convenient fiction. That being granted, the immediate subsequent problem was to explain how things human would not degenerate into solipsism, selfishness, terror, and death, as Shakespeare had predicted in Ulysses' famous speech in *Troilus and Cressida*. Adam Smith claimed that an "invisible hand" would intervene and, as if automatically, turn individual actions of selfishness into a big picture of compatibility with the common good. Twenty years after Smith wrote those lines, France was giving some indication that individual passions might not turn out so benignly after all. If there was an invisible hand at work in France during the 1790s, its most significant characteristic was its invisibility. "It was only a constructive revolt which the *philosophes* had desired";

Lester Crocker writes, "but they were unable to halt the dynamics of revolu-tion, even as the men of '89 could not prevent the coming of '93."[37] The tra-jectory from Enlightenment to death had two salient characteristics: it was impossible to deny the consequences, and it was just as impossible (at least among those who deemed themselves progressive) to relinquish the illusion of "liberation" which led to those consequences. Mary Shelley's *Franken-stein* was born out of her inability to resolve that contradiction.

The potential of using vice as a form of control, as Barruel made clear, was part of human nature:

> Any fool may attract the people to the theatre, but the eloquence of a Chrysostom is necessary to tear them from it. With equal talents, he who pleads for license and impiety will carry more weight than the most elo-quent orator who vindicates the rights of virtue and morality.[38]

Classical Christian writers had always realized that there was an asym-metry in social motivation. It was always easier to convince people to do what their passions were telling them to do anyway, rather than to convince them to resist in favor of some higher good. The act of persuading people to gratify illicit passion was known as pandering. It was the illusion of the En-lightenment, as illustrated in texts like Bernard Mandeville's *Fable of the Bees,* to see passion as the engine for prosperity. Weishaupt took the same idea and molded it to his own ends. Passion would not only be the cause of the Enlightenment; it would be its vehicle as well. Weishaupt was associ-ated, like the fictional Victor Frankenstein, with the University of Ingolstadt. Frankenstein was a student of medicine, and Weishaupt a professor of law. Mary Shelley got her image of Weishaupt from Barruel, who saw him as:

> An odious phenomenon in nature, an Atheist void of remorse, a profound hypocrite, destitute of those superior talents which lead to the vindication of truth, he is possessed of all that energy and ardour in vice which gener-ates conspirators for impiety and anarchy. Shunning, like the ill-boding owl, the genial rays of the sun, he wraps around him the mantle of dark-ness; and history shall record of him, as of the evil spirit, only the black deeds which he planned or executed.[39]

Unlike Shelley, Weishaupt was not an aristocrat, but the rest of the de-scription, including his nocturnal habits, corresponds uncannily to Hogg's description of Shelley at Oxford. There are other similarities as well. Barruel tells us that "but a single trait of his private life has pierced the cloud in which he had enveloped himself," namely, that he had incestuous relations with his sister-in-law, got her pregnant, and then tried to thwart the ensuing scandal by attempting unsuccessfully to abort the baby.

> Incestuous Sophister! it was the widow of his brother whom he seduced. – Atrocious father! it was for the murder of his offspring that he solicited poison and the dagger. – Execrable hypocrite! he implored, he conjured

both art and friendship to destroy the innocent victim, the child whose birth must betray the morals of his father.[40]

"I am on the eve of losing that reputation which gave me so great an authority over our people," Weishaupt wrote to his co-conspirator Hertel, "My sister-in-law is with child. . . . How shall I restore the honour of a person who is the victim of a crime that is wholly mine? *We have already made several attempts to destroy the child*; she was determined to undergo all; but Euriphon is too timid."[41]

With Nietzsche and later Freud, who appropriated his "Oedipus Complex" surreptitiously from *The Birth of Tragedy*, incest would take on a numinous significance for sexual revolutionaries, becoming a way to force nature to reveal her secrets, but it had already taken on a similar significance in Shelley, who made it the centerpiece of his attack on Christianity in "The Revolt of Islam," which is dedicated to Mary Godwin and her sexual daring:

> How beautiful and calm and free thou wert
> In thy young wisdom, when the moral chain
> Of Custom thou didst burst and rend in twain,
> And walked as free as light the clouds among.

By the time Shelley and Mary and Claire Clairmont linked up with Byron at the Villa Diodati, their menage was known as "the league of incest," a description that refers to "The Revolt of Islam" and the sexual congress Byron and Shelley were having with two half sisters. There is every indication that the expression of the gossipmongers corresponded to Shelley's intention as well. Shelley knew that Illuminism meant controlling people through the manipulation of their passions because he read this in Barruel. There is every indication that Shelley tried to use this Illuminist technique, in combination with a double incest, to ensnare the most famous poet of the day to his revolutionary cause.

With the concatenation of incest and abortion, we come to the heart of the esoteric gnosis of the Enlightenment. The similarities between Weishaupt and later revolutionary adepts is too great to ignore. To begin with the situation closest at hand, there was Shelley's sexual relationship with his sister-in-law Claire Clairmont. When she first met Byron she confided to the great poet that she had already slept with Shelley, gotten pregnant by him and aborted the child. Then she proceeded to say that since she believed in free love, Byron could do the same with her if he wished. Byron seems to have been taken in by the offer, having sexual relations and eventually a child by Claire, but before long revulsion overcame any attraction he might have felt. Byron would later refer to Claire as an "Atheist and Murderer," in reference to both the Illuminist ideology she adopted under Shelley's tutelage and the abortion she claims to have carried out on Shelley's child. In the letter in which she proposed becoming Byron's mistress, Claire also held out her half sister Mary as an added inducement to sleeping with her. "You will, I daresay, fall in love with her," she wrote. "She is very handsome and very amiable, and you will no doubt be blest in your attachment; nothing could afford me more pleasure. I will redouble my attentions to please her . . . do everything she tells me, whether it be good or bad."

Byron was the most important poet in England at the time, and Shelley seems to have taken a page from Barruel by using Claire and the possibility of sex with Mary as a way of at first ingratiating himself with Byron and then controlling him by controlling his dominant passions. What Claire proposed in her letter to Byron was a sort of double incest *á la Weishaupt*; Byron and Shelley would share the same half-sisters. It was Weishaupt, after all, who proposed that initiates to the Illuminati should first give a secret autobiography and then be controlled by a combination of blackmail and "*secretly gratifying their passions, durch begnugung ihrer leidenschaften im verborgenen. . . . And this association might moreover serve to gratify those brethren who had a turn for sensual pleasure.*"[42] Byron was already notorious for his affair with his half-sister Augusta. The possibility of sleeping with the same half-sisters Shelley had slept with offered numinous possibilities, based on the secret life of Adam Weishaupt, founder of the revolutionary cell Shelley hoped to resurrect as a prelude to Promethean upheavals in the mode of the French Revolution. Shelley's poem about the French Revolution, the "Revolt of Islam," originally had as its two main characters Laon and Cythna, brother and sister, who engaged in incestuous sexual relations as a way of producing good occult/revolutionary juju.

Incest, as a result of Weishaupt, took on numinous significance in the secret gnosis of global revolution. In the *Birth of Tragedy*, Nietzsche refers to "the mother-wooing, riddle-solving Oedipus," who brings about "through oracular and magical powers, the force of both present and future, the rigid law of individuation as well as the magic of nature are broken."

"The preconditioning cause" of domination of nature, Nietzsche tells us,

> is the fact that beforehand a monstrous act against nature – *something of the order of incest* – [my emphasis] must have taken place; then how is one to force nature to reveal her secrets other than by victoriously going against her, that is, though an act contrary to nature. I see this recognition sketched out in that hideous trinity of Oedipus' fate: the same man who solves the riddle of nature – that double-edged Sphinx – must also violate the most holy order of nature as both parricide and spouse of his mother. Indeed, the meaning of the myth seems inescapable, that wisdom, and especially Dionysian wisdom, is an unnatural horror, and that the man who through his knowledge plunges nature into the abyss of annihilation experiences in his own being the disintegration of nature. "The point of wisdom turns against the wise; wisdom is a crime against nature."[43]

If the goal was the domination of nature through some violent unnatural act – as Nietzsche said, "wisdom is a crime against nature" – then incest was the first step for the Gnostic, revolutionary initiate, as well as a staple of English romantic poetry. The goal in each instance was to overturn the moral order and, thereby, God's hegemony on earth. The esoteric understanding went a bit deeper. Since the moral law is the only thing that guaranteed man's autonomy and inviolability, man without morals was easily controlled, and those who broke the law in the first place were the most likely candidate for the controllers of mankind. It was precisely this system of control which emerged from Weishaupt's writings. In fact, Barruel's reading of Weishaupt goes out of its way to explain the Illuminist cell as based on the arousal and systematic management of passion. The precondition for this sort of "liberation" was the systematic overthrow of the moral order, another term for revolution. It was to become the vehicle for revolution for the next 200 years.

Shelley took Barruel's reading of Weishaupt as his model for the revolutionary cell, and there is evidence that Byron was to be brought into this cell by seduction. Weishaupt's goal was, according to Barruel, "the most absolute, the most ardent, the most frantic vow to overthrow, without exception, every religion, every government, and *all property whatsoever.*, He pleased himself with the idea of a distant possibility that he might infuse the same wish throughout the world; he even assured himself of success." "*The French Revolution,*" he said at another point, "*is but the forerunner of a Revolution greater by far, and much more solemn.*"[44]

The means to this revolutionary end involved first finding the adept among the powerful: "Seek out also those who are distinguished by their power, nobility, riches or learning, *nobiles, potentes, divites, doctors, quaerite* – Spare no pains, spare nothing in the acquisition of such adepts. If heaven refuse its aidance, conjure hell. *Flectere si nequeas superos, Acheronta movebo.*"[45] Then after identifying the adept's dominant passion through study and the adept's confession, manipulating that passion as an instrument of control: "Study the peculiar habits of each; *for men may be turned to any thing by him who knows how to take advantage of their ruling passion.*"[46]

Weishaupt admired Ignatius of Loyola, and so the Illuminati were in many ways an imitation of the Jesuits and their recruiting and control practices a parody of the *Spiritual Exercises*. Where faults are identified by the Jesuit superior through examination of conscience to be then confessed and their power over the novice thereby broken, the Illuminist parody of the examination of conscience first ferrets out dominant passions to be preserved and manipulated by the Illuminist controller, rather than extirpated through repentance and confession. Examination of conscience in the Illuminist sense of the word is used by the Illuminist confessor as an instrument of control. Once the adept has confided his vices to his superior as part of the initiation rite, his passions will be used as a way of controlling him. If he discovers the ploy and objects, his past sins will be used against him in a form of blackmail that is in many ways a demonic perversion of the seal of the confessional. "Study the peculiar habits of each; *for men may be turned to any thing by him who knows how to take advantage of their ruling passions.*"[46]

"Now I hold him," Barruel writes of the newly initiated Illuminatus, *"I defy him to hurt us; if he should wish to betray us, we have also his secrets."*[47] It would be in vain for the adept to attempt to dissimulate. He will soon find that the most secret circumstances of his life, those which he would most anxiously wish to hide, are known by the adepts. Barruel maintains that the French Revolution happened after the French Masonic lodges became illuminized, i.e., taken over by Weishaupt's revolutionary cells. The interaction between the lodges and the Illuminati was, however, a two way street. From the lodges, Weishaupt learned that the main "advantage to be reaped from SECRET SOCIETIES" was "the arts of knowing men and governing them without constraint."[48] The goal of the Illuminati was three fold: "to teach the adepts the art of knowing men; to conduct mankind to happiness, and to govern them without their perceiving it."[49] In reality all three goals involved the same thing: the release of passion and the subsequent control of those who had abdicated self-control through adherence to the moral order.

Shelley, in other words, had a great plan. The only problem is that it didn't work. The culmination of the plot involved a seance at the Villa Diodati of the sort that used to unhinge Jane Clairmont after Mary had gone to bed. Byron began the evening by reciting Coleridge's poem "Christabel." In the course of a previous discussion of Coleridge's poem, which the poet used to recite at the Godwin household as Mary cowered behind a sofa, Mary told Shelley that the original idea for the lamia's deformity was that she had "two eyes in her bosom." The idea became an obsession for Shelley and on the night of the seance caused what would have to be termed a mental breakdown on his part at the crucial point when Byron was to be absorbed through the league of incest into Shelley's power. Shelley couldn't shake the hallucination that the nipples on Mary's breasts had become eyes. Since eyes are traditionally considered the windows to the soul, the image bespoke a self-consciousness at the moment of physical pleasure that could only bespeak a guilty conscience. As the monster would predict in the yet-to-be-completed *Frankenstein*, "I will be with you on your wedding night." Guilt over Shelley's treatment of his first wife Harriet, in other words, derailed his attempt to revive Illuminism and bring Byron under his control. Shelley was thwarted, as Weishaupt had been before him, by his own guilty conscience.

It was the beginning of the end of the first sexual revolution. When Mary and Shelley returned to England in the fall, they were greeted first by the suicide of Mary's other half-sister Fanny Imlay and then by the suicide of Shelley's first wife Harriet, who was fished from the Serpentine after a six-week immersion in early December. *Frankenstein* is the psychic protocol of that fall, when the dream of sexual liberation collapsed into the reality of guilt, a guilt from which neither Shelley nor Mary Godwin could escape.

In *Gothic*, Ken Russell's film version of the famous Shelley-Byron seance, Mary Godwin is off in a room by herself leafing through a book when suddenly she comes across a page of pornographic drawings. The book is obviously *Justine* by the Marquis de Sade. We know that Byron had a copy in April of 1816, and we know he linked up with Mary Godwin in May of 1816, so chances are he had the book with him. There is also the internal textual evidence which links *Frankenstein* with *Justine*, including the maid of the same name in the former book who is executed for a crime she doesn't commit just as Justine dies innocent in Sade's novel. In *Frankenstein*, we see the fulfillment of Sade's fantasies, not in a sexual utopia, as Shelley had planned but in a monster born of guilt and horror. What began in sexual desire ended in horror, which was the inchoate recognition of a moral order which Mary Godwin Shelley could never acknowledge openly. Guilt is the rock on which the first sexual revolution foundered.

"I am torn to pieces by Memory," Mary wrote on February 12, 1839, twenty-three years after she began writing *Frankenstein*. "Poor Harriet to whose sad fate I attribute so many of my own heavy sorrows as the atonement claimed by fate for her death. . . There are other verses I should well like to obliterate for ever," namely Shelley's sad poems of 1818–1822. "One looks back with unspeakable regret and gnawing remorse to such periods," she wrote in her note, "fancying that had one been more alive to the nature of his feelings and more attentive to soothe them, such would not have existed."[51] Shelley couldn't exorcise Harriet's ghost either, writing in one of his poems, about "the wandering hopes of one abandoned mother." On another occasion, Mary wrote to her half-sister: "O happy are you, dear Claire not to be devoured by humiliating and remorseful thoughts."[52]

On July 8, 1822 Shelley set sail in the Gulf of Spezia in northwestern Italy with an American John Williams and their boat boy Charles Vivian. Shelley, true to the principles he had espoused in *Queen Mab*, was about to embark on an adulterous affair with Williams' wife. Like the narrator in his "Ode to the West Wind," Shelley identified with the forces of nature that resembled his own unruly passions. A storm was rising, and Shelley had already rendered the boat dangerously top heavy by adding more sail than it could safely carry. Nevertheless, when the storm hit from the southwest the last thing an observer saw was Shelley unfurling more sail. "Be thou me," Shelley might have said, when the storm hit. But no one will know for sure. His body washed up lacerated and unrecognizable onto the rocky beach ten days later.

On August 4, 1822, the *Examiner*, an English paper, ran a laconic account of his death: "Shelley, the writer of some infidel poetry has been drowned; now he knows whether there is a God or no."[53]

When Shelley died, the first sexual revolution died with him. What followed was the repudiation of sexual liberation that has come to be known as the Victorian age. His widow dedicated the rest of her life to effacing their sexual experiment from public memory. Shelley became at the hands of his wife a Victorian angel and would remain so for another 150 years until another sexual revolution made another interpretation of his life possible.

Part I, Chapter 7

Paris, 1821

One year after Abbé Barruel's death and one year before Shelley's, on May 3, 1821, a young man by the name of Auguste Comte was walking through the Palais Royale enjoying the weather and admiring the young couples walking along its paths when a young woman caught his eye. Her name was Caroline Massin, and she was used to catching the eye of strolling young men. She was, in spite of her fresh looks, a prostitute, although the young man did not know that at the time. He got her address and asked if he could see her again.

Comte was five months younger than Mary Godwin, having been born on January 19, 1798, or the first day of Pluviose in the year VI, since France, then under the rule of Napoleon, still reckoned that time began with the founding of the French Republic. Comte's parents were ardent Catholics and Royalists, and wanted their child to be baptized, but the churches had been closed since 1793, and the baptism of children was still against the law. Even if his parents were devout Catholics and Royalists, Comte was very much a child of the French Revolution. If his parents wanted to transmit the Catholic faith to their child, they did so, but not in the way they most probably had hoped. Comte was a devout anti-revolutionary, and his philosophical system, which came to be known as Positivism, came into being as a reaction to the revolutionary chaos of his youth. By the time Comte reached manhood, he had lived under four separate governments and had seen his country, the most powerful in Europe when his parents had been born, ravaged by blood-thirsty mobs of Frenchmen and marauding foreign armies. Comte and his fellow high school students formed their own military brigade to defend the fmotherland against the invading Russian army, and on March 30, 1814, the Russian dragoons marched into town and dispersed them like the schoolboys that they were. Twenty students were wounded and a number were also taken prisoner.

Yet Comte, for all of his hatred of Napoleon and revolution, couldn't accept the religion of his parents, and this meant he couldn't become part of a resistance movement like the Vendee. Comte was an atheist by the age of fourteen. Having rejected both Catholicism and the Revolution, the only two political forces in France at the time, Comte would go on to fashion a philosophy, and ultimately a religion, which was a weird combination of both. Positivism might be called the Church of the Enlightenment, and through it,

Comte attracted a following that would make a significant contribution toward turning sociology, in the broadest sense of the term, which is how Comte intended it, into a system of control which would become the world's dominant regime by the end of the twentieth century. Aldous Huxley would call Comte's Positivism "Catholicism minus Christianity," and in this it was similar to Weishaupt's appropriation of Jesuit spirituality in the service of Freemasonry. Both men took what they found appealing in the Catholic Church and ripped it out of its matrix and introduced it to a radically different context which changed its meaning completely. Both took what were essentially mechanisms of self-control based on Catholicism's understanding of the moral order and turned them into essentially heteronomous instruments of social control whose goal was the betterment of "humanity" and whose validating principle was "science." Herbert Croly, who had been baptized into Comte's Church of Positivism by his Irish newspaperman father in the 1880s in America, would go on to implement Comte's ideas as editor of the *New Republic*, which among other things would orchestrate America's entry into World War I and the subsequent rise of the American empire. Domestically, Croly and the *New Republic* were avid supporters of Watsonian Behaviorism and Advertising, which meant the creation of national markets, which would, in turn, extinguish ethnic loyalty and local government in the interest of a national consensus that had much in common with the General Will so praised by French revolutionaries. Croly and the *New Republic* also supported John Dewey's attempt to turn the public school system into a national entity whose main goal was not the transmission of skills but the inculcation of attitudes they found congenial to national consciousness and the general will.

Comte almost went to America himself. In preparation for his trip he immersed himself in the language and political thought of what he thought was going to be his new home, but at the last moment the job fell through, and he became secretary to Claude-Henri Saint-Simon instead. It was from Saint-Simon that he would make contact with what Marx and Engels would later call utopian socialism or critical utopian socialism. Like Saint-Simon, Comte's intellectual trajectory was the result of a parallelogram of intellectual and cultural forces which involved revolution and Catholicism. Both lived to see the disillusioned aftermath of the revolution that failed, yet neither was able to return to the Catholic social order which preceded the revolution. The same was true of Charles Fourier, another utopian socialist closer in age to Comte.

With the dissolution of the *ancien régime*, morals were cast adrift. Revolutionary appeals to "virtue," Comte's generation had learned, invariably meant murder in some form or other, and the utopian socialists were realistic enough to see that revolution didn't lead to any improvement in France. In fact, to a large extent it had blighted their lives. Of the three, Saint-Simon was the least affected because he was the most revolutionary. Having fought alongside George Washington in the campaign against Cornwallis on the Yorktown Peninsula, Saint-Simon returned to play a leading role in the French Revolution and lived to see the dreams he espoused go up in smoke when Napoleon declared himself emperor and then went on to defeat at the hands of the Russians. Fourier was twelve years younger than Saint-Simon, and even more so than Comte, who was twenty some years his junior, Fourier's life was ruined by the upheaval the revolution caused. Each man, in his way, saw the passions which the Revolution aroused spin out of control; each man sought a mechanism whereby that passion could be brought under control, and yet each man was incapable of placing faith in the tradition which preceded the Enlightenment, the movement which had brought about the revolution in the first place.

It was from Saint-Simon that Comte got the idea that Industrialism was to be the new form of social order that would replace the old order which had been swept irrevocably away by the revolution. The new order was to be based on science, not the now discredited religion, because no one could argue with science, which as Shelley has said, was based on fact, not hypothesis. "*Hypothesi non fingo*," Newton had written, and Shelley had quoted the passage in a footnote to *Queen Mab* as the marching orders for the New Man who would bring about heaven on earth. To substantiate Shelley's revolutionary pedigree, Friedrich Engels would arrange to have *Queen Mab* translated and distributed during the revolution of 1848. Saint-Simon's idea of heaven on earth meant using the factory, or Phalantasery, as the basis of social order. Young people of both sexes were to be interned in factories where they would produce useful goods, be kept under control, and be diverted from any idea of rebellion by the sexual attraction which co-workers of the opposite sex would exert over them. It was, *in nuce*, the workplace of the late twentieth century, and it was the first concrete proposal of how to use sex as a form of control by integrating it into the emerging factory system.

Comte entered into a sexual relationship with Caroline Massin shortly after he met her in 1821. One year later, Comte issued the pamphlet "Plan for Scientific Studies Demanded by the Reorganization of Society," published in 1822. Three years later, he issued an expanded version of that pamphlet with Massin's assistance as editor, under the title *System of Positive Polity*. That book was in effect the core of his ideas and the core of the six volumes of the *Cours de philosophie positive* and the four even heavier volumes of the *System de politique positive* added only details to the original idea. On February 19, 1825, which is to say around the time his most important work was published, Comte married Massin in a civil ceremony at the city hall of the 4th arrondissment in Paris. From the outside, it might have seemed to be the consolidation of his personal and his intellectual life, but there was evidence that looks were deceiving. To give one such instance, the witness for the bride was a certain M. Cerclet, one of her first and best customers. The marriage did little to change the fact that Comte, for all his involvement in the laws of human society, could never be sure his wife was being faithful to him. She would disappear periodically, and then return to his life as if nothing had happened, creating the nagging suspicion in his mind that she had returned to her previous *métier*, either for fun or profit.

It may have been the insecurity which Massin's conduct engendered which led Comte to his periodic bouts of insanity, and ultimately to his suicide attempt. Comte eventually went to see Dr. Esquirol, the man who had shut down the Marquis de Sade's theatrical performances at Charenton, and Esquirol, suspecting that Massin was the cause of his problems and that Comte would not leave Massin, was unable to cure Comte. Comte, however, associated his mental illness with Massin in a different way. "Now I will be cured, because I am with her," is what he said as she picked him up in a cab from the hospital.[1] Given her proclivities, however, any cure based on her faithful presence could only be considered temporary. Still suffering from bouts of depression, Comte decided to take the matter into his own hands in April of 1827 by throwing himself into the Seine and putting an end to his life. The minute he hit the cold waters, however, he was struck by a profound desire to go on living, and was cured of his illness as well.

The pathos of Comte's personal situation mirrors in many ways the lives of future reformers who would also try to formulate the fundamentals of social organization (i.e., control) while in the throes of sexual passion. John B. Watson springs to mind. Psychically plagued by sexual insecurity, Comte created by way of compensation a scientific universe that was unable to change. He rejected, for instance, the discovery of Neptune because that would mean that the laws of astronomical science were not complete at the time he had formulated the tenets of Positivism. As a result, science could not provide the stability that the post-revolutionary order demanded. "Comte's true ambition," according to his biographer, "lay in the scientific organization of society, the bringing about of a scientific heaven on earth – and what is a heaven if not a perfect and definitive order of things and conditions?"[2] Again the pathos of the personal life of the great scientific reformer intrudes. Comte may have been saved from incurable mental illness by love, but love had no place in the system he created to bring order to a revolutionary world which had spun out of control. The man who needed to be loved in order to be sane, erected a system which had no place for love. Hence, both he and his system were suffused with an pervasive air of insanity.

The same could be said, *mutatis mutandis*, of the other utopian socialists. Like Comte, their project was born of the same need for order in the face of widespread social breakdown. Like Comte, they sought in science what the previous regime had sought in the Church. Like Comte, Charles Fourier sought the antidote to revolution in the Enlightenment, which had caused the

revolution in the first place, because he couldn't conceive of finding that solution anyplace else. Fourier based his social theories on a system which cast
passion as the human equivalent of Newton's force of gravity. As a matter of
fact, the opposite was sooner the case, since Fourier claimed that "everything, from the atom to the galaxies, was an imitation of human passion"[3] As
a result of this reduction of the driving force of human life to the psychic
equivalent of the subatomic particle, passion is alienated from the human
soul, and reason is disinherited as the instrument which brings passion under
control, being replaced by will either individual or collective, as in the case
of class interests. As a result, morality, which was traditionally reason's ability to apprehend the truth in the practical order, gets cut adrift from its rational matrix and forced to find a home in "science." All oughts now have to
justify themselves as ises, since fact is the only validator in any Positivist
system. When morals were cast adrift, sexual behavior was cast adrift with
them. It was up to the utopian socialists to find a new home for sexual morals.
Unfortunately, all of them shared the Enlightenment's essentially voluntarist
view of morals, later adopted by the Communists, which claimed that family,
along with religion, was an engine of oppression created by the propertied
classes to insure their grip on the levers of power. Once passion was reduced
to an abstract physical force like gravity, sexual morals become a function of
broader forces as well, like the means of production, and as a result sexual
"customs" were to become fluid and a function of something other than the
moral determination of the people who got married. In this Fourier had much
in common with the critique of Marx and Engels, who pretty much adopted
what he had to say.

By locating marriage and the family in a matrix of economic forces, Fourier and the Marxists placed "liberation" at the center of family life. Given
their economic premises, certain sexual conclusions were unavoidable. If,
for example, marriage was in its very essence asocial and based on the domination of women as property, then the only real criterion of genuine social
liberation was the extent to which women could emancipate themselves from
marriage. But what did that mean? Fourier is clear on the matter. Emancipation from marriage means the integration of women into the production process, which means, of course, getting a job in a factory. Once again liberation
upon closer inspection showed itself as a form of control. Women were to be
delivered from the tyranny of their husbands only to be handed over to the
tyranny of their bosses in the cotton mills, who now would exploit them for
their profit. *Le plus ça change*, as the French would say. There were other
similarities as well. Since marriage, from the traditional point of view, was
synonymous with sexual morality, then emancipation meant "liberation"
from the moral law. It was, in other words, the same Enlightenment formula
which had led to revolution fifty years before.

Therefore, it is not surprising that it should lead to revolution once again, which is what happened in 1848. Traditional French culture, already wearied by the revolution, proved resistant to utopian schemes during the nineteenth century, but America, already populated by a rootless group of immigrants whose very immigration showed they were sympathetic to some form of social experimentation, soon became home to a number of utopian social communities, some of which were based on the French model. Like Brook Farm, which Nathaniel Hawthorne immortalized in his novel, *The Blithedale Romance*, all of them failed.

In the fall of 1824, shortly before Comte married Caroline Massin, a Welshman by the name of Robert Owen, who had become famous in England for establishing a model factory and community in New Lanark, Scotland, arrived in America to start another more ambitious community in New Harmony, Indiana. Whereas New Lanark had succeeded, New Harmony failed, and Owen, after trying to persuade the Mexican government to let him try to found a still more ambitious community on the banks of the Rio Grande, returned to England to figure out why it had failed. Marx concluded that the experiment had failed because of "the deeply hidden conspiracy of the upper classes against the rights of the poor and the working class." When Owen suggested workmen's compensation and higher wages as the solution to the ongoing labor crisis in England, the Malthusians responded by saying that those measures would only lead to overpopulation. With the defeat of Owen and the moderate evolutionary approach of the utopian socialists, the field was left with only two major players: the Malthusian/Manchester School defenders of the unjust status quo and the Marxist proponents of revolution. With Marx's verdict on Owen's failed experiment, the world was ripe for revolution, and in 1848, as in France sixty years earlier, the revolution took place once again. And once again it failed.

One of the participants this time around was a young conductor and composer by the name of Richard Wagner. Wagner had manned the barricades with Mikhail Bakunin in Dresden, and when the revolution of 1848 collapsed there, Wagner went into exile in Switzerland. Wagner used the opportunity to rethink his revolutionary priorities. His thoughts were published in a book called *Art and Revolution*, and in the process of writing that book, he changed from being an unsuccessful political revolutionary into being a very successful cultural revolutionary by the creation of an opera, *Tristan and Isolde*, and a new musical form, chromaticism, which would become the anthem for sexual liberation for the next fifty years.[4] One of the people most affected by Wagner's *Tristan* was a young gymnasium student by the name of Friedrich Nietzsche, who dedicated his life thereafter (some said by deliberately infecting himself with syphilis) to promoting sexual passion as a form of cultural terrorism. By the latter half of the nineteenth century, when Victoria was on the throne in England, and France had yet to recover from its revolution, sexual liberation was almost exclusively a German phenomenon, one centered largely around performances of *Tristan und Isolde*, as Thomas Mann, no stranger to sexual liberation himself, makes clear.

By the turn of the twentieth century there were a number of small groups of people who devoted themselves to the writings of Nietzsche, which was Wagner's sexual liberation in a more toxic, philosophical form. In addition to Bayreuth, where the faithful could see Wagner performed each year, another place which drew those interested in sexual liberation and its Germanic rationalizations was the northern Italian resort of Ascona, where an ongoing German version of Woodstock was in session for the first decade of the twentieth century. One of the famous habitués of Ascona during this period was the son of a policeman by the name of Otto Gross, a man characterized by Richard Noll as

> the great breaker of the bond, the loosener, the beloved of an army of women he had driven mad – if just for a short time. He coaxed one lover/patient to suicide, and then another patient died under similar circumstances. His contemporaries described him as brilliant, creative, charismatic, and troubled. He was a Nietzschean physician, a Freudian psychoanalyst, and anarchist, the high priest of sexual liberation, a master of orgies, the enemy of patriarchy, and a dissolute cocaine and morphine addict. He was loved and hated with equal passion, an infectious agent to some, a healing touch to others. He was a strawberry-blond Dionysos.[5]

He was also an influence on C. G. Jung, even as his patient, and it was through Jung and Freud and their resurrection of Illuminism as psychoanalysis that we return to the main thread of our story.

Part II, Chapter 1

Paris, 1885

In October 1885, one year before his marriage, a young Viennese medical doctor by the name of Sigmund Freud went to Paris to study with Jean-Marie Charcot, the famous French neuropathologist. Freud was not a religiously observant Jew, but he was a politically active Jew, a Zionist, as well as socially ambitious, and as such he could not have been unaware of the anti-Semitism that was sweeping France at the time. This anti-Semitism was part and parcel of the conservative reaction to the spirit of 1789 and the secret societies which purportedly spread the spirit of revolution throughout Europe. The most famous explication of what has come to be known as the conspiracy theory got its start with the publication in England of Abbé Augustin Barruel's *Memoirs Illustrating the History of Jacobinism*, in the years 1796–99, the book which turned the tide against revolution in England. Young Mary Godwin modeled Dr. Frankenstein, the "modern Prometheus," on both Shelley, the revolutionary manqué, and Adam Weishaupt, professor of Canon Law at the University of Inglolstadt, and founder of the Illuminati, one of the three groups who along with the *philosophes* and the Freemasons brought about the French Revolution, the most effective overturning of throne and altar to date.

Nesta Webster in her book *World Revolution* produces a chart which traces the influence of the Illuminati throughout the nineteenth century all the way up to the Russian Revolution of 1917. In promoting what has come to be called the conspiracy theory, Webster proposed what amounts to a revolutionary version of Apostolic succession, making the transmission of the idea dependent on an interlocking chain of revolutionary organizations. Shelley's use of Barruel proposes a different paradigm of transmission. Instead of organizations begetting the idea, we have, in the case of Shelley, a case of literary influence in which the idea begot the organization. Shelley's example is telling because the influence of the Illuminati in this instance is more literary than organizational. By writing the book that he did, Barruel created a following for Adam Weishaupt and his ideas that his organization never could have achieved on its own. "Illuminist ideas," James Billington writes, "influenced revolutionaries not just through left-wing proponents, but also through right-wing opponents. As the fears of the Right became the fascination of the Left, Illuminism gained a paradoxical posthumous influence far greater than it had exercised as a living movement."[1] Filippo

Buonarotti, the Illuminist heir presumptive in Italy, was a *bona fide* revolutionary, but he got the idea by reading Barruel, not by joining Weishaupt's organization. Sigmund Freud was just one more example of the fascination of the Left being based on the fears of the Right.

Daniel Pipes accuses Barruel of what one would have to term post-hoc anti-Semitism on the basis of the Simonini letter. He also cites Webster extensively in his book but ignores her claim that Barruel in no way implicated the Jews in the French Revolution:

> We should require more than such vague assertions to refute the evidence of men who, like Barruel and Robinson, devoted exhaustive study to the subject and attributed the whole plan of the Illuminati and its fulfillment in the French Revolution to German brains. Neither Weishaupt, Knigge, nor any of the ostensible founders of Illuminism were Jews: Moreover, as we have seen, Jews were excluded from the association except by special permission. None of the leading revolutionaries of France were Jews, nor were the members of the conspiracy of Babeuf.[2]

Barruel's *Memoirs* may have been the source of the conspiracy theory, but his followers modified his thinking at will, and one of the major modifications which took place during the course of the nineteenth century was the conflation of Illuminatus, Freemason, and Jew. Throughout the course of the nineteenth century, the conflation continued. Biberstein cites the Simonini letter in his history of the conspiracy theory but claims that the major impulse for the conflation of Jew and conspirator happened thanks to Napoleon when in 1806 he called a meeting of Jewish notables in Europe and gave that assembly the name of the Sanhedrin.[3] In addition to giving credence to the belief that Napoleon was the Antichrist, this gesture also gave the impression that a secret Jewish regime was already in existence and that its loyalties were firmly within the revolutionary camp.

France was a hotbed of anti-Masonic thought throughout the period of reaction to revolution in the nineteenth century. As a result of the conflation of Jew and Freemason, anti-Semitism became part of antirevolutionary thought. Since Jews were connected in the reactionary mind with secret societies like the Freemasons as the major proponents of the revolution of 1789, the rise of counter-revolution meant the rise of anti-Semitism. The drumbeat which continued in the wake of Barruel's book (even though it contradicted Barruel) reached a crescendo around the time Freud arrived in Paris to study with Charcot. The conflation of Jew-Freemason-Revolutionary was given considerable impetus with the publication of the Roger Gougenot des Mosseaux's book *Le Juif, le Judaisme et la Judaisation des Peoples Chrétiens* in 1869. Gougenot des Mosseaux took as the epigraph of his book a quote from Disraeli's *Coningsby*: "So you see, my dear Coningsby, that the world is governed by very different personages to what is imagined by those who are not behind the scenes." Gougenot des Mosseaux hints that Freemasonry and secret societies of this sort have as their purpose the destruction of Christendom and the erection in its place of a worldwide Jewish regime.

Five years later, from 1874 until 1876, the Rev. Nicolas Deschamps, S.J. published his *Les Societés secretes ou la philosophie de l'histoire contemporaine*, in which he mentions Barruel's *Memoirs* explicitly. By 1881 Deschamps's book was in its fourth edition. In July 1878 the Paris review *Le Contemporain: Revue Catholique* published Father Grivel's reminiscences on Barruel, further increasing his stature among the counter-revolutionaries. In 1881 Abbé Chabauty published his book, *Les Francs-Mâçons et les Juifs*, in which he wrote that a Judeo-masonic conspiracy was then at work preparing the way for a Jewish Antichrist who was going to bring into being Jewish hegemony throughout the world.

Three years later, which is to say one year before Freud arrived in Paris, Eduard Drumont stated in his pamphlet *La France Juive: Essai d'histoire contemporaine* that the Jews were exploiting the revolution for their own purposes, that Adam Weishaupt was a Jew (!) and that Freemasonry was just a front for Jewish influence. In 1893 the Most Rev. Leon Meurin, archbishop of Port Louis on Mauritius published a pamphlet entitled *La Franc Mâçonnerie: Synagogue de Satan,* in which he mentions Barruel explicitly as well as the Jewish-Christian lodge in Frankfurt "*Zur Aufgehenden Morgen*" and Simonini's letter. Meurin's conclusion – that "*En vérité, tout ce qui trouve dans la franc-mâçonnerie est foncièrement juif, exclusivement juif, passionément juif, depuis le commencement jusqu'à la fin*" – shows that by the time Freud reached Paris as a young medical student the conflation of Jew and Freemason (Freemason being a synonym for Illuminatus) was complete.[4] It was to continue unabated for the next ten years. In 1903, one year after the publication of *The Psychopathology of Everyday Life,* Abbé Isidore Bertrand stated in his pamphlet *La Franc Mâçonnerie: Secte Juive* that the Jew and the Freemason were united by their hatred of Christ and the gentiles, "and by that last word we mean Catholics."[5]

Eventually the Catholics took cognizance of the agitation sweeping Europe concerning secret societies, and on April 4, 1884, Pope Leo XIII issued his encyclical *Humanum Genus*, also known as the encyclical on Freemasonry. In 1883 Armand-Joseph Fava, bishop of Grenoble issued a pamphlet entitled *Le secret de la franc-mâçonnerie*, in which he accused the Freemasons of satanic worship, sacrilegious violation of the eucharistic host and other crimes. Fava was a friend of Leo XIII and known as the "hammer of the freemasons" and, according to Biberstein, influenced the pope in his writing of *Humanum Genus*.[6] If so *Humanum Genus* is as significant for what it did not say as for what it did. Leo XIII does not mention the Jews, and one gets the impression that in *Humanum Genus,* Leo XIII sought to take control of the secret society mania and bring it back to its *locus classicus*, i.e., Barruel's *Memoirs*. In *Humanum Genus*, Leo XIII purged the anti-Masonic,

antirevolutionary movement of the anti-Semitic accretions which had become attached to it during the course of the nineteenth century.

Humanum Genus makes clear that "the society of which we speak" is the
"Masonic sect" which "produces fruits that are pernicious and of the bitterest
savor . . . namely, the utter overthrow of the whole religious and political order of the world which the Christian teaching has produced and the substitution of a new state of things in accordance with their ideas, of which the
foundations and laws shall be drawn from mere Naturalism."[7]

So much for the ends of the Masonic sect. The means whereby they
achieve their ends are, according to Leo XIII, the corruption of education, the
corruption of culture, and, common to both, the corruption of morals. In a
world corrupted by Original Sin, Leo XIII sees the Masonic sect preaching
its "gospel of pleasure" as the main weapon in their arsenal. The Masons
preach the "gospel of pleasure" as part of a concerted plan to gain political
hegemony over Christian Europe:

> Wherefore we see that men are publicly tempted by the many allurements
> of pleasure; that there are journals and pamphlets with neither moderation
> nor shame; that stage-plays are remarkable for license; that designs for
> works of art are shamelessly sought in the laws of a so-called realism; that
> the contrivances of a soft and delicate life are most carefully devised; and
> that all the blandishments of pleasure are diligently sought out by which
> virtue may be lulled to sleep. Wickedly also but at the same time quite
> consistently, do those act who do away with the expectation of the joys of
> heaven, and bring down all happiness to the level of mortality, and, as it
> were, sink it in the earth. . . . For since generally no one is accustomed to
> obey crafty and clever men so submissively as those whose soul is weak-
> ened and broken down by the domination of the passions, there have been
> in the sect of the Freemasons some who have plainly determined and pro-
> posed that artfully and of set purpose, the multitude should be satiated
> with a boundless license of vice, as, when this has been done, it would eas-
> ily come under their power and authority for any acts of daring.[8]

Sexual liberation, to use a later term for what Leo XIII calls the "domination of the passions," is a form of political control. In this Leo XIII is consistent with Barruel's reading of Illuminism, which was, according to Adam
Weishaupt's plan, a form of ruling people without their knowing it by secretly manipulating their passions. Leo XIII mentions neither Barruel nor
Illuminism, but his encyclical is beholden to the former for his explication of
the strategy of the latter-day Illuminists. In explaining the destructive effect
of uncontrolled passion on the soul, Leo XIII has recourse to classical psychology, which is to say, the classical explanation of the relationship between passion and rational control. Weakened by Original Sin and,
therefore, more disposed to vice than virtue, man must reconcile himself to a
life of constant vigilance and strenuous moral effort:

> For a virtuous life it is absolutely necessary to restrain the disorderly

movements of the soul, and to make the passions obedient to reason. In this conflict human things must very often be despised, and the greatest labors and hardships must be undergone, in order that reason may always hold its sway. But the Naturalists and Freemasons, having no faith in those things which we have learned by the revelation of God, deny that our first parents sinned, and consequently think that free will is not at all weakened and inclined to evil. On the contrary, exaggerating rather our natural virtue and excellence and placing therein alone the principle and rule of justice, they cannot even imagine that there is any need at all of a constant struggle and a perfect steadfastness to overcome the violence and rule of our passions.[9]

We have here an expression of the psychology which is the diametrical opposite of the one which Freud would choose fifteen years later as the epigraph for *The Interpretation of Dreams*: "*Flectere si nequeo superos, Acheronta movebo*," If I cannot bend the higher powers, I will move the infernal regions. Leo XIII, as the supreme representative of the higher powers, was proving particularly immobile, as was the Austro-Hungarian Empire at the time of the writing of Freud's first two books, and so Freud conceived of a "revolutionary" psychology, according to which the passions would at first subvert and finally overwhelm rational control. Once again, as in revolutionary France, repression, and not sinful passion, became the enemy. Reason, representing the King, was at first to be subverted and weakened and finally swept away by the unruly mob that man's passions had always been. That Freud was consciously part of the revolutionary tradition is also indicated by the *Acheronta movebo* quote. Peter Swales claims that Freud got it from Ferdinand Lassalle, another Jew and revolutionary. As Freud's use of the quote as the epigraph to his first book indicates, psychoanalysis was a covert reaffirmation of the revolutionary tradition, which was now reawakening as the alliance which defeated Napoleon and restored order to Europe in the aftermath of twenty-some years of revolution started to unravel.

Part II, Chapter 2

Chicago, September 1900

In the summer of 1900, the same year in which *The Interpretation of Dreams* appeared in print, John Broadus Watson, a young teacher from Greenville, South Carolina, wrote to William Rainey Harper, the president of the University of Chicago, asking for either a full scholarship or a job that would allow him to pay his tuition. Watson, who had received his undergraduate degree at the distinctly lesser known Furman College, a religious institution for the education of Southern Baptist preachers, now wanted to attend what he termed "a real university" because he wanted to make his way in the world, and, at the dawn of the twentieth century, it was becoming obvious that education was the key to success.

Watson had grown up in what might be termed the archetypal American family if *The Adventures of Huckleberry Finn* can be termed the archetypal American novel. His mother, who had died on July 3, 1900, right around the time he wrote his letter, had the moral fervor of the Widow Douglas, while his father resembled Pap, not only because of his heavy drinking but also because he would periodically disappear into the wilderness to spend time with one or the other of his Indian concubines. Then when John was thirteen, Pickens Watson, his father, disappeared for good, leaving his son to be raised by a mother steeped in the emotional religion typical of that region. Both parents would leave their mark on Watson, who would become a heavy-drinking womanizer who was dedicated with all of the fervor of a Southern Baptist preacher to the new religion of science in general and behaviorist psychology in particular. In many ways, Watson, who was born in 1878, was the typical man of the 1880s generation, the prototypical generation of "moderns," who came into their own in the decade following World War I as a result of the social dislocations that war wrought. All of the "moderns" were fervent believers in scientific materialism and tried to shape the world to their new-found faith with all of the zeal of the early apostles. "You will find me an earnest student," Watson wrote to Harper, and in this he was telling the truth.

Perhaps because a Baptist seminary provided him with a background in Latin and Greek, Watson initially hoped to study philosophy under John Dewey. We know this because he wrote to Dewey at around the same time he wrote to Harper. By the time Watson's application landed on the president's desk, John Dewey was in the middle of a ten-year stay at the university and at the apogee of his influence there. Under Dewey, Watson took a course on Kant – twice, as a matter of fact – and at the end of both could make neither heads nor tails of the *Critique of Pure Reason*. The only lasting effect of Watson's exposure to Kant was an abiding animus against philosophy of the German school and "introspection," which was the method of the new science of psychology, a science which had come into existence at the university only eight years before Watson arrived. To be a psychologist then meant becoming, in effect, a German, as G. Stanley Hall, the father of American psychology had done, when he left for Germany in the 1880s to study under Wilhelm Wundt in Tübingen.

Germanic introspection is a long way from the disinterested contemplation of the truth, which was the goal of the classical philosophical tradition, but it was still too far removed from the American penchant for action and results that characterized both John Dewey and John Watson. Americans had always tended to be a superficial lot, fumbling among the patrimony of the Western tradition like a cargo cult without a can-opener. And this same impatience characterized the founding of modern psychology. People like Dewey were known as pragmatists for good reason. They were interested in the truth about the human psyche only insofar as that truth produced results. Like the physical sciences, which were not so much a means of understanding nature as they were a means of controlling it, the new science of psychology, as conceived by John Dewey, would be a way of controlling the human mind. Dewey was one of the architects of twentieth-century liberalism, and one of the goals of liberalism was social control.

Liberalism, in this respect, was both arsonist and fire department. Science was the solvent which was to dissolve all of the old bonds associated with morals, religion and tradition, and once that dissolution had been accomplished and the culture was on the verge of social chaos as a result, science, specifically the new science of psychology, would provide the culture's mandarins a way of controlling the unruly masses along new, more "rational" lines, which also, by the way, would benefit the controllers both politically and financially. Psychology, according to Dewey, was to become the scientific arm of democratic reform, and the public school was to be the institution wherein the democratic science found its application to life.[1] Dewey was, of course, reacting to the waves of immigration which were sweeping over America's shores from southern and eastern Europe at the time. Dewey saw the schools as the main instrument of socialization, an instrument which would produce a homogenized American citizen, purged of ethnic and familial affiliation, who identified with progressive, national goals as articulated by the masters of public opinion in a mass-media age. Schools would be "managed on a psychological basis as great factories are run on the basis of chemical and physical science."[2] The schools would create Americans as Dewey defined them, which is to say, people who believed in science but shared a skepticism about the institutions created by the founding fathers. This skepticism would find its way into the writings of fellow liberals like Walter Lippmann, Herbert Croly, and the rest of those who found their apotheosis with the founding of the *New Republic* and the coming of Woodrow Wilson's war.

The University of Chicago had come into being the year before the Chicago Exposition of 1892 with the financial backing of John D. Rockefeller, and like its patron, the university was more interested in results than disinterested contemplation. Watson, because of his temperament, imbibed the imperatives of Enlightenment science with an avidity which soon impressed his teachers. He abandoned his career in philosophy almost immediately and substituted in its place an interest in psychology, which was being defined in almost exclusively mechanistic terms. Under the tutelage of Jacques Loeb, who experimented with the artificial insemination of sea urchin eggs, he learned that man was an "organic machine" which would soon be replicated in the laboratory, as soon as a few physiological details had been worked out. It was Mary Shelley's vision of *Frankenstein* purged of all of the humanist misgivings and the sad lessons which the sexual revolutionaries of eighty years before had learned in the expensive school of experience. Since man was a biological machine with no "instincts," much less an immortal soul, he was a complete *tabula rasa*, completely formed by the intersection of his experiences with his biology. Man had gone from a being informed by a rational soul, whose potentialities developed by exposure to the world as received by the senses, a being which could discern the order in the universe and thereby order his own life according to that reason, to being an organic machine, completely plastic, whose impulses were a direct response to stimuli outside his control. Since man possessed no soul, no mind, and eventually – according to Watson, at least – not even consciousness and since his biological make-up was a given, man was nothing but what his environment made him. From there it was only a short step to concluding that he who controlled the environment controlled the man. Given this radically truncated view of man, the key issue was understanding the mechanism whereby the imperatives of the environment were transformed into the imperatives of the mind. The man who unlocked that secret would become the ultimate pragmatist; he would know the science of controlling his fellow man.

The preceding worldview takes into account both the thought of the early Watson and the intellectual milieu he imbibed from his teachers. Watson's ability to embody and advance the spirit of his age was either enviable or unfortunate depending on your point of view. If he were time-bound and his faith in science now sounds hopelessly dated, that very same quality allowed him to move with ease to the forefront of a new profession which thought it was going to finally unlock the age-old secrets about human behavior and regulate them in a way which had proven impossible to both philosophy and religion. Like Dr. Frankenstein, like Shelley upon whom Frankenstein was modeled, modern Prometheans like Watson hoped to create the galvanized corpse of the new man out of unacknowledged body parts pilfered surreptitiously from the graveyard of their own personal and (more often than not) sexual biographies. Since Watson would eventually go on to assert that there was no such thing as consciousness, it isn't all that surprising that he would have a dim view of autobiography. "I don't see how anyone but a very naive person," Watson wrote at the height of his fame in 1928, "could write up his own life."

> Everyone has entirely too much to conceal to write an honest [autobiography] – too much he has never learned to put into words even if he would conceal nothing. Thinking of chronicling your adolescent acts day by day – your four years of college – your selfishness – the way you treat other people – your pettiness – your daydreams of sex! Autobiographies are written either to sell the good points about oneself or to vanquish one's critics. If an autobiographer honestly turned himself inside out day by day for six months, he would either commit suicide at the end of the time or else go into a blissful oblivescent depression.[3]

The last article John B. Watson ever wrote (one which never got published) was on why he and other famous men of his acquaintance didn't commit suicide. As the foregoing passage indicates, Watson's life as a young man was characterized by emotional and moral turmoil. After reading Hume at the University of Chicago around the same time that he abandoned philosophy in favor of psychology, Watson became convinced that reason was "the slave of the passions."[4] Hume, in this instance, was probably only confirming what Watson was learning from first-hand experience of a life which seemed to alternate between acting on irascible and concupiscible passions with little rational mediation in between. As a young man in Greenville, South Carolina, Watson was an avid participant in what he called "nigger fighting," something which was probably tolerated by the authorities. The fact that Watson got arrested for doing it gives some indication that he let this passion get out of hand, as do the circumstances surrounding his second arrest for firing a gun in the middle of the town.

The same is true of the concupiscible passions. Watson became sexually active at around the time he entered Furman College, which is to say by the age of seventeen or eighteen. By the time he graduated he had had an affair with an older woman and had developed what would become a life-long habit of lack of self-control in sexual matters. During the fall of 1903, while at the University of Chicago, he suffered a nervous breakdown which caused him to "watch his step." The breakdown was apparently related to sexual matters because he would say that it led to his acceptance of a large part of Freud's thought later in life. Now even a superficial analysis of Freud and Behaviorism indicates that they have little in common. Yet, when it came to matters sexual, Watson was a Freudian who felt that things like the Oedipus Complex could be traced to bad habits acquired in the infant's earliest conditioning. If this sounds implausible now, it didn't sound much more plausible then.

Watson's biographers have noted the incongruity as well. Watson felt that Freud was useless to the "laboratory psychologist,"[5] but he agreed with his idea of the "sex references of all behavior."[6] Freud had retained the vocabulary of classical science (id = passion; superego = reason) in revolutionary form. Watson was to abolish all of that in favor of what might be termed dramatized physiology, according to which love was memories of sexual stimulation and "thought" was a function of the motion of the larynx, a form of talking out loud. Love, according to the behaviorist point of view, was tumescence. Yet when it came to explaining his own sexual behavior, Watson found Freud more satisfying than his own behaviorism. The reason is simple enough. Ultimately the congruity between Freudianism and Behaviorism was political and not scientific. Both Watson and Freud were revolutionaries using science as a cover for their war on the moral order, as manifested in their minds by Victorian society:

> What behaviorism and psychoanalysis ultimately had in common was a belief in the plasticity of human nature and in the temporality of social institutions. This signified a break with the values of Victorian society. Standards of conduct that had been set and enforced by community and church were being replaced by an ethos that stressed self-fulfillment and personal gratification. Far from being liberating, however, this shift had the effect of casting the individual adrift in a sea of shifting values that were determined more and more by styles of consumption.[7]

After his nervous breakdown in the fall of 1903, Watson attempted to resolve the sexual conflicts in his life by getting secretly married to a nineteen-year-old undergraduate by the name of Mary Ickes on December 26 of the same year. Watson was always a sucker for adoring undergraduates and apparently married Ickes on the rebound from being spurned by Vida Sutton, another student. When Sutton returned to say that she was having second thoughts about Watson's proposal, an affair ensued. Ickes's brother Harold, who would later become Secretary of the Interior in the Franklin Roosevelt administration (his son would occupy a similar post in the Clinton Administration), was apparently a good judge of character. He never approved of the marriage and, after hearing the rumors, hired a detective, who presented the evidence to Mary. It was not an auspicious beginning for a marriage which would eventually end seventeen years later, but the incident does provide some insight into the man who would achieve fame for promising to come up with a technology which would not only predict but also "control" human behavior. Watson was never in control of his own sexual behavior, and, as a result, he was always being controlled by other people. He was controlled by the "stimulus" whenever he saw an attractive woman; he was controlled by remorse, an emotion he failed to explain convincingly according to behaviorist principles, and he was controlled by people who were willing to use the details of his sexual life as a form of blackmail. It is not surprising therefore that control of human behavior was one of the goals he announced in his famous lectures of 1913. In the book based on them known as *Behaviorism*, Watson insisted that psychology was a "purely objective experimental branch of natural science," with its "theoretical goal" being nothing less than the "prediction and control of behavior."[8]

Watson's interest in controlling behavior was rooted in his own life, primarily his sex life, which was, more often than not, out of control. God, Sigmund Freud once said, was an exalted father. Watson must have taken this dictum to heart. He abandoned religion because his father had abandoned it before him. Morals were associated with religion, which Watson associated with his emotional mother. Morals had failed both in his father's life and his own as a normative guide to behavior. Science, then, was the only option that could offer the control of behavior which Watson so desperately sought. Psychology would provide a technology of control, once Watson had jettisoned the philosophical baggage of the past and had discovered an empirical law based on animal behavior. Control of nature would then lead to control of human nature, since humans were organic machines like rats anyway. Watson's sexual impulses were, in ways he cared not to admit, closely analogous to the responses he could measure in rats. They were completely other-directed. Rather than admit that he had no self-control, Watson decided to create a psychology where the concept of self-control had no meaning. "I get rather disgusted sometimes," Watson wrote to Robert M. Yerkes, the famous primatologist, "with trying to make the human character amenable to law."[9] The statement is either poignant or arrogant depending on how it is taken: poignant if seen in response to his own lack of self-control, arrogant when seen as an attempt to project his own failings onto mankind as a whole.

Harold Ickes was correct in his assessment of Watson. Watson had no character, if by character we mean the ability to take rational control of passion on a consistent and dependable basis. Rather than admit his own failures, Watson decided to remake mankind in his own image. Man was now remade in the image of the superficial American, a man with no interior life, no morals, nothing but a seething mass of desires and fears that could be manipulated at will by those who knew how to control his passions. Man was an empty vessel, a *tabula rasa* upon which advertisers could write their texts. In the name of freedom, his passions could be manipulated into a bondage congenial to those who controlled the instruments of public opinion. Science was the mantra which *Homo Americanus* chanted to himself to assure himself that his bondage was really freedom. This should not be surprising, given Watson's view of what psychology was and what man was. Ultimately, John Watson was what he described: a response to a stimulus. His sex life was the model for behaviorism. *Homo Americanus* gave up inner-directedness and rejoiced in becoming, like Watson, simple reaction to sexual stimuli. Once certain influential classes of Americans made this decision to jettison sexual morals, science was the only way of gaining control where morals had failed.

There was only one problem. For both Watson the behaviorist and Watson the man, there was no such thing as self-control. This meant that behaviorism could explain reaction, but it could never explain action. In this it laid bare the ultimate stupidity of American pragmatism, a philosophy which eschewed what it considered to be outdated "metaphysical" concepts like truth in exchange for results based on action, but then was unable to explain what action was because action, as opposed to reaction, was always based on reason and its ability to apprehend transcendental values like the true and the good. In addition to being a tacit admission of the moral failures which Watson the man had accumulated during his life of sexual indulgence, behaviorism was a contradiction in terms as well. It could never explain the thing it was based on. It could never explain action. It only made sense in a world of controllers, which is why it proved congenial to the liberals and the world they would eventually build on the ruins created by World War I.

John B. Watson, in spite of rejecting the South, its religion, and its traditions, would remain forever the farm boy from South Carolina, no matter how sophisticated his environment became. Shortly after he got his job on Madison Avenue, he bought a farm in Connecticut. His definition of happiness was being lost in activity, a fitting description for an American pragmatist, and he soon lost himself in the activity of raising animals and building barns, all of the things he had left behind as a boy. Watson was always more at home with animals than he was with human beings, and during the first decade of the twentieth century, he spent much of his time studying animal behavior. In addition to rats in the lab, he studied birds on the Dry Tortugas. His goal was to get at the basic building blocks of human behavior and begin creating out of them a psychology which would explain the things he found so troubling in his own life. "Emotions," according to Watson, "when properly used, can be made to serve us rather than to destroy us." This statement leads one of his biographers to opine:

> The terrifying specter of annihilation that he posed as the grim alternative
> to the subordination of emotions helps to explain his obsession with their
> control. . . .Watson especially feared the unbridled release of mass emo
> tion. One of his favorite targets for criticism was evangelical Christianity,
> especially as manifested in the increasing number of large, urban centered
> revivals. "Every psychopathic clinic and hospital in the city feels the
> strain of a big revival meeting," Watson remarked to sociologist William
> I. Thomas. . . . Watson, who had so ostentatiously discarded those values

when he embraced modern urban life, registered his disapproval in clear, shrill tones. Religion, after all, Watson argued, was but an outmoded form of social control.[10]

Watson felt that religion was a form of social control because, in a world where there is no action, everything is a form of social control. Given his psychology of stimulus/response, a psychology which can't explain action because it can't admit reason, reaction is the only thing a man can do. And if all man can do is react, his life is nothing but response to stimuli controlled by others. Behaviorism is, therefore, not a psychology at all; it is a technology of psychic control. It doesn't explain why men act, but it does give a seemingly plausible explanation of how men may be controlled, which is why it proved congenial to the powers that were seeking to transform America from a republic of yeoman farmers into an empire of mindless consumers. Watson rode the crest of that political wave. Modernity needed, in the words of T. J. Lears, an "instrumental rationality that desanctified the outer world of nature and the inner world of the self, reducing both to manipulable objects."[11] If there is no inner world, no consciousness, then there is no reason, and if there is no reason, man cannot act. Practical reason is the science of action which explains how all action is predicated on man's perception of the transcendental good. If there is no inner world, then there is no psychology, and what goes under that name is nothing more than a technology of control, "an instrumental rationality for manipulating the control of emotions."[12]

In 1914 Watson published *Behavior: An Introduction to Comparative Psychology*, an introductory textbook he hoped would also interest the general reader. The "technological" aspects of new psychology were apparent almost from the beginning of the book: "The interest of the behaviorist in man's doings," Watson wrote, "is more than the interest of the spectator – he wants to control man's reactions as physical scientists want to control and manipulate other natural phenomena. It is the business of behavioristic psychology to be able to predict and to control human activity."[13] Man, according to the view Watson learned under Loeb at the university of Chicago, was best thought of "as an assembled organic machine ready to run."[14] And the mind or soul? The answer is equally glib: "We can throw all of our psychological problems and their solutions into terms of stimulus and response."[15]

Yet even in Watson's rush to turn psychology into the psychic equivalent of chemistry and physics, the personal still intrudes. In *Behaviorism*, Watson describes "Wives 'who do not understand,' sex hungers from which there is no escaping (for example, marriage to an invalid or insane husband or wife), malformations of the body (permanent inferiorities), and the like"[16] as problems now well within the realm of the solvable. By the end of his book, Watson tells us that "Some day we shall have hospitals devoted to helping us change our personality because we can change the personality as easily as we can change the shape of the nose, only it takes more time."[17] Until that time, however, "The reactions that we now make to the permanent stimuli are often abortive, inadequate for adjustment; they wreck our constitutions and may make us psychopathic."[18]

Watson here refers to his own nervous breakdown, his wife "who does not understand" and conditioning as an escape from his "sex hungers from where there is no escaping." The personal, however, takes a back seat to the political. Behaviorism will solve social problems by making psychologists into social engineers. And it is to this possibility that John Dewey reacted so enthusiastically, announcing that he was a "well-wisher" of behaviorism. Dewey welcomed the political implications of behavioral psychology, seeing in it not only a refutation of those who claimed there was a fixed human nature – "the ultimate refuge of the standpatter" – but also the fulfillment of Condorcet's prophecy of a "future in which human arrangements would be regulated by science."[19] Ultimately, it was the liberal social science establishment, with its interlocking network of grant-giving foundations and organs of public opinion, which spread Watson's ideas, and Watson made contact with this network early on.

In the fall of 1908 Watson joined the faculty of Johns Hopkins University in Baltimore, Maryland. Shortly after his arrival, Watson's mentor and co-worker in the nascent science of behaviorist psychology, John Mark Baldwin, was caught, quite literally, with his pants down when police raided a Negro brothel he was frequenting. Baldwin was soon thereafter forced to resign, and, as a result, Watson became head of the one of the most prestigious psychology departments in the country and editor of the equally prestigious *Journal of Animal Behavior,* which he founded with Robert M. Yerkes.

Yerkes was two years older than Watson and, like Watson, was raised on a farm. Like Watson, Yerkes turned his early interest in animals into a scientific career after majoring in psychology. Both abandoned the Christian faith in favor of science. In an unpublished autobiographical manuscript entitled "Testament," Yerkes wrote that "the assumptions, methods, and daily experiences of the natural scientist make for objectivity, disinterestedness, breadth and independence of mind, whereas those of the religionist make rather for subjectivity, bias, limitation of view, authoritarianism, and an attitude of dogmatic certainty."[20] Like Watson, Yerkes was convinced that science offered a "way of life" superior to any moral system that religion had to offer.

Yerkes graduated with a Ph.D. in psychology from Harvard in 1902 and immediately joined the faculty there. Over the 1916–17 academic year, Yerkes was elected president of the American Psychological Association. Because he had become deeply involved with psychological testing by that time, he was asked to head the Army's psychological testing program in

1916. During that same year, the National Research Council was created by Congress as the working arm of the National Academy of Sciences. In 1917 Yerkes secured a position with the NRC in Washington, D.C., where he demonstrated both his administrative skills and his ability to foster the work of others in the same field. In 1924 Yerkes left the NRC and returned to academic life, this time at Yale, and in 1929 his research work culminated in the crowning achievement of his scientific career, the publication in 1929 of his book *The Great Apes: A Study of Anthropoid Life*.

In 1910, at the height of Yerkes's collaborative friendship with Watson, when the latter was involved with the experiments that would lead to the 1913 lecture in New York at Columbia and the 1914 book *Behaviorism*, John D. Rockefeller, Jr., had been asked to serve as foreman on a grand jury in New York City that was looking into what was termed the "white slave traffic" at the time. The lurid tales of respectable young white women lured into prostitution made for sensational headlines at the time, but they also propelled the richest family in the world to become involved in sex research. In the winter of 1911, Junior, as he was known in the Rockefeller family, and several other civic leaders organized the Bureau of Social Hygiene. The social hygienists, according to James H. Jones,

> were looking to science to explain why people behaved as they did sexually, thereby furnishing reformers with the data needed to understand and control human sexual behavior. Ultimately, however, the joke would be on the social hygienists. Just as the shattering of the conspiracy of silence had led to a public dialogue on a host of sexual questions, with far-reaching consequences no one could have foreseen, the decision to impress science into the service of social control eventually backfired. Social hygienists failed to recognize that scientific data could be used to support sexual liberation as easily as social control, a point that Kinsey would demonstrate repeatedly in the decades ahead.[21]

Jones fails to see that the matrix of sex research, as the Yerkes-Watson connection makes clear, was behaviorism, which did not believe in morals and had always been intended as a technology of social control. As a result, Jones comes up with a false dichotomy, seeing sexual liberation as the antithesis of social control, when it was really an instrument of social control, one which would become absorbed into communications theory/psychological warfare research when the Rockefeller Foundation began funding Kinsey – at Yerkes's recommendation – in 1941.

Part II, Chapter 3

Bremen, 1909

In August of 1909 Sigmund Freud embarked upon a fateful journey. He, along with his psychoanalytic heir apparent, Carl Gustav Jung, had been invited by G. Stanley Hall, the father of American Psychology, to give a series of lectures at Clark University in Worcester, Massachusetts. Hall was also the man who thought nature was more important than nurture and as a result ended up being the occasion for Margaret Mead's famous book to the contrary, *Coming of Age in Samoa*. Freud's voyage to America had an inauspicious beginning. Jung got drunk and started talking in a confused way about the prehistoric bog corpses which he mixed up with the mummies in the lead cellars of Bremen, the city from which they were departing by ship to America. Freud felt that the talk of mummies was a veiled attack on fathers in general and him and his authority in particular and in the middle of their conversation Freud suddenly fainted.

Things then went from bad to worse. Freud and Jung agreed to analyze each other's dreams during the voyage, but when Jung confronted Freud about a dream involving Freud's wife and sister-in-law, Freud shut down the analysis, claiming that he could go no further. "I cannot risk my authority," is how Freud framed the issue.[1] Which is exactly how Jung saw it as well. Freud's authority involved keeping something secret, and that secret involved his relationship with his sister-in-law, Minna Bernays. If the true nature of that relationship came out, Freud would lose his authority – presumably over Jung, of course – but one gets the impression that the issue was bigger than that and that Freud was worried about losing it over the rest of his followers and over his nascent following throughout the world as well.

Jung, of course, knew something that Freud didn't know. On his first trip to Vienna to meet Freud in person, he claimed that Minna Bernays, Freud's sister-in-law, confided that she had been having an affair with Freud. Biographers like Peter Gay have found the claim implausible, but the very fact that Jung was pressing the issue on the sea voyage to America argues in favor of believing that it happened. Jung, of course, brought his own sexual baggage to the meeting. He had been having an affair with a patient by the name of Sabina Spielrein and had gone to Freud for what amounted to absolution, an act which confers power on the absolver. If Freud were involved in the same sort of illicit sexual activity as Jung, then the act of absolution might seem more than a little bit hypocritical, and this probably fueled Jung's resentment toward his mentor and his determination to find out whether in fact Freud was involved in the same sort of thing. A candid admission of guilt might have cleared the air, but it might also have taken the wind out the sails of the psychoanalytical movement. Whether it would or wouldn't have is beside the point now. Freud clearly felt that he could not take the chance, that the risk was too great, that Jung was onto something, and that if he admitted the affair, Jung, and not he, would have had the upper hand in the relationship.

The relationship collapsed anyway. Jung later said that Freud lost his authority by not confessing. "Freud," he said, "was placing personal authority above truth."[2] The truth, in other words, were it known, would destroy whatever authority Freud had. The simplest explanation of Freud's reticence, the one I pursued in *Degenerate Moderns*, is that what Freud called the Oedipus Complex, the fact that "all men" desire sexual relations with their mothers or sisters, is really nothing but the projection of Freud's guilt away from his affair with Minna Bernays.[3] Instead of admitting that he had done something wrong, Freud engaged in a massive instance of rationalization. He subordinated the truth to his desires. If his followers were to uncover the details of his transgression, they would hold the key which explained his theory in terms of his behavior. As a result, the theory would lose its power to explain the psyche, and Freud would lose his authority along with his failed theory.

All of that is true as far as it goes, but as much as it explains the personal sources of the Oedipus Complex, it barely begins to explain the political ramifications of that idea. Both Freud and Jung could read the signs of the times. Both were aware that they had discovered in psychotherapy not so much a medicine for healing people as much as a tool for manipulating them. Psychotherapy was a way of managing guilt, as Jung understood first hand, and both Freud and Jung knew that wealthy patients were, in the name of psychotherapy, willing to pay large sums of money to be absolved of guilt while at the same time allowed to hold onto the vices which caused the guilt in the first place. Both Freud and Jung understood how powerful and how profitable this new discovery could be, and the break between them is best understood in this light. It wasn't over ideas, but over control of a movement, over the control of rich patients and their financial resources, that Jung broke with Freud. Jung knew where the source of Freud's power lay, and he wanted that source in his own right and not as somebody's gentile heir apparent.

At around the same time that Freud first received his invitation to speak at Clark University, Jung received a visit from a wealthy American patient by the name of Medill McCormick, scion of the wealthy Chicago family which owned *The Chicago Tribune* and International Harvester. "Fate," Jung wrote,

> which evidently loves crazy games, had just at this time deposited on my doorstep a well-known American (friend of Roosevelt and Taft, proprietor of several big newspapers, etc. . . .) as a patient. Naturally he has the

same conflicts I have just overcome, so I could be of great help to him, which is gratifying in more respects than one. It was like balm on my aching wound. This case has interested me so passionately in the last fortnight that I have forgotten my other duties.[4]

McCormick was suffering from alcoholism and depression, and Jung, bolstered by Freud's absolution of his affair with Sabina Spielrein, decided that he had the cure. Jung prescribed polygamy. "He rather recommended," McCormick wrote later, "a little flirting and told me to bear in mind *that it might be advisable* for me to have mistresses – that I was a very dangerous and savage man, that I must not forget my heredity and my infantile influences and lose my soul – if women would save it."[5] Noll explains Jung's infatuation with polygamy as part self-exculpation of his own behavior but also as stemming from his increasing interest in "Aryan" mysticism, an infatuation which grew in direct proportion to his alienation from the Jew Freud and what he perceived as the "Jewish" psychoanalysis of the Freudian school.

The Aryan/Jewish conflict, much like the mystical/atheist polarity of an earlier age, was at root a pretext for a struggle which was over control of a new psychic technology and the financial benefits that went with that control. Freud had discovered a way of controlling people by alternately manipulating guilt and the passion that caused the guilt, and Jung, after experiencing first of all how powerful it was first-hand, and then discovering in Freud's biography the source of that power, wanted to control it himself. He first treated Medill McCormick in Zurich in late 1908, then again in March of 1909, and then again, this time in America, in September of 1909 on the same trip with Freud to Clark University.

Jung had just made contact with one of the wealthiest families in America and was rubbing his hands in anticipation of the rewards which might accrue from that contact. After the break with Freud, Jung was beating the master at his own game. Freud, as Swales documents, was obsessed with money throughout his career. In a letter to Fliess in 1899, he wrote, "My mood also depends very much on my earnings. Money is laughing gas for me." Freud's best explanation of his relationship to his patients came in the form of a cartoon which appeared in the *Fliegende Blätter*, a popular humor magazine of the time, in which a lion looks at his watch and mutters, "Twelve o'clock and no Negroes." Freud was the lion, and in his letters to Fliess thereafter he referred to his patients as "Negroes," which is to say, something to eat.[6] Freud had already established the predatory nature of psychoanalysis in his relationship with Jung. Patients were to be either people of wealth or influence. The latter instance applied to Jung, who was the Aryan heir apparent who would ensure that psychoanalysis would become something other than a simply Jewish affair.

Jung learned his lesson well – too well, in fact – and the struggle between the two men quickly became the struggle for who would control this emerging technology of psychic control. Jung could apply the exculpation Freud had wrought on him to the wealthy young American and bring this man under his control by simultaneously manipulating his vices and absolving him of the guilt which flowed from those actions, just as Freud had done with him. The conflict may have been inevitable, but the immediate context is also relevant. The rise of Jung's quarrel with Freud corresponded with Jung's introduction to wealthy American patients. The struggle wasn't primarily over ideas but rather over influence. Who would get to eat the "Negroes"?

By the time the break between Freud and Jung was complete in 1913, it looked as if Jung were winning. After making contact with the McCormicks, one of the wealthiest families in America, Jung had just made contact with the Rockefellers, *the* wealthiest family in America when Edith Rockefeller McCormick, Medill's sister-in-law, showed up in Zurich for treatment for depression. When word got out that Jung had received a grant in 1916 amounting to $2 million in current funds, Freud was both envious and bitter. The Aryans were triumphing over the Jews once again.

In order to soften the blow that Jung's defection inflicted on the psychoanalytic movement, the "Jewish" faction of the psychoanalytic movement came up with an idea of forming a secret society around Freud. Its purpose was to maintain orthodoxy, to insure that the movement would continue after Freud was gone, and, in Ernest Jones's words, "to monitor Jung."[7] In his partisan biography of Freud, Jones said, "The idea of forming a brotherhood of initiates came from his boyhood memories of 'many secret societies from literature.'" L. J. Rather thinks that Jones is referring here to the novels of Benjamin Disraeli, specifically *Coningsby* and *Tancred*, both of which talk about a Jewish conspiracy to topple the thrones and altars of Europe. "You never observe a great intellectual movement in Europe," Disraeli wrote in *Coningsby*,

> in which the Jews do not greatly participate. The first Jesuits were Jews: that mysterious Russian Diplomacy which so alarms Western Europe is organized and principally carried on by Jews: that mighty revolution which is at this moment preparing in Germany, and which will in fact be a second and greater Reformation . . . is entirely developing under the auspices of Jews, who almost monopolize the professorial chairs of Germany.[8]

The fact that Disraeli was himself a Jew lent a credibility to his fictions that was both ironic and compelling. Cosima Wagner thought it ironic that a Jew would make such a statement and said so to her husband. The novels of Disraeli, with their purported revelation of Jewish conspiracies revolving around the concept that "all is race" (Houston Stewart Chamberlain picked up the idea from Disraeli) continued to be a topic of conversation four years

later when *Tancred* appeared. Since Nietzsche was part of the Wagner
household at the time, he was probably in on the conversations about Jews
and secret societies. Rather traces Jones's proposal to initiate a secret society
at the heart of psychoanalysis to Disraeli's novels and indicates that psychoanalysis was at root a Jewish conspiracy whose goal was the overthrow of
Christendom. Phyllis Grosskurth, however, indicates that the idea of creating a secret society at the heart of the psychoanalytic tradition might have
come from Freud himself. She cites the official explanation of the secret society as it appeared in Jones's biography along with the crucial passages
Jones left out. Jones, she writes,

> suggested that a secret committee be formed as a Praetorian guard around
> Freud. The unstated aim, of course, was to monitor Jung, to maintain a
> watching brief in which they would report to Freud. Freud's response
> (August 1, 1912) was highly enthusiastic: *What took hold of my imagina-
> tion immediately is your idea of a secret council composed of the best and
> most trustworthy among our men to take care of the further development
> of and defend the cause against personalities and accidents when I am no
> more. You say it was Ferenczi who expressed this idea, yet it may be mine
> own shaped in better times, when I hoped Jung would collect such a circle
> around him composed of the official headman of the local associations.
> Now I am sorry to say such a union had to be formed independently of
> Jung and of the elected presidents. I daresay it would make living and dy-
> ing easier for me if I knew of such an association existing to watch over my
> creation.* I know there is a boyish, perhaps romantic element too in this
> conception but perhaps it could be adapted to meet the necessities of real-
> ity. I will give my fancy free play and leave to you the part of the Censor.[9]

In the italicized section, which Grosskurth restored, Freud makes clear
that the idea of psychoanalysis as a secret society was part of his concept
even during his association with Jung. After the break, however, the Jewish
nature of the secret society became more apparent. Eventually, the idea was
made reality during a secret ring ceremony in 1913, when Freud gave Hanns
Sachs, Karl Abraham, Sandor Ferenczi, and Otto Rank and Ernest Jones
Greek intaglio rings embossed with an image of Zeus. The fact that Freud acceded so readily and enthusiastically to the idea and even had rings made to
consummate it indicates that Grosskurth's suspicions are justified. It was
probably Freud's idea from the beginning. The same idea is also developed
by Rather, who says Freud had already been drawn to secret societies as a
young man. Freud admired his physiology teacher Ernst Bruecke, who came
together with Emil du Bois-Reymond and Hermann Helmholtz in 1852 to
"form . . . a kind of scientific freemasonry . . . whose goal was to destroy
completely whatever remained of the old vitalist ideology." In addition to
that, as a student at the Sperl Gymnasium Freud came under the influence of
fellow student Heinrich Braun, who "awakened a multitude of revolutionary
trends in me." Freud was also a member of B'nai B'rith, and so it is not sur-

prising that his idea of a secret society revolved around the role of the Jew in a Christian and, more specifically, Catholic world, the Austro-Hungarian empire, where conversion to Christianity, as in the famous case of the composer Gustav Mahler, was the necessary condition for a career in the arts or sciences. Freud was a non-observant Jew who hated all religion and saw it as an "illusion," but he deeply resented the hegemony of Christianity in Vienna as well as its chilling effect on his ambitions. Christianity may have been an illusion, but that hardly changed the fact that it was thwarting his career.

The resentment comes out clearly in a famous passage in the *Psychopathology of Everyday Life,* in which two Jews meet by chance on the Croatian coast, where they are vacationing. One of them is Freud, and the other a younger man who is familiar with his works and wants to know why he can't remember a certain word from a famous line in the *Aeneid*. The line is *Exoriare aliquis nostris ex ossibus ultor* ("Raise up from our bones an avenger") and the word which the young man can't remember is "aliquis," which he breaks down into "a - liquis" and from which, after a long involved analysis, Freud deduces, like a latter-day Sherlock Holmes, that the man is worried that his lady friend is pregnant. The inability to remember bespeaks an ambivalence on the young man's part which stems from repression: He wants an heir to be his avenger against "Rome," but he is afraid that the heir might come from some unwanted source and endanger his career. That the young man is concerned about his career comes out when the conversation turns to "race," i.e., the Jewish question: "We had fallen into conversation – how I have now forgotten – about the social status of the race to which we both belonged; and ambitious feelings prompted him to give vent to a regret that his generation was doomed (as he expressed it) to atrophy, and could not develop its talents or satisfy its needs."[10]

The "Exoriare" line has direct relevance here. Taken from the *Aeneid* it is Dido's curse on the founder of Rome, Aeneas, for betraying her, and was used by Jewish revolutionaries like Ferdinand Lassalle as the rallying cry against "Rome," which is to say the Catholic Church and the states where Catholicism was the established religion. The conflict between Rome and Carthage had special meaning to Freud, who saw himself as a revenant of Hannibal, the Semite who attempted to conquer Rome. Rather sees in Freud someone influenced by Moses Hess, the proto-Zionist and proto-socialist and teacher of Karl Marx, whose book *Rom und Jerusalem* gave early expression to rising Jewish expectation in Christian Europe.[11]

The fact that the young Jew can't quite bring himself to utter Dido's curse leads Freud to return to the Jewish issue and elicit more associations, and as a result, the psychoanalysis again returns to the issue of Jewish social and political aspiration: "I am thinking," the young man continued, "of Simon of Trent, whose relics I saw two years ago in a church at Trent. I am thinking of the accusation of ritual blood sacrifice which is being brought against the Jews again just now, and of Kleinpaul's book in which he regards all these supposed victims as incarnations, one might say new editions of the Savior."[12]

Rather claims this is a reference to accusations of Jewish blood ritual murder in general and the Tisza-Eszlar affair of 1882 in particular. However, the phrase "just now" could just have easily referred to the Dreyfus affair. Alfred Dreyfus, a French army officer, was convicted of treason in 1894, and the conviction was overturned in 1906. The simple truth of the matter is that concerns about Jewish conspiracy were quite common during the entire last quarter of the nineteenth century. Disraeli's novels gave expression to a common obsession, a fear of a Jewish-Masonic conspiracy which aspired to overturn both throne and altar on its way to establishing a Jewish worldwide regime that many thought would bring about the reign of the Antichrist. These fears reached a crescendo in the Dreyfus affair and beyond that found further substantiation in the Zionist congress in Basel in 1896, called in reaction to the Dreyfus affair, at which Theodor Herzl called for the creation of a Jewish state.

Eventually Freud brings the psychoanalysis to a conclusion by tracing the young man's ambivalence and forgetfulness to a suspicion that he both wants an heir to avenge him and at the same time does not because the avenger would come from an unpleasant and unexpected source "The contradiction," Freud concludes, "has its roots in repressed sources and derives from thought that should lead to a diversion of attention."[13]

But diversion of attention from what? In *Degenerate Moderns*, I discuss Swales's explanation of this passage in *The Psychopathology of Everyday Life*, according to which there is no young man. Freud is psychoanalyzing himself and making, in what I termed an expression of the Dimmesdale Syndrome, a veiled confession about his affair with Minna Bernays, which was consummated near Trent in September of 1900. That affair is the psychic source of the Oedipus Complex, which avers that "all men" have a desire to sleep with their mothers or sisters. So Freud is the young man, and the young man is very aware of his position as a Jew in society and the fact that he can't make it in a Christian world unless he capitulates to "Rome" and converts to Christianity. Just as the Oedipus Complex is Freud's guilty conscience projected into a "scientific" principle, a discovery of the real nature of man, which absolves him of all guilt in the matter, so the inability to remember a key word in the line from the *Aeneid* beginning with "Exoriare" is Freud's covert expression of his Jewish animus against Rome and, perhaps, a just-as-covert attempt to tell the reader what he plans to do about that unacceptable state of affairs. In typical fashion, Freud makes use of a literary reference to indicate his intentions, but as always in covert fashion. Like the young man who is really a disguised version of himself, Freud is full of ambivalence. He wants an avenger and is afraid of an avenger. He wants to both reveal and conceal the source of his resentment and his plan for revenge.

Freud may have used the Oedipus Complex to justify his affair with Minna Bernays, but the idea did not originate with him. He got the idea for the Oedipus Complex, not from self-analysis as he said – Jones launched this myth in his biography – but rather from Nietzsche's *Birth of Tragedy*:

> with regard to the mother-wooing , riddle-solving Oedipus, an immediate interpretation comes to mind, that where through the oracular and magic powers the force of both present and future, the rigid law of individuation as well as the magic of nature is broken, the preconditioning cause is that beforehand a monstrous act against nature – something on the order of incest – must have taken place; then how is one to force nature to reveal her secrets other than by victoriously going against her, that is, through an act contrary to nature. I see this recognition sketched out in that hideous trinity of Oedipus's fate: the same man who solves the riddle of nature – that double-edged sphinx – must violate the most holy order of nature as both parricide and spouse of his mother. Indeed the meaning of the myth seems inescapable, that wisdom and especially Dionysian wisdom is an unnatural horror, and that the man who through his knowledge plunges nature into the abyss of annihilation, experiences in his own being the disintegration of nature. "The point of wisdom turns against the wise; wisdom is a crime against nature."[14]

Freud corresponded with Nietzsche as a student, and so we know he was familiar with his work. Torrey claims that "Freud was indebted to Nietzsche for the concept of the id,"[15] without mentioning the above-cited passage from *The Birth of Tragedy* as the source of the Oedipus Complex. We know as well that Freud never mentioned Nietzsche because he was obsessive about covering his intellectual trail. In the passage from the *Birth of Tragedy*, we see much more clearly than in Freud's heavily censored version of the "Oedipus Complex" a way out of the young man's dilemma, a way for an ambitious Jew to achieve his goals without kowtowing to "Rome" or more particularly the Catholic Hapsburg monarchy which ruled the Austro-Hungarian empire at the time. Incest had long been part of the Illuminist, revolutionary tradition. Shelley made incest the centerpiece of his revolutionary poem, "The Revolt of Islam." Incest, as Nietzsche makes clear, has a political application. By killing the father and/or becoming spouse of his mother, the Oedipal revolutionary "forces nature to reveal her secrets." Knowledge, especially illicit carnal knowledge, means power, the power to bring off a revolution like that of 1789 in France and, perhaps, even greater. The epigraph for his first book *The Interpretation of Dreams* indicates in Freud's typically cryptic way the political program of psychoanalysis: *Flectere si nequeo superos, Acheronta movebo* ("If the powers above ignore me, I will move the powers of hell").

Freud is proposing here a revolutionary psychology in which the passions, before kept under the control of reason, now act as secret agents betraying reason's control by seemingly inconsequential things like forgetting foreign words or substituting names. The id, Freud's word for what the classical world called the passions or appetites, corresponds to the powers of hell Dido calls on to avenge Carthage. Unable to make use of the powers from above in the Austro-Hungarian empire to foster his career, Freud in his veiled way begins to propose a revolutionary psychology which will allow him to harness the id for political and economic purposes. The secret society is the vehicle for the political program of psychoanalysis, whose power lies in being able to manipulate the confessional relationship for personal, financial, and, ultimately, political gain. In keeping with the classical allusion to Dido and her desire for revenge against Rome, Freud described himself in his letters to Wilhelm Fliess as a latter-day Hannibal, a "Semite" who crossed the Alps (as Freud would have to do) on his way to Rome. Like Hannibal, Freud planned to approach Rome by indirection and thereby conquer it unawares. The Oedipus Complex and the psychoanalysis which it was based on had a political purpose from the beginning. The purpose was to conquer Rome, i.e., to subvert the influence of the Catholic Church and the confessional states like the Austro-Hungarian Empire based on that religious order.

It is not surprising, therefore, that Freud would turn psychoanalysis into a secret society. The destruction of Rome, the overturning of throne and altar, had been the purpose of secret societies since their heyday in the eighteenth century. Psychoanalysis had always been the "Jewish" (at least in Freud's eyes) conspiracy to mobilize the powers of Acheronta against Rome and Vienna. It had always been a revolutionary organization; when Freud's hope for a gentile heir died with Jung's defection, it became even more explicitly so by adopting all of the tropes and paraphernalia attributed to secret societies by nineteenth-century writers. Psychoanalysis became, in their words, a Judeo-masonic conspiracy to overthrow throne and altar.

On September 11, 1899, Freud wrote to Fliess to say that he was "saddened and embittered" by the Dreyfus affair.[16] "There is no question," he concluded, "on whose side the future lies."[17] Since Alfred Dreyfus wasn't acquitted until five years later, Freud must have meant that the anti-Semites were winning. Or did Freud have something else in mind? By the time Freud mentioned the frustration of Jewish ambitions in 1902 in the *Psychopathology of Everyday Life,* the conflation of Jew and Freemason was complete. If he were familiar with any of the arguments of the anti-Semitic tracts – and there is every indication he was – he was aware of the conflation as well. Jew and Freemason had taken on an interchangeable character in the anti-secret society, anti-revolutionary literature of the day. By the time Freud wrote *Psychopathology*, Adam Weishaupt, the student of the Jesuits and the professor of Canon Law in Catholic Bavaria, was regularly called a Jew. If

Freud was aware of the rising tide of anti-Semitism and the conflation implicit in the commonly used term *"judeo-mâçonnerie"* then he must have been aware of Barruel because Barruel was mentioned in virtually all of the anti-Judeo-masonic tracts as their ultimate source. (In addition to the French sources, two German sources on Illuminism appeared at around the same time: Ludwig Wolfram's book *Die Illuminaten in Bayern und ihre Verfolgung* appeared in 1899–1900, the same year as *Interpretation of Dreams*. Leopold Engel's book *Geschichte des Illuminaten Ordens* appeared in 1906.)

In his book, *The Mythology of Secret Societies*, J. M. Roberts, who is no admirer of Barruel (he calls the *Memoirs* a "farrago of nonsense") grants Barruel primacy of place as the *fons et origo* of the conspiracy theory, calling his *Memoirs* "the bible of the secret society mythology and the indispensable foundation of future anti-Masonic writing.[18] '*Toute la politique anti- mâçonnique du XIXe siècle à ses sources dans le livre de l'abbé Barruel,*' remarks a standard authority on "French 18th century [*sic*] thought."[19] If Freud were at all familiar with the controversy surrounding the "social status of the race to which we both belong" he knew that Jews were being accused of belonging to a secret society based on the Freemasons or the Illuminati; he knew that that secret society was revolutionary in intent, seeking to overturn both throne and altar, and he knew that the man that all of the anti-Semitic writings cited as their source was the Abbé Barruel. That Barruel never mentions the word "Jew" in his 2,200 pages does not change the fact that those who called upon his name did. By the time Freud wrote the *Psychopathology of Everyday Life* in 1902, the conflation of Jew and Freemason had been expanded to include the triad Jew-Freemason-Satanist. Vitz says Freud made a pact with the devil 1888, on *Walpurgisnacht* in direct imitation of the corresponding scene from Goethe's *Faust*.

As all of the foregoing, but especially the allusion to Vergil and Goethe indicates, Freud operated not primarily as a natural scientist but as a literary man under the conscious influence of literary models. He got the Oedipus Complex from Sophocles by way (unacknowledged, of course) of Nietzsche, and it is precisely as a literary figure from the pen of the Abbé Barruel that Adam Weishaupt, founder of the Illuminati, exerted most of his influence. Nesta Webster in *World Revolution* claims a direct organizational connection between the Illuminati and the Bolsheviks, a claim which has caused the so-called conspiracy theory to fall on hard times. A stronger case can be made for literary influence. By publishing the secret papers of the Illuminati in 1787, the prince of Bavaria granted Weishaupt an immortality that his organizational skills could never have achieved on their own. That fame was spread even farther by Barruel's *Memoirs*, a best-seller in just about all of the countries of Europe where it appeared at the turn of the nineteenth century. Mary Godwin Shelley immortalized Weishaupt as Dr. Frankenstein, after reading Barruel. Even a *bona fide* revolutionary like Buonarroti learned about the Illuminist conspiracy not by any direct initiation into its secrets but by reading Barruel as Shelley did. We are talking about literary influence here, not, as the Germans put it, *"Drahtziehertheorie"* (manipulator theory). Freud like Shelley and Buonarotti most likely found out about the Illuminist-Jewish-Masonic- Satanist conspiracy by literary influences, all of which led back to Barruel.

That Freud does not mention Barruel is not surprising. He doesn't mention Nietzsche either, and certainly not as the source of the Oedipus Complex. As a matter of fact, Freud never mentions the things most important to him in any direct way. He is a master of covering his intellectual trail. In a letter to Fliess dated December 3, 1897, a time of great turmoil for Freud, he connects his Jewish animus against Rome with his boyhood hero Hannibal and then abruptly breaks off any more associations lest he reveal either his sources or his intentions too clearly. "My longing for Rome," Freud writes, "is, by the way, deeply neurotic. It is connected with my high school hero-worship of the Semitic Hannibal, and this year I did not reach Rome any more than he did from Lake Trasimeno. Since I have been studying the unconscious, I have become so interesting to myself. A pity that one always keeps one's mouth shut about the most intimate things: *"Das beste was Du weisst,/ Darfst du den Buben nicht sagen."* The quote "The best of what you know, you dare not tell the boys." is from Goethe's *Faust*, and again we are given a cryptic reference to something Freud would rather not say out loud, lest he lose his authority. Goethe's influence on Freud is hard to underestimate, and cited by many. Most commentators, however, fail to mention that Goethe was an Illuminatus, whose code name was Abaris. Goethe is one of the literary figures who became a member of the organization while it was still in existence and not, like Shelley and others, as a result of literary influence, chiefly Barruel's book. Goethe was intimately involved in trying to find a sinecure for Weishaupt after he had to flee Bavaria. (W. Daniel Wilson claims that Goethe was in fact a double agent, spying on the Illuminati for Duke Karl August of Weimar as a way of keeping them under control.) Goethe wrote about secret societies explicitly in his novel *Wilhelm Meisters Lehrjahre,* but the arcana of *Faust* stems from that tradition as well.

Freud, in his letter to Fliess, adverts to his desire to conquer Rome, his identification with the Semite Hannibal, and then, with a reference to Goethe, says he can tell us no more, the implication being that he would lose his authority if he did. If we really knew what Freud were up to, then he would have no power over us. Psychoanalysis, in other words, can only function as a form of manipulation from behind the scenes. Because of this, it is quintessentially conspiratorial. Conspiracies work only if they are kept secret. If their real intentions were clear, they would be ineffective. Freud, Vitz tells us, burned his personal papers, not once but twice, as a way of throwing future investigators off the scent. The only safe conclusion one can draw from Freud's use of the line from Goethe is that if an idea or source is important to Freud ("*Das Beste was Du weisst*") Freud will not tell us what it is ("*Darfst Du den Buben doch nicht sagen.*").

This, of course, does not mean that there is no evidence that Freud read either Barruel or the Illuminist manuscripts. The evidence is in the text itself. In describing the code names of the conspirators, Barruel explains that Zwack, because of his hatred for kings, took the name "Philip Strozzi, after that famous Florentine Conspirator, who having murthered Alexander de Medicis was afterwards taken in open rebellion against his sovereign, and plunged a dagger into his own breast reciting that verse with all the cry of vengeance: *Exoriare aliquis nostris ex ossibus ultor.*"[20]

In a description of recruiting techniques that has direct relevance to Freud's penchant, already discussed, of seeking out wealthy patients, Weishaupt instructs his followers to seek out

> the dextrous and dashing youths. We must have adepts who are insinuating, intriguing, full of resource bold and enterprising; they must also be flexible and tractable, obedient, docile and sociable. Seek out also those who are distinguished by their power, nobility, riches or learning, *nobiles, potentes, divites doctors, quaerite* – Spare no pains, spare nothing in the acquisition of such adepts. If heaven refuse its aidance, conjure hell.
> *Flectere si nequeas superos, Acheronta movebo.*[21]

The similarities between Freud's secret society and Adam Weishaupt's become even more striking if we look at the incident which threatened to bring both institutions down, namely, incest. When challenged by Jung to explain his relationship to his sister-in-law, Freud retreated, saying by way of explanation, "But I cannot risk my authority." In a letter to his co-conspirator Hertel, Weishaupt admits to having had an affair with his sister-in-law, who is now pregnant. Barruel relates the incident in the following way:

"Now," says Weishaupt to his adept, "let me, under the most profound secrecy, lay open the situation of my heart. It destroys my rest, it render [*sic*] me incapable of every thing. I am almost desperate. My honor is in danger and I am on the eve of losing that reputation which gave me so great an authority over our people. My sister-in-law is with child."[22]

Weishaupt goes on to ask Hertel's assistance in procuring an abortion ("it is not too late to make an attempt, for she is only in her fourth month") but the thing that troubles him the most is the fear that admitting that he committed incest with his sister-in-law will destroy his authority: "What vexes me the most in all this is that my authority over our people will be greatly diminished – that I have exposed a weak side, of which they will not fail to advantage themselves whenever I may preach morality and exhort them to virtue and modesty."[23]

Incest may have been coincidental to Weishaupt's scheme, but it became part of the occult revolutionary program thereafter. It played a key role in Byron's and Shelley's writings and in their lives as well. As part of his Illuminist cabal, Shelley first had sex with his sister-in-law, Claire Clairmont, and then sent her to seduce Byron as well. The "league of incest," as contemporary gossip termed their menage, was to become complete when Byron seduced or was seduced by Mary Godwin, but Shelley had a psychotic breakdown before the incestuous circle could be completed. Taking his cue from Nietzsche, Freud saw incest as a way of forcing nature to reveal her secrets and therefore her power to him, but he also understood that the secret which was the source of his power over nature must be guarded if he were to retain his authority. If people like Jung were ever to find out about his relationship with Minna his sister-in-law, they would have the key to Freud's sphinx-like riddle and that would mean the end of his authority and, therefore, his power. They would also understand the real source of the Oedipus Complex in Freud's guilty conscience.

But even more striking than the literary influences and the connection between incest and loss of authority is the similarity between Illuminism and psychoanalysis. Both Illuminism and psychoanalysis claimed that they could plumb the depths of the soul by carefully observing seemingly random lapses and gestures. Both were based on having the patient or adept give in-depth, quasi-confessional "examinations of conscience" during which they told the Illuminist controller or psychotherapist details of their personal lives which could later be used against them. Both Illuminism and psychoanalysis ended up as covert forms of psychic control, whereby the controller learned of the adept's dominant passion and manipulated him accordingly. Illuminism claimed to be a kind of "*Zucht*" or training, a way to perfection, but Agethen, in comparing Illuminism to its roots in the German pietist tradition, makes it clear that "self-knowledge was not the final goal of a religious-transcendental longing for salvation; rather, self-knowledge and human knowledge served as forms of control which were to bring about the creation of a utopian heaven on earth."[24]

Psychoanalysis and Illuminism were, in effect the same project – the Illuminist term *Seelenanalyse* is simply the Germanified term of psychoanalysis or vice versa – with the details changed to suit the sensibilities of a later age, an age which believed that "science" and "medicine," rather than secret societies, would lead to heaven on earth. Both psychoanalysis and Illuminism engaged in what a later critic called "*Seelenspionage*," spying on the soul. Both made use of what might be called a Masonic doctrine of two truths as part of their very nature. What the adept knew was not the same as what the controller knew. The patient saw psychoanalysis as a form of liberation; whereas the therapist fostered this illusion as a form of control. Psychoanalysis adopted all of the essential characteristics of Illuminist mind control, but Illuminism can just as easily be seen as an early form of psychoanalysis, a project long cherished by the Enlightenment. Christian Thomasius, writing at the very beginning of the Enlightenment in 1691, describes the "new discovery of a science that is both well-grounded and highly necessary for the common good," a science, namely, that "is able to recognize the hidden things in the hearts of other men even against their will out of the details of their daily conversation."[25]

At the heart of psychoanalysis we find Freud, as the paradigmatic analyst acting out, in his own words, the role of "father confessor." The manipulation of both confession and examination of conscience as the heart of Illuminism is a well-established fact. Adam Weishaupt was a student of the Jesuits for eight years. In creating his secret society, Weishaupt simply took the Spiritual Exercises of Ignatius of Loyola, most specifically the examination of conscience and illuminized them. Weishaupt was a case study in ambivalence when it came to the Jesuits. He hated them and yet told Friedrich Muenter that as a young man he almost became one himself (*dass er als junger Mann "selbst nahe dabey war, Jesuit zu werden"*).[26] By stripping the examination of conscience of all supernatural content and removing the controls on the confessional established by the Church (most notably the notion of confidentiality intrinsic to the seal of the confessional), Weishaupt turned confession into an instrument of manipulation and control. Examination of conscience taken out of the confessional became *Seelenspionage*. Instead of liberating the penitent from sin, it rendered him bound to his controller, liable to blackmail, but more often than not manipulated according to the passions he described in detail to his "confessor." Illuminism is not the adoption of the spirituality of Ignatius; it is its perversion.

According to Barruel, Weishaupt "detested the children of Benedict, Francis or Ignatius, [but] he admired the institutions of these holy founders, and was particularly charmed with Ignatius, whose laws directed so many zealous men dispersed throughout the world toward the same object and under one head." Weishaupt, according to Barruel, "conceived that the same forms might be adopted, though to operate in a sense diametrically opposite."[27] Agethen cites the influence of the Jesuit Balthasar Gratian in his 1647 book *Orocula manual y arte de prudencia*, in which he explains "how to control others, how to have influence on their will, by knowing their inclinations and their weak points. Observation of another and knowing as much about him as possible becomes the central means of power."[28] Weishaupt's co-conspirator Knigge called their technique of manipulating lower rank Illuminati a "semiotics of the soul": "From the evaluation of all these characteristics," Knigge wrote, "even the smallest and least significant appearing, one can draw the most glorious conclusions in terms of both general results and human research, and gradually thereby work out a reliable semiotics of the soul."[29]

Weishaupt was convinced that his psycho-techniques held the key to understanding human beings by paying attention to what otherwise seemed like insignificant lapses, coincidences or gestures, the same type of the thing Freud purported to explain in the *Psychology of Everyday Life*. Weishaupt also felt that his system of controlling people without their knowing it involved in an "exemplary" form of "education." Weishaupt was able to train his Areopagites "how one can consciously organize a large group of people without much effort." He understands the art of "operation and manipulation" better than "anyone else in the [Illuminati] organization" because he paid attention to the smallest nuances: "O! Everything depends on that. I study each glance and gesture . . . and train my people to go in response to a wave of my hand, and so that I can without speaking read the meaning in their faces."[30]

Weishaupt concludes his enthusiastic description of his power over his the underlings in the Illuminati order by mentioning the case of his pupil Alois Duschl, also of Ingolstadt. "I keep him on as short a leash as possible, give him much work. He is so compliant, like the best novice in any Cloister. I lead him without him noticing it."[31] Here as elsewhere, Weishaupt thanks the Jesuits for revealing to him the techniques of noncorporal compulsion. "In his mind," Barruel wrote, "[Weishaupt] combined the plan of a society, which was at once to partake as much as convenient of the movement of the Jesuits, and of the mysterious silence and secret conduct of Masonry."[32] Barruel who was both Jesuit and (for a time) Illuminist, is quick to point out the difference between "the illuminized and the religious obedience":

> Of that immense number of religious who follow the institutes of St. Basil, St. Benedict, St. Dominic or St. Francis, there is not one who is not thoroughly convinced that here exists a voice far more imperious than that of his superior, the voice of his conscience, of the Gospel, and of his God. There is not one of them who, should his superior commend any thing contrary to the duties of a Christian, or of an honest man, would not immediately see that such a command was a release from his vow of obedience. This is frequently repeated and clearly expressed in all religious institutes, and no where more explicitly or positively that in those of the Jesuits. They are ordered to obey their superior, but in cases only where such obedience is not sinful, *ubi non cerneretur peccatum.*[33]

Just as Freud's unacknowledged appropriation of Nietzsche reveals the true source and real meaning of the Oedipus Complex, so his unacknowledged appropriation of Illuminist psychotechniques reveals that at its root psychoanalysis was not medicine or therapy but a form of psychic control. It was a covert way of controlling people through the manipulation of both guilt and passion in a quasi-confessional relationship. It is precisely in removing confession and examination of conscience from their religious matrix that Weishaupt changes them from an instrument of spiritual liberation and turns them into an instrument of psychic control. Once the Church is seen as the enemy and the moral order a form of repression, there are no controls on the controller. The controller can do with his adept whatever he wants. Not only is there no seal of the confessional, obliging the confessor to keep secret what he has heard; Illuminism is based on the systematic sharing of information. The information, however, only moves upward; what the controllers have learned from their adepts is passed on to the top. Information never descends in a secret society.

Both Illuminism and Psychoanalysis are in many ways the fulfillment of Bacon's dictum, so cherished by the Enlightenment, that knowledge is power. Knowledge of the in-most perturbations of the soul, now liberated from the seal of the confessional and the moral order established by the Christian religion, was seen as a form of psychic control. Illuminism naturally leads to exploitation and manipulation, and it was precisely these psycho-techniques of controlling people as if they were machines that caused the most outrage when the Illuminist manuscripts were published in 1787. The French Revolution two years later only added to the suspicion that people were being controlled from without by secret manipulators.

In his recent attack on Freud, *Why Freud was Wrong*, Richard Webster makes much of Freud's role as father confessor. Freud, in his own words, stood "as the representative of a freer or superior view of the world, *as a father confessor, who gives absolution, as it were, by a continuance of his sympathy and respect after the confession has been made*" (Webster's italics).[34] He might just as tellingly emphasized the first half of the quote because Freud's Illuminist departure from the tradition of auricular confession is every bit as significant as his imitation of it. Freud is "the representative of a freer or superior view of the world," and it is from this position that he gets his power over his clients, for the clients who came to Freud for healing were for the most part wealthy people whose psychic troubles revolved around illicit sexual desires and the guilt which followed from acting on those desires, a fact which Webster misses completely. Instead Webster claims that psychoanalysis is a "religion," using the word in an obviously pejorative sense. But by locating the source of this religion in Catholic confessionals of the Middle Ages, Webster overshoots the mark by about six hundred years. Freud's use of confession is Illuminist, not Catholic. Freud was not interested in freeing people from the slavery of sin. He was much more interested in giving people permission to sin and then reaping financial benefits by absolving them of guilt (or claiming to do so) in psychoanalysis and thereby gaining control over them.

Like Illuminism, psychoanalysis became a form of social control whose purpose was the overturning of throne and altar by the corruption of morals. Until the day when the final revolution arrived, psychoanalysis fulfilled its purpose by providing "Negroes" or "goldfish" whose money was to line the pockets of their therapist liberators. Confession done in the manner promoted by Illuminist therapists was a form of covert control, not a form of medicine. That confession can have salutary psychic effects, no one will deny. In psychotherapy Freud discovered a "scientific" form of Illuminism, one based on the mythology of his own day and not that of the eighteenth century, but it remained, as Freud's ring ceremony in 1913 made clear, a secret society with all of the same goals that secret societies from the Illuminati onward shared. Freud, like Weishaupt, proposed the exploitation of the human desire for confession for his own personal benefit, but he also proposed it as part of a revolutionary strategy, consonant with what he learned about the "*judeo-mâçonnique*" secret societies from the anti-Semitic literature of the late nineteenth century. In Freud, the fears of the right became the fascination of the left. In creating psychoanalysis out of his unacknowledged borrowing from the revolutionary tradition, Freud became the subversive Judeo-Mason the anti-Semites had been warning the world about. Freud created a "Jewish" secret society to bring them to fruition in a conspiracy whose goal, like that of the Illuminati before him, was the toppling of throne and altar throughout Europe. In exploiting his wealthy patients for financial gain by playing the "father confessor," Freud also promoted "liberation" from moral norms, the Nietzschean "transvaluation of values," and the subversion of a social order based on Christian principles. The only rules established for psychoanalysis are those of Freud's making, and they are there primarily, if not solely, for Freud's benefit. Guilt is a reality of human existence, something which Webster seems not to understand. By fostering behavior that begets guilt, the psychoanalyst binds his patient to himself in vampire-like exploitative relationship that is the exact opposite of sacramental confession but very similar to Illuminism, Weishaupt's attempt to control people through the manipulation of their passions.

Greenwich Village, 1913

The year 1913 was an *annus mirabilis* of sorts. The year before the Great War was the year during which modernity surfaced, and it can only be compared with 1921, the year when *The Waste Land* and *Ulysses* appeared, the year when the forces of dissolution freed by the war's dislocation of mores and morals began to be implemented on a wide scale. It was during 1913 that John B. Watson gave his lectures on behaviorism at Columbia University, in competition with Henri Bergson, who was speaking downtown, but the paradigmatic event of that year was the Armory Show, which introduced New York and America to the trends which would dominate the art world after the war. The most famous picture at the Armory Show was Marcel Duchamps's "Nude Descending a Staircase," an importation of the cubist techniques which Braque and Picasso had developed, but which one American perceived as an explosion in a shingle factory.

Plato said that changes in musical form presaged changes in the state. The same could be said of painting. Cubism was, of course, a revolt against morals, but the new forms were so bewildering that few people understood it as such. The few who did lived in Greenwich Village, and felt that the rest of New York, the city above 14th Street, was "cut off from the Village like the Ego from the Id."[1] The comparison gives some indication of how Freud's theories took America's Bohemia by storm during the first decade of the twentieth century. As perhaps the opening shot in the publicity campaign that would make Freudian terminology part of the cultural *lingua franca* by the 1920s, Max Eastman wrote two long articles on Freud in 1915 in *Everybody's Magazine*, which at the time had a circulation of 600,000 readers. Eastman, who would go on to become a Communist and then an anti-Communist, described psychoanalysis as a new treatment "which I believe may be value to hundreds of thousands of people," a method for dissecting out "mental cancers . . . [which will] leave you sound and free and energetic."[2] The one thing Eastman never abandoned was his sexual libertinism, and before long it became clear that this was the force driving the acceptance of Freud's theory of psychoanalysis among the bohemians in Greenwich Village. In 1916 fellow radical Floyd Dell, also associated with Eastman on the editorial board at *The Masses*, went into psychoanalysis. He would say later that "everyone at that time who knew about psychoanalysis was a sort of missionary on the subject, and nobody could be around Greenwich Village without hearing a lot about it."[3] Dell's psychoanalyst was Samuel A. Tannenbaum, an early proponent of sexual liberation who felt that sexual abstinence was psychologically dangerous. Tannenbaum also advocated the legalization of prostitution, feeling that if young men frequented prostitutes they would dissipate dangerous amounts of "frustrated excitement."[4]

Another early convert to the gospel of Freud was a young journalist by the name of Walter Lippmann, a man who would later be called "the prophet of the new liberalism." Reading Freud was for Lippmann an almost religious experience, something significant for someone who did not believe in religion, organized or otherwise. Lippmann, the young Harvard graduate, when searching for the epiphany which might be commensurate to his discovery of Freud could only compare it to the feeling his father's generation might have felt on discovering Darwin.

In 1914 Lippmann was named associate editor of the *New Republic*, the flagship of the new liberalism, and with this new journal as his platform Lippmann and his friend Alfred Booth Kuttner, one of the first people to be psychoanalyzed by Freud's American student A. A. Brill, began to pump out flattering accounts of Freud's new theory. Freudianism through Lippmann would become a constitutive part of American liberalism as well as one of the intellectual constructs Lippmann would use to analyze social problems. Lippmann also brought the Freudian gospel to Mabel Dodge's salon, where it quickly spread further among the intellectuals there. Dodge was so taken with the new theories as a possible explanation of her own bisexual behavior that she immediately began analysis with Brill. Brill, a man with his own set of sexual compulsions and a penchant for smutty jokes, was if anything more forthright than Freud when it came to advocacy of sexual liberation. "With a normal sexual life," he is quoted as saying in a Lippmann article, "there is no such thing as a neurotic."[5]

This excuse for sexual indulgence was just what the boho crowd in the village wanted to hear, and during the second decade of the twentieth century Freud's ideas were adopted by them as their own. According to one observer, Freudian theory, which implicitly encouraged sexual freedom, became a wedge used "to liberate American literature from pruderies and other social restrictions. . . . It may well be that the freedom to write about sex, which was linked with other freedoms, would have been won without the intervention of Freud. But the literary exploitation of Freud was a heavy reinforcement at a decisive moment and materially assisted the coming of age of our literature."[6]

Right around the time of the Armory Show, a twenty-one year old by the name of Eddie Bernays had, at the urging of a friend, taken over the editorship of an obscure journal known as the *Medical Review of Reviews*. Eddie had always had a perceptive ear for what people were saying, and perhaps because the Freudian id was successfully seeping uptown from the village, sex was on people's minds, and Eddie saw an opportunity to make money out of it. Eddie understood the words of one New York editor who announced on March 15, 1913, that it was "sex-o'clock in America." In the early months of 1913, Bernays received a review of a play called *Damaged Goods*. Written by the French playwright Eugène Brieux, *Damaged Goods* told the story of a man who contracts syphilis, then marries, then fathers a syphilitic child. The review was a frontal attack on the sensibilities of the times and perceived as such by the magazine's conservative audience.

Far from being cowed by the reaction, Bernays approached an actor who had indicated a desire to produce the play, pledging the magazine's support. "The editors of the *Medical Review of Reviews*," Bernays wrote to Richard Bennett, "support your praiseworthy intention to fight sex-pruriency in the United States by producing your play *Damaged Goods*. You can count on our help."[7]

Bernays was so gratified by Bennett's favorable response that he immediately agreed to underwrite the costs of the production, an ambitious undertaking for someone who was making $25 a week. Bernays understood intuitively that there was a market for sexual liberation and that he could tap that market financially by turning the play into a *cause célèbre*. *Damaged Goods* could stand for freedom of expression on sexual matters, and in order to make his point he began to enlist the support of a group of influential New Yorkers who shared his point of view. One of the first people to come on board the *Medical Review of Reviews* Sociological Fund Committee to help in the fight against prudery was John D. Rockefeller, Jr., who explained to the young Bernays that "the evils springing from prostitution cannot be understood until frank discussion of them has been made possible."[8] Hundreds of checks poured in from people like the Rockefellers and Mr. and Mrs. Franklin D. Roosevelt, and Eddie was on his way to becoming, as he would call himself later in what would prove to be a very long life (he died at the age of 103), "the father of public relations." Eddie Bernays had parleyed his interest in sex into the creation of the first front group and a career that would ride the crest of the advertising and public-relations wave that would break over the United States, transforming the country into what it is today. The front group as a technique for manipulating public opinion would dominate cultural life during the twentieth century, and the subterfuge whereby economic interest would camouflage its manipulation would become increasingly sophisticated to the point where "today. . . it takes a detective to unmask the interests behind such innocuous-sounding groups as the Safe Energy Communication Council (antinuclear), the Eagle Alliance (pronuclear), and the Coalition Against Regressive Taxation (trucking industry)."[9]

"It all started with sex," Eddie would say, describing his remarkable career. If so, the beginning was not auspicious financially. As soon as Bennett acquired the rights to the play, he told Bernays to get lost. "I don't need your damn [*sic*] sociological fund anymore," he wrote to Bernays.[10] Not one to brood, Bernays decided that the money he hadn't earned was ancillary to the lessons about manipulating public opinion which he had learned, and so in the summer of 1913 he decided to escort a young man to Europe to talk over the psychological implications of what he had learned with his uncle. His decision was not based simply on familial ties. Eddie Bernays's uncle was Sigmund Freud.

The details of their conversation as the twenty-one-year-old Bernays tramped through the woods surrounding Carlsbad, in what was soon to become Czechoslovakia, with his by then famous fifty-seven-year old uncle have been lost to posterity. The general tenor of their conversation, however, was clear. Bernays had made his first foray into manipulating the public mind by appealing to its sexual interests, and since his uncle was famous as an authority on sex, Eddie wanted to know what he knew so he could apply it to mass man. "Whatever the specifics of their conversation," writes Tye, "it is clear that when Eddie returned to New York in the fall of 1913 he was more taken than ever with the Viennese doctor's novel theories on how unconscious drives dating to childhood make people act the way they do. And Eddie was convinced that understanding the instincts and symbols that motivate an individual could help him shape the behavior of the masses."[11]

In trying to understand the intellectual connection between Eddie and his famous uncle, Tye is hampered unfortunately by certain misconceptions about Sigmund Freud and psychoanalysis. "Bernays's ideas," Tye tells us,

> reflected the profound influence of his uncle Sigmund. He talked about the use of symbols, as Freud did, and of the centrality of "stereotypes, individual and community, that will bring favorable responses." He was as driven as his uncle to know what subconscious forces motivated people, and he used Freud's writings to help him understand. But while the esteemed analyst tried to use psychology to free his patients from emotional crutches, Bernays used it to rob consumers of their free will, helping his clients predict, then manipulate, the very way their customers thought and acted – all of which he openly acknowledged in his writings.[12]

At another point, Tye repeats the same misconception of Freud:

> Bernays is a philosopher, not a mere businessman. He is a nephew of that other great philosopher, Dr. Sigmund Freud. Unlike his distinguished uncle, he is not known as a practicing psychoanalyst, but he is a psychoanalyst just the same, for he deals with the science of unconscious mental processes. His business is to treat unconscious mental acts by conscious ones. The great Viennese doctor is interested in releasing the pent-up libido of the individual; his American nephew is engaged in releasing (and directing) the suppressed desires of the crowd."[13]

And again, in the same vein, Tye claims that "while Freud sought to liberate people from their subconscious drives and desires, Eddie sought to exploit those passions."[14]

As with James Jones in his analysis of the relationship between Kinsey and the Rockefeller interests, Tye proposes a dichotomy where none exists. Eddie Bernays did not have a different goal in mind when he proposed exploiting sexual passion for financial gain. Bernays's uncle Sigmund, as the case of Horace Frink makes clear, had been doing this for some time. In fact, even Freud himself admitted that psychoanalysis wasn't really medicine. In his more candid moments with his friend and confidant Wilhelm Fliess, Freud referred to patients as "goldfish" and "Negroes," making it quite clear that psychoanalysis was a form of psychic control for the financial benefit of the analyst. The transaction was quite simple and transacted many times in places like Greenwich Village. In exchange for permission to gratify his sexual passions, the patient would receive "absolution" from the psychoanalyst acting as crypto-confessor for a financial consideration. Bernays and his famous uncle were both involved in exploiting sexual passion for financial gain. The only difference was the medium the younger man chose. Freud bilked his patients individually in psychoanalytic sessions; Bernays tried to manipulate the country collectively through the mass media, by means of advertising and public relations.

In both instances, the technique was pure Illuminism, something which Bernays makes clear in his writings, specifically his 1928 *magnum opus, Propaganda*, where he tells us that "we are dominated by the relatively small number or persons – a trifling fraction of our hundred and twenty million – who understand the mental processes and social patterns of the masses." America was now ruled by a group of "invisible governors," composed of PR professionals like Bernays, who "pull the wires which control the public mind, who harness old forces and contrive new ways to bind and guide the world."[15] These "invisible governors" were necessary to "the orderly functioning of group life"; in fact, the "invisible governors . . . help to bring order out of chaos." Democratic man, in other words, needed control as soon as he was liberated.

Part II, Chapter 5

Zürich, 1914

Five years after Jung treated Medill McCormick, Medill's sister-in-law Edith Rockefeller McCormick showed up in Zurich to be treated for a depression stemming from the death of her daughter Editha. Over the course of the next ten years, Jung corrupted Edith with a steady diet of astrology and spiritualism, turning her into an agoraphobic woman who never left her hotel room. All of this was done in the name of first therapy and then training, after Jung convinced Edith to become a therapist in the Jungian mold. Eventually her withdrawal from the world brought about her divorce from her husband and her death in poverty in a hotel in Chicago, but not before Jung exploited his doctor/patient relationship with her by persuading her to give Jung's organization the equivalent of $2 million.

With the break with Jung and the formation of his secret society, Freud not only brought about a permanent schism at the heart of the psychoanalytic movement, he also, in terms of financial influence, seemed to come out on the losing side of the break, for psychiatry was now split between Aryan and Jewish practitioners, and all of the wealthy patients, especially those coming from America, were "Aryans," specifically wealthy Protestants whose grasp on Christian principle was becoming looser year by year. By granting Medill McCormick permission to gratify his passions, Jung gained a foothold with one of the wealthiest families in America. By treating Edith, he was now parlaying that foothold into contact with *the* wealthiest family in America. When Edith Rockefeller McCormick showed up at Jung's door, her father's personal fortune comprised about 2 percent of the gross national product of the United States of America.[1]

In 1916 Freud, hardly able to control his envy, wrote to Ferenczi complaining that Jung had latched onto a rich American who had given him a building in Zürich. Freud had often said that Americans were good for one thing, money, and now the pupil was proving himself superior to his master in exploiting rich Americans for financial gain. Freud was no stranger to the idea of exploiting his patients for financial gain. "Freud," according to Peter Swales,

had in psychotherapy some of the richest women in the world. On August 1, 1890, he wrote to Wilhelm Fliess, declining an invitation to visit him in Berlin and certainly he was alluding to Anna von Leiben, whom he would dub his "prima donna" when he explained, "My chief woman client is now undergoing a kind of nervous crisis and during my absence *she might get well.*" [my emphasis].[2]

Freud feared that his patient "might get well" during his absence, a curious attitude for a doctor to have. However, the attitude is not curious if psychoanalysis is nothing more than crypto-Illuminist psychic control. To say that Freud was involved in medicine belies his real intention. Patients, Freud told Ferenczi toward the end of his life, are "trash," "only good for making money out of and for studying, certainly we cannot help them"; psychoanalysis as a therapy, he concluded, "may be worthless."[3] Swales goes on to say that several members of the von Leiben family regarded Freud as a charlatan who kept Anna in a state of permanent "hypernervosity" by means of the "interminable daily seances" that Freud called therapy. Freud's biggest fear was that his patient "might get well." The "disease" was iatrogenic. The purpose of therapy was not cure but control, control in this instance for financial gain.

Five years after Freud expressed his envy of Jung and the money he was receiving from the Rockefeller family, Freud had his own chance to fleece a wealthy American, although not someone as wealthy as John D. Rockefeller's daughter. By 1921, the Austro-Hungarian empire was history, and Austrian money barely worth the paper it was printed on. Since Freud charged his patients in dollars, he was always happy when a wealthy American showed up at his door. Horace Frink showed up in 1921. He was not wealthy – he was an aspiring psychoanalyst who had come to Vienna for the analysis with the master which was necessary for certification – but like most analysts of the time he treated wealthy patients. Frink was a physician and aspired to be a psychoanalyst in the Freudian school and in order to do that he had to lie down on the couch and bare his soul to the master. During the course of the analysis, Frink described his erotic attraction to one of his wealthy patients, a woman by the name of Angelika Bijur. Sensing a financial killing, Freud capitalized on the situation by telling Frink to dump his wife and marry Bijur. Frink initially resisted but, after six months, finally came around to Freud's point of view, eventually divorcing his wife. But the analysis wasn't over yet. Freud then persuaded Frink that he had a homosexual attachment to Freud, which expressed itself in Frink's desire to make Freud "a rich man." "Your complaint that you cannot grasp your homosexuality," Freud wrote to Frink, "implies that you are not yet aware of your phantasy of making me a rich man. If matters turn out all right, let us change this imaginary gift into a real contribution to the Psychoanalytic Funds."[4] Once again Freud was exploiting the doctor/patient relationship for financial gain. In her account of the Frink affair, Edmunds says that "Freud openly encouraged this sexual liberation."[5] In a letter to Bijur's ex-husband, Freud explains his analysis of Frink in the following terms:

I simply had to *read my patient's mind* [my emphasis] and so I found that he loved Mrs. B., wanted her ardently and lacked the courage to confess it to himself . . . . I had to explain to Frink, what his internal difficulties were and did not deny that I thought it the good right of every human being to strive for sexual gratification and tender love if he saw a way to attain them, both of which he had not found with his wife.[6]

Freud first discovered the dominant passion of his client through therapy; then, he urged the patient to gratify that passion, absolving him of all guilt in his role as "father confessor"; then, when the patient had succumbed to the temptation and was in most need of absolution, Freud exploited the situation by trying to extort a financial contribution from the patient. The procedure was pure Illuminism.

It was most certainly not medicine. That becomes evident by the effect this therapy had on Frink, who succumbed almost immediately after his divorce and remarriage to a guilt-induced depression which he could not shake. The situation was made even worse when his wife died of pneumonia after being driven from their home and spending years on the road in one hotel after another with their two small children. Frink, in spite of Freud's absolution, never recovered from his wife's death. Less than one year after being re-elected to the presidency of the American branch of the Psychoanalytic Society, Frink ended up in a mental hospital himself, unable to shake the depression into which his guilt-ridden soul had fallen. Eventually his second marriage fell apart under the strain, and Angelika Bijur began to suspect Freud's motives, feeling that he had arranged the marriage for his own financial benefit. Her suspicions were confirmed when she received a telegram from Freud after the marriage collapsed: "Extremely sorry," Freud wrote, "the point where you failed was money."[7]

Swales claims that the problem of "undue influence . . . is virtually endemic to a profession which, after all, owes its very existence and propagation to a plethora of credulous individuals ready and able to pay out good money for the luxury of abdicating their mental sovereignty to another, all too often in a desperate bid to unburden themselves of moral responsibility for the wreckage of their lives."[8]

The "abdication of mental sovereignty to another" is the heart of the Illuminist project; however, the sovereignty lies not with the patient but with the doctor. The thing which motivates the "patient" in a relationship like this is the gratification of illicit passion, the permission to transgress the moral law with impunity, with, in fact, the tacit approval of the therapist. That technique of control is pure Illuminism, but the real motivation to place the power to control in the hands of the Illuminist therapist is sexual liberation. Psychotherapy rode to its position of power in America in particular on the back of sexual liberation because people wanted permission to transgress the moral law and the Freudian therapists were willing to grant that permission – for a price. Liberation, in this instance, became a form of bondage, as people who acted out their passions – often at the behest of their therapists, often with their therapists – quickly learned that they had to pay for the privilege of absolution, and that the price they paid was an interminable and expensive regimen of therapy. Sexual liberation, it turns out, was a form of financial control. "Rumors," Torrey writes,

> that psychoanalysts occasionally recommended sexual intercourse as a treatment for their patients proved to be true, and as early as 1910 Freud tried to quiet such accusations with an essay titled "Wild Psychoanalysis." A physician had told a woman who had left her husband, said Freud, "that she could not tolerate the loss of intercourse with her husband and so there were only three ways by which she could recover her health – she must either return to her husband, or take a lover, or obtain satisfaction from herself." In discussing the case Freud acknowledged that "psychoanalysis puts forward absence of sexual satisfaction as the cause of nervous disorders," but he said the physician in question had failed to point out a fourth possible solution – psychoanalysis. Freud did *not* say in this essay, however, that a recommendation to take a lover was necessarily wrong."[9]

Torrey documents Freud's seduction of America in detail, beginning with the years following his lectures at Clark University:

> Between 1909 and 1917 Freud's ideas spread rapidly among New York's intelligentsia. According to one observer, Freudian theory, which implicitly encouraged sexual freedom, became a wedge used "to liberate American literature from pruderies and other social restrictions. . . . It may well be that the freedom to write about sex, which was linked with other freedoms, would have been won without the intervention of Freud. But the literary exploitation of Freud was a heavy reinforcement at a decisive moment and materially assisted the coming of age of our literature."[10]

The nomenklatura wanted to be seduced, and the seduction, which succeeded beyond their wildest dreams, had as its ultimate outcome, the destruction of one American institution after another. Promising liberation to the gullible while granting covert control to the manipulators, Illuminism has proved the most durable of conspiracies.

Part II, Chapter 6

New York, 1914

"Civilization's going to pieces," broke out Tom violently. "I've gotten to be a terrible pessimist about things. Have you read 'The Rise of the Colored Empires' by this man Goddard?"

"Why no," I answered, rather surprised by his tone.

"Well, it's a fine book, and everybody ought to read it. The idea is if we don't look out the white race will be – will be utterly submerged. It's all scientific stuff; it's been proved."

"Tom's getting profound," said Daisy, with an expression of unthoughtful sadness. "He reads deep books with long words in them."

The Great Gatsby
F. Scott Fitzgerald

The year 1914, it turns out, was a crucial turning point in the life of Margaret Sanger. Having married a Jewish architect by the name of William Sanger in 1902 at the age of 23, Margaret Higgins Sanger moved with him to Greenwich Village in 1910, where they were almost immediately swept up into the social and intellectual ferment that was brewing there at the time. Shortly after arriving there, the Sangers joined the Socialist Party, and one year later Bill ran for office, an unsuccessful attempt to become a municipal alderman.

More significant that any political education was the Sangers' introduction to the intellectual theories of the socialist cultural avant garde. The Sangers became regular habitués at the salon of Mabel Dodge, where they met people like John Reed, Carlo Tresca, and Emma Goldman, who introduced Margaret, in Ellen Chesler's words, "to a Neo-Malthusian ideology then fashionable among European Socialists, who disputed Marxist orthodoxies that condemned contraception as hopelessly bourgeois and encouraged a high proletarian birth rate."[1] In Sanger, Goldman found an apt pupil, one who in fact appropriated her message and later refused to give her credit.

But advocacy of birth control and free love was more than an intellectual exercise for Margaret Sanger. Before long, she began acting on the theories she espoused, to the chagrin of her husband, who unwittingly introduced her to the intellectual toxins that would destroy their marriage. In the Dodge salon, Margaret became acquainted with Nietzsche, whose attack on religion and morality fit in congenially with the life she was espousing, if not practicing. Then during the summer of 1913, theory, as it usually does, led to practice. While vacationing at John Reed's house in Provincetown, Margaret would occasionally travel to Boston to do research on birth control at that city's libraries. During that summer, Margaret had an affair – if not the first since she married, then the first one documented – with a magazine editor by the name of Walter Roberts. When husband William found out about it, it seems to have changed his view of Greenwich Village. Within a period of three years, the avant garde had changed in his eyes from being the cutting edge of a movement calling for social justice for the working classes into a "saturnalia of sexualism, deceit, fraud and Jesuitism let loose."[2]

It's difficult to know which Jesuits he had in mind, but it is not difficult to see why his wife's hands-on experience with free love changed his view of the revolutionary worker's movement. What he previously saw as high ideals now seemed nothing more than a "hellhole of free love, promiscuity and prostitution masquerading under the mantle of revolution."[3] Revolutionary politics, Sanger had to learn the hard way, was nothing more than a thinly disguised rationalization of sexual promiscuity. "If Revolution means promiscuity," he said, stating the same idea in a different context, "they can call me a conservative and make the most of it."[45]

His disillusionment with socialism, though all but complete, came too late to save his marriage. Margaret was now committed to a life of sexual and drug-fueled self-indulgence which would continue until her death. When her son Grant refused to increase the dosage of the Demerol his seventy-year-old mother would crave, Margaret would say, with a lifetime of experience behind it, "I am rich; I have brains; I can do anything I want."

As the hedonism in her life increased, so did Margaret's attachment to the cause of birth control, so much so that it is virtually impossible not to see a correlation between the two. Birth control was the cause which absolved promiscuity of whatever baseness it retained in her mind. Without the cause of birth control, there was nothing but the base selfishness of her actions left confronting her, a prospect she found intolerable, especially when the reproach was brought by her children.

Her third child Peggy had contracted polio during the summer of 1910 at around the same time the Sangers moved to Greenwich Village. The more Margaret got swept up in revolutionary politics and the affairs of the men who pursued those ideals, the more she neglected her children. During the summer of 1913, Margaret's affair with Walter Roberts coincided with a worsening of Peggy's situation. In spite of her husband's admonitions that something needed to be done about Peggy's leg, nothing got done, and she then decided that a trip to Paris might allow him to pursue the career in painting he had chosen to the detriment of his family's financial security and beyond that draw Margaret out of the clutches of free love disguised as revolutionary politics.

Neither hope was fulfilled. Margaret, in spite of the opportunity to research Parisian methods of contraception, was no scholar and after tiring of Paris abruptly returned to New York, abandoning her husband and children.

Peggy's condition seems to have weighed heavily on her mind at the time. She wrote letters to her daughter, assuring her of her love and even started dreaming about her as well, dreams associated with the number six. On the way back to New York, Sanger conceived a journal which she would call the *Women Rebel*, a journal whose values included a woman's "right to be lazy" and her "right to destroy." Gradually the idea of a new ideology based on something more immediately appealing than struggle for the social justice of the working class began to take root in her mind.

But in 1914, Mrs. Sanger was still a creature of the left and so when in April of that year detectives in the employ of the Rockefellers rampaged through a tent city populated by the families of striking miners in Colorado, killing women and children, she reacted in a fashion that bespoke more her uncritical allegiance to the left than anything else. She called for the assassination of John D. Rockefeller, Jr. When later in life, she would explain the indictments that forced her to leave the country in 1914 she would only mention sending birth-control material through the mails, not the call to murder the scion of the Rockefeller family.

The fact is not surprising because by the time she was famous enough to be interviewed by the press, she was also the beneficiary of Rockefeller money as well. Within a period of ten years, Sanger went from a position calling for Rockefeller's murder, to having him as one of her major benefactors. Of all the benefactors she had during her lifetime, only one gave her more money than John D. Rockefeller, Jr., and that man was her second husband Noah Slee, who devoted his entire fortune to Sanger's cause. The philosopher's stone that worked this alchemy was contraception, and the alliance between the left and the wealthy which contraception forged has proved enduring indeed. They say that politics makes strange bedfellows, and if so sexual politics makes bedfellows even stranger. But the alliance between John D. Rockefeller, Jr., and the woman who once urged Americans to rise up and assassinate him is stranger than most. Yet after a little thought not so strange at all. In fact, the alliance is with us still because of the mutual needs it resolved.

The Ludlow Massacre precipitated a chain of events that would have far-reaching consequences for both Margaret Sanger and John D. Rockefeller, Jr. Sanger would eventually flee the country to escape arrest for the article in which she urged her readers to "Remember Ludlow." In her exile in England, Margaret lacked nothing in terms of sexual or intellectual fulfillment (although sleeping with Havelock Ellis hardly seems to qualify on either count), but she did miss her daughter, and in many respects felt guilty of abandoning her.

"Dear Peggy," she wrote "how my heart goes out to you. I could weep from loneliness for you – just to touch your soft chubby hands – but work is to be done dear – work to make your path easier – and those who come after you."[6]

As the letter makes obvious, the cause of birth control had become a panacea if not for the world's problems, then at least for Margaret Sanger's guilty conscience. Sanger had abandoned her ailing daughter to follow a life of sexual self-indulgence, and the only thing that made this act tolerable to her guilty conscience was her crusade for birth control. Peggy, according to Sanger's guilty imagination, would eventually benefit from the liberation that her mother was carving out for all womankind.

Unfortunately, Peggy never lived long enough to reap the benefits of her mother's crusade for birth control. Sanger's only daughter died unexpectedly of pneumonia on November 6, 1915. It was an event which would haunt Sanger for the rest of her life. Even Ellen Chesler, who applauds just about everything Sanger did, no matter how selfish, as necessary for liberation, perceived the devastating effects that the death of her daughter had on Sanger's psyche:

> Margaret never fully stopped mourning Peggy or exorcised the guilt over having been absent during the final year of her brief life. For years later, she could not sit across from another mother and daughter on a train, or in any other public setting, without losing control. She wrote in her journal of recurrent sleeplessness, reporting that images of a child slipping away from her haunted her dreams and left her to awaken in tears.[7]

The death of Peggy had two principal effects: It got Sanger involved in the occult, and it turned the birth-control crusade into something even more personally necessary to her psychic well-being – a personal obsession, in other words. Both effects were related to guilt. The main purpose of her seances was to talk to Peggy, something she found consoling primarily because the mediums she consulted invariably told her what she wanted to hear. Chesler's reading of the connection between guilt over Peggy's death and the cause of birth control is fairly straightforward as well. Sanger "could now satisfy a sense of maternal obligation without deviating from her chosen path, since Peggy remained with her – in effect, if not in reality – as the justification for her own professional preoccupations."[8]

The cause of birth control served the same purpose on a less personal level. Chesler again makes the same point, citing Sanger's claim "that personal feelings were a necessary sacrifice to 'ideals that take possession of the mind.' Even in Bill's letters from the winter of 1914, clearly she had already invented a calling out of her work, which rationalized her disobedience as a wife and a mother."[9]

Or as Chesler puts it at another point: "Through her work for birth control, [Sanger] would translate personal, painful circumstances into public achievements, and no one would stop her."[10] In the absence of repentance, the most common way to assuage guilt feelings is by transmuting vice into a political cause. The birth-control crusade seems to have fulfilled just this need in the lives of Margaret Sanger and the women she inspired. When the cause failed to do its work, Sanger could fall back on the occult and attend seances where Peggy would tell her that everything was okay, and if her conscience proved particularly imperious, there was always Demerol and alcohol, anodynes she used with increasing regularity late in life. "I am rich," Margaret would repeat mantra-like, "I have brains. I can do whatever I like."

But sexual sin is not the only thing that weighs on the conscience. There are seven deadly sins, and although lust seems to dominate the twentieth century as its vice of choice, avarice did well during the nineteenth. In fact, liberalism's attack on the moral order began by undermining the connection between the moral order and economics. Having accomplished that, the undermining of sexual morals was only a matter of time. Economics, it should be remembered, comes from the Greek for household or family, an institution which has both a monetary and a sexual dimension. The *oikos* was what suffered under both regimes.

The Ludlow Massacre in this regard provided a crucial nexus. Ensor and Johnson, Rockefeller's biographers, indicate that Junior was troubled by Ludlow, even to the point of traveling to Colorado, there to dance with the wives of his workers, just to defuse the disastrous publicity which resulted from the killing of over 700 people, many of them women and children. The symbolic gestures, however, did not deter Junior from his determination to bring the strikers to heel, which happened in December of 1914.

The Ludlow Massacre also brought about the birth of public relations. William H. Baldwin, a pioneer in the field of public relations, didn't deny the role Eddie Bernays played in the rise of that field, but he located its beginning in another event. "I date the emergence of public relations," he told Bernays's biographer, "from the work that Ivy Lee did for John D. Rockefeller Sr. in the Colorado strike."[11] Baldwin was referring to the Ludlow Massacre.

The Ludlow Massacre is important because it is the starting point of a permutation that would have long-reaching political consequences. In the world of economics and population, there are only two alternatives: the Catholic and the eugenic, and these two alternatives would constitute the two opposing sides in the culture wars surrounding sexual liberation in the twentieth century. Faced with want, faced with poverty on a widespread scale, faced with the girl holding the empty bowl in the Planned Parenthood overpopulation ads, we can either increase the amount of food or decrease the amount of people. The Catholics advocated the former alternative; the Malthusians the latter.

In 1914 the picture was made a bit more complicated because the distribution side of the equation was represented more by the revolutionary workers movement, which in America was under the leadership of bohemia, headquartered in Greenwich Village. As socialists, their agenda went well beyond the condition of the workers, which was their ostensible *raison d'être*. The "liberals" in this situation, as represented by Margaret Sanger, were compromised by their commitment to sexual liberation; while at the same time, the "conservatives," as represented by John D. Rockefeller, Jr., were compromised by their attachment to an unjust social order. Then, as now on a world-wide scale, inequitable distribution was the cause of scarcity, but then, as now, it was easier to grasp at a panacea than face up to the real problem.

Contraception was that panacea, but it was also the device which allowed the convergence of the left and the propertied classes, which would become the basis of the New World Order which emerged in the 1990s after the fall of Communism. Contraception allowed the left to hold onto its desire for sexual liberation, just as it allowed the wealthy to hold onto the benefits accruing from an unjust social order by thwarting economic reform. Once there was widespread acceptance of the liceity of contraception, the poor could be blamed for their own lot in life, especially if they refused to go along with the eugenic measures of the powerful. The tying of World Bank loans to the acceptance of "population policies" based on contraception, abortion, and sterilization was the ultimate expression of this belief. Contraception was the invention which made the alliance of the wealthy and bohemia not only possible but a reality. The New World Order, as manifested in meetings like the United Nations-sponsored conference on population in Cairo in 1994 was Pocantico Hills and Greenwich Village united in imposing its Neo-Malthusian ideology on the entire world. Once the United States government became involved in the promotion of contraception, an event which happened over the summer of 1965, a radical redefinition of the role of government was the inexorable result. When the influence of Msgr. John Ryan was determinative in Washington, government was there to aid in development. When that influence was replaced in the '60s by the spirit of Margaret Sanger, government's main role became the suppression of population.

Even an observer as sympathetic to Sangerism as Ellen Chesler had to admit that it was impossible to have it both ways:

> Margaret attempted to reconcile her new vision of a society purified by the efforts of women with the social ideals that had fueled her energies as a radical. She did not intend birth control to replace "any of the idealistic movements and philosophies of the workers. . . . It is not a substitute – it precedes. . . . It can and it must be the foundation upon which any permanently successful improvement in condition is attained." Yet she could not have it both ways. By identifying birth control as a panacea, she cer-

tainly undermined the objectives of the revolutionary labor struggle, and by housing her abstract arguments in a practical political framework focused wholly on one issue, she implicitly challenged the value of even a more moderate agenda of progressive social reform.[12]

Contraception, more than anything else, defeated economic development because it defined people and not maldistribution as the source of the problem. Yet, in framing the issue that way, its supporters made contraception attractive to both sides in the class struggle in the United States. The left got sexual liberation, and the rich got to preserve economic privilege, and people like Margaret Sanger got both in a convergence that would eventually subordinate the left's desire for social justice to its desire for sexual license. The effect of this convergence on people like Sanger and her lover H. G. Wells is evident to even devotees of contraception like Chesler, who indicates that once they became famous as promoters of the new world order by making the contraceptive the *sine qua non* of progress, nay, identical with progress itself, Sanger and Wells "seemed reluctant to condemn the maldistribution of wealth, goods and services that gave rise to widespread discontent in the economies of the West."[13]

Thus it comes as no surprise that the Rockefellers became so amenable to the funding requests of the lady who called for their assassination. Birth control, it turns out, created the racial fears of the '20s, the ones which found expression in *The Great Gatsby*. The more the upper classes engaged in non-reproductive sex, the more they became concerned about those who didn't. Thus, out of their behavior was born the fear of "differential fertility rates." Taken at its most basic form, the fear over differential fertility meant the fear that somewhere, someone was having more children than the upper classes were. Eventually, the fact that all the best people were limiting the size of their families meant that those who were not limiting the size of their families were not good people. Hence, eugenics was the solution to the troubled Malthusian conscience of the wealthy classes during the early part of the century. Contraceptive use, once established, became a moral imperative for all humanity, at least according to the views of those who were using it.

With the depression and the efforts of people like Msgr. Ryan the contraceptive/Malthusian ideology suffered a setback, a setback that was only confirmed by general repugnance at the Nazi ideology, which took the eugenics movement to its logical conclusion. But as contraceptive use persisted and increased, so would the pressure to use it as the panacea for all social problems. The Birth Control League changed its name to Planned Parenthood in 1942, and after the war people like Bernard Berelson, using money from John D. Rockefeller III's Population Council, would take a different tack, and use the newly burgeoning communications media to persuade people to do to themselves what hitherto the state had to do to them with the threat of coercion.

Similarly, the discovery of the pill and the IUD in the early '60s was followed almost immediately by the fear that the world was overpopulated. Contraception once again was being proposed as the social panacea, and this time the Catholic Church, subverted from within by people like the Rev. Theodore Hesburgh, C.S.C., who used Rockefeller money to fund secret conferences on contraception at the University of Notre Dame from 1962 to 1965, was unable to stem the tide. The Malthusian ideology was back in business, with government funding now, and one of the ironies is that it was the Democrats, the party of John A. Ryan and the working man, who put it there. That shift to the Malthusian ideology as the cornerstone of both domestic and foreign policy was the essence of the cultural revolution of the 1960s. The Democrats, who once believed in fostering development by defending the interests of the working man, at some point converted to the point of view of their opponents and adopted the Rockefeller view that population was the problem. With the triumph of the Malthusian ideology in the '60s, the role of government changed as well from an entity which promoted the welfare of its citizens to one committed to increasing its control over them by limiting their numbers.

Baltimore, 1916

In the 1930 edition of his famous book which first appeared when Europe dissolved into war, John B. Watson tried to allay any fears his readers might have concerning social experimentation. "First we all," he assured them, "we all must admit that social experimentation is going on at a very rapid rate at present – at an alarmingly rapid rate for comfortable, conventional souls. As an example of social experimentation . . . we have war."[1]

When America entered the war in 1917 John B. Watson tried to enlist as a line officer. He was turned down because of his eyesight, but a year later he would get another chance. In July of 1917, the psychologist E. L. Thorndike, now on the War Department's Committee on Personnel, wrote to President Goodnow of Johns Hopkins asking him to release Watson for military service with half pay. Watson, who was thirty-eight years old at the time, was commissioned as a major in August of 1917 and put to work administering aptitude tests to aspiring pilots. The tests he devised eventually proved worthless, and given his temperament and his drinking habits, it was inevitable that Watson would soon be quarreling with his superiors, which landed him a job training carrier pigeons, whose value was rendered dubious by the improvements in the wireless. He was then sent to England to interview British pilots, but when he arrived, they were too busy to talk to him. He was then sent to the front near Nancy in France, where he remained within hearing distance of the war for three months with nothing much to do until he got disgusted and asked to be shipped home. On that voyage he came as close to war as he would ever be as he watched a torpedo go sailing past the stern of his ship. While away from home Watson also met with British psychologists and had numerous affairs.

The war may not have been particularly beneficial to Major Watson but it was good for psychology. War and behaviorism were made for each other. Unlike Germanic introspection, behaviorism was pragmatic and American, and it promised results. Its greatest triumph during the war, if one can call it that, was intelligence tests, which were promptly used by the racist eugenics crowd after the war as an indication that the great majority of Americans, especially those of immigrant stock, were feeble-minded idiots. A wave of sterilization laws swept the country's legislatures as a result, the most famous of which got contested at the Supreme Court level in *Buck v. Bell*, the case which prompted Chief Justice Holmes to opine that "three generations of imbeciles" were "enough."

The man more responsible than anyone else for the promotion of intelligence tests in the military was Watson's friend and collaborator, Robert M. Yerkes, who was commissioned as a major in 1917, the same year he was elected head of the American Psychological Association, and the same year he was appointed head of the National Research Council. War was the catalyst that brought big government and big business and big science together in the project of social engineering, a project that would be applied to the civilian sector as soon as the war was over. In March of 1919, in his "Report of the Psychological Committee of the National Research Council," Yerkes could announce with a certain amount of self-satisfaction and pride that "two years ago mental engineering was the dream of a few visionaries, today it is a branch of technology which, although created by war, is evidently to be perpetuated and fostered by education and industry."[2]

If that were in fact the case, it was the result largely of Yerkes's efforts and of his collaboration with John B. Watson. In the spring of 1916 Yerkes had received a letter from a jubilant Watson, announcing that he had just been hired as a personnel consultant by the Wilmington Life Insurance Company. Watson was involved in negotiations for a similar contract with the Baltimore and Ohio Railroad and sure that a similar contract with them would be soon to follow. The merger of business and academe seemed promising for both parties but especially for the university, which could now demonstrate its usefulness to the business community in a concrete way while at the same time bolstering its prestige on campus with increased funding. Watson was already offering a course in the "Psychology of Advertising" at Johns Hopkins and hoped to expand future course offerings in the business economics major to include courses which would explain to future managers how they could apply the insights of psychology in controlling their employees.

The establishment of the NRC created the precedent that government should be involved in funding scientific research, and it also established the premise that scientists like Yerkes and Watson, and not politicians, would say how that money was going to be spent. The war also did much to win over the public mind – especially the business sector – to appreciating the value of psychology. Having given the impression that psychology was instrumental in the managing of a million men in uniform at a time of rapid change, Yerkes and Watson went on to claim that behavioral psychology would now help businessmen choose the right employees, control crime, and keep men "honest and sane and their ethical and social life upon a high and well-regulated plane."[3] Rather than have employers change the working environment to suit clamorous (and increasingly unionized) employees, behaviorism offered the promise of changing employees to suit their jobs. It was an offer that the plutocrats found hard to resist. The Goodyear Tire and Rubber Company showed an interest in the practical side of "mental engineering," and the psychology committee of the NRC received a large grant from the Rockefeller Foundation for the development of intelligence tests. The NRC under Yerkes and in collaboration with Watson played a crucial role in insinuating behaviorism's vision of social control throughout the emerging but already interlocking complex of big government, big business, and big science. A confidential memorandum outlining the purpose of the NRC emphasized the need to stimulate the "growth of science and its application to industry." According to its founders, the NRC was organized "particularly with a view to the coordination of research agencies for the sake of enabling the United States, in spite of its democratic, individualistic organization, to bend its energies effectively toward a common purpose."[4] Mental engineering would allow employers to find trainable workers among the unskilled, allowing the employers to bypass the trade unions and pay lower wages. Behaviorism was always seen as an instrument of control by its founder, and now it was being implemented as such by those who controlled the means of production. While the first generation of psychologists – people like G. Stanley Hall and William James – still retained the morals of the Victorian era, Watson felt that morals were simply the response to a stimulus and that that stimulus was the prevailing social order. "Behaviorism," according to Buckley, "would make techniques of social adjustment available to those who wished to determine that order."[5] Might made right – that much was clear. Behaviorism was simply a way to put that Nietzschean order into practice.

As a result, behaviorism began to be seen as an instrument of political control as well. Just as Dewey, Lippmann, Croly, and the crowd at the *New Republic* wanted a war because they were interested in social engineering, they were just as interested in promoting behaviorism as a way of continuing that engineering in peacetime. Just what that meant became clear from their writings. In *Public Opinion*, Walter Lippmann described a "Melting Pot Pageant," which had probably taken place on July 4, 1918, when George Creel's campaign to undermine the identity of ethnic groups in America reached its high point:

> It was called the Melting Pot , and it was given on the Fourth of July in an automobile town where many foreign-born workers are employed. In the center of the baseball park at second base stood a huge wooden and canvas pot. There were flights of steps up to the rim on two sides. After the audience had settled itself, and the band had played, a procession came through an opening at one side of the field. It was made up of men of all the foreign nationalities employed in the factories. They wore their native costumes, they were singing their national songs; they danced their folk

dances and carried the banners of all Europe. The master of ceremonies was the principal of the grade school dressed as Uncle Sam. He led them to the pot. He directed them up the steps to the rim, and inside. He called them out again on the other side. They came, dressed in derby hats, coats, pants vests stiff collar and polka dot tie, undoubtedly , said my friend each with an Eversharp pencil in his pocket and singing the Star-Spangled Banner.[6]

The anecdote gives an accurate view of the liberal project of social control which began during the war and was carried over into civilian life during the '20s when the population at large was asked to abandon its allegiance to the ethnic neighborhood and the small town and conform its habits to national markets, brand names, and "science" as the ultimate arbiter of behavior. Lippmann, Croly, Dewey, and the *New Republic* saw behaviorism continuing what the war had started, a consolidation of power in a strong central state.

As the United States edged closer to the brink of World War I, an influential group of American progressives seized upon the conflict as a means of transforming American society. Herbert Croly, who championed a strong central state to promote economic and political freedom, and his co-editor at *The New Republic*, Walter Lippmann, saw the war as a "rare opportunity" to advance democracy abroad and begin social reconstruction at home. By social reconstruction, Croly and Lippmann meant the substitution of rational planning for the old authorities that had been discredited or destroyed by the advent of modern industrial life. Lippmann and Croly were essentially articulating the position put forth by John Dewey, "who urged that the war be used as an efficient means of achieving intelligent control over the economic and political process."[7] The same group of people saw the war as their best ally in undermining Victorian mores and re-establish in its place "a modern way of life" since "it was the first time in history that an entire society was mobilized for total war."[8]

In the theories of Lippmann and Harold Lasswell we have the beginnings of modern psychological warfare. Lasswell's theory of communication – "who says what to whom and with what effect" – could also be used to suppress rival visions of communication, and this was precisely how it was used in the rise of the age of modern advertising, which began around the time of the war. Mass marketing, as Eddie Bernays realized, was an all-or-nothing proposition. It meant replacing one set of values – ethnic, traditional, religious – with another – impulsive, suggestible, "scientific." It meant, in other words, the erosion of traditional societies by mass media and the substitution of local products by national brand names. Mass-media advertising worked only with brand names in mass markets served by an infrastructure like the railroad system.

Watson was at one with Lippmann and Lasswell in the vision they shared of technocratic state in which, according to Lippmann, "science" would provide the bond that would make democracy cohesive and effective. Behaviorism was crucial to that vision because behaviorism gave man the ability now to shape the psychic and, therefore, social world, just as physics had given him the ability to shape the material world. Lippmann saw the development of an "infinitely greater control of human invention" in sciences that were "learning to control the inventor."[9] Dewey, likewise, saw in behaviorism the ability to control the most crucial environment, the human mind. Once man could do that – and Watson had shown it could be done – man could take control of the future. All that man had to do was to "press forward . . . until we have a control of human nature comparable to our control of physical nature."[10] Missing from these utopian accounts of the future was the fact that behaviorism had been used during the war – as Lippmann's account of the Melting Pot Pageant made clear – as a form of psychological warfare against recalcitrant ethnic groups. In this respect, the liberal state which Dewey, et al., envisioned was also a state in a constant state of covert ethnic warfare. The triumph of man over nature meant the triumph of some men over other men using "science" as their weapon.

Herbert Croly completed the liberal vision of the future by revising American history and coming up with a politics more suitable to a scientific age. Jefferson, Croly felt, was too committed to the maintenance of local communities. Instead of the division of powers proposed by the founding fathers, Croly proposed a vastly strengthened presidency, which, responding directly to public opinion, would give embodiment to the General Will of the national community. In Croly, we see the link between the French Revolution and the Clinton Administration. His repudiation of the system proposed by the founding fathers saw the creation of a "direct democracy" as its goal, a goal which would find fulfillment in a president who could bypass the legal system and rule directly by manipulating the passions of the masses and then present himself as the embodiment of their will. Like Watson and Lippmann, Croly had faith in science. He, however, unlike them, got it from his parents who venerated Auguste Comte. Together they embarked on a project to destroy the American republic and erect in its place an empire based on the most sophisticated manipulation the world had ever known.

Part II, Chapter 8

Paterson, New Jersey, 1916

Around the time John B. Watson got drafted into the army, a Russian émigré by the name of Alexandra Kollontai was settling into life in Paterson, New Jersey. She had moved there to be near her son, Misha, who had just enrolled in a course in automotive engineering. Madame Kollontai was in a unique position to study traditional American life on the brink of the war which would destroy that life forever. She talked about the women, bored or doing stupid housework, sitting on the porches of their monochrome wooden bungalows on straight streets lined with maple trees.

Madame Kollontai talked so contemptuously of housewives because she was a revolutionary. The year before her stay in Paterson, she had joined the Bolsheviks and, under the leadership of V. I. Lenin, she would devote her life to the overthrow of the Czar in Russia as a prelude to worldwide revolution on the part of the working class. The year before she took up residence in Paterson, Kollontai had come to the United States for the first time to give a series of anti-war speeches. Her audiences were, for the most part, German and, for the most part, uninterested in revolution. She found even the American socialists hopelessly undisciplined when it came to revolutionary work. Apparently seeing in Kollontai a political organizer of rare linguistic and editorial ability, the Communist newspaper in New York asked her to stay on as its editor, but she refused. She wanted to be back in war-ravaged Europe, since it was obvious that no revolution was imminent in the United States. And for some time now, revolution had been the sole reason for her life and work.

In fact, only her son could countermand her desire for revolution, and so planning to renew the contacts she had made the year before with American socialists and Russian émigrés, she was back in the United States because of the promptings of "a mother's heart," as one of her Soviet biographers put it. As a revolutionary, Kollontai hated the family. As a mother, she was devoted to her son, even to the point of taking herself out of the heart of the revolutionary struggle when it was on the brink of achieving its greatest success since the revolution of 1789 in France. Her life revolved in many ways around the contradiction implicit in those terms. Kollontai hated the family, and yet she never stopped seeking the love that most people find there and there alone. At the mid-point in her career, but at the end of her life as a revolutionary writer and thinker, she framed the issue thus: "Love with its many disappointments, with its tragedies and eternal demands for perfect happiness still played a very great role in my life. An all-too-great role! It was an expenditure of precious time and energy, fruitless and, in the final analysis, utterly worthless. We, the women of the past generation, did not yet understand how to be free."[1]

Kollontai was forty-four years old when she arrived in Paterson and fifty-four when she wrote the above-cited lines about her failed quest for love. The situation, however, is simpler than Kollontai portrays it. Freedom for women, according to Kollontai's reading of socialism, meant work outside the home. Since her life was full of such work, she should have considered herself "liberated." Yet the actual dialectic of her life was much more complicated than that. In the years between her departure from Russia in 1898 and the Russian revolution nineteen years later, Alexandra Kollontai led the life of the quintessential rootless cosmopolite. Based in Berlin, she would travel from city to city and congress to congress using her impressive language skills to propagandize for revolution. Yet, in spite of her fierce and total commitment to revolutionary struggle, she would inevitably succumb to a loneliness which would drive her into the arms of yet another man for the consolations of love which she claimed could not be found in the family. The love affair would inevitably turn sour, leaving Kollontai longing once again for the freedom from attachment, which would quickly turn to loneliness, which is what drove her to the love affair in the first place. And so the cycle from loneliness and longing to bondage and disgust would start all over again. It was a dialectic which Kollontai attempted many times to explain, but one which she never understood herself and one which she most certainly never learned to transcend, as the quote from her autobiography indicates. Kollontai had dedicated herself to a life of study and activism in the service of revolution, and yet even after the revolution arrived, the comradeship in sexual matters which it promised would recede forever before her eyes like the mirage of the promised land which she, like Moses, would never occupy. She would carry this contradiction with her for the rest of her life (she died in 1952 in her eightieth year at the end of Stalin's reign of terror). By 1937, the revolution's failed promise of universal love still weighed heavily on her mind. Writing to an aging comrade in 1937, at the height of Stalin's purges, Kollontai wrote that

> our romantic epoch is completely finished. With us, we could take the initiative, stimulate the administration, make suggestions. Now we must be content with executing what we are ordered. Between my colleagues and me there is neither camaraderie nor friendship. Moreover the activity of each of us is strictly compartmentalized. Our relations are cold and distrust is everywhere.[2]

The dream of "winged Eros," to use Kollontai's term for the sexual liberation which the Revolution promised, died long before Stalin's purges of the

1930s. In fact, it died within ten years of the revolution itself, and Kollontai watched it expire in spite of her efforts to keep it alive. Just why it died has been the subject of debate ever since. Wilhelm Reich devoted his book *The Sexual Revolution* to answering this question, and subsequent generations of sexual revolutionaries, following his example, have been unable to give this corpse a decent burial, attaching it to any number of intellectual life-support systems that keep it twitching with galvanic energy but are unable to restore it to life. Not even Kollontai's biographers seem able to see that the second sexual revolution, the one associated with the October Revolution in Russia, died of its own excesses, every bit as much as the first one did. Faced with the unprecedented social upheaval which sexual liberation had caused in Russia, the commissars themselves had to end it, for in allowing it to continue they ran the risk of completely destroying what little social order was left in the Soviet Union. Perhaps no one life epitomizes the rise and fall of the second sexual revolution better than Alexandra Kollontai.

Kollontai's hatred of domestic life came naturally. Which is another way of saying that she brought it on herself by her own decisions early in her married life, decisions which set the course for her subsequent life and laid the intellectual foundations for a feminism which could never reconcile love and work. Born in 1872 to an aristocratic but indulgent liberal father and a mother who had divorced her first husband to be with him, Kollontai established a reputation for rebellion early in life by marrying an impecunious engineer against the express wishes of her mother. Alexandra was appalled at the marriage of her elder sister, at the age of nineteen, to a man fifty-one years her senior, and vowed that this sort of marriage for money would never happen to her. And yet according to her own account, the marriage for which she incurred family opprobrium, lasted "hardly three years" in spite of the birth of a son in 1894. Kollontai's account of her early life in her autobiography is written, like all autobiographies, as a justification of the choices she made:

> Although I personally raised my child with great care, motherhood was never the kernel of my existence. A child had not been able to draw the bonds of my marriage tighter. I still loved my husband, but the happy life of a housewife and spouse became for me a "cage." More and more my sympathies, my interests turned to the revolutionary working class of Russia. I read voraciously. I zealously studied all social questions, attended lectures, and worked in semi-legal societies for the enlightenment of the people. These were the years of the flowering of Marxism in Russia (1893/96).[3]

Just why a "happy life" should become a "cage" is something Kollontai never explains. She comes close, however, by telling us close on the heels of that revelation that she "read voraciously." The "emancipation" of Alexandra Kollontai led to unhappiness via socialist writings. Socialism was, at the same time, the justification for her unhappiness in love. It led her on a quest for love that was such a dramatic failure that she could only term it a "fruitless" and "utterly worthless" waste of time when she looked back on her life in her mid-fifties.

It didn't start out that way though. Early in their marriage, Kollontai's husband was assigned to install a new ventilating system in one of the cotton mills near Moscow, and accompanying him on that trip she was given a tour of the factory and quickly became appalled at the working conditions she found there. Her state of mind was compounded by the fact that they were staying in a pleasant hotel not far away, where she was expected to dance in the evening after seeing the appalling conditions in the factory during the day. Under Czar Nicholas II, Russia was undergoing the rapid industrialization that England had experienced a century before, and the social dislocation caused by industrialization, especially among women, was devastating the social fabric of the country. No longer an integral part of the peasant family, women were herded into factories in the cities, where they were often seen as desirable because they were more docile than male employees, a situation in which sexual exploitation was also rampant. In the first two years of the twentieth century, the number of women in the workforce in Russia increased by 12,000 while the number of men in the factories decreased by 13,000. During the first decade of the century, the industrial workforce in Russia increased by 141,000 workers, and of that number 81 percent were women. There are a number of ironies associated with the situation. The Czar was unwittingly revolutionizing Russia by bringing about its industrialization, and he and those who profited the most from that industrialization would soon reap the whirlwind of their own greed. But those who overthrew the Czar would continue the same policy of forcing women from their homes into the country's factories, now owned by the state, which is to say, by and for the benefit of the Communist Party.

Having seen the social dislocation caused by the factory system first-hand, Kollontai turned to the socialists for answers, breaking with the ameliorist liberalism of both her husband and her father. In 1895 Kollontai read an abridged Russian translation of August Bebel's *Woman and Socialism*, a book which she described as the "woman's bible," when she wrote her own introduction to the unabridged version in 1918. Bebel, like Marx and Engels and the Utopian Socialists like Fourier and Saint-Simon before them, saw marriage and the family as an essential part of the capitalist system of ownership and exchange. Women, according to this view, were considered property, and morals were simply a system whereby women were kept under control for the benefit of their exploiters. Religion, following this line of thinking, simply reinforced morals, which in turn reinforced the unjust exploitation of the worker. Women were, according to this line of thought, especially susceptible to exploitation via their religious feelings. According to

Bebel, woman "suffers from a hypertrophy of feeling and spirituality, hence is prone to superstition and miracles – a more than grateful soil for religion and other charlataneries, a pliant tool for all reaction."[4] Given this state of affairs, the socialist solution was clear. Abolish property and everything else will take care of itself. This meant that only in the absence of property would relations between the sexes or "marriage" be based on love, something which Bebel saw as a "natural instinct" which man would satisfy as simply he would other natural desires such as hunger and thirst.

Once marriage had been separated from economic exchange by the abolition of property, man would base his sexual relations on love alone, and a true system of sexual morality would come into existence, one based not on property but rather "spiritual affinity." To have intercourse without spiritual affinity and oneness was immoral. That meant the erection of a completely new moral system at the heart of which lay subjective states of mind which determined the morality of all sexual action. Other consequences flowed just as inexorably from this premise. If a man suddenly ceased having this sense of spiritual unity, then he was no longer "married," and free to seek sexual gratification elsewhere, especially from a woman who engendered the feelings anew. Just how this spiritual affinity differed from passion of the turbulent, traditional sort never got explained. Indeed, in the new age without property, there was no need of explanation, for as Shelley had said in *Queen Mab*, passion and reason at this point were one. This, of course, also meant that a man could rationalize the most brutal selfishness as well, as indeed Shelley had done, but any consideration of the actual state of sexual affairs was usually postponed until after the revolution. Kollontai did the same sort of postponing. The difference in her life derived from the fact that she was around when the revolution actually arrived. It also derived from the fact that she, as the newly named Bolshevik minister of social welfare, was expected to make sense of the contradictions the socialists had engendered in their forays into sexual politics.

In the pre-Revolutionary meantime, liberation for women meant abandoning the family. "To be truly free," Kollontai wrote, following Marx, Engels and Bebel, "woman must throw off the contemporary, obsolete, coercive form of the family that is burdening her way."[5] Kollontai wrote this after she had become a Bolshevik, but the principle was there in Marx and Engels and Bebel, which is what she began reading as a young wife and mother in the mid-1890s.

In his *Economic and Philosophic Manuscripts of 1844*, Marx had written that "one can judge the entire stage of development of the human being" on the basis of a man's relationship with a woman. "From the character of this relationship one can conclude how far the human being, as a species and as an individual being, has become him/herself and grasped him/herself."[6] If this were the case Marx and Engels had never developed very far. Marx had an ongoing and exploitative affair with his servant, who bore him an illegitimate son whom he never recognized. Engels likewise was sexually attracted to working class girls and would flit from one to the other. Because morals had been subsumed into economics, they had been denied any ontological validity of their own. As a result, it should not be surprising that the revolutionaries behaved badly when it came to their relations with women. Revolution became the justification for personal sins of sexual exploitation and that is what it became, *mutatis mutandis* for Kollontai, who became both victim and victimizer. The revolution promised to change everything because it would change the property relations which were the basis of all other relations, especially marriage. Women were to be "liberated" from marriage, which meant being liberated from morals, which invariably meant a kind of bondage. But no one saw it that way at the time. "After the dictatorship of the proletariat," one of Kollontai's biographers wrote, "the universal destruction of private property would remove both the basis for male supremacy and the economic functions of the family. Women would then work as full equals; through their labor they would become free. Public organizations would assume all services previously performed in the home, including child rearing."[7] Marriage would continue as an institution based on "sex love" between equals, unlimited by any restrictions save those the couple themselves established. When love ended, the marriage was over. "If only marriages that are based on love are moral, then, indeed only those are moral in which love continues," Engels wrote.[8]

Since Engels arranged to have *Queen Mab* translated for the 1848 revolution, it is not far-fetched to see him here echoing Shelley, who was in turn echoing Godwin's idea that marriage was only valid as long as the partners were in love with each other. This was the new morality, and Shelley had practiced it in an especially brutal way on his first wife Harriet. Now all those who had done similar things to their spouses – Margaret Sanger, Kollontai, Inessa Armand, Max Eastman, Claude McKay, Carl Van Vechten – could use it as a justification after the fact and see it as the beginning of a new world. The Marxists were more susceptible than most in this respect because their lives were based on the emergence of a future state in which all contention would cease. In many ways, this use of the future to justify sins in the present is the main reason they were Marxists.

Sexual intercourse should be "judged" as "legitimate or illicit" by determining "whether it arose from mutual love or not." In a passage which gives some insight into its author's sex life, Engels wrote, "The duration of the impulse of individual sex love differs very much according to the individual, particularly among men; and a definite cessation of affection, or its displacement by a new passionate love, makes separation a blessing for both parties as well as for society."[9] Sexual morality in the socialist mode was a projection of the sexual practices of the men who authored socialist theory. It was also a function of the guilt they felt for acting on those sexual imperatives. "Separation" in this instance is a blessing for "society" only from the point of view of the man who has grown tired of his sexual partner.

Kollontai, like Engels and Bebel, claimed that in bourgeois society woman could choose only between marriage and prostitution, two forms of the same bondage. "In the sight of the whole," Kollontai wrote with ill-disguised glee, "the home fire is going out in all classes and strata of the population, and of course no artificial measures will fan its fading flame." Liberation from the family meant getting a job, and that meant the introduction to factory work. The whole project of revolutionary "liberation" came full circle – in theory at least – when Engels announced that "women's liberation becomes possible only when women are enabled to take part in production on a large, social scale."[10] Women can only become liberated, in other words, by working outside the home. "Liberation" for women meant transferring the benefits of women's labor from her immediate family to the benefit of the factory owners, be they the capitalists or, as in the case of Russia after the revolution, the state. Women's liberation, as conceived by Marx and Engels and as put into practice by Kollontai, was, as a result, a form of control. The system of transferring women's labor was already in place theoretically in the writings of the Utopian Socialists and then simply appropriated by Marx and Engels. Those theories would then be put into practice by the Marxists in Russia under Lenin, and ironically by the feminists in the United States under late capitalism. When the Russian peasant women heard about the new system which Kollontai and her intellectual friends had concocted for them in 1918, they were less than enthusiastic. What they wanted was not social engineering in the name of liberation, but rather support for the lives they were trying to live in support of their families. But Kollontai and her supporters were adamant in their refusal to entertain anything less than the destruction of the family as their ultimate goal, no matter how willing they were to compromise in terms of effectiveness on intermediary measures. Why this was so can only be understood in the context of the decisions they had made concerning their own lives and families.

The fish, according to the French proverb, rots first at the head. After this young and impressionable member of the cultured classes immersed herself in the reading of Marx, Engels, and Bebel, it was not surprising that she would come to consider marriage "a cage." It is also not surprising that she would act on what she knew. Action follows naturally from intellectual conviction. And, as was the case with Margaret Sanger, introduction to the doctrines of socialism meant introduction to the doctrine of free love as well. At some point during the mid-1890s, Kollontai asked her governess and mentor Lyolya Stasova to introduce her to the Russian equivalent of Greenwich Village, the revolutionary underground, which treated her as a dilettante and source of easy money rather than the "intellectual," writer, and party theoretician she aspired to be.

Ironically, it was with one of her husband's colleagues that she found the intellectual respect she sought from the radicals who failed to take her seriously. One gets the impression that Kollontai's husband treated her intellectual theories with a certain amount of condescension, although probably no more condescension than they deserved. On the other hand when she told him she wanted to be a writer, he was willing to hire the extra help she needed to devote herself more completely to her work. So he can't have been completely averse to her intellectual aspirations. On the other hand, he was probably not as sympathetic to them as was the colleague of her husband whom Alexandra identifies only as "the Martian." As his name implies, the Martian wasn't particularly handsome, but he was deeply versed in the intellectual currents of the day, and was willing to flatter Kollontai that she was just as abreast of the issues as he was. The suspicion that the Martian may have had ulterior motives in this regard is confirmed by the fact that he eventually ended up having an affair with Kollontai, something which complicated her life much more than what she had been reading, although the socialist denigration of marriage and morals in the books she was reading probably contributed directly to the affair. Like the Victorian writers in England who were forever trying to decide between sensual and spiritual women, Kollontai now had to decide which man she really loved: the practical engineer who was her husband and the father of her child but was fatally compromised by his relations with the state and the now equally discredited state of marriage, or the sympathetic intellectual revolutionary who flattered her intellectual pride as a way of getting in bed with her. "Did we really love both [men]?" Kollontai wrote, trying to understand this crossroads in her life. "Or was it the fear of losing a love which had changed to friendship and a suspicion that the new love would not be lasting?"[11]

Instead of choosing one over the other, Kollontai left both men when in August 1898, she left Russia to study political economy under Professor Heinrich Herkner in Switzerland. "Therewith," she would later say, "began my conscious life on behalf of the revolutionary goals of the working-class movement. When I came back to St. Petersburg – now Leningrad – in 1899, I joined the illegal Russian Social Democratic Party."[12] The laconic account in her autobiography belies her emotional state at the time. Taking the fast train from St. Petersburg to Zürich, Kollontai, then a young mother of twenty-six, was plagued by the thought that she was destroying a perfectly good marriage for no good reason. She was also tormented by the thought that she might never see her four-year-old son again. Kollontai was so overcome with guilt and grief that it was only with the greatest psychic effort that she was able to stay on the train each time it stopped. Her natural inclination was to return to her family, but she stilled that natural inclination by assuring herself, in her letters to her childhood friend Zoya, that she was called to something more important than marriage, and that study in Zürich, which had become a Mecca for syndicalist radicals and émigré revolutionaries, was essential to that end. She hadn't bothered to tell her husband that she was leaving for a year of studies, and the fact that she didn't indicates that the studies were seen as a way of dissolving the marriage, or of resolving the fact that she was sexually involved with two men at the time and unable to choose between them. Instead of admitting the sexual dimensions of the situation for what they were, she chose to dramatize them as a pretext for her quest for "freedom." "But I was not as happy as he," she wrote referring to her husband. "I longed to be free."[13] When Zoya responded by asking her what she meant by freedom, Kollontai responded by naming what was bothering her the most: "I hate marriage. It is an idiotic, meaningless life. I will become a writer."[14] The fact that Kollontai's husband was willing to do whatever it took to facilitate her career as a writer belies her assertion that marriage was a cage. Kollontai was the daughter of an indulgent liberal father and the wife of a man of the same mold. No matter how much the economic conditions of the time cried to heaven for vengeance, they were never more than symptomatic of a deeper spiritual crisis which revolved around what Augustine would call the essence of all sin, namely, the desires of the "autonomous self," which men shared with fallen angels. We are talking about rebellion in its most basic sense, which is to say, rebellion against God and the nature of his creation. "Rebellion," Kollontai wrote, trying to justify her actions in 1898, "flared in me anew. I had to go away, I had to break with the man of my choice, otherwise (this was an unconscious feeling in me) I would have exposed myself to the danger of losing my selfhood. . . . it was life that taught me my political course, as well as uninterrupted study from books."[15]

Man's desire to be unhappy on his own terms rather than happy on God's is the essence of Satan's rebellion: "Better to reign in hell than serve in Heaven," is how John Milton put it in the famous line from *Paradise Lost*. Acting on that impulse has significant consequences in terms of human freedom, one which Clements is quick to perceive. Kollontai wanted both freedom and love, but she wanted them on her own terms, a fact which imprisoned her in a dialectic of behavior which meant that she would flee from human relationships into loneliness and then from loneliness into the anodyne of sexual love, which she found degrading and imprisoning, which would force her to flee to "freedom" and concomitant loneliness once again. Clements writes that Kollontai "would return again and again to the theme of the individual seeking relief from solitude in a love relationship, then fleeing possession, in a fruitless attempt to find solace in a 'collective.' Kollontai was obviously generalizing from her own experience; she was an individualist who could not reconcile independence and dependence and who therefore looked for a solution in a communal future."[16]

To say that Kollontai generalized from her own experience is another way of describing her projection of her own internal moral and spiritual conflicts onto the working class, which was supposed to be grateful for the attention. Kollontai could not accuse herself of infidelity, so she indicted the institution of marriage as oppressive and inimical to the interests of women. "When I was appointed as Russian envoy to Oslo," she wrote in her autobiography, "I realized that I had thereby achieved a victory not only for myself, but for women in general and indeed, a victory over their worst enemy, that is to say, over conventional morality and conservative concepts of marriage."[17] Because Kollontai had broken with marriage and morality, they were now women's "worst enemy."

In 1899 Kollontai returned to Russia, only to find that her husband had found someone new and wanted a divorce. Had he welcomed her back to their home, Kollontai's story might have been different, but as it was, the rejection only confirmed her in her belief that morals and marriage were the enemies of women, and she plunged into her revolutionary work to ensure that history would affirm that she was right in the path she had chosen. In the uncanny way that students of this period of history have already noticed, especially in the spell Rasputin seems to have cast over Czarina Alexandra, the Czar seemed to collaborate with a chain of events which was destined to bring about his demise. In January 1905 a crowd of 100,000 peasants and workers marched to the Winter Palace in St. Petersburg, carrying religious banners and portraits of the Czar, convinced that if he only understood their plight he would bring about the changes they sought. Instead the Cossacks who guarded the palace charged the crowd on horseback and then fired on the unarmed demonstrators. When the day was over 3,000 people were dead, and Russia was one step closer to revolution. Kollontai was there when the Cossacks charged and remembered well the unbelief of the peasants and workers. She also says that she was well known as a revolutionary at the time.

Perhaps because she was so well known, she was forced to flee Russia once again in 1908 and go into revolutionary exile, an exile from which she would return only after the revolution had toppled the Czar. In December 1908 Kollontai, still a Menshevik, crossed the frontier into Germany, where she made contact with revolutionaries there. The German socialists were ahead of the Russians in most things, and this was true as well of their efforts to mobilize women for revolution. The SPD, the German socialist party, had begun publishing a paper for female workers called *Die Gleichheit* as early as 1891. In Germany Kollontai met Rosa Luxembourg and Karl Liebknecht, who would become martyrs to the revolutionary cause when the German army, unlike the army in Russia, turned against the revolution at the end of World War I, and they were murdered after presiding shortly over a Soviet republic in Berlin.

It was in Germany in 1908 that Kollontai also met Helene Stocker, a collaborator of the world's first sexologist Magnus Hirschfeld, who would go on to found the *Institut für Sexualwissenschaft* in Berlin in 1920. Stocker was head of the *Bund für Mutterschutz*, and Kollontai was much impressed with the German women's movement, and modeled the Soviet women's bureau, the *Zhenodtel*, on this German model. In doing that, however, Kollontai opened herself to charges that she was a "feminist," i.e., someone who put the interests of sex above those of class and revolution. It was a label that would stick, in spite of her zeal in promoting revolutionary causes as a Menshevik, and from 1915 as a Bolshevik under Lenin.

Shortly after her arrival in Germany, Kollontai, who was by this time a strikingly beautiful thirty-six-year-old woman who still retained the aristocratic taste, bearing, and speech of her childhood, fell in love with another Russian émigré, an economist by the name of Petr Petrovich Maslov, and an affair ensued which lasted for two years. It must have been a numinous period in Kollontai's life because twelve years later, in 1922, as she was just about to go into diplomatic exile and her plans for the sexual reorganization of the Russian family were about to go up in flames, Kollontai wrote a novel describing both the affair and the world as it existed in 1910. Actually, the book, *A Great Love*, was a conflation of Kollontai's affair with Maslov and fellow revolutionary Inessa Armand's affair with Lenin. Armand was two years younger than Kollontai, the daughter of an English mother and a French father, both of whom were actors. When the father died, Armand's mother took her to Russia, where she took a position as governess with the wealthy Armand family. Inessa aspired to be a governess too but instead married Alexander, the eldest son of the Armand family, by whom she bore four children. Inessa actually had five children before she converted to the revolutionary cause, but the fifth was most probably fathered by her husband's younger brother, Vladimir, who moved in with his erstwhile sister-in-law after her marriage broke up. Vladimir was also a committed revolutionary, and it is most probably through him that she made contact with the revolutionary underground. Like Kollontai, Inessa Armand had abandoned a happy, child-filled marriage as the result of a sexual affair, in this instance with her husband's younger brother, who also introduced Armand to political revolutionary radicalism.

Like Kollontai, Armand regarded marriage thereafter as a cage which needed to be smashed if women were to be free. Like Kollontai, Armand projected her own psychic needs onto the peasant women she longed to "liberate" after the revolution. Unlike Kollontai, Armand didn't live long enough to see any of her policies put into effect. Shunted from one city to another during the chaos of the civil war which broke out in 1918, Armand succumbed to cholera and died in 1920. Lenin attended her funeral, his face swathed in a scarf that he hoped would hide his tears. Kollontai wrote *A Great Love* three years after Armand's death when Lenin was dying and with him the revolution's commitment to "winged eros," which had characterized the first years of the revolution. Kollontai's book, written in the disillusionment of exile, was a frank description of how liberation felt from the inside; it also granted a candid look into the psyches of those who had liberated themselves from morals only to find themselves, as a result, the slaves of passion.

The book begins with Natasha, a revolutionary with important Party work, now living in France in the aftermath of the brutal czarist reaction to the abortive 1905 revolution, reminiscing about the end of her affair with the head of the party, Semyon Semyonovich. Semyon, like Maslov, is married to a sickly wife who cares for their sickly children. He is obviously drawn to the vivacious Natasha, and on one out-of-town congress, they consummate the longing by having an affair. In spite of his contempt for "bourgeois morality," Semyon is unable to leave his wife, and half out of scruple and half out of the exigencies of a life in which both are at the beck and call of the party, they break off the affair. Natasha rejoices in her newfound ability to get work done, but then, out of the blue, Semyon writes to say that he wants to resume the affair. He has been granted access to a professor and his archives in G'ville in the South of France, along with three weeks to study. Would Natasha like to join him there? And, by the way, would Natasha also like to pay for this three-week interlude? The element of exploitation is there from the beginning, and Kollontai does little to disguise it. Semyon Semyonovich is the typical radical intellectual who exploits his comrades both sexually and financially and then goes on to rationalize his behavior by appealing to the cause of revolution. It is the end which justifies any means, no matter how exploitative, and Natasha, fully aware of the exploitative nature of the relationship, is unable to resist getting enmeshed in its coils. She is vulnerable to this sort of exploitation precisely because she has abandoned the moral law as some bourgeois construct whose purpose is her subjugation, but before long she begins to see "liberation" as every bit as subjugating.

Eventually Natasha jeopardizes her work and borrows money to subsidize their rendezvous, only to be disappointed when she finally meets Semyon at the designated city by his coldness, his deviousness, and his sexual brutality. The anticipation of their moments alone is destroyed by the dull reality of Semyon's imperious lust. He can't even wait until she takes off her hat and the pins holding it to her hair.

> By this time Natasha had abandoned the struggle to remove her hat and
> was lying across the double bed. She felt awkward and uncomfortable.
> Lying there underneath him, his hot breath burning her face, her hat drag-

ging at her hair and the pins digging into her scalp, she suddenly felt once more, and quite terrifyingly, that he was a complete stranger to her. That unique and powerful joy which had given wings to her journey here broke into a thousand pieces, crushed by Semyon's rough and brutally hasty embraces.[18]

Semyon falls asleep after gratifying his lust, and Natasha is left lying awake wondering why she came. Liberated from reason in matters sexual, Natasha begins to see that her motivation in acting has become a mystery. She no longer understands why she does what she does. "And to think," she ruminates sitting next to the sleeping Semyon,

> it was for him that I left work, ran into massive debts, rushed here, there, and everywhere organizing this trip, one moment out of my mind with joy, the next moment worried sick about the whole thing – to think it was he who gave me something to live for, and believe, and look forward to. . . . What a fool I've been, what a fool![19]

Natasha now realizes that male and female are hopelessly out of sync. He wants to sleep when she wants to talk. He is not interested in her ideas after all. Realizing that "his interest in her was obviously so crudely sexual," she wonders why she had come. It is a question she never gets around to answering because to answer it would call into question her entire life. Natasha left work and incurred massive debts to gratify her lust, and in gratifying it she made lust her master. Her "liberation" became, in other words, a form of bondage. She is now ordered around by her passions to do things she finds humiliating, but at the same time she finds herself unable to resist passion's demands no matter how demeaning. Gradually, the idea begins to dawn on her that the freedom she coveted so greedily is really a kind of prison: "Natasha's stay in G'ville," Kollontai writes, after it becomes apparent to her that she has been brought along to be a sexual appliance for the time when Semyon is not occupied with the professor, "was rapidly turning into a kind of voluntary incarceration."[20]

Kollontai stumbles here upon the essence of sexual liberation as a form of control; it is "voluntary incarceration." Because the will is more important than reason to the revolutionary, because in effect will is the essence of reason for both the Marxist and the Nietzschean, the revolutionary is unable to see how he is enslaved by his own will because he is unable to see the role that passion plays in that self-subversion. All the revolutionary can see is his passion, and because his only thought is how to gratify those passions – morals having been discredited as "bourgeois" – he is blind to how his passions control him. When Natasha reproaches Semyon for his selfishness, he responds with a question. "Tell me," he asks, "have I ever forced you to do anything you didn't want to do?"[21] Semyon, in other words, manipulates Natasha by manipulating her passions. As a result the manipulation remains invisible, disguised behind the choices which Natasha made. Natasha, hav-

ing been educated by socialist writings, lacks the psychological sophistication to explain how passion leads to bondage when it is gratified outside of
reason's, which is to say morality's, command. Believing that all is will,
Natasha fails to understand how Semyon has colonized her will by manipulating her passions. All Semyon wants is "there to be complete equality between us." Natasha is dumbfounded by the appeal to revolutionary rhetoric
and so can only respond by saying "Well, let's not go into all that now. I expect you're right."[22] Natasha is, in other words, completely defenseless
against the manipulation of her passions because she has so completely internalized the revolutionary rhetoric about freedom and equality, which is
two-thirds of the revolutionary triad bequeathed to the Communists from the
French Revolution. Her reason has been lamed by her acceptance of revolutionary ideology, which is nothing more than rationalized desire. By giving
in to that desire, she becomes captured by it and subject to the sort of exploitation, both sexual and financial, which she never would have tolerated as a
married woman.

Unable to escape from what she now terms "this ridiculous imprisoned
existence,"[23] she agrees to yet another tryst in yet another town, this time involving still more money which she doesn't have. On her way there, Natasha
bumps into a stranger at the train station who articulates the very things
which Natasha cannot bring herself to say, namely, that sexual "liberation" is
more constraining than marriage. Waiting for Semyon to arrive, she strikes
up a conversation with a tall man with a small square-cut beard and dark,
lively eyes which seem "most sympathetic." The man begins by talking
about his mother, who is on the same train with Semyon, and the conversation moves from there to his assertion that the only love he can respect is a
mother's love "because it's the only unselfish love." The tall stranger then
goes on to say what Natasha can't admit, not even to herself, namely, that "I
actually think that living with someone you're not married to imposes many
more chains than any legal marriage."[24]

"People," he continues, "are still bound to each other by the same emotional chains, don't you agree?"[25]

Instead of giving the standard line about human relations being redeemed at some unspecified future date by the revolution and the abolition of
property, Natasha finds herself agreeing with what he had to say. In fact,
"Natasha, equally vehemently, began pouring out to this complete stranger
everything she'd been thinking and suffering these past months."[26]

In their final confrontation, Semyon silences Natasha's reproaches by
asking her if he has ever forced her to do something she didn't want to do.
She has no answer to that question because the life she has led, based on the
impulsive gratification of illicit passion, admits no answer. Freedom of this
sort is bondage. Natasha understands that intuitively, but she can't articulate

it because both her ideology and her life deny it. So she remains silent, even though "she knew that by staying silent she was courting her own slavery to another's moods."[27]

The best she can do in the end is assure herself that love isn't ultimately all that important.

"The great love which had made her heart beat all these years, which she thought would never fade, had gone forever. It was dead, extinguished, and nothing, no tenderness, no prayers, not even understanding could reawaken it. It was too late." But in its place, Natasha now has her "work." "Now she belonged body and soul to her work."[28]

"Kollontai," according to her biographer, "said years later that she had been drawn to Maslov by his intellect and that her sexual longing for him grew out of a need for spiritual closeness to an admired comrade. She felt that his interest in her was only sexual; when he was physically satisfied, he could no longer understand her need to be with him. Nor would he treat her as an intellectual equal, preferring to discuss economics with male colleagues."[29]

In "Sexual Morality and the Social Struggle" and "On an Old Theme," articles she wrote around the time of the breakup of her affair with Maslov, Kollontai blamed erotic love as the cause of women's inferiority with the same vehemence she used to level against bourgeois marriage. By the time she wrote her autobiography in the mid-'20s, the attack on love as the cause of women's bondage had mellowed a bit, but the bitterness resulting from her affairs is still palpable:

> I could still find time for intimate experiences, for the pangs and joys of love. Unfortunately, yes! I say unfortunately because ordinarily these experiences entailed all too many cares, disappointments, and pain, and because all too many energies were pointlessly consumed through them. Yet the longing to be understood by a man down to the deepest, most secret recesses of one's soul, to be recognized by him as a striving human being, repeatedly decided matters. And repeatedly disappointment ensued all too swiftly, since the friend saw in me only the feminine element which he tried to mold into a willing sounding board to his own ego. So repeatedly the moment inevitably arrived in which I had to shake off the chains of community with an aching heart but with a sovereign, uninfluenced will. Then I was alone. But the greater the demands life made upon me, the more the responsible work waiting to be tackled, the greater grew the longing to be enveloped by love, warmth, understanding.[30]

We are talking here about a vicious circle. Life as a rootless, unmarried cosmopolite led inevitably to loneliness, which led to an affair, which led to an even greater sense of alienation after it was consummated, which led to a desire to be free from the chains of love, which led to more work, which led to more loneliness. Kollontai's new woman is a slave to her own passions, a slavery which is all more effective because she can never identify its source, blaming instead "the slavery" of marriage, "bourgeois morality," and the extant social order. The one thing Kollontai will not relinquish is her sexual passions:

> But when the wave of passion sweeps over her, she does not renounce the brilliant smile of life, she does not hypocritically wrap herself up in a faded cloak of female virtue. No, she holds out her hand to her chosen one and goes away for several weeks to drink from the cup of love's joy, however deep it is, and to satisfy herself. When the cup is empty, she throws it away without regret and bitterness. And again to work.[31]

Kollontai, as the paradigmatic new woman, breaks off the affair, seeks solace in revolutionary work, which means rationalizing her own behavior, and working toward creating a world that reflects her experience. Work becomes the solution to guilt, just as it had earlier become the justification for abandoning her husband and son. But what exactly does work, especially intellectual work of the sort she was engaged in, mean in this context? Work is little more than rationalization of the bad choices she has made, and persuading others to accept them as well. Just as love is robbed of its meaning by ripping it from its matrix in morality, so work is denied its meaning as well by ripping it away from any connection with the truth. The ultimate expression of the projection of personal desire that work had become was revolution. And before long, if enough people participate in the disruption of the moral order that their disordered desires create, revolution becomes a reality.

On February 28, 1917, Alexandra Kollontai was returning home by train after a day's work promoting revolution among the Norwegians in Christiania (now Oslo) when she looked up and read the headline which announced that the revolution had finally come to Russia. Her heart immediately began to pound. Since the train had already left the station, making it impossible for her to buy a paper of her own, Kollontai leaned as calmly as she could toward her fellow passenger and asked, "When you finish, could you lend it to me? I am a Russian, naturally I am interested in the news." On March 2, she learned from a Norwegian friend that the Czar had abdicated, and after an impromptu celebration in the hall which involved hugging her revolutionary comrades, Kollontai made plans to return to Russia after nine years in exile. Her dream of revolution had finally come true. Kollontai was greeted at the Finnish border as a liberator and quickly plunged into the debates about the *novus ordo seculorum*.

During the war years, while lecturing the Scandinavian countries, Kollontai met another Russian revolutionary by the name of Aleksandr Shliapnikov, a man of proletarian origins who was much younger than she, and another affair ensued. It was Shliapnikov who introduced Kollontai to Lenin, who in turn persuaded her to join the Bolsheviks. Lenin, for his part, was glad to have someone of her linguistic abilities working for the party, especially since he seems to have lacked any ability in foreign languages in spite of spending years in exile. By the time Kollontai arrived in Russia after the first revolution of 1917, her reputation as a sexually liberated lady had preceded her, to her detriment. Piritim Sorokin, who went on to become a sociologist of antirevolutionary sentiments at Harvard University, locked horns with Kollontai in debate, and perhaps because he came out on the losing end described her in terms of the reputation her liberated sexual life had acquired. "As for this woman," he wrote,

> it is plain that her revolutionary enthusiasm is nothing but a gratification of her sexual satyriasis [*sic*]. In spite of her numerous "husbands," Kollontai, first the wife of a general, later the mistress of a dozen men, is not yet satisfied. She seeks new forms of sexual sadism. I wish she might come under the observation of Freud and other psychiatrists. She would indeed be a rare subject for them.[32]

Tiring of debate, the Bolsheviks decided to seize power in October of 1917. After an all night meeting, the Bolsheviks responded to Kerensky's attempt to close down their newspaper by planning to seize Petrograd's communication and transportation centers. In *Ten Days that Shook the World*, John Reed describes the meeting as ending with Kollontai joining in the singing of the *Internationale* and blinking back the tears "as the immense sound rolled through the hall, burst out of the windows and doors and soared into the quiet sky." Kollontai would later say that the number of Bolshevik conspirators was so small that they would all have fit onto one sofa, but in spite of their numbers they succeeded in seizing power, and after seizing power they set about to remake Russian society.

On October 28, Lenin appointed Kollontai commissar of social welfare. Since she couldn't even persuade the doorman to let her into the building, the appointment had little immediate effect, but that would change as the Bolsheviks consolidated their hold on power. In December of 1917, the Bolsheviks legalized divorce. Gradually, Kollontai began to take control of the bureau of social welfare. When the original employees walked out with the keys to the safe, she threatened to have them thrown in jail if they didn't return. Since the bureau's main source of revenue was the monopoly it had been granted in the production of playing cards, she increased the price of a dozen decks from 30 to 360 rubles, and since the country was in a gambling mood, the money began to roll in, and as the money came in she began to implement reforms in child labor, maternity leave and medical care. On December 19, 1917, on the same day the Bolsheviks legalized divorce, Kollontai announced that her commissariat would be reorganizing children's homes to accommodate the 7 million homeless children that the revolution and subsequent civil war had created by 1921.[33]

On January 20, 1918, Kollontai ordered all maternity hospitals opened to all women free of charge. Since the country was full of wounded and disabled soldiers, she decided on her own to expropriate the Alexander Nevsky monastery as a veterans hospital. The decision caused a major church-state incident, and she was rebuked by Lenin for being too precipitant with the monks. Lenin had planned to confiscate Church property but not then and not in that manner. The incident brought out the strains which were developing in Kollontai's relationship with Lenin. Kollontai was in many ways a more doctrinaire leftist than Lenin, who was always open to pragmatic consider-ations in pursuing revolutionary goals. When Lenin initiated the New Eco-nomic Policy in the early '20s, allowing a certain amount of private owner-ship and entrepreneurial freedom, Kollontai again opposed him on ideologi-cal grounds. She also opposed him on the role unions would play in relation to the party, a role which would earn her Lenin's enmity and her de facto ex-pulsion from party life.

Her actions also earned her a reputation for recklessness, a reputation which was only enhanced by her affair with a sailor seventeen years her ju-nior by the name of Pavel Dybenko. Dybenko was born into a peasant family in the Ukraine in 1889. In 1911 he was conscripted into the navy and one year later he became a Bolshevik. In 1917 he was, in John Reed's words, "a giant bearded sailor with a placid face,"[34] who met Kollontai when she came to Helsingfors in the spring to raise the revolutionary consciousness of the sailors there. "Our meetings," Kollontai wrote describing the tumultuous summer of 1917, "always overflowed with joy, our partings were full of tor-ment, emotion, broken hearts. Just this strength of feeling, the ability to live fully, passionately, strongly, drew me powerfully to Pavel."[35]

If there were ever an example of "winged eros," it was Kollontai's rela-tionship with Dybenko. Born in the passions of revolution it followed the tra-jectory of historical events for the next five years until it finally burnt itself out when Kollontai ended up in diplomatic exile back in Norway. By No-vember of 1917 virtually every one in a position of leadership knew they were lovers. Stalin had to be rebuked by Trotsky for listening in on their phone conversations and mocking their conversations to fellow party mem-bers. It may have been party gossip or it may have been Dybenko's peasant roots or it may have been enthusiasm for the new regime, but Dybenko de-cided that he and Kollontai should be the first to register their union under the new marriage law which Kollontai helped draft. Kollontai reacted with am-bivalence, apparently discussing it with Zoya, her childhood friend, who re-sponded in typically sexual revolutionist terms: "Will you really put down our flag of freedom for his sake? You who all your life have always fought against the slavery which married life brings, and which inevitably comes into conflict with our work and achievements."[36]

In spite of Zoya's warning, Kollontai and Dybenko registered their un-ion and the marriage caused a sensation even in that revolutionary age, pri-marily because of the difference in age and class between Kollontai and her much younger peasant husband. Albert Rhys Williams wrote in the *New*

York Evening Post that "we were astounded to find one morning that the versatile Kollontay [hsic] ad married the sailor Dybenko."[37] The marriage also gave rise to the rumor that Kollontai was sexually insatiable and that her sexual appetites could only be satisfied by numerous lovers from the younger and more vigorous lower classes. Zeth Hoeglund, who had worked with Kollontai when she had her affair with Shliapnikov in Scandinavia during the war, said that the seventeen-year age difference had caused "a sensation." Louise Bryant, John Reed's lover, wrote that many Bolsheviks "looked with disapproving eyes upon Kollontai's infatuation for Dubenko [*sic*]."[38] The fact that the marriage caused so much attention is in itself remarkable, for at this moment in Russian history there were many other more pressing matters to think about.

Ever since the Kaiser had sent Lenin and his Bolshevik comrades back to Russia in a sealed train in the spring of 1917, like some political bacillus to lame the Russian war effort, the Russian people harbored the suspicion that the Bolsheviks were foreign agents, interested more in weakening Russia than achieving peace or perhaps more interested in weakening Russia by achieving peace at any price. When Lenin agreed to the ruinous conditions of the Treaty of Brest-Litovsk in May of 1918, ending Russia's participation in the war, the worst suspicions of the Russian patriots were confirmed, and a civil war broke out which threatened to sweep the Bolsheviks from the pages of history. Rather than wait for a commission, Dybenko left Moscow for his native Ukraine, where he organized his own army to battle, not without some success, the white armies, which were now backed by the British and French governments.

During the summer of 1918 Dybenko was arrested as a deserter and thrown in jail. It was only because of Kollontai's strenuous efforts on his behalf that he was released on bail, but then, making matters even worse, Dybenko and Kollontai jumped bail for a trip to Petrograd to visit Kollontai's son. The Party leadership was furious and wanted Dybenko shot; Lenin, on the other hand, is claimed to have said that the most appropriate punishment would be sentencing both Dybenko and Kollontai to live with each other for five years. Since that is the approximate duration of their marriage, Lenin seems to have been something of a prophet. It was most probably the bail-jumping incident that led to the rumor that Dybenko and Kollontai had become so passionately involved with each other that they ran off to the Crimea for a honeymoon during the October Revolution.

In fact, the pair were together only sporadically during this tumultuous period of Russian history. Part of the explanation lies with the social chaos which the Civil War created, but there were deeper causes as well. Dybenko and Kollontai found it impossible to live with each other for an extended period of time. "Winged Eros," love on the run, was more than just making a virtue out of necessity during the tumult of the civil war; it was the only way the relationship could survive as long as it did. Given the premises which Bebel, Marx, and Engels had proposed for the establishment of "truly moral" relations between the sexes, the revolution was bound to impose a psychic burden on those who believed that the new era was going to bring about a new morality. Now that property had been abolished, there was no excuse for failures in love. Her affair with Dybenko, however, was proving the opposite to be the case. The more passion was freed from the constraints of bourgeois morality, the more imperious it became, the more contentious the relationships of the liberated became. By 1918, a year into her marriage with Dybenko, it had become clear that the revolution was not solving problems associated with relations between the sexes. In fact it was making them worse.

"The new women," Kollontai wrote around the same time she was embroiled in the relationship with Dybenko, "do not want exclusive possession when they love."[38] It was easy to say, but less easy to put into practice when Kollontai traveled to Odessa to find that Dybenko had moved in with a nineteen-year-old orphan.

> The modern woman can forgive much to which the woman of the past would have found very difficult to reconcile herself: the husband's ability to provide for her material maintenance, lack of attention of an external kind, even infidelity, but she never forgets or forgives the non-esteem of her spiritual "ego," of her sensibility.[39]

Had this been the only instance of infidelity on Dybenko's part, Kollontai might have been able to overlook it as stemming from the conditions imposed by the civil war. But Dybenko was more than a little compulsive about his infidelities, even to the point of sleeping with Kollontai's secretary while he was staying at Kollontai's apartment. Given the calculated affront this was to their love, Kollontai could only make a virtue of necessity by claiming that fidelity wasn't important after all, and that the only thing that really counted was the autonomy of self, which had caused the break-up of her first marriage and launched her on her career as a revolutionary in the mid-'90s. "For the woman of the past," Kollontai wrote, again presuming to speak for the "new woman,"

> the infidelity or the loss of her beloved was the worst possible disaster, in imagination and in fact. But for the heroine of our day what is truly disastrous is the loss of her identity, the renunciation of her own "ego" for the sake of the beloved, for the protection of love's happiness. The new woman not only rejects the outer fetters, she protests "against love's prison itself," she is fearful of the fetters that love, the slumbering atavistic inclination in her to become the shadow of the husband, might tempt her to surrender her identity, and to abandon her work, her profession, her life-tasks.[39]

By now it should be obvious that for the new woman, love and identity are mutually exclusive. A woman can have love or she can have an "ego," but she can't have both. At this point the similarities between the new woman and the old woman become equally obvious because Kollontai is proposing here the same thing she rebelled against under the Czar. Love means the extinction of personality. A woman can only be herself if she renounces love. Since Kollontai can give up neither her quest for love nor her autonomy of self, she condemns herself to alternating forever between those two irreconcilable poles. The new woman is a self that is forever lonely, drawn to a love that is forever devouring and humiliating.

Dybenko was eventually expelled from the party because of his lack of discipline. Kollontai's career suffered for the same reason. "Little by little," she wrote, "I was freed also of all other work. I lectured again and went over my ideas about 'the new woman' and 'the new morality.'"[42] It was in this frame of mind, when the initial passion of her infatuation with Dybenko had begun to fade, that Kollontai decided to throw herself back into her work. Like John B. Watson, Kollontai saw work, first and foremost, as activity begetting self-forgetfulness. Work took Kollontai's mind off the pain which her relationship with Dybenko caused, but, more than that, work was the implementation of revolution, which meant the projection of her desires and those of other disaffected intellectuals onto the working class which supposedly embodied their ideals. Kollontai's desire to "reform" marriage corresponded to the difficulties and eventual break-up of her marriage with Dybenko. "Work" was always a compensation for personal failure. When the marriage finally broke up in 1923, Kollontai threw herself into negotiating the sale of herring and sealskins. "I work to the utmost. It is better this way. It is essential." Work in 1918, however, meant "reforming" the Russian family.

On November 16, 1918, Kollontai welcomed over 1,000 delegates to the First All-Russia Congress of Worker and Peasant Women. Since the civil war was in full swing, it was not clear that anyone would or could show up, given the chaotic state of soviet transportation. Kollontai planned on 300 delegates and was stunned when four times that many showed up, hungry and cold, dressed in the sheepskins and traditional garb of the countryside. The purpose of the conference was evident in its slogan – "through practical participation in Soviet construction – to communism." And it soon became apparent from the tenor of Kollontai's opening address that she didn't consider raising a family "participation in Soviet construction." Privately, she had expressed her own fears to Jacques Sadoul. She had been away from Russia since 1908. She had never been a peasant, and as a result, she wondered if what she had to say would have any purchase on the minds of the women who had braved the civil war to come to hear her talk. Kollontai would soon find out. She proposed in her speech the destruction of the individual household and what amounted to taking away these women's children to be educated in state schools. Kollontai asked the Russian peasant women to open themselves up to a life in which they would no longer be dependent on men. In short, Kollontai was asking them to become like her. Even her feminist biographers, who are certainly more sympathetic to what Kollontai was proposing than her audience at the time, come to the same conclusion. Kollontai was projecting her own needs onto her audience. In order to become "liberated," they had to become like her. "Her speech," Beatrice Farnsworth writes,

> was as much a reflection of her own past and of her need to fight the emotional ties of the family, as it was a guide for Russia's women. In a fascinating way, her speech followed the outlines of her own liberation, which began with divorce. It was no accident that she started by discussing the right to divorce, which had been decreed shortly after the October Revolution and by urging women not to fear their new freedom.[43]

The "withering away of the family" was, in other words, "a projection of Kollontai's own fight for independence against conventional marriage and domesticity."[44] Kollontai's program for the Russian family was an attempt to control Russian women based on her own psychic needs. Divorce was essential to their liberation because it had been essential to her own. The Russian woman needed to be liberated by work outside the home – just as she had been liberated by work outside the home. Kollontai's proposals were, in this regard, no more radical than what was being proposed by other Bolsheviks. Bukharin had called the family a stronghold of conservatism. Zlata Lilina, Zinoviev's wife, wrote that children needed to be rescued from their families: "In other words we must nationalize them. They will be taught the ABCs of Communism and later become true Communists. Our task now is to oblige the mother to give her children to us – to the Soviet State."[45] Lenin, who also addressed the women at the congress, took a more pragmatic stand, arguing that the family was necessary for child rearing. A radical pamphlet, probably written by Sabsovich, insisted that "one of the first results of the socialization of our education must be that children shall not live with their parents. From . . . birth they are to be in special children's homes in order to remove them . . . from the harmful influence of parents and family. We ought to have special children's towns."[46] Kollontai avoided the word, but her program was just as authoritarian. The New Child would grow up under rigorous state supervision, spending most of his time in state institutions where intelligent educators would make him a communist.

At this point one begins to notice similarities between what Kollontai was proposing in Soviet Union and what John B. Watson was proposing in the United States. Both had been influenced by Pavlov into believing that the infant came into the world a *tabula rasa*, upon which conditioners could write whatever text they saw fit. Since there was no human nature, children were essentially what their conditioners made them. Once that matter got settled, the only question that remained was who would condition the children, and on this issue the Bolsheviks were of one mind. The family was a retro-grade, atavistic, conservative influence that now had to be replaced by the state. The only real questions in this regard among the Bolsheviks were tacti-cal. How could the children be removed from their parents without causing rebellion among the parents? In both instances, reform of childrearing prac-tices was a covert form of social control. The Bolsheviks, who were good be-haviorists, wanted to control the upbringing of children so that they could create out of them docile communists for the future. But they also wanted to convince women to work for their benefit in factories, rather than for the ben-efit of their children and husbands in the home.

The reaction of the peasant women was predictable. They thanked the Bolsheviks for redistributing the land. They also said the equal rights were fine, but they would not hand over their children to state-run kindergartens or nurseries. "Peasant women," according to Clements, "simply wanted to be left alone to get on with their lives. They had no time to go to meetings, nor did they see any particular reason to do so. They certainly had no intention of turning their children over to strangers."[47] What the peasant women didn't understand was that liberation was a form of control, and that exerting that control over peasant women was the purpose of the 1918 conference and the women's bureau which sponsored it. Perhaps because they share Kollontai's feminist liberationist bias, most of her biographers fail to see the women's bureau as an instrument of control even though the evidence is clearly there. Clements writes that once the party had established Zhenodtel sections in the provinces under Bolshevik control, they then focused their attention "on in-volving women in socialist construction, *which meant convincing women to cooperate with the program of compulsory labor which the government had recently ordered*" (my emphasis).[48] She writes this without a note of irony.

In 1920, the Bolsheviks decriminalized abortion, and this too is noted without irony, even though the Bolsheviks themselves were worried that in doing this they were capitulating to the ideology of eugenic social engineer-ing that the communists called Malthusianism. Kollontai applauded the de-criminalization of abortion as a liberating and long-overdue measure. Yet, she seemed unaware that the main justification for abortion in Malthusian countries like England was the elimination of inferior classes of people. If the working class was by that definition inferior, why was the workers' para-dise allowing the extermination of its own people? Lenin tried to square this circle in 1918 when he said that "freedom from medical propaganda is one thing, the social theory of neo-Malthusianism is quite another."[49] But that did not change the fact that workers were now using the tactics of their op-pressors. If, according to Marxism there can be no overpopulation because the worker is the source of all wealth, then why were the Soviets implement-ing Malthusian ideas like abortion, especially when the combination of World War I, the revolution, and the civil war had killed off 11 million workers whose labor was so urgently needed? The answer is simple: abortion is the *sine qua non* of sexual liberation, and in 1920, sexual liberation was still alive and thriving in the workers' paradise, and under people like Commissar Kollontai, it was proving to be normative in matters sexual – at least for the time being.

Part II, Chapter 9

New York, 1917

"My life," Max Eastman wrote in his diary at the time, "began in January 1917."[1] Eastman, who was thirty-four years old when his life began, saw the world at the time as "on the brink of a new epoch of history,"[2] after which nothing would be the same. Eastman listed America's entry into the war and the revolution in Russia as two events which would change the world forever, but the really momentous event in Eastman's life, the reason he dated January 1917 as the date of his rebirth, had nothing to do with politics in the conventional sense of the word. The date commemorated the beginning of his affair with the movie star Florence Deshon. As the United States was preparing to plunge into the First World War, and Russia into a revolution that would dominate world politics for the rest of the century, Eastman and Deshon were lying "side by side in the corner bed by the big moonlit window" of his newly purchased country home in Croton-on-Hudson experiencing "for the first time the ideal rapture and the physical achievement of love." Eastman had finally achieved liberation from the Christian morals of his forebears, most especially his Congregationalist minister parents. "I had won my long war of independence . . ," he wrote, "I had fallen wholeheartedly in love. After much preaching and philosophizing and many academic vows of consecration to it, I had at last stepped forth into the enjoyment of living. It was possible for me now to use in a grown up way whatever wisdoms I possessed."[3]

It is, unfortunately, difficult to discern much wisdom in Eastman's subsequent conduct. Max Eastman married Ida Rauh, his childhood sweetheart from Elmira, New York, on May 4, 1911, in what was supposed to be a new arrangement where both partners kept their names and separate identities. In order to foster his career as a writer, Eastman and Rauh moved to Greenwich Village, where the same solvent that dissolved the Sangers' marriage began to work its corrosive effect on theirs. The circumstances were in many respects identical. Both the Sangers and the Eastmans became involved in the revolutionary workers' movement, and for both it functioned, as Bill Sanger had said, as an excuse for free love. Neither marriage survived the Village. In Eastman's case, the effect was almost immediate, which is not surprising since he viewed the relationship as "casual" from the beginning. "I had lost," he wrote, "in marrying Ida, my irrational joy in life. I had lost my religion. I had committed – irrevocably it seemed to me – the Folly of Growing Up.

How poignantly I remember the effort it required to lift my will, against the drag of her indifference to a state of normal interest in examining that ship."[4]

Since the ship in question is the one they sailed off on for their honeymoon, the marriage did not seem to be off to an auspicious beginning. That beginning was only made worse by the ideas they discovered when they moved to Greenwich Village. Eastman later described his marriage as a convenient way of getting a traveling companion for a trip to Europe. It is difficult to discern, however, whether these were his views at the time. At one point in the first volume of his autobiography, he claims that

> He who looks back, however, is one person; he is the one who triumphed and survived. He will inevitably tend to read himself back into the whole picture. The other, the rejected one, will fight a losing battle even to be remembered.
>
> The "I" who accepted her as intimate friend and child and mother, resolutely adapting himself to her rich if unsuitable nature and the achievement in happy hours innumerable, is dead and gone. The rebel against that kind of happiness, which in truth could never rise to joy, took full possession finally and lived to tell the tale. Had the battle gone the other way, or could we with some psychical engine dredge up the recollections of a defeated self, the tale would wear a different color.[5]

Whether the younger Eastman felt the same way is impossible to tell. The man who recounts the tale is other than the man who could have written the tale of his fidelity to wife and child. That man was eliminated long before the story got told, and the story, as Eastman makes clear, is essentially Eastman's justification of the life he chose to live. According to the later Eastman, "marriage always seemed to me a gauche intrusion on the part of the state and society into the intimacies of a private romance."[6] Eastman had decided that he didn't "want to be tied. Only with a sister, a mother with another boy, only with irresponsible freedom, can I have the full taste of any adventure."[7]

When the young married couple returned to New York after a long and disappointing European holiday, they decided to set up their household under two separate names, a practice which has become common of late but was considered newsworthy at the time. So newsworthy in fact that a reporter was dispatched from the *New York World* to get the story. When the reporter arrived, Mrs. Eastman gave her view like a good German dug in confidently on the sexual front. Under the title, "No 'Mrs.' Badge of Slavery Worn by the Miss/Wife," "Miss-Mrs Rauh-Eastman," as she was termed in the article, opined that "Our attitude toward the marriage service is that we went thought with it; then we can say afterward we don't believe in it. It was with us a placating of convention, because if we had gone counter to convention, it would have been too much of a bother for the gain. . . . There may be some who still feel that marriage is a sacrament, but the idea is passing away."[8]

Copy like that might have played well in New York City, but it caused a storm of indignation in Elmira, New York, the Eastmans' home town. "Against the entrance of this serpent of lust and falsehood," opined one Methodist minister, "let every man's hand be raised, and let every sword of manly and fatherly honor flash death to the intruder who would mar the tree of life."[9] Less floridly, one prominent citizen wrote that "'Professor' Eastman and Miss Rauh defy the bonds of the sacred marriage service which they swore to reverence while at the very hour of its taking they knew their oath was false."[10] With over thirty years of hindsight, Eastman could chuckle over the effect his nascent feminism had on the hometown crowd, but at the time it must have been a serious affront to his parents, both of whom were still ministers there.

The really painful repercussions were to come later when Eastman decided to act on his convictions concerning the un-sacredness of the marriage vow. During the summer of 1913, Eastman became sexually involved with one of his wife's friends and then, perhaps because of his upbringing or his view of himself as a fearless seeker after truth, confessed. The effect on his wife was devastating. It turned out that she really didn't believe what she had been willing to tell the New York tabloids. His wife had earlier confided to this same friend how much the marriage meant to her, which the friend in turn conveyed to him in a letter which he received while on their honeymoon. "My foolishly cherished opinion," he wrote, "that we were merely protecting by this public act the private enjoyment of a trip to Europe, or at the most an experiment in living together, had not been her opinion at all."[11] Ida had taken the marriage seriously. "Max," she said when he told her, "I can't bear it. I can't bear it." He describes her as gasping "as though I had put her body on the rack." Eastman for his part was filled with remorse. "I was appalled at what I had done. I lost all poise, all pride, all self-identity, all simple common sense in an overwhelming Conviction of Sin."[12]

Eastman should have known better; however, there is no indication that he would have acted differently had he known. Perhaps this is because his memoir was written by the man formed by the choices he made. Eastman, in spite of his religion of antimarriage, could not break with his wife and child immediately. His attempts to free himself from them lasted about four years. During that time he became involved with more than one woman, but more importantly, he was involved with his peers in Greenwich Village in heavy conversations over the meaning of freedom from "bourgeois" institutions like monogamy and marriage. It was also during this time that Eastman became a public devotee of Sigmund Freud, deriving from his discipleship the same salve for this conscience that Freud's wealthy patients had discovered. Eventually Eastman was considering moving out but needed to talk it over with his friends, Eugen and Inez Boissevain, who were married but "to ensure each other the whole wealth of experience, had taken a vow of unpossessive love." Given their attitude toward marital fidelity, the outcome of the conversation was a foregone conclusion. Eastman characterized "this boldly idealistic talk" as being:

> like an Act of Emancipation. It released me from the clutch of a force that was stronger even than Ida's will, my sense of guilt. It knew now, and could remember forever, that I am not an abject, abnormal, morbid, immoral or irredeemable sinner – there is a beauty and a potentiality in my sexual constitution and a possibility of companionship for it.[13]

In other words, the Village was full of people just like him, who wanted the same sort of liberation from the exigencies of the moral law that he did. The Village had become a support group for people who were tired of being married. Max could not discuss the issue with his sister Crystal, who, he would discover later, was experiencing the same sort of restlessness herself. She too would abandon her spouse and seek absolution in psychoanalysis. Her way of coping with divorce was to go to Europe and study with "Dr. Jung in Zürich." Crystal thought that Max should be psychoanalyzed as well, which prompted Max to plunge into Freud and read "every book on Freud then available." Eastman anticipated the American vogue for Freud by ten years, but the matrix for both conversions was the same, namely, the guilt which accrued from transgressions against the moral law, sexual morality in particular. This was the matrix of virtually all of the ideologies and trends which would emerge from the Village during this period. Within a few years of Eastman's decision to leave his wife, these forces would be marshaled under the red flag of Bolshevism. Communism was, in effect, the control mechanism which people like Eastman sought out – if not as a punishment for their sins – then as a mechanism which anesthetized guilt and one where party discipline kept these people's lives from spinning out of control. The communism of the '30s was the totalitarian reaction to the sexual license of the '20s. Communism was the twentieth century's quintessential form of political control, and it derived its power in Greenwich Village from the sexual mores of the Left. Arthur Koestler said much the same thing about his motivation in joining the party, describing the disgust he felt at a one night stand as the immediate cause.

Eastman, who was to go on to become a fervent anti-Communist in later life, expended a lot of effort spinning a hedonistic philosophy out of his desire to pursue sexual liberation. However, the thought that it may all come down to nothing more than rationalization was never far from his mind:

> Perhaps I am so tormented because all this "confession" about not "loving" her is but a rationalization of the desire of having other physical and semi-romantic gratifications without losing her love. At this moment, in a stupendous way, even the whole of our intercourse presents itself to my remorseful heart as a long-headed cunning eternal ruse of my Machiavellian intellect to attain that end without moral reprobation![14]

Eastman always states the case against himself more effectively than his denials, which for the most part end up as just that without any convincing justification. His prescription is true not only of himself but of the whole generation of radicals whose aspirations he so successfully articulated as editor of both *The Masses* and *The Liberator*. Eastman was a successful editor precisely because he could extrapolate from his own experiences to the desire for sexual thrills without "moral reprobation" among his readership. At another point in his long struggle to separate from Ida, he reduced the whole ideological question to one convincing bottom line: "I am not happy with Ida *because I want to be free to satisfy other sexual desires* [emphasis in original]. There I have said it. Now the question remains: is it the essential truth?"[15]

Eastman quickly says that it is not, but he just as quickly backs down on that assertion as well. At another point, he continues the debate with himself, and as if to justify himself once and for all to the reader and, more importantly, to himself, asserts, "I know that the substance of the book is true. It is not a rationalization."[16] But almost immediately he is consumed with doubts. It turns out that his philosophy, which is based on his own reading of his anti-monogamous constitution, is in turn based on a simple act of the will: He wants what he wants – sexual desire, to be sure – but beyond that Eastman discerns simple selfishness:

> Yet even so – the sense of guilt comes back – why not renounce for her sake a thing that pains her? I can only answer, though it makes me desperately sad and sick with scruples: I know that I will not do it. I am not unselfish enough. So then I will have the other virtue. I will at least strongly and candidly, like a man grown up in the daylight, go and have my way.[17]

Eastman's consecration to selfishness and hedonism has all the trappings of a religious conversion. Henceforth, he is to be "the creature of successive alarms of passion."[17] Beyond that, he feels called like some St. Paul of the Libido, to spread this gospel: "My own reconquest of freedom," he writes, "fanned up my zeal to extend it to all men."[18] His conversion to the religion of libido, which coincided with his deconversion from Christianity, takes on the character of a second birth. Eastman is born again but born again into a completely different religion. Which is why he can say that his life "began in January 1917," the rebirth corresponding with his affair with Florence Deshon.

The new dispensation did not bring happiness, however. The affair with Deshon most certainly did not end happily. Each was tormented with fits of jealousy and possessiveness alternating with fear of losing new-found independence. Deshon was called to Hollywood in December of 1919 and put under contract to one of the studios there. She also met Charlie Chaplin, and an affair ensued, while Eastman on the East Coast pursued an affair with the dancer Lisa Duncan, sister to the more famous Isadora. Eastman claimed to be undisturbed by the prospect of sharing Florence with Chaplin because "what I wanted more than any love just then was freedom from loving. I wanted to be selfish."[20]

That is, of course, a wish that is easy to fulfill. Its fulfillment, however, was not as fraught with enjoyment as Eastman anticipated. Eastman claimed that "there was a kind of famousness about our relationship, it was so unhampered by convention and seemed so perfect"[21]; however, perhaps because of that very freedom from convention, Eastman had to admit later that "we were both a little insane – at war with ourselves as well as with each other."[22]

> I spoke of my own dividedness as insane, and when Florence was gone my conduct came near to proving it. Though a mere chance had brought us together again, love now lived in me with the old intensity – also the implacable rebellion against it. I was torn in two and instead of taking refuge in the daily life I had been living before she came, I stayed like a hermit in the small house in Croton, living in the little rooms where we had lived together, inviting and entertaining my grief.[23]

Eastman's religion of enjoyment wasn't faring well on its maiden voyage. Eastman, who had abjured Christianity to become "the creature of successive alarms of passion," was now being torn apart by precisely those conflicting passions:

> I am in love and yet I can not love. I am out of love and yet I can not cease from loving. . . . All day my heart aches with longing, and yet when I imagine your coming here again it is with positive terror. And when I come up the stairs into the sweet house in Hollywood, the Black Panther is there too. And I know that it is going to be my death to be in her power.[24]

The relationship hadn't proven especially enjoyable to Deshon either. Over the winter, she had got pregnant by Chaplin and then had had a miscarriage. In addition to that, she was faced with the prospect of throwing her lot in with either Eastman or Chaplin. When Chaplin insisted that she return with him to the West Coast and she refused, the relationship was over, and, although she didn't realize it at the time, her career was over too. She had chosen to spend some time with Eastman, but when she returned to Hollywood she learned that Chaplin wasn't interested in her anymore. His pride had been wounded. Beyond that, she had to face the fact that her sudden rise to stardom the previous winter was more the result of her affair with Chaplin than of her own talent or beauty. The promised movie roles never materialized. For a while she was paid to sit in Hollywood and do nothing, but before long that contract expired as well, leaving her worse off than when she left for Hollywood the previous fall.

Eastman titles the second volume of his autobiography *Love and Revolution*, but he never tells us exactly how the two parts of the title fit together. That they were connected seems obvious from the simple fact that they are juxtaposed so readily and frequently. "During this time of sorrow," he writes, referring to his affair with Deshon, "I was taking an optimistic part in winning American socialists to bolshevism."[25] In the May and June 1920 issues of *The Liberator*, the equally sexually liberated Bertrand Russell announced his conversion to communism. Russell then went on a pilgrimage to the holy land of his conversion that summer, an event which brought about a deconversion – one of the quickest on record, according to Eastman – of equal vehemence. Although many, including Eastman himself, would follow the same path, Russell's *volte-face* seemed at the time an irrelevant aside to the Left, which seemed determined to see in Moscow a vehicle for overthrowing the status quo in morals as well as in economic matters.

Eastman, as we have indicated, never specified the exact relationship between love and revolution. However, his autobiography makes clear that as troubles in the former area increased the attraction to the latter area increased in direct proportion. Eastman, the economic materialist, was convinced that with the changing of economic relationships, personal relationships would take care of themselves. He had learned the theory, ironically enough, from Ida Rauh, his first wife, who went on to be hoist on her own sexual petard. "I remember that conversation so distinctly," he wrote describing his talk with Ida Rauh

> because it was the turning point in my intellectual life. My impulse toward an extreme social ideal and my obstructing sense of the hard facts of human nature were reconciled in a flash by this Marxist idea of enlightened class struggle toward socialism. Here was a method of attaining the ideal based upon the very facts of what made it seem unattainable. I need no longer extinguish my dreams with my knowledge. I never need again cry out: "I wish I believed in the Son of God and his second coming!"[26]

As Eastman's troubles with Deshon increased, so too did his interest in the Communist revolution. Perhaps he saw the latter as some sort of consolation for the troubles he was experiencing in love. At any rate, both reached the crisis point at around the same time. In late 1921, Deshon, having lost her studio contract in Hollywood, had moved back to New York City. Eastman, perhaps as a way of keeping his options open, was keeping his distance. He bought her a copy of his newest book in February 1922 but delayed delivering it. Delayed too long, it seems. He was awakened by the news that she had committed suicide. In April of the same year, Eastman left New York for Moscow. Domestic troubles had propelled him eastward just as unerringly as they would propel his Negro poet protégé Claude McKay in the same direction a few months later. It was in fact to McKay that Eastman turned in mid-Atlantic to unburden himself once again on the issue of personal freedom:

> By the way of a declaration of inward independence, or of the right of free thought and feeling, I wrote from mid-ocean to my friend Claude McKay: "I feel sometimes as though the whole modern world, capitalism and com-

munism and all were rushing toward some enormous nervous efficient machine-made doom of the true values of life."[27]

Eastman was right again, but in a way that he couldn't understand at the time. In terms of this century's penchant for mass destruction, the best was yet to come. But by the time he arrived on the continent, Eastman was too intent on the proceedings of the Genoa conference and the swath that the Bolsheviks were cutting there to explicate the connections between his love life and his penchant for revolution. His interest in international politics did not prevent him, however, from indulging in another affair of the heart. If he had been crushed by the death of Deshon, it was not apparent to one of the female interpreters who was attached to the Soviet delegation. But that may have been because Eliena Krylenko was having romantic problems of her own in the midst of the revolution as well. "We were busy enough," wrote the woman who was to become the second Mrs. Eastman, "but not too busy for passionate flirtations. Everybody, from the heads of the delegation down, was having a love-affair. But the most engrossing and tearful affair was a real love that sprang up between me and Vladimir Divilkovsky, a young Russian attaché of the Rome Embassy."[28]

Eliena and Max sat on a rock and stared out over the sea. She taught him the Russian word for silver. Eastman had "the sadness of lost love in my heart, and yet a springtime thirst for a new experience," which he would slake with the liberated Soviet ladies in their brave new world. After checking into the situation in Moscow, Eastman set off for Yalta, where he decided to learn Russian by seducing the first woman he found. Given his good looks and the relaxed sexual standards in newly revolutionary Russia, Eastman's crash course was doomed to success. Before too long he met Nina, a beautifully formed, brown-haired, twenty-seven-year-old wife of an engineer from Kharkov, who was at the seaside while her husband was away on a long construction job. The seduction was especially easy because

> among the intelligentsia in general the restrictions upon freedom of choice in sex relations were much relaxed in those beginnings of the "new world" of socialism. No ghost of the Seventh Commandment, no wraith of marriage vow, not even, I think, the memory of a talk about fidelity between Nina and her husband, haunted the sky-covered scenes of our embraces. The October Revolution, whatever it was going to do for the proletariat, had already done some liberating for the culture classes. It had cut down a number of artificial barriers between the beautiful and the good – one of them the habit of putting on clothes to go swimming.[29]

Part II, Chapter 10

Versailles, 1919

When Eddie Bernays was about to be drafted in 1918, George Creel wrote a letter to his draft board saying that "Mr. Bernays's current position [at the Committee for Public Information] is far more important to the Government than any clerkship that he might fill." Creel would live to regret his letter when Bernays, ever the self-promoter, announced that he was going to the Versailles peace conference "to interpret the work of the Peace Conference by keeping up a worldwide propaganda to disseminate American accomplishments and ideals."[1] Now that the war was over the Republicans in Congress didn't want any more Wilsonian propaganda paid for with taxpayers' money. The lesson that Bernays was learning – partially from his uncle and partially from his experience doing propaganda for George Creel at the Committee for Public Information during the war – was that man was a function of his passions, which he does not control. "The Freudian theories upon which Mr. Martin relies," he wrote in *Crystallizing Public Opinion* after the war, "very largely for his argument led to the conclusion that what Mr. Henry Watterson has said of the suppression of news applies equally to the suppression of individual desire. Neither will suppress."[2] Man is motivated not by reason but by passion; civilization, meaning tradition, morals, and religion, had fought a losing war with the passions throughout history. This much he had learned from his uncle. In a revolutionary age, however, and Uncle Sigmund was nothing if not a revolutionary, the passions could be mobilized for social change by anyone who knows how to manipulate them successfully. This had been the lesson of the Enlightenment and the French Revolution. The lesson of the war, a lesson soon to be transferred to the advertising agencies of the 1920s, was that these passions could be liberated by the manipulation of public opinion and redirected into channels congenial to those who control public opinion, but in order for this to work, it had to operate on a large scale, of the sort that was occurring in the aftermath of World War I in Russia in the wake of the October Revolution. Everyone had to be involved in the subversion of morals, in other words, or at least everyone had to be perceived as being involved. Otherwise, the aberrant individual would be ostracized for antisocial behavior:

> The tendency, however, of the instincts and desires which are thus ruled
> out of conduct is somehow or other, when the conditions are favorable, to
> seek some avenue of release and satisfaction. To the individual most of

these avenues of release are closed. . . . The only release which the individual can have is one which commands, however briefly, the approval of his fellows. That is why Mr. Martin calls crowd psychology and crowd activity "the result of forces hidden in a personal and unconscious psyche of the members of the crowd, forces which are merely released by social gatherings of a certain sort." The crowd enables the individual to express himself according to his desire and without restraint.[3]

But pan-cultural liberation can only take place with the assistance of pan-cultural instruments of persuasion. It could only take place with the emergence of mass-media, and it was precisely those instruments – magazines with a national circulation, cinema, radio, television – which emerged during the course of Bernays's long life. It was Bernays, taking his cue from this famous uncle, who wrote the book on how to manipulate the masses through those instruments.

In order to re-engineer man, the "invisible governors" had to create a world populated by "mass man," rootless individuals cut off from ethnic and religious affiliation who relied not on religion or tradition or the moral codes they propagated, but rather on the opinion of what seemed to be everyone else as propagated by the mass media. The new authority which everyone followed in this regard was science. Science broke taboos; science gave rational permission whereas tradition proposed only irrational restraint. In formulating his theory, Bernays drew on his experience promoting the play *Damaged Goods*, which was able to make the American public accept the word "syphilis" because "the counsel on public relations projected the doctrine of sex hygiene through those groups and sections of the public which were prepared to work with him."[4]

In expressing these thoughts, Bernays was following not only the lead of his Illuminist uncle, he was also following the lead of one of Freud's most influential American disciples, Walter Lippmann. Bernays's book *Crystallizing Public Opinion* was published one year after Lippmann's *Public Opinion* appeared in 1922, and in it Bernays developed many of the same ideas. Lippmann had also served under George Creel, who had been appointed to head the Committee of Public Information, which was made up of the secretaries of the war, navy and state. According to Harold Lasswell, who like Lippmann would become a major figure in communication theory/psychological warfare, the CPI was "the equivalent of appointing a separate cabinet minister for propaganda . . . responsible for every aspect of propaganda work, both at home and abroad."[5]

When the war ended, Lippmann, Lasswell, Bernays, and Creel took the insights they had gained from mobilizing a nation for war and offered those insights to the business community, which in turn set about to mobilize the nation into an army of consumers. Advertising was an essential part of liberalism, as defined by Lippmann, Dewey, and Croly, the crowd which founded the *New Republic* at least in part as a way of getting the United States into the war. In advertising, Bernays and Lippmann saw the practical application of the lessons they had learned in the CPI during the war. The rise of advertising meant the erosion of parents, tradition, and religion as authority figures and their replacement with "science" and brand names, endorsed by scientists. It meant idolizing Wilson and destroying ethnic enclaves in the interest of national, as opposed to local and regional, concerns. It might have happened all by itself, but Wilson's war certainly facilitated its arrival.

In his work at the CPI during the war and in advertising and public relations later on, Bernays with the help of Lippmann internalized the contradictions of liberalism and its view of mass man, and the main contradiction revolved around the dichotomy of freedom/control. Liberalism freed men from superstitions like belief in God. Yet, once there was no God, once the moral law had been discredited as equally superstitious, then social control becomes a necessity because the object of self-control, the passions, now had nothing to give them direction or keep them under control. Just as social chaos was the natural result of liberalism's philosophy, so social control was the natural result of its politics; the one flowed inexorably from the other. The paradox of liberalism lay in the fact that it promoted passion as liberation from traditional morals and belief in God, but only as an intermediary stage followed by the imposition of another more draconian order which it established for the benefit not of priests but of scientists and their wealthy backers in industry and the regime.

"Bernays's fundamental faith," according to Marvin Olasky who interviewed him extensively, "has been his lack of belief in God." Bernays was acutely aware that "a world without God' rapidly descended into social chaos. Therefore, he contended that social manipulation by public relations counselors was justified by the end of creating man-made gods who could assert subtle social control and prevent disaster. . . . Pulling strings behind the scenes was necessary not only for personal advantage but for social salvation."[6]

Liberalism, by the inner dynamic of its logic, was forced to become an instrument of social control in order to avoid the chaos which it created by its own erosion of tradition and morals. Democratic man could not be left to his own devices; chaos would result. The logic was clear. If there is no God, there can be no religion; if there is no religion, there can be no morals; if there are no morals, there can be no self-control; if there is no self-control, there can be no social order; if there is no social order, there can be nothing but the chaos of competing desire. But we cannot have chaos, so therefore we must institute behavioral control in place of the traditional structures of the past – tradition, religion, etc. Abolishing tradition, religion and morals and establishing "scientific" social control are one and the same project. As soon as the liberal cabal abolished morals, religion, tradition, etc., they needed something to control the passions of the masses they had just "liberated." As

Bernays said in *Propaganda*, "Intelligent men must realize that propaganda is the modern instrument by which they can fight for productive ends and help to bring order out of chaos."[7]

Once it became obvious that liberalism led to, in fact, required the imposition of social control, all that remained was finding the most effective instrument of control. This meant finding something compatible with the American temperament. This meant focusing more on the carrot than the stick, in contradistinction to places like the Soviet Union. Fresh from his work at the CPI, Harold Lasswell in collaboration with Walter Lippmann came up with the idea of communication as domination, an idea he considered more humane than conventional tactics. "Propaganda," he argued, was superior to brute force because it was "cheaper than violence, bribery, and other possible control techniques."[8] The war gave people like Creel, Lippmann, Lasswell, and Bernays the opportunity to experiment on the manipulation of public opinion; the peace gave them opportunity to experiment further on the American public for the benefit of industry. Wilfred Trotter, in his book *The Instincts of the Herd in Peace and War*, claimed that Bernays "saw the crowd as governed by the same Freudian instincts that drove individuals, and the way to rein it in, he said, was to master and manipulate those instincts. That, Trotter believed, could best be done not by the press, as Tarde proposed, but by an elite group of intellectuals able to exploit the same sorts of psychological symbols Freud was using with his patients."[9]

Bernays was obviously influenced by his famous uncle but to say that that was the only influence in his life ignores Bernays's genius in picking up new trends which might be serviceable in helping the "invisible governors" restrain the passionate masses in their headlong plunge toward social chaos. "The basic elements of human nature," Bernays wrote after the war which found him on the opposing side of the conflict from his famous uncle, who never really liked Americans, "are fixed as to desires and instincts and innate tendencies. The directions, however, in which these basic elements may be turned by skillful handling are infinite. Human nature is readily subject to modification."[10]

The talk about the "infinite" possibility subjecting human nature to "modification" is not the sort of talk one would get from an old man living in the truncated remnant of a defeated empire. Eddie's belief in conditioning is typically American and typically pragmatic, and it did not come from his famous uncle. Eddie is not borrowing from Freud here; he is talking about John B. Watson.

Part II, Chapter 11

Baltimore, 1919

Major Watson was demobbed in 1918. By 1919 he was back at work in his laboratory at Johns Hopkins, this time with an attractive nineteen-year-old graduate student by the name of Rosalie Rayner. The experiments this time involved human beings, specifically an infant who would go down in the history of psychology known as "Little Albert." Watson would expose little Albert to animals like rats or to fire and observe his reaction, which was no reaction at all. Then Watson would expose Little Albert to the same stimuli and simultaneously bang a metal bar behind the infant's head. Little Albert would immediately react to the noise and burst into tears. What is more, the memory of the noise would return whenever Little Albert was shown the previous visual stimuli, causing now the same fearful, tearful response which the metal bar had created, but now without the noise being made. Watson got the idea from Pavlov, but he claimed it as his own, saying that he had now discovered the psychological equivalent of the atom, the basic building block – stimulus/response – out of which the human personality was made. It was the discovery of the conditioned reflex which now allowed Watson to move behaviorism from a psychology of prediction to a psychology of control.

Beyond that, Watson would claim that the Little Albert experiments proved that human nature was completely malleable. There was no such thing – be it a snake or a rat – which elicited fear in the infant. All emotional reaction was extrinsic and purely the result of association with stimuli which inspired fear, love or rage, the three basic emotions out of which the human personality was constructed. So the child would love not his mother in particular, but rather anyone who stimulated his erogenous zones. Similarly, he would fear anything that was associated with loud noises, and he would become enraged at anything he associated with constriction of his movements. Man was what his environment made him, and now Watson, the behaviorist psychologist, had isolated the method whereby man was conditioned by his environment. The Little Albert experiments proved that – or so Watson thought. All of the problems in the world, therefore, are attributable to faulty conditioning, and that conditioning was faulty because it was conducted by non-professionals with no training in behaviorist psychology, i.e., mothers. "Parenthood," Watson would write after he had become famous as an expert on raising children, "instead of being an instinctive art, is a science, the details of which must be worked out by patient laboratory methods."[1]

If there was a sense of urgency behind the experiments, it was because the social order seemed to be on the verge of collapse as a result of the dislocations caused by the war. The Little Albert experiments corresponded chronologically with the Red Scare of 1919–1920 and the Palmer Raids, which were in turn based on the fear that the Bolshevik revolution was spreading throughout Europe and heading toward the United States. The Little Albert experiments corresponded as well to an unprecedented wave of labor unrest. In the conditioned reflex, Watson now had a scientific solution to all of those social problems, one which eliminated the messy give-and-take of the political process, the legal system, and collective bargaining. The unrest which the Wilson administration had created by abrogating the democratic process during the war could now be solved scientifically by conditioning the workers. The war had already established the precedent for social engineering. All that remained was to continue the experiment under different auspices.

Watson was never really able to implement behaviorism as a way of solving the social unrest plaguing the country at the time because another kind of unrest entered into his experiments. He became sexually involved with his assistant. "I get rather disgusted sometimes," he wrote to his friend and colleague Robert Yerkes, "with trying to make the human character amenable to law."[2] The Little Albert experiments were in many ways the culmination of Watson's disgust at "trying to make the human character amenable to law." At the very moment when he felt he had succeeded in making the human character amenable to law by discovering the conditioned reflex as the basic building block of the personality and the key to behavioral control, his own behavior spiraled out of control, as he lost whatever tenuous grasp he had maintained till that time on his sexual impulses.

Rosalie Rayner was the daughter of one of Maryland's most influential families, a family with a fortune in railroads, mining and shipbuilding, and at least some of that fortune went to Johns Hopkins University. Rayner had graduated from Vassar in the spring of 1919. By the Spring of 1920, Watson was writing her notes in which he declared that "every cell I have is yours," the highest compliment a psychologist who didn't believe in the existence of the soul could pay someone.[3]

Mary Watson at first thought that this infatuation would pass as Watson's other affairs had done. When it didn't she decided to take action. Since the Watsons were on social terms with the Rayner family, Mary arranged a dinner date. Then excusing herself by saying that she had a headache and that she was sure that her husband and Rosalie would like to discuss their work together, Mary Watson adjourned to Rosalie's bedroom, where after a perfunctory search, she found her husband's love letters. Armed with the letters, she confronted Rosalie's parents and suggested that they send their daughter away to Europe. When Rosalie refused to cooperate, Mary turned to her brother John Ickes, who attempted to use the letters to blackmail the Rayner family. When that failed and it became clear that John was not going to stop seeing Rosalie, Mary filed for divorce. The potential for scandal was quite significant then; professors, after all, can still get in trouble for sleeping with their interns, but Watson seems to have felt that his reputation in the psychological profession was so great that Johns Hopkins's President Goodnow couldn't afford to fire him. That belief came to an abrupt end in October of 1920 when Goodnow called Watson into his office and demanded his resignation. If Watson had hoped to get a job at another university, those hopes were dashed when the press got wind of the divorce proceedings, including the love letters, in November of 1920. Just when he thought he had discovered the psychological equivalent of the atom, Watson's academic career crashed and burned around him as a result of his uncontrollable sexual impulses. It is no wonder then that he said he became a believer in Freud at around the same time.

Just as his experiences terrorizing infants had rendered Watson an expert in childrearing, so his adultery rendered Watson an expert on sex and marriage. Sex was certainly on his mind. He talked about it at home a great deal, and he wrote about it in the popular press. In 1928 he announced on the pages of *Cosmopolitan* that by 1978 men would no longer marry. This would mean the end of matrimony, but that, of course, would signal the advent of real sexual freedom. In 1920, at the height of his affair with Rosalie Rayner, Watson told a New York newspaper that the young people of 1920 were "too alert and too wise to follow the dictates of their parents in sexual matters."[4] Watson favored contraception and suggested strongly that men in their prime should marry women in theirs. This meant that men in their forties should marry women in their late teens, which just happened to be the case of John Watson and Rosalie Rayner. As with most experts in sexuality in the twentieth century, Watson was simply proposing his own morally aberrant behavior as a norm for mankind. Watson was convinced that the home, the family, and traditional sexual morality were going to wither away, as they had in his own life, under the white heat of scientific truth. Watson, according to Cohen, wanted to bring into being "a new individual who needed no country, no party, no God, no law, and could still be happy, – a free individual. The American child was unlikely to be elevated into this emancipated creature for that infant was nothing but 'layers of obsolete religious and political bandages wrapped round the semblance of life.'"[5] By May 1930 Watson was giving talks entitled "After the Family – What?" as a way of hastening the coming of that day. Scientific sex education like scientific child rearing became a way of taking authority away from parents and handing it over to psycho-technicians, "experts," who provide "services formerly provided by families themselves" often times in the schools.[6] As Simpson perceptively notes, this undermining of the family, in reality, "only broadened the *application* of psychological techniques as instruments of control. Actual control passed into the hands of the new psychological technicians."[7]

In 1926 Watson wrote an introduction to a book called *What Is Wrong with Modern Marriage?* in which he claimed that "sex is admitted to be the most important subject in life."[8] Unfortunately, no one had undertaken a scientific study of sex. Watson then revealed that he had been recently invited to work on a committee on sexual research.

Shortly after World War I, Robert Yerkes in his capacity as the director of the NRC's Research Information Service, received a query from the American Social Hygiene Association wondering if the NRC might be interested in getting its scientists involved in doing sex research if the Bureau of Social Hygiene, under the auspices of the Rockefeller Foundation, would pay for the research. In 1921, while he was still with the NRC in Washington, Yerkes's life fused irrevocably with that of the Rockefeller family and their interests when he decided, after consulting with colleagues in and out of the NRC, to become head of the Committee for Research on the Problems of Sex.

Had Watson remained at Johns Hopkins after his friend Robert Yerkes became head of the CRPS, it is almost certain that Watson would have got involved in sex research, given his personal predilections and the interests of the Rockefeller Foundation. The only thing that prevented this from happening was the moral indignation of the American public when Watson got fired from Johns Hopkins. Because of that, Robert Yerkes would have to wait another twenty years before he got involved in sex research, but when he did it was still in the context of the behaviorist project of controlling behavior – not in the interest of the moral order, an order which the behaviorists thought outmoded anyway, but in the interest of winning yet another war.

As it was, Watson was a victim of his own ideology. He fostered the erosion of morals; he urged people to people throw off restraint; he was ready to apply the social control of behaviorism if their passions got out of control, but he couldn't apply that medicine to his own life because in the psychological lexicon of behaviorism there is no word for self-control. Man is always controlled from without. Watson couldn't apply the lessons of behaviorism to his own life because a man can't be at the same time controller and controlled. Watson couldn't control his responses to sexual stimuli. As a result he lost his job. When his divorce hit the papers in November 1920, he became all but unemployable in academe.

Part II, Chapter 12

Berlin, 1919

In 1919, right around the time John B. Watson returned to Johns Hopkins to work on what would come to be known as the Little Albert Experiments, a medical doctor by the name of Magnus Hirschfeld founded the *Institut für Sexualwissenschaft* in Berlin. Born before there was a Germany, in 1869, Magnus Hirschfeld followed in his father's footsteps and was a physician himself when he first met with the publisher Max Spohr in August of 1896 and brought out his book *Sappho und Sokrates oder Wie erklärt sich die Lieber der Männer und Fraue zu Personen des eigenen Geschlechts?* the first of a series of pro-homosexual, quasi-scientific tracts that would establish him in the public mind, even more so than Sigmund Freud, as the Weimar Republic's premier example of moral decadence and *Kulturbolschewismus*.

Less than a year later, on May 15, 1897, Hirschfeld met with Spohr, the lawyer Eduard Oberg, and the writer Franz Josef von Bülow to found the world's first homosexual-rights organization, the *Wissenschaftlich-humani-täres Kommittee*. It was as head of this committee that Hirschfeld, who was homosexual himself, known in the gay milieu of Berlin as "Tante Magnesia," would work for the next thirty-three years for the overturn of Paragraph 175, the law criminalizing sodomy, until 1930 when he went on a world tour, or less euphemistically, exile in anticipation of the Nazis' rise to power. (Ironically, for all its reputation for decadence, the Weimar Republic never decriminalized sodomy.)

Hirschfeld's magazine for sexual research was titled *Die Aufklärung* or, in English, *The Enlightenment*, giving some indication of its intellectual orientation and, beyond that, the Enlightenment's hidden sexual agenda as well, an agenda that now espoused homosexuality as its *cause célèbre*. When Hirschfeld addressed the First International Conference for Sexual Reform Based on Sexual Science, held in Berlin in 1921, he reminded his audience that the term "sexual science" derived from Charles Darwin's *The Descent of Man* and Ernst Haeckel's *Natürliche Schöpfungsgeschichte*. "Nothing which is natural," he told his audience "can escape the laws of nature." The statement situated Hirschfeld as the link which connected the Marquis de Sade to Alfred Kinsey, in the Enlightenment's continuing attempt to destabilize morals and replace them with biology and hygienic technology. During the Weimar years, Hirschfeld's name was synonymous in the popular mind with the moral decline of Germany, often because of the fact that he testified as an expert at high-profile sodomy trials, like the Eulenberg affair, but in no small measure because the Institute for Sex Science in Berlin had become a Mecca for anyone of homosexual persuasion throughout Europe and North America.

One of the young people who made the trip to Berlin as a sexual pilgrim was a young Englishman by the name of Christopher Isherwood, who traveled there because his friend and former classmate, Wystan Hugh Auden, had recommended the gay bars from his personal experience. After founding the *Institut für Sexualwissenschaft* in 1919, Hirschfeld would periodically hold international congresses for sexual reform. Because he lived in Berlin, which was the capital of the movie industry at that time, and because he was interested in sex, Hirschfeld became acquainted with the German film director G. W. Pabst, and together they frequented the gay bars of Berlin, a collaboration which eventually resulted in the Pabst film *Geheimnisse einer Seele*, inspired by their visits to the Eldorado, a transvestite bar.

In January 1921, Hirschfeld was made an honorary Member of the British Society for Sexual Psychology, with corresponding publicity, but "the greatest event of the year," according to his biographer, was the First International Conference for Sexual Reform based on Sexual Science, which took place from September 15 to September 20 in Berlin while Carl Theodore Dreyer, the Danish director who would portray Hirschfeld as a vampire, was working on *Love One Another*, a film set in the newly-formed Jewish quarter in North Berlin where the newly arrived Jewish emigrants from Poland and Galicia were trying to cope with the rising anti-Semitism created by Hirschfeld's sex congresses and testimony at sodomy trials. While in Paris in the fall of 1921, Dreyer and Christen Jul composed a vampire script after seeing Tod Browning's *Dracula*. "I could damn well make one of those too,"[1] Dreyer reportedly said, and sent his assistant Ralph Holm to recruit a cast. After looking under Seine bridges and at the Salvation Army, Holm returned with a Polish journalist by the name of Jan Hieronimko, who then got remade in the image of Magnus Hirschfeld.

But more than Hirschfeld's tireless advocacy for the overturn of sodomy laws drew Dreyer's attention to Hirschfeld. On May 24, 1919, Hirschfeld became a movie star himself, in fact playing himself as the sympathetic, enlightened, sexually condoning doctor in Richard Oswald's pro-homosexual film *Anders als die Andern*. Based on the life of the violinist Paul Koerner (played by Conrad Veidt, who would pay for his role by his forced emigration to Hollywood and gain his revenge by playing the malignant Nazi officer in *Casablanca*), Veidt is courted by two women but is really in love with one of the women's brothers who is threatened with blackmail and about to commit suicide, when Magnus Hirschfeld appears on screen, *in persona propria*, and not only dissuades the young man from following in the Veidt character's footsteps by killing himself, but, playing "the great doctor he was," as his adulatory biographer put it, saved "the youth's life through his empathy with his predicament" and persuaded him to join in the crusade to overturn "the nefarious Paragraph 175" as well.[2]

Christopher Isherwood remembered seeing the film at the Institute or at least some of it:

> Three scenes remain in my memory. One is a ball at which the dancers, all male, are standing fully clothed in what seems about to become a daisy chain. It is here that the character played by Veidt meets the blackmailer who seduces and then ruins him. The next scene is a vision which Veidt has (while in prison?) of a long preocession of kings, poets, scientists, philosophers, and other famous victims of homophobia, moving slowly and sadly with heads bowed. Each of them cringes, in turn, as he passes beneath a banner on which "Paragraph 175" is inscribed. In the final scene, Dr. Hirschfeld himself appears. I think the corpse of Veidt, who has committed suicide, is lying in the background. Hirschfeld delivers a speech – that is to say, a series of subtitles – appealing for justice for the Third Sex.[3]

As films went it was an outrageous example of homosexual agit-prop, and Wolff, in spite of her sympathetic identification with Hirschfeld's goals and claims that the film was part of the flowering of art and culture during Weimar, can't help but notice that the film evoked a powerful reaction as well.

On August 18, 1920, after making cinematic history in Germany, the film was banned by government censors who saw it as a romantic exercise in homosexual propaganda whose purpose was to undermine public morals. In addition to bringing the topic of homosexuality to the public, *Anders als die Andern* had as its other main effect an increase in anti-Semitic attacks against Hirschfeld in particular and Jews as decadent purveyors of *Kulturbolschewismus* in general. "The Weimar Republic," even Hirschfeld's unfailingly sympathetic biographer must concede,

> which had promised a new freedom to the German people, had its roots in the air. The mass of the population, particularly the middle classes and the monarchists, resented the revolution. Anti-Semitism became more rampant than ever, as Jews were, as usual, made the scapegoats for discontent.[4]

Wolff's reading of the times overlooks the fact that anti-Semitism was not historically a characteristically German phenomenon, but was, in fact, fanned into a white heat by the perception that Jews were in the forefront of corrupting German morals through *Kulturbolschewismus* and the stranglehold they had on the instruments of culture. No one was more responsible for giving this impression than Magnus Hirschfeld, who seemed to embody everything wrong with the Weimar Republic in the eyes of the average German. If Hirschfeld hadn't existed, Hitler would have had to invent him as a way of coming to power.

Less than a month after *Anders als die Andern* had been banned, *Das Hamburger Echo* called for a disruption of a lecture Hirschfeld was to give on September 16 in Hamburg. Hirschfeld gave his lecture in spite of the threat and escaped unharmed. He was not so lucky when he tried to do the same thing in Munich, by then a Nazi stronghold. Hirschfeld had become a lightning rod for Nazi agitation and, in 1920, was attacked and brutally beaten by a group of Nazi students, prompting the publisher of his autobiography to remark that

> The Nazis had chosen him from the very beginning as a symbol of everything they hated, and it was Hitler himself, who, after the fascist students attacked Hirschfeld in Munich in 1920 and left him badly injured, declared him in many public speeches as the very epitome of the repulsive Jew and enemy of the German people.[5]

Hirschfeld's vampiric nature was fairly apparent not only to Carl Dreyer but to most of those who knew him intimately. Actually, in *Vampyr*, Hirschfeld is portrayed not as a vampire but as the medical doctor who functions as the vampire's assistant, in other words, a doctor who uses his office as a way of serving the vampire, a fairly accurate summary of Hirschfeld as scientist, the man who placed science at the service of desire. Hirschfeld's appetites were insatiable, and everything he did was a way of justifying them both to himself and to the world at large. Guenter Maeder told Charlotte Wolff that Hirschfeld's "sensuality was such that he could not keep his hands off attractive youths."[6] Hirschfeld had two sexual relationships of long standing in addition to the numerous anonymous encounters typical of the homosexual lifestyle. One was a boy he picked up in China, the other a German youth by the name of Karl Giese, who became his assistant at the *Institut für Sexual Wissenschaft*. Isherwood recounts meeting Giese in his memoir, remembering him as having a "long handsome face" that was melancholy in repose.

> But soon he would be giggling and rolling his eyes. Touching the back of his head with his fingertips, as if patting bobbed curls, he would strike an It-girl pose. This dedicated, earnest, intelligent campaigner for sexual freedom had an extraordinary innocence at such moments. Christopher saw in him the sturdy peasant youth with a girl's heart who, long ago, had fallen in love with Hirschfeld, his father image. Karl still referred to Hirschfeld as "Papa."[7]

Hirschfeld liked to be called Papa by his homosexual friends, rather than Tante Magnesia, because, in some intuitive way, he understood that he could expand his sexual gratification by appealing to the qualities these young men sought in their own fathers but could not find. "As a consequence of his early sense of rejection by father and resulting defensive detachment from masculinity," Nicolosi writes,

> the homosexual carries a sense of weakness and incompetence with regard to those attributes associated with masculinity, that is, power, assertion, and strength. He is attracted to masculine strength out of an unconscious striving toward his own masculinity. At the same time, because of his hurtful experience with father, he is suspicious of men in power. Homosexual contact is used as an erotic bridge to gain entry into a special male world.[8]

Giese, of course, could no more "draw off" the masculinity he craved from Hirschfeld than Hirschfeld could siphon it off from him, and so, like most homosexuals, he attempted to derive from quantity what he failed to derive from quality.. He also found himself drawn into other forms of perversion. Wolff writes in her typically empty-headed way that

> Karl Giese . . . loved Hirschfeld, but needed masochistic satisfaction in the form of flagellation which he could not get from him. Hirschfeld apparently did not mind. Erwin Hansen, a sturdy communist, supplied the need by beating him.[9]

Things did not turn out well for Giese. The man he called Papa turned out to be a vampire, and turned him into one as well. Giese always wanted to go to medical school, but a boisterous course of events intervened. As Isherwood said, "There was terror in the Berlin air – the terror felt by many people with good reason – and Christopher found himself affected by it." Isherwood felt that he may "have been affected by his own fantasies" or, perhaps, stated with more psychological coherence, his fantasies brought on the terror. He started hearing heavy wagons drawing up to the house late at night and started seeing swastika patterns in the wallpaper. Everything was beginning to look brown, Nazi brown. Once again, Nemesis seemed just over the horizon, and this time his name was not Robespierre but Adolf Hitler.

In thinking back on his days at the Institute, while in exile in France, Hirschfeld remembered a day, three years before the Nazis came to power, when the institute treated a patient who had had a sexual encounter with SA chief and NSDAP founder, Ernst Roehm. "We were on good terms with him," Hirschfeld wrote of this patient,

> and he told us quite a bit of what happened in his circle. But at that time we hardly took notice of his accounts. He also referred to Adolf Hitler in the oddest possible manner. "Afi is the most perverted of all of us. He is like a very soft woman, but now he makes great propaganda in heroic morale."[10]

Guenter Maeder described the conversation as "Tuntengeschwaetz," or queer gossip, but Hirschfeld was obviously having second thoughts as did

Maeder, who wrote that, "after careful reflection about the matter, and in the view of prominent psychologists, Hitler had something feminine about him. He was perhaps sadomasochistic, with some homosexual inclinations. These instincts did not seem strong enough to resist repression and sublimation through an iron will."

Far from persecuting homosexuals, the Nazi leadership was almost exclusively homosexual, and struggles in the Weimar Republic during the '20s amounted, according to Abrams and Lively's reading, to a battle between two groups of homosexuals: the "butch" faction under SA leader Ernst Roehm, and the "femmes" under Magnus Hirschfeld. Because the courts referred violators of Paragraph 175 to him for treatment, Hirschfeld came into possession of large amounts of incriminating evidence concerning the sex lives and homosexual proclivities of prominent Nazis. Hirschfeld, apparently no respecter of professional confidentiality, worked hand-in-glove with the SPD, the Social Democrat Party in Germany, during the Weimar Republic, releasing to their newspapers selected details about the perverted sex lives of Nazi luminaries. Ernst Roehm had to make an impromptu trip to Bolivia as the result of Hirschfeld's sexual-science archives making their way into SPD newspapers. The Nazis bombed in the next elections, as a result, and Hitler was furious. Hirschfeld, as a result, became not only the essence of everything Hitler hated – the Jew, the phony scientist, the queer, the *Kulturbolschewist*, and social engineer – he became a potent political enemy as well, and denunciations of Hirschfeld, as the typical Jew, began to figure prominently in Hitler's speeches from then on.

Hitler, according to Igra, was a homosexual prostitute in Vienna. The Nazis were also notoriously homosexual, so much so that Mussolini was scandalized by their behavior. As a result the homosexual issue was something that Hitler would have to use against his opponents lest his opponents used the issue against him. Politically, however, the situation was unambiguous. The major parties of the Left, the SPD and the Communists, both espoused gay rights and came close to fulfilling Hirschfeld's dream in the late '20s of abolishing Paragraph 175. This left Hitler only one option in exploiting the average German's revulsion at the Weimar Republic's version of gay liberation. In addition to that, Hitler, largely as the result of his stay in prison following the abortive Munich Beer Hall putsch, had decided that he needed to come to power in Germany by democratic means, not by military force. That meant taking into account public opinion and manipulating it to his advantage. That meant tapping the huge amount of resentment against the punitive Versailles Treaty, the threat of Communist revolution, and *Kulturbolsche- wismus* or modernity of the sort practiced by Schoenberg in music, Gropius in architecture, and, most of all, Hirschfeld in sexology.

As a result of these exigencies, Hitler embarked on an anti-gay rights campaign that focused obsessively on Hirschfeld and quickly shaded over into smearing all things modern as Jewish, foreign, internationalist, and racially degenerate. The fact that Berlin had become a magnet for homosexuals lent force to Hitler's claim that modernity and degeneracy were synonymous. If anyone doubted Hitler's charges, there was always the high-profile example of Magnus Hirschfeld testifying at another sodomy trial or organizing one of the international congresses for sexual reform to prove him right. In this respect, Hitler used Hirschfeld as a way of solidifying his support among the middle-class Germans scandalized by the sexual excesses of Weimar and their effect on a nation already weakened by revolutionary threats from the East and the onerous financial burdens exacted by the West through the ruinous Versailles Treaty.

Even Max Hodann, who was sympathetic to the cause of "sexual reform," saw Hirschfeld as a catalyst for reaction. Hirschfeld, in this regard, was even more notorious than Sigmund Freud as a sign of decadence. Erwin Haeberle, another avowed proponent of homosexual rights, claims that "according to Hodann, Hirschfeld provoked the reactionary opposition by being a Jew, a leftist, and an advocate of homosexual rights."[11] The Nazis persecuted Hirschfeld, not only on account of his "non-Aryan" extraction but also "because of his open acknowledgment of pacifistic and socialistic tendencies and his work in sexual science."[12]

Homosexual rights, as practiced by Jewish homosexual advocates like Magnus Hirschfeld, was made to order for Hitler's rise to power, a rise to power that was based, at least until 1933, to a large extent on the revulsion the German population at large felt at the sexual excesses of the Weimar Republic. German Jews had homosexual activists like Hirschfeld to thank for the rise of Hitler. Haeberle claims that, "indeed, the very concept of sexology, was the work of German Jews"[13] without understanding or being willing to admit the role that homosexual decadence would play in creating and fostering anti-Semitism in the Weimar Republic and, in effect, in bringing Hitler to power. In the hands of an unscrupulous political manipulator like Hitler, *Kulturbolschewismus,* as epitomized by someone like Hirschfeld, became synonymous with Jewish influence, which, in turn, became an excuse for anti-Semitism, an all-embracing explanation of why things were not right in Germany and how they could be put right once Hitler had been granted enough power by the German people to expunge Jewish influence.

On May 14, 1928, in response to a request for a formal statement from a German homosexual rights organization, the Nazi Party issued a statement in which, among other things, they averred that:

> Might makes right. And the stronger will always prevail against the weaker. Today we are the weaker. Let us make sure that we will become the stronger again! This we can do only if we exercise moral restraint.

> Therefore we reject all immorality, especially love between men, because
> it deprives us of our last chance to free our people from the chains of slav-
> ery which are keeping it fettered today.[14]

Everything needed a Darwinian justification in the Weimar Republic,
and this meant both homosexuality, as justified by Hirschfeld's appeal to
Darwin at the first Congress for Sexual Reform in 1921, and the attack on homosexuality which Hitler promoted. The fact that Hitler called Roehm back
to Germany one year later to suppress a rebellion in the SA ranks gives some
indication that the rejection of homosexuality was nothing more than a cynical public-relations ploy. Lively and Abrams make it clear that the Nazi party
leadership was more than a little like Queer Nation when it came to both sexual orientation and political tactics. But the resentment among the population
at large, which the Nazis exploited so effectively, was just as real too, and, as
a result, the irony of the pink triangle room in the Holocaust Museum becomes too large to ignore. Historically, Germany was not known as an
anti-Semitic country. Proof of this is the fact that so many Jews lived in Germany at that time. Germany was enlightened, cultured, and, therefore, to
Jews who bought into the Enlightenment, a bulwark against prejudice. The
decadence of the Weimar Republic changed all that, primarily because of its
own excesses. As with their manipulation of the revulsion at homosexuality
among the population at large, so also the prosecution of homosexuals became, under the Nazis, a matter of political expedience. To begin with,
prominent homosexuals who were helpful to the Nazis were left unmolested.
Conversely, homosexuality became a convenient way of getting rid of incon-
venient members of the opposition, oftentimes Catholic priests.

In 1935 the Nazis amended Paragraph 175 by including a provision
which criminalized any type of behavior that could be construed as indicating homosexual inclination or desire. The results of, as well as the intention
behind, this change in the law, which, not coincidentally, dropped reference
to homosexuality as unnatural, are easy enough to see. The Nazis, in the
name of upholding sexual morality, could now eliminate, without judicial restraint, anyone who disagreed with them. This new law provided the Nazis
with an especially potent legal weapon against their enemies. It will never be
known how many non-homosexuals were charged under this law, but it is in-
disputable that the Nazis used false accusations of homosexuality to justify
the detainment and imprisonment of many of their opponents. "The law was
so loosely formulated," writes Steakley, "that it could be, and was, applied
against heterosexuals who the Nazis wanted to eliminate. . . . the law was
also used repeatedly against Catholic clergymen."[15] Kogon writes that "The
Gestapo readily had recourse to the charge of homosexuality if it was unable
to find any pretext for proceeding against Catholic priests or irksome critics."[16]

So the largely homosexual Nazi leadership now could eliminate its opponents by charging them with the crime of homosexuality, which also served as a way of defaming their character. If any actual homosexuals ended up in concentration camps, it was simply because they happened to be at the wrong end of the political equation, and not because of their homosexuality, a tactic which the contemporary homosexual movement evidently learned as well, recently "outing" a congressman who voted against recognizing homosexual marriages.

Part II, Chapter 13

New York, 1921

In October 1920, after submitting his resignation to President Goodnow, John B. Watson went home, packed his bags, and took a train to New York City, where he moved in with sociologist William Thomas, who had just been dismissed from the University of Chicago for transporting a woman across state lines for immoral purposes. They say that misery loves company. If so, there was lots of company in the nascent profession of behaviorist psychology caused by the reckless sexual adventurism of its major proponents. Thomas and Watson had followed Mark Baldwin to a position of prominence followed by a hasty exit from a profession which specialized in social control but whose leaders had little in the way of self-control in matters sexual. On the last day of 1920 Watson married Rosalie Rayner, and in the first month of 1921 he began a new career as an advertising executive with the J. Walter Thompson company.

Watson's arrival at J. Walter Thompson was fortuitous in many ways. The war was over; business had been impressed by the role psychology had played in the armed forces, no matter how peripheral that role was to winning the war, and now they wanted to implement the civilian version of the same lessons in measurement, prediction, and control – both on employees, who had grown restive at wages frozen by war-time controls, and on consumers, who could now be organized into national markets organized around the promotion of brand names. The same forces which had promoted the Melting Pot Pageant at the behest of the CPI under George Creel as a way of winning the war now focused their attention on further crippling the same ethnic communities by discrediting their traditions, morals, and religion as unscientific and old-fashioned. The industry could hardly admit that the citizens of the United States were being subjected to an extension of the psychological warfare that had been applied during the war, but there was some sense that an attempt to homogenize the American population in the interest of marketing certain products was afoot. In 1920, a headline in *Printer's Ink*, the trade sheet of the publishing industry, announced that "People Have Become 'Standardized' by Advertising."[1]

"Skillful advertising," according to Pope,

> was to teach workers how to consume effectively. At the same time, advertising could be employed directly for ethnic acculturation and "Americanization" of immigrants. Even Albert Lasker, president of Lord &

Thomas and one of the few Jews to reach the top in the advertising business, told his staff in the 1920s, that "we are making a homogeneous" people out of a nation of immigrants. Meanwhile, national media carrying ads for nationally-distributed brands were said to weaken regional distinctions and peculiarities. These themes were expounded with varying intensity. During World War I, for example, "Americanization" through advertising was a favorite topic of advertising writers. During the Red Scare of 1919–20, advertising as a means of soothing worker discontent and breeding consumer consciousness was stressed. Throughout, the hope was for unity and for mass consumption of advertised, branded merchandise.[2]

The J. Walter Thompson agency got its start in the late nineteenth century as a broker for space in Methodist magazines when the product advertising promoted most was nostrums or medicines which promised to cure just about anything from cancer to backache. These patent medicines may not have cured any of the customer's ailments, but they often made people feel better almost immediately, since many of them contained as their main active ingredient opium, cocaine, or a high-proof alcohol. Coca Cola began its life as a tonic whose kick came from cocaine. When John B. Watson needed to cram for finals at the University of Chicago, he would fortify himself for his all-nighters by taking a bottle of cocaine-based Coke syrup with him to his room to study.

The rise of advertising not only reflected the change from America as a nation of rural island communities into a nation of nationally organized consumers, it brought about that change. In 1850 only 10 percent of the bread consumed by the nation was baked in bakeries, and the overwhelming majority of that bread was specialty items which were not considered the staff of life. By 1930 that percentage had risen to just about 60 percent, a remarkable change but still modest by comparison to a nation which would soon get a large amount of its sustenance from fast food restaurants. America's "consumers" during the nineteenth century largely bought raw materials like flour and did their own manufacturing in the home. Given a nation which consumed raw materials locally produced, the generic took precedence over the particular in terms of products people bought, and the merchandiser held the upper hand in the distribution system. When Abraham Lincoln worked as a clerk in a store in Illinois he stocked one brand name on his shelves, namely, Baker's chocolate. Everything else was the raw materials out of which housewives and husbands fashioned the infrastructure of their daily lives. Living in a world in which even bananas have brand names and their skin is looked upon as packaging, it's difficult to imagine stores in which just about everything, including crackers, came in barrels or sacks.

By the end of the nineteenth century, however, with the completion of a railroad grid connecting the island communities, it became feasible to think of national markets for finished products. The National Biscuit Company –

even the name is significant – was one of the first companies to capitalize on the national market by coming up with a cracker in distinctive packages known as Uneeda biscuits. Uneeda was eventually so successful that the company that came to be known as Nabisco had its own fleet of trucks delivering to stores. With the rise of brand names, however, the balance of power began to shift in the retail system. With advertising now possible in mass-circulation magazines and a rail system that could distribute goods relatively quickly to major markets across the country, the manufacturer could use brand-name recognition as leverage to force grocers and other retailers to stock their products. Eventually, large national manufacturers had so much leverage they could dispense with their own system of distribution and concentrate on cranking out their products in higher and higher volume. The retailer would have to stock their products because the customer demanded it, and the customer demanded certain products because advertisers had manipulated their desires to do so. The rise of advertising was tied to the rise of national markets, and the rise of national markets fit in nicely with the desire of the Wilsonian advocates of empire, as expressed by the liberals at the *New Republic* – Dewey, Lippmann, Croly, et al. – to abandon the separation of powers and abolish the particularities of local government as envisioned by the founding fathers in favor of a strong president who could embody the General Will by manipulating the passions of the masses directly through the burgeoning mass media.

The rise of advertising and nationally recognized brand names was also tied to new technologies with large economies of scale which could produce unprecedented amounts of goods and, therefore, needed some instrument which would keep demand commensurate with supply. The tobacco industry is a good example. At around the end of the nineteenth century, tobacco was a product which was consumed by men, largely in the form of cigars, which were rolled by hand by skilled workers working with the tobacco a leaf at a time. In 1904 the value of cigar production was still thirteen times larger than cigarette production, which again was done largely by the consumer, a population which was largely made up of immigrants from Eastern Europe. In 1885 James Buchanan Duke acquired the rights to use the Bonsack cigarette-rolling machine for a royalty of $.24 per 1,000 cigarettes and The American Tobacco Company began spewing out cigarettes in quantities that necessitated a new system of marketing. The result was Lucky Strike, the brand name in a distinctive package, that could be marketed aggressively to get rid of the excess capacity created by the Bonsack rolling machine. Once the system of production became coordinated with the nascent advertising industry in a conglomerate which had sufficient financial mass, the next logical step was to engineer the consumer by psychological manipulation. In order to do this, cigarettes had to be associated with certain values which were antithetical to the values associated with cigars. The war played a role in this. Cigarettes were portable in a way that cigars were not. The exigencies of life in the field could be used to restructure soldiers' smoking habits. After the war, the consumer was persuaded that cigarettes were modern whereas cigars were not, and this attempt at consumer engineering would culminate in one of the classic public-relations campaigns of all times.

John B. Watson arrived at the J. Walter Thompson agency in January of 1921, just as advertising was emerging as the key whereby large-scale manufacturing enterprises could gain access to national markets by promoting brand-name products. Since behaviorists like Watson promised a "science" which would both predict and control behavior, he was precisely the sort of man the advertising agencies were looking for. If Watson had believed in God, he could have seen his firing from Johns Hopkins as providential because it allowed him to arrive on Madison Avenue just as advertising was poised to incorporate both behaviorism and psychological warfare into its assault on the American public.

It is not clear whether Stanley Resor believed in God, but he knew an opportunity when he saw one. Resor graduated from Yale University in 1900 after majoring in history and economics. After reading the historian Thomas Buckle, Resor became convinced that human behavior in the aggregate could be described and predicted according to observable statistical laws, and, under Resor's guidance, after he acquired a controlling interest in the company, J. Walter Thompson became a leader in compiling demographic data from census reports. Since Watson had been peddling his theories to big business since 1916, Resor saw an opportunity to integrate behaviorism and advertising as a way of controlling and homogenizing an increasingly unruly population in the interests of the business community. Liberalism had to come up with a solution to the social chaos its policies created, and Watson's behaviorism combined with the propaganda techniques evolved during the War seemed like the answer.

But there was another reason Resor found the prospect of hiring Watson appealing. The industry had its own ethos, which was overwhelmingly liberal. Advertising executives were a remarkably homogeneous lot, oftentimes the sons of Protestant ministers, who had the fervor of their fathers without their faith. These were men who believed that science was a better guide in life than morals, and they were enamored of the possibilities it offered for creating a brave new world in the image of their passions. Man was what the conditioners made him. There was no soul, no essence, no human nature. Man was nothing but responses to stimuli, which were increasingly under the scientist's control, first of all because Watson had discovered the conditioned reflex as the "building block" of personality, but secondly because powerful new instruments for manipulation, like the cinema, were now waiting to be used to their full potential. The rise of advertising was more than just the exploitation of a new psychological technique. That technique was predicated on a world-view which most advertisers shared, and the rise of advertising corresponded to the rise of that view of the world as ultimately normative. In many ways the connection was causal because the rise of advertising meant above all else supplanting traditional authority. The traditional criteria according to which one made choices – parents, ethnicity, tradition, religion – had to be supplanted on a massive, pan-cultural scale before mass advertising would work. Advertising was a form of social engineering which required the creation of a new man if it were to be successful. Unlike nineteenth century man, who was frugal, bound by the traditional constraints of the local community and willing to deny himself certain things in the interest of a greater good, the new man envisioned by advertising was to be, in Pope's words, "reactive, suggestible, and impulsive."[3]

By about 1920, the institutional arrangements that still characterize American advertising were already set in place. By then, too, an ideology of advertising had appeared. Its exponents portrayed advertising as a force that would reconcile social harmony with personal freedom of choice. Persuasion would replace coercion. The ideals of liberal individualism could be realized in a society dominated by large-scale enterprises. "Reputation monopolies," otherwise known as brand names, would bring about the abeyance of social tension in a way that was both painless to the consumer and profitable to the controller. The new social order may not have been altruistic, but it was more humane, as Harold Lasswell had said, than assassination. In 1920 the day had arrived when "the gentleman who awoke to a Big Ben alarm clock, and shaved with a Gillette razor, washed with Ivory Soap, breakfasted on Kellogg's Corn Flakes, and continued through his daily routines depending on advertised brands" was completely within the purview of values acceptable to the new liberalism and the corporate elite.[4]

Advertising soon became a laboratory in which business tested the often-overstated claims of the behaviorists against the reality of human nature. In spite of what behaviorists like Watson said, the advertisers soon came to realize that consumers were not "infinitely malleable." Advertisers might claim that they could sell "dirty dishwater," and in some instances they might, but they could not do so over the long haul. As they became more and more convinced that the consumer was motivated by nonrational and even irrational buying appeals, they were forced to consider the nature of desire and where those desires came from. As they explored the age old distinction between want and need, which Plato had discussed in the *Republic*, they began to realize that consumption patterns varied widely from the objective circumstances dictated by a real world and were more influenced by unacknowledged desires. These desires, however, were radically limited in number and had only a tenuous connection to a product, but that connection could be strengthened by conditioning. It was at this point that the advertisers began to see sex as a marketing strategy. Man was not "infinitely malleable";

he was a rational creature with a tenuous hold on his passions, which were limited in number, sex being one of the most easily manipulated. Success in advertising meant, therefore, using the conditioned reflex to attach a particular product to the consumer's sexual passion.

By 1957, the connection between sexual passion and the products Madison Avenue wanted to sell was so well known that Vance Packard could write a best-seller *The Hidden Persuaders* based on widespread fears of loss of autonomy in the face of manipulation of desire. "The most serious offense many of the depth manipulators commit, it seems to me," Packard concluded, "is the that they try to invade the privacy of our minds."[5] Wilson Bryan Key addressed the same fears in a more specifically sexual sense in his books *Subliminal Seduction, Media Manipulation,* and *The Clam-Pate Orgy*. One needn't agree with Key's analysis of ice cubes in whiskey ads to appreciate the sense of sexual seduction that advertising was arousing in the consumer by the end of the century.

John Watson managed specific ad campaigns for J. Walter Thompson, but his main contribution to the industry during the 1920s was as a guru of scientific technique, specifically in the realm of childrearing. It was his job to function as the scientific expert who would tell the public that they had got it all wrong up till then in just about everything they had done – including, and especially, the raising of their children – and that now it was time to stop being old-fashioned and unscientific and start listening to what the experts had to say. Watson, according to Buckley, "became a popularizer of psychology as a means of self-help for those who had difficulty adapting to the new social order and an advocate of psychological engineering to an emerging class of social planners and corporate managers who sought scientific methods for social control."[6]

The ironies of the world proposed by Resor, Bernays, and Watson would become evident with hindsight. Watson's need to replace "traditional guides for human conduct" was inevitably followed by a regimen of social control. The consumer, who was seen as driven by irrational passion, most notably sex, could only be manipulated by appealing to authorities which were "scientific" as opposed to the practical reason which had been distilled by tradition, but was now portrayed as "irrational." Science was the solvent which dissolved the traditional bulwarks against the passions and allowed them to be manipulated as a form of behavioral control. The campaign would continue throughout the rest of the century in America and in pre-technological societies throughout the world. Liberalism would continue to be both arsonist and fire department, dissolving traditional cultures in the name of "science" and "liberation" and substituting in their place forms of social control based on manipulation of the passions.

Part II, Chapter 14

New York, 1922

In the Spring of 1922, Harcourt, Brace and Company brought out a small book of verse by a Jamaican writer by the name Claude McKay, called *Harlem Shadows*. McKay had already made a name for himself as the founding writer of what came to be known as the Harlem Renaissance with his novel, *Home to Harlem*. Now he was trying to expand his literary reputation by bringing out a book of verse with the help of Joel Spingarn, a Jewish patron of Negro causes. McKay characterized the book of verse as a *succès d'estime*, which meant it brought in a number of flattering reviews – enough to "make a fellow feel conceited about being a poet" – but not enough money to allow McKay to get caught up in the feeling for too long.[1] In addition to attracting the attention of a number of sympathetic reviewers, the book brought attention from unexpected quarters. Shortly after the publication of *Harlem Shadows*, when McKay was taking some time off with a group of friends, "consuming synthetic gin," his estranged wife showed up at his Fourteenth Street apartment. McKay's friends were shocked. "Why I never knew you were married," one exclaimed. McKay for his part was annoyed, not only at the intrusion of someone he felt had been safely consigned to the past but at the reaction of his friends as well. McKay responded by saying that "nobody knew" about his marriage "except the witnesses" and "that there were many more things about me that he and others didn't know."[2]

McKay, born Festus Claudius on September 15, 1890, named after the Roman governor and emperor mentioned in the Acts of the Apostles, was the youngest of eleven children born to a member of Jamaica's agricultural black middle class. McKay referred to his father as "a Presbyterian Calvinist ... a real black Scotchman," who was "strict and stern."[3] McKay clearly preferred his mother, describing her as "much more elastic and understanding."[4] McKay remembers his father as telling African tales, but opposing the African-based nature religions that were rampant in rural Jamaica at the time. McKay's memories of childhood, of course, are all filtered through the mind of the man he became. His biographer claims that "he never identified with the harsh disciplinarian and the dour Old Testament moralist who towered over his childhood."[5]

If the conflict between son and father seemed destined to explode, it was defused when young Claude was sent to live with his oldest brother U'Theo, at the age of six or seven. Claude lived with him during the next seven years and imbibed during this time U'Theo's rejection of the faith of their father. Like many of his contemporaries in the British Empire at the end of the nineteenth century, U'Theo had fallen under the influence of Darwin and considered him and his rationalist followers, people like Herbert Spencer, an antidote to the Christian faith that had become obsolete in the light of scientific discoveries. Like many of his Victorian contemporaries, U'Theo wanted to throw off the dogmas of Christianity without threatening the mores which had grown up under their influence. "An agnostic," he told his younger brother, "should so live his life that Christian people would have to respect him."[6] U'Theo wanted "to expel the preternatural elements from Christianity, to destroy its dogmatic structure, and yet to keep intact its moral and spiritual results." "Try as I may," U'Theo said at another point, "I cannot regard the teachings of priest and prophet as anything but superstition."[7]

Given his early training, it is not surprising that McKay soon began to consider himself a freethinker too. McKay's Christianity was the harsh and unbending faith of his father, subtly undercut by his equally father-like older brother, who would undermine that faith as pious superstitions. As a young Jamaican, McKay was confronted with three religious alternatives: There was the puritanical religion of the middle-class, the African-based animist religion of the field hands, and the rationalism of the professional classes and expatriates. These three alternatives were to provide McKay with his constellation of religious options until he visited Spain in the 1930s and became exposed to Catholicism. Implicit in these options is an all but insurmountable antinomy between faith and reason and nature and grace. It would come to the fore in McKay's later fiction, in which one finds characters in pairs, both of which represent McKay's inability to unify these dichotomies in one coherent human nature. McKay was both the intellectual character Ray and the sensual character Jake in his novel *Home to Harlem*. In his fiction, however, he was never able to come up with one character who possessed the qualities of both. His intellectuals were always wondering if their thinking were achieved at the expense of their vitality. His lower-class characters, on the other hand, could enjoy life, but are unable to understand it. The impasse in McKay's fiction mirrored the impasse he found in the religious options presented to him as a child.

As McKay matured, however, the religion that was suitable to his career aspirations began to seem more and more attractive. He aspired to be a poet, and the religion of the freethinkers seemed most suitable to that vocation. His choice was also influenced by the people he met. Perhaps more than most writers, McKay was a man who needed mentors. For the most part, those who fulfilled this role were older white men. When McKay was a seventeen-year-old apprentice to a Jamaican wheelwright, he met an English expatriate by the name of Walter Jekyll, the first of a number of important white mentors in his life. Jekyll had met Robert Louis Stevenson in the early 1890s.

Jekyll, like the Dr. Jekyll of Stevenson's famous story, was a rationalist with a scientific bent. Jekyll, like McKay's older brother, was a confirmed free-thinker and, according to McKay, "opened up a new world to my view . . . the different writers of the rationalist press." In addition to the works of the so-cial Darwinist Spencer, Jekyll introduced McKay to the writings of Kant, Schopenhauer, Spinoza, and Nietzsche.[8]

Unlike U'Theo, however, Jekyll was not interested in maintaining Christian morals in the light of decaying dogmas. Those who were most vo-ciferous in undermining Christian belief often had a hidden moral agenda as well. This seems to have been the case with Jekyll, who was a homosexual who seems to have provided McKay with, if not his first introduction to ho-mosexual activity, then at least with an introduction to rationalizing that be-havior by construing it in the light of rationalist thought. Cooper puts the matter in the following way:

> The evidence about Claude's sexual orientation is much more clear cut. Although McKay had sexual relations with women, he also had many ho-mosexual affairs, particularly in the United States and Europe. The evi-dence indicates his primary orientation was toward the homosexual end of the spectrum of human sexual inclinations, not too surprising in view of the difficulties he had in relation to his father and the strong identification with his mother. A homoerotic component was most likely to underlay the relationship Claude developed with Jekyll. This did not necessarily mean they developed a physical relationship. Nothing in Claude's writings ever hinted that their friendship took such a turn, but he did once indirectly sug-gest that Jekyll introduced him to the reality and to the moral legitimacy of homosexual love.[9]

Jekyll not only helped McKay get his early Jamaican dialect poetry pub-lished, he also provided McKay with enough money to study agriculture at Booker T. Washington's Tuskegee Institute. McKay arrived in Charleston, South Carolina, in the late summer of 1912, at the age of 22, and was exposed to the system of segregation in the United States for the first time. "I had heard of prejudice in America," McKay wrote, "but never dreamed of it be-ing so intensely bitter."[10]

McKay's introduction to America was also his introduction to the rheto-ric of the race struggle, for the terms in which that issue was framed were those proposed in the United States and not Jamaica. In order to become a Negro in terms that would make sense to the reading public in the West, McKay, like fellow-Jamaican Marcus Garvey, first had to come to the land in which the racial issue was defined. McKay's intellectual odyssey recapit-ulates in a way the various philosophies of race relations that were being pro-posed at the time. His first stop was at Tuskegee, where he proposed to learn Booker T. Washington's accommodationist philosophy of training the Ne-gro to be an artisan and small-scale mechanic or farmer.

After a short while, McKay discovered that the Tuskegee approach was not to his liking and he moved on to Kansas State University in Manhattan, where he moved to the next phase of race relations. While at Kansas State, McKay joined a small group of white students with a socialist bent and read W. E. B. Du Bois's classic, *The Souls of Black Folk,* a book that he later reported "shook me like an earthquake."[11] Like James Weldon Johnson and Langston Hughes and a whole generation of other black thinkers, McKay was impressed with Du Bois's criticism of Booker's accommodation to segregation. McKay was also evidently inspired in a literary direction by the example of Du Bois, who showed that Negroes didn't have to become farmers or mechanics. Du Bois was the pre-eminent Negro man of letters in the United States at the time, having studied at Harvard and Berlin. James Weldon Johnson called *Souls of Black Folk* "a work which had had a greater effect upon and within the Negro race in America than any other single textbook published . . . since *Uncle Tom's Cabin.*"[12]

Perhaps it was the influence of Du Bois and the fact that he was now living in New York, but after two years in Kansas, McKay, with the help of a few thousand dollars from Jekyll, abandoned Kansas and moved to Harlem, where he began an ill-starred career as a restaurateur. In addition to starting a business in New York, McKay also got married to a Jamaican girlfriend by the name of Eulalie Imelda Lewars in Jersey City, New Jersey, on July 30, 1914. McKay was twenty-three at the time, and his restaurant was in Brooklyn, but the fascination which New York exerted on him was emanating pre-eminently from Harlem. Like many blacks who arrived there from the small towns and farms of the South, McKay found himself intoxicated by the big-city atmosphere of freedom from moral restraint. Harlem had become the focal point of black artistic and intellectual endeavors in the United States; however, McKay proved to be more interested in the good times that surrounded the cultural endeavors. "Vice of all kinds,"[13] Cooper writes, flourished around the restaurant with predictable results. "High living and bad business" soon swallowed all his money. The restaurant failed. There are, of course, any number of reasons why businesses fail, many of which involve no culpability on the part of those involved. That this was not the case with McKay is implied in a letter to James Weldon Johnson of March 10, 1928, asking that mention of the restaurant be stricken from his biographical sketch that Weldon had submitted to Harper & Row: "There are certain details concerning it," McKay writes referring to the restaurant, "that might be aired and make a very embarrassing situation for myself and others."[14]

Shortly after McKay's business failed, his marriage broke up as well. Describing the situation from the vantage point of 1918, McKay wrote, "My wife wearied of the life in New York in six months and returned to Jamaica,"[15] where she gave birth to their only child, Rhue Hope McKay. McKay would never see the child. In the late '40s, McKay's daughter was enrolled as a student at Columbia University. McKay planned to meet her for the first time when he came to town to give a talk in honor of James Weldon Johnson. But he died before he could accomplish either goal. His daughter never saw him alive, although she did attend his funeral.

Once his family had abandoned him, McKay would refer to morals as "the white man's law." "Spiritually," McKay wrote of himself in the auto-biographical story "Truant," "he was subject to another law. Other gods of strange barbaric glory claimed his allegiance and not the grim frockcoated gentleman of the Moral Law of the land."[16] It should be remembered that the only reason McKay was in the United States and in a position to get married and start a business was because of the financial largesse of a white benefac-tor. Beyond that, this white man, who was most probably a homosexual and most certainly a freethinker, was hardly representative of the Christianity that McKay was bent on rejecting as the white man's law. His father, on the other hand, a staunch adherent of the Christian moral law, was hardly white. Why then this gratuitous dragging of race into a fairly clear-cut case of sex-ual dereliction? Perhaps it was because McKay was determined to exploit the racial situation to his own advantage and as a cover-up of his own sexual misbehavior. "At the heart of McKay's own marriage dilemma, of course," Cooper writes,

> lay his homosexuality. New York, with its great concentration of popula-tion and teeming impersonality, tolerated the existence of a large though officially repressed homosexual community whose members found regu-lar, if illicit, outlets for the exercise of their sexual and social tastes. McKay enjoyed this almost clandestine aspect of New York life, and after the dissolution of his marriage he pursued a love life that included partners of both sexes.[17]

The term "white man's law" signals the beginning of McKay's use of the racial situation as a exculpation for his own sexual misbehavior. As the mis-behavior intensified, so did McKay's preoccupation with race as a way out of the guilt his misbehavior created in him. In a sense, McKay needed the racial situation in the United States to justify his rebellion against the moral law. Without it, he would have been confronted by the morality which he had learned from his father, which was certainly Christian, and perhaps exagger-ated and harsh, but in no sense "white." Arriving in a "white" country with a large and economically exploited Negro proletariat provided McKay with just the set of characters he need to justify his own break with the religion of his family.

During the initial period of McKay's rebellion, World War I broke out and, as a result of the labor shortage in the United States, enormous numbers of Negroes were drawn up from the South to the now-booming armaments industries of the North. In 1917, McKay found a job as a dining-car waiter on the Pennsylvania Railroad. His job enabled him to spend the next two years visiting the uprooted Blacks from the South, who were discovering new-found freedoms and prosperity in the Black Belt neighborhoods of the principal cities of the industrial Northeast. World War I provided, in E. Franklin Frazier's words, "a third terrible crisis in the cities of the North, a crisis as severe as those of slavery and Reconstruction." The rootlessness of the Reconstruction Period, when the slaves were freed, often only to wander from one turpentine camp to another, with correspondingly disastrous consequences for the black family, was replicated on an even larger scale as the war industries drew blacks to the ghettos of the North. McKay was able to witness this drama first-hand. Gradually, he began to define himself in the terms propounded to him by the race situation in the United States. McKay, whose father was the strict Presbyterian and his brother the freethinker who wanted to outdo the Christians in morality, began to view himself as a split personality. In terms propounded in his novel *Home to Harlem,* he was simultaneously Ray, the Negro intellectual from Haiti who tries to write poetry while sharing his racially grounded *Weltschmerz* with anyone who will listen, and Jake, the happy-go-lucky, sexually liberated darky. Here as later, e.g., during the brouhaha over the Moynihan Report in the '60s, race became a code word for an essentially sexual problem.

Perhaps because McKay was so influenced by the racially tainted writings of the social Darwinists, Ray, his intellectual Negro stand-in in *Home to Harlem,* tends to see culture in racial terms. Ray is a misfit because he is a black man with a "white" education. "The fact is Jake," Ray broods, "I don't know what I'll do with my little education. I wonder sometimes if I could get rid of it and go and lose myself in some savage culture in the jungles of Africa. I am a misfit."[18] Civilization, in other words, is the possession of the white race, and Negroes are naturally irresponsible when it comes to sex. Ray comes to the idea when he broods over the prospects of having a family with his wife Agatha. "Soon," he writes describing a view of procreation that is essentially homosexual in its disgust at women's procreative powers and progeny, "he would become one of the contented hogs in the pigpen of Harlem, getting ready to litter little black piggies. If he could have felt about things as Jake, how different his life might have been. Just to hitch up for a short while and be irresponsible! But he and Agatha were slaves of the civilized tradition."[19]

Ray's envy of Jake could only come from an intellectual with sexual problems. Jake, according to this scheme, is a real Negro because he is sexually irresponsible. Ray, on the other hand, is cut off from the genius of the Negro race because he thinks too much. In his determination to link race and sex, McKay comes perilously close to the views espoused by the Ku Klux Klan of his day, a fact not unnoticed by reviewers of the time. "He shares with his brothers of the Klan," one of his reviewers noted, "a dangerous proclivity to generalize – only he reverses the values. To him, the Negro is superior in all that appears important: a capacity to feel and enjoy, to be generous and expressive, to be warm and irresponsible, to live without shame and inner repression. . . . Are Negroes . . . the uninhibited children of joy that Claude McKay believes?"[20]

There is some evidence that they were not. "Ray," for example, "felt more and his range was wider and he could not be satisfied with the easy, simple things that sufficed for Jake."[21] However, he never seems to be able to act on these moments of insight. Ray's intellectual paralysis is not difficult to understand. His intellectual goal seems to be the extinction of thought; he would like to be the way he perceives Jake to be: instinctive, sexually irresponsible, free of guilt and "white" inhibitions. Whether the people he fanta-sizes are indeed like this is another matter. For the purposes of the novel, Jake is defined as such, and that is that. Ray, like McKay, aspires to be a poet. He aspires to have some grasp of the situation. And he enjoys being admired by Jake for his accomplishments. When Ray decides to leave Harlem and take a job as a seaman, Jake, who had been to Europe during the war, waxes philosophical about the effect of traveling and concludes, "when you hits shore it's the same life all ovah." Ray concedes that he may be right, and can't resist saying that "Goethe said the same thing in *Werther*." Needless to say, Jake has not read Goethe, but the quote impresses him nonetheless. "I wish I was edjucated mahself," he opines. But all that Ray can say is, "Christ! What for?"[22]

In one sense, Ray's question is legitimate; in another it is not. The type of rationalism which McKay saw as the intellectual life was in many ways as deracinated as the Negro intellectual he was to vilify in his later work, *Banjo*. In addition to the standard social Darwinist challenges to late nineteenth century beliefs, McKay's mentor Jekyll introduced him to the early modern justifications of homosexuality. In an article published in *Pearson's* in 1918, McKay listed as among the famous authors he discussed with Jekyll: Oscar Wilde, Edward Carpenter, and Walt Whitman. Carpenter published a pro-homosexual tract in 1894 entitled *Homogenic Love and Its Place in a Free Society*. "For those in 1918," Cooper concludes, "who were possessed by 'the love that dared not speak its name,' the stringing together of the names Wilde, Carpenter, and Whitman would have left no doubt about McKay's meaning. It was there, so to speak, written between the lines."[23]

So when Ray cries, "the more I learn the less I understand and love life. All the learning in this world can't answer this little question, 'Why are we living?'" it is not hard to sympathize with him. The intellectual tradition he was raised in was defective and incapable of answering such questions. It was at its root rationalization of desire and so incapable of leading Ray beyond those desires. However, the image of the happy-go-lucky, guilt-free darky is one which McKay would have to admire from afar. Since he could not be one "naturally," he could only approximate that sort of ideal by intellectual means, but, the more he was thrown back on the intellect, the more he became alienated from a goal which was the extinction of intellect in general and conscience in particular. Ray was in a no-win situation, and leaves the scene with all of the major issues unresolved.

McKay resolves the issue symbolically instead. Jake meets the prostitute he had lost during the first pages of the novel, and together they walk along 113th Street, "passing the solid gray-grim mass of the whites' Presbyterian church."[24] The church is construed as a bulwark against "the black invasion" from Harlem. The invasion can, of course, be construed in two ways. First of all, there is the white neighborhood, the "Block Beautiful," which is threatened by the Negroes who have already taken over the previously all-white Harlem and are now threatening to move south. But McKay goes beyond this image to portray the black invasion in moral terms as well. The invasion involves "black" sexual immorality overwhelming gaunt, white Presbyterianism, and the avant garde is represented by Jake and Felice, whose primitive love is a threat to the "white" establishment: "desperate, frightened, blanch-faced, the ancient sepulchral Responsibility held on. And giving them [the whites] moral courage, the Presbyterian church frowned on the corner like a fortress against the invasion."[25]

Jake and Felice are the advance units of an invasion of sexually liberated blacks who are going to bring about a revolution of values and the demise of the Protestant culture: "But groups of loud-laughing-and-acting black swains and their sweethearts had started in using the block for their afternoon promenade. That was the limit: the desecrating of that atmosphere by black love in the very shadow of the gray, gaunt Protestant church! The Ancient respectability was getting ready to flee."[26]

McKay was, of course, right. "Ancient Respectability," represented by the Protestant churches, was getting ready to flee in a number of ways. To begin with, they were about to abandon the traditional Christian moral teaching on sexuality in general and contraception in particular, and, in a quite literal sense, the members of their congregations were preparing for a flight to the suburbs, one which would intensify in the years following the Second World War. Eventually race relations would replace sexual morality as an issue of prime concern to the mainline Protestant churches, causing a major destabilization of the social order in the United States, and one of the prime agents in this destabilization was the Negro. Lenin was right in seeing the Negro as the prime locus of revolutionary activity in the United States. And the Left followed his lead unerringly throughout this century. The revolution the Communists sought would be impossible without the collaboration of the Negro or without the Negro as the first wave in the assault on "ancient respectability." If the church could be portrayed as "white," then it could easily be discredited. And the Protestant churches, born as national churches after their break with Rome, were particularly vulnerable in this regard. Many whites of Protestant stock – people like Max Eastman – no longer believed in the religion of their fathers (they were in New York City for this very reason) and were looking for a graceful way out. The Negro, who had suffered injustice at the hands of white Protestant culture, provided not only a way to atone for past sins, but also a way to rationalize future sins in the sexual arena.

That McKay chose a Presbyterian church as the emblem of "Ancient Respectability" is not surprising. His father was a Presbyterian, and McKay's rebellion against Presbyterianism is a rebellion against the moral order his father represented in his life. In order to rationalize his rejection of family responsibility when he moved to Harlem and abandoned his wife and let his business go down the drain, McKay had to necessarily paint the church "white" as a way of undermining its authority. McKay's father would hardly have approved of what his son Claude was doing, and Claude had no way of responding to the charges of moral dereliction on their own terms. He was, in effect, guilty as charged. Instead of pleading guilty, McKay indicted the standards of judgment. If it could be shown that Presbyterianism was a corrupt, racist, "white" organization, then his father's implicit reproach against McKay's failures in the family arena – his failed marriage and business – would lose their sting. McKay knew that the values he was attacking were in no specific way "white," since they are the values of his father. However, he was simply not in a position to espouse sexual liberation, which in his case meant homosexuality, openly. Playing the race card allowed McKay to indulge in his homosexual desires while at the same time cloaking that behavior in the morally exculpating garments of racial injustice. The race card indicted the guardians of the sexual moral order of injustice and as a result put them on the defensive. If whites are wrong, McKay's burdened conscience argued, then blacks were right. Racial injustice became then the indictment which paved the way for the overturning of sexual morality. Before long, others would take their cue from McKay's characters.

McKay concludes *Home to Harlem* with both Jake and Felice fleeing New York for Chicago, if not exactly ready to get married at least ready to face life together. By the end of the novel, Ray has already left New York and his wife Agatha to be a mess boy on a trans-Atlantic freighter. Leaving the home had become a literary convention in American literature, a way of giving a dramatic resolution to issues which remained essentially unresolved. Huck Finn lit out for the territories; Rip Van Winkle walked out of his home and headed for the mountains when domestic stress got to be more than he could handle. It was a literary convention which fit well with McKay's needs. Life was imitating art. After slipping out of the bonds of matrimony and business, McKay was getting ready to imitate his own characters.

The sudden appearance of his wife crystallized plans which McKay had long held in abeyance. Now he would light out for the territories too. However, for a young man of loose life and socialist inclinations, the territories in 1922 lay in the exact opposite direction – to the east and not to the west.

McKay decided to go on one of the most venerable of this century's intellectual pilgrimages. He decided to go to Moscow, to witness the implementation of the Bolshevik Revolution first-hand. In his autobiography, McKay makes it clear that his attraction to the Bolshevik Revolution clearly had domestic roots. He was escaping from his newly returned wife and the prospect of supporting her and his child, and he was escaping as well from the round of sexual dissipation which precipitated the estrangement of his wife in the first place. "All my planning was upset," he wrote of the disruption which his newly appeared wife introduced into his "quickly fading conceit about being a poet":

> I had married when I thought that a domestic partnership was possible to my existence. But I had wandered far and away, until I had grown into a truant by nature and undomesticated in the blood. There were consequences of the moment that I could not face. I desired to be footloose, and felt impelled to start going again.
>   Where? Russia signaled. A vast upheaval and a grand experiment. What could I understand there? What could I learn for my life, for my work? Go and see, was the command. Escape from the pit of sex and poverty, from domestic death, from the cul-de-sac of self-pity, from the hot syncopated fascination of Harlem, from the suffocating ghetto of color consciousness. Go, better than stand still, keep going.[27]

McKay was not alone in this feeling. In fact, the details of his life described a trajectory that was shared by the majority of radicals at the time. In all essential details, race was irrelevant. Race was used as a pretext for attacking Christian morality and the Protestant culture which embodied it. McKay's life was in many ways identical in this regard to the life of the ten-year-older white Harlem Renaissance writer Carl Van Vechten, author of *Nigger Heaven*. Like Van Vechten, McKay came from a rural middle-class, stable Protestant family. Like Van Vechten McKay married his hometown childhood sweetheart. Like Van Vechten, McKay abandoned his wife shortly after arriving in New York, and began a career as a literary purveyor of modern trends. Both McKay and Van Vechten were bisexual and first gave rein to their homosexual impulses after they became acclimated to the freer life that was being increasingly openly promoted in New York City. Both McKay and Van Vechten were drawn to modernity as the justification for their domestic dereliction. McKay was drawn to socialism and then communism, Van Vechten to more literary forms of decadence, including the music of Schoenberg and Stravinsky. Van Vechten also became literary executor of the estate of Gertrude Stein. Like Van Vechten, who was white, McKay, the black Jamaican, was drawn to race as an ideological justification for sexual license. Van Vechten wrote his contribution to the race-inspired destabilization of Christian mores, *Nigger Heaven* ,in 1926. McKay followed suit two years later with the publication of *Home to Harlem*, which the black press in general condemned as a black *Nigger Heaven*. Both Van

Vechten and McKay were drawn to the Greenwich Village radicals of the so-called Innocent Rebellion of 1912–1916 – Emma Goldman, Margaret Sanger, Eugene O'Neill, John Reed, Mabel Dodge. A good number of these people, including Claude McKay, were absorbed into communism after the Bolshevik Revolution in 1917.

It was this initial alliance between Harlem Negroes and Village radicals that spawned the Harlem Renaissance. In fact the seminal meeting for this alliance took place at McKay's going away party in September of 1922 when McKay left for Russia. *The Liberator* collaborated with "a select list of persons connected with the NAACP" in raising enough money to send McKay off to attend the Fourth Congress of the Third Communist International to be held in Moscow in November of that year. "Wc often speak of that party back in '22," James Weldon Johnson wrote to McKay years later,

> Do you know that was the first getting together of the black and white literati on a purely social plane. Such parties are now common in New York, but I doubt any has been more representative. You remember there were present Heywood Broun, Ruth Hale, E. P. Adams, John Farar, Carl Van Doren, Freda Kirchwey, Peggy Tucker, Roy Nash – on our side you, Dubois, [*sic*] Walter White, Jessie Fauset, Arthur Schomburg, J. Rosamond Johnson – I think that party started something.[28]

What it started, of course, was the alliance of the Left and the Negro which eventuated, after a sojourn in the hands of the Communist Party, in the civil rights movement of the '50s and '60s, followed by the cultural and sexual revolution which swept through this country's institutions during the '60s and '70s. McKay's farewell party "started something," to use James Weldon Johnson's term: It brought about the race-based re-engineering of the social order that had been based on the Protestant reading of the moral tradition of the West. The thing, however, which made the party possible was McKay's relationship with Max Eastman, then the handsome editor of the left-wing radical magazine, *The Liberator* and in McKay's words, "an ikon for the radical women."[29]

In 1919, while working in the dining cars of the Pennsylvania railroad, writing poetry when his hectic schedule would allow, and at the same time steeping himself in the life of the new black ghettos of the urban northeast, McKay met Eastman through Eastman's sister Crystal, who in 1919 was co-editing *The Liberator* with him. After publishing one of his poems, Crystal invited McKay down to *The Liberator*, offices to discuss his work with her. Crystal, like her brother, was a feminist and socialist; she was, in addition, one of the co-founders of the ACLU. McKay described her as "the most beautiful white woman I ever knew."[30] (Ever ready to express his opinions on the relative beauty of white women, McKay wrote to Eastman in 1937, giving him his opinion of Lenin's wife: "There can never be any question about Krupskaya's ugliness. She was the most awfullest ugliest Russian woman I ever saw and gave me the impression of an alligator half-asleep.") When McKay met the Eastmans he was introduced to the heart of American radicalism, as proposed by *The Masses*, the magazine Eastman was editing when he met McKay. Eastman, listed its primary tenets as "the struggle for racial equality and woman's rights, for intelligent sex relations, above all (and beneath all) for birth and population control."[31]

Eastman was not convinced that the socialist millennium was going to come in the manner in which its most fervent devotees awaited its arrival, but he was, nonetheless, in agreement with its goals, and Claude McKay was impressed with Max Eastman. Eastman was thirty-six years old at the time they met and one of the handsomest figures of his generation. His tall, lean good looks in the American manner, and his prematurely white but full head of hair, insured a steady stream of female admirers. Eastman, according to his own testimony, was not loath to take advantage of their attention. During the fall and winter of 1921, when Eastman was on the rebound from his affair with movie star Florence Deshon, he carried on affairs with three other women. "It was then, I believe," he wrote, "in the recoil from my too aspiring love, that I began to acquire the legendary reputation as a sort of Byronical professional lovemaker – a Don Juan or Casanova – which has long pursued me, and stood somewhat in my way as a real lover."[32]

Claude McKay, whose aspirations for literary fame and sexual liberation paralleled Eastman's, could not help but be impressed by the older, more successful version of what he himself wanted to become. In the summer following their first meeting, McKay wrote to Eastman to tell him, "I love your life – more than your poetry, more than your personality. This is my attitude to all artists. It may be unhealthy, but life fascinates me in its passions."[33] McKay was about to embark on another of his mentor relationships with another older white man. Like Jekyll, Eastman would provide a sort of fatherly guidance and financial assistance, as well as help in editing his poetry for the rest of McKay's life. Unlike his relationship with Jekyll, there was no hint of homosexual contact. As was the case with the homosexual rationalist Jekyll, McKay made steady progress in his ideology of negritude under the tutelage of white radical father figures. His most famous poem, "If We Must Die," which went on to inspire generations of blacks, was published in the July 1919 issue of *The Liberator* under Eastman's editorship. Over sixty years later, the poem was found among the writings which inspired the black inmates who took over the Attica State Prison in upstate New York. *Time* magazine described one of the seven pieces that McKay wrote for the July 1919 *Liberator* as "a poem by an unknown prisoner, crude but touching in its would-be heroic style, entitled 'If We Must Die.'"[34]

Like McKay and Van Vechten, Eastman married a childhood sweetheart and brought her to New York City. There talk of the sort that he described at the editorial meetings of *The Masses* combined with what is usually termed concupiscence, destroyed his marriage. With the October Revolution in Russia, Eastman and McKay saw a world revolution that seemed intent on implementing their own beliefs in sexual liberation. Neither could resist the temptation to travel there and experience the revolution first hand, just as Mary Wollstonecraft and the English radicals had done 130 years earlier when they visited Paris.

"I tried," Eastman wrote of the time before his rebirth as the sexual revolutionary,

> making a declaration of temperamental independence, asserting my right to be the volatile and inconstant poet that I am. It was the beginning of a war that the scattered, ragged, and ill-armed guerrilla forces-of-character in the command of such a poet could never possibly win. With her traditional morality and my ancestral load of virtue to back her, Ida plowed through my fitful volitions and frail theoretical defenses like a battle tank.[35]

In the Soviet Union, "the new land of freedom," however, the moral tables were turned. Now the burden of proof was on the woman who wanted to reassert traditional values like monogamy and fidelity and care of offspring. Sexual morality had been relativized as belonging to one class and thereby discredited as part of the communist program to abolish all class distinctions. Eastman noticed the connection immediately. And beyond that, he noticed the drive to universalization implicit in it as well. If abolishing "restrictions upon freedom of choice in sex relations" in one country could have this salutary effect upon his troubled conscience, just think what a paradise would ensue if that revolution could spread throughout the entire world! That would mean a world in which no wife could inflict guilt on an errant husband. This promise of moral legitimacy was enough to convert the cause of Bolshevism into a holy crusade for sexually troubled pilgrims throughout the West, where the memory of unhappy love was still fresh. All the workers of the world had to lose were their bathing suits. "At home," Eastman continued, "I had been a little squeamish about this kind of liberation when indulged in by radical friends on sequestered beaches," but Eastman soon grew accustomed to "this Garden-of-Eden-like freedom" in the Soviet Union because it had the sanction of the regime which aspired to bring liberation of this sort to the entire world.[35] The paradise of sexual liberation was only plausible insofar as it aspired to universality. It could only calm the troubled conscience in an effective manner when it was legitimized by the regime in power. In this regard, what better conscience machine could there be than one which confidently banned God and His law from public life and then went on in the name of high moral purpose to make this vision normative for the entire world? An entire world without bathing suits, without nagging wives and despondent lovers, a world without guilt! No wonder, then, that Eastman and the constituency of sexual revolutionaries he represented underwent mass conversions to the cause of bolshevism. It was their best hope.

By traveling to "the new land of freedom," Eastman even got the type of wife he wanted in America but could never find. He eventually moved in with Eliena Krylenko in her Moscow apartment and began a relationship which "came as near to anything in the Soviet Bohemia of those days to being a marriage."[37] When Max told her about Nina and the sky-covered embraces outside Yalta, Eliena was sad for a bit but eventually got over it, giving Eastman permission to have as many affairs as he chose to. According to Eastman's account, Eliena was so devastated by her father's suicide that she made "a childish vow . . . that when she grew up she would marry a man like her father and let him love all the other women he wanted to."[38] Eastman was hardly going to argue with her on this score. It was, as far as he was concerned, a dream come true. And if he could ascribe it to some quasi-Freudian kink in Eliena's relationship with her father, so much the better. Then his infidelities could be construed as therapeutic for both of them. Eastman indicates the importance of the regime in legitimatizing sexual liberation: "The destabilizing of the social order that communism had brought about had destabilized everyone's sexual conscience as well, for a while at least."[39] Before long, the world would learn that the converse of that statement was true as well.

Part II, Chapter 15

Moscow, 1922

Claude McKay noticed the same loose morals that Eastman had when he arrived in Moscow. McKay left the United States in mid-September 1922 as a stoker on a merchant steamer bound for England. After a short stay in England, where hc tried to make contact with his radical friends of the year before as a way of getting credentials for the Fourth Congress of the Third International, he moved on to Berlin. While waiting to get credentials, he visited cabarets which "seemed to express the ultimate in erotomania," where "youngsters of both sexes . . . were methodically exploiting the nudist colony indoors."[1] McKay arrived in Moscow in late October, one week before the beginning of the Fourth Congress on November 5, 1922, and he was caught up in the festive atmosphere of the times. Max Eastman would later attribute the feeling among the population to the revival of prosperity, which came about when private enterprise was given a new lease on life under Lenin's New Economic Policy. The fact that McKay was black only increased his popularity among the communist politicians, who favored him over the light-skinned delegate from the official communist delegation from the United States and among the population in general. "Never in my life," McKay wrote in his autobiography,

> did I feel prouder of being an African, a black, and no mistake about it. Unforgettable that first occasion upon which I was physically uplifted. I had not yet seen it done to anybody, nor did I know that it was a Russian custom. The Moscow streets were filled with eager crowds before the congress started. As I tried to get through along the Tverskaya I was suddenly surrounded by a crowd, tossed into the air, and caught a number of times and carried a block on their friendly shoulders. The civilians started it. The soldiers imitated them. And the sailors followed the soldiers, tossing me higher than ever.
>
> From Moscow to Petrograd and from Petrograd to Moscow I went triumphantly from surprise to surprise, extravagantly feted on every side. I was carried along on a crest of sweet excitement. I was like a black ikon in the flesh. The famine had ended, the Nep was flourishing, the people were simply happy. I was the first Negro to arrive in Russia since the revolution, and perhaps I was generally regarded as an omen of good luck! Yes, that was exactly what it was. I was like a black ikon.[2]

McKay was also noticing that his fortunes as a writer rose as well. He received fees well above those paid to Soviet writers for articles, stories, and poems which appeared in *Izvestia*. Beyond that, he was kept in a constant state of activity, making public appearances, visiting soviet military facilities, and giving speeches. "The photograph of my black face," he recounted in his autobiography,

> was everywhere among the most highest [*sic*] Soviet rulers, in the principal streets, adorning the walls of the city. I was whisked out of my unpleasant abode and installed in one of the most comfortable and best-heated hotels in Moscow. I was informed: "You may have wine and anything extra you require, and at no cost to you." But what could I want for, when I needed a thousand extra mouths and bellies for the importunate invitations to feast? Wherever I wanted to go, there was a car at my disposal. Whatever I wanted to do I did. And anything I felt like saying I said. For the first time in my life, I knew what it was to be a highly privileged personage. And in the Fatherland of Communism! Didn't I enjoy it![3]

Although it did not go by that name at that time, McKay was the beneficiary of the Soviet version of affirmative action. Then as now there were strings attached. He would be promoted beyond other writers in exchange for his support of the Soviet regime. In exchange for the royal treatment he got in Moscow, McKay was expected to criticize the United States in an attempt to entice the Negro to the cause of communism. McKay, at the beginning at least, was only too happy to oblige. *Negroes in America* was McKay's way of holding up his end of the bargain. "Our age," he wrote in that work, "is the age of Negro art. The slogan of the aesthetic art world is 'Return to the Primitive.' The Futurists and Impressionists are agreed in turning everything upside down in an attempt to achieve the wisdom of the primitive Negro."[3] The Bolsheviks shared the same interest, as their promotion of McKay showed; however, before long McKay began to wonder, as beneficiaries of affirmative action often do, whether he was indeed worthy of the attention the communists lavished on him.

He was noticing that sexual liberation had its downside too. "In 1922, he wrote, "I left America in perfect health and more completely whole than the day on which I was born."[4] The term "whole" has a curious ring to it. It is difficult to discern whether this is simply one of McKay's Jamaicanisms or whether he is hinting at some other metaphysical quality, like integrity, when he discusses it. Whatever the reason for his choice of words, McKay goes on to give an account of his failing health as a result of going to Russia. In the spring of 1923, he experienced "a deadness in his left side" and "once my face gradually became puffed up like an enormous chocolate soufflé."[5] After having a tooth extracted in Petrograd, he characterized his condition as "quite ill." By the time McKay arrived in Germany during the summer of 1923, he was suffering from intermittent fevers and headaches, a condition which plagued him for three months. His condition, however, did not prevent him from visiting the same cabarets he had visited a year before, this time in the company of Charles Ashleigh, a Communist and homosexual he had met in England. In October 1923, he left Berlin for Paris, where he "consulted a French specialist, who advised me to enter a hospital immediately."[7] McKay never tells us the diagnosis of the French specialist, only that after he was better he was told: "You are young, with a very wonderful constitution, and you will recover all right if you will live quietly and carefully away from the temptations of the big cities."[8]

McKay had contracted syphilis. Although he never mentions it in his autobiography, he did mention it in letters to both Alain Locke, editor of *The New Negro,* and Max Eastman. McKay's biographer expresses some puzzlement at McKay's departure from Moscow at the height of his fame there:

> He had political success within his grasp in Moscow, but it seemed incompatible and somehow insignificant when compared with the purely literary success he sought. His poems seemed to him insufficiently important for the fame they had brought him. He felt the need to push on with his literary career, to prove himself.[9]

McKay never explains why he left Russia, but it is clear from his letters that he left Berlin for Paris to get medical treatment. It is also reasonable to assume that he left Russia for the same reason. Medical treatment for venereal disease at the time consisted in extremely precise doses of toxic metals like mercury and arsenic. If the dosage was not exact, either it did nothing at all to check the spread of the disease, or it resulted in a case of poisoning or death. The incubation period for syphilis is nine to ninety days. Secondary symptoms, such as the fevers McKay experienced in Berlin in the summer of 1923, can appear at any time from four to six months after the initial contact. This means that McKay in all likelihood contracted syphilis in the Soviet Union, while being feted as a "black ikon" by the Communists. In all likelihood he sought treatment in Russia as well but, given the state of medicine there five years after the revolution, was given inexact dosages which brought on partial paralysis and swelling of the face, symptoms consonant with arsenic and/or mercury poisoning. The skill of the doctor was of paramount importance in such cases. We know that McKay left Berlin for better treatment in Paris. In all likelihood he left Moscow, with its much more primitive medical facilities, for the same reason. McKay left a promising career as a black apologist for communism, most probably to avoid dying from venereal disease or being poisoned by the doctors who were treating him there.

McKay never mentions the disease in his autobiography, but he alludes to it and the state of mind it produced in him by reprinting in that work a poem he had written at the time, he tells us, "while I was convalescing in the hospital." It was entitled "The Desolate City," and was, he continues, "largely symbolic: a composite evocation of the clinic, my environment, condition, and mood":

> My spirit is a pestilential city,
> With misery triumphant everywhere,
> Glutted with baffled hopes and human pity.
> Strange agonies make quiet lodgment there:
> Its sewers bursting ooze up from below
> And spread their loathsome substance through its lanes,
> And blocking all the motions of its veins:
> Its life is sealed to love or hope or pity,
> My spirit is a pestilential city. . . .
> And all its many fountains no more spurt;
> Within the damned-up [*sic*] tubes they tide and foam,
> Around the drifted sludge and silted dirt,
> And weep against the soft and liquid loam.
> And so the city's ways are washed no more,
> All is neglected and decayed within,
> Clean waters beat against its high-walled shore
> In furious force, but cannot enter in:
> The suffocated fountains cannot spurt,
> They foam and rage against the silted dirt. . . .[10]

The imagery of venereal disease is obvious throughout the poem, yet McKay seems determined to deny the obvious in his autobiography. Significant here is not so much the fact that he omits mentioning his venereal disease or admits it in an oblique way that bespeaks what we have called elsewhere the Dimmesdale Syndrome.[11] Significant is the fact that, two pages earlier, McKay claimed that he was "entirely unobsessed by sex." Responding to the claim of Communist critics that *Home to Harlem* was thinly veiled autobiography, McKay claimed that

> I have never wanted to lie about life, like the preaching black prudes wrapped up in the borrowed robes of hypocritical white respectability. I am entirely unobsessed by sex. I am not an imitator of Anglo-Saxon prudery in writing. I haven't arrived at that high degree of civilized culture where I can make a success of producing writing carefully divorced from reality. Yet I couldn't indulge in such self-flattery as to claim Jake in *Home from Harlem* as a portrait of myself. My damned white education has robbed me of much of the primitive vitality, the pure stamina, the simple unswaggering strength of the Jakes of the Negro Race.[12]

One has the impression that McKay doth protest too much. His poem is full of remorse at the consequences of his sexual life as well as nostalgia for a pre-sexual, pre-diseased childhood:

> There was a time, when, happy with the birds,

The little children clapped their hands and laughed;
And midst the clouds the glad winds heard their words
And blew down all the merry ways to waft
The music through the scented fields of flowers.
Oh sweet were children's voices in those days,
Before the fall of pestilential showers.[13]

McKay may or may not be "obsessed by sex" depending on how we define that term; however, his mind is preoccupied by "suffocated fountains" which "cannot spurt" and all the other imagery of venereal disease. His assertion that he is "unobsessed by sex" is about as credible as his claim that *Home from Harlem* is not autobiographical. Beyond that, there is the gratuitous introduction of race into the question of his sex life. He refers to "Anglo-Saxon prudery in writing" and "hypocritical white respectability" and then goes on to complain that "my damned white education has robbed me of much of the primitive vitality, the pure stamina, the simple unswaggering strength of the Jakes of the Negro Race."

The claim that the white race is somehow prudish when it comes to sexual relations is difficult to understand in light of McKay's own experiences. Walter Jekyll, McKay's first white mentor, in all probability introduced McKay to homosexual activity, and if not to the activity itself then surely to the rationalization of it. Jekyll was also one of McKay's most ardent supporters. It was through his financial support that McKay could travel to the United States and eventually set himself up in Harlem.

McKay's second important mentor, Max Eastman, was equally ardent in his support of sexual liberation. McKay received most of his "damned white education" at the hands of both of these men. His education led him directly into the sexual excess whereby he contracted venereal disease. Syphilis is, of course, precisely the thing which "robbed" McKay of the "primitive vitality, the pure stamina, the simple unswaggering strength" which he attributes to "the Negro Race." McKay's racial ideology, in other words, is nothing more than a covert protest against the sexual morals of his adopted father-figure mentors. McKay had followed the example of his white mentors and suddenly realized that all it got him was a debilitating venereal disease. His "damned white education" at the hands of Jekyll and Eastman had "robbed" McKay "of the primitive vitality . . . of the Negro Race," which in this particular instance is probably a reference to his father's beliefs and his own childhood .

The phrase means either that or it is something which makes no sense, for sexual liberation, as McKay learned in the cabarets of Bérlin and in the worker's paradise of the Soviet Union, was hardly the monopoly of the black race. In fact, race in this regard was only something which took on importance in light of their desire for liberation. McKay, every bit as much as Lenin and Carl Van Vechten, wanted to use race as a tool for destabilizing morals. McKay hardly needed the concept of race to destabilize his own morals, but it was a handy device for justifying his deviations from conduct he had learned from his middle-class, black Christian parents. If McKay could show that sexual behavior flowed from race, then it was something over which he had no control, and as a result he could not be held culpable for what he had done, beginning with the estrangement from his wife in New York City. The more deeply McKay became involved in sexual misbehavior, the more appealing the whole notion of "racial" sexual values became to him because of the subtle exculpation they wrought.

In describing the cultural situation in Paris in 1923, the setting for "The Desolate City" and the place where he was recuperating from venereal disease and its equally deleterious treatments, McKay brings up the subject again. "Sex," he claims, roughly ten pages after he has treated the reader to a description of the "suffocated fountains" which "cannot spurt,"

> was never much of a problem to me. I played at sex as a child in a healthy harmless way. When I was seventeen or eighteen I became aware of the ripe urge of potency and also the strange manifestations and complications of sex. I grew up in the spacious peasant country, and although there are problems and strangeness of sex also in the country, they are not similar to those of the city. I never made a problem of sex. As I grew up I was privileged to read a variety of books in my brother's library, and soon I became intellectually cognizant of sex problems. But physically my problems were reduced to a minimum. And the more I traveled and grew in age and experience, the less they became.[14]

McKay then goes on to divert the reader's attention to race:

> What, then, was my main psychological problem? It was the problem of color. Color-consciousness was the fundamental of my restlessness. And it was something with which my white fellow-expatriates could sympathize but which they could not altogether understand. For they were not black like me. Not being black and unable to see deep into the profundity of blackness, some even thought that I might have preferred to be white like them. They couldn't imagine that I had no desire merely to exchange my black problem for their white problem. For all their knowledge and sophistication, they couldn't understand the instinctive and animal and purely physical pride of a black person resolute in being himself and yet living a simple civilized life like themselves. Because their education in their white world had trained them to see a person of color as either an inferior or as an exotic.[15]

Again McKay doth protest too much, using race as a cover for sexual guilt. The fact is that his problems with sex did not diminish "the more I traveled and grew in age and experience." The plain fact, which he withholds from the reader of his autobiography, is that the opposite took place. He contracted syphilis as a result of his travels and experience, and it oppressed him severely as shown in his poem, which he himself included in his biography as a way of letting the reader read between the lines to the heart of his own troubles. His explanation of "color-consciousness" as "the fundamental of my restlessness" is equally unconvincing. No one can deny that racism was a problem in the 1920s, and McKay experienced both segregation in the South and the rise of Nazism in Germany first-hand. However, even granting all that, McKay was hardly a victim of racism; in fact the exact opposite was true. He was promoted by whites throughout his career, often, as in the case of the Soviet Union, simply because he was black. If anything, McKay was the beneficiary of preferential treatment rather than the victim of discrimination. Warned not to go back to Germany because of the Senegalese troops which had just been stationed in the Ruhr, McKay found that he could enter pubs and cabarets with impunity in Berlin. He detected not the least bit of anti-Negro sentiment in Germany. The same is true of his treatment at the hand of the American radicals, like Eastman, who helped McKay out financially and professionally for his entire life.

Race and sex are inextricably linked in McKay's thinking. At first glance, he seems to be proposing nothing more than the Ku Klux Klan's view of race with the polarities reversed. "White" civilization is bad; the sexually liberated "black" race is good. However, the situation is more complex than that. Behind the bluster about race, McKay's disillusionment with sexual liberation emerges. McKay had followed the example of his white mentors in sexual revolution, and all it had earned him was a bad case of VD. McKay, however, seems determined not to face the problem, which is, at root, his own choice of sexual irresponsibility. Instead, he chooses to blame "white" civilization for his own derelictions. In this, he was blazing a trail that many were to follow. The more sexual dysfunction came to characterize the black ghetto, the more black leaders would attempt to blame white racism as its cause. Afrocentricity arrived on the cultural scene at the same time as family melt-down in the ghetto. Negritude, like patriotism, was oftentimes the last refuge of a scoundrel. And McKay was no exception to this rule. However, understanding the particular dynamic of race and sex is crucial, and McKay's philosophy was in many ways its *locus classicus*.

In November 1923, McKay left the hospital in Paris as cured as one can be by taking precise dosages of various poisons. In December, he was earning a living by posing naked in Paris studios. McKay describes the situation in his second novel, *Banjo,* through Ray, the same character who was his autobiographical *Doppelgänger* in *Home to Harlem.* The students, Ray tells Banjo, the eponymous hero of the novel, "were all fierce moderns." As a consequence, they were interested in Ray as a "black ikon" as much as the Communists had been interested in McKay in Moscow. Among the "fierce moderns" of Paris, the Negro had come to represent "primitive simplicity." That this primitive simplicity had a distinctly sexual edge to it became evident in what was to become the seminal modern painting, Picasso's *Les*

Demoiselles d'Avignon, which had been painted almost twenty years before McKay's session with the art students but had only recently become accessible to the public. Picasso had been inspired by African sculpture and masks but, in a manner dear to white Europeans who were looking for a way to ditch their moral heritage, had placed the masks on the bodies of prostitutes. *Les Demoiselles d'Avignon* was named after the red light district in Barcelona and not the French city that had been home to the papacy; it is only fitting that that quintessentially sexual movement should find its inception in a whorehouse. Africa was appropriated to make the setting more interesting and to give a veneer of cultural relativism to the voyeurism implicit in the painting. Africa, Picasso seemed to be saying, was the place close to nature, where extramarital sexuality occurred naturally and without the guilt and hang-ups that accompanied its exercise in Europe and America.

Since Ray was not unaware of the attraction of the primitive himself, he found that he could enhance his money-earning potential in Paris as a black ikon if he augmented his black body with the appropriate critical theories. "Some of them," Ray recounts in *Banjo,*

> asked if I had seen the African Negro sculptures. I said yes and that I liked them. I told them that what moved me most about the African sculpture was the feeling of perfect self-mastery and quiet self-assurance that they gave. They seemed interested in what I had to say and talked a lot about primitive simplicity and color and "significant form" from Cézanne to Picasso. Their naked savage was quickly getting into civilized things.[16]

McKay's success with the "fierce moderns" was to a large extent not only a function of his skin color but also a function of telling them what they wanted to hear, which was that Africa was indeed the repository of primitive virtues. That these virtues were almost exclusively sexual is clear from Picasso's appropriation of African imagery for his protomodern rendition of a Spanish whorehouse. McKay makes clear that he was not above trading on this aspect as well. "I got extra money for private appointments," Ray tells us, "which paid better than the school."[17] The passage is surrounded by ellipses, leaving the reader to fill in his own blanks and suspicions. In addition to hinting that he was paid for sexual favors, McKay tells us flat out that he was paid for intellectual favors of the same dubious sort. He was paid to represent the moderns' notion of primitive uninhibited sexuality, not only in drafty Parisian studios, but in Moscow by the Communists and in New York by the publishing industry, which brought out *Home to Harlem* as a black sequel to *Nigger Heaven.* The *New York Times* called *Home to Harlem* "the real stuff, the lowdown on Harlem, the dope from the inside." Louis Sherwin of the *New York Sun* saw in the novel's publication an expression of "the jig-chasing passion that has obsessed the literati of this village for years."[18]

Modernity, it turns out, was nothing more than intellectual jig-chasing. In order to be truly black, McKay had to adopt the ideology of sexual primitivism that the fierce moderns in Paris were seeking. Picasso, it turns out, was a Spanish jig-chaser who introduced the genre to France and in the process started the movement that was known as modern art. And McKay was a jig who wasn't averse to being chased – and caught, for that matter, as the fierce modern epigone, who were imitating Picasso in the '20s found out. McKay was being paid to represent sexual liberation. Being its "black ikon," however, which meant in effect being a sort of male prostitute for the white moderns, aroused mixed feelings in McKay, feelings which are best traced in all their ambivalence in his novel *Banjo*, set in the vieux port of Marseilles.

Like *Home to Harlem, Banjo* is populated by various Negro characters who represent the split in McKay's personality between the black intellectual poet and the lower-class Negro, who lives simply according to his passions. Ray, the same character who represented McKay's intellectual side in *Home to Harlem,* debates with Lincoln Agrippa Daily, otherwise known as Banjo, the novel's paradigmatic black free spirit. In addition, Jake, an earlier manifestation of the Banjo type from *Home to Harlem,* shows up at the end of the novel too. Both Ray and Jake have abandoned their respective wives and children for a vagabond life. "Ray had undergone a decided change since he had left America. He enjoyed his role of a wandering black without patriotic or family ties."[19] They had become the sort of men that then Undersecretary Moynihan would talk about forty years later.

Jake told Ray of picking up Felice again and their leaving Harlem for Chicago. After two years there, they had had a baby boy. And then they decided to get married. Two years of married life passed, and he could no longer stick to Chicago, so he returned to Harlem. But he soon found that it was not just a change of place that was worrying him. "I soon finds out," he said, "that it was no joymaking business for a fellah like you same old Jake, chappie, to go to work reg'lar every day and come home ehvrah night to the same ole pillow."[20] The problem was basic sexual wanderlust. "It was," Jake tells Ray, "too much home stuff."[21] Jake eventually reconciled with his wife, although, if that is the case, it is not clear what he is doing in Marseilles. But Ray can identify because, it turns out, he was having the same sort of feelings. "You're a thousand times a better man than me, Jake. Finding a way to carry on with a family and knuckling down to it. I just ran away from the thing." At this point Ray admits that he has abandoned his wife and child and changes the subject by suggesting that they both have another drink.

Ray is McKay's mouthpiece for sorting out his complicated feelings on sex and race. When it comes to sexual liberation, Ray is a divided man. On the one hand he likes the loose living he finds among the lower-class blacks. On the other hand, he is not free from the qualms of conscience that arise from that sort of life. He is clearly ill at ease when he has to admit to Jake that he abandoned his wife and child. Ray solves the sexual problem, much as McKay did in his autobiography, by projecting it onto a racial arena. "Ray," we are told, " . . . hated civilization."[22] The thing that bothers Ray the most about civilization is, of course, "the used-up hussy of white morality."

> I don't think I loathe anything more than the morality of the Christians. It is false, treacherous, hypocritical. I know that, for I myself have been a victim of it in your white world, and the conclusion I draw from it is that the world needs to get rid of false moralities and cultivate decent manners.[23]

In place of "white morality" McKay proposes "the richness of fundamental racial values" of the sort he claims to find in black Africa:

> He did not feel that confidence about Aframericans, who, long deracinated, were still rootless among phantoms and pale shadows and enfeebled by self-effacement before condescending patronage, social negativism, miscegenation. At college in America and among the Negro intelligentsia he had never experienced any of the simple, natural warmth of a people believing in themselves, such as he had felt among the rugged poor and socially backward blacks of his island home. The colored intelligentsia lived its life "to have the white neighbors think well of us," so that it could move more into nice "white" streets.[24]

It is not difficult to sympathize with McKay's dissatisfaction with the deracinated condition of the Negro in the urban ghettos of the industrial Northeast in the United States. However, the alternative he is proposing is never as clear as his condemnation of what he is rejecting. Just what exactly are "fundamental racial values"? Around the same time McKay was writing, Hitler was trying to derive a morality from race as well. His failure was more spectacular but no less predictable than McKay's, who seems to be saying that a person's behavior is deducible from his race. The credulity of the reader is strained even more when it becomes apparent that McKay has had no more first-hand contact with black Africa than Pablo Picasso or Carl Van Vechten had. In each instance, we are dealing with projection of the most patent sort.

    In McKay's ideology, race provides an inadequate foundation for morality. However, the desire that sets the system in motion is moral at its cause, and, in this instance, since McKay shares the sexual vices of Van Vechten and (with the exception of homosexuality) of Picasso and Eastman, he is attracted to Africa for the same reason that they are. The color of his skin in this regard is not nearly as important as the content of his character. McKay turned Africa into a religion because he saw it as the antithesis of Christian Europe. In this he was no different from any of the white moderns, who were interested in the same moral (or better, immoral) ends. "Negroes are never so beautiful and magical as when they dance to that gorgeous sublimation of the primitive African sex feeling. . . . this dance is the key to the African rhythm of life," says Ray, who is willing to impugn the morals of an entire continent and race in order to justify his own sexual behavior to himself.

Of course, McKay possessed at the time, as he would admit later, a less than perfect notion of Christianity. This is understandable since he gathered it from the outscourings of Marseilles's red-light district. A typical representative of the Christianity McKay finds unpalatable is the black American Pentecostal, Sister Geter, who announces, "I belongs to the Pentecostal Fire Baptized Believers and I ain't studying no lang-idge but the lang-idge of faith. I was fire baptized in the gift of tongues and when I deliver this heah Gawd's message . . . people heahs what I say and just gotta understand no matter what lang-idge they speks."[25]

Sister Geter's main concern is to preach against "fohnication," and although there is plenty of that to preach against, her anti-intellectual approach turns Ray off. Langston Hughes described a similar experience in his autobiography, *The Big Sea.* "My aunt told me that when you were saved you saw a light, and something happened to you inside. And Jesus came into your life! . . . so I sat there calmly in the hot, crowded church, waiting for Jesus to come to me."[26] In criticizing Sister Geter, McKay forgot to mention that he is only interested in a particular type of anti-intellectualism, the type manifested by Banjo, his archetype of the "real" Negro, "who in all matters acted instinctively." Ray, on the other hand, is trying to figure out how "he could bring intellect to the aid of instinct."

Intellect to the aid of instinct is, of course, the classical notion of the intellectual life turned upside down. It is also the classic description of both ideology and rationalization. If we put all of these elements together, we have some sense of the ideology that was modernity and the role that the Negro played in symbolizing it. McKay's fundamental racial values turn out to be a pretext for something that is transracial, the modern's desire to rationalize sexual misbehavior.

Throughout most of his career as a writer. McKay found himself caught in a dynamic which he understood imperfectly, if at all. Claiming to be a victim of white racism, he was in fact promoted by a series of white mentor-father figures. Western society had become a combination of greed, religious weirdness, and Darwinian ideologies, all of which McKay construed as "white" and, therefore, Christian. His sexual rebellion had made him hostile to Christian morality, but his guilt-induced attraction to Africa left him with no workable code of action. Just what were "fundamental racial values" anyway? McKay had no more idea what that meant than Hitler, other than the rejection of Christianity that it meant for both.

There is a way in which McKay's behavior makes perfect sense, though. As a result of his choosing sexual liberation, primarily through becoming estranged from his wife and child, McKay threw his lot in with the white moderns who were his intellectual foster fathers. However, the more he acted out this modernity, the more alienated he became. Modernity was essentially rationalized sexual misbehavior, a notion he learned from both Jekyll and Eastman. The more he acted modernity out, the more alienated he became and the more disappointed in the direction his white "fathers" were giving him. Rather than break with them, he began to hold a grudge against the white race, and white education as sapping his native vitality. And as the case with his venereal disease has shown convincingly, there is a sense in which this was perfectly true. In reference to what he had learned from Jekyll and Eastman about the rationalization of sexual vice, it was perfectly true to say that "my damned white education has robbed me of much of the primitive vitality . . . of the Negro race." Venereal disease has a way of doing just that.

Part II, Chapter 16

Moscow, 1922

In the fall of 1922, around the same time that Claude McKay was being feted as a "black ikon" in the Soviet Union, Alexandra Kollontai, the first woman minister in the revolutionary government, where she took the post of minister of social welfare in 1917, was getting ready to leave Russia once again, this time to accept a diplomatic post in Oslo, as the Soviet ambassadress to Norway. After almost twenty years of exile abroad under the Czar, Kollontai was now going into diplomatic exile under the Communists. Considering what happened to the other critics of Bolshevik policy, her punishment was mild by comparison, but it was punishment nonetheless. Kollontai had just fought a losing battle against Lenin and Trotsky in favor of an increased political role for labor unions – a battle which would earn her the epithet "syndicalist" in orthodox Marxist circles, but the cause for which she had become famous, and for which she would be vilified even more than for her syndicalism, was feminism and sexual liberation. The name Alexandra Kollontai was to become synonymous with the sexual liberation which drew people like Max Eastman and Claude McKay to the Soviet Union during the early years of the revolution. And now in the face of five years of unremitting hardship and chaos, including 7 million orphans, over 11 million dead, venereal disease in epidemic proportions, and more prostitution than under the Czar, sexual liberation was getting a bad name. The attitude of Kollontai's successor as the head of the Zhenodtel, Sofia Smidovich, gives one indication of the change in the air. "Why among us, in the North," she wondered, making perhaps an oblique reference to Claude McKay's fifteen minutes of fame during the fall of 1922, "such African passions have developed is beyond my knowledge."[1]

Kollontai left for Oslo in late 1922, thinking it would allow her a chance to do some writing, and at the beginning of her stay this was true. Unfortunately, most of what flowed from her pen in 1922 and 1923 simply sealed her fate as the advocate of an idea which had become associated with another time and another class of people. Sexual revolution had become not only passé; it was looked upon with positive hostility by the women it was supposed to liberate, those who now had an illegitimate child to care for or a disease to cure or a job in a factory which made housework seem idyllic by comparison. In addition to that, the newly "liberated" peasants were faced with the prospect of selling a cow or a horse or something else essential to their livelihood in order to pay for a divorce. Sofia Smidovich may or may not have learned about the downside of sexual liberation in the expensive school of experience. At one point she told a reporter that she loved her children but didn't see them very much because they were in a state-run nursery. But Smidovich, as head of Zhenodtel, had the unenviable task of taking care of the casualties created by the sexual revolution, and in 1922 that seemed like an insurmountable task.

Kollontai used her first few months in Oslo as a way of coming to grips with the sexual liberation with which her name had become associated in the Soviet Union. Her assessment was not without ambivalence. While there she wrote *A Great Love*, giving some expression to her disillusionment at the fact that the revolution did not change the exploitative nature of relations between the sexes. However, even granting the pain which sexual liberation had caused in her own life, Kollontai still spoke in its favor, urging her fellow revolutionaries not to return to the morality of the past but to press on toward a revolutionary future. Given the state of sexual affairs as they actually existed in the Soviet Union at that time, the future held Kollontai's only hope. As if to contradict the lesson she had already learned by writing *A Great Love*, Kollontai wrote a futuristic piece set in 1970 entitled *Soon (In 48 Years)* about children raised in a commune. Like John B. Watson, who was writing the same thing at around the same time, Kollontai assumed that the family would have died out by the 1970s. Being a Marxist meant having an unswerving faith in the future, no matter how disappointing the immediate aftermath of the revolution had been in bringing about better relations between the sexes, and so her pessimism about sexual matters was confined to historical fiction.

At around the same time, Kollontai also published *The Love of Three Generations*, a story which closely paralleled the relationship between Alexandra's generation and that of her liberal mother and that of the even more radical daughter she never had. Olga, the Kollontai character, is committed to "free love." Olga's mother is committed to monogamous marriage, even if it is to two different men at two different times during her life. Embodying the love of the third generation is Zhenia, Olga's daughter, who has an affair with Olga's lover and justifies it in Marxist terms as the logical extension of the abolition of private property now applied to sex. She then gets pregnant and has an abortion, all apparently without the slightest remorse. In Zhenia we see Kollontai fantasizing the woman she always wanted to be but could never become. The Zhenia fantasy was part of Kollontai's Marxist reliance on some future age when the state would wither away and along with it the family and all guilt relating to matters sexual. Zhenia embodies the woman Kollontai's ideology told her she should have been. Kollontai, being both a behaviorist and economic determinist, imagined a generation to come which had no guilt-induced psychic pain because it had no conscience.

Zhenia would go on to become famous as the representative of "the glass of water theory," which Kollontai had not coined but which nonetheless became associated with her name, the idea being that one could satisfy the sex drive as simply as one quenched one's thirst.

In her writings of 1922–23, Kollontai remained true to her vision of "winged Eros," which meant erotic love with any number of people but without possessiveness. But by the time her articles reached print in 1923, her Communist sisters were beginning to see that this justification for promiscuity held little in store for them in terms of benefits. Women were now routinely shaken down for sexual favors on the job; the number of prostitutes had reached the same level it had under the Czar, and because of the liberal divorce laws which Kollontai had drafted and then got passed into law, women were abandoned with no prospect of supporting their children. Disillusionment had become the main legacy of the sexual revolution, and before long disillusionment turned to anger, and the anger sought out Kollontai as its focal point, at least in part because she had become so visible in print. With her elegant prose and equally elegant clothing, Kollontai was seen as the representative of a bygone era and a hated class, the independently wealthy bohemian intellectual, who could escape the consequences of her promiscuity because of her wealth and family connections. If that weren't bad enough, Kollontai then went on to preach that same gospel of promiscuity to women who could not escape its consequences. Beyond that she sought to make her own bad experiences normative by incorporating them into the new marriage law which condoned the divorce which enabled their husbands to abandon them. If the divorce law of 1917 meant liberation, it did so on terms that excluded the interests of the very women it was supposed to liberate. Kollontai's arrogance now seemed inexcusable. And soon women started saying just that.

On July 26, 1923, Polina Vinogradskaia, one of Kollontai's former colleagues at the Zhenodtel, published an attack on her that was the first of many, claiming that "Comrade Kollontai . . . occupies herself now with purely intellectual literary exercises about the 'winged, wingless, etc., Eros'"[2] when the average woman cared far more about feeding her children than about reforming love. Kollontai was guilty of "George Sandism,"[3] which meant if anything that she was trying to impose the fantasies and guilt she had acquired while leading the rootless life of the revolutionary on people whose lives not only had completely different needs, but which were also being damaged beyond repair by the sexual adventurism Kollontai both preached and practiced.

During the summer of 1922 Kollontai's relationship with Dybenko had deteriorated beyond repair. At her suggestion, he had taken a younger mistress, but Kollontai was still jealous. Earlier that year she had received a letter from a young Communist asking her for the specifics of Communist morality. Were there, he wanted to know, any hard and fast rules when it came to sexual behavior? In her answer Kollontai responded by saying that there was no Communist equivalent of the Ten Commandments. Moral behavior was simply whatever the collective determined to be moral behavior. "So long as a member of a collective he loves (nation, class, party) depends on that collective, the commands of that collective will be compulsory for him."[4] It was a touching piece of advice, coming as it did from someone who was now at odds with her "collective." In spite of the fact that all of her writings of 1922 and 1923 were published in officially sanctioned Communist publications, the tide of Communist opinion was turning against Kollontai because it was turning against the sexual liberation which had become associated with her name. The very fact that she had so many pieces published in 1922–23 meant the end of her ability to get published thereafter and the end of her influence as a political and sexual liberationist thinker.

Sofia Smidovich, Kollontai's successor as the head of the Zhenodtel and the lady who wanted to protect Russian women from African sexual passion, has earned the reputation of a sexual demagogue among Kollontai's feminist biographers, but what they describe as her "prejudices" seem more like the sexual version of common sense in light of the devastation sexual liberation was wreaking on Russian women at the time. In response to Lida, a nineteen-year-old *Komsomolka* who had written to her for advice on sexual matters, Smidovich said that for a woman love was "not transient passion, but an extended process of birth, nursing, and childrearing."[5] Smidovich went on to say that the idea of marriage without children wasn't worth discussing because it was so rare. Smidovich also rejected recourse to abortion in all instances save where the life of the mother was threatened. In every other instance, abortion was dismissed as the irresponsible rationalization of young men eager to be rid of their responsibility toward the children they had fathered. "The more Smidovich wrote," complains an obviously unsympathetic Beatrice Farnsworth, "the more it became apparent that she rejected the idea of female sexual freedom. . . . She drew pathetic pictures of abortion waiting rooms where pale, haggard girls yearned hopelessly for maternity. If abortions were illegal, men would not feel justified in 'forcing' them on their wives."[6]

The culmination of the attack on Kollontai took place in 1925 when an interview which Lenin had granted to Klara Zetkin in 1920 was resurrected and republished. It was in this interview that Lenin both articulated and condemned the "glass of water theory," something which by then had become clearly associated with Kollontai's writings and life.

"You must be aware of the famous theory," Lenin told Zetkin, "that in communist society the satisfaction of sexual desires, of love, will be as simple and unimportant as drinking a glass of water. This glass-of-water theory has made our young people mad, quite mad. It has proved fatal to many young boys and girls. Its adherents maintain that it is Marxist. But it is completely un-Marxist. Of course, thirst must be satisfied. But will the normal man in normal circumstances lie down in the gutter and drink out of a puddle, or out of a glass with a rim greasy from many lips? But the social aspect is most important of all. Drinking water is of course an individual affair. But in love two lives are concerned, and a third, a new life arises. It is that which gives it its social interest, which gives rise to a duty towards the community."[7]

Lenin concluded his attack on the "glass-of-water theory," by saying that in his opinion, "the present widespread hypertrophy in sexual matters does not give joy and force to life, but takes it away. In the age of revolution that is bad, very bad."[8]

Lenin's views on sex reflected his pragmatism on other political issues. Just as he was willing to grant a certain measure of entrepreneurship and ownership of private property in order to pull the country out of the chaos caused by eight years of war and revolution, so he was also willing to tolerate a certain amount of sexual common sense for the same reason. Promiscuity was causing chaos, and chaos was threatening the very existence of the revolution. Lenin was in his way the supreme opportunist; his ideas were certainly not based on any traditional view of morals. When pressed for his own views on sexual morality, Lenin told Zetkin: "So we simply take advantage of the few short hours of release that are granted to us – there is nothing binding, no responsibility . . . Of course, there is always the danger of contracting disease. But no man will lie to you about that – no comrade, that is – if you look straight into his eyes and ask for the truth."[9]

Apparently the comrades weren't looking each other straight in the eye when they asked intimate questions because venereal disease rates soared during the early '20s to epidemic proportions, and since there was no cure at the time, that meant a large population of more or less debilitated workers unable to work who continued to spread their disease. Syphilis was becoming a major cultural preoccupation in Europe during the 1920s, one that would have an impact on political events. It loomed large, to give just one example, as a threat to the German nation in Hitler's *Mein Kampf*, a book which appeared in Germany at the same time that the reaction to sexual liberation was building in Russia.

In his interview with Zetkin, Lenin had returned from the grave to condemn Kollontai, and now Kollontai lacked access to party organs to give a response. As if the situation weren't bad enough, events conspired to bring Kollontai's theories into disrepute as well. Kollontai was blamed for a wave of brutal rapes that swept the country during 1925–26, which were precisely the years when the debate over the sexual revolution was taking place. In Leningrad a girl was raped by fifteen students, who then tried to justify what they did by appealing to the withering away of family and morals that communism was supposed to bring about. As a sign that the Communists were appalled by the implementation of their own theories, the defendants were given a show trial, accused of perpetrating "petty bourgeois debauchery" and "sexual chaos," and in the end five of them were sentenced to death. Commenting on the trial in his autobiography, Victor Serge blamed the rapes on "books like those of Alexandra Kollontai," which "propagated an oversimplified theory of free love."[10] Even sympathetic biographers have to concur. "Although she did not openly condone it," Clements writes, "her writings were nevertheless the chief cause of young people's promiscuity in Russia."[11]

In response to articles which Kollontai had published in *Komsomolskaya Pravda* and the legal journal *Worker's Court*, Smidovich renewed her attack on "half-baked notions of Comrade Kollontai"[12] and tried to direct them to a sexual morality that was less toxic than the morality of the "new woman." Since the Communists couldn't really mount an attack on Kollontai's theories based on traditional morality, they chose to frame the discussion in Marxist/materialist terms. Emelian Yarloslavksy claimed that Kollontai's promotion of sexual liberation encouraged the workers of the Soviet Union to "fritter away precious nervous and sexual energy,"[13] energy that might better be put to use building cement factories and hydroelectric plants. Like Lenin, the Communists had to smuggle sexual morality in by the back door, which they did during the marriage debate of 1926. This debate became Kollontai's last-ditch attempt to defend the sexual revolution and the last time she would be allowed to express herself openly on sexual matters. When Kollontai returned to Moscow from Oslo in late December 1925, her life's work hung in the balance. The regime was planning to revise the marriage law she had helped write in 1918.

The marriage debate of 1926 brought the conflict of interest at the heart of the revolution out into the open. The revolution was waged by bohemian intellectuals who lived lives based on bohemian morals but who justified what they were doing by saying it was in the interests of the working class and peasants. When the revolution finally succeeded and they were thrust into a position of power, the bohemian intellectual class immediately imposed its moral system on peasants and workers whose economic existence was threatened by the chaos which sexual liberation wrought in their already fragile and beleaguered lives. Again, the testimony of Kollontai's feminist biographers is especially telling: "Since 1918," Clements writes,

> evidence had been growing that the law enacted with such fanfare during the early days of the revolution had actually increased women's burdens. Community property had been abolished, allowing men to walk out on their wives and take all the family's assets with them. The lack of a clear statement of the father's financial responsibility for his children meant that he could abandon them, and the wife could receive restitution only though litigation. Women who had not registered their marriages with the

government – and there were many such women – were in even greater
difficulty, for they had no legal recourse. A marriage code that had been
designed to liberate was thus enabling some men to victimize dependent
women. By 1925 the government had decided that the law had to be re-
written to reinstitute alimony.[14]

As Clements indicates, the crucial issue was alimony. Alimony was the fault
line which exposed the glaring difference in class interests between the bohemian revolutionaries on the one hand and the women and peasants they
purported to liberate on the other. To give the simplest instance of abuse,
men could avoid paying alimony simply by refusing to register their marriages. This in turn created a welfare burden for the state which it simply
could not bear.

If the absence of alimony was unjust to women, forcing peasants to pay it
on the other hand, in the case of divorce, was unfair to peasants because it
threatened the existence of the entire family and the farm which supported it.
Because the peasants operated to a large extent outside the money economy,
forcing a peasant to come up with 100 rubles in cash meant in effect destroying the farm and impoverishing the entire extended family to pay the divorced wife a pittance that wouldn't support her anyway. Divorce may have
liberated people like Kollontai, but it threatened the very existence of the
peasants in whose name she waged revolution. This became clear in an exchange between a peasant delegate and Public Prosecutor, N. V. Krylenko.

"I divorce my wife," the peasant said. "We have three children. My wife
immediately appeals to the court and I am ordered to pay for the children."

"As there is a common household," the peasant continued referring to
the fact that the *dvor,* or family farm, housed the peasants' extended and not
just immediate family, "the court decides that my entire household must contribute. Why should my brother be punished?"[15]

Krylenko objected that the brother would not be called upon to subsidize
his brother's divorce. This forced the peasant to explain once more the communal nature of the *dvor*, something a Communist should have understood
but evidently didn't, and the devastating effect divorce had on it.

"If we live together," the peasant continued, "the whole family suffers. If
I am ordered to pay 100 rubles and the family owns two cows and one horse,
we shall have to destroy the whole household" to make the alimony payment.
According to Farnsworth, "To many delegates the law still seemed fair neither to peasants nor to workers but only to Nepmen, profiteers of the partial
restoration of capitalism, who alone under the New Economic Policy had the
money for alimony."[16]

Eventually the conflict between the proletariat, especially the Russian
peasants, who wanted property preserved from dissolution by threat of divorce and alimony, and the sexual liberationist engineering of Kollontai,
who wanted to project her own needs onto the proletariat, was resolved by

the new marriage law of 1926 which gave both sides something. Divorce was actually made easier by allowing it on petition from one party instead of two, but peasant property was exempted from alimony claims, thereby preserving the *dvor* from dissolution. The divorce bill of 1926 was one of the last pieces of Soviet legislation which took the interests of peasants into account. Soon Stalin would embark on the forced collectivization of agriculture and his attack on the "Kulaks," a term no one could define with any precision but one which allowed the wholesale driving of the peasants from their land. The marriage bill was no victory for the sexual liberationists either. As Plato had said, tyranny always follows democracy. Like Hitler in Germany, Stalin would use his countrymen's widespread revulsion at the sexual excess of the '20s as a way of imposing a draconian order of undreamt-of severity on the Russian people, one which would last more than twice as long as Hitler's. As with Hitler in Germany, revulsion at the excesses of sexual liberation enabled the imposition of that draconian order.

Kollontai had her say during the debate as well. She urged the party to press on with sexual liberation and not to cling to the morality of the past. She appealed once again to the future, claiming that current difficulties were symptomatic of a transitional age. Society should press on until a generation of Zhenias had come of age. Kollontai defended a system that wasn't working and urged more of the same. But by 1926 the nation had learned the lesson of sexual morality in the expensive school of experience, and no one was listening anymore. The second sexual revolution was now over, and Kollontai retreated into her diplomatic work defeated, never again to say anything publicly on sexual matters.

Kollontai remained defiant in her autobiography: "No matter what further tasks I shall be carrying out, it is perfectly clear to me that the complete liberation of the working woman and the creation of the foundation of a new sexual morality will always remain the highest aim of my activity, and of my life."[17] Well, almost defiant. After writing the above passage, Kollontai ordered it deleted from the published version lest these sentiments get her in trouble with Stalin.

Just as the Germans' defeat in World War I was so unexpected that it generated the myth, exploited by Hitler, that their otherwise invincible military had been stabbed in the back, so the defeat of sexual liberation in Russia engendered its own version of the *Dolchstosslegende*. The sexual revolution had been betrayed by party bureaucrats who betrayed the sexual revolution from within. Wilhelm Reich dedicated his book *The Sexual Revolution (Die Sexualität im Kulturkampf)* to this thesis, and the sexual revolutionaries of the 1960s, the time of the Reich revival, adopted his explanation of the otherwise inexplicable, namely, why anyone would turn against sexual "freedom" and tried sexual revolution once again, with equally predictable results.

Writing in 1970, the year in which Kollontai had fantasized there would

be no more families, but only smiling communist children raised in benevo-
lent Communist nurseries, Germain Greer cites Reich and accuses the Communist Party of betraying the real revolution, which is always sexual:

> The extreme opprobrium which already attached in 1926 to theories of
> sexual and ethical revolution did not diminish as the years passed. Wil-
> helm Reich was excluded from the German Communist Party in 1932,
> and the Institute for Marxism/Leninism in Berlin has omitted all mention
> of the Sexpol movement from its massive historical study of the German
> workers' movement. Some insight into the pressures behind this oblitera-
> tion may be got from Reich's *The Sexual Revolution*, which implies what
> Kollontai would not let herself believe, that repression of the movement
> towards a new sexual morality is the first symptom of betrayal of the revo-
> lution.[18]

What the sexual revolutionaries could never admit to themselves is the
role their heroes – people like Magnus Hirschfeld in Germany and
Alexandra Kollontai in Russia – played in bringing both Hitler and Stalin to
power on the tide of revulsion which swept both countries in reaction to the
social chaos which sexual liberation had created. Sex liberated from the
moral order invariably led to social chaos and personal horror, and social
chaos was always the excuse which the tyrant needed to impose his own
form of draconian order in the place of the moral order which the populace
refused to impose on itself.

In 1936 Stalin recriminalized abortion; In 1937 Volfson attacked the
"coarse animal anti-Marxist views" of Kollontai and proposed in their stead
monogamous marriage.[19] In 1937 Kollontai wrote to Body that "our romantic epoch is completely finished."[20] One year later Dybenko was shot by the
NKVD. "Our relations are cold and distrust is everywhere," she continued. It
was a world that was the opposite of one she proposed, but Kollontai would
never understand how much she had contributed in bringing it about.

Part II, Chapter 17

Moscow, 1926

As if determined to prove Hitler right, in June 1926, Hirschfeld accepted an invitation from the Soviet government and made the sexual version of the Potemkin tour of Russia. Like George Bernard Shaw who toured the Ukraine in the '30s and determined that everyone was happy and well fed, Hirschfeld returned with nothing but praise for the sexual freedoms which the Russians, out of social necessity, were at that very moment in the process of abolishing under Stalin. Now in addition to *Kulturbolschewismus*, Hirschfeld was promoting *Ehebolschewismus*, or marital bolshevism, direct from the capital of the garden variety *Bolschewismus*, which, as Hitler had announced, now had the conquest of Germany as its next goal. Now, one year later, Hirschfeld traveled to Russia as if trying to prove that Hitler was right when he said that "in Russian Bolshevism we see the attempt in the twentieth century on the part of the Jews to gain control of the world."[1] Oblivious to the wind he was putting in Hitler's sails, Hirschfeld returned to Germany singing the praises now of "marital bolshevism" in the Soviet Union, oblivious as well to the fact that the Russians were dismantling the sexual revolution which he praised as the wave of the future:

> We who have seen with our own eyes the consequences of the new marriage law in Russia, find the word "*Ehebolschewismus*" an affront. We in Germany are still ruled by the inequality of the sexes and material conditions in allowing a marriage. I think it right that men and women in Russian need no banns, but can just register their marriage. And either the woman or the man is allowed to register divorce when the marriage is at an end, either because the partners do not love each other any more, or find the menage unsuitable. A so-called "concubinage" is not punishable in Russia either. The Soviets have also nothing against marriage on the basis of friendship [*Kameradschaftsehe*], but the partners have to inform each other about venereal and mental diseases in either family. False reports would be punishable, not with prison sentences, but work in a factory, or a fine of 1000 rubles. This strictness in a *Kameradschaftsehe* seems to me unbelievably out of place. The prescription would be more suitable for a "real" marriage, where apparently it is not demanded.[2]

We have here, of course, the fulfillment of Shelley's dream as articulated in *Queen Mab*. That it should be advocated by a homosexual is not surprising because what it amounted to was the homosexualization of marriage.

Marriage would be reduced to the level of couplings at the Cozy Corner, one of Isherwood and Auden's favorite gay bars in Berlin.

Hirschfeld's view of homosexuality in the Soviet Union was just as out of touch with reality as his views on marriage. In 1930 he was still claiming, in the pages of *Sexology*, that homosexuality was freely expressed in the Soviet Union, when, in fact, it had been recriminalized under Stalin in 1928.[3] Hirschfeld was also fond of saying that homosexuals were constitutionally incapable of cruelty and sympathetic to a fault, a claim which earned him the scorn of fellow sexologist Albert Moll, who cited the Haarmann case, a Weimar version of the homosexual mass murders that have since become household words with names like John Wayne Gacy and Jeffrey Dahmer attached to them. Slowly but surely, Hirschfeld was slipping into the realm of caricature and, with him, the whole idea of sexual science as well. It was fast gaining the reputation of homosexual special pleading. Kinsey would learn that lesson from Hirschfeld, and, as a result, the homosexual bias of the Kinsey Institute was rigorously camouflaged.

Christopher Isherwood, the English author of *Goodbye to Berlin*, which eventually got made into the musical *Cabaret*, described Hirschfeld as "notorious all over Western Europe as a leading expert of homosexuality. Thousands of members of the Third Sex, as he called it, looked up to him as their champion because, throughout his adult life, he had been campaigning for revision of Paragraph 175 of the German Criminal Code."[4] Isherwood not only visited the Institute, he lived there for a while as part of his pilgrimage to the holy land of sexual liberation, as Berlin then was for sodomites in the know. Isherwood's reaction to living at the Institute is a complex mixture of prurience and disgust. "Christopher," Isherwood writes referring, to himself in the third person,

> giggled because he was embarrassed. He was embarrassed because, at last, he was being brought face to face with his tribe. Up to now, he had behaved as though the tribe didn't exist and homosexuality were a private way of life discovered by himself and a few friends. He had always known, of course, that this wasn't true. But now he was forced to admit kinship with these freakish fellow tribesmen and their distasteful customs. And he didn't like it. His first reaction was to blame the Institute. He said to himself: How can they take this stuff so *seriously*?[5]

Such was the reaction of even homosexuals to "sexual science" of the sort popularized by Hirschfeld in Berlin in the '20s. Hirschfeld's institute, as Isherwood and others would learn, was in reality simply a scientific cover for a homosexual bordello. Isherwood makes the same point in his memoir *Christopher and His Kind*:

> Live exhibits were introduced, with such comments as: "Intergrade. Third Division." One of these was a young man who opened his shirt with a modest smile to display two perfectly formed female breasts. [French

novelist and homosexual André] Gide looked on, making a minimum of polite comment, judiciously fingering his chin. He was in full costume as the Great French Novelist, complete with cape. No doubt he thought Hirschfeld's performance hopelessly crude and un-French. Christopher's Gallophobia flared up. Sneering, culture-conceited frog! Suddenly he loved Hirschfeld – at whom he himself had been sneering, a moment before – the silly solemn old professor with his doggy mustache, thick peering spectacles, and clumsy German-Jewish boots. . . . Nevertheless, they were all three of them on the same side, whether Christopher liked it or not. And later he would learn to honor them both, as heroic leaders of his tribe.[6]

Hans Blueher, another homosexual-rights activist at the time, discovered that science was the cover for desire in much the same way. Blueher describes meeting Hirschfeld at the Institute, "sitting on a silk covered fanteuil, legs under him like a turk." Hirschfeld introduced Blueher to a beautiful young man. "A Hermaphrodite," said Hirschfeld. "Why don't you come to me during my office hours tomorrow, you can see him naked then." During the same meeting, an older gentleman in his sixties recited a poem to a sixteen-year-old youth full of yearning. This and the rest of the "scientific" goings-on at the institute convinced Blueher "I was in the middle of a brothel."

Isherwood came to the same conclusion, although he was considerably less appalled by the fact since homosexual contact was the reason he came to Berlin in the first place. When he first passed through German customs, the thought occurred to Isherwood that "This might even become an immigration." When the German passport official asked him the purpose of his journey, he could have truthfully replied, "I'm looking for my homeland and I've come to find out if this is it."[7] His new homeland *in potentia* was so exciting precisely because of the possibilities it offered for engaging in anonymous sex. Isherwood was specific in his memoir about the need to have sex outside his class and found it even more exciting when he was unable to speak the language of the person he had sex with. "Christopher," he writes, after returning to Germany with a greater facility for the language, "found it very odd to be able to chatter away to him in German – odd and a little saddening, because the collapse of their language barrier had buried the magic image of the German Boy."[8]

There is magic in the image of the boy because it seemed to possess what Isherwood lacked, namely, a sort of masculine self-confidence. Sex, as a result, fulfilled a very special need in Isherwood's life, one that made it pointless to seek sexual gratification with women because – and this is the gist of homosexual activity – there is nothing of value he can "draw off" from women. They are not "romantic." Isherwood asked himself:

> Do I now want to go to bed with more women and girls? Of course not, as long as I can have boys. Why do I prefer boys? Because of their shape and

their voices and the smell and the way they move. And boys can be romantic. I can put them into my myth and fall in love with them. Girls can be absolutely beautiful but never romantic. In fact, their utter lack of romance is what I find most likable about them. They're so sensible.[9]

Joseph Nicolosi, in his book *Reparative Therapy of Male Homosexuality*, sees homosexuality as essentially a "male deficit,"[10] which results from family problems, specifically an estrangement between father and son at a crucial stage of the son's psychic development. As a result of this failure to receive the father's approval, the homosexual seeks that sense of masculinity from sexual contact with men who seem to embody what the homosexual feels he lacks. "After years of secrecy, isolation and alienation," Nicolosi writes, describing the psychic odyssey of one of his patients but describing Isherwood's odyssey from Victorian England to decadent Berlin as well, "most young men find the gay world powerfully alluring, with its romantic, sensual, outrageous, and embracing qualities."[11] This psychological need for the father's approval becomes, generally through seduction by an older man, attached to sexual behavior which quickly becomes compulsive and self-destructive. The homosexual, according to Nicolosi, is attracted to "Mysterious men. . . those who possess enigmatic masculine qualities that both perplex and allure the client. Such men are overvalued and even idealized, for they are the embodiment of qualities that the client wishes he had attained for himself."[12]

Women, on the other hand, represent neither beauty nor pleasure, as they do to normal men, but a strange sense of heteronomous duty. Women become a challenge to which the homosexual does not feel adequate, and, with that, comes the sense that liking women and going out with them and having sex with them or marrying them are duties imposed from without by forces alien to the "real self." Whenever Isherwood thinks of "girls," he

> would become suddenly, blindly furious. Damn Nearly Everybody. Girls are what the state and the church and the law and the press and the medical Professional endorse, and command me to desire. My mother endorses them, too. She is silently, brutishly willing me to get married and breed grandchildren for her. Her will is the will of Nearly Everybody, and in their will is my death. My will is to live according to my nature, and to find a place where I can be what I am. . . . But I'll admit this – even if my nature were like theirs, I should still have to fight them, in one way or another. If boys didn't exist, I should have to invent them.[13]

Since sex for the homosexual is essentially an attempt to appropriate the masculinity that he feels lacking in himself from someone who seems to embody it, sex with girls has no purpose, since girls do not have what he lacks. Once it gets construed in this way, sex becomes an essentially vampiric act. It is either sucking the desired object to obtain its male essence, or being sucked for the same purpose. Isherwood makes this vampiric character clear, but in a slightly veiled manner, when he talks about Bubi, the first object of his homosexual attentions in Berlin: "Christopher wanted to keep Bubi all to himself, forever, to possess him utterly, and he knew that this was impossible and absurd. If he had been a savage, he might have solved the problem by eating Bubi – for magical, not gastronomic, reasons."[14]

Again, Isherwood refers to magic, this time to a magic form of cannibalism that will allow him "to keep Bubi all to himself forever, to possess him utterly," in other words, to appropriate forever from Bubi what Isherwood himself lacks. Cannibalism, as the case of Jeffrey Dahmer showed, is nothing more that an extreme form of homosexuality. Both actions involved a "magical" ingestion of the desired characteristics of the other. In this regard, cannibalism is but one term in a series of psychic linkages that radiate out from the vampire, the prime representative of Weimar Republic culture. With the breakdown of the family, the son does not get the needed affirmation of his own masculinity from the father. As a result, sex becomes an attempt to alleviate this male deficit. It becomes an exercise in feeding on another person, which gets fantasized sometimes as cannibalism but, more often than not, as a sucking off of the liquid essence from the desired object in the actual act of fellatio or in the symbolic act of vampirism. (Hirschfeld, by the way, in his *magnum opus* listing all the sexual variants, lists vampirism as one and cites the specific case of a man who could not reach orgasm without first ingesting the blood of his spouse. The Marquis de Sade lists a similar instance in *Justine*.)

In either case, the point of the act is to assuage the hunger-like feeling that is the physical manifestation of the deficit nature of homosexuality, but also of lust. As one of Nicolosi's clients explains about his sexual involvement with a male he admired: "That power and control – I've always wanted to draw off of that, to be so together."[15]

Like a vampire, the homosexual "draws off" that power by sucking, by draining the desired object of its lifeforce and absorbing it into himself in some ritualistic "magical" banquet. Of course, this magic never works; in fact, it only exacerbates the loneliness and inadequacy which drove the homosexual to this form of sexual activity in the first place, and so, what arises in place of the "magic" is a compulsive, addiction-like, vicious circle, in which the homosexual tries to compensate for a sense of masculine inadequacy by engaging in homosexual activity, which, once it's over, only makes the sense of inadequacy seem even worse.

"Immediately after every homosexual experience," one of Nicolosi's clients explains, "it feels like something is missing. The closeness I wanted with another man just didn't happen. I'm left with the feeling that sex is just not what I wanted."[16]

And once again, the vampire provides the best explanation of the cyclic nature of this pseudo-sexual activity. There is the depletion of death, the

craving, the hunger for what the vampire lacks, which is temporarily alleviated by the sucking of fresh blood, but the transformation is eternally temporary, forcing the vampire, or, in this case, the homosexual, to engage in a
never-ending search for new partners/victims so that he can draw off from
them a momentary escape from his feeling of isolation and inadequacy.
"Considering the habit-forming nature of sexual behavior," Nicolosi writes,
"the more homosexually active the client is, the more difficult the course of
treatment."[17]

Hitler, who most certainly saw Murnau's *Nosferatu* conflated the Jew
and the Vampire and the cultural revolutionary and the homosexual into one
figure, symbolized best by Magnus Hirschfeld, as the essence of what was
ailing Germany at the time. Hirschfeld fought back in his way by releasing
confidential information on homosexual Nazis to the SPD newspapers at the
time. But the dynamic of this relationship was more than Hirschfeld could
handle with leaks from the files that the courts sent to his institute for treatment. By his ceaseless campaigning for the abolition of paragraph 175,
Hirschfeld did more than Hitler could have done alone in assuring his rise to
power.

Part II, Chapter 18

Vienna, 1927

On January 30, 1927, Wilhelm Reich, a promising young psychoanalyst of the Freudian school, had a nervous breakdown and had to be taken to the sanitarium at Davos made famous by Thomas Mann's novel *Magic Mountain*. While Reich was at Davos, a group of World War I veterans, who were members of the predominantly Catholic *Heimwehr*, an Austrian militia group, fired on a group of Social Democrats, killing a man and a child. On July 14, the defendants were acquitted, and one day later, the workers in "Red" Vienna organized a strike. After the collapse of the dual monarchy, Austria had been polarized into two, oftentimes armed, camps, fighting for control of the culture. The countryside was controlled by Catholic groups like the *Heimwehr*; the city of Vienna by Reds of various shades ranging from the Social Democrats to the Communists. When the protesting Reds set fire to the courthouse where the acquittal had just been handed down and then prevented the firemen from extinguishing the blaze, violent confrontation became inevitable, and it began just as Reich arrived on the scene with his wife. As Reich approached the courthouse, a police officer gave the order to open fire on the crowd. Three hours later, 89 people were dead and 1,000 had been wounded. It was the worst civil violence to hit Austria since the revolution of 1848, and on the day after the shooting, Reich joined a medical group affiliated with the Communist Party.

Born March 24, 1897, in Galicia in what was then the easternmost end of the Austro-Hungarian empire, Wilhelm Reich was raised by his nonobservant Jewish father to identify with the Empire on a country estate where his father's word was law. He was not allowed to play with peasant children, nor was he allowed to play with Yiddish-speaking Jewish children. As part of his education to the elite land-owning class (Reich's father managed an estate owned by one of their relatives), Reich had a personal tutor for his early years who conducted experiments in biology and animal reproduction.

Reich's own experimentation in the realm of biology and reproduction took on a personal dimension when at the age of eleven and a half he had sexual intercourse with one of the household maids. Shortly thereafter, he discovered that his tutor's interests were more than theoretical as well, when he discovered that he was having an affair with Reich's mother. Reich, who discussed the incident in an early psychiatric article in which he disguises himself as one of his patients, seems to have been torn at this point between an impulse to use his secret knowledge as a way of blackmailing his mother into having intercourse with him or informing his father about his mother's behavior. Eventually, the latter impulse won out and after the predictable calamity which followed the exposure, Reich's mother committed suicide. It was a death for which Reich bore much guilt, but as was his custom throughout his life, Reich took the guilt and projected it onto institutions, in this case sexual morality, for which he blamed whatever evil followed as the consequence of his actions.

Shortly after his mother's death, Reich was packed off to a Gymnasium in Czernowitz, the capital of Bukovina, where the sexual habits he learned at the hands of the chambermaid were transposed to sexual intercourse with prostitutes, which he frequented in the town's whorehouses, where, he noted later, he saw many of his Gymnasium teachers as well. Then in 1915 the world Reich knew as a child collapsed forever when Russian troops overran the family estate where he grew up. He joined the Austrian army, fought on the losing side of that war, and in 1918 found himself demobbed and living in Vienna, the capital of the now-truncated empire, and studying medicine. There, in medical school, not surprisingly given his sexual history and his troubled relationship with his mother, Reich ended up falling under the spell of another dispossessed Jew from the eastern fringe of the Empire with an equally irregular relationship with his mother by the name of Sigmund Freud. On March 1, 1919, Reich wrote in his diary: "Perhaps my own morality objects to it. However, from my own experience and from observation of myself and others, I have become convinced that sexuality is the center around which revolves the whole of social life as well as the inner life of the individual."[1]

Reich quickly immersed himself in the heady atmosphere of post-W.W. I Vienna. He joined Schoenberg's musical society at just about the time that Schoenberg was claiming authorship of the twelve-tone system. Walter Gropius was in Vienna, about to leave for Weimar, where he would take over the Bauhaus school of design, and come up with the definitive modern building. And then there was psychiatry. Reich became a rising star in the new psychoanalytic movement, and perhaps having inherited his father's ability to relate to people from the commanding heights, soon began seeing patients on a regular basis. One of his patients was a wealthy Jewish girl by the name of Annie Pink, with whom he began having sexual relations while she was his patient. When Pink's parents discovered the relationship, Reich married Pink but never seems to have given any indication that his exploitation of his position as therapist was in any way unethical.

Instead of settling Reich down, marriage made him more unhappy. Reich spoke frankly later in life of how multiple sexual partners before marriage increased the likelihood of adultery after marriage, but he seemed incapable of drawing conclusions about his own moral behavior from that otherwise astute observation. Reich instead began to talk about the "sexual dulling" which occurred whenever a man (or a man like Reich) found himself confined within a monogamous relationship. Reich, true to a pattern which would follow him through his life in increasingly bizarre ways, exonerated his own behavior by discovering hitherto unknown principles of human nature, which indicated that everything that had been known up until that time as sexual morality was in fact a vast conspiracy whose intent was the psychic crippling of otherwise healthy individuals. Reich once told Richard Sterba that he experienced sharp feelings of physical discomfort when deprived of sexual intercourse for any length of time.

Even his otherwise totally sympathetic biographer Myron Sharaf is forced to admit that Reich's theories were at heart justifications of his behavior. According to Sharaf, Reich was bitterly critical of the institution of "lifelong, compulsive monogamy," partly on the grounds that a partner chosen in one's twenties may be incompatible with one's psychic development at thirty. "It is clear," Sharaf concludes, "that when he formulated this criticism, he had his own experiences much in mind."[2]

Not surprisingly, Reich began to have affairs with other women, including another patient who died as the result of an abortion he procured for her. As Reich's sexual transgressions increased, so also did his desire to project the guilt which flowed therefrom. This manifested itself in a number of ways. He would fly into fits of jealous rage, accusing his wife of the behavior he himself had engaged in. His behavior became so noticeable that even the sympathetic Sharaf, who even has positive things to say about Reich's later experiments with orgone boxes, claims that "a psychotic process dated from that time."[3] Reich was a man who was constitutionally incapable of ever admitting that he had done something wrong, and so as his transgressions with their burden of guilt increased, so too did his mania for rationalization. The case of his invalid grandmother is instructive in this regard. When his sister-in-law Ottilie asked Reich for some financial assistance for his aged grandmother, fearing that if it were not forthcoming, she might end up in the poorhouse, Reich flew into a rage and denounced his grandmother as a "meddlesome parasite."[4] The normally sympathetic Sharaf gives the following interpretation of Reich's outburst, by saying that Reich

> insisted on making a principle out of what others considered a "failing." To have an affair was one thing; to make a principle of it another. Not to help out a relative was one thing; to assert that it would be wrong to help a "parasite," that one's money was better spent elsewhere, was different. Then there was Reich's anger toward the target of his disapproval. Not only did the grandmother not deserve his support; she merited the "poorhouse."[5]

The more guilt Reich felt, the more he insisted on some theoretical justification for the behavior which caused the guilt. As a result, his devotion to the role of orgasm in psychic health took on proportions that quickly became an embarrassment to the psychiatric profession, leading to the alienation of Paul Federn, his one-time mentor, and eventually to his expulsion from the psychoanalytic profession in the mid-'30s.

It also led to an ever-deepening involvement in politics. The logic is simple enough. The more resistance Reich encountered to his selfish behavior and the theories he generated to rationalize it, the more global he saw the problem. The cause of his dis-ease was not simply blockage in his own psyche; it arose from a culture where blockage was pandemic. Psychic blockage based on the mystical inhibition of healthy orgasm was, in fact, the universal condition of mankind, and as such it could only be combated effectively on a political level and not, as psychoanalysis was attempting, on a personal level. Faced with the choice of conforming his desires to the truths of the moral order, or restructuring the world to suit his illicit desires, Reich unhesitatingly chose the latter course with a consistency that led to megalomania and psychosis as unerringly as night followed day. Reich's life ended in a federal prison in Lewisburg, Pennsylvania, in 1957. It could just as easily have ended in a mental hospital. In fact during the winter of 1927, five years into a marriage made unhappy by compulsive infidelity, Reich landed in Davos, ostensibly to be cured of tuberculosis, but showing at the same time signs of mental breakdown, ostensibly as the result of his conflict with Freud over the role of orgasm in psychic health. Perhaps it was his position as the coddled child, the scion of the landed gentry who could take chambermaids *ad libidum* that led him to feel that the world would capitulate to his disordered desires just as willingly. Whatever the reason, Reich soon concluded that sexual problems (his own and those of other people) required a political solution.

Sensing this early on, Reich became a member of the Social Democratic Party's youth movement almost as soon as he arrived in Vienna, where he became known for the radicality of his views and his vociferous arguments with more moderate colleagues. Reich would eventually get expelled from the Communist Party too, for pretty much the same reason he got expelled from the psychoanalytic association, but along the way he invented something which he called the "sex-pol" movement, which the feminists later expanded to the more familiar term, sexual politics. By the late '20s, Reich was dissatisfied on two fronts. On the personal, psychoanalytic front, he was becoming increasingly impatient with the long, tiresome, and often fruitless regimen of psychoanalysis; on the political front, he was becoming increasingly irked by obtuse Communist officials who held forth on Marxist dogma, in speeches which bored the masses who attended their rallies. Sharaf claims that:

> In the interrelation between actual neuroses and psychoneuroses, Reich
> believed he had found some way of short-cutting the long involved pro-

cess of resistance analysis he had elaborated in the technical seminar. This particular direction would lead him later into very active social efforts, counseling of the young, birth control clinics, and mass meetings dealing with the connections between politics and sexual suppression.[6]

With the messianic glow of a man who had discovered the one truth which is the secret of the universe, Reich started to travel around Vienna from one workers' meeting to another giving lectures not on class conflict but on orgasm. Good orgasm was the basis of psychic and physical well being; the role of government, therefore, should be to insure good orgasm by providing the litany of improvements the neo-Reichians have made a familiar part of our world and government policy by now: sex education, contraception and abortion.

By talking dirty, Reich found that he could hold the attention of even the most distracted crowd. It was a lesson the Americans would learn at around the same time from Freud's nephew Edward Bernays, when that worthy took what he learned by cranking out propaganda during World War I and applied it to the nascent science of advertising. During the spring and summer of 1928 and 1929, Reich took his sex act on the road. The sex-pol team would arrive in a van at some prearranged site, usually at a public park, where they would talk to local workers' groups not about class conflict or the more theoretical aspects of psychoanalysis but rather "the concrete problems of people's sex lives."[7] Reich would talk with the adolescents and men, and Lia Lasky, Reich's lover at the time, would talk to the children, and a gynecologist would talk to the women and either prescribe contraceptive devices or fit the women with them on the spot. Reich had taken his own sexual compulsions and had turned them into a powerful new way to organize the masses. Reich had discovered that one way of mobilizing people was by mobilizing their passions.

Part II, Chapter 19

New York, 1929

On March 31, 1929, a woman by the name of Bertha Hunt stepped into the throng of pedestrians in their Sunday-best clothing marching down Fifth Avenue that was known in New York as the Easter Parade and created a sensation by lighting up a Lucky Strike cigarette. Her action would not have created the reaction it did had not the press already been alerted to what was going to happen in advance. Hunt then told the reporter from the New York *Evening World* that she "first got the idea for this campaign when a man with her in the street asked her to extinguish her cigarette [*sic*] as it embarrassed him. 'I talked it over with my friends, and we decided it was high time something was done about the situation.'"[1]

The press, of course, had been warned in advance that Bertha and her friends were going to light up. They had received a press release informing them that she and her friends would be lighting "torches of freedom" "in the interests of equality of the sexes and to fight another sex taboo."[2] Bertha also mentioned that she and her friends would be marching past "the Baptist church where John D. Rockefeller attends" on the off-chance that he might want to applaud their efforts. At the end of the day, Bertha and her friends told the press that she hoped they had "started something and that these torches of freedom, with no particular brand favored, will smash the discriminatory taboo on cigarettes for women and that our sex will go on breaking down all discriminations."[3]

What Miss Hunt did not tell the reporter is that she was the secretary of a man by the name of Eddie Bernays, nor did she tell him that Mr. Bernays was now a self-styled expert in the new discipline of public relations, who had just received a handsome retainer from the American Tobacco Company to promote cigarette consumption among women. What billed itself as a feminist promotion of the emancipation of women was in reality a public-relations ploy to open a new market for tobacco by getting women addicted to cigarettes. Once again what purported to be a form of sexual liberation was in reality a form of control.

Years later Eddie would wax philosophical about the "torches of freedom" campaign. "Age-old customs, I learned, could be broken down by a dramatic appeal, disseminated by the network of media," he wrote in his memoirs.[4] Eddie failed to note that he had given the essential definition of public relations and advertising as practiced during the 1920s. Like the behaviorists, Eddie might have felt that human beings were infinitely malleable when subjected to orchestrated public opinion, but his insight needs its proper historical context to be understood correctly. What he was really talking about was the erosion of custom by the manipulation of passion. Throughout the century, tradition and morals would prove vulnerable to publicity campaigns which gave "scientific" justification for succumbing to passion. Feminism was no exception to this rule. It entailed the systematic re-engineering of the morals of women as a way of moving them out of the home and into the workforce, thereby lowering wages and weakening the power of organized labor and the working-class family.

Like Ida Rauh-Eastman, Eddie Bernays's wife belonged to the Lucy Stone League, which argued that women should be able to keep their own (i.e., their fathers') names after marriage. Bernays was a fervent feminist, but his was a feminism with an ulterior motive. Eddie, like the feminists of the '70s, wanted to break women's connection with tradition and the home because once that connection was broken women were more open to suggestions emanating from the mass media and those who controlled it – the people, in other words, who paid Eddie's handsome retainers. Eddie promoted smoking among women because he was paid to do so by American Tobacco, but promoting smoking was also a way of breaking tradition's hold over women's minds, and this was important because once that hold was broken these women were more amenable to his suggestions. The "torches of freedom" campaign was a classic instance of using sexual liberation as a form of control. It proposed addiction as a form of freedom. In this, it was an early version of the Virginia Slims, "You've come a long way, baby" campaign, which made repeated reference to the suffragette movement as a way of associating cigarettes with freedom.

In this regard, Eddie's feminism would be consistent with the feminism of the 1970s which was orchestrated for similar reasons. The operative word was, of course, "freedom." Eddie called his attempt to introduce a whole new market segment, namely, women to the joys of nicotine, the "torches of freedom" campaign. Bernays got the term from his Uncle Sigmund's New York disciple A. A. Brill. Bernays had been hired by George Washington Hill, head of American Tobacco, in 1928 for an annual retainer of $25,000. Hill, according to Bernays, "became obsessed by the prospect of winning over the large potential female market for Luckies. 'If I can crack that market, I'll get more than my share of it,'"[5] he told Bernays. Getting women to smoke cigarettes would be "like opening a new gold mine right in our front yard."

At Bernays's suggestion, Hill paid for a consulting session with the Psychoanalyst A. A. Brill, who established the psychological parameters of the campaign. In a manner more Watsonian than Freudian, Brill linked cigarettes with the new woman. Cigarettes stood for liberation from children and child-rearing. Cigarettes were like contraceptives; they were associated with sex without issue. They appealed to women who were willing to neuter themselves sexually in their admiration of masculine qualities. "It is perfectly normal for women to want to smoke cigarettes," Brill told Hill. "The emancipation of women has suppressed many of their feminine desires. More women now do the same work as men do. Many women bear no children; those who do bear have fewer children. Feminine traits are masked. Cigarettes, which are equated with men, become torches of freedom."[6]

Since American Tobacco's revenues jumped by $32 million in 1928 alone after Bernays was hired, Hill was eager to proceed in opening up yet another market, this time women. Perhaps in no campaign were the issues linked more closely than in American Tobacco's torches campaign. In order to sell more cigarettes, Bernays intuitively understood that he had to attack traditional sources of authority. Since the taboo against women smoking was largely sexual – women who smoked were seen as sluts and whores – the way to expand the market was to denigrate sexual morality as repressive. All the gullible consumer saw was women wanting to be free, whereas in reality the women who marched in the parade smoking their Luckies were being manipulated by the tobacco industry into a sort of bondage that was both literal, in terms of physical addiction, and moral in the sense that it was motivated by a subliminal understanding of sexual liberation.

By 1929 neither advertising nor behaviorism thought of man as completely malleable in the hands of the omnipotent conditioner. Instead, they began to understand man in a sense which was much closer to the understanding of traditional rational psychology, with a heavy dose of Augustinian pessimism. Man may have been a rational animal, but his choices were motivated more often than not by passion and not by reason, and since the vocabulary of passion was nothing if not limited, the advertisers had recourse to the same themes over and over again. "The behavioral approach," according to Buckley,

> ignored questions of the rationality or irrationality of mind and emphasized instead the malleability of human behavior. In the emerging field of public relations, no less a figure than Freud's nephew, Edward Bernays, underlined this assumption. "The group mind," he wrote, "does not *think* in the strict sense of the word. In place of thoughts it has impulses, habits, emotions." Bernays urged advertisers to "make customers" such as any other commodity is produced by transforming the raw material of emotions into habits of consumption.[7]

The secret was to associate a product in some subliminal way with the consumer's sexual desires. Just as Freud had learned that he could exploit the sexual desires of his rich patients for financial gain, so Eddie was now learning how to do the same thing to large groups of people through advertising. The contribution behaviorism made was that just about any commodity could be associated with sexual desire with the correct application of conditioned reflex. Gradually, the idea of infinite malleability gave way to the use of conditioned reflex in associating a particular product with one of the passions that the classical writers had known about all along. Since the advertisers hadn't and couldn't create another human being, they were forced to deal with human beings as the Creator had made them and as people like St. Augustine had explicated their weaknesses. Public relations and advertising meant making use of the insights of Augustine about fallen human nature, while at the same time denying his authority in the matter. "A man," Augustine had written, "has as many masters as he has vices." Since advertising was not dealing with an infinitely malleable creature, people like Bernays and Watson would eventually have to implement any real form of control on Augustine's terms and not on their own, and that meant getting involved with sexual passion as a form of control.

Brill's input figured not only in the "torches of freedom" Easter Parade but also in the advertising campaign which followed on its heels. Before the billboards went up advertising Lucky Strikes for women, Brill would have his say. The original idea of two men and one woman was scratched as too confusing. "Two people should appear, one man and one woman. That is life," Bernays recalled the psychologist saying. "Nor should a woman offer two men a package of cigarettes. The cigarette is a phallic symbol, to be offered by a man to a woman. Every normal man or woman can identify with such a message."[8] Brill's analysis of the cigarette billboards was, according to Bernays, the first instance of Freudian advertising. Brill's input was a concrete example of what Bernays described in his 1928 book, *Propaganda*, when he claimed that "The use of psychoanalysis as the basis of advertising is common today." Brill's "lightning analysis" of the cigarette poster, however, "may have been the first instance of its application to advertising."

Bernays clearly had Brill (and himself) in mind when he claimed in *Propaganda* that "we are dominated by the relatively small number of persons – a trifling fraction of our hundred and twenty million – who understand the mental processes and social patterns of the masses."[9] These are the people who "pull the wires which control the public mind, who harness old forces and contrive new ways to bind and guide the world."[10] These "invisible governors" are necessary "to the orderly functioning of our group life."[11] Without them there would be no one to "bring order out of chaos."

Part II, Chapter 20

Berlin, 1929

By the time Wilhelm Reich arrived in Berlin in 1929, the Weimar Republic was in its last days. Wilhelm Reich was also a father by this time, and in keeping with his already established program of mobilizing youth for sexual liberation, his sex-pol work, Reich sent his daughter off to be educated in a Communist children's collective. Eva, his daughter by Annie Pink Reich, disliked the collective, with its poor food and dirty living conditions, intensely. Eventually, she returned to Reich's apartment with the ultimatum: "You are the Communist. You go live at the center. I'm staying here."[1]

The incident did not quench Reich's ardor for using children for political causes. Reich continued to send Eva to Communist summer camps and to take part in Communist marches with other children. During one march, Eva and the other children were chanting "Hunger! Hunger! Give us bread," when someone came up to her and pinched her cheek and told her that she wasn't hungry, prompting Reich's daughter to admit to herself then and others later that what the passerby said was true. "I'm not hungry. I am lying."[2]

In *The Mass Psychology of Fascism*, Reich relates a similar incident, so similar in fact that it may be a disguised version of the same story, just as the patient Reich wrote about in his article on incest was in fact a disguised version of himself. "A girl of some seven years of age," Reich writes,

> who was consciously brought up without any idea of God suddenly developed a compulsion to pray. It was compulsive because she really didn't want to pray and felt it to be against her better judgment. The background of this compulsion to pray is as follows: The child was in the habit of masturbating before going to sleep every night. One night, for some reason, she was afraid to do so; instead she had the impulse to kneel down in front of her bed and to recite a prayer similar to the one quoted above. "If I pray, I won't be afraid." *It was on the day she renounced masturbation for the first time that fear appeared.* Whence this self-renunciation? She told her father, who had her complete confidence, that a few months earlier she had had an unpleasant experience while on vacation. As so many children, she and a boy had played at having sexual intercourse ("had played Mommy and Daddy"). Another boy had suddenly come upon them and had shouted "shame" at them. Though she had been told by her parents that there was nothing wrong with such games, she felt ashamed and, in place of the game, masturbated before going to sleep. One evening, shortly before the appearance of the compulsion to pray, she had walked home from a house party with several other children. Along the way they

had sung revolutionary songs. An old woman passed them who reminded her of the witch in Hänsel and Gretel. This old woman had called out to them: "May the Devil take you – you band of atheists." That evening, when she wanted to masturbate again, it struck her for the first time that perhaps there really was a God who sees and punishes. Unconsciously, she had associated the old woman's threat with the experience with the boy. Now she too began to struggle against masturbation, became afraid, and to allay her fear began to pray compulsively. *Prayer had taken the place of sexual gratification.*[3]

Reich's daughter Eva was between the ages of six and nine during her years in Berlin. She was living through the collapse of her parents' marriage as well as the collapse of the Weimar Republic and was intimately involved in both catastrophes. Sharaf says she was "suffering from certain symptoms" at the time "night terrors, temper tantrums and obsessive ideas."[4] Like the girl in the report, Eva had been exposed to the same sort of sexual stimuli, but ultimately her identity is beside the point. What Reich discovered in the girl's behavior was a fundamental truth of sexual politics, one discovered by the Catholic Church long ago. It can be formulated in either of two ways: either masturbation destroys your prayer life, or prayer destroys your ability to enjoy masturbation. The two forms of activity are psychically mutually exclusive. Anyone interested in changing the default settings of the culture would notice that the settings are binary as well: either/or. There are only two cultural options. Either the state fosters prayer, belief in God, the authority of the father as God's representative, and the social order based on morals, or it fosters masturbation, which is to say, illicit sexual activity, which brings about an inability to pray, the "death" of God, the loss of authority by the father, revolution, and – the evidence from the Russian Revolution which Reich ignored – social chaos.

Reich felt that "sex economy" was "self-regulating." If repression were lifted, in other words, a healthy, happy, peaceful world would follow. It was the same sort of thinking his followers promoted during the '60s, until Altamount and the Manson murders, when Plato's view reasserted itself and horror films, like *Alien* and *Halloween*, became popular as part of the inchoate cultural reaction to the sexual revolution.

In the *Mass Psychology of Fascism*, Reich never lets us forget that in promoting masturbation, he has ulterior motives. He was at war with the Catholic Church over whose values would control the culture. His attempt to conflate fascism and Catholicism, something which Paul Blanshard and Theodor Adorno would attempt at a later date, belies the reality of the situation since Nazism was a homosexual, pagan revival cult. In *The Sexual Revolution*, Reich cites Gorki, who gives some indication of the reputation the Nazis had internationally, when he writes, "In Germany, there is already a slogan: 'Exterminate homosexuality and Fascism will disappear.'"[5] Recent sexual politics has found it expedient to expunge the truth about the homosexual proclivities of the Nazis from the historical record. The view of Mussolini, that homosexuality was "*il visio tedesco*" can still be found in artifacts like Lucino Visconti's film *The Damned*. Trying to preserve a united sexual front, apologists for the regime now claim that homosexuals were victims of the holocaust instead of, as the case of SA chief Ernst Roehm makes clear, members of the party which perpetrated it. Following Reich's direction (but ignoring simultaneously the anti-homosexual evidence in his books), the Left decided after the war that mysticism meant Catholicism, and that fascism was just a particularly virulent form of Catholicism, a view which still has widespread currency among the Left to this day. The Catholic Church, as Reich predicted in *The Mass Psychology of Fascism*, remains the villain in this psychodrama because it inhibits masturbation.

"In all cases treated by character analysis," he wrote, "it was clearly shown that mystical sentiments develop from the fear of masturbation in the form of a general feeling of guilt. It is difficult to understand how this fact could have been overlooked by analytic research until now. One's own conscience, the internalized admonitions and threats of the parents and teachers, are objectified in the idea of God."[6]

The truth Reich discovered is that both systems – the mystical and sexual liberationist – are of one piece and are at the same time mutually exclusive. There can be no pluralism here. The state must come down with both feet in favor of one or the other form of government: either the rule of reason and self-control or the rule of sexual revolution – either prayer or masturbation. It can't promote both. What Reich discovered is the mechanism whereby sexual deviance, especially among the young, can be used for political effect. "Let us return to our little girl," Reich writes:

> The compulsion to pray disappeared when she was made aware of the origin of her fear; this awareness made it possible for her to masturbate again without feelings of guilt. As improbable as this incident may appear, it is pregnant with meaning for sex-economy. *It shows how the mystical contagion of our youth could be prevented* [my emphasis].[7]

The separation of Church and State could be seen as a way of avoiding this conflict, but the closer one examines the respective historical instances, the more irrelevant such legal fictions become. To begin with, we are talking primarily about morals, and the moral order is the possession of no one religion, although some adhere to it more faithfully than others. Whether it took place in Berlin in rebellion against Prussian Protestantism or in Austria against the Catholic Church or in the United States against a government which claimed to be neutral when it came to religion, the essential outline of the struggle remained the same. The crucial political struggle, according to Reich, was over who controlled sexual mores because Reich understood, like Nietzsche and Euripides before him, that he who controls sex controls the state. The state can tolerate only those mores compatible with its system of values, and there are only two sets of mutually exclusive values to choose from, those symbolized in the life of the Communist girl by the poles of prayer and masturbation. What Reich understood as the result of his sex-pol work is that belief follows from behavior, and that the social order of the classical state can only maintain its existence under certain conditions. The classical state must foster virtue; the revolutionary state must foster vice. The revolutionary can foster vice as a way of bringing down the classical state, but vice leads sooner or later to the demise of the revolutionary state as well, as the Soviets found out, in the short run in 1926 when they attempted to stem the tide of decadence, and in the long run when the Soviet empire collapsed for good in 1989.

The counter-revolutionary who attempts to practice virtue violates, whether he knows it or not, the established religion of the revolutionary state, which is the worship of Dionysos. The illusion of the Enlightenment, the illusion which Reich shared when he formulated his idea of some self-regulating sex economy, is that vice may be harnessed for the general good. Reich's contribution to the political ends of revolution was a technique based on a knowledge of psychology unavailable to revolutionaries like Marx, Engels, and Lenin. "We concur," Reich writes, "with the opinion of many researchers that all forms of religious mysticism mean mental darkness and narrow-mindedness. . . . We differ from them only in terms of our serious determination to combat mysticism and superstition successfully, and to convert our knowledge into hard practice."[8]

Reich here is most probably drawing on his own disappointing experiences as a Communist, wasting time debating things like the existence of God. If, as Marx said, the goal of communism was to change the world, not to understand it, Reich was now claiming that he had discovered the *élan vital* which was the source of all social change, namely, sex. Once he discovered how effective sexual liberation was in combating "mysticism," the revolutionary could dispense with all debate and concentrate simply on changing behavior – sexual behavior, to be specific. To do that, since everyone is inclined to act on sexual impulses anyway, all the sexual revolutionary need do is discover a rationalization for what everyone wants to do anyway: "We do not discuss the existence or nonexistence of God," Reich writes, "we merely eliminate the sexual repressions and dissolve the infantile ties to the parents."[9] Once a person can be persuaded to act in a certain way sexually, all debate is unnecessary. Thought follows naturally from action, especially actions as intimately rooted as the sexual. "The inescapable conclusion of all this," Reich concludes, "is that a clear sexual consciousness and a natural regulation of sexual life must foredoom every form of mysticism; that, in other words, natural sexuality is the arch-enemy of mystical religion. By carrying on an anti-sexual fight wherever it can, making it the core of its dogmas and putting it in the foreground of its mass propaganda, the church only attests to the correctness of this interpretation."[10] By getting people to act contrary to the Church's teaching on sexual morals, Reich and his followers automatically limited its political influence. The logical conclusion of this is also clear: the total sexualization of a culture would mean the total extinction of the Church and the classical state based on the moral law. The real revolutionaries could triumph over repression – and this was the program of the '60s – just by having a good time, by smoking dope, getting laid and listening to subversive music. Their political agenda came directly from Reich.

So, in the final analysis, the sexual options the little girl faced became a paradigm for the political options of control faced by the state: either masturbation or prayer. If the sexual revolutionary can get a significant number of the young involved in masturbation – through either sex education or the widespread dissemination of pornography – the political reach of "reaction," as in, say, the influence of the Catholic Church, is dramatically shortened. "The process of the *uprooting* of mysticism" is accomplished more effectively, in other words, by deviant sexual behavior than by debate over the existence of God or the nth thesis of the Sixth International. Reich felt that sexual license would win out over self-control in every instance, and he probably felt that way based on his own experiences, where self-control lost consistently. But he also was empirical enough to see the same phenomenon in others. He mentions "clerics" who find it impossible to continue in their vocation once they have "felt on their own body" the "physical consequences" of sexual license.[11]

> The uncovering of the sex-economic processes, which nourish religious mysticism, will lead sooner or later to its practical elimination, no matter how often the mystics run for tar and feathers. *Sexual consciousness and mystical sentiments cannot coexist.* Natural sexuality and mystical sentiments are the same in terms of their energy, so long as the former is repressed and can be easily transformed into mystical excitation.[12]

The political implications of this insight are clear, but they can be put into effect only after a cultural revolution has taken control of the instruments of culture. In other words, most people will not act out sexually in any consistent fashion on their own. They will be cowed by social convention into inhibition or brought by it to repentance. Reich noticed the inhibiting effect of culture on his patients. He was also quick to draw a conclusion which was the converse of the one he discovered. If women are inhibited sexually by culture, changes in the imagery promoted by the culture will bring about a change in behavior, which will in turn bring about a change in values.

> When I talk to a sexually inhibited woman in my office about her sexual needs, I am confronted with her entire moralistic apparatus. It is difficult for me to get through to her and to convince her of anything. If, however, the same woman is exposed to a mass atmosphere, is present, for instance, at a rally at which sexual needs are discussed clearly and openly in medi-

cal and social terms, then she doesn't feel herself to be alone. After all, the others are also listening to "forbidden things." Her individual moralistic inhibition is offset by a collective atmosphere of sexual affirmation, a new sex-economic morality, which can paralyze (not eliminate!) her sexual negation because she herself has had similar thoughts when she was alone. Secretly, she herself has mourned her lost joy of life or yearned for sexual happiness. The sexual need is given confidence by the mass situation; it assumes a socially accepted status. When the subject is broached correctly, the sexual demand proves to have far more appeal than the demand for asceticism and renunciation; it is more human, more closely related to the personality, unreservedly affirmed by everyone. Thus, it is not a question of helping, but of making suppression conscious, of dragging the fight between sexuality and mysticism into the light of consciousness, of bringing it to a head under the pressure of a mass ideology and translating it into social action.[13]

"Bringing it to a head under the pressure of mass ideology" means that in order to succeed, the sexual revolutionary must sexualize public life by the mass dissemination of sexual imagery. Pornography is an important educator in this regard. It defines what is permissible by expanding the idea of what is possible. One thinks also of the music festivals of the '60s, where at places like Woodstock, the women literally danced naked on the mountainside, as Euripides explained in *The Bacchae*. Widespread dissemination of pornography was crucial in breaking down "mystical" inhibition among women. Only when these women had the impression that many other people were engaging in the same form of deviant behavior did it become plausible for them to engage in such behavior themselves.

Lisa Palac says as much in her recent memoir, *The Edge of the Bed*. She was raised a Catholic in a Polish family in Chicago ("I tell them I was raised Catholic. We all have a good yuk over that one. Ah, Catholicism. Where sex is dirty and the thrill of transgression is endless!"[14]), but before long it becomes clear that her real teachers were the sexualized post-'60s mass media. As Reich said, "It is clear that such an atmosphere of sexual affirmation can be created only by a powerful international sex-economic organization" and that organization in this instance was not the Catholic Church. It was "pop culture" as the purveyor of transgressive imagery: "Pop culture," Palac tells us,

> glued me to my friends, expanded my vocabulary and, of course, tipped me off to the big world of sexual possibilities. It was the type of sex education where I learned through suggestion and nuance. But if I wanted more than nuance, all I had to do was dig through the neighbor's trash to find it, or under my older brother's bed, or in the basement where my father had a couple copies of *Hustler* hidden above his fishing tackle.[15]

Music, as Plato warned in the *Republic*, was also a "teacher" who could corrupt or edify. Palac, under the sway of popular culture, listened to nothing but corrupting music. She mentions Alice Cooper, in particular, which " exposed me to a cornerstone idea of modern sexual philosophy: Gender is a construct." Television was the medium which made this education possible: "Like music, television – in addition to being my baby-sitter, dinner date, humanities professor, political adviser and late-night companion – was another sexual secret agent."[16] Ultimately the TV morphed into the computer monitor, which became the medium for the dissemination of hard-core pornography, which is an aid to masturbation, which is what Palac promotes in her book as liberation from repression under the name of cybersex.

In Palac's book we find the mirror image to the story that Reich recounts in the *Mass Psychology of Fascism*. Lisa Palac is a Catholic girl who stopped praying when she started masturbating; the girl Reich mentions was a Communist girl who stopped masturbating when she started praying. In both instances, the sexual dimensions of this political struggle between the Enlightenment and the Catholic Church are clear. Whoever determines sexual mores rules the state. Those things remain constant. The details change but the big picture remains. The cultural revolution in the United States in the '60s was a replay of the cultural revolution in the German-speaking world between the wars. Reich and his followers, according to Sharaf, "wanted to wrest education from Catholic hands and influence the minds of the young. The idea was to develop the whole person; the aim, to build a 'socialist man.'"[17]

The battle there was simply transposed to American soil when many of the cultural bolsheviks were expelled by the Nazis and found asylum in the United States. The "bitter political polarization between the Christian Socialists with their rural Catholic constituency, many still devoted to the monarchy, and the urban, secularly oriented Social Democrats"[18] simply got transposed to America, where representatives of the declining Protestant elite opened up their institutions to people like Reich, and Paul Tillich and Walter Gropius and the other cultural bolsheviks as a way of waging war on American Catholics, who were reaping the political fruits of long-term demographic expansion, one which would accelerate over the baby boom years of 1946–64 after the war. The sexual revolution of the 1960s was the cultural counterattack against that Catholic resurgence. During the '60s, the purpose of sexual liberation was to convince Catholic women to use contraceptives. During the '90s, the purpose of sexual liberation was to convince their daughters to masturbate and consume pornography. The goal in both instances is control. In the first instance, the purpose was to wrest the sexual lives of Catholic women from the hands of the Church as a way of weakening Catholic political power, which was based on Catholic demographics. The fact that the Church lost that battle meant that the sexual exploitation of women would expand in both degree and kind. By the 1990s, the daughters of women who took the pill were being exploited financially and sexually in a more extreme and explicit fashion. The only thing that changed during those thirty years was the extent of the bondage. "The ideological project of "liberation from repression by exposure to transgressive imagery," according to Joseph McCarroll, "is to be found in the media with its continuous contraction of the boundaries of the impermissible in what can be depicted, said, sung, discussed and approved, and in the schools, universities and training institutions where technique and programmes are used to induce students to by-pass rational self-control of emotions, imagination, desire, choice and behaviour."[19]

This "liberation from repression" is "being transformed in the new education by a socialised, collectivised type of groupwork into a covert form of social control and psychic homogenisation" of the sort promoted in sex education classes, whose purpose is to promote masturbation under the guise of "safe sex." No matter what the guise, the result is the same, morals are portrayed as an instance of "repression," thereby robbing the child of reason, his first line of defense against exploitation:

> Self-control, especially modesty, chastity and fidelity in the sexual area, are regarded as "repression," an emotional disorder from which the public and school-children need to be "liberated." One of the principal tools proposed to bring about this "liberation" is exposure to transgressive imagery which invites the participant to suspend or bypass the form of rational self-control proposed by Judeo-Christian and philosophical traditional moral knowledge and virtues.[20]

If morality is a form of repression, then reason is repressive, and if reason is repressive, then man can become free only by becoming irrational, but once he becomes irrational, the only thing that drives him to act is his appetites, his impulses, and his passions. But once man is driven by his passions, he loses all control of his actions. Thus freedom of this sort, as the ancients rightly saw, becomes a form of slavery. Those who advocate freedom of this sort are promoting, whether they understand it or not, a form of social control because the motive for action which previously lay in reason has now been replaced by the stimulation of passion. Those who control the stimuli now control the stimulated. The purpose of transgressive imagery is social control. Those who relinquish reason are controlled by their passions, which are exploited financially and politically by those who control the flow of transgressive imagery. The people who profit financially from promoting the imagery contribute to the election of those who will protect it politically, and so a form of political control evolves from a system of financial exploitation.

But more consequences follow as well. One of the lessons of the past 2,000 years is that passions can be manipulated from without. Plato understood the role that music could play in manipulating the emotions and as a result felt that in the ideal republic certain modes should not be played in the presence of the young, those who had not had sufficient experience in governing the passions. The same thing is true of certain images. The rise of technology has not changed human nature, but it has made it possible to manipulate people in ways unimagined in the past. Muzak calls itself "musical engineering," which is to say, that technology has now made it possible to manipulate people musically to get them to work faster or buy more. Technology has enabled the unscrupulous to turn the warnings of Plato on their head and use music as a way of controlling people's behavior.

The same is *a fortiori* true of "transgressive imagery." It blinds reason by inflaming the passions. To say that a man who follows his appetites beyond the boundaries of the moral law is then liberating himself from repression is the same thing as saying he is enslaving himself. As with the girl who either prays or masturbates, there are only two options here. Either a man imposes self-control on himself by adhering to the moral order, which is reason applied to behavior, or he submits to his passions, which means he submits to control from the outside, either to the passion itself or to the people who exploit the passion for their own benefit, either economic or political.

Now those who identify with their desires, people like Wilhelm Reich, do not see things that way, but all this means is that they do not see things correctly. If a horse gallops off toward a cliff with a man on his back, it is only in some analogous sense of the word to say that the man is riding the horse. The horse is in charge and will bring both itself and its "rider" to their deaths unless the man reasserts control. The same is true of unbridled passions, which also tend toward death as their ultimate end. Appetites belong to man only if he asserts rational control over them. If the opposite holds true, the man belongs to his appetites. Addiction is the only word which seems to convey this truth in our culture. And so just as Joe Camel can induce children to smoke, sex education and pornography can induce them to masturbate. Both are forms of social control, but only the former is recognized as such. The latter is invariably construed as "liberation from repression," not because it is so, but because the regime wants us to believe it is so. Unless passion is under rational control, it is invariably under the control of someone else, especially in an advertising culture like ours, which is based on manipulation. These are the only two options; either you control yourself according to the moral law or your passions control you in the absence of moral control or – and this is the modern variant on the latter possibility – someone controls you through the manipulation of your passions. It took Reich's evil genius to see how passion could be mobilized politically to bring about the revolutionary society.

Reich, of course, being an heir of the Enlightenment, felt that in the discovery of what he called "sex-economy" he had discovered a self-regulating form of sexuality, in other words a middle way between the moral order as proposed by Moses and the Catholic Church and the social anarchy which was tearing the Soviet Union apart at the time. Upon closer examination, however, sex economy turns out to be a thinly disguised rationalization of whatever desires Reich felt most deeply. So Reich tries to distinguish between the essentially bipolar options surrounding adultery in the following way. Not for Reich the simple dichotomy of either being faithful or not faithful. Instead he proposes a third way, which upon closer analysis turns out to be special pleading for his own personal derelictions: "There is a difference," Reich tells us, "between a man irresponsibly deserting his wife and children because of a superficial relationship and the man who, because he is sexually healthy, makes an unbearably oppressive marriage which he cannot dissolve more bearable by maintaining a secret happy relationship with another woman."[21]

The above passage could have been written when he left Annie Pink Reich for Elsa Lindenberg or when he left Elsa Lindenberg for Ilse Ollendorf or when he cheated on Ilse Ollendorf by having an affair with one of his American admirers. Or it could have been based on a whole lifetime of experience of this sort. What is obvious is that there is no difference, especially when one eliminates the exculpating adjectives. Just as obvious is the fact that Reich's principles were in fact thinly disguised rationalizations of his actions, and he was too blind to see the obvious. As soon as one understands that his notion of a self-regulating sex economy is nothing more than rationalized sexual misbehavior, the perceptive reader is left back at square one with the two alternatives Plato adumbrated in the *Republic*. There is either reason or social chaos. Liberation from oppression turns out to be a transitional period from the former to the latter condition.

Reich is, of course, the philosopher of "liberation from repression," having forged his ideology out of materials garnered from Marx and Freud. Reich remains the one writer who understands the practical consequences of using sexuality as a form of revolutionary politics best. "He who has once seen the intense eyes and faces at sex-economic assemblies;" Reich tells us, describing his own experience doing sex-pol work, "he who has heard and has had to answer the hundreds of questions relating to the most personal sphere of human existence – that man has also arrived at the unshakable conviction that social dynamite lies buried here."[22]

What Reich failed to see is that when the social dynamite goes off, the social order gets destroyed in the process. He could have learned that lesson from the Soviet commissars when he visited the Soviet Union in 1929, but his desires were so imperious they would not let him listen. Instead, he goes on to say, that only those who are willing to promote childhood masturbation will be able to set off this social dynamite. Reactionaries who shy away from exploiting sexuality in this fashion, even those who hide behind the labels of Marxism and Leninism, will never be able to put this social dynamite to its full destructive use.

As should be obvious by now, the full use of Reich's "social dynamite" didn't take place in his lifetime. It took place during the '60s, when the Reich revival brought about widespread dissemination of his writings. In 1968 revolution swept through Berlin, but this time it happened over here in America, Reich's new home too, and his books helped make it happen.

On August 19, 1939 Reich boarded the *Stavanger Fjord*, the last ship out of Norway before World War II broke out on September 3. Theodore Wolfe and Walter Briehl, two American students of Reich, had persuaded the New School for Social Research to put up several thousand dollars guaranteeing his salary. Reich had previously tried to get financial support from the Rockefellers for his bion research, but they turned him down. By landing a position at the New School, he got that support indirectly anyway.

From there Reich made contact through Alexander Lowen with the Settlement House connected with the Union Theological Seminary in New York City, then home to Paul Tillich, another refugee from Nazi Germany. Lowen arranged a speaking engagement for Reich to the people of the Union because he felt that Reich "could change the world" by explaining the social implications of the sexual problems of youth. Reich was now doing sex-pol work in New York City connected with the staff of the most prestigious Protestant seminary in the country.

His influence expanded from there, often through Reichian therapy. One by one, the prominent New York-based cultural revolutionaries made contact with Reich's ideas about how to bring down the state by changing sexual mores. Paul Goodman, author of the immensely influential book, *Growing Up Absurd*, was in therapy with Alexander Lowen around 1945. Goodman, who was if anything more licentious than Reich, wrote a glowing review of Reich's work, which prompted Reich to meet with him personally. Saul Bellow was in therapy with one of Reich's students during the '40s as well and wrote both *The Adventures of Augie March* and *Henderson the Rain King* under Reich's spell. Norman Mailer was never in Reichian therapy, but anyone who has read his essay "The White Negro" can see Reich's influence in Mailer's insistence on good orgasm as the *summum bonum*.

Part II, Chapter 21

Berlin, 1930

On December 4, 1930, Magnus Hirschfeld addressed the American Society for Medical History on the topic of sexology, a lecture arranged by Dr. Harry Benjamin, who would soon play a pivotal role in bringing Hirschfeld's ideas to America. Hirschfeld was introduced by Victor Robinson, son of Hirschfeld's friend, Dr. William Robinson, who was to become, like Benjamin, a colleague and early supporter of Alfred Kinsey, who would establish the American version of the *Institut für Sexualwissenschaft* in Morrison Hall, at the University of Indiana in Bloomington and go on to become famous with the publication of his Kinsey reports on human sexuality in 1948 and 1953. Hirschfeld's fame by 1930 was certainly world-wide, if for no other reason than because of his involvement in the World Congresses for Sexual Reform, and this most certainly guaranteed him an audience in New York, where German émigrés like Benjamin had made their mark in the medical profession.

But there were other reasons to embark on a lecture tour as well, the most pressing, of course, being the increasingly dangerous political situation in Germany, which did not abate while Hirschfeld was away. As a result, one lecture in New York expanded into a lecture tour that would take in the entire country. Hirschfeld spent six weeks in New York, and then four weeks in both Chicago and San Francisco. In addition to that, he spread his pro-homosexual message to auto workers in Detroit, as well as audiences in Philadelphia, Newark, and Los Angeles. When it came time to leave, Hirschfeld decided to go home the long way and embarked on a lecture tour in China, which led him to other ports in the Far East and eventually to India, where, in addition to speaking on homosexuality, he made a pilgrimage to see Annie Besant, then head of the theosophy movement.

It was in China that he picked up Tao Li, the young man who would eventually accompany him for the rest of the trip, which, because of the worsening political situation in Germany, never ended up being a trip home but rather a trip into exile in France. In his biography of Hitler, Joachim Fest talked about "an overwhelming sense of anxiety" pervading Europe at the time. "It was," he concluded, "above all and immediately, fear of the revolution, that 'grande peur,' which had haunted the dreams of the European bourgeoisie from the time of the French Revolution throughout the entire nineteenth century."[1] Isherwood had talked about it in his memoir. Mary Wollstonecraft had mentioned the same thing. Now fear that revolution always begat was stalking the streets of Berlin.

On May 6, 1933, Nemesis arrived at the doors of the *Institut für Sexual Wissenschaft* wearing a brown uniform. Magnus Hirschfeld was not there to receive him; he watched the newsreel version of the Nazi sacking of the institute and subsequent "book burning" from the relative security of a movie theater in France. Erwin Hansen, the "sturdy Communist" who used to beat Karl Giese to fulfill his masochistic needs, was at the Institute when the Nazis arrived early in the morning. Since the arrival of the truck-loads of Nazi students was accompanied by the playing of a brass band, in keeping with Hitler's penchant for public theater, Hansen went down to open the door for the invading army, but the Nazi youth decided to break it down anyway.

Isherwood, who describes the raiding of the institute in his memoir, was struck by the fact that the Nazis seemed to know what they were looking for. The point of the raid was not so much the destruction of Hirschfeld's institute and his dirty pictures but rather the removal of the incriminating evidence which had accumulated at the institute, documenting the homosexual behavior of leading Nazis. Ernst Roehm, in this regard, was a prime suspect, as Hirschfeld had mentioned in his already cited letter. Roehm would eventually pay the price for his homosexuality as well, when, a year later, he and his homosexual friends were gunned down in a German resort by SS men carrying out Hitler's orders. Hitler was only responding to pressure from Mussolini and other sources and saw at the time a political opportunity to consolidate his power that was too tempting to pass up. With the dissolution of the Institute and the arrival of the Nazi nemesis at the pinnacle of power in Germany, *Kulturbolschewismus* began to fold its tents and disappear, heading more often than not to the West, and ending up in the United States in general and, for people like Isherwood, Schoenberg, Thomas Mann, Franz Werfel, Peter Lorre, Conrad Veidt, and Berthold and Salka Viertel, in Hollywood in particular. The same monster that had come from England to Germany was on the move again; like Christopher Isherwood, who came to Berlin because of boys, it left Berlin because of boys as well, and like, Isherwood, when it left Berlin, it went to Hollywood as its new abode. Isherwood's ticket to Hollywood had a German connection. He went there as Berthold Viertel's assistant because he spoke German. Isherwood would stay in Hollywood for other reasons, and his stay there would have other consequences. As Isherwood was escaping from Germany, he met one of his gay friends from Berlin who had a new boy and a fresh case of syphilis. Isherwood escaped unharmed by either disease or the police, who were now hunting down foreigners.

Karl Giese, on the other hand, was not so fortunate. He escaped to France with much of the Hirschfeld archival material, only to commit suicide there in 1938. The archival material, however, did not remain in France. It ended up at the Kinsey Institute in Bloomington, Indiana.

Part II, Chapter 22

Moscow, 1930

In 1930 Wilhelm Reich traveled to the Soviet Union. Reich's success in attracting crowds with his sex-pol work created as much consternation in the Communist Party as it had in the psychoanalytic profession. One of the main reasons for the consternation was the recent experiences of the Communists in the Soviet Union. Following the revolution of 1917, Russia became a Mecca for devotees of free love from the West, who traveled to the Soviet Union during the heyday of sexual liberation there during the brief time of relative prosperity brought about by Lenin's New Economic Policy. By the time Reich was promoting sex-pol in Vienna and Berlin, the pendulum was swinging in the opposite direction. Lenin was dead, and Stalin was ushering in the tyrannical reaction to sexual license which Plato had discussed in the *Republic*. Sharaf tries to paint a picture of political cowardice on the part of Communist officials but fails to take into account the devastating effect that government-fostered sexual liberation had on Soviet society. Reich devoted a large part of his book *The Sexual Revolution*, to explaining why the sexual revolution had failed in the Soviet Union. When Reich finally got to the Soviet Union, the signs of retreat from the earlier days of sexual liberation under Lenin were everywhere apparent and only increased with time. What Hitler was to the Weimar Republic, Stalin was to the Communist regime under Lenin. The "freedom" of unfettered passion had led inexorably to tyranny and reaction.

Reich spends much time in his book recounting the evidence of sexual reaction and even more time trying to refute it. By the early '30s, the commissars all sounded like Catholic priests in their condemnation of sexual immorality, not because they believed in the Gospel of Jesus Christ but because they had discovered the social utility of sexual morality the hard way, in the expensive school of experience: "Not even the peasants have been spared the sexual crisis," wrote one Soviet thinker discussing the outcome of sexual liberation in the Soviet Union. "Like an infectious disease which knows neither rank nor station, it pours down from castles and villas into the drab dwellings of the workers, glances into peaceful homesteads, rushes into the numb Russian village. . . . There is no defense against the sexual crisis."[1]

Reich, who became a Communist for sexual reasons, was stunned by the reversal of sexual revolution that was taking place in the Soviet Union. What he saw as moral cowardice, a failure to be consistently revolutionary, which is to say revolutionary in personal as well as economic matters, the Soviet authorities saw simply as a matter of social survival. Sexual revolution had unleashed so much chaos in the Soviet Union that the very existence of the social fabric was threatened, and that, in turn, necessitated reaction, a retreat to within the bounds of the moral order, an order whose existence had been discovered in the hard school of necessity.

The evidence kept mounting, and Reich kept denying it as fast as the Soviets decided that they had to act on it. "On June 16, 1935," Reich writes,

> the Norwegian newspaper *Arbeiderbladet* reported that the Soviet government had resorted to mass raids against delinquent children. In addition to describing acts of theft, burglary, and looting, *Arbeiderbladet* reported that these children were infected with venereal diseases: "Like a pestilential flood, these children carry the infection from one place to another."[2]

In the same year, Soviet citizens could read in *Pravda* that "in the Soviet Union, only great, pure, and proud love should be cause for a marriage" as well as articles by medical experts describing the damage abortion did to the female body. "I have to compare work in the field of abortion," wrote a Dr. Kirilov in 1932 in Kiev, "with the extermination of the first-born in ancient Egypt who had to die because of the sins of their fathers who devastated man and society."[3] All of the above quotes are cited in Reich's book with increasing rage on his part.

On his visit to the Soviet Union, Reich asked one doctor how the People's Commissariat for Health dealt with masturbation among adolescents and was told that one tried to "divert" them from this sort of behavior. When Reich responded by explaining the medical point of view, "which in Austrian and some German sexual-counseling centers had become a matter of course, that a guilt-ridden adolescent should be counseled so as to enable him to experience gratification in masturbation," the idea was rejected as "horrendous."[4] Similarly, the famous "glass of water" theory, which postulated that satisfying sexual urges should be as uninhibited, simple, and as inconsequential as drinking a glass of water had also undergone some revision. Lenin's criticism of the "glass of water theory," concluding that love takes three, was almost a verbatim account of marriage from the Catholic priests who would assure the young couple that a successful marriage needed three people – man, woman, and God. Now it was coming from the mouths of Communist officials, who were complaining about "African passions." Whatever the cause, the antidote was clear enough: "Abstinence!" Reich can hardly contain his disgust at this point. Abstinence was nothing more than "a slogan which was as convenient as it was catastrophic and impossible to realize."[5] At least Reich found it impossible to realize.

Reich's alternative was to pour more gasoline on the fire. His solution was more sexual liberation, an idea which was so out of line with recent experience in the Soviet Union that it probably hastened his expulsion from the Communist Party. Reich never really backed off from his insistence that the Soviet Union hadn't gone far enough. In the late '40s, in a subsequent introduction to *The Sexual Revolution*, Reich wrote that "what Soviet Russia tried to resolve by force within a brief time span during the 1920s, is being accomplished today throughout the whole world in a slower but far more thorough manner."[6] The Soviets, according to Reich, made a big mistake by thinking that an economic revolution would change sexual relations automatically. In other words they thought that the cultural revolution would follow from the economic revolution automatically. When it did not, they retreated on the social front into reaction. The perceptive observer might say at this point that the Soviets discovered the moral order the hard way, but Reich was never that perceptive. According to Reich, the Communists simply didn't understand sex and how the transformation of society demanded first of all transformation of the citizens' sexual lives. Sexual revolution could not just be left to take care of itself in the aftermath of the revolution as a merely private matter: "Just as the economic and political revolution, so the sexual revolution must be consciously understood and guided forward."[7] .

In other words, according to Reich, the Communists in the Soviet Union got it backwards. Their revolution failed because "the carrier and cultivator of this revolution, the psychic structure of man, was not qualitatively changed by the social revolution."[8] An economic revolution is the necessary but not sufficient condition for "liberation." What the Russian revolutionaries should have done after the fall of the Czar was use the revolution as an attempt to work for the abolition of the family, in other words, the abolition of sexual morality, which is the main hindrance to good orgasm and, therefore, human happiness. Reich reveals himself as a bit obtuse here. He fails to see that this is precisely what happened in the Soviet Union during the '20s, and that it was precisely this attempt to engineer human nature that created the resulting chaos and the reaction which followed. Reich's desires were so imperious that he never questioned them. Since sexual desire itself is above question, then the source of the problem must lie elsewhere; it must lie with the inadequacy of Communist thinking on sexuality. "Since the Communist Party," Reich wrote, "had not formed any opinion on the sexual revolution, and since they could not master the revolutionizing upheaval of life with the historical analysis of Engels alone (which furnished merely the social background but not the essence of the problem), a struggle broke out which will show all future generations the birth pangs of a cultural revolution."[9]

For Reich, in other words, the Russian Revolution was to pave the way for sexual revolution, but the two events were two different things, and the first in no way led necessarily or automatically to the second. Neither Marx nor Engels knew enough about sex to bring about the cultural revolution that would bring about man's ultimate "liberation." Trotsky was no better than the rest, and "therefore . . . the Soviet sexual revolution had no theoretical basis."[10] "Lenin, himself," Reich stressed, "emphasized that the sexual revolution as well as the process of social sexuality in general had not been understood at all from the viewpoint of dialectical materialism, and that it would take enormous experience to master it."[11]

Given his megalomania, it is not surprising to learn that Reich felt that he was the man to master what Lenin failed to understand. And, in a certain sense, he was. Reich was going to be the Joshua who would lead the chosen people into the sexual version of the promised land while Moses – in political terms Marx and in sexual terms Freud – watched from the other side of the Jordan River. We see here an example of Reich, the Freudian, lecturing his left-wing fathers, just as we saw Reich the political operative lecturing Freud. In explaining the state of sexual revolution in the Soviet Union in the '20s in this fashion, Reich held out hope to the left-wing revolutionaries of the '60s, when the Reich boom began, that they could succeed where their revolutionary fathers had failed by simply being more liberated sexually.

At the same time, Reich was offering another, more dangerous insight into how sexual passion could be used as a way of mobilizing the masses and ultimately controlling them. The new revolution would be based not on economic grievance but on sexual grievance. Reich was smart enough to see that by pandering to the sexual passions of the masses he was also on his way to creating out of them a political movement which he, as the guarantor of their illicit desires, could control. In other words, forget about grilling young Communists with questions like, "What was the nth thesis of the Sixth World Congress?" The best way to mobilize children politically is to get them to become sexually active. Actions speak louder than words, and sexual actions spoke loudest of all. Sexually active children were natural revolutionaries, and so to bring about the real revolution, then, all that people like Reich and his followers had to do was make children sexually active:

> In contrast, a child whose motor activity is completely free, and whose natural sexuality has been liberated in sexual play, will oppose strictly authoritarian, ascetic influences. Political reaction can always compete with revolutionary education in the authoritarian, superficial influencing of children. But it can never do so in the realm of sexual education. No reactionary ideology or political orientation can ever accomplish for children what a social revolution can with respect to their sexual life. In terms of processions, marches, songs, banners, and uniforms, however, reaction undoubtedly has more to offer. We thus see the revolutionary structuring of the child must involve the freeing of his biological, sexual motility. This is indisputable.[12]

A careful reading of this passage makes certain things clear. For one, it is virtually impossible to tell whether Reich is trying to liberate young people sexually or control them politically because in allowing them to gratify their sexual impulses he is also turning them into foot-soldiers for his revolution.

Reich can only mobilize the masses by appealing to their sexual passions. It is their desire for sexual liberation that moves them politically. So Reich can only "liberate" them by controlling them. He can only free them by mobilizing them politically, and he can only mobilize them politically by unleashing their passions. Ultimately, this paradox can never be resolved because liberation and control are one and the same thing when it comes to freeing sexual passion from rational control. Passion can be mobilized to bring down a regime, as in the case of the French Revolution, but once the moral order had been abandoned, the destruction of the social order would soon follow, as Plato said it would. So within ten years of the Russian Revolution, the Soviet leadership was faced with a choice: they could either continue to foster revolutionary sexuality and watch the social order disintegrate, with all of the dangers that entailed in light of a looming conflict with Germany, or they could repudiate their "revolutionary" principles and institute the reaction that would restore social order. The Communists chose the latter way; Reich chose the former, and as a result, a parting of the ways was inevitable.

In 1930 Reich moved to Berlin, partly as an expression of his disappointment with Freud and the psychiatric profession, but also as a way of becoming more politically involved through his sex-pol work with the workers in this increasingly decadent city. He arrived in Berlin just in time to see the decadence of the Weimar Republic reach a shrieking crescendo and its simultaneous denouement at the hands of the Nazis who came to power by telling the average German that they would put an end to *Kulturbolschewismus* of the sort Reich was promoting. Reich, in other words, brought about the very reaction he sought to thwart by his promotion of sex-pol. *Kulturbolschewismus*, in other words, brought Hitler to power. It was a fact which neither Reich nor his left-wing epigones could ever admit. Perhaps this was why he was so keen on finding a scapegoat for what he brought about. Just as *The Sexual Revolution* sought to explain how the Soviets betrayed the sexual revolution, so *The Mass Psychology of Fascism* attempted to explain why the German workers chose reaction over sexual progress of the sort Reich was promoting. Instead of seeing Hitler as the German version of Stalin, putting into effect the dictum of Plato that democracy always begat tyranny, Reich laid the blame for Hitler at the feet of "mysticism," i.e., Christianity, which inhibited orgasm by its promotion of sexual morality and thereby, according to what was essentially plumbing psychology, created a vast pool of resentment which eventuated in the sadistic excesses of the Nazis. Reich postulated a theory whereby sexual repression led to totalitarianism, when in fact the exact opposite was the case. The Weimar Republic, with its *Kulturbolschewismus* and sexual decadence, brought Hitler to power, not sexual morality. Subsequent apologists for the left made the same intellectual mistake, if we can call something this willful a mistake. By the late '40s when Erich Fromm, Theodor Adorno and Richard Hofstadter joined in the same chorus, a consensus had all but formed among the left. In his book *The Authoritarian Personality*, Adorno created the definitive post-war left-wing explanation of Fascism, by claiming that it came about as a result of "repression," i.e., conservative forces which were increasingly identified with the Catholic Church. It wasn't as Plato might have said, sexual excess leading to tyrannical reaction. According to Reich, Adorno, and Fromm, it was repression, a verdict which set the stage for the sexual revolution 20 years later, as once again, the Left tried to overthrow repression through sexual excess.

In Reich's scenario, the father was the villain. Because, as Reich had learned from Freud, God was an exalted father, any attack on the father was an attack on God and vice versa. "The strict father," according to Reich, "who denies the fulfillment of the child's desires, is God's representative on earth and, in the fantasy of the child, is the executioner of God's will."[13] Reich discovered through his sex-pol work, especially in Berlin, that the best way to attack the social system which rested on the authority of the father, who represented the authority of God the father on earth, was to persuade the young person to engage in sexual activity before marriage. Intercourse was preferred, but masturbation was just as good, and in fact in many ways it was better because it was easier to accomplish. Once the child engaged in illicit sexual activity, he was immune to the allure of reaction, Reich's term for morality. "Children," he wrote, "do not believe in God. It is when they have to learn to suppress the sexual excitation that goes hand in hand with masturbation that the belief in God generally becomes embedded in them."[14] Reich was, of course, not slow to draw political implications from this truth. Encouraging children to masturbate was simply another way of blocking their ability to believe in God. Once God was out of the picture, the authority of the father disappeared, and with that the whole social order based on the moral order, which is to say social order in any real sense of the word. Masturbation, in other words, was a way of bringing down the state. It was an instrument for revolution, no matter what the Communists said to the contrary. The Communists betrayed the revolution when they repudiated sexual liberation, which the Soviet Union had to do to prevent the slide into anarchy. Widespread sexual immorality brought the Soviet Union to the brink of anarchy and social collapse because sexual morality was, as the Catholics had always maintained, the cornerstone of social order. The fact that the commissars were now saying the same thing only increased Reich's chagrin and made him more determined to prosecute the real revolution, which was at its heart sexual:

> With the elimination of the spastic condition in the genital musculature, the idea of God and the fear of the father always lose ground. Hence, the genital spasm not only represents the physiological anchoring of religious fear in the human structure, but at the same time it also produces the pleasure anxiety that becomes the core of every religious morality. . . . Genital

shyness and pleasure anxiety remain the energetic core of all anti-sexual patriarchal religions.[15]

According to Reich, sex was the best tool for revolution. Illicit sexual activity was also the best prophylaxis against belief in God, and with God and the family out of the picture, revolutionaries like Reich were guaranteed success in their political struggle. By exploiting sexual passion, Reich could mobilize the masses in ways unheard of in the past. The Soviets found that doing this exacted a steep price in terms of social disorder, but Reich simply ignored what they were saying, as did the generation which came of age during the '60s and attempted to put Reich's theories into practice. The '60s were in effect the Reichian revolution. It was this revolution which put the current regime in power. Which is why the regime promotes this kind of behavior by encouraging the dissemination of pornography, and why the office of surgeon general has become inextricably tied to the promotion of abortion, contraception, and, under the Clinton Administration, masturbation. Joycelynn Elders made perfectly clear at the end of her tenure as surgeon general of the United States, that sex education and masturbation were one and the same thing. They serve the same purpose, namely, the prohibition of prayer and a social order based on morals and the father's authority. Masturbation is simply the act of putting sexual enlightenment and, therefore, social revolution into practice. It was an insight she could have gained from Reich. "We cannot enlighten children and adolescents," Reich wrote in *The Sexual Revolution*,

> and at the same time prohibit sexual games and masturbation. We cannot keep the truth about the function of sexual gratification a secret. We can only tell the truth and let life run its course completely free of interference. Sexual potency and physical vigor and beauty must become the permanent ideals of the revolutionary freedom movement.[16]

Part II, Chapter 23

Washington, 1930

In 1930, in a ruling known as *Young's Rubber Corporation v. C. I. Lee & Co., Inc.,* the United States Supreme Court in adjudicating what was a trademark dispute between two condom manufacturers seemed to affirm the legality of interstate commerce in contraceptives. "Seemed" seemed to be the appropriate word because just a few months earlier the same Court had affirmed the so-called Comstock Act's definition of obscenity when it ruled against the distribution of a sex education pamphlet distributed by Mary Ware Dennett. The ambiguity arising from the disparity between the two decisions was seen as a window of opportunity by the birth controllers, and they lost no time in attempting to capitalize on it.

On November 5, 1930, Eleanor Dwight Jones, head of the American Birth Control League, wrote to Lawrence B. Dunham, then director of the Bureau of Social Hygiene, announcing that "the time is ripe for us to launch throughout the country a systematic campaign against the present disgenic [*sic*] multiplication of the unfit." "The public," Mrs. Jones continued, "is beginning to realize that scientific, constructive philanthropy does not merely care for the diseased, the poor and the degenerated, but takes steps to prevent the birth of babies destined to be paupers, invalids, degenerates, or all three."[1]

Mrs. Jones never got around to saying how she knew that certain babies were "destined to be paupers, invalids, degenerates, or all three." But, in a sense, she didn't have to. The instrument which allowed Mrs. Jones to peer crystal-ball-like into the future and discern the moral character of as yet unborn infants was known as the eugenics movement, and the tenets of that movement were held just as firmly by the Rockefeller foundations, from whom Mrs. Jones was soliciting a large donation. Latter-day feminists, from biographers of Margaret Sanger to filmmakers who sanitized her life to delegates to the various United Nations's conferences on population, like to portray the birth-control movement as somehow different from the eugenics movement, but the simple fact of the matter is that they were one and the same thing. Contraception was a form of ethnic warfare from its inception, and the promoters of it were very aware of that fact and willing to fund it on precisely those terms, terms which Mrs. Jones makes abundantly clear in her letter, and terms which, since the Rockefellers gave her $10,000 during the Depression in response, they must have found acceptable as well.

"The second half of our program," Mrs. Jones continued, again hammering on the eugenics issue,

> is to secure the cooperation of the social agencies in these cities in getting the women of the lowest social and economic class to avail themselves of the contraceptive advice offered them. . . . We . . . are concentrating on the practical work of making it possible for the lower social classes to practice birth control. For the good of the race, people of poor stock – incompetent and sickly – should have few or no children, and fortunately they want few or no children. In this matter private interest is in accord with public interest. That is the strength of the birth control movement.[2]

"We are not planning any legislative work," Jones wrote in conclusion, "because we do not feel that it is urgent. The federal law does not prohibit physicians from prescribing contraception orally, but only the mailing and expressing of contraceptive information and supplies and this is not enforced. . . . only two states, Pennsylvania and Mississippi, prohibit physicians from giving birth control information, and the Pennsylvania law is so dead that three birth control clinics are now being publicly operated in that state with no interference, even from Roman Catholic police."[3]

Mrs. Jones's dismissive reference to "legislative work" was a disguised dig at her rival at the Rockefeller funding trough, Margaret Sanger, who had been ousted as head of the American Birth Control League after a two-year absence in Europe in 1928 and was now running a clinic and heading an organization called The National Committee on Federal Legislation for Birth Control, which was trying to overturn the federal ban on importing and/or transporting information on contraceptive devices or the devices themselves which was part of the Comstock Act of 1873. By 1930 the NCFLBC had been able to get bills introduced into both houses of Congress, and a showdown was in the offing as a result.

The eugenics movement was based on a simple fact of life: Once the upper classes became habituated to the use of contraception, they became equally aware that other groups were not using contraception at all, and the long-term result of having few or no children while other ethnic groups were having many – the term they used for it was "differential fertility" – was the gradual loss of political and economic ascendancy, a fact which was not lost on one of the most politically active groups of undesirables, namely, the Catholics.

Msgr. John A. Ryan, a professor of moral theology at Catholic University and head of the National Catholic Welfare Conference, used to end his speeches attacking contraception with the following peroration:

> More than seventeen centuries ago the great Christian writer, Tertullian, addressed the superior classes of his day, the rulers of the Roman empire, in these words of triumph: "We are but of yesterday, yet we fill your cities, islands, forts, towns, councils, camps, tribes, decuries, the palace, the sen-

ate, the forum; we have left you only the temples." Paraphrasing the statement, those who reject birth control might thus challenge the superior
classes of today: "We, too, are of yesterday, but tomorrow we shall be the
majority. We shall occupy and dominate every sphere of activity; the
farm, the factory, the countinghouse, the schools, the professions, the
press, the legislature. We shall dominate because we shall have the numbers and the intelligence, and above all, the moral strength to struggle, to
endure and to persevere. To you we shall leave the gods and goddesses
which you have made to your own image and likeness, the divinities of
ease and enjoyment and mediocrity. We shall leave to you the comforts of
decadence and the sentence of extinction."[4]

Born on May 25, 1869 in Vermillion, Minnesota, twenty miles south of
St. Paul, Ryan was ten years older than Margaret Sanger, but like her he was
born into a large immigrant Irish family. Ryan was raised on a farm in the
sort of immigrant community which advertising as an instrument of national
consciousness was supposed to obliterate. "The members of the farm community where I was born and reared," he wrote in his autobiography:

> were all Irish immigrants and all Catholics. In the district school which I
> attended there was at no time in my experience even one non-Catholic pu-
> pil. The adjoining community to the south was composed entirely of Ger-
> mans, likewise all Catholic. With them the people of our Irish settlement
> got along very well. There were no quarrels, enmities or friction between
> the two groups, although we Irish regarded our German neighbors as
> somewhat inferior. As a matter of fact, they were superior to us in some
> respects. In those days, however, we shut our eyes to these qualities and
> kept our attention only on the characteristics we thought marked us as a
> superior race.[5]

The disparity between the "superior race" of the Irish and their position in
nineteenth-century America as despised menials created in Ryan an acute
awareness of social justice issues. Ryan cast his first vote for the populist
candidate for governor of Minnesota and defended that vote in his autobiography at the end of his life. As the Democratic Party, however, began to import populist planks into its platform, Ryan shifted his allegiance, becoming
in the end such a firm supporter of Franklin D. Roosevelt that one biographer
referred to him as the "Right Reverend New Dealer." Along the way, Ryan
found confirmation and support for his views in the epoch-making encyclical
Rerum Novarum issued in 1892 by Pope Leo XIII. Consistent with that encyclical, and its sequel *Quadragesimo Anno*, issued by Pope Pius XI forty
years later, Ryan condemned both communism and socialism on the left and
the Manchester School of laissez-faire economic thought on the right, and
proposed instead the primacy of the worker as person, with all of the spiritual
rights that went with that status, and not simply as a means of production according to some materialist anthropology which benefited factory owners,
be they capitalists or commissars. Ryan's first book was entitled *The Living*

Wage, and in it he attacked the Malthusian desire for low birth rates coupled with low wages. Margaret Sanger was in many ways the paradigmatic example of what he opposed. As soon as she began promoting birth control, she stopped talking about wages. The solution to every instance of economic injustice was reducing the birthrate.

The issue was twofold for Ryan: Birth control was intrinsically evil, and he wasted no opportunity saying that. On April 8, 1924, ten years before his showdown with Margaret Sanger, Ryan testified before Congress that the Catholic Church held that contraception was "immoral – everlastingly, essentially, fundamentally immoral . . . more so than even adultery, because adultery does not commit an outrage upon nature, nor pervert nature's functions."[6] But Ryan also felt that birth control was against the interests of the working man because as soon as it was given legitimacy it would be used, as it had always been and as Margaret Sanger was using it during the '30s, as an excuse to stifle pressure for higher wages.

Writing for the 1906 edition of the *Catholic Encyclopedia*, Msgr. John Ryan explained how Malthus's theories mirrored the pessimism of his age. In doing this he also explained how population control went hand in hand with economic oppression. By 1798 the bloom was off the French Revolution. The euphoria of Wordsworth and Coleridge, of their walking tour of France, had given way to reaction and to Robespierre's reign of terror. "The French Revolution," according to Ryan's analysis, "had caused the downfall of the old social system without improving the condition of the French people."[7] In addition to that a series of bad harvests had impoverished the agricultural districts of England, to the point where she was forced to import food from abroad causing an imbalance in trade payments and an increase in debt.

Most significantly, however, English textile industries were becoming mechanized and, as a result, increasingly productive, creating not only new employment but also whole new towns of Englishmen working in the new factories. The new technology in effect created an increase in the population, but the material benefits accruing from the new mechanization of industry accrued solely to the owners of the machinery. The Luddites were just one form of protest against this new development. Instead of protesting the unequal distribution of wealth, the Luddites smashed the mechanized looms that were putting them out of work.

The first edition of Malthus's essay was written in response to William Godwin's utopian tract on political justice, which claimed that poverty was traceable to defective social institutions. The solution to poverty, according to Godwin, was equitable distribution of the world's goods, a process that could be set in motion by political revolution. We see, in other words, in the Godwin-Malthus exchange the first hazy outline of the forces that would lead to the Russian Revolution and the bi-polar political landscape of much of the twentieth century: socialism, on the one hand, arguing for revolutionary changes in the social order, and the Malthusian ideology, which became the dominant ideology in England and America, arguing that these social changes would make no difference because increases in population would always outstrip increases in the food supply, as it was doing at that particular period in England. The former system proposed a human nature that was completely malleable, and the latter a social order that was the immutable result of "iron" laws, which invariably benefited the wealthy classes.

Malthus generalized from the economic system in England at the time and came up, in the second edition of his book, with his famous "law" that population always increases geometrically while food increases only arithmetically. Hence, Malthus claimed that there would always be too little food to go around following any increase of population. Given a situation in which the wealth of a nation increases as a whole, but one at the same time in which the working classes receive none of the benefits of that increase in wealth, increased production will always seem to mean simultaneously an increase in population and a decrease in the amount of resources available to that population. Ryan claimed that this was simply another way of saying that the increase in productivity was not shared equitably. The increase in wealth went to the expansion of industry, which involved hiring more workers, but the wages of the workers remained fixed and low, causing the population of the workers to increase but with no concomitant increase in purchasing power. As a result, farm prices remained low and as a result of that farm production did not increase. Before long the wealth will become so concentrated in the hands of so few people that economic exchange will collapse, as it did periodically throughout the nineteenth and well into the twentieth century.

Malthus's "law," Ryan argued, was both an ideology, tailored to the interests of the ruling class in England, and a self-fulfilling prophecy. It became the lens through which economic injustice was rationalized in both England and America. Transmuted into a "law" of the sort proposed by Newtonian physics, the unequal distribution of wealth was transformed from a case of injustice into an inescapable scientific fact, and therefore a justification for maintaining an intolerably unjust status quo. Malthus may not have intended it as such, but his ideas quickly took on a life of their own and were adopted by the wealthy classes of both England and America as the rationale for their essentially unjust business practices. Malthus was, in fact, eventually to repudiate his belief that human populations would inevitably follow the growth trajectory of animal populations, but by then his ideas had taken on a life of their own, primarily because of their benefit to those who wanted to maintain the status quo.

As Scrooge had shown in *A Christmas Carol*, the Malthusian ideology had always been used by the plutocrats as a way of diverting employees who wanted higher wages into thinking about ways to "decrease the surplus population." Birth control had always been the Malthusian answer to the worker clamoring for higher wages, and in 1930 Margaret Sanger, sensing a new window of opportunity, tried to use the Depression as a way of promoting birth control. The Rockefellers and the ethnic interests they represented funded Sanger to do just this: promote birth control as the solution to the poverty of the Depression and divert the working classes thereby from asking for higher wages. One of the examples Sanger used before Congress is telling in this regard.

"My husband," Sanger began citing a letter from an anonymous woman impoverished by the Depression, "has been gone for more than 2 weeks looking for work, and I don't know where he is. I am almost barefoot and have only 2 badly worn dresses . . . and my 15 yr. old girl has been in the hosp. since Jan. So, Mrs. Sanger, if my poor miserable letter that comes from bitterness and want can help other wives and mothers to have less babies and more common sense and comfort then for God's sake use it."[8]

Touching as we may find this letter, it is not self-evident that this woman's poverty came from the number of children she had, nor is it self-evident that if Margaret Sanger sent her birth control that her husband would get a job, or if he did get a job that it would pay him a decent wage, one whereby he could support his family. In fact, as the Malthusian ideology developed, it became, more often than not, an excuse not to pay a decent wage to the worker, since any increase in his well-being would only urge him to procreate more fervently, thereby once more outstripping the resources available to him. Ever since Malthus argued with Godwin, the world had been divided between those who thought that the world was overpopulated and wanted to reduce the number of people and those who thought it was underdeveloped and wanted to increase the worker's wages.

In the early 1930s, after the stock-market crash, the discussion broke out anew with Margaret Sanger taking the former position and Msgr. John Ryan taking the latter. In 1934 both Margaret Sanger and Msgr. John A. Ryan testified before the Congress of the United States on a bill that would make it legal to distribute contraceptives. By the 1930s, Margaret Sanger had become completely attached to the goals of the eugenics movement, partially because she was being funded by the plutocrat aristocracy who wanted wages kept low, partially because they were involved in a covert *Kulturkampf* against the Catholic Church and partially because of the exigencies of her own sexual life, which was rescued from the guilt she felt at the death of her daughter by transmuting birth control into a sacred cause. *The Birth Control Review* adopted the language of eugenics as its rationale for the spread of birth control. Sanger proposed a "nation of thoroughbreds" as well as "more children from the fit, less from the unfit," the latter category being defined in chiefly racial terms, "Hebrews, Slavs" Catholics and Negroes. She was also an enthusiastic supporter of Hitler's eugenic policies, offering the pages of

The Birth Control Review to Ernst Rudin of Hitler's Kaiser Wilhelm institute.

Not surprisingly Sanger in her testimony before Congress touted birth control as the solution to the country's economic ills. "Population," she testified, "is pressing upon the relief agencies, upon the dole, upon the other fellow's job. . . . What is to become of the children of the millions whose parents are today unemployed?"[9]

The answer to that question is now apparent, just as apparent as the answers to the dire questions raised by those fearing a "population explosion" in the '60s are now answered as well. The children of the unemployed got enough to eat as soon as their fathers got a decent wage, which came about generally as the economy recovered after the United States entered World War II.

Ryan in his rebuttal argued that the Depression was caused by low population growth and low wages, in other words, population implosion not explosion. Not only was the U.S. population dropping but the purchasing power of a diminishing population was further aggravated by low wages, which compounded the problem of "underconsumption" into a vicious circle whose final result was the contraction of the economy and subsequent lowering of the general standard of living. Birth control, in this regard, would only accelerate the forces causing this vicious circle. It would not solve the problem of poverty; it would intensify it, and so it should come as no surprise that Ryan reserved his sharpest condemnation for the panacea that would only make the economic disease worse. In his testimony before Congress, Ryan defined the terms of the argument in no uncertain terms:

> To advocate contraception, as a method of bettering the condition of the poor and unemployed, is to divert the attention of the influential classes from the pursuit of social justice and to relieve them of all responsibility for our bad distribution and other social maladjustments. We simply cannot – those who believe as I do – subscribe to the idea that the poor are to be made responsible for their plight, and instead of getting justice from the government and a more rational social order, they are to be required to reduce their numbers.[10]

Over the next seven decades, the population issue would be brought forth with various justifications but always by the same ethnic group with the same political ends in mind. During the '60s, people like Paul Ehrlich, the Paddocks, and Garrett Hardin explained with a specificity that would make a Millerite blush, just when and how the world was going to come to an end by starvation. "The battle to feed all of humanity is over," Paul Ehrlich wrote in 1968 in tones that gave new meaning to the word dire. "In the 1970s the world will undergo famines – hundreds of millions of people are going to starve to death in spite of any crash programs embarked upon now."[11] Emphasis on contraception was always a way of relieving the wealthy of their responsibility for bad distribution.

On June 13, 1934, the last day of that congressional session, Sanger's bill came up for a vote, along with 200 other bills, and passed. The bill, however, was recalled by Senator Pat McCarran of Nevada, and then killed. The notion of government involvement in contraception would remain dead for another thirty years, but its vampire-like resurrection in the spring of 1965, this time at the behest of the Supreme Court, would signal the official beginning of Sexual Revolution III. For now the idea of contraception as the solution to the economic woes of the Depression was dead.

But the Plutocrats had the ability to keep it alive in secret. On March 1, 1934, at the height of the Ryan/Sanger debate in Congress, John D. Rockefeller III, scion of the Rockefeller family, wrote to his father urging him, in spite of shutting down the Bureau of Social Hygiene, to continue his support of both the American Birth Control League, which was to get $10,000, and Sanger's National Association for Federal Legislation, which was to get $1,000. He also announced that he had "one further statement in regard to my interest in birth control. I have come pretty definitely to the conclusion that it is the field in which I will be interested, for the present at least, to concentrate my own giving, as I feel that it is so fundamental and underlying."[12]

Sanger's defeat at the hands of Ryan led to John D. Rockefeller III's conversion to a full-time warrior in the eugenics crusade. It also led him to understand just how powerful the Catholics had become and how it would be impossible to defeat them without some technological advantage of the sort that lots of money could buy. The Rockefellers' official biographers make JDR III's conversion sound more mysterious than it was. John D. Rockefeller III, according to John Ensor Harr and Peter Johnson,

> never could explain exactly why he had developed such a strong interest in the population field long before it came into vogue or was generally recognized as an area of concern. . . . In fact, it was Junior's decision to terminate the Bureau that led his oldest son to volunteer to make the population field a major focus of his interest and to do what he could to carry on the work. In a letter to his father in 1934, he expressed concern that the support of population studies and projects would not be picked up by any of the other Rockefeller organizations, including the foundation, because of "the element of propaganda and controversy which so often is attached to endeavors in birth control."

Far from being a repudiation of what his father had done, JDR III's conversion to eugenic warfare was perfectly consistent with the aspirations of his ethnos to remain in power and its fear that the Catholics were going to deprive them of that power by demographic means. In addition to that, JDR III had come to the conclusion that population control, including sterilization, contraception, and abortion, had become the *conditio sine qua non* of solving problems like hunger and development in the Third World. JDR III spent much of the late forties and early fifties traveling around the Far East at the behest of John Foster Dulles, a fact which earned him the name Mr. Asia at The *New Yorker*. His travels there only reconfirmed what he had concluded in his late twenties. Population was the problem.

Eventually John D. Rockefeller III would go on to create the Population Council in the early '50s, which would fund the research that would come up with both the pill and the IUD. But the plans, as his letter to his father indicates, were laid long before that. During the mid-'30s, the Rockefeller foundations and those funded by other plutocrat families worked hard at breaking down resistance to contraception among medical doctors by focusing their attention through Robert Latou Dickinson on the AMA.

On June 9, 1937, Arthur W. Packard, head of the Davison Fund, wrote to JDR III to discuss long range plans:

> Where do we go from here? Now that the subject has been opened up professionally and with legal sanction, the question of promulgating standards concerning methods of study for the discovery of better techniques, of the areas where contraception could be used and should not be used, and of the attitudes of public health instrumentalities seem to assume first importance. . . . The Rockefeller Foundation, the Carnegie Corporation, the Macy Foundation, the Milbank fund and possibly the Davison Fund will, by the fall, have agreed upon some formula for the financing of a new program by the Committee which will represent the biggest stake which has yet been planted in the field of research for new techniques.[13]

The plutocrats realized that the biggest barrier to widespread use of contraception was the primitive nature of the methods then available. That shortcoming would be remedied by what amounted to a Manhattan Project for contraception funded by the foundations which drew their wealth from the WASP establishment. As one can guess, knowing who sponsored the research, the purpose of birth control was eugenic warfare waged in the ethnic interests of the WASP establishment. As Packard's letter to JDR III makes clear, the rationale was and would remain eugenic, in spite of the fact that that term had become associated with Hitler, with whom the United States, at the urging of the Anglophile establishment, would soon fight a war. Packard makes his eugenic sympathies perfectly clear in his letter to JDR III. In fact, this ethnic group was so committed to eugenic measures, it made them the cornerstone of their philanthropy. "I am inclined to think," Packard continued,

> that the one constructive propaganda agency which is showing signs of insight and intelligent strategy is the Eugenics Society, and I feel quite confident that over the next few years this organization will make a very

substantial contribution to what might be termed the philosophy of contraception as a matter of national significance. The Eugenics Society, at least, is the only agency I see which along positive lines is undertaking to say contraception knowledge must be available to all families, *but not all families at all times should use it,* though some families at all times should · use it. It is the one agency which is trying to feel its way through to the point where, among other things it can develop a set of principles which can be used by Public Health workers, social workers, doctors and laymen in delineating an intelligent basis for the prescription of contraception among great numbers of people [his emphasis].[14]

As the italicized passage makes clear, the WASP establishment ran a risk in promoting the use of contraception, and the risk was that the very people Packard and Rockefeller wanted least to limit their families were most likely to limit their families. Despite the risk, the Rockefellers pressed on expanding their efforts to spread the use of contraceptives among the lower classes.

Three months after his note to JDR III, Packard received a letter from Mrs. Richmond Page, a society matron from Philadelphia, who announced that the American protectorate of Puerto Rico had just legalized contraception. "It is interesting to note," she wrote in her letter of September 21, 1937, "that the entire membership of both Houses is Catholic and that the bill was signed on May 1st by acting Governor Menendez Ramos with the full approval of Governor Winship. I have recently learned that it was intentionally arranged that Mr. Ramos should sign the bill in Governor Winship's absence for this reason that, as a Puerto Rican and a Catholic, his approval would carry more weight on this particular issue."[15]

Mrs. Page went on to say that the Puerto Rican plutocrats, which is to say the owners of the sugar companies, were fully behind the birth-control campaign. In fact, "In August Mr. Roig, head of one of the wealthiest and most powerful of the Puerto Rican sugar companies, opened two contraceptive clinics on company grounds."[16]

The point of this letter is, of course, money. Mrs. Page wants to know whether the Rockefellers are interested in funding more birth control clinics in Puerto Rico, which is visualized as a laboratory for the same sort of thing on the continental United States in the not too distant future. If the Rockefellers have the money, Mrs. Page has a group willing to staff the clinics, namely, the Quakers from Philadelphia, who had already proven themselves in the field of eugenics by setting up birth control clinics in the Appalachians. "Under the direction and supervision of the Friends Health Service," she continued, "a birth control clinic was started in 1933 in Logan, West Virginia, one of the largest and most benighted of the coal mining centers."[17] This may have been of interest to the Rockefellers because they had coal mines in this benighted area themselves and were probably interested in the same benefits for their workers that Margaret Sanger had promised to the country at large by giving them contraception instead of a decent wage. Mrs.

Page closed her letter by proposing a meeting between Packard and Clarence Gamble, heir to the Proctor & Gamble fortune and a notorious population controller, and Mr. Clarence Pickett, the head of the Friends Service Committee and the man who had brought birth control clinics to the benighted coal miners of West Virginia.

In 1942, in reaction to the bad name that eugenics had got by its association with National Socialism in Germany, the American Birth Control League changed its name to Planned Parenthood. Reading PP material, however, makes it clear that the change was in name only. The organization was still pursuing the same eugenic goals with the same people funding it for that purpose. In February 1943, Planned Parenthood launched its "Negro Program," a "nation-wide educational program" whose purpose was "creating among Negroes a greater understanding of the importance of Planned Parenthood to their health and welfare and economic security" and, of course, to reduce their birthrate by persuading them to use contraception. On November 2, 1944, D. Kenneth Rose, national director of Planned Parenthood, wrote to Arthur W. Packard soliciting money for the "Negro Community Organization Program," which had "programs in Nashville Tennessee and three rural counties in South Carolina." The NCOP "proved that Negro families in the lowest economic and intelligence levels would use birth control information if made available through regular Public Health services."[18]

On December 26, 1945, Packard wrote to Morris Hadley of Planned Parenthood, informing him that John D. Rockefeller III had made a contribution of $2500 to support PP's Harlem Project, which was "to provide an example for other Negro populated communities" on how to reduce their numbers through the use of contraception. Earlier in 1945, Planned Parenthood, anticipating the return of American military personnel after the war, issued its pamphlet "For the Man who Comes Back – and for all his generation." Again, in spite of the war and the bad name Hitler had given eugenics and the name change to evade association with it, Planned Parenthood was still talking the eugenic line.

"Selective Service," the pamphlet begins, "estimates that 8,000,000 of our 22,000,000 young men of military age are not fit to fight for their country." These men were rejected because "they are the children of parents who are unfit for reproduction." And under the subheading "Work with Negroes," we learn that Negroes are twice as unfit for reproduction as white people. "Although little more than 10 percent of the population," the pamphlet continued, "Negroes account for almost 20 percent of men rejected for the armed forces."[19] In order to help the Negro become more "fit," Planned Parenthood – at the urging of Negro leaders, of course – had launched the "Harlem Mothers' Health Center," funded generously by the Rockefellers.

Throughout all of the name changes and turmoil caused by the war, the Rockefeller foundations' adherence to eugenics remained constant. In a memo dated June 29, 1943, Packard listed four jobs still to be done. In addition to "contraception promotion" goal number one, and "contraception research," goal number two, Packard discussed "birth promotion," which meant the promotion of births from certain people. Packard urges

> promoting and propagandizing on the subject of more births on the part of certain cultural groupings where sterility is an important factor or where contraception is practiced with dysgenic effects in terms of population differentials or where contraception is practiced as a matter of personal convenience and not from medical indications with the occasional result of sterility in mid-life when children are desired.[20]

The irony of course is that Planned Parenthood was promoting contraception as a matter of personal convenience among precisely the class of people that Packard wanted to have more children. Despite that fact, Packard never deviated from the eugenic party line, no matter how inexpedient it had become to support it publicly, nor did the Rockefellers ever stop funding PP's eugenic programs. On March 13, 1947, Packard wrote to Junior, explaining once again the rationale he was using in dispensing his money:

> We have in America today a population differential between different social and cultural groupings which from the eugenic point of view tends to make the practice of birth control a disgenic [sic] factor in American life, i.e., our population trends within various cultural groupings reflect the fact that some of those groups who do practice birth control are not reproducing themselves at replacement levels, whereas other groups are reproducing themselves considerably above the replacement requirement. Such groups do not practice birth control and those groups in many instances might wish to do so, and constitute considerable drain upon the social and cultural resources of the country because they do not. This consideration gives rise to two important points in connection with the current campaign. On the one hand, it is a well considered serious effort to get an understanding of birth control before those who do not now have it. On the other hand, it points up the need for more substantial and effective research in the field of contraception. The groups which need birth control the most also stand in need of a simple, cheaper and more effective technique than modern science has yet developed.[21]

The paradox was that the groups that needed birth control most, from Packard's point of view, wanted it least, and those that wanted it the most, needed it the least – at least from Packard's point of view. Packard and the ethnic group he represented were in a bind, but like all good Enlightenment thinkers, Packard felt that all he needed to solve his dilemma was a new invention and a better technique. When they were in place, the third sexual revolution would begin in earnest.

Part II, Chapter 24

New York, 1934

On February 1, 1934, around the same time that Margaret Sanger was debating John Ryan before Congress, a sadder but wiser Claude McKay returned from his self-imposed exile, when he stepped off the *SS Magallenes*, the ship which had brought him from Spain, onto the dock in New York City. As one might expect of the man whose most famous book was *Home to Harlem,* McKay headed immediately north and checked into a room at the YMCA on 135th Street. The return to Harlem of the man who in many ways started the Harlem Renaissance was still newsworthy enough to merit an article in the *Amsterdam News*, where Henry Moon wrote that McKay's ten-year exile had turned him into a "reserved individual with a cynical twinkle in his eye." When asked why he had come back, McKay said that "the Negro intellectuals have been boasting for years that I could not come back." He then added that he had returned "to prove them wrong."[1] McKay then left Harlem to spend the weekend with his friend Max Eastman in Croton-on-Hudson.

Throughout his career as a writer, McKay found himself caught in a dynamic which he understood imperfectly, if at all. Claiming to be a victim of white racism, he was in fact promoted by a series of white mentor-father figures like Max Eastman. In this he was typical of virtually all of the writers and artists of the Harlem Renaissance. Langston Hughes was promoted by Mrs. Van de Vere Quick, who took Hughes as the vessel of some mystical consciousness emanating from the Black race. He was then promoted by the homosexual Carl Van Vechten, who introduced him to the publishers who brought out his first book of poetry. Henry Crowder, the musician, became the pet of Nancy Cunard. Zora Neal Hurston was so eager for the same kind of patronage she attempted to steal Mrs. Van der Vere Quick from Langston Hughes. And Claude McKay, of course, had Max Eastman. In each instance, there was a sexual element to the exchange. In each instance, the black artist symbolized dark sexual forces which had evaded the enervating effect of "white" Christianity. But in each instance the patronage involved a sort of bondage as well, either financial bondage or cultural bondage or sexual bondage. In each instance the black partner in this unwritten covenant agreed to embody the white man's fantasy of a sexual life liberated from "Christian" guilt. And more often than not, the Negro who agreed to the terms of the agreement understood them as little as the white people who proposed them. The situation of bondage was compounded by the fact that the rich white patrons were promoting contraception among the Negroes at the same time they were promoting "negritude." This tradition would reach its culmination at the end of the century in a figure like Ali Mazrui of the SUNY system, who would get paid handsomely to promote Afrocentricity to whites in America and then paid again to promote contraceptives to blacks in Africa. Being a black "leader" meant pretty much what the Planned Parenthood brochures describing them meant, namely, a man who took money from the whites to deliver his fellow blacks into some form of eugenic or cultural bondage.

Perhaps because he participated so avidly in the liberation from sexual morality which was the heart of the Harlem Renaissance, McKay began to resent it and what it did to him. The initial reaction in the '30s was much like the black reaction to the same sort of sexual engineering when it got practiced in the '60s, namely, black nationalism, negritude, and blaming the white man's religion for engineering the bondage that was brought on by the systematic exploitation of passion. The "white" civilization which McKay accused of being Christian in the 1930s was in fact a mix of Nazi/racist neo-paganism, Communist materialism, social Darwinism, and the last gasp of a dying Protestant ruling class, which had succumbed to hedonism and was in the process of putting itself out of business politically by the widespread practice of contraception. Once he understood the predatory nature of the culture which had promoted him as a black cultural icon, McKay turned to racial politics, separatism, and moral relativism as the answer.

Western society had become a cultural battleground in which two competing forms of social Darwinism would soon lock horns in another world war. Looking on this mishmash of rationalized greed, decadent morals, and eugenic "science," McKay construed all of it as "white" and, therefore, Christian. His sexual rebellion had made him hostile to Christian morality, but his guilt-induced attraction to Africa left him with no workable code of action.

Toward the end of the novel, the eponymous Banjo is taken out of "the Ditch," the old port in Marseilles which symbolizes the "white," modern world and all its mean venality, and taken to a hospital which "loomed up like a great gray Rock of Refuge on the hill above the Ditch. The ultimate hope of salvation for the afflicted. Below it was a Church with a wooden Christ nailed to a cross in the yard."[2] Given the Church's location and the fact that McKay's writing is largely autobiographical, McKay's meditation on the crucifix indicates that his stay in France got him thinking about Catholicism. In the French hospital, Ray, the black intellectual, and Banjo, who lived according to his instincts, found refuge in a building which provided a neat counterpoint to the Presbyterian Church, which rose up at the end of *Home to Harlem*, like a fortress for the "Ancient Respectability," which McKay "was getting ready to flee."

On June 25, 1943, McKay, who had never been in good health since he returned to the United States in 1934, suffered a stroke while working as a riveter in a federal shipyard in Port Newark, New Jersey. Tom and Mary Keating, a Catholic couple McKay had met at Friendship House in 1942, offered him the use of their country cottage near New Milford, Connecticut, as a place to recuperate. While recuperating, McKay "had plenty of time to read many pamphlets and books on Catholicism." What he read convinced him that the Church possessed what he had been looking for in communism – "the one true International of Peace and Good Will on earth to all men."

> My study of the Catholic church led to the discovery of important facts of which I was not formerly aware. For example, when Catholicism conquered Rome, in its infinite wisdom it abolished the tribune and usury. It put priests in the palace of the tribunes and as Jesus Christ had chased the money-changers out of the temple, the Catholic Church, following in his footsteps, did likewise. But fifteen hundred years later the money-changers were apotheosized and permitted to rule the world by the Protestants. As I continued to get enlightenment, it just flashed upon me that Agnosticism, Atheism, Modernism, Capitalism, State Socialism and State Communism were all children of the Pandora Box of Protestantism.[3]

By the time of his stroke, McKay had become disillusioned with modernity in all its manifestations. Just about everything bad in the modern world seemed to flow from the Protestant Reformation; however, his special contempt was reserved for the Communists, who had grown increasingly powerful under the shielding alliance with the Soviet Union that World War II had brought about. McKay felt that the Communists had blocked virtually all of his efforts to get work published after he returned to the United States. He had become similarly disillusioned with the Negro literati. "When I returned from abroad in the middle of the nineteen thirties," McKay wrote, "the 'Niggerati' (as they delighted in calling themselves) and their white admirers thought that I was a loose and lewd person, because I had written *Home to Harlem*. . . . Anyway when the 'Niggerati' discovered that I was not what they thought I was, they dropped me like a hot potato."[4]

In an earlier letter to Mary Keating, he assured her that the "colored intellectuals" were not "against me. But they feel that they cannot offend any powerful group of whites who claim to be friends of colored people." By the time McKay was willing to talk about the alliance between the liberal intelligentsia and the Negro, no one was willing to publish what he had to say. In "Right Turn to Catholicism," which remained unpublished, McKay talked about an editor who wanted a story on the isolationist Congressman Hamilton Fish receiving $25,000 a year from the dictator of the Dominican Republic. When McKay replied that he would rather do a piece on the editor of the *New Republic* receiving the same amount of money taken from "the naked rumps of the black natives of the neighboring Haitian Republic," he got turned down cold. According to McKay, "the Negro editor who wanted the story was appalled because the *New Republic* was 'progressive' and a 'friend of Negroes,' but Hamilton Fish was reactionary."[5] The Negro/Liberal alliance was to continue well beyond McKay's death, but the terms of the agreement remained the same, as Eldridge Cleaver found out when he became a born-again Christian in the '80s or Clarence Thomas found out when he was nominated to the Supreme Court.

On June 1, 1944, McKay wrote to Eastman to inform him that he was planning to become a Catholic because "I know that the Catholic Church is the one great organization which can check the Communists and probably lick them." Then as if a bit embarrassed to be talking about spiritual things with Eastman, McKay added almost apologetically, "but there is also the religious angle." Eastman, who was by then a staunch anti-Communist himself, was appalled:

> All these years at such cost and with such heroism you resisted the temptation to warp your mind and morals in order to join the Stalin church. Why warp it the other way now for the Catholics? Why not die firm, free and intelligent as you have lived? To see you go the way of Heywood Broun would be so ugly – so sickly a finish disproving, so far as you can, everything you've stood for – *handing the Stalinists just what they want* [his emphasis]. Can nobody stand fast for the truth?[6]

Eastman's stand prefigures the position that Paul Blanshard would take five years later when he referred to Catholicism and Stalinism as equally totalitarian and equally inimical to "American freedom." On June 30, McKay responded by saying that he had always been religious, "as my poems attest." At another point he claims that he had never been a Communist. In light of poems like "Petrograd: May Day, 1923," which he wrote after viewing that year's May Day celebration, standing next to Zinoviev and other party functionaries from the viewing stand in Uritsky Square, it is difficult to understand what McKay meant: "Jerusalem," he wrote then, "is fading from men's mind,/ And sacred cities holding men in thrall/ Are crumbling in the new thought of mankind/ The pagan day, the holy day for all."[7]

Like Langston Hughes, who would repudiate his poem "Good-bye Christ" before a Congressional hearing, McKay was re-writing his past in light of his most recent conversion, no matter how genuine that conversion might have been. In McKay's case, there was no external pressure or threat of retaliation as there was in the case of Hughes' recantation. McKay was simply expressing his views to an old friend in a private letter. Like Max Eastman, subsequent writers found McKay's conversion so distasteful they had to attribute it to ulterior motives. Arnold Rampersad, author of a two-volume biography of Langston Hughes, claims, "The one-time radical had died in the arms of the Roman Catholic Church. Illness, poverty, and isolation had driven him there."[8] Cooper calls his conversion "ambivalent" but "genuine." The ambivalence can be gleaned from McKay's letters. In the already mentioned letter to Eastman, McKay claimed that "had I remained in

Morocco, I most certainly would have become a Muslim, because I felt so utterly lost in not being in one of the religious groups, when Religion was such an intense thing in Morocco." Even granting the ambivalence, it is clear that McKay was drawn to Catholicism for personal reasons – his experiences in Spain and France, the kindness of the Keatings, his contact with "Baroness" Catherine de Hueck, the White Russian émigré who founded Friendship House to combat the inroads of Communism among the Negroes – but there were intellectual reasons as well, one of them an incisive understanding of the unique role that Catholicism played in the world, especially in distinction to the various Protestant national churches. McKay came to the conclusion that the world needed a universal church and that when that need was repressed by national churches, the repressed returned in the form of the Communist International. After his experience with communism and other political movements, McKay also concluded that the world needed a pope:

> I do believe that the ancient and medieval world had a wonderful asset which we lack today, when a Pope of Rome, with the authority of Jesus, could say to a stubborn ruler: Stop! For what you do is contrary to the Will of God! Stop or you will be excommunicated! Even if the pope might be wrong, I think it was better for him to err on the spiritual side than a monarch on the temporal. I don't think Protestantism has made an enviable progress in the spiritual field of Wisdom and Restraint.[9]

Missing from all of the accounts of his conversion was the powerful cultural position the Catholic Church had achieved in America in the 1940s. To cite just one example of cultural power, Catholicism dominated Hollywood during the 1940s. *The Song of Bernadette* beat out *Casablanca* as the best film of 1941. Hollywood may have been reacting to the stick wielded by the Legion of Decency and their influence over the Production Code, but they were also enticed by the carrot of a large homogeneous audience and sought to lure them into the theaters by having Bing Crosby and Barry Fitzgerald and Pat O'Brien give sympathetic portrayals of Catholic priests that would seem all but incomprehensible considering the point of view which dominated post-code Hollywood. McKay was reacting to Catholic cultural influence at a time when it was at an all-time high.

On October 16, 1944, McKay wrote to Eastman from Chicago to announce that five days earlier he had been "baptized into the Catholic (Roman) faith." In that letter he continued the apologia for his conversion, and continued his critique of Protestantism, charging them with an "inordinate flair for Modernism."

> If I accept the Catholics in a Christian country, it is because I do sincerely believe that the Roman Church is the traditionally true church and that the Catholics are superior to any of the Protestants in religious unity and strength. The Protestants have been over eclectic in their attitude towards life and progress, jingoistically pushing ahead in their inordinate flair for

Modernism, even at the expense of trampling underfoot the millions of humanity. You yourself have exposed the trick in your statement on the Federal Church of Christ and their endorsement of Soviet Russia.[10]

The charge is, perhaps, an implicit reproach against Eastman and McKay's other white mentors. McKay criticizes Eastman for abandoning the Christianity of his youth. "Unlike you," he wrote, "I have never had any religious experience, because my brother educated me without religion. I was pretty well versed in the Bible but it was like reading any historical or philosophical book, and in my adolescence I came under the influence of the Englishman who sent me to America to be educated, and who was an agnostic. I used to have great faith in Agnosticism, up until World War I when the German and British Agnostics or rationalists lost all sense of reason, became rabid nationalists and began denouncing one another."[11]

Eastman's life expresses as well as anyone's the declension of liberal Protestantism into radical liberationism of the political and sexual sort. McKay had followed Eastman's guidance as well as Jekyll's, the Englishman of the letter, and all the advice had got him ultimately was a case of VD. If there is a sense of rebellion against these figures, however, it is moderated by a critique of the historical situation in which Catholicism stands as the only viable alternative to the racism, economic exploitation, and doctrinal decay which McKay felt flowed from the Reformation. Catholicism was the implementation of the International, which inspired his move toward Communism. It was also the antidote to the racial nationalism which McKay proposed on the rebound from communism and its mendacity in professing concern for the Negro. "Jesus Christ," McKay wrote in his unpublished ms. "Right Turn to Catholicism,"

> rejected the ideal of any special, peculiar chosen race or nation, when he charged his apostles: Go ye into all the world and preach the gospel. Not the gospel of Imperialism, Feudalism or Capitalism, or Socialism, Communism, or a National Church. It was Protestantism that started the movement of national churches. The Catholic Church superseded the tribal religions in the days when kings and emperors were gods. I find in the Catholic Church that which does not exist in Capitalism, Socialism or Communism – the one true International of Peace and Good Will on earth to all men. And as a child of Christendom that suffices for me. Even though many white folks may regard me as an outcast child.

The white folks were not alone in regarding McKay that way. By the time McKay had converted to Catholicism, the Niggerati were through with him too. McKay characterized Harlem as a "melange of pagans and Protestants." At the time of McKay's conversion, the balance of power in Harlem was shifting away from Communist domination and into the hands of the Negro organizations which would dominate the civil-rights movement during the '50s and '60s. It was also devolving into the hands of the sexual liberationist WASP foundations which funded the civil rights movement. By the early 1950s, the Communists were gone, and taking their place were the great foundations – Ford, Rockefeller, and Carnegie. As a result the Negro organizations never transcended the Protestant roots of the plutocrat foundations which funded them, and, as a result of accepting that funding, they were absorbed into the eugenic campaign that sought to lame them politically by driving down their birth rate. The new eugenic movement had names like Planned Parenthood and the Ford Foundation, and it would reach its goal during the sexual revolution of the '60s when the War on Poverty became a front for the distribution of contraceptives.

As a result, the Negro organizations which McKay criticized never really transcended their Protestant roots. In fact, through their absorption into the neo-eugenic movement they became willing victims of the same racism. The racial issue was caused, according to McKay's critique, by the creation of national churches. And the blacks, confronted by this Protestant fact of life, went on to create national churches of their own by way of compensation. The pendulum swung from communist internationalism to black nationalism in the late '40s and early '50s. The civil-rights movement could only transcend its roots in the black national Protestant churches by appealing to the Left, which was always willing to accommodate its internationalist aspirations – for a price. In the '30s, the price was support for the Soviet Union; in the '60s, the price was support for sexual liberation. As a result, McKay saw the Negro as condemned to oscillate between two equally counterproductive poles – their own national churches or the internationalism of left-wing politics. McKay knew the dangers so well because he had succumbed to both of them. For McKay, Catholicism was the only way out of ethnocentric national churches and leftist internationalism. McKay felt that it was a secret kept from the Negro rank and file who, according to McKay, are the prime victims of this dilemma:

> Our white liberal and radical "friends" will not tell Negroes the truth as they see it, for they are white and diplomatic. When the liberal and late Senator Borah attempted to tell us the truth, he brought the wrath of Negrodom down on his head. But being one of them I can say without worrying about the reaction that we Negroes of the New World are not merely a lost remnant of a race, we are also a lost people. We have no soul we can call our own, for we are running away from ourselves and whither we are running, God only knows. . . . Our leaders will sell the Negro people to any group of whites for a price and social intercourse.[12]

McKay's warnings went unheeded. By the time the '60s arrived, the man who saw the Catholic Church as the antidote to both communism and national churches both black and white had been forgotten and replaced by Catholic priests who could think of nothing better to do than fill buses for the next civil rights march and claim that the Catholic Church was "a white racist institution." By using race as a way of subverting morals, the sexual revolutionaries would wage a successful *Kulturkampf* against the Catholic Church during the 1960s and in the process of suppressing morals would turn places like Harlem into increasingly violent ghettos where children were raised without fathers by mothers who were wards of the state. "This here Harlem," said Gin Head Suzy in McKay's *Home to Harlem*, "is a stinking sink of iniquity. Nigger hell! That's what it is."[13] And that's what it would remain.

On December 1, 1944, less than two months after Claude McKay became a Catholic, Arthur W. Packard received a call from Kenneth Rose, director of the Planned Parenthood Federation. Rose was in regular contact with Packard, who, as the administrator of the Davison Fund, was the man in charge of disbursing Rockefeller money for contraception. Rose began the conversation by relating an incident on a train during which he was told that "there were too many Catholics managing the [Rockefeller] enterprise." Packard denied the allegation, which must have struck him as bizarre, but then "very quickly," according to the account which Packard wrote of the conversation a few days after it took place, Rose got to what was bothering him. "I wondered," he said to Packard, "if you people had not about decided that it was time to take on the Catholic Church."[14] Rose hung up before Packard had a chance to reply, but the impertinent question stuck in his mind, and on December 12, when Packard ran into Rose at a conference, he brought up the telephone conversation and took the occasion "to state in polite language that we not only resent the method that he used but also the presumption which seemed to us to underlie his observation on the telephone."[15] Rose, perhaps fearing that he had just killed the goose that laid the golden eggs, backed off immediately, claiming that Packard had misunderstood what he had said. All Rose really meant to do was "'wonder' if we were in any way actively taking issue with the Catholic Church." Packard took the opportunity to tell Rose that " it was a free country" and "that we accorded to every individual the right of freedom of religious choice, which we expected for ourselves and that we believed that only through tolerance, understanding and cooperation would the American ideal survive."[16] Duly chastised, Rose abandoned that line of questioning. To make matters even more clear, Packard wrote a follow-up letter to Rose on December 26, after showing it to board member Thomas M. Debevoise, who told him not to tone it down, and to add for emphasis "that only through tolerance, understanding and cooperation can the American ideal survive."

Rose of course was only giving expression to the misgivings about Catholics that would reach full expression after the war in books like Paul Blanshard's *American Freedom and Catholic Power,* in which Blanshard mentioned that Bertrand Russell's greatest fear was that America was going to become a Catholic country and that the Catholics were going to accomplish this by the numbers, which is to say by demographic increase, which is pretty much what Msgr. Ryan was saying too. During the postwar period, birth control was to become the prime area of contestation between the rising power of the Catholics and the equally demographically based political decline of the still powerful WASP aristocracy. Planned Parenthood, as its eugenic pamphlets and its letters to the Rockefellers indicate, was heavily involved in the campaign against the Catholic Church and Catholic political influence, a campaign which would reach its culmination in the sexual revolution of the '60s.

If the Rockefellers were as upset with Rose's impertinent remarks as Packard was, their donations do not indicate that fact. During their first nationwide campaign of 1947 alone, the Rockefeller family gave $35,000 to Planned Parenthood. This contribution placed them, in Packard's words "close to being at the top of the list but not embarrassingly out of line."[17]

Part II, Chapter 25

New York, 1932

In 1931, the CRPS's budget was shifted from the Bureau of Social Hygiene to the Rockefeller Foundation. From the outset, the foundation's officers pressured Robert Yerkes with little success to concentrate on human problems. Yerkes, responding to that pressure, wrote to Watson in 1932 urging him to return to academic research, but by that time Watson had become too habituated to the good life and the emoluments which accrued to him as an advertising executive. As a result, the whole project of psychic engineering through sex languished during the 1930s as it drifted away from Watson, and Watson drifted away from it. Yerkes's letter on why he didn't commit suicide was his last correspondence with Watson. After completing the article in 1933, Watson sent it off to the editor at *Cosmopolitan* who had commissioned it. The editor, however, rejected it as too depressing and a few months later, as if to confirm his original feelings about the article, committed suicide himself.

Even though Watson, the creator of the behaviorist project for social control, was of little use to Yerkes, Yerkes continued to write to Watson during the early '20s urging him to continue his research. In 1924 Watson finally linked up with what he termed "the Rockefeller interests." In 1924 the Laura Spelman Rockefeller Memorial Fund (LSRM) awarded a grant of $15,000 to the Teachers College of Columbia University so that Watson could continue the work on infants that he had begun at Johns Hopkins. The LSRM was a major player in the field of behavioral research in the '20s, and foundation director Beardsley Ruml made it clear that he was not interested in the disinterested contemplation of the truth. He was interested in research that had social results and that meant, more than anything else, formulating strategies of social control under the guise of scientific childrearing. The LSRM viewed scientific childrearing as the first step in the engineering of social relationships, and far from being put off by the prospect of conducting experiments on little human beings, Ruml jumped at the chance to fund an experiment whose point was, in Watson's terms, to devise methods of controlling human behavior "without having the parents as the main conditioning factor."[1] If schools were to become, as Dewey had predicted, factories which engineered the minds of their pupils away from the views of those children's parents and toward the interests of the large corporations and other purveyors of the liberal ideology, someone would have to come up with an explanation of how children learned. Watson, according to Buckley, was "attempting to create techniques that would reduce child rearing to standardized formulae."[2]

Eventually, the research would end up in Watson's 1928 book on child rearing, *Psychological Care of Infant and Child*, which Watson co-authored with Rosalie Rayner Watson. The book was dedicated to "the First Mother Who Brings up a Happy Child" and it coincided neatly with the disintegration of the extended family which liberalism was accomplishing by its assault on the local, for the most part, ethnic community in the wake of World War I. Cut off from the childrearing mores of their own hopelessly old-fashioned parents, "modern" mothers were urged to turn to science as the guide in raising their children, specifically the science of behavioral psychology as explicated by Dr. Watson. Watson lost no time in beginning his assault on "traditional guides for human conduct." "A great many mothers," Watson writes, "still resent being told how to feed their children. Didn't their grandmothers have fourteen children and raise ten of them?" Watson counters by saying that the fact that "many of grandmother's children grew up with rickets, with poor teeth, with under-nourished bodies, generally prone to every kind of disease means little to the mother who doesn't want to be told how to feed her child scientifically."[3]

Watson addresses his book to "the modern mother who is beginning to find that the rearing of children is the most difficult of all professions, more difficult than engineering, than law, or even medicine itself."[4]

"No one today knows enough to raise a child," Dr. Watson informed modern mothers. "The world would be considerably better off if we were to stop having children for twenty years (except those reared for experimental purposes) and were then to start again with enough facts to do the job with some degree of skill and accuracy. Parenthood, instead of being an instinctive art, is a science, the details of which must be worked out by patient laboratory methods."[5]

Watson's book is full of instances where the laboratory is taken as the model for the nursery. Mothers should relate to their children the way Dr. Watson related to Little Albert. Mothers should treat their children "as though they were young adults." This means:

> Never hug and kiss them, never let them sit in your lap. If you must, kiss them once on the forehead when they say good night. Shake hands with them in the morning. Give them a pat on the head if they have made an extraordinarily good job of the difficult task. Try it out. In a week's time you will find how easy it is to be perfectly objective with your child and at the same time kindly. You will be utterly ashamed of the mawkish, sentimental way you have been handling it.[6]

No matter what Watson's intention was in writing this sort of thing, the net result was to make mothers feel shame for exhibiting affection because affection was not scientific, nor was love, an emotion which Watson felt, probably drawing from his own experiences, was based on stimulation of erogenous zones. Mothers should not even be seen by their children any more than was necessary to administer feedings – by bottle, of course – and change dirty diapers because too much maternal contact fostered an unhealthy dependence in the child. For those mothers whose heart was "too tender" and felt, all of Watson's exhortations to the contrary, that they had to peek in on their child, Watson recommends: "make yourself a peephole so that you can see it without being seen, or use a periscope."[7] Even while peering through her periscope, however, the modern mother should show no emotion; she should instead "handle the situation as a trained nurse or a doctor would and, finally, learn not to talk in endearing and coddling terms."[8]

Watson spoke as an expert about a world where the school was taking over more and more of the education and socialization which the family had formerly done. By internalizing the dictates of the technocratic society and implementing them in the nursery, the modern mother would facilitate her child's success in the world later on. "The modern child," according to Buckley, "would soon learn that real authority lay not in the family but in the marketplace and in its supporting social institutions. Achieving success depended upon internalizing the values of the corporate order. Success itself came more and more to be seen as the ability to emulate a style of living defined and exemplified by mass advertising."[9]

No matter how promising scientific methods of child-raising seemed, they placed an enormous burden on the mother, who now had two options: she would be culpable of neglect if she ignored the modern methods, or she would be culpable for every quirk of the child's personality if she didn't implement them correctly. This was clear for a very simple reason. There was no God, no nature, no culture, and no tradition to fall back on in Watson's universe. There was only the raw material of biology and conditioning, and the mother was the main conditioner. If there were any failures, she was responsible.

"If you start with a healthy body," Watson told young mothers, "the right number of fingers and toes, eyes, and the few elementary movements that are present at birth, you do not need anything else in the way of raw material to make a man, be that man a genius, a cultured gentleman, a rowdy or a thug. . . . You are completely responsible for all the other fear reactions your child may show."[10]

Whether admonitions like this were intended to cause guilt is hard to say. That they did seems almost certain as modern mothers strove to be as scientific as possible by adopting the commands of experts like Watson. The guilt simply increased the social control, which was congenial to those who were promoting the experts.

Because his ideas dovetailed so closely with the interests of the mass media, Watson's thought appeared in one mass market magazine after another during the 1920s. In addition to writing for *Harper's, The Nation, The New Republic, The Saturday Review of Literature, McCall's* and *Liberty,* he was profiled in *The New Yorker*. In 1930 Horace Kallen wrote an article on Watson and behaviorism in the *Encyclopedia of the Social Sciences* in which he foresaw a world according to Watson's principle producing human beings "as equal as Fords." Neither Kallen nor Watson seemed upset by the conflation of the assembly line and human reproduction. In fact both seemed to see it as a step forward, especially since Watson was predicting that marriage would be gone by 1978.

During the first ten years of their marriage, Rayner and Watson had two boys, which he raised according to behaviorist principles, under the approving eye of the media, which would report periodically that "they seem[ed] normal." Billy Watson would eventually commit suicide, so appearances were evidently deceiving, but by then he was grown and the media had other stories to occupy their attention.

In 1922, it looked as if Watson might be able to have the best of both worlds. In addition to his advertising job, he received a teaching appointment at the New School for Social Research, an institution founded in 1917 by Charles A. Beard and John Harvey Robinson to disseminate the ideas of Lippmann, Croly, Dewey, and Thorstein Veblen. Watson gave a series of weekly lectures at the New School from 1922 to 1926 when his character, or lack thereof, caught up with him. He was fired in 1926, according to the testimony of Beard's daughter, for sexual misconduct.

That incident pretty much ended Watson's academic career. By 1930 he had reached the height of his influence, but he had run out of things to say. All he could think to write about was a story on why people don't commit suicide. The topic probably gives some insight into Watson's frame of mind at the time. Cohen thinks Watson was suicidal at the time and resolved the crisis by moving out of New York City to a farm in Connecticut where he could lose himself in the details of caring for animals.[11] Watson, it should be remembered, once said any attempt at autobiography would probably lead to suicide, so maybe he was thinking about his own life at the time.

Whatever the reason, Watson wrote to 100 prominent people and asked them why they went on living. He got responses from everyone he wrote to, including a letter from Robert M. Yerkes, who replied that "despite psychological ills, difficulties and disappointments, I find life intensely interesting, a game in which by matching my wits against the universe I may oftener win than lose and enjoy the risk."[12] Yerkes had written to Watson in 1932 urging him to take up observational work again. Watson, however, had no desire to get back into laboratory work. "I am afraid there is too much water under the dam for me ever to be able to think of going back to university work," Watson wrote to Yerkes.[14] Cohen tells us that Yerkes had no practical suggestions, which seems odd since returning to research was Yerkes's idea.

In 1932, the first reaction to Watson, and his British popularizer Bertrand Russell, began to appear. In a novel called *Brave New World*, Aldous Huxley attacked behaviorism as the ideological basis for the "soft" totalitarian regime of the future. Huxley was no stranger to America and clearly had it and Watson's vision in mind when he recognized that sexual passion was an especially effective form of social control because it was so effectively internalized. In defending his passions, the victim thinks he is defending his very self when in fact he is defending the interests of those who give him the permission to gratify them. The government, then, that incites and protects the gratification of these passions will gain a hold over its citizens in a way more deep-seated than any other. As a student of the Enlightenment, Aldous Huxley recognized the same phenomenon and described it in the writings of the Marquis de Sade, who

> regarded himself as the apostle of the truly revolutionary revolution, beyond mere politics and economics – the revolution in individual men, women and children, whose bodies were henceforward to become the common sexual property of all and whose minds were to be purged of all the natural decencies, all the laboriously acquired inhibitions of traditional civilization. Between sadism and the really revolutionary revolution there is, of course, no necessary or inevitable connection. Sade was a lunatic and the more or less conscious goal of his revolution was universal chaos and destruction. The people who govern the Brave New World may not be sane (in what may be called the absolute sense of the word); but they are not madmen, and their aim is not anarchy but social stability. It is in order to achieve stability that they carry out, by scientific means, the ultimate, personal, really revolutionary revolution.[15]

Huxley could write this way because in the period from 1795 sexual liberation had gone from the force which toppled the *ancien régime* to being the force which maintained the revolutionary regime in power. "A really efficient totalitarian state," Huxley continued, "would be one in which the all-powerful executive of political bosses and their army of managers control a population of slaves who do not have to be coerced, because they love their servitude. To make them love it is the task assigned, in present-day totalitarian states, to ministries of propaganda, newspaper editors and schoolteachers."

Since the best way to make slaves love servitude is to make servitude pleasurable, all that remains in turning sex, which is certainly pleasurable, into a form of control is to make the state the arbiter of sex, freeing it up to be enjoyed on the terms established by the state and not by the moral order, and a population of slaves will quickly swear its allegiance to what it sees as the source and guarantor of its pleasures. By taking control of the sexual lives of its citizens, in other words, the state takes control of the citizens at their most vulnerable point. What makes the control so effective is that it is not seen as control as all but rather as "freedom," which is defined as the ability to gratify illicit desire. "The most important Manhattan Projects of the future," according to Huxley, "will be vast government-sponsored enquiries into what the politicians and the participating scientists will call 'the problem of happiness' – in other words, the problem of making people love their servitude." Huxley sees this transformation already happening in America:

> Nor does the sexual promiscuity of *Brave New World* seem so very distant. There are already certain American cities in which the number of divorces is equal to the number of marriages. In a few years, no doubt, marriage licenses will be sold like dog licenses, good for a period of twelve months, with no law against changing dogs or keeping more than one animal at a time. As political and economic freedom diminishes, sexual freedom tends compensatingly to increase.

Huxley was prophetic if a bit dated because he was more influenced by the totalitarian governments of the '30s. What Huxley failed to see was that the American system making use of market forces was more effective in creating the servitude he warned against because it was less obtrusive, therefore more invisible, to its victims. The persistent illusion emanating from this system was that there was nothing more to it than an individual and his insistent desires. Hidden away behind the scenes were the foundations and all of the other forces influencing the supposedly naked market place to their own advantage. The book's pessimistic ending may reflect personal weakness or simply a realistic assessment of the average man's inability to resist sexual temptation without supernatural help. Either way, the net result of succumbing to this world-wide net of technological temptation was bondage.

During the early summer of 1936, Rosalie Rayner Watson contracted dysentery and on June 19, she died. Shortly before her death, her two children were sent off to camp, so she never saw them before she died. After her death, Watson's drinking increased, as did his silence on matters psychological, leaving a vacuum that was felt at the CRPS and elsewhere. By the late 1930s, the CRPS was deeply involved, in Yerkes's words, with "studies of neural and behavioral mechanisms as facts in the control of sexual activity and reproduction."[16] Once again, however, infrahuman studies predominated, leaving nagging questions about human behavior unsettled. This disappointed Yerkes, who had never abandoned his goal of using the CRPS to support scientists who could provide reliable data that would help society understand and control human sexual behavior.

With war clouds gathering over Europe, however, the need for social engineering became more urgent. Joseph Goebbels, it turns out, was a fan of Eddie Bernays and made use of his book *Crystallizing Public Opinion*, in Bernays's words, "as a basis for his destructive campaign against the Jews in

Germany."[17] And Austria, he might have added. One of those Jews was his. Uncle Sigmund, who was lucky enough to escape to England in the late '30s. Eddie's aunts were not so fortunate.

If the Nazis could influence public opinion to such a degree simply by reading Eddie's book, then the Americans were clearly going to have to take the study of propaganda to a new level if they were going to defeat them in the next war. During the latter part of the 1930s, the Rockefellers got increasingly interested in communication theory and its military application, psychological warfare, and began funding studies that involved the people who had been involved in the CPI under George Creel during World War I. Harold Lasswell was working on a Rockefeller-funded study of content analysis at the Library of Congress, Hadley Cantril was doing similar work at Princeton for the Public Opinion Research Project. Paul Lazarfeld was working at the Office of Radio Research at Columbia University. Watching the Nazis, the Rockefellers became convinced that the mass media had only increased their power to influence the public mind since World War I, and now they wanted to set the media to the same task as the CPI had done then. The Rockefellers were interested in a campaign of "democratic prophylaxis" that would target ethnic communities in the United States and make them immune to the effects of Axis and Soviet propaganda. In 1939, the Rockefeller Foundation organized a series of secret seminars with men it regarded as leading communication scholars to enlist them in an effort to consolidate public opinion in the United States in favor of war against Nazi Germany. The America First movement under the leadership of people like Charles Lindbergh tried to prevent entry into a new war by reminding the country of the devastation the last one had caused, but ultimately their protests were of no avail. The isolationists were simply outgunned when it came to influencing the media and as a result in forming public opinion. If they hadn't written it yet, the Rockefeller interests were writing the book on psychological warfare, combining the insights of behaviorism, advertising, and communication theory into a potent weapon that would have far-reaching consequences for the country long after the war was over.

Harold Lasswell felt that the Rockefeller Interests representing the Anglophile elite in the United States should "systematically manipulate mass sentiment in order to preserve democracy from threats posed by authoritarian societies such as Nazi Germany or the Soviet Union."[18] Not everyone agreed. Certainly the America Firsters were of another opinion on the matter of whether America should enter the war, but some of the communications theorists objected too. Donald Slesinger, a former dean at the University of Chicago and a Rockefeller seminar participant, felt that in resorting to the methods of psychological manipulation, the Rockefeller interests were no better than those they hoped to oppose: "We [the Rockefeller Seminar] have been willing, without thought, to sacrifice both truth and human individuality in order to bring about given mass responses to war stimuli." Slesinger contended. "We have thought in terms of fighting dictatorships-by-force through the establishment of dictatorship-by-manipulation."[19] As a result of his outspoken criticism, Slesinger, according to Simpson, "drifted away from the Rockefeller seminars and appears to have rapidly lost influence within the community of academic communication specialists."[20]

That lesson was not lost on Robert M. Yerkes. By 1940, it was clear that the war was not going well for the British, and the Anglophile establishment was clearly looking for a way to get into the war to help them out. They were also interested in upping the ante in psychological research, and that meant they were becoming increasingly impatient with Yerkes and his emphasis on infrahuman studies. As a result, Alan Gregg, the director of the Rockefeller Foundation's medical division, decided to pressure Yerkes into funding sex research that involved human beings. In January of 1941, he informed Yerkes that the CRPS could look forward to funding for at most two more years. His grant for the 1943–44 year was "a terminating grant."[21]

Watson, the most likely candidate to do sex studies, was completely out of the picture now. Yerkes, however, had no intention of retiring, and he made this clear in his "Twentieth Annual Report of the Committee for Research in Problems of Sex," when he called for a new role for the committee. "Henceforth," he began, "we have concerned ourselves with knowledge and its extension through research. Scant attention has been given to the effects of current knowledge of sexual and reproductive phenomena on [the] individual and society."[22] To date, the CRPS had limited itself to promoting "the extension of knowledge disinterestedly, in accordance with the scientist's ideal and almost regardless of social values, applications and risks." Much of the knowledge that scientists had accumulated with such pains would become useless, he warned, unless some way was discovered to apply it with wisdom and insight to society. Many scientists, he continued, believed that disinterestedness was a menace. They insisted that "biological engineering" should become the teammate of research. "Lifting our eyes from the details of vital processes," he declared, "we discover that life itself needs guidance."[23] In order to get involved in "biological engineering," the CRPS needed to know more about human sexuality. They needed someone who could discover the basic structure of the sexual mechanism just as Watson had come up with the conditioned reflex as the basic building block of learning in infants.

In December 1940, an obscure entomologist by the name of Alfred Kinsey wrote to Yerkes about the surveys he had been conducting among students at the University of Indiana at Bloomington, where he was a professor. The conjunction was fortuitous. Kinsey needed money, and, more than that, he needed the respectability which an organization like the Rockefeller Foundation could confer. Yerkes, on the other hand, needed someone who was actually involved in sexual research on human beings as a way of saving his job at the CRPS. "Kinsey's request for funds," according to Jones, "offered Yerkes an opportunity to marry the human studies sought by the Rockefeller Foundation with the behavioral focus favored by the CRPS in the 1930s."[24] Watson had always wanted to do sex research but the exigencies of the times and his career never allowed him to proceed. Now the lessons of advertising which had emerged from psychological warfare after the last war and had been refined during the 1920s and '30s were about to be reabsorbed into their original scientific matrix once again. The lesson of advertising's refinement of behaviorism was clear. Man was not infinitely malleable. He was a rational creature whose reason could be overruled by his passions, which were limited in number, the most passionate of which was sex. If sex could be used to make the consumer buy products, it could also be used in other forms of "biological engineering" of the sort envisioned by Yerkes. Just as Watson had been funded to explain the fundamental building blocks of personality in stimulus-response, now Kinsey would be funded to explain how sex could be used as a form of control. It was a lesson he was eager to teach. It was a lesson which Alan Gregg and Robert M. Yerkes would learn the hard way by falling under Kinsey's control. Yerkes and Gregg would find out first-hand how successfully sex could be used as an instrument of control, after Kinsey took their sexual histories.

In May of 1941, Yerkes informed Kinsey that the CRPS had approved a grant of $1,600 for the fiscal year beginning July 1, 1941. Yerkes strongly advised him to acquaint the committee with his methodology over the next several months through personal discussions or printed material. Kinsey replied that he would be delighted to have any or all of the committee members come to Bloomington and observe his operation.

Part III, Chapter 1

New York, 1940

On April 2, 1940, a man by the name of William Stephenson entered the United States. Stephenson, a British citizen, had ostensibly come to this country on an official mission of the British Ministry of Supply. Britain was now in the middle of a war with Germany, a war which Winston Churchill, who would become prime minister on May 10, had concluded they simply could not win – without, that is, outside help – and the only place with enough sympathy and materiel to help Britain win the war was the United States. Stephenson was sent to the United States as a secret agent whose job it was to get America into the war on the side of England.

To do this, Stephenson had to overcome considerable opposition. The Democrats had been excluded from the White House for the entire decade of the 1920s once the horrendous cost of the First World war became apparent to the American people. The Republicans, who benefited from the backlash against Wilson's foreign adventurism, were, however, divided into two camps: the conservative, isolationist faction which had the base of its power in the Midwest, and the Anglophile, East Coast WASP plutocrats, who, as the description implied, saw their ethnic heritage as English and their allegiance to a group that was similar to them in both income and ethnicity which transcended national borders. Their sympathies were with England in the war then raging in Europe. Perhaps because the elitist practice of American government differed so radically from its democratic theory, the WASP establishment spent much of its time and effort denying its own existence. The facts, however, spoke otherwise. The United States had a ruling ethnic group which acted with surprising unanimity. That ethnic group had converted to Darwinist eugenics as its core belief and the contraceptive as the *sine qua non* of marital virtue at some time before the 1920s. In 1930, as a ratification of this shift in behavior, the Lambeth Conference of the Anglican Church announced the liceity of the contraceptive, after having declared it immoral twenty years earlier. As a result of this combination of ethnic affinity, intellectual corruption, and sexual degeneracy, the ruling class in the United States had become a fifth column bent on empire in the English mode and, therefore, the subversion of the American republic. "Though the American people are largely foreign, both in origin and in modes of thought," Lord Cecil had written after World War I, "their rulers are almost exclusively Anglo-Saxons, and share our political ideals."[1]

When he arrived in this country, Stephenson knew that President Roosevelt's sympathies lay with those of his ethnic group. He also knew that certain families had more clout than others. Which is why he ended up establishing his headquarters on the 38th floor of Rockefeller Center, prime office space for which he paid no rent. Stephenson knew as well that American history could be characterized not only by its source in English culture but by its desire to escape from that influence. That struggle did not end with the successful completion of the Revolutionary War. America and Britain found themselves fighting on the North American continent in the War of 1812, during which Britain succeeded in burning both the Capitol and what came to be known as the White House to the ground.

This struggle did not end with the cessation of military activity in the early nineteenth century. Throughout the nineteenth century, when the American system of protected manufactures brought about a spectacular rise in this nation's wealth, it lay dormant, but in the early twentieth century with the arrival of Irish Catholics and Southern and Eastern Europeans in great numbers, it reasserted itself, and the war was prosecuted by other means. At the heart of this intra-American struggle lay the question of whether America was to become an empire, on the British model, or remain a republic as conceived by the founding fathers, who warned against entangling European alliances. The Anglophile establishment got its first big break with the presidency of Woodrow Wilson, the professor who not only got America into World War I, but who also tried to rearrange the map of Europe according to his own preconceived ideas. Woodrow Wilson, according to Michael Hunt,

> was . . . certain of the universal relevance of Anglo-American political institutions and values. As a student of government, Wilson had long celebrated liberty as the flower of the Anglo-American tradition, its evolutionary advance the benchmark of progress, and constitution-making one of man's great accomplishments. The British parliamentary system was his institutional ideal, and the American Revolution stood for him as an epochal event that made "the rest of the world take heart to be free."[2]

Wilson, like Franklin Delano Roosevelt, was a Democrat. Being a conservative at this time meant being isolationist and being dedicated to the preservation of America as a republic. This Anglophobe tradition, based largely in the Midwest, had as its leaders people like George Norris, a Republican from Nebraska, and Robert LaFollette, Sr., a Republican from Wisconsin. But then as now the Republican Party was divided and the party's Anglophile eastern wing, representing the country's plutocrats, wanted war with Germany even if it wasn't on Wilson's terms. This group, according to Hunt, was:

> self-consciously Anglo in their ethnic orientation and without exception

Protestant (usually Anglican or Presbyterian).The emergent twentieth century variant of this type was usually a Northerner or Easterner and increasingly from Northeastern cities. His formal education at private schools and Ivy League colleges and law schools was supplemented by an informal education in foreign affairs promoted by trips to England and the Continent. He practiced corporate law until gaining public office, usually by appointment. His soundness on foreign-policy questions was insured by the values inculcated in elite social circles, in exclusive schools and in establishment clubs and organizations of which the [Rockefeller sponsored] Council on Foreign Relations (established in 1921) was the most important.[3]

Woodrow Wilson's legacy was the income tax, the hated Versailles Treaty, and an increasing penchant for social engineering of the sort which the *New Republic* under Lippmann, Dewey, and Croly applauded. Wounded by their association with the stock market crash and the subsequent Depression, the Republican isolationists were swept from the White House but regrouped when it became apparent that Roosevelt, like his predecessor Wilson, was determined to lead the United States once more into a European war. Like Woodrow Wilson, Franklin Roosevelt had a hard time separating ethnicity and value. If the Anglo-Americans were the repository of freedom and democratic institutions, then Germans must be bad. Hunt tells us that for Wilson "it was not enough to defeat Germany. He wanted also to defeat those banes of humankind that Germany stood for – imperialism, militarism, and autocracy. A victorious war would be for him only the prelude to global reform. And enlightened peace would redeem the bloody sacrifices of the war and break the grim cycle of suspicion, hatred and conflict."[4]

Things didn't turn out as Wilson planned. The ascendancy of the "Anglo-America" internationalist faction created a crisis of major proportions for this country. Perhaps frightened by the arrival of immigrants from southern and eastern Europe, the eastern Anglophile establishment attempted to change the idea of what it meant to be an American. Now the prime designation was racial and/or ethnic rather than intellectual assent to a series of propositions, foremost among which was the idea that all men were created equal. Americans were now not so much those who accepted a set of propositions and agreed to live according to them: Americans were people of a certain stock, namely white, Protestant Anglo-Saxon. Once this decision was made, ethnic interest replaced citizenship as the primary tie of allegiance. National solidarity took a back seat to race and class. This meant that the Cabots and the Lodges and the Rockefellers identified more with people of their class in England than they did with, say, a Jew or an Italian in New York, which is to say their own newly arrived fellow citizens. This reordering of allegiance meant a transition from republic to empire would follow naturally if this group ever got its hands on the levers of power.

The last great battle came on the eve of World War II. Embittered by the cost of Wilson's War – $100 billion and over 100,000 lives – America turned isolationist in the '20s. The Anglophiles were out of power until the stock market crash of 1929 brought the Democrats back to the White House, and, like President Wilson before him, Franklin Delano Roosevelt was an Anglophile who orchestrated America's entrance into another war. His great opponent in this regard was Charles Lindbergh, head of the America First committee.

Throughout the 1930s Charles Lindbergh and the America Firsters, with many supporters in the Midwest, posed a significant threat to the Anglophile hegemony in foreign policy. That threat disappeared in a matter of minutes on December 7, 1941, when Japan attacked the U.S. fleet at Pearl Harbor and the United States entered the war against the Axis powers on the side of England. From that moment until the present, foreign policy was in the hands of the Anglophile establishment.

Thomas Mahl's book *Desperate Deception* shows that the defeat of the America Firsters wasn't just the result of superior debating skills. William Stephenson, a British millionaire, became head of an entity known as British Security Coordination in 1939. The BSC was an arm of British intelligence whose purpose was to get America into the war on the side of England. In order to do that, the BSC, in the words of Ernest Cuneo, the Roosevelt Administration liaison with BSC,

> ran espionage agents, tampered with the mails, tapped telephones, smuggled propaganda into the country, disrupted public gatherings, covertly subsidized newspapers, radios and organizations, perpetrated forgeries . . . violated the alien registration act, shanghaied sailors numerous times, and possibly murdered one or more persons in this country.[5]
>
> BSC headquarters in New York occupied two full floors of the Rockefeller Center. The fact that Stephenson paid no rent for such prime real estate gives some indication that the Rockefeller family and its wealthy foundations sympathized with his goals and were willing to support him no matter how treasonous or illegal those activities were. The goal was clear. In the first of his seven wills, Cecil Rhodes, founder of the Rhodes Scholarship, called for the creation of a secret society whose aim (in Rhodes' words) is "the extension of British rule throughout the world . . . and the ultimate recovery of the United States of America as an integral part of the British Empire."[6]

Although the Rockefellers were Republican and Roosevelt was a Democrat, in foreign policy both acted on their common ethnic interests. On June 14, 1940, three months after Stephenson's arrival, Nelson Rockefeller wrote to Harry Hopkins to suggest the creation of an intelligence operation that would later, after its official establishment by executive order on August 16, 1940, be known as the Rockefeller Office. By the end of August, the Rockefeller Office was working on a "voluntary program by which American businesses would eliminate all their Latin American representatives who were Germans or German agents."[7] The existence of the Rockefeller Office, otherwise known as the Office of the Coordinator of Commercial and Cultural Relations Between the American Republics, or later the Coordinator of Inter-American Affairs, came to light in 1976, thirty years after the war's end, and only then was it revealed that it had been an intelligence operation.

Stephenson's collaboration with the Rockefellers made a number of things clear. First of all, it showed that the Anglophile establishment, as represented by one of its wealthiest and most influential families, put ethnic identification above citizenship when it came to their primary allegiance. Secondly, it showed that the Rockefeller family was not above supporting illegal activities to attain their ends. Thirdly, it showed that the Rockefeller family was in direct contact with British intelligence, a significant fact when it came to implementing the latest developments of psychological warfare, and finally, the collaboration with Stephenson showed that the Rockefeller family was willing to use that psychological warfare against their fellow Americans. Stephenson brought about the political demise of isolationist Republicans like Hamilton Fish, and those politicians whom they couldn't defeat in political campaigns were defeated by less orthodox methods, including sexual seduction. In addition to conducting phony opinion polls, something which the John D. Rockefeller III's Population Council would refine during the '50s and '60s, the BSC was involved in its own form of sexual engineering. Mahl recounts the fate of Senator Arthur Vandenberg, the once isolationist stalwart from Michigan whose votes, which secured crucial concessions to the British, were brought about by the sexual wiles of Mitzi Sims, wife of British attaché Harold Sims and "Cynthia," the BSC code name for Betty Thorpe, another wife of another British diplomat. The Vandenberg case showed that sex was part of the arsenal of psychological warfare, and the Rockefellers' concurrent interest in supporting Professor Kinsey of Indiana University gave every indication that they were planning to use that weapon in dealing with new enemies.

In May of 1941, Robert M. Yerkes informed Kinsey that the CRPS had approved a grant of $1,600 for the fiscal year beginning July 1, 1941. Kinsey, who had been funding his study out of his own pocket up to that point, was already deeply involved in collecting histories on his own. The promise of financial assistance from the Rockefellers allowed him to expand his efforts by hiring other investigators. In early 1941 Kinsey hired Glenn V. Ramsey, a newly graduated IU Ph.D. who had given his history to Kinsey when he was doing his marriage course, to take histories for him. Ramsey was employed at the time as a high-school teacher in Peoria, Illinois and so naturally began to use his contacts at the high school for Kinsey's benefit, something which would cause trouble before long.

By the middle of the summer of 1941, Ramsey was earning $30 a week from Kinsey for taking histories of high-school students in Peoria, and what is more important, offering them advice on sexual matters if they happened to have questions. Buoyed by his initial grant from the CRPS, Kinsey planned to bring Ramsey onto his staff full time in 1942, providing that a second, larger grant was approved as expected.

But then trouble arrived. Perhaps encouraged by the prospect of full-time employment, Ramsey outdid himself during the fall of 1941 in both pestering his students for the details of their sexual behavior and counseling them in sex matters according to the Kinsey school of sexual ethics. Eventually word of Ramsey's activities got to the students' parents, who then informed the Peoria board of education what was going on and demanded Ramsey's dismissal. The parents were especially outraged that Ramsey was giving what amounted to clandestine sex education to their children, and when Ramsey didn't deny the charge, his fate was sealed. In December 1941, in emergency session, the school board voted to suspend Ramsey. Kinsey, who would later use Rockefeller money as part of Ramsey's legal defense fund, was furious, and he minced no words in either expressing that fury or in letting it be known who he felt was responsible for this attack on sexual freedom. "If we let them get away with this in Peoria now," Kinsey wrote in a letter dated January 23, 1942, "this precedent will encourage Catholics elsewhere, perhaps here in Bloomington or anywhere else, to try the same tactics against us here and against the entire research program."[8]

Kinsey's animus toward Catholics was well known and based on a few simple ethnic facts. The WASP establishment had adopted science, Darwinism, and the contraceptive as their deepest beliefs and the main obstacle to the implementation of a social order based on those values, as the intervention of Msgr. Ryan before Congress in 1934 had shown, was the Catholic Church. Paul Blanshard's book on the "Catholic Problem" was still seven years in the future, but Kinsey's reaction showed that his class had achieved a remarkable amount of unanimity on just who the enemy was. Over the coming decades they would also achieve unanimity on how to solve the problem. Catholics, according to Kinsey's most recent biographer, "struck [Kinsey] as the most wretchedly conflicted group around. In words tinged with both anger and pathos, he noted that the Catholic Church 'has always emphasized the abnormality or the perverseness of sexual behavior which occurs outside of marriage.'"[9] Since Kinsey was "a son of the Enlightenment"[10] whose sexual deviance had led him to a position of "radical antiessentialism,"[11] Kinsey had come to the conclusion that religion was the "root cause of sexual repression" and that science, therefore, had to displace religion as the ultimate arbiter of morality. By the time he was famous in the early '50s, Kinsey would rarely give a lecture without mentioning in throwaway fashion that the Kinsey Institute had the second largest collection of pornography in the world. With the audience's curiosity thus piqued, he would then announce dryly that the largest collection of pornography could be found at the Vatican. Thirty-three years after Kinsey's death, John Barbour, religion writer for the Associated Press, was not only still repeating this canard, when questioned about his source he even said that some anonymous AP writer had seen the collection "in a basement somewhere." Kinsey Report co-author Paul Gebhard would later admit with a laugh that Kinsey had picked up the idea of the Vatican's pornography collection at around 1940 from Robert Latou Dickinson as a sort of insider joke which he would use to get a rise out of audiences.[12] Kinsey was not known for his sense of humor, and the oft-repeated remark about the Vatican's pornography collection betrays more than just a desire to get a laugh. It bespoke the deepest concerns of Kinsey and his class about the growing political power of their main opponents in the culture wars which would follow the successful completion of the shooting war then in progress in Europe. Once the Rockefeller interests defeated the America Firsters, they turned their interests on their next domestic opponents after the war, namely, the Catholics.

Part III, Chapter 2

New York, 1941

In 1941, the feast of the Assumption of the Blessed Virgin Mary's body and soul into heaven fell on Friday that August 15, and in New York City the weather was hot and humid with light rain in the afternoon. It was into this rain that Thomas Merton emerged out of the subway at Lenox and 135th Streets in the heart of Harlem, carrying, incongruously enough, a large bouquet of flowers. Merton, who, seven years later, with the publication of his best seller *The Seven Storey Mountain*, would become the world's most famous monk, was now a young layman, recently converted to Catholicism, and also recently graduated from Columbia University. During the summer of 1941, he was trying to make up his mind whether he was being called to a vocation as a writer or a priest. In April of the same year, he had gone to a retreat at Gethsemane, the Trappist Monastery near Bardstown, Kentucky, which would eventually become his home for the next twenty years. But during the summer of 1941, he was teaching courses in English Literature at Saint Bonaventure's, a Catholic college, and trying to pursue a career as a writer. It was at Saint Bonaventure's that Merton had almost unwillingly attended a lecture given by a Russian émigré by the name of Catherine de Hueck, better known as the Baroness, or simply "the B."

The Baroness had lost her family to the Communists and was now trying to counter their efforts to mobilize the Negroes in Harlem to their cause. Her solution was a radically Catholic social-action project known as Friendship House, which called on her co-religionists to "renounce the world, live in total poverty, but also doing very definite things, ministering to the poor in a certain definite way." The description is Merton's, as entered in his journal, and the attraction of that way of life to this idealistic young man was immediate. Merton, at the time, was emerging in more than one sense of the word. Merton was a second-generation modern, a bohemian by birth, son of an artist and born in 1915 in the middle of the cataclysm that was modernity's defining event. His mother died when he was six years old and after being first placed in the care of his grandparents, he was then dragged around France by his artist father. After his father died, he was placed, along with his younger brother, in the care of his grandparents once again. Merton came by his modernity naturally, so to speak, and spent his time reading its literature, books whose titles he refuses to divulge in *The Seven Storey Mountain*, and living the life that corresponded to the literature and the biographies of the first-generation moderns. As a result he became involved in a number of affairs, one of which (it was rumored) led to an illegitimate child who was killed along with its mother during the blitz in London. A blasphemous mock crucifixion at a drunken party got Merton expelled from Cambridge University and sent back to the New World and New York City, where he enrolled as an undergraduate at Columbia University in the mid '30s.

Unlike the Baroness, who lived with the Communists for a year to learn their strategy for the Negro so that she could better counter it at Friendship House, Merton arrived at Columbia University in the winter of 1935 ready to become a Communist himself. In *The Seven Storey Mountain*, Merton described both the attraction of communism to a promiscuous twenty-year-old and why he ended up rejecting it. "Having decided," Merton wrote, "that God is an invention of the ruling classes, and having excluded Him, and all moral order with Him," the Communists "were trying to establish some kind of a moral system by abolishing all morality in its very source."[1] "Most Communists," he would recount after he had definitively rejected them, "are, in actual fact, noisy and shallow and violent people, torn to pieces by petty jealousies and factional hatreds and envies and strife." At another point he recounted the story of a meeting of Communists at "a Park Avenue apartment" which "was the home of some Barnard girl who belonged to the Young Communist League." "Her parents had gone away for the weekend," Merton recounted; however, the book cases were full of "volumes of Nietzsche and Schopenhauer and Oscar Wilde and Ibsen." Even worse than the literature, Merton found particularly annoying a young man who saw one of the apartment's windows as the ideal place for a machine gun nest.[2]

As in England so in New York. Sexual immorality led to social activism as its palliative. Bloomsbury decadence during the 1920s and before had provided the most fertile soil for the growth of Communism in the '30s. Kim Philby had just left Cambridge when Merton arrived for his short and unhappy term there. Philby and fellow Cambridge students Guy Burgess and Anthony Blunt, William Stephenson's colleagues in Section D, were to go on to make names for themselves as this century's most famous Communist traitors. Merton, who was ripe for the same type of recruitment into the Communist cause, walked up to the brink of commitment and then in a dramatic *volte face* chose Catholicism instead. The appeal in either case was moral. Stephen Spender in *The God That Failed* talked about the "doubly secured Communist conscience"[3]: "A conscience which tells us that by taking up a certain political position today we can attain a massive, granite-like superiority over our own whole past, without being humble or simple or guilty, but simply by virtue of converting the whole of our personality into raw material for the use of the Party machine!"[4]

"For the intellectual of good will," Spender concludes, "communism is a struggle of conscience. To understand this explains many things."[5] Merton never became as committed to communism as Spender did, but he was just as much in need of something to calm his conscience. So much so in fact that he had an episode on the train back to Long Island, during which it seemed "as if some center of balance within had been unexpectedly removed, and as if I were about to plunge into a blind abyss of emptiness without end."[6]

> I had refused to pay any attention to the moral laws upon which all our vitality and sanity depend: and so now I was reduced to the condition of a silly old woman, worrying about a lot of imaginary rules of health, standards of food-value, and a thousand minute details of conduct that were in themselves completely ridiculous and stupid, and yet which haunted me with vague and terrific sanctions. If I eat this, I may go out of my mind. If I do not eat that, I may die in the night. . . . I had at last become a true child of the modern world, completely tangled up in petty and useless concerns with myself, and almost incapable of even considering or understanding anything that was really important to my own true interest.[7]

Catholicism and communism were two spiritual poles in Merton's life which, for a while at least, exerted an equal attraction on him. By the time he arrived in Harlem to work with the Baroness, Merton saw the effects of the same force field on the soul of the Negro. Modernity's rejection of the moral order, which began with the economic liberalism of the nineteenth century, was the matrix out of which all of the twentieth-century ideologies grew. Confronted with the decay of Protestantism's version of Christendom, Merton was forced to choose between a religion of the past, Catholicism, which sought to restore the moral order in its completeness, or a religion of the future, Communism, which chose to abolish it completely. From his description in *The Seven Storey Mountain*, Merton saw the Negroes of Harlem as confronted by the same choices he had already made.

> Here in this huge, dark, steaming slum, hundreds of thousands of Negroes are herded together like cattle, most of them with nothing to eat and nothing to do. All the sense and imagination and sensibilities and emotions and sorrows and desires and hopes and ideas of a race with vivid feelings and deep emotional reactions are forced in upon themselves, bound inward by an iron ring of frustration: the prejudice that hems them in with its four insurmountable walls. In this huge cauldron, inestimable natural gifts, wisdom, love, music, science, poetry are stamped down and left to boil with the dregs of an elementally corrupted nature, and thousands upon thousands of souls are destroyed by vice and misery and degradation, obliterated, wiped out, washed from the register of the living, dehumanized. What has not been devoured, in your dark furnace, Harlem, by marihuana, by gin, by insanity, hysteria, syphilis?[8]

Merton was taken by the Baroness's plea to save Harlem from the Communists. However, his contempt for the culture which created Harlem was tempered by the recognition of the fact that much of the vice that went on there was committed by the inhabitants themselves, often against one another. There is, in other words, a sort of double edge to Merton's early writing on race that seems to have all but dropped out by the end of his life, when his writings reflect an absorption of a specifically Catholic point of view into the concerns of the civil rights movement.

> Now the terrifying paradox of the whole thing is this: Harlem itself, and every individual Negro in it, is a living condemnation of our so-called "culture." Harlem is there by way of a divine indictment against New York City and the people who live downtown and make their money downtown. The brothels of Harlem, and all its prostitution, and its dope-rings, and all the rest are the mirror of the polite divorces and the manifold cultured adulteries of Park Avenue: they are God's commentary on the whole of our society. Harlem is, in a sense, what God thinks of Hollywood. And Hollywood is all Harlem has, in its despair, to grasp at, by way of a surrogate for heaven.[9]

Harlem may have been "a divine indictment"; however, it was also "full of vice," a place

> where evil takes place hourly and inescapably before their eyes, so that there is not an excess of passion, not a perversion of natural appetite with which they are not familiar before the age of six or seven: and this by way of an accusation of the polite and expensive and furtive sensualities and lusts of the rich whose sins have bred this abominable slum. The effect resembles and even magnifies the cause, and Harlem is the portrait of those through whose fault such things come into existence. What was heard in secret in the bedrooms and apartments of the rich and of the cultured and the educated and the white is preached from the housetops of Harlem and there declared, for what it is, in all its horror, somewhat as it is seen in the eyes of God, naked and frightful.[10]

Merton adverts to the sexual vice in Harlem in a way which places virtually all the blame on the dominant white culture. At certain points he descends into unwarranted sentimentality as when he claims "that if Our Lady were to act according to her usual custom, Harlem would be one of the first and only places I would expect her to appear."[11] Yet in spite of lapses into sentimentality, Merton never loses his moral compass. Hollywood is bad, but Harlem is also bad in its way. Both are manifestations of modernity in their way. Hollywood may be a surrogate for Harlem insofar as it manifests money and glamour. However, Harlem is every bit as much a heaven for Hollywood in so far as it epitomizes sexual liberation.

Implicit in Merton's analysis of Harlem is a certain element of moral condemnation, not just of white racist society with its jejune ideals but also of the inhabitants of Harlem who have been taken in by those ideals. Catholic action of the sort proposed by the Baroness had a dual value to the inhabitants of Harlem. It was an antidote to communism, but it also testified to the necessity of following the moral law. Harlem may not be as culpable for its "furtive sensualities" as Hollywood; however, Merton condemns the sexual misbehavior of both. Merton seems to be saying that Harlem was aping Hollywood, when in fact the opposite seems to be the case. Beginning with the twenties, white cultural brokers saw jazz and the Negro as a type to symbolize their liberation from small-town mores and Christian morals. This portrayal was as accurate as the respective media would allow. It could be as sleazy as Van Vechten's *Nigger Heaven* or as innocuous as Hollywood's *Mr. Bojangles*.

By the time Thomas Merton arrived at Columbia, Harlem had evolved its own cultural lingua franca, commonly known as jazz, a form of music to which virtually every Columbia student in the 1930s and '40s was exposed willy nilly. Merton the would-be mystic, talks about taking the subway with his fraternity brothers to the nightclubs on 52nd street and

> letting yourself be deafened by the jazz that throbbed through the whole
> sea of bodies binding them altogether in a kind of fluid medium. It was a
> strange, animal travesty of mysticism, sitting in those booming rooms
> with the noise pouring through you, and the rhythm jumping and throb-
> bing in the marrow of your bones.[12]

At about the same time that Thomas Merton was emerging from the subway on his way to Friendship House, a Columbia sophomore from Massachusetts was all but fully recovered from a broken leg sustained in a football game the previous fall. Jack Kerouac, like Merton, was a Catholic. Unlike Merton, he was not a convert; he had been Catholic from birth, coming from French-Canadian stock which had settled in the mill town of Lowell. In fact, it might be said, that the two young men, seven years apart in age, were being exposed to the same stimuli and as a result propelled in radically different directions. Columbia, which had been a step down from Cambridge, was the scene of Merton's conversion. The same university, which had been more than one step up for the proletarian from Lowell, was the scene of what might be called Kerouac's deconversion from Catholicism. Both spiritual events took place in the shadow of Harlem with jazz playing in the background. Roughly a year before, one of Kerouac's student friends had taken him to the Apollo Theater in Harlem to hear Jimmy Lunceford. It was the first time that Kerouac had heard a black musician in a live performance, and Jack was, in the words of his biographer Dennis McNally, "instantly swept up in the whirlwind known as American race relations."[13] Jack became one of those "alienated whites who at least verbally reject racism and become respectfully interested, sometimes obsessed with, Afro-American culture."

Both Merton and Kerouac were contemptuous of "white" culture, which is to say the prevailing mores in America in the 1940s. However, Kerouac, perhaps because he grew up within the Church, was less able to separate it from the culture at large. Even if Merton was able to slip into sentimental idealizations of the Negro at times, he still shared the opinion of the Baroness that the Negro needed the spiritual resources of the Catholic Church. For

Merton and the Baroness, Catholicism and communism, the forces of good and evil respectively, were fighting for possession of the Negro's soul. If the outcome was in doubt, that was only because the will was free, not because either the Baroness or Merton had any doubts about the good or evil of the respective alternatives.

With Kerouac, at this stage of his life at least, the situation was different. Catholicism was part of the "white" culture which included Columbia University and Hollywood. Given the times, it was not hard to see how the confusion could take root in an impressionable nineteen-year-old. Universities founded under Christian auspices, often as seminaries, still functioned *in loco parentis*, and while modernity had taken root among the cultural elites, those elites had not completed their march through the institutions which supported them. Beyond that, the culture of the time showed a remarkable ability to accommodate Catholic piety, an open-mindedness which would have been unthinkable fifty years earlier – or fifty years later for that matter. In 1928, the Ku Klux Klan had flexed its political muscles and marched against Al Smith, whose famous line after losing the presidential election, "tell the Pope to unpack his bags," memorialized the bigotry that contributed to his defeat. In 1989, using tactics which made the Klan seem tame by comparison, homosexuals in New York City had attempted to shut down a talk given by Joseph Cardinal Ratzinger, the Vatican's prefect for the Congregation of the Doctrine of the Faith. One year later, the same group of homosexuals, in an outburst reminiscent of the nativist riots of over one hundred years earlier, invaded Saint Patrick's Cathedral in New York City during the celebration of Mass, and after shouting down the celebrant, John Cardinal O'Connor, chewed up communion wafers and spat them on the floor.

But in the '40s things were different, and Catholicism enjoyed a public esteem that was unprecedented in American history. In the early '40s, two of Hollywood's biggest box-office successes were *Going My Way* and *The Song of Bernadette*. However, the flip side of this unprecedented esteem was guilt by association. Both Kerouac and Merton, but especially the former, assumed a linkage that was only apparent. In this respect both men followed opposite trajectories. Kerouac was unable to distinguish Catholicism, especially its redaction of the Christian moral code, from what he considered "white" culture at large at the beginning of his career. However, he began to identify himself as more and more Catholic toward the end of his life as he became more and more alienated from the counter-culture he helped launch. Merton, on the other hand, followed virtually the opposite path, especially in regard to the Negro issue. The moral critique of Harlem in *The Seven Storey Mountain* has all but disappeared by the time a late work like *Conjectures of a Guilty Bystander* appeared. Merton's critical faculties were conquered by the categories of the emerging counter-culture. If in the mid-'40s Hollywood was to come under Merton's condemnation, then a good deal of American

Catholicism was going to suffer from guilt by association. In 1964 Merton was to write:

> The confusion modern Catholics can fall into is to treat whatever culture they are born into as if its traditions – although they have nothing to do with Christianity at all – were part of our religion. One clear instance of this is the acceptance, by some Catholics, of the American social tradition of race prejudice, in complete and *sinful* contradiction of the doctrine of the Mystical Body of Christ.[14]

Condemning something as multifarious as a culture is a tricky business, the main danger being throwing the baby out with the bathwater, for each culture is a mixture of both good and bad. Merton's balanced assessment of Harlem in the '40s degenerated by the '60s into a critique that was in no way uniquely Catholic and in many ways indistinguishable from the civil-rights liberalism of the time. If Merton succumbed to Bohemian *ressentiment* against the established order, it is not surprising that Kerouac did the same at an earlier date. In fact, at the same time that Merton along with the Baroness was proposing Catholicism as the antidote for Harlem, Kerouac was adopting Harlem as the cure for "white" culture, if not specifically Catholicism. By the 1940s, the Harlem Negro, primarily through the medium of jazz, symbolized the antipode to the values espoused by the dominant culture. As early as 1929, Claude McKay could write that "The American darky is the performing fool of the world today."[15] With the end of World War II, New York became the cultural capital of the world, and the Negro's symbolic value increased correspondingly.

In 1941, around the same time that Thomas Merton was working at Friendship House in Harlem, Alfred Kinsey was also showing an interest in the Negro. "Late in 1941," writes Kinsey co-worker Wardell Pomeroy in his biography of Kinsey,

> Kinsey went to Gary, Indiana, where he secured seventy-one histories of blacks, nearly all of them females, and in the process had his first brush with the police, who were highly alarmed when they heard rumors of what he was up to in the black neighborhoods. Unable to make the patrolmen understand, Kinsey was taken to the station house, where he made his explanation to the night captain, who called the University. As soon as Kinsey's identity was established, there were no further objections.[16]

Pomeroy neglects to tell the reader that the police were interested in Kinsey because virtually all of his histories of black females were taken from prostitutes. At another point in the same book, Pomeroy mentions going with Kinsey to Indianapolis to measure the clitorises of black prostitutes there. The fact is significant. Kinsey was drawn to the Negro ghetto for the same reason Jack Kerouac was. He was intrigued by sexual pathology, which he construed, like Kerouac, as a sort of liberation from Christian morality. As early as 1942, Kinsey had heard of the homosexual demimonde of Times

Square from prison inmates at the Indiana State Penal Farm. When he arrived to take his sex histories, Kinsey ran into Jack Kerouac and his crowd of "white Negroes" down slumming from Columbia University. "Kinsey," Kerouac wrote in *On The Road*, "spent a lot of time in Ritzy's bar, interviewing some of the boys; I was there the night his assistants came, in 1945. Hassel and Carlo were interviewed."[17]

Carlo was the homosexual poet and countercultural icon Allen Ginsberg; Hassel was the homosexual prostitute and petty criminal Herbert Huncke. The man who proved to be the key link between Times Square and Columbia was the homosexual drug addict William Burroughs, author of *Naked Lunch*, which Burroughs characterized as a kind of "catharsis where I say the most horrible thing I can think of."[18] Kerouac typed the manuscript and thought it exceeded the efforts of the French homosexual playwright Jean Genet, the Marquis de Sade, and the Satanist, Aleister Crowley.

It was among people like this that Kinsey came to his conclusions about the sexual behavior of the average American male. According to Pomeroy's account, Kinsey

> came to Times Square with no contacts whatever, and hung around the bars on Eighth Avenue that he recognized as gay. Observing for hours at a time on different occasions, he noticed a man who also seemed to be constantly hanging around. Going over to him, he said, "I am Dr. Kinsey, from Indiana University, and I'm making a study of sex behavior. Can I buy you a drink?"

Pomeroy concludes that "it was impossible . . . to doubt this clear-eyed, earnest, friendly man from the Midwest." According to his own account, Huncke only agreed to give his sex history after Kinsey agreed to pay $10 for it. After listening to Huncke's story in his hotel room, "a sexual history that must have stood out for its rich variety, from his first experience at the age of nine," Kinsey asked to measure the size of Huncke's penis. He took out a card with a phallus drawn on it and explained how he would mark the length first when soft and then erect. Kinsey then said he would pay Huncke $2 for every interviewee he could produce. Ted Morgan goes on to say that Burroughs "may be the only writer of renown to have his sexual history on file, including his penis size soft and erect, at the Kinsey Institute for Research in Sex Gender, and Reproduction, in Bloomington, Indiana."[19] Perhaps Morgan doesn't consider William Faulkner a writer of renown, but Faulkner's history is on file at Bloomington as are those of other literary figures, who felt the need to show and tell all to "this clear-eyed, earnest friendly man from the Midwest."

Kinsey was driven to the ghetto, to prisons and to gay bars – his three favorite sources for sexual histories – for two reasons: first of all, he liked the variety he found there, being especially avid for homosexual deviance, and secondly, because this sort of person was the only sort who would talk to him. Given the particulars involved in his interviews, something over which he and his co-workers still maintain a veil of secrecy, it becomes obvious that only a certain type of person is going to be willing to be interviewed. Psychologist Abraham Maslow brought out this "volunteer bias" in an article which appeared in *The Journal of Abnormal and Social Psychology* in April 1952, maintaining that

> the bias introduced into a sex study by the use of volunteers is, in general, in the direction of inflating the percentage reporting unconventional or disapproved sexual behavior - such as masturbation, oral sexuality, petting to climax, premarital and extramarital intercourse, etc. The more timid and retiring individuals, evidently, are apt to be privately, as well as socially conforming. They are likely, it seems, to refrain from volunteering for sex studies in which they are asked embarrassing questions. The present study would lead us to conclude that the percentages reported are probably inflated and that they should be discounted to some extent for volunteer-error until reexamined.[20]

Maslow, who worked with Kinsey at the time he was gathering histories, made his findings known to Kinsey while he was preparing his first volume, but Kinsey ignored the objections. In a letter written in 1970, Maslow said that he warned Kinsey about volunteer error but Kinsey "refused to publish it and refused even to mention it in his books, or to mention anything else that I had written. All my work was excluded from his bibliography."[21] According to Maslow, "the whole basis for Kinsey's statistics was proven to be shaky,"[22] by the findings on volunteer bias, which Kinsey willfully ignored.

This self-selection bias was true of both whites and Negroes, but Kinsey found out that this was true of the Negro first-hand when he tried to get interviews from "educated Negroes" at Howard University. According to Pomeroy's account, Kinsey and Co. "were surprised to find a great deal of resistance to giving histories, a rare occurrence. Kinsey quickly understood why. These students thought Whitey was delving into their lives in his own interest, not theirs; white researchers encounter the same reaction today when they attempt to make ghetto studies."[23]

This is the first of many contradictions in Pomeroy's account of Kinsey's inclusion of Negro material in his reports. Pomeroy begins his section on the Negro by saying that as of 1945 "Kinsey was acutely conscious that his Negro sample at that point was too heavily loaded with poorly educated and economically lower groups, and he was afraid that too many people might take that picture as typical of Negroes as a whole."[24] Pomeroy goes on to say that "[i]n time, however, we did get enough histories of upper-level Negroes to compensate for the others." However, he concludes the section by quoting Kinsey's claim that "our first published volume was confined to the white male."

On page 79 of the female volume, published in 1953, Kinsey, et al., write that "[s]ome small portion of the discrepancy between our female and male data may be accounted for by the fact that these interracial contacts were included in the male volume but are not accounted for in the present volume, because no Negro females are included in this volume." That disclaimer would seem to indicate that the Negro material did make it into the first Kinsey Report. On p. 213 of the same volume, Kinsey writes concerning "sex dreams" that "some 13 percent of the females in the sample (Negro and white) who had ever dreamed, had had sex dreams which went beyond their actual experience," again indicating that the Negro material has been included in the female volume as well.

One Kinsey scholar reconciled this apparent contradiction by saying that in the matter of race, Kinsey "wanted to have his cake and eat it too." Kinsey included the material on ghetto Negroes to tilt the norm toward sexual deviance while claiming to have excluded it because he wanted to insure the respectability of his data in the face of white suspicions about Negro sexuality. Kinsey included the Negro material, which, as his experiences at Howard University showed, was primarily drawn from prisoners and prostitutes, because it weighed the reports' results in favor of deviance and helped in destabilizing moral norms. Kinsey deliberately sought the ghetto as the locus of sexual pathology, every bit as much as he sought out the denizens of gay bars and prisons. And when he sought out whites in New York City, it was almost exclusively among those with a heavy penchant for deviance. They were the only people willing to talk to him, as Maslow had proven to his dismay.

If, as Kinsey claimed, there was no difference between the mores of black and white, class being equal, then there was no more reason to exclude blacks than whites from his database. The only thing which affected the sample was volunteer bias, which Kinsey ignored, but which affected both races equally. Furthermore, his sample of Negroes was more than ten times the size of his sample of Orthodox Jews, a fact which in no way prevented him from the most grandiose generalizations about the latter group's sexuality. Taken as a whole, Kinsey's data were drawn overwhelmingly from the pool of the sexually liberated, precisely the alliance between ghetto-dwelling black and white bohemian described by Kerouac in his novels. Both groups needed each other. Kinsey, et al., had a craving for deviance, and the deviant groups he interviewed, especially the homosexuals according to Pomeroy, needed to confess to the all-enabling, all-approving "scientist" from the Midwest. "Not far from the hotel," Pomeroy writes, describing a session of taking sex histories around Times Square, "a towering Negro male prostitute came running after us, having recognized Kinsey" as the "sex doctor" and then wanting to know "why ain't you come around to get my history."[25]

Kinsey proved to be the role model of a whole generation of subverters of sexual morality, including Masters and Johnson and Hugh Hefner, who mentioned Kinsey as the inspiration behind the founding of *Playboy*. Since only the sexually liberated would talk to him, Kinsey's reports proved to be an expression of the hip-ghetto alliance in one of its purest forms. When Kinsey tried to portray these results as an expression of what everyone did, the sexually liberated culture brokers accepted it with an avidity that bespoke a guilty conscience. After describing his own instincts as essentially "lecherous," Max Eastman went on to add "that I experienced no glimmer of surprise or disbelief when Dr. Kinsey published his book of statistics about *Sexual Behavior in the Human Male*"[26] – something which should have come as no surprise since Kinsey was basically describing the behavior of people who behaved just like Eastman. Norman Mailer's description of the "White Negro" could be just as easily applied to Kinsey and Pomeroy's nocturnal ramblings around Times Square. Both were "urban adventurers who drifted out at night looking for action with a black man's code to fit their facts."[27] Beyond that, Mailer saw the emergence of the "hipster," the "White Negro," as a crucial watershed in the history of the Left in this century. Describing the decade which began with the publication of the Kinsey Report in 1948 and ended with the publication of Kerouac's *On the Road* and the emergence of the beatnik as a mass cultural phenomenon, Mailer opines that

> the rise of the hipster represents the first wind of a second revolution in this century, moving not forward toward action and more rational equitable distribution [i.e., communism], but backward toward being and the secrets of human energy, not forward to the collectivity which was totalitarian in the proof but backward to the nihilism of creative adventurers. . . . that first revolution . . . was conscious, Faustian and vain, enacted in the name of the proletariat but more likely an expression of the scientific narcissism we inherited from the nineteenth century. . . . the second revolution . . . would be to turn materialism on its head, have consciousness subjugated to instinct. The hipster, rebel cell in our social body, lives out, acts out, follows the close call of his instincts as far as he dares.[28]

At some time during the late '40s or early '50s, the sexual revolution, as epitomized by the ghetto Negro and his white imitators, had succeeded the Communist revolution as the Left's preferred vehicle of social change. Instead of Negroes having to become Communists – the status quo in the 1930s as demonstrated by people like Richard Wright, Langston Hughes, and Paul Robeson – now the true left-wing revolutionary had to become a Negro – as evidenced by people like Jack Kerouac and Neal Cassady. The economic revolution had been superseded by a cultural revolution of primarily sexual dimensions, with the ghetto Negro as its avant garde.

Part III, Chapter 3
Bloomington, Indiana, 1942

Kinsey may have lost his battle with the Peoria school board in early 1942, but his stature with the Rockefeller Foundation and its surrogates continued to rise. In December 1942 Robert Yerkes and two of his colleagues at the NRC made a trip to Bloomington "to get fully acquainted with Dr. Kinsey and his methods of work."[1] Kinsey was now at the height of his power as a sex investigator, and he used that power to ensnare the people who held the purse strings which supported him, ensuring a steadily increasing flow of foundation money for the next twelve years. Kinsey, according to Jones, "had no intention of becoming an agent of social control."[2] However, Kinsey's behavior following the arrival of the "three wise men from the east," indicates otherwise. It also indicates that Jones can't read his own text, for the visit to Bloomington – what later became known as "the treatment" – was an exercise in the use of sexual liberation as a form of control from the very beginning, something which becomes clear from Jones's own description of it.

No sooner had his visitors checked into their rooms at the IU student union than Kinsey had them over at Morrison Hall looking at pornography, which was a prelude to taking their sexual histories. According to Jones, "Yerkes, Corner and Reed agreed to give Kinsey their sex histories so that they could evaluate his ability to secure accurate data." But it is clear, even from Jones's account, that Kinsey had ulterior motives, motives which Jones can admit to himself only reluctantly. Kinsey, according to Jones, "would control and they would react; and at the end of the interviews, he would possess their secrets ,but they would not know him. . . . Kinsey had built a life on the principle that knowledge is power. He understood full well that taking their histories would give him leverage. . . . Once they contributed their histories, they would surrender their privacy, an act of trust that would force them to rely on his pledge of confidentiality."[3]

Jones describes Kinsey's encounter with the three wise men using all the rhetoric of psycho-sexual control without once admitting the most obvious fact, namely, that once the foundation executives had told Kinsey the most intimate details of their sex lives, they could now be blackmailed if they ever had second thoughts about continuing their support. Kinsey was using the sex histories as a form of control. Just as the people most likely to fall into a scam are people who have perpetrated one themselves, so those most likely

to be controlled by sex are those interested in using sex as a way of controlling others. In this instance, Yerkes and the other scientists were easy pick-
ings. Yerkes and his colleagues entered the trap with their eyes wide open.
Kinsey later told a friend that Yerkes, et al., "everywhere made it apparent
that this is the study they have been waiting for more than twenty years."[4]
According to Jones, Yerkes "had never abandoned his goal of using the
CRPS to support scientists who could provide reliable data that would help
society *understand and control human sexual behavior* [my emphasis]."[5]
Kinsey not only allowed Yerkes to broaden the CRPS studies to involve sexual research on humans at a time when it was considered taboo, he also allowed him to save his own job by moving from "the extension of knowledge
disinterestedly, in accordance with the scientist's ideal and almost regardless
of social values, applications and risks," into something dearer to the heart of
the Rockefeller Foundation at the moment, namely, "biological engineering."

As Christopher Simpson makes clear in his *Science of Coercion*, the immediate goal of this sort of research was the defeat of the Axis powers, and
shortly thereafter the defeat of international Communism during the Cold
War. But unlike World War II, the Cold War was not a declared war. It may
have had a middle and a clearly defined end in 1989, but it would have been
troubling to Aristotle because it had no clearly defined beginning, other than
a speech by Winston Churchill which served that role with more of the benefit of hindsight than anything else. As a result, it was the liberal cabal which
inhabited the OSS/CIA, the foundations, the media, and academe which determined more often than not how this research got put to use and against
whom. The Communists were the obvious targets, but as the '50s proceeded,
it was also becoming increasingly apparent that many of the black operations
begun by this cabal also targeted segments of the United States population
which were from the point of view of the psychological warriors needed to
be subverted or enlightened.

The personal, in other words, is only half the story here. Professor
Kinsey, with all of his homosexual compulsions, would have remained just
one more geek with a bow-tie and crew cut if the Rockefellers hadn't paid his
way to fame. Kinsey "had emerged at precisely the right moment to capitalize on the foundation's desire to use science as a tool for controlling human
behavior."[6] Jones goes on to say that "the decision to impress science into the
service of social control eventually backfired. Social hygienists failed to recognize that scientific data could be used to support sexual liberation as easily
as social control," but that is simply because Jones fails to understand that
sexual liberation *is* a form of social control, and it is precisely for this reason
that the Rockefeller Foundation was interested in learning more about it.
Sexual liberation fit in with the rest of the research they were sponsoring on
psychological warfare at the time, and if the information didn't get used dur-

ing the '40s or the '50s, it most certainly got used during the '60s, when John D. Rockefeller III and the Population Council under Bernard Berelson orchestrated what has come to be known as the Sexual Revolution, beginning with *Griswold v. Connecticut*, through *Roe v. Wade*, up to Henry Kissinger's NSSM 200 in 1974, which established population control as the pillar of United States foreign policy. Not surprisingly, since they subsidized the research that went into the book, Jones's biography of Kinsey amounts then to an exculpation (perhaps unwitting) of the Rockefeller Foundation; Kinsey is made the fall guy, for something that would and in fact did take place without him.

Jones documents Kinsey's use of sex as a way of controlling people throughout his book, but he seems strangely incapable of understanding all of its ramifications. "I think [Kinsey] liked secrets, that their possession gave him a sense of power," said one source who felt that Kinsey "could have figuratively blown up the United States socially and politically" if he had chosen to reveal the sexual histories of the "political, social and business leaders of the first rank" he had interviewed during the course of his research.[7] Jones omits the fact that Kinsey threatened to do just this, a fact mentioned by Wardell Pomeroy in his 1972 Kinsey biography. The control was a two-way street. Kinsey controlled the men who controlled the purse strings at the Rockefeller Foundation, and they in turn hoped to capitalize on his insights by implementing instruments of sexual control throughout the culture at large.

In this regard the controllers at the Rockefeller Foundation – Yerkes, Corner and Gregg – got more than they bargained for in Kinsey, whose *modus operandi* capitalized on the ideological commitment to science they shared. To begin with, all of the above-mentioned men had jettisoned religion in favor of science as a guide to life. That naturally led them to see sex as just one more field of study, which led them to ignore its power over them. Hence when Kinsey jerked their chains, they were unaware of what was going on until it was too late. In this Kinsey played Dionysos to their Pentheus .(see Euripides' *The Bacchae*.) All the while they thought he was in their power, when all he had to do was ask if they wanted to see the women dancing naked on the mountainside to turn the tables on them.

Which is precisely what Kinsey refined into the standard treatment for VIPs who came to visit the Institute in Bloomington. "I want you to see our library and our collections of erotic materials in sufficient detail to understand what bearing they have on the research project as a whole," Kinsey wrote to Alan Gregg, director of the Medical Science Division of the Rockefeller Foundation and the man who held the purse strings.[8] On February 6, 1947 Gregg arrived in Bloomington. "Kinsey," Jones tells us, "took obvious delight in showing his visitor various books, photographs and drawings."[9] Kinsey's delight is not hard to understand when one considered the amount of both money and approval the Rockefeller Foundations would shower on his compulsions. Kinsey understood how sex could be used as a way of controlling Gregg and through him the virtually unlimited financial resources he controlled.

The culmination of every trip to Bloomington was, of course, the moment when Kinsey took his victim's sexual history. (Actually, many of Kinsey's willing victims then went on to allow themselves to be photographed while engaged in sexual activity, but this was the exception and not the rule.) Yerkes had given his history before Gregg arrived in Bloomington and afterward no matter how shabbily Kinsey treated him, Yerkes felt obliged to support him. The word "blackmail" springs most immediately to mind. Kinsey took sexual histories as a way of gaining power over people, and scientists, those who felt that sexual morality was an outdated remnant of a bygone era, were his easiest picking in many ways. The threat of blackmail was never far from the practice of taking sexual histories, which is probably, in addition to his prurient interest in the subject matter, why Kinsey was so avid to take them. Once he had taken their sexual histories, Kinsey had a record of the most intimate details of the lives of men in the public eye, men who could have been easily brought down by scandal. Beyond that, he could also use the information as a way of working on their weaknesses, something especially true of homosexuals.

Kinsey's use of sex as a way of controlling people was not limited to foundation executives. He did the same thing to the press in preparation for the release of the male volume. Reporters were invited to Bloomington, softened up by being shown pornography, then asked to sign a "contract" which would allow Kinsey to read any article they wrote before it was published – in the interest, of course, of scientific accuracy. To insure final control over this willing group of Enlightened thinkers, Kinsey persuaded them to give their sexual histories. Then in the event that one of the journalists would somehow come to his senses and write something unfavorable, Kinsey had a wealth of information on the most intimate details of his life that could be used against him.

Kinsey tried the same tactic on the statisticians who came to Bloomington to rip apart his claim that what he was doing was in any way representative of the American population at large. In October of 1950, under extreme pressure from the people at the Rockefeller Foundation, who by this point were convinced that Kinsey's data was statistically bogus, Kinsey agreed to meet with a panel of experts from the American Statistics Association which arrived in Bloomington for days of meetings. In this particular meeting Kinsey was like a deer caught in the headlights. He quite simply could not provide the statistical proofs for the arguments which had appeared in the male volume two years before. Facing almost certain humiliation, Kinsey could only save the day by shifting the conversation to sex. "Things did not take a turn for the better," according to Jones, "until the statisticians gave their sex histories. For the first time since they had arrived, Kinsey finally had them where he wanted them – on his turf."[10]

Kate Mueller, the dean at IU who eventually got Kinsey removed from teaching and contact with students, was subjected to the same kind of pressure . When Kinsey failed to persuade Mueller to back down, he became enraged. "I was quite frightened," Mueller recounted later. After the threat of physical violence subsided, Kinsey told Mueller that she "was unsuited for the job I had; *he thought I ought to give him my own history*" [my emphasis].[11] Given Kinsey's success with the people at the Rockefeller Foundation, it's not hard to understand why he wanted Mueller's history as well, nor is it hard to understand how the fact that IU president Herman Wells gave Kinsey his history virtually insured support from the top for his entire tenure there.

In the end, the only people at the Rockefeller Foundation who were capable of pulling the plug on Kinsey funding were the people who had not given him their histories. Those who had were completely under his control even when it jeopardized their standing among their peers and even after the controversy surrounding Kinsey's project had introduced unprecedented dissension into the group. The three wise men from the Rockefeller Foundation – Yerkes, Corner, and Gregg – never knew what hit them. The same premise undergirds contemporary phenomena like SAR (Sexual Attitude Restructuring) of the sort that psychologists and medical professionals are forced to undergo for certification as experts in the field of sex. SAR means looking at pornography, and the sex educators who have followed in Kinsey's footsteps understand that if you look at enough pornography, you will become desensitized; your attitudes will change; you will be more likely to act on what you see and less likely to object to what you see. If you follow the trajectory to its logical conclusion, you will become someone enslaved to passion – a sexual addict, to use the contemporary term. This is the strategy behind porn on the Internet; it is a variant of the CIA psy-op strategy of targeting elites. TV is for lowbrow propaganda. Computers for elites.[12] Kinsey did the same thing with foundation executives, academics, and journalists, insuring that the publication of the male volume would be greatest PR coup in American history. The success of this coup was insured by sexual manipulation, but it was also engineered by the psychological warfare network, which would later put his work to effect in the '60s. Sexual manipulation was the *sine qua non* of a whole new advance in the power of social control which the psychological warriors had developed during World War II; however, it would work only in a society whose sexual mores were more liberal than the law permitted in the '50s. Hence, the need to change the laws on obscenity and contraception during the '60s.

In January 1943, Robert M. Yerkes returned to New York to sing

Kinsey's praises to Alan Gregg. Kinsey's web of control was so light at this point that none of the people caught in it knew that it existed. Yerkes was full of enthusiasm for Kinsey's work and hoped that Gregg would approve long-term funding, something which Yerkes found especially appealing since long-term funding for Kinsey would also be long-term funding for the CRPS. At around the same time that Yerkes met with Gregg, Kinsey met with Dr. Robert Latou Dickinson, an early devotee of sexual liberation and author of a book on contraception, who had contact with Magnus Hirschfeld's world congresses on sexuality. Since Dickinson too, independently of Yerkes, sang Kinsey's praises into Gregg's ear, an increase in funding seemed like a foregone conclusion. In May of 1943, the NRC announced that Kinsey had been awarded a grant of $23,000 to continue collecting his sex histories. Before long that money would increase to $40,000 per annum. By the time it cut him off in 1954, the Rockefeller Foundation would pour hundreds of thousands of dollars into the coffers of the Kinsey Institute, which by special agreement became an independent entity on the IU campus in 1941 shortly after their first big grant. The Kinsey Institute would then go on to have its cake and eat it too for the next fifty years and more, taking in money from the public trough – by 1990 they would get $500,000 per annum from the Indiana legislature alone – but all the while behaving as if the materials which the state paid for could be kept from the eyes of all but a few within the charmed circles of Kinsey Institute certified experts.

Kinsey, in the meantime, continued to use his sex histories as a form of controlling influential people and consolidating his power. In August 1943 the CRPS sponsored a conference on primate sexuality for Kinsey's benefit at the Hotel Pennsylvania in New York City. After introductory remarks by Yerkes, in which he claimed that Kinsey's research would "contribute to the understanding and wise control of human sex behavior,"[13] Kinsey got down to business, which, in spite of the conference's avowed purpose, was not talking about monkeys, but rather getting the sex histories of the scientists in attendance. Kinsey then lost no time in putting what he found out to personal use. When Yerkes hinted that there may be too much homosexuality in his survey and that it might skew and nullify the applicability of the results, Kinsey shut Yerkes up by informing him that there was no such thing as "normal" sexual behavior. Kinsey then informed Yerkes that he knew whereof he spoke because he had interviewed all of the scientists at the recent primate conference and that of the eighteen attendees, only two or three could be considered normal. "I speak with some knowledge for I have the histories of most of that group," Kinsey informed Yerkes.[14] As he expanded the web of his control, Kinsey paralyzed all those who objected by claiming to be in possession of knowledge which they subsidized but could only access through Kinsey and his secret code.

While in New York for the same conference, Kinsey met Alan Gregg in person for the first time. Since Gregg had been hearing his trusted advisors sing Kinsey's praises for months now, it was not surprising that he was completely won over by Kinsey in person, when he arrived at his office on the morning of September 3, 1943. What followed was non-stop "treatment" as Kinsey pressed all of the buttons which would elicit the proper responses from a fellow WASP eugenicist who believed that science should replace religion as the arbiter of morals. After so many years of disappointment, after Watson's defection to Madison Avenue and years of Yerkes's pointless subsidy of animal studies, Kinsey must have seemed to Gregg like the answer to a prayer, if he had been disposed to pray. Gregg was favorably impressed. Kinsey, as usual, had his own agenda. In courting Gregg, he was conspiring to cut out Yerkes, the middle man, and thereafter get all of this funding directly from the Rockefeller Foundation, or if that failed, he at least assured that the funds wouldn't dry up at their source, now that he had Yerkes firmly under his control.

Alan Gregg, however, had a similar agenda of his own. His position at the head of the medical division was secure, so the control he was interested in was the control he saw flowing from Kinsey's survey into the foundation which controlled the purse strings for the benefit of the ethnic group which it represented, a group which was now locked in struggle with the Axis powers and would become, after their demise, locked into another, less visible struggle with the Catholics and the Communists in its continuing quest for world domination.

In February 1943, a social worker from South Bend, Indiana, by the name of Wardell Pomeroy joined the Kinsey Institute staff. Pomeroy would later become one of the administrators of the sex education and certification empire, but in the fall of 1943 he had run into trouble. In the fall of 1943, Wardell Pomeroy was told to report to Draft Board #6 in South Bend to prepare for induction into the armed services. Kinsey was attached to Pomeroy for a number of reasons. He had just trained Pomeroy in his questioning techniques and secret codes, and, since it was difficult enough to get anyone at all to work during the war, Kinsey was faced with the prospect of a severe labor shortage just when the money started to flow in abundance and the Rockefellers were looking for results. Kinsey was also interested in Pomeroy because of his unconventional sex history, something which made him "nonjudgmental" in Kinsey's eyes, which meant that Pomeroy would just as resolutely promote deviant sexual behavior as Kinsey would. Pomeroy was also a willing participant in sexual experiments, episodes that sometimes involved sex with Kinsey himself but more often than not involved sex with willing participants which Kinsey would observe first-hand. "The beauty of sex research," according to Jones, "was that it allowed Kinsey to transform his voyeurism into science."

To term what Kinsey did "science" required a large stretch of the imagination, but the Rockefeller Foundation was willing to make that stretch, and so it was to them and to Gregg in particular that Kinsey turned in his hour of need, asking Gregg to write a letter to Pomeroy's draft board. Gregg obliged and would do so for other Kinsey assistants when asked. In each instance the letter he wrote gave the rationale for Rockefeller's support of Kinsey's activities. Far from promoting "liberation," the Kinsey Institute was providing a form of control. On October 21, 1943, Alan Gregg contacted Draft Board #6 in South Bend to inform them that Wardell Pomeroy was engaged in "providing information of quite exceptional value to persons responsible for the control of soldier and civilian personnel."[15] After giving the rationale for Rockefeller subsidy of the Kinsey project, Gregg continued by adding, "No investigative work in several years has produced as much valuable information as the project employing Mr. Pomeroy and I am in considerable measure depending on his experience with its methods."[16] The local draft board ignored Gregg's request, but Pomeroy's classification was reversed when it reached Washington, probably because at the time the Rockefeller interests had more clout on the national than on the local level.

In December 1943 Dr. Dickinson visited the Kinsey Institute in Bloomington where he was given "the treatment," which meant extensive exposure to pornography in a world where it was rare because owning it meant the threat of criminal prosecution, with all of the predictable results. Dickinson, as a result, began sharing his contacts with Kinsey and as a result, Kinsey met the man Jones identifies only as Mr. X, and the Kinsey people as "Mr. Green." Mr. X, identified elsewhere as a government employee by the name of Rex King, was an omnivorous sexual deviant who had, among other sexual contacts, molested according to his own account 800 children.[17] The fact that he had recorded his crimes in some detail made him even more interesting to Kinsey, who was writing to him in May of 1944 to tell him in no uncertain terms "You must not, under any condition, destroy your materials."[18]

Kinsey was interested in Mr. X for other reasons as well, not least of which was the fact that he seemed to embody Kinsey's ideal of the "natural man," i.e., the man in whom moral inhibition had evaporated completely. In Mr. X, Kinsey saw "a scientific treasure,"[19] which is to say, the living proof that his theory of sexuality was not only theoretically possible, it had actually been lived by a man who was now willing to share his records of sexual molestation with Kinsey. It was as though "the second Darwin" had discovered the sexual equivalent of "the missing link."[20]

Contact with Mr. X, however, brought up some unsettling issues as well. Chief among these was the fact that Kinsey was involved at the very least in promoting criminal activity and at worst in committing it himself. Victor Nowlis had begun work at the Kinsey Institute in June of 1944 with his wife and two children. Nowlis was a Catholic, and he was also a protégé of Yerkes. Because of the latter fact, Kinsey had to overlook the former fact and hire Nowlis in the name of preserving his funding. Perhaps because of that fact, Helen Nowlis was the only staff wife who did not give her sexual history to Kinsey, and the only one to object to the "degree of control which somehow or other [Kinsey] felt he needed over his colleagues."[21]

In October 1944, Nowlis accompanied Kinsey, Clyde Martin, and Wardell Pomeroy on a sex history collecting trip to Columbus, Ohio, during which Kinsey "seemed to be setting up some kind of homosexual activity."[22] Nowlis was amazed that even he hadn't seen how the others were already engaged in this kind of behavior with Kinsey.

Because he wasn't sexually involved with Kinsey, Nowlis was able to see other things as well. Nowlis considered Mr. X a "monster," and counseled against including his material in the male volume, but Kinsey was determined to proceed. With that decision, which involved Mr. X's ongoing molestation of children, Kinsey became still more deeply involved in criminal activity. Jones claims that had Yerkes got wind of what was going on, the NRC and the Rockefellers would have cut off financial support. However, since Yerkes was Nowlis's mentor, and since Yerkes himself had been to the institute and had seen the material, which at that time probably included material on children, it seems clear that the Rockefellers knew that Kinsey was involved in illegal activity and either ignored it or felt that it was necessary to advance their agenda.

In March of 1945, Kinsey offered to pay Mr. X's salary, with Rockefeller money, so that he could take a leave of absence to organize his materials. Jones admits that Mr. X was a "predatory pedophile"[23] and that Kinsey exhibited "a huge moral blind spot,"[24] by employing him, but goes on to say that "Kinsey took the records of Mr. X's criminal acts and transformed them into scientific data."[25] Just how scientific the data were which were acquired in the midst of perverted sexual activity would be subject to later debate, specifically when questions on the source of the child sexuality data began to be asked. All the while the involvement of the Rockefeller Foundation in criminal activity deepened. Much of the outrage against it has vanished with the laws against sexual deviancy which the Kinsey reports helped to overturn, but the animus against child molestation remains, and as Table 34 on Kinsey's study attests, someone was heavily involved in molesting children during the gathering of data which led up to the book's publication.

Kinsey began writing the male volume during the summer of 1945 and would continue that work for the next two years. He would claim that his report was "first of all a report on what people do,"[26] but he never really got around to telling the nation which people were doing what. By claiming that his report was simply an account of what the average person did while basing it on his personal fascination with the mores of people like Mr. X, Kinsey provided the perfect vehicle for the destabilization of morals and the subsequent increase in political control which flowed from that change.

On April 3, 1946, the trustees of the Rockefeller Foundation met and, after hearing about Kinsey's work in detail, approved an unprecedented three-year grant of $120,000. As soon as Kinsey got the grant, he went out and hired photographers Clarence Tripp and William Dellenback as "permanent members of the Institute staff." He also purchased expensive camera equipment, which both Dellenback and Tripp used to photograph Kinsey and other staff members as well as outside volunteers in sexual activity. The Kinsey Institute was now in the pornography business, and the Rockefeller Foundation was footing the bill. One person who found this unpalatable was Warren Weaver, a member of the foundation board who would go on to become a determined foe of Kinsey. In a letter dated May 7, 1951, when the board was fatally polarized over Kinsey and ready to cut him loose, Weaver reminded his colleagues that he had opposed the funding for pornography, which means that they were aware that that was what the money was being used for at the time. Weaver complains that Kinsey's "library of erotic literature has become sufficiently important so that they have installed and equipped a complete photographic laboratory, and have a full-time photographer (I almost said full-time pornographer) who receives $4,800 a year."[27]

Weaver concludes his letter by contending "that it is perfectly realistic to say that the RF is paying for this collection of erotica and for the activities directly associated with it. And I say further that I don't think we need to, or ought to."[28]

Just what "the activities directly associated with it" entailed would come out later. In 1980, in an article which appeared in the homosexual magazine *The Advocate* Samuel Steward discussed being filmed while engaged in sadomasochistic homosexual activity.[29] On October 8, 1998, England's Channel 4 ran a documentary directed by Tim Tate entitled "Secret History: Kinsey's Pedophiles," during which Clarence Tripp, the man Kinsey hired with Rockefeller money, described an incident during which Mr. X (or Mr. Green) had sexual relations with a child "who agreed to sexual contact." Tripp failed to mention that no child can legally agree to sexual contact with an adult. Tripp goes on to say that the child "yelled out when it actually took place" because "they were very young and had small genitalia and Green was a grown man with enormous genitalia and there was a fit problem."[30] If Tripp was observing the encounter, as his testimony implies, then he was most probably filming it as well, since that was his job. This means that the Rockefellers were funding, as Weaver implies with considerable trepidation, the filming of the molesting of children.

As Kinsey's use of the Rockefeller name increased and their involvement with him deepened, his benefactors would become increasingly nervous – evidently with good reason. In spite of their desire to remain anonymous behind-the-scenes agents of social change, the Rockefeller Foundation was being lured into an unwanted public position primarily by Kinsey's manipulation, which was based in turn on his desire to legitimate what he was doing. On March 27, 1943, Senator Harry S Truman of Missouri stood up in the United States Senate and accused the Rockefellers of treason because of their business dealings with the German firm of I.G. Farben. Before long, the same call would be heard again in the same halls, largely as a result of Kinsey's obsessive desire to drape the mantle of social approval over his hunched shoulders.

Part III, Chapter 4

New York, 1947

In the summer of 1947 both Thomas Merton and Jack Kerouac had completed books, and both books would end up with the same editor, Robert Giroux, who was then with Harcourt, Brace and Company and fresh out of a stint in the U.S. Navy. Within a year, Merton's autobiography would go on to become the bestseller of 1948 and the biggest-selling book of Giroux's career. Kerouac's novel, *The Town and the Country*, wouldn't appear until one year later and then only to modest sales and politely respectful reviews. But in the summer of 1947, the 25-year-old Kerouac decided to embark on a cross-country hitch-hiking adventure that would prove to be the basis for his one and only bestseller, *On the Road*, which would not appear until 1957. Both books were to prove to be immensely influential in their way. *The Seven Storey Mountain* was an enormously sympathetic portrayal of Catholicism at a time when the world was weary of modernity and its destructive ideologically fueled wars. *The Seven Story Mountain* was a Catholic best-seller in a country in which, according to Michael Mott, "Catholics in the public eye, with a few exceptions, had been anxious to underplay the fact that they were Catholics." The book coincided with the rise of Bishop Fulton J. Sheen in the equally improbable role of a Catholic bishop as an American TV star. *The Seven Storey Mountain* inspired a series of conversions among the intellectuals and caused an overnight housing shortage at Gethsemane, the Trappist monastery outside Bardstown, Kentucky, where Merton had sought refuge from the modern world.

There is no indication that Kerouac read Merton's autobiography or that he was interested in what it proposed. At the same time that Merton was writing about the "dark furnace" of Harlem with its "marihuana, gin, insanity, hysteria, syphilis," Kerouac was on his way to making what Merton perceived as Negro vices into a new religion of hedonism that would ultimately eventuate in the beatnik and hippie phenomena. Unlike Merton who saw Christianity as the cure for the malaise of Harlem, Kerouac saw negritude as the cure for white alienation. Both books began in the shadow of Harlem and then proceeded in opposite directions in a way which indicated how American culture found itself at the crossroads in the 1940s.

On February 6, 1947, Alan Gregg arrived in Bloomington for the "treatment." Kinsey had written to him earlier telling him: "I want you to see our library and our collections of erotic material in sufficient detail to understand what bearing they have on the research project as a whole." Since Alan Gregg was a human being, and since what Kinsey had to show was hardly available on street corners at the time, the unhinging of the chairman of the Rockefeller medical division was likely now reinforced from what he had first seen as one of the three wise men from the east five years earlier. Whatever his immediate reaction might have been, Jones tells us that Gregg was "hooked,"[1] and that meant that Kinsey was insured funding for the foreseeable future. Gregg's decision may have been based on prurient interest or it may have been based on the potential for blackmail as well, but even admitting all that, what Kinsey was proposing was what the Rockefellers had been seeking all along. From the point of view of the Rockefeller Foundation, which had used Yerkes as a way of funding Watson's behaviorism as a way of understanding and controlling human behavior, Kinsey was the man who was to deliver what others had only promised. "He had emerged," according to Jones, "at precisely the right moment to capitalize on the foundation's desire to use science as a tool for controlling human behavior." The Rockefeller interests may have promoted Kinsey in the name of science, but their subsequent behavior makes clear that they were not interested in the truth when it came to sexuality. When it became obvious that Kinsey's statistical methods were fatally flawed, the Rockefellers arranged for a meeting with the American Statistical Association so that Kinsey could regain some credibility by the time the female volume appeared, but they did nothing to disabuse the public that what Kinsey presented as a picture of the way Americans behaved sexually was in reality nothing of the sort. In fact, at the same time that it had become obvious to the Rockefeller board that the statistics were just plain inaccurate, the Rockefeller interests were promoting changes in laws across the country based on what they knew were bogus statistics.

In addition to a secure base of financial support at the Rockefeller Foundation, Kinsey had traded on the Rockefeller name with such skill that the New York publishing world was beating down his door for the privilege of publishing his book. Kinsey eventually settled on Saunders, the medical publishing house from Philadelphia. In late 1947, W. B. Saunders Company, a Philadelphia-based medical publishing house, did a market survey to decide how large their first printing of a book on sexual behavior by an Indiana University entomologist should be. They originally settled on a first run of 10,000 but upgraded that figure to 25,000 by the publication date of January 5, 1948. By January 15, Saunders had ordered its sixth printing, bringing its initial run to a total of 185,000, an unheard of number for a medical publisher. The title of the book was *Sexual Behavior in the Human Male*, but it came to be known as the Kinsey Report. Two hundred thousand copies of the first Kinsey Report were sold in the first two months following its publication. Perhaps nothing makes the moral choices faced by this nation more strikingly apparent than the fact that both a Catholic convert who eschewed the world for a monastery in Kentucky and a notoriously anti-Catholic bigot who did probably more than any one man in the postwar period to undermine sexual morality could both achieve bestsellers by appealing to the same conflicted readership.

Over the summer and fall of 1947, Kinsey took the instrument of control which he had forged so successfully in dealing with the foundations and applied it to the press, and in so doing he engineered what has been called the greatest public relations coup in American history. The technique was simple: invite the reporters to Bloomington, show them pornography, then get them to give their sexual histories. Lawrence Sanders found Kinsey's skill at handling the press little short of miraculous.[2] Then as if that weren't enough, Kinsey got the reporters to sign a thirteen-point written contract that allowed Kinsey final say over the articles they were writing.

In retrospect it has become clear that few people actually read the Kinsey Report when it came out. Journalists were vetted before being given access to it, and then had to clear their stories with Kinsey before he allowed them to publish them. The result was a series of adulatory articles that overlooked virtually all of the book's shortcomings. In 1954, a group of statisticians showed with devastating accuracy just how thin and unrepresentative Kinsey's samples were. To give just one example, Kinsey based his statement that orthodox Jews are the least sexually active of all religious groups in the United States on a sample of 59 Orthodox Jews in the entire U.S., all of college level. Kinsey was portrayed as a thoroughly conventional family man who was dedicated to nothing but scientific truth. One of the unwittingly true things said of him is that he "possessed none of the conventional vices." Since Kinsey was fond of inserting, among other things, a toothbrush into his urethra, and was filmed from the waist up while doing it, one could hardly say that his vices were conventional. The result, however, was a glaring case of journalistic oversight. Not until 32 years later did anyone seem to notice that Table 34 of the male volume involved what had to be criminal activity involving the torture of children.

Just why the more than normally perceptive people at the *New York Times* either ignored or suppressed or missed this fact may be traceable to the behind the scenes connections the paper had with the report. Since Arthur Hays Sulzberger, the publisher of the *New York Times,* had been on the board of trustees for the Rockefeller Foundation during the time it approved money for Kinsey's experiments, it would have been embarrassing, to say the least, to notice that that money had been put to use for criminal activity. So it was not noticed. And in the New York Times-Rockefeller-Kinsey connection we have just one instance of conflict of interest, that allowed the book to become a bestseller.

On January 4, 1948, the Sunday before the male volume was published, the *New York Times* ran an adulatory review of the book by Howard A. Rusk, director of the medical center at New York University. Rusk ignored the plain evidence of criminal behavior in the book and went on to tell the American public that everything that they had been taught about sex was wrong and had been proved so by "science," as indicated by Kinsey's statistics. That statement was clearly false, but Rusk did have some true things to say too. He informed the *Times'* readers that the "nation was in for a major overhaul of its mores."[3] This truth bespoke first of all the intentions of the social engineers who were plotting that overhaul with the Kinsey Reports as their front. The Rockefellers were interested in social engineering through the manipulation of sexuality, and the Kinsey Report was the vehicle which would make that possible in the near future, with the collaboration of a supine mass media culture.

Shortly after the Kinsey Report appeared, riding on the crest of a tidal wave of covertly manipulated positive press, the Carnegie Institute made a grant creating the American Law Institute as the educational arm of the American Bar Association. The main function of the American Law Institute was to promote something it referred to the as the "model penal code," and one of the purposes of the model penal code was the abolition of sex crimes. In the year the Kinsey Report appeared and the ALI was funded to implement its sex findings by changing laws in every state in the union, Morris Ernst, a lawyer for the ACLU published a book based on Kinsey's findings that, given the time lag in book publishing, could have only come from inside information. Ernst's book, *American Sexual Behavior and the Kinsey Report,* targeted 52 sex crimes for removal from the country's penal codes, including sodomy and the distribution of pornography. "It is fair to say," writes Judith Reisman, that Ernst's book "could not have reached the public so quickly without prior arrangements and collaboration with powerful individuals and institutions, including the influential media agents of the Rockefeller Foundation."[4] Ernst, who spent the rest of 1948 trying to get the ACLU to support his proposed changes, made it clear that Kinsey was essential to the destabilization of the moral order which he was proposing. "The whole of our laws and customs in sexual matters," he wrote, "is based on the avowed desire to protect the family and at the base of the family is the father. His behavior is revealed by the Kinsey Report to be quite different from anything the general republic had supposed reasonable or possible."[5] Rene Guyon, a French jurist and pedophile, also published a book calling for the restructuring of sexual morals in 1948. Like Ernst's book, it was also to include material from the Kinsey Report which was released prior to the KR's publication date. The introduction was written by Kinsey promoter Harry Benjamin. Over and over, the same truth was drummed into the heads of an unsuspecting American public. "Unless we want to close our eyes to the truth or imprison 95 percent of our male population, we must completely revise our legal and moral codes." When people hear the same thing from different sources, they tend to perceive it as true. As a result of the combined PR expertise of the Kinsey Institute, the Rockefeller Foundation, the *New York Times*, and all of the alumni of the OSS who were now involved in psychological warfare at either the foundations, academe, or the mass media, people began to hear the same thing over and over again and gradually their attitudes began to change away from traditional morals and toward the biologist eugenicist views of the mandarins who controlled the culture from behind the scenes.

Part III, Chapter 5

New York, 1947

Kenneth Rose was so chagrined by Arthur Packard's rebuke over the "Catholic problem" that he lost no time in writing back to him to assure him that his contribution of Saucony stock would be used exclusively for Planned Parenthood's Negro Program. Launched in February 1943, the Negro Program was:

> A nation-wide educational program [which] was launched simultaneously to acquaint Negro leaders with the existence and purpose of these programs and to enlist their active cooperation in creating among Negroes a greater understanding of the importance of Planned Parenthood to their health and welfare and economic security.[1]

The Rockefellers were avid supporters of the Negro Program, and Planned Parenthood regularly received large infusions of Saucony Oil stock to keep it going. On March 6, 1943, Jeannette Jennings Taylor wrote to Mrs. John D. Rockefeller, Jr. to thank her for her contribution, noting that "at this time especially it is very important to give every parent medically directed birth control so that they may plan a strong and healthy family, thereby improving the quality instead of the quantity of our race."[2]

By funding programs like the Harlem Project, the Rockefellers hoped to cut Negro fertility. Influencing Negro ministers would prove relatively easy; however, there was no clear cut connection between what the ministers preached and how their congregations behaved. The connection between what the preachers preached and the unchurched was even more tenuous. The Catholics, the other main dysgenic group in the United States according to the Rockefeller interests, posed the opposite problem. The connection between Catholic preaching and Catholic sexual behavior was closer, but the opposition to contraception was adamant and all but universal among Catholic priests. Both situations would change during the '60s, the former as a result of government programs inserted into the War on Poverty and the latter as a result of the subversion of Catholic intelligentsia through payments to Catholic colleges and universities.

By 1947 the ruthlessly imperialist nature of Soviet communism had been exposed. Communism had dominated intellectual circles in the United States with increasing authority since 1917 when the until-then-socialist magazine *The Masses*, under the editorship of Max Eastman, came out in support of Bolshevism. By the 1930s, that domination was virtually com-

plete. Then came the Hitler-Stalin Pact in 1939, causing widespread disillu-
sionment, and the denunciation of communism by both Churchill and
Truman after World War II. As a result, for the first time in thirty years the
Left found itself without a clear champion. The so-called Negro question had
been a large part of the left-wing agenda in the United States ever since John
Reed, at the behest of Lenin, invited Claude McKay to address the Third
Communist International in 1920. McKay wouldn't arrive in Moscow until
two years later, and their collaboration never really got off the ground. However, this failure does not change the fact that advocacy of the Negro question fell solely within the agenda of the Left during this period. In 1933,
Nancy Cunard wrote that "the more vital of the Negro race have realized that
it is communism alone which throws down the barriers as finally as it wipes
out class distinctions. The communist world order is the solution of the race
problem for the Negro."[3]

Beginning with a 1928 Comintern decision which decided that the Negro race constituted a separate nation within the United States, the Communists gave major priority to working with blacks. The Communists were
behind the massive publicity campaign in 1931 and the following years to
save the "Scottsboro boys"; they also helped create the National Negro Congress. However by the late '40s their dominance was on the wane. This was
partially the result of international politics; the Soviet Union was no longer
an ally in the war to defeat Hitler. But it was also a result of the heavy-handed
way in which the Communists attempted to control the Negro issue. Richard
Wright was expelled from the party during the '30s. Ralph Ellison gives
some indication of Communist duplicity and manipulation in his book *Invisible Man*. Harold Cruse in *The Crisis of the Negro Intellectual* claims that
"the profound ineffectiveness of [communist] social action did not strike me
forcibly until around 1950–51."[4] The event which crystallized Cruse's discontent with the party's policies was a left-wing-inspired boycott of the
Apollo Theater for showing the anti-Communist satire *Ninotchka*, with
Greta Garbo in the starring role. The decision had been ordered "by the communist hierarchy downtown" and forced onto "the captive Negro leadership
in Harlem." Cruse found the whole incident "ludicrous" because it showed
how little the concerns of the Communists coincided with those of the average Negro in Harlem, who couldn't have cared less about the Garbo film.

By the late '40s a significant realignment in Negro-Left relations was
ready to occur. The Communists who had dominated black-white relations
were in the process of being swept aside as irrelevant to the concerns of both.
The Negro could see nothing to gain from picketing *Ninotchka*, and the
whites in the United States were more interested in what the image of the Negro could provide culturally than in the contribution he could make to the
Communist Party, which was seen as an increasingly irrelevant middle man

in the cultural sphere. Michael Harrington describes the change in political terms:

> There was . . . a brief period in the thirties when it seemed that the Communists and [Brotherhood of Sleeping Car Porters, President A. Phillip] Randolph had the same idea: a class movement of black and white workers. Norman Thomas, Randolph's comrade, was playing a critical role in organizing an integrated union of sharecroppers and poor farmers in the South, and Randolph himself had emerged as a key black trade unionist. But when Randolph organized the March on Washington Movement and forced Roosevelt to decree an antidiscrimination measure in the war industries, the Communists, now supporting World War II with a fanatic intensity since the Soviet Union was under attack, denounced him as a "fascist." After World War II, the Communists were viciously persecuted by Democratic liberals, such as Harry Truman and Hubert Humphrey, as well as by Joe McCarthy; the crimes of Stalin were partially acknowledged by Khrushchev; and the party lost almost all of its previous influence, in white America as well as black.[5]

What was true on the political front was *a fortiori* true on the cultural front. The policies of the Communist Party in the United States were seen as increasingly irrelevant to both blacks and whites. The blacks wanted amelioration of Jim Crow, not revolution, and the white intelligentsia, like their prototypes Margaret Sanger and Max Eastman, decided they were more interested in sexual liberation than economic improvement for the working class. In effect, the two parties decided to eliminate the irrelevant middle man that the Party had become. Communism had become irrelevant, because with the advent of the Cold War, neither racial integration nor sexual liberation were going to go anywhere under a Communist banner. The Negro who had been proposed as a paradigm of sexual liberation by the moderns in the '20s and then virtually taken over by the communists in the '30s, as evidenced by the career of Richard Wright and as portrayed in Ellison's *Invisible Man*, suddenly found himself in a position where his weight as symbol outweighed the Left's ability to control it.

Sensing in a perhaps-inchoate way the change in the balance of power and the new mood of the postwar period, Jack Kerouac stepped into the situation and seized the day. The Negro had liberated himself from Communist patronage and was increasingly free to dictate his own terms in the cultural marketplace and hearken back to the images created during the Harlem Renaissance, which were at once more relevant to the cultural scene in the United States and more immediately appealing to what the Left now wanted. In cultural terms, the Communist tail had stopped wagging the dog. The Left opted out of its allegiance to the Communist Party and began to throw in its lot more and more with the Negro, whose cause showed the most promise of discrediting the social and moral status quo that needed to be delegitimatized in their eyes. As Norman Mailer said in 1957 in "The White Negro," "the only revolution which will be meaningful and natural for the 20th Century will be the sexual revolution one senses everywhere."[6] And then drawing the conclusion that was forming in mind of the Left during the late '40s, "the source of Hip is the Negro."[7] Jazz, the "working philosophy in the sub-worlds of American life" has made "its knifelike entrance into culture, its subtle but so penetrating influence on an avant-garde generation" whose main tenets are "a disbelief in the socially monolithic ideas of the single mate, the solid family and the respectable love life."[8] It was a transformation which took place over twenty years. By the '30s it hadn't started; by the late '50s it was complete.

The pivotal point was the late '40s when Jack Kerouac hit the road. Instead of Bigger Thomas, the Negro hero of *Native Son* who aspires to become a Communist, we have Sal Paradise, the white hero of *On the Road*, who aspires to become a Negro.

"At lilac evening," Kerouac wrote of his stay in Denver, where he was visited by Robert Giroux, the same editor who worked with Thomas Merton on *The Seven Storey Mountain*, who discussed changes in Kerouac's first novel *The Town and the Country*,

> I walked with every muscle aching among the lights of 27th and Welton in the Denver colored section, wishing I were a Negro, feeling that the best the white world had offered was not enough ecstasy for me, not enough life, joy, kicks, darkness, music, not enough night.[9]

Roughly twenty years later, a convicted rapist by the name of Eldridge Cleaver, professing to be impressed by both Kerouac and Merton, cited both the lilac evening quote from *On The Road* and the dark furnace quote from *Seven Storey Mountain* in his book *Soul on Ice*. Cleaver, who was himself a Catholic once, found himself confronted by two Catholics who were using the Negro as a way of proposing Catholic moral teaching and sexual liberation respectively as the way out of the collapse of "white," i.e., Protestant, ideals. In 1968, when *Soul on Ice* came out, Cleaver chose the sexual liberationist point of view with a vengeance; however, ten years later after exploring leftist, liberationist, and terrorist options, he chose the Christian alternative in his book *Soul on Fire*.

Kerouac in Denver in the late '40s finds himself wishing that he were anything, even "a Denver Mexican, or even a poor overworked Jap," anything but a "'white man disillusioned."[10] He faults himself for having "white ambitions," and having had them all his life. As the antithesis of "white ambitions" he fantasizes "the dusky knee of some mysterious sensual gal." When a "gang of colored women" pass by, he almost gets his wish; one of them approaches him and mistakes him for someone named Joe, perhaps because of the dwindling light, but scurries back to the group when she recognizes her mistake. This gives Kerouac another occasion to bemoan his "whiteness." "I wished I were Joe," he continued. But unfortunately, "I was only myself, Sal Paradise, sad strolling in this violet dark, this unbearably sweet night, wishing I could exchange worlds with the happy, true-hearted, ecstatic Negroes of America."[11]

Writing in the late '50s, when Kerouac's novel had just spawned the beatnik fad, Norman Podhoretz felt that "Kerouac's love for Negroes and other dark-skinned groups is tied up with his worship of primitivism," which seems fair enough, but then he goes on to call this Melanophilia "an inverted form of keeping the nigger in his place."[12] With the benefit of thirty some years of hindsight, however, it would be more accurate to say that Kerouac was expressing the exact opposite attitude. Kerouac was advocating the "negrification" of American culture. "Black" mores were proposed as the new norm in America in a cultural revolution that had at its heart the overturning of the moral order and the hegemony of the Judeo-Christian God who created it. Here, as in the Harlem Renaissance twenty years earlier, the Negro who believed in God and sexual morality and was involved in raising a stable family was simply written out of his race by those bent on implementing the de-Christianization of American culture.

If we take Merton, Kerouac, and Cleaver, all at least one-time Catholics, as three separate representatives of rebellion who maintained a sympathetic view of Christianity, it becomes easier to define what "white" meant. White culture was essentially secularized Protestantism. Cleaver talked about going to Mass in prison, as opposed to Protestant services, even though that would have been a closer approximation of his own background (his grandfather being a minister) because that was where the Mexicans worshipped. He wanted non-white worship. Merton had similarly unflattering things to say about the "progressive" Zion church congregation of his grandparents on Long Island. Each of the three men was attracted in variously coherent ways to the universality of Catholicism because Catholicism was an internationalized Christianity in ways that Protestantism was not. And because it was international, it was not "white" in the way that the Protestant sects were. The Protestant churches, by the facts associated with their inception, had become de facto national churches. The Church of England was a national and therefore "white" church in the way that the Catholic Church in Spain was not and could never become. "The Catholic Church in the United States," writes Cyprian Davis in *The History of Black Catholics in the United States*, "has never been a white European church. The African presence has influenced the Catholic church in every period of its history."[13] The consequences for the slave trade in the new world were striking. In Protestant North America, the Negro slave was never assimilated into church or society because that society was based on a "national" church. Beginning with Luther, who established a rigorously German national church in the sixteenth century, Protestantism could only propose a particularly ethnocentric brand of Christianity which lacked the cultural flexibility to absorb members of other races. The French Jesuits arrived in the New World to convert the Indians. The English Puritans who arrived at about the same time, arrived, with some notable exceptions (John Eliot, the "Apostle to the Indians," comes to mind), to conquer and not convert.

Because of their close alliance with secular authority, the reformed churches were similarly unable to resist the pressures of the Zeitgeist. R. H. Tawney and others talk about the gradual retreat of the Protestant churches on the issue of usury, but this was only emblematic of changes in doctrine across the board. This in combination with its voluntarist bias – Luther's position on free will is a good example – rendered most denominations helpless when it came to preserving the historic intellectual patrimony of the faith. As a result, the various churches found themselves in a position where they could either be doctrinally "pure" or faithful to the facts of human existence. Puritanism in America collapsed before the end of the seventeenth century. Jonathan Edwards attempted a return to Calvinist doctrinal purity and succeeded in a way that cut him off from any effect on his peers. In the nineteenth century, Emerson imbibed enough German idealism to lead an already etiolated Unitarianism to its logical conclusion outside the bounds of Christianity. By the late nineteenth century, Protestant belief in the United States had reached a state of crisis, similar to the one in Victorian England. Belief had lost its connection to mores, leaving those who believed open to the charge of hypocrisy, and making a revolution of mores all but inevitable. During the course of an intimate conversation with a female friend during which Mark Twain explained what he believed, the woman asked why he didn't publish these beliefs. Mark Twain responded by asking a question of his own:

> I asked her if she had ever encountered an intelligent person who privately believed in the Immaculate Conception – which of course she hadn't; and I also asked her if she had ever seen an intelligent person who was daring enough to publicly deny his belief in that fable and print the denial. Of course, she hadn't encountered any such person.[14]

The passage appears in the first volume of Max Eastman's biography. Eastman is instructive for our purposes. He began his career as a socialist and editor of *The Masses*, then converted to Bolshevism only to be disillusioned by what happened to the Russian revolution. By the late '40s, Eastman was a committed anti-Communist who would later write for both *Reader's Digest* and *National Review*. Throughout all his political permutations, however, Eastman remained a strong supporter of sexual revolution. Eastman was the son of two Congregationalist ministers. Twain's wife attended their church. Born in the 1880s, Eastman was part of the proto-modern generation which carried the loss of belief into the public arena. When Eastman and his generation advocated free love or birth control or Bolshevism, he could be chided by intellectual elders like Mark Twain as being indiscreet but not for advocating anything that they thought was morally impossible.

In addition to being born under the sign of ethnocentrism, the "white" Protestant Churches fought a losing battle against the Zeitgeist to maintain doctrinal integrity. Since the Enlightenment, which Protestantism had absorbed as avidly as other cultural phenomena, believed in "progress," which is to say morals which were historically relativized, the sins of the past could easily become the virtues of the future. Since virtually all American blacks came from that same Protestant/Enlightenment culture, and since most of them only knew Christianity through the medium of one or the other Protestant denominations, it was inevitable that they would make connections between "whiteness" and Christianity. Christianity had become "white" through its association with Protestant national churches. At the same time it had become "white," it had become secularized as well, leaving it prey to pseudo-scientific racialist ideologies. Christian doctrine was succumbing to ideologies like Darwinism and the related beliefs of racial superiority that would flourish in the late nineteenth and early twentieth century. In each instance, one had not only a "white" religion, i.e., one associated with an ideology of race, one had likewise a hypocritical "white" religion, which had proven incapable of maintaining doctrinal orthodoxy in both faith and morals. When belief failed, pressure to change mores was sure to follow. And the Left's exposure of the ethnocentrism of the Protestant churches was the surest way to undermine their credibility.

Part III, Chapter 6

Dartmouth, 1947

In 1947, a little over two years after Kenneth Rose of Planned Parenthood called Arthur W. Packard to goad him into action against the Catholics, a middle-aged writer by the name of Paul Blanshard had just finished a book on the Caribbean for Macmillan and was browsing through the stacks in the Baker Library at Dartmouth University when he came across *Moral and Pastoral Theology*, a four-volume work by an English Jesuit by the name of Henry Davis. Blanshard was especially impressed by the sections on what he called "priestly medicine," so much so, in fact, that as he read, his "eyes bulged with astonishment," as Davis described "the most detailed and viciously reactionary formulas for women in childbirth" as well as prescriptions for "sexual intercourse without contraception."[1] "Did the public really know about this amazing stuff?" Blanshard wondered. And then, as if to answer his own question by concluding that it did not, Blanshard decided to embark upon "a deliberate muckraking job, using the techniques that Lincoln Steffens and other American muckrakers had used in exposing corporate and public graft in the United States."[2] Blanshard was going to do an exposé on the Catholic Church.

Lincoln Steffens went on to become famous for his trip to the Soviet Union, where he announced that he had seen the future and concluded that "it works" a few decades before the Soviet Union, if not the future, collapsed. Blanshard was evidently having similar thoughts. He was looking at the demographic future of the United States, and he decided that he didn't like what he saw. Because the WASP aristocracy had adopted the contraceptive as an integral part of their married lives, America was on its way to becoming a Catholic country. As a result, Blanshard got on a train shortly after his visit to the Baker Library and set himself up at a table at the Library of Congress where he promptly devoted the next few months of his life to immersing himself in the arcana of Catholic moral theology. "I realized," he said later, "that I had the best story of my journalistic career."[3]

What Blanshard doesn't tell us in his memoir is that what he would go on to term "the Catholic Problem" in his 1949 best-seller, *American Freedom and Catholic Power*, was on the minds of many other people of his class and background as well. The immediate catalyst for all this concern was a 1947 Supreme Court decision which goes by the name of *Everson v. Board of Education*, in which the Court, in a 5-4 majority ruling written by Justice Hugo

Black, affirmed that the State of New Jersey could reimburse the parents of Catholic schoolchildren for the cost of their bus transportation to and from school. The decision provoked outrage among groups already concerned about the rising political clout of American Catholics and provoked articles and editorials in newspapers across the country which saw therein the demise of American democracy, since American democracy was predicated on the socialization which its citizens received, as John Dewey had shown, in the halls of its public schools.

Everson eventually spawned a group known as Protestants and Other Americans United for the Separation of Church and State (a name which Blanshard ridiculed as "clumsy" and which was eventually changed to the less unwieldy Americans United for the Separation of Church and State). Blanshard would eventually become its spokesman in fighting what the group perceived as a Catholic takeover of the country. Using the vocabulary of the recently concluded war, Blanshard claimed that the Catholic Church was sympathetic to fascism, if not itself a crypto-fascist organization, and Blanshard cited concordats the Church had signed with Franco's Spain, Mussolini's Italy, and Hitler's Germany as evidence. In his second book on the same topic, *Communism, Democracy, and Catholic Power*, Blanshard also attacked the Church as totalitarian in the Stalinist sense of that term, calling the Vatican and the Kremlin, "the two greatest dictatorships in the world."[4] and calling in question as well the *bona fides* of one of America's partners in the anti-Communist crusade. "One of my basic purposes in writing the book," Blanshard would recall later, "was to deprive the Catholic Church in the United States of its shopworn claim that because it was such a bitter enemy of communism it was therefore entitled to respect as a friend of democracy. My rather transparent conclusion was that democracy should eschew both manifestations of totalitarian rule."[5]

In addition to spawning organizations like Protestants and Other Americans, *Everson* prompted the American Unitarian Association to stage an elaborate tribute to Thomas Jefferson in Washington, which was attended by four Supreme Court justices and broadcast across the nation on the NBC radio network. Jefferson, as both a Southerner and a slaveholder, was an unlikely hero for Unitarians from Boston, but Jefferson was crucial to their efforts because of the phrase which the Unitarians took from one of his letters in 1801 which spoke about "a wall of separation between church and State." The main speaker at the 1947 Jefferson pageant in Washington was Frederick May Eliot, a Unitarian spokesman who pleaded fervently for a Christianity "free of all autocratic ecclesiastical control over the mind and conscience of its individual members."[6] Fearing perhaps that his reference proved too oblique to his audience, Eliot later explained that "although I have named no names, I have no doubt that what I meant was clearly understood by the members of the hierarchy," i.e., the Catholic bishops.

Blanshard's articles on Catholic power appeared in the November 1947 issues of *The Nation,* a leftist journal which had taken sexual liberation as one of it perennial themes. It should come as no surprise then to learn that the real issue in the aid to nonpublic education debate which *Everson* spawned was sexual, something which Blanshard makes clear in his memoir. Conceding that "on the surface the Catholic arguments" in favor of school aid were "persuasive," Blanshard quickly got to the heart of why "enlightened and progressive parents . . . should not support a Catholic school system." The reason is sexual: "That system is part of a great conservative complex centering in Rome which, without giving American Catholics the power to disagree effectively, stands for no birth control, no divorce, no abortion and the promotion of many anti-scientific ideas which liberals find repugnant."[7]

If the separation of Church and State as applied to education, both Catholic and public, had a distinctly sexual subtext, Paul Blanshard's life had one too. Blanshard was born in Fredricksburg, Ohio, in 1892, minutes before his twin brother Brand, to a preacher father and into a family which he characterized later in life as "afflicted with too much religion."[8] That Blanshard did not feel so at the time of his youth is evident from the fact that he, like his father, became a minister himself. Like Max Eastman, who came from the same milieu and underwent the same sort of conversion to sexual libertinism, Blanshard can only view his early life in the light of the choices which created the person he later became, choices which made his early vocation to the ministry seem all but incomprehensible. "It is hard for me now to understand why I chose the ministry as a career," Blanshard wrote in his autobiography at the end of his life. Then, as if to answer his own question, he adds a few sentences later, "I think sexual continence had something to do with it."[9] As with most sexual revolutionaries, Blanshard has difficulty reading his own texts. Unlike Wilhelm Reich, who saw clearly in his sex-pol work in Berlin and Vienna that the idea of God evaporated from the minds of seminarians who became enmeshed in sexual vice, Blanshard never understood that the absence of chastity in his own life brought about his deconversion from Christianity and caused his ultimate abandonment of the pulpit.

Blanshard would later write that his life had been dominated by three themes: religion, sex, and politics. As his Christian namesake had said in another context, the greatest of these was love. Sex was the driving force behind Blanshard's animus against the Catholic Church. He became famous attacking the Church at the precise moment in history when the Catholic Church in the United States was powerful enough to stand athwart the eugenic Protestant juggernaut and say 'no,' and make that 'no' stick by thwarting birth control legislation in every state in the union. Blanshard was not a Protestant, in any religious sense, when he became a spokesman for Protestants and Other Americans United for the Separation of Church and State – by then he didn't even believe in the existence of God – but he was very much a Protestant in the ethnic sense of the word, and since many of his peers had undergone the same sort of deconversion he had, he could represent their ethnic interests without hesitation. Blanshard, more importantly, was still committed to sexual liberation, and the separation of Church and state as promoted by "Protestant" groups was simply a front for sexual liberation. "Protestant" theology à la Blanshard was essentially negative. It was the antithesis of what Catholics believed. This becomes obvious in the case of birth control. "Blessed be the pill!" Blanshard wrote as an old man. "Perhaps some future historian will hail it as our century's greatest contribution to happiness – and also the dissolution of Christian monogamy."[10] By 1950 no one seems to have noticed anything anomalous about the fact that Blanshard, the "Protestant" spokesman, was promoting the demise of Christian marriage.

It was a task which came naturally to him since he worked avidly to undermine his own marriages. As a young man, Blanshard married a co-ed from the University of Michigan. Like Shelley and Engels and Max Eastman, Blanshard took a page from *Queen Mab,* and both he and his bride pledged "to live together only as long as love should last."[11] After giving up his pulpit in Tampa, Florida, Blanshard arrived with his wife, virtually penniless, in New York in 1917, where they, like Margaret Sanger and Max Eastman before them, got swept up into left-wing politics and free love, as espoused by *The Nation*. As some indication of what *The Nation* stood for at the time, Blanshard cites Joseph Wood Krutch's book *More Lives than One*, in which he describes the "gay crusaders" (a term which has taken on a different sexual connotation) at *The Nation* as "all Liberals but even more conspicuously Libertarians or Libertines – in the Eighteenth Century sense of the term, as well as, frequently at least, in the modern sense also."[12] That meant, of course, "complete frankness in [the] marital relationship,"[13] which was a euphemism for rationalized adultery. Krutch would later advocate more discretion and less forthrightness in practicing adultery, but Blanshard found that he and his wife never had to hide anything from each other. "After our children were born," Blanshard wrote describing his arrangement with his first wife Julia, "we became utterly typical samples of the sexual revolution of the 1920s, unashamed and joyous in our defiance of orthodox sexual taboos." By the end of his life, Blanshard could play the role of prophet, claiming that "the world has caught up with us – or gone down the moral drain with us."[14]

Blanshard had been married three times by the time he wrote those words. In addition to that he had had numerous extramarital affairs, and in carrying out these affairs, Blanshard developed what has to be called a certain amount of callousness, even brutality, in interpersonal relations:

> I cannot say that my own sexual life outside of marriage was altogether sensible or inspiring or even civilized. The male animal when sexually aroused is not naturally a kindly animal. There is something very cruel in

the selfish masculine impulse to woo the desired female with breathless
ardor, take her, then discard her. In this instinctive process I occasionally
was guilty of inflicting deep wounds without being entirely conscious of
my perfidy.[15]

The passage is crucial if we want to understand the connection between sex
"liberated" from the bonds of matrimony and sex as a form of control. The
libertine, if he persists in his sexual self-indulgence becomes, as the above
passage indicates, a sexual predator, preying on members of the opposite
sex, inflicting "deep wounds" on them, in fact, to gratify his passions. Once
that state of affairs becomes accepted, as it was by the time Blanshard wrote
his autobiography, it becomes only a short step from personal domination of
the other for pleasure to systematic domination of other groups for political
gain. The latter form of exploitation and control is already implicit in the former. Since adultery, in effect, "engineers" the consent of the other party – if it
did not, it would be known as rape – it opens the door for social engineering
on a larger scale.

This, at any rate, is the trajectory that sexual liberation took in Paul
Blanshard's life. Blanshard ultimately backed away from his commitment to
socialism, but he never backed away from his commitment to sexual liberation. In fact, the more he committed himself to sexual liberation, the more its
scope expanded from the personal to the political. Sexual engineering in the
form of adultery soon led Blanshard to the political form of sexual engineering that came to be known as eugenics. The one led naturally to the other,
both for Paul Blanshard personally and for the *ethnos* he represented in his
writings – the ministers' sons who had lost their faith through decadence and
now feared they would be shoved aside from their position as the ruling class
by an upstart group that still believed the Gospel they abandoned and were
outprocreating them as a result. The anti-Catholic crusade was a war on sexual morals waged by people who had learned sexual engineering in their
dealings with the opposite sex and now were intent on applying those lessons
globally for political advantage. "After birth control, voluntary sterilization,
liberal abortion laws, and easier divorce – all developments of my life span
–" Blanshard wrote, "there must come, I believe, the planned tailoring of the
human gene to produce a superior form of human life. I am still so much enamored of the possibilities of this new eugenics that if I had my life to live
over again I would be a geneticist."[16]

Like Margaret Sanger, who was a guest speaker at the Maverick Church
in Boston when Blanshard was assistant pastor there, Blanshard began his intellectual life as a socialist and a libertine in New York city in the period of
social upheaval before World War I. Like Sanger, Blanshard was deeply affected by the Ludlow Massacre. But just as in Sanger's life, libertinism gradually won out over Blanshard's concern for workers' rights in Blanshard's
life as well. By the end of his career, Blanshard, like Sanger, thought of so-

cial justice totally in sexual terms. Like Sanger and Alexandra Kollontai, he projected his desires onto mankind as a whole and determined that they needed to be liberated just as he had been liberated, which is to say, they needed to be subjected to the same form of domination. He would dominate them in the same way that he was dominated by his unruly passions.

Like Margaret Sanger, Blanshard found that sexual liberation led directly to social engineering. Once eugenics replaced socialism as the prime coordinate of his intellectual life, the Catholics replaced the capitalists as the chief enemy of human happiness. "My interest in eugenics," Blanshard writes with disarming frankness, "was closely bound up with my interest in Catholicism and my increasing doubts about the validity of my earlier and rather naive socialism."[17] As evidence of his disillusionment with socialism, Blanshard cites a quote from Romain Gary's novel, *The Roots of Heaven*: "The only revolution I still believe in is biological revolution. One day man will became a possible thing. Progress can only come from the biological laboratories."[18] In explicating Gary's text, Blanshard claimed that he still wanted a socialist society, "but I could not visualize a successful socialist society unless the population problem could be solved first."[19] The terms Blanshard used to explain the problem were taken directly from the lexicon of the eugenics movement, which he referred to euphemistically as the "movement for human quality." Eventually Blanshard would sign a contract with Beacon Press for a book whose tentative title was Preface to Human Quality, which would explain the deleterious effect of "the qualitative overproduction of inferior types."[20] But the book never got written perhaps because Blanshard didn't "know enough even to popularize the thought of other men,"[21] as he indicates, but perhaps because he couldn't face the implications of his eugenic theory as squarely in the immediate postwar period as he could twenty-five years later when he embraced the eugenic philosophy of the Nazis without apology. "Hitler," he wrote, "had set back the movement for human quality for a generation by advocating the extermination of the 'unfit' and by defining unfitness in such a way as to include Jews and liberals."[22] Like the Rockefellers, Blanshard accepted all of the tenets of the eugenic movement, but like the Rockefellers he also accepted the change in tactics which Hitler's imprudent embrace of the same principles necessitated. Now the new methods of mass-media persuasion as refined by Watson and Bernays and a whole host of Rockefeller-funded experts in "communications theory" would persuade the unwitting to do to themselves voluntarily what Hitler had tried to foist on them by force. Blanshard wanted to prevent the "unfit" from procreating every bit as much as Hitler did, and in order to bring this end about he had at his disposal both Watson's behaviorism and Dewey's pragmatism, which was the political application of Watson's psychology.

Blanshard met Dewey when he enrolled as a graduate student at Colum-

bia University in 1917, and he got involved in a form of Dewey-inspired social engineering almost immediately. During the spring of 1918 Blanshard
and his brother Brand had been chosen to attend "a very special seminar in
advanced philosophy under John Dewey at Columbia."[23] One of their fellow
students was a wealthy eccentric from Philadelphia by the name of Albert C.
Barnes, who had amassed a fortune producing Argyll ointment for the eyes
and then amassed an equally impressive collection of impressionist art,
which he held under lock and key in his estate in Bala Cynwyd, Pennsylvania, allowing only a fortunate elite to see it. Barnes was so taken with
Dewey's theories of social engineering that he offered to set up the entire
seminar in a house in Philadelphia where they could experiment on Polish
Catholics. Blanshard describes Barnes as "a fanatical, almost unbalanced admirer of both John Dewey and Bertrand Russell" and the project as "the establishment of a temporary settlement house." Inaugurated over the same
summer as the Melting Pot Pageant which Walter Lippmann described in
Public Opinion, Barnes's project failed to divert Polish Catholics from either
their ethnic allegiance or their loyalty to their priests and both Blanshard and
his brother Brand walked away from the ill-conceived experiment with an
abiding animus against ethnic Catholics and a taste for social engineering
which would receive ample gratification during the rest of the century which
coincided with its rise as a social science.

In 1925 Blanshard traveled to Russia to see one of the twentieth century's biggest attempts at sexual social engineering first hand. Later in life,
Blanshard would describe Stalin, who was then attempting to foment revolution in China and as a result competing with Christian missionaries from the
West for the Chinese soul, as "an unrealistic fundamentalist of the left; the
missionaries from the other Georgia were unrealistic fundamentalists of the
right."[24] At the time, however, Blanshard was much more sympathetic to
what was going on in Russia, especially "the revolution in sex and family
standards," a subject which "fascinated" him precisely because everything
seemed "wide open" once the regime began promoting sexual liberation.[25]
Blanshard was especially impressed with the efforts of Alexandra Kollontai,
who was then holding up the losing end in the debate over sexual morals.
Blanshard claimed that the Russian sexual revolution ended in 1936, but it
was ending when he was there; he didn't recognize the fact because he could-
n't speak the language. All that he saw as the sexually sympathetic outsider
was that "Russia had become the first great country in the world to attempt a
quick change in 'bourgeois' sex and family life by official action."[26] It was
obviously a project in social engineering which appealed to him as a student
of Dewey and as a liberal socialist. Had he listened more closely to the debate
he might have learned about the casualties which sexual liberation had
caused, but given his already stated attitude toward getting his way with
women no matter what wounds he inflicted, there is little reason to believe he

would have taken the lesson to heart. What is clear from his memoir is his admiration for the Russian experiment and his complete omission of any evidence which might prove embarrassing to the cause of sexual liberation. Unlike Reich, Blanshard did not agonize over why the Soviet sexual experiment failed. If that blindness were the case in 1973, when all of the evidence against it was in, then it was *a fortiori* the case in the late '40s, when Blanshard was instrumental in launching the anti-Catholic campaign as another form of sexual engineering, one which would culminate in the sexual revolution of the 1960s. "The thing that impressed me most about the new sexual code of the revolution," Blanshard wrote, "was the utter frankness with which the young people discussed serious sexual issues. They were developing some of the same kind of frankness about sex which appeared in the United States in the late 1960s, but there was at that time less exhibitionism about it."[27]

Following hard on the heels of Blanshard's disillusionment with socialism, the anti-Catholic campaign offered another chance at social engineering but one in which the Americans had much more sophisticated "engineering" tools at their disposal than the Russians had during the early '20s. The anti-Catholic campaign coincided with the creation of the CIA as the cold war sequel to the OSS, which was in its way a more sophisticated revival of the World War I CPI. Even more crucial than the CIA itself and its ongoing funding of "communications theory" at universities across the country was the fact that the OSS alumni who did not graduate into the CIA had dispersed into positions of influence in the mass communications elite; these were people who shared the values and concerns of Paul Blanshard. Recruited from elite clubs like Skull and Bones at elite universities like Yale and now staffing both the communications industry and the tax-exempt foundations, the psychological warriors came from Blanshard's ethnic group, and they shared Blanshard's liberal biases when it came to sex and Catholics.

The Catholics were becoming resentful as a result. Conflict was inevitable. At the 1947 commencement at Fordham University, Francis Cardinal Spellman, ordinary of the Archdiocese of New York, spoke of a resurgence of nativism claiming that "bigotry is once again eating its way into the vital organs of the greatest nation on the face of the earth, our own beloved America." Although Spellman's attack preceded the appearance of Blanshard's articles in *The Nation*, Blanshard would later credit Spellman's attack on *American Freedom and Catholic Power* as the incident which turned it into a best-seller. Spellman recognized that anti-Catholicism was in the air and that it was fueled by WASP unhappiness over the rise in Catholic political power. That political power was driven by demographics, and the baby boom which had begun in 1946 and would continue for the next sixteen years threatened, as the election of John F. Kennedy made clear, to wipe the WASP aristocracy off the political map if it played by strictly democratic rules. The Catholics counterattacked when Blanshard's articles appeared by arguing for a boycott of *The Nation*, which begat a counter-counterattack, an ad-hoc committee to defend *The Nation* chaired by poet Archibald MacLeish and having as members a host of liberal luminaries including Eleanor Roosevelt and Leonard Bernstein. Bowing to Catholic pressure in general and alluding to pressure from Cardinal Spellman in particular, Cyrus Sulzberger refused to allow the book to be advertised in the *New York Times*. The culture war was now on, but in keeping with the tenor of the times, it was a covert war between ostensible allies in the anti-Communist crusade. Then as later it was a covert psychological war, in which the sexual issues which provided the subtext for this *Kulturkampf* were never in the headlines but never far from the surface either. "I felt even in those days," Blanshard wrote in his autobiography, "that the most serious flaw in Catholic policy was sexual hypocrisy and suppression."[28] At the time, Blanshard would defend the recently released Kinsey report by saying that the National Council of Catholic Women denounced it in 1948 as "an insult to the American people."[29] He also adverted to the legislative battles that were heating up across the country, describing the defeat in 1948 of a "birth control amendment" which "was described throughout Massachusetts as immoral legislation and an 'anti-baby law.'" All of this led Blanshard to conclude that the "Church's opposition to birth control has now become the most important part of its sexual code." At least it seemed that way to him.

Blanshard gives the impression that he came up with the idea of an anti-Catholic crusade on his own, but it is clear that he was part of a larger movement and in no way its initiator. It is also clear with hindsight that the representation of OSS alumni and other psychological warriors in the media made the battle in the press over sexual morals and which educational system would determine which morals got taught a foregone conclusion. The Catholics were simply outgunned. The fight can only seem fair by comparison with the situation twenty years later when even Catholic organs of opinion had been subverted from within. Simpson makes clear that the intelligence community in the United States was a very specific group of people with a very specific set of goals. Drawn largely from Yale University in general and often from secret societies like Skull and Bones in particular, the OSS drew much of its science of psychological warfare from studies funded by the Rockefeller Foundation in the '30s. Many of the OSS alumni stayed with the agency when it became the CIA, but many of its alumni drifted into the fields of communication theory, which was a euphemism for psychological warfare, in either the theoretical fields, as academics, or in more practical areas. In 1953 one OWI alumnus described how his colleagues became

> the publishers of *Time, Look, Fortune*, and several dailies, editors of such
> magazines as *Holiday, Coronet, Parade* and the *Saturday Review*, editors
> of the *Denver Post, New Orleans Times-Picayune*, and others; the heads

of the Viking Press, Harper & Brothers, and Farrar, Straus and Young; three Hollywood Oscar winners, a two time Pulitzer prizewinner, the board chairman of CBS and a dozen key network executives; President Eisenhower's chief speech writer; the editor of *Reader's Digest* international editions; at least six partners of large advertising agencies, and a dozen noted social scientists.[30]

More importantly, OSS alumni also became the staff and oftentimes the directors of the major foundations – Ford, Rockefeller, Carnegie – which in turn funded most of the communications and social-science research at the time. In 1939 the Rockefeller Foundation funded a series of secret seminars on ways to "find a 'democratic prophylaxis' that would immunize the United States' large immigrant population from the effects of Soviet and Axis propaganda."[31] The use of vocabulary taken from the field of social hygiene is instructive. The psychological warriors all valued science highly and felt that the advances in physical hygiene might be matched by similar psychological advances that would help them win the war. In 1939, the Rockefeller Foundation organized a series of secret seminars with men it regarded as leading communication scholars to enlist them in an effort to consolidate public opinion in the United States in favor of war against Nazi Germany. In these secret seminars, one sees a consistent *modus operandi* which stretched from the work of the Bureau of Social Hygiene to the Kinsey surveys of the '40s to the secret conferences on contraception at Notre Dame University in the early '60s. In each instance, university based "science" was used as a cover for psychological warfare against certain targeted ethnic or religious groups.

Although the members of the interlocking network of psychological warriors which staffed the CIA, the foundations and university communications departments came to be as fervently anti-Communist during the '50s as they had been anti-fascist during the '40s, this same group was equally suspicious of the Catholic Church. In fact, they often saw Rome as every bit as dangerous a foe to American freedoms as Moscow, and said so publicly no matter how severely it jeopardized the common front against communism. "To be honest," said Karl Barth, a leading Protestant theologian who had a large following in the United States, "I see some connection between them." He was referring, of course, to Catholicism and Communism. "Both," he continued, "are totalitarian; both claim man as a whole. Communism uses about the same methods of organization (learned from the Jesuits). Both lay great stress on all that is visible. But Roman Catholicism is the more dangerous of the two for Protestantism. Communism will pass; Roman Catholicism is lasting."[32]

Thoughts like this made it clear that the anti-Communist alliance between the Church and the United States was just as fragile as the alliance between the United States and the Soviet Union against fascism. Americans, it was by now clear, were a diverse group of people who had to be mobilized in

certain ways to achieve certain goals, the war against fascism being a good
example. What emerged from the defeat of fascism in 1945 was a complex
alliance involving three parties who were determined to fight a Cold War on
two fronts. Each party got maneuvered into various alliances depending on
the exigencies of the moment. So after the successful conclusion of the Great
Patriotic War in 1945, the Soviet Union found itself at war with both the
United States (and its allies) and with the Catholic Church, whose influence
it sought to extirpate from Eastern European countries like Poland and
Croatia. The Catholic Church for its part found itself in a two-front war as
well, whose lines of battle could have been predicted by a close reading of
the Church's social encyclicals beginning in 1891 with *Rerum Novarum*, but
as recently as 1931 with *Quadragesimo Anno*. Leo XIII stated quite explicitly in the former document that both liberalism, of the sort practiced in England in the nineteenth century, and communism were antagonistic to a sound
social order; in fact, the pope would go on to claim liberalism was the cause
of bolshevism. Pius XII's concern with communism, a concern which went
back to his days as nuncio in Munich in 1919 when he was almost murdered
by a Bolshevik mob, led him to strategic alliances with the liberals, but even
he never confused their interests with those of the Catholic Church.

If the Communists were at war with both the Catholic Church and the
capitalist powers – even if they conflated the two in the early days of the Cold
War – the situation in the United States was even more complex, because a
large number – 18 percent in the late '40s – of Americans were Catholic and
had also fought in the war as patriotic Americans. The dominant class in
America, the WASPs, which is to say the ruling elite which came from the
mainline Protestant denominations, however, had never viewed Catholics
without suspicion, and after the close of World War II, their suspicions reasserted themselves as the Catholic birthrate started to surge in what came to be
known as the baby boom.

As a result, the rise of the CIA, with its penchant for psychological warfare, coincided with the rise of anti-Catholic animus on the part of the people
who were staffing the intelligence community. A look at the personnel involved makes it quite clear that the intelligence community, the people running the anti-Communist crusade, were virtually the same people concerned
about the "Catholic problem." Blanshard was very aware of the communist
threat, but he was far from willing to subordinate his animus against Catholics to bring about a common front against the Soviets. In fact, as even a superficial reading of *American Freedom and Catholic Power* makes clear,
Blanshard regards the Catholics as every bit as dangerous to "American
Freedom." Hence, his conclusion early on in the book:

> Some readers who accept every fact that I have recorded in these pages
> may still question the wisdom of discussing these matters in public at the
> present time, because of the critical international situation which finds the

Western democracies pitted against a Russian communist aggressor. These critics would keep silent about the antidemocratic program of the Vatican until the present crisis is resolved, because they regard the Catholic Church, with all its faults, as a necessary bulwark against militant Communism. I respect the sincerity of this view, and I share with most Americans the conviction that Russian aggression must be met with determined resistance. But I do not believe that fear of one authoritarian power justifies compromise with another, especially when the compromise may be used to strengthen clerical fascism in many countries. Certainly in this country the acceptance of any form of authoritarian control weakens the democratic spirit; and one encroachment upon the democratic way of life may be used as a precedent for others. In the long run, the capacity to defend American democracy against a communist dictatorship must be based upon a free culture.[33]

Blanshard misconstrued the Church's willingness to work under just about any form of government as "opportunism" and wondered if at some point in the future the Church might change its mind and decide to collaborate with the Communists. "If we are to judge by the writings of the outspoken apologists of Catholicism in Europe and America," writes Sidney Hook with Blanshard's obvious approval, "they are just as ready, if necessity arises, to baptize Marx as they once baptized Aristotle." Hook correctly predicted the rise of liberation theology in the '70s and '80s, but he failed to understand that the emphatic condemnation of communism in *Quadragesimo Anno* would carry the day in terms of theory and eventually in terms of praxis as well.

But both Blanshard and Hook were right in their way. The Church was committed to no one form of government, and certainly not to democracy of the American variety, no matter how sacred that was in Blanshard's eyes. Nor was the Church committed to Fabian Socialism, where Blanshard's real political allegiance lay. What Blanshard failed to see was that his book was in many ways a self-fulfilling prophecy. The rising anti-Catholic animus among the elite, liberal classes in the United States, almost guaranteed that the anti-Communist alliance would fall apart by the end of the '50s – and certainly by the mid-'60s – because the Church began to realize that the most pressing danger to its well-being came from its "friends."

Blanshard cheered on the Masonic persecution of the Church in Mexico, and he was galled by the Church's ability to impose a weapons embargo against Republican forces in Spain. Doubly galling in this regard was the fact that Archbishop Fulton J. Sheen had a prime-time TV show which allowed him "to broadcast, free of charge, innuendoes and pronouncements against political and religious liberalism, birth control, reasonable divorce laws, the government of Yugoslavia, and any other target that inspires his wrath." "Neither Monsignor Sheen nor the other Catholic speakers on this program are censored," Blanshard argued, evidently proposing the same sort of censorship he decried when it was practiced by Catholic priests.

Blanshard's book was prompted proximately by the *McCollum* and *Everson* Supreme Court decisions, which seemed to give aid to Catholic schools, but his real concern was demographic, sexual and moral. Catholics did not believe in artificial birth control; whereas their more established and better off Protestant countrymen did. The result was what people like Blanshard euphemistically referred to as "differential fertility." The ethnic Catholics were outprocreating the Protestants, and, if this state of affairs continued, the United States would soon become a Catholic country, a prospect which filled the dominant WASP class with dread. "What are the actual prospects for Catholic control of the United States?" Blanshard wonders:

> Bertrand Russell said twenty years ago that he thought the Roman Catholic Church would dominate the United States "in another fifty or one hundred years" and "by sheer force of numbers." Many Catholic leaders have echoed that prophecy. Father James M. Gillis, editor of the *Catholic World*, predicted in 1929 that "America will be predominantly Catholic before the present younger generation dies."[34]

Blanshard's fears of Catholic power came not just from the number of children they were having but from the fact that Catholics seemed so "monolithic," to use '60s cultural-revolutionary Leo Pfeffer's term, when it came to values and organization, and that caused Blanshard concern because "in our individualistic nation a closely knit political organization does not need a majority of the people to control the government." That being granted "the hierarchy's most substantial hope for transforming a Catholic minority into a majority lies in a differential birthrate." Blanshard then goes on to cite Catholics who seem to confirm his deepest fears:

> The Right Reverend John J. Bonner, diocesan superintendent of schools of Philadelphia, boasted in 1941 that the increase in the Catholic births in Philadelphia in the preceding decade had been more than fifty per cent higher than the increase in the total population, and that Philadelphia "will be fifty percent Catholic in a comparatively short time." . . . If the disparity in birth rates which he claimed should continue indefinitely, it would not be long before the United States became a Catholic country by default.[35]

After reading this sort of thing, McGeorge Bundy joined John Dewey, Albert Einstein and Bertrand Russell in praising Blanshard's book, calling it "a very useful thing."[36] Bundy was a professor at Harvard at the time he made the comment, but he had been a member of Skull and Bones at Yale and would go on to head the Ford Foundation, and oddly enough join the administration of John F. Kennedy, the first Catholic president of the United States. Bundy would eventually become responsible for investigating Kennedy's assassination and was a key figure in the interlocking circles that would make up the liberal establishment in the United States that was at war with communism and Catholicism as twin threats to American freedom.

During the early '50s, the United States government spent as much as $1 billion annually on psychological warfare. Simpson makes clear that much of this money was used illegally in "black" operations against American citizens. What he doesn't make clear, but what was obvious from an examination of the interlocking nature of the groups which made up the CIA, foundation, and academic establishments is that the psychological-warfare community and the people concerned about the Catholic problem were effectively the same group of people. This meant that when Rome collaborated with the United States in the anti-Communist crusade, it also collaborated in its own demise in the United States as a political power. This became more and more obvious as first the Rockefeller-controlled foundations and then the United States government and then the United Nations got more heavily involved in the promotion of population control. By the mid-'60s, Catholics who had identified themselves as patriotic anti-Communists found themselves caught up in promoting something that was in direct contradiction to Church teaching. The only thing that made the contradiction less than obvious was the gradual way in which it had come about.

Dr. Tom Dooley is just one example of the kind of anti-Communist Catholic who was being promoted by the CIA at the time. His connection with Notre Dame, another front for foundation money which was being used to subvert the Catholic Church's teaching on contraception, was memorialized in an engraved letter from Dooley to then-Notre Dame president Theodore Hesburgh at the Notre Dame replica of the grotto at Lourdes. On the other side of the coin, the same CIA which was involved in promoting Dooley was equally involved in the assassination of Ngo Dinh Diem, a man who was the anti-Communist President of Viet Nam but the wrong kind of Catholic. By the beginning of the '60s, anti-communism had become in effect a way of managing the "Catholic Problem." As the United States became more aggressive in promoting population control throughout the world, Rome slowly came to the conclusion that it had more to fear from its friends than its enemies. The result was a change of heart as Rome got out of the anti-Communist crusade and got into *Ostpolitik*.

Back in the United States, the hopes of Catholics were raised by *Everson* in 1947 only to be dashed by *McCollum v. School Board* one year later in 1948. Hugo Black again wrote the opinion, but this time concluded that the use of pubic school buildings by religious groups constituted a breach in the wall separating church and state. In his memoir Blanshard praised the Supreme Court as "the one institution in Washington which faced the issue of the separation of church and state."[37] If Blanshard admired the Court, the feelings were mutual. Hugo Black was an avid reader of Blanshard's books, and his personal library included a well-marked copy of *American Freedom and Catholic Power*. "He suspected the Catholic Church," Black's son wrote in a 1975 book on his father. "He used to read all of Paul Blanshard's books exposing power abuse in the Catholic Church."[38] Together with William O.

Douglas, who dumped his first wife around the time Kinsey's and Blanshard's books came out and embarked on a career of libertinism thereafter, finally marrying an eighteen-year-old waitress when he was in his seventies, Hugo Black would become the intellectual leaders of the Warren Court, and, as Blanshard indicated, the court would become the political vehicle for the third sexual revolution, the one which began – judicially, at least – with the *Roth* decision in 1957, continued with *Griswold v. Connecticut*, the 1965 decision striking down the ban on the sale of contraceptives, and would culminate in *Roe v. Wade* in 1973. One year later in 1974, when Henry Kissinger wrote NSSM 200, the state department document making population control the central pillar of our foreign policy, the revolution would be complete.

Part III, Chapter 7

Bloomington, Indiana 1950

In spite of the avidity with which the fourth estate promoted the sexual liberation for which Kinsey proselytized in his male volume, Kinsey's book had antagonized a wide spectrum of influential Americans from Norman Vincent Peale on the right to Lionel Trilling and Geoffrey Gorer and his girlfriend Margaret Mead on the left. Once the media applause died down, the reaction set in. Beginning in 1950 the FBI began looking into the sexual habits of prospective civil servants, and this brought about the creation of what amounted to a database on homosexuals. Since Kinsey was without a doubt the country's leading connoisseur of homosexual activity, his name began to surface in FBI reports along with the suspicion that he was "anti-FBI."[1] In 1950 Kinsey received a note from J. Edgar Hoover, FBI director, informing him that "I would like to have one of my assistants see you on the occasion of your next visit to New York."[2] Kinsey was clearly shaken by the announcement. He was involved in all sorts of criminal activity, everything from trafficking in pornography (for which the institute would be prosecuted unsuccessfully) to child molesting. In addition to that he was now as famous as any of the people whose sexual histories he had taken and, therefore, just as vulnerable to blackmail as they were. If the true nature of his activities had been made public in 1950, when his name was well known and the reaction against him mounting in intensity, his work would have been strangled in the cradle. Hoover, however, seemed reluctant to publicize what he knew, leading Jones to believe that Kinsey cut a deal with him, opening his confidential files and giving him sexual ammunition that Hoover could use to blackmail his enemies.[3] Whatever the reason, Hoover did not move on Kinsey when he could have damaged him most.

The fact that he indicated that he might, however, made the people at the Rockefeller Foundation extremely nervous. Weaver had objected when the Rockefeller Foundation got into the pornography business in 1946 by giving Kinsey the money to hire Tripp and Dellenback and the movie cameras they needed to film people engaged in sexual activity. Now Weaver wrote to the board again in 1950 reminding them that he had told them four years earlier that "it is perfectly realistic to say that the R[ockefeller] F[oundation] is paying for this collection of erotica *and for the activities directly associated with it*" [my emphasis].[4] The Rockefeller Foundation, Weaver was telling the board, was involved in promoting criminal activity, and now the FBI was looking into Kinsey and his work.

In October 1950, at around the same time that the FBI was getting ready to investigate Professor Kinsey in Bloomington, a gorgeous southern belle by the name of Bettie Page was walking along the beach at Coney Island, New York, when she noticed a black weightlifter whose body she found attractive. The feeling was clearly mutual because Jerry Tibbs, the weight-lifting policeman who was also an amateur photographer, asked Page if she had ever modeled before. Page said she hadn't, but the alacrity with which Page accepted his offer to do so must have indicated that she wasn't telling the truth. Since the result was the same, Tibbs didn't press the matter when she agreed to come to his studio. Lower Manhattan was full of second-story lofts which could be had cheaply because of the post-war recession. The war had created other dislocations as well, and New York was willing to capitalize on them too. Just as the Civil War had created an opportunity to exploit the sexual longings of soldiers, one which led then President Lincoln to pass the nation's first obscenity law, so World War II had spawned a business in pin-ups, pictures of Hollywood actresses more or less clothed which would be shipped to soldiers around the world. The demand for this sort of thing did not cease with the end of the war. In fact, fueled by things like the Kinsey report, the demand increased and, as it did, the demand for more and more nudity increased as well. What would become a flood of pornography by the 1970s did not look like that at its beginning any more than the mouth of the Amazon looks like its source, but the trajectory was there even in its inception. The problem, however, was that the numbing which this sort of obscenity brought about blinded the culture to its effects. The more it saw the less it could understand.

Writing at around the same time that Bettie Page was on her way to becoming the most popular pin-up model in New York City, which is to say in 1948, Richard Weaver wrote in *Ideas Have Consequences* that

> our most serious obstacle is that people traveling this downward path develop an insensibility which increases with their degradation. Loss is perceived most clearly at the beginning; after habit becomes implanted, one beholds the anomalous situation of apathy mounting as the moral crisis deepens. It is when the first faint warnings come that one has the best chance to save himself; and this, I suspect, explains why medieval thinkers were extremely agitated over questions which seem to us today without point or relevance. If one goes on, the monitory voices fade out, and it is not impossible for him to reach a state in which his entire moral orientation is lost. Thus in the face of the enormous brutality of our age we seem unable to make an appropriate response to perversions of truth and acts of bestiality. . . . We approach a condition in which we shall be amoral without the capacity to perceive it and degraded without means to measure our descent.[5]

Bettie Page's photos, so innocuous looking by later standards, would be an important index of that descent. Eventually one of them ended up in the hands of a man named Irving Klaw, who had made his fortune selling pin-ups to soldiers. Klaw recognized Page's potential and was soon doing his own studio sessions with her. After the war, the demand increased for what Klaw would call "Damsel-in-distress" photos, which is to say pictures of women bound and gagged for the sadomasochist crowd. Soon Page was posing in costumes like this for Klaw. Klaw didn't do nudes, but, the times being what they were and the network of "photographers" being resourceful, Page was soon doing that kind of posing as well. She was also soon acting in 8mm movies with titles like "Jungle Girl Tied to Trees." Those who look at the Bettie Page photos fifty years later wonder what the big deal was all about without realizing that the big deal lies in the very fact that the viewer can no longer feel the passion the photos were intended to incite. Pornography is something based on transgression, and the boundaries of 1950 have been so often and so thoroughly transgressed, that no one can see that they were once boundaries. This numbness has become the prime political problem of our age. It has also become the main tool whereby the oppressors maintain their hold on political power.

Richard Foster, author of *The Real Bettie Page,* mentions the phenomenon of numbing but never really explains it in any coherent fashion because the author himself has been numbed. "After a while," Page's biographer writes without really understanding the implications of what he is saying, "the impact of all that flesh is numbing."[6] Foster is writing here about the editor of a girlie magazine which featured Bettie's photos, but he just as well might have been writing about the culture at large. He might have been writing about himself as well, but the main issue here is the fact that people who get numbed never realize that they are getting numbed. They just notice that the imagery that was once so powerful now seems quaint. They then go off on a search of more transgression, and what follows is the trajectory of lust leading to death as one taboo after another falls by the wayside. The mandarins of the liberal regime have unleashed a historically unprecedented amount of transgressive imagery into the culture, hoping that they will be able to profit from the dislocation it creates, by focusing the isolation in economically profitable ways, i.e., pornography, but no one seems to know how to stop this chain reaction once it starts, and so as a result, people get murdered or go crazy when these unfettered desires get the upper hand.

Which is what happened in the case of Bettie Page. Bettie led a dissolute life beginning with her eighteenth year. While in high school she was one of the top students in her class and planned at the time to become a teacher. By the mid-'50s, when she was approaching forty, she had descended into psychosis. She had become incapable of finishing any of the many Bible courses she enrolled in and was a threat to the life and well-being of those around her.

Foster gives all of the usual Freudian explanations, including the most plausible – the one, by the way, which Freud rejected as the Seduction Theory – namely, that she had been molested by her father as a child. No one should minimize the trauma associated with events like that, but by the same token, the trauma in this instance took on psychic importance the further away it receded in time, which is a good indication that it functioned as a screen memory for something more closely associated to the present, namely, her sexual behavior as an adult.

If the particulars of modesty are culturally relative, the consequences of lust are not. The final consequence of promiscuity, according to the order of being, is the dissolution of the self. The self is constituted by its relationships; the trauma of a father transgressing those boundaries might have been healed by an understanding husband in a permanent monogamous relationship, but that was not Bettie's fate. The easy money from the photo sessions must have made easy relationships seem equally inconsequential, but at a certain point psychic reality caught up with Bettie, and when it did the passions the self aroused at will began to assert their hegemony over a self that was no longer in a position to control them.

On August 1, 1951, the Honorable E. E. Cox of Georgia stood up in the United States House of Representatives and announced that he had "introduced a resolution to create a special committee to conduct a full and complete investigation and study of education and philanthropic foundations and other comparable organizations which are exempt from Federal income taxation."[7] Getting down to specifics, Cox cited the case of "the Negro poet, Langston Hughes," one-time protégé of Carl Van Vechten and one of the products of the Harlem Renaissance, which had been fueled by prurient white interest in the sex lives of blacks there. Hughes, Cox informed his colleagues, was the "author of the poem, 'Good-bye Christ,' which urges Jesus to 'beat it on a way from here now' and to 'make way for Marx, Communist Lenin, Peasant Stalin, Worker me.'" Cox announced that Hughes had been "last heard of as a 'poet in residence' at the Rockefeller supported University of Chicago." In addition to that Hughes was also "the recipient of a Guggenheim fellowship in 1935, and of fellowships from the Rosenwald fund in 1931 and 1941" and Cox wanted to know why foundations with names associated with the country's leading capitalist families were giving grants to Communists like Langston Hughes. Cox denounced in particular the Rockefeller Foundation, "whose funds have been used to finance individuals and organizations whose business it has been to get communism into the private and public schools of the country, to talk down America and to play up Russia." As a result, the Rockefeller Foundation "must take its share of the blame for the sending of the professors and students in China to communism during the years preceding the successful Red revolution in China."[8]

Mr. Cox would spend the short time remaining to him on this earth barking up the wrong tree. By the time his poem achieved the fame which it did not deserve, Langston Hughes was no longer a Communist. In fact, he had never been anything more than an opportunist. Seeking patronage from the wealthy and the influential – whether it was his first patron Mrs. Van de Vere Quick, who used to commune with his African soul by mental telepathy or the Communists who ran the Negro literati in the 1930s – Hughes would tell them what they wanted to hear. Preoccupation with communism would also obscure the eyes of the Congressional inquisitors like Cox to what was really going on with the foundations, which were most certainly involved in sub-version but not of the sort he imagined. In fact the main problem with the Cox and subsequent Reece investigations was precisely failure of imagina-tion. They simply could not conceive of a conspiracy other than one run by Communists. To say that the wealthiest families in the country were engaged in sexual subversion in the interest of ethnic hegemony was an idea beyond Cox's ken. And soon he would be dead. This situation improved somewhat with Cox's successor, Carroll Reece of Tennessee, but the Reece Commis-sion was handicapped with the same set of ideological blinders. If subversion were taking place, the Communists had to be behind it. Neither the Cox nor the Reece Committees had the vocabulary to describe the type of subversion the foundations were funding, and as a result their efforts where tinged with an ineradicable hue of implausibility. This implausibility was exaggerated by the media, who were in turn influenced by the network of OSS alumni who drifted into the new media to practice the psychological warfare they had learned there on their unsuspecting fellow citizens.

Because it lacked the vocabulary of sexual control, neither the Reece nor the Cox commissions could make a compelling argument about the subver-sion that was actually taking place. The Reece Committee at one point re-ferred to evidence produced by its predecessor, the Cox Committee, which showed "that there had been a Moscow-directed, specific plot to penetrate the American foundations and to use their funds for Communist propaganda and Communist influence upon our society." It went on to claim that there was also evidence "this plot had succeeded in some measure."[9] If anything the emphasis on communism let the foundations off the hook, giving the im-pression that they had been subverted by foreign influence, when they were simply implementing an agenda for a class of people, a stealth *ethnos*, which remained invisible to the investigators. At one point, the Reece Committee even claimed that the Rockefeller Foundation trustees "were not fully aware of what was happening."[10] The Rockefeller Foundation had, in other words, no idea how its money was being spent. "Like the trustees of so many large foundations," the Reece Committee surmised at one point, "they left most decisions to their employees, the officers of the foundation."[11] If this argu-ment applied at all to other wealthy families, it most certainly did not apply to the Rockefeller family, whose scion, John D. Rockefeller III had dedicated his life to the cause of eugenic population control and would administer the family's funds and his own money through the Population Council with a micromanager's avidity for the next forty years. The argument may have had some plausibility in the case of Rockefeller support for the Institute for Pacific Relations, but it was most certainly not the case with the money they gave to Kinsey. Kinsey was not a Communist, and the Rockefeller Foundation supported him with their eyes wide open – including their knowledge of his involvement in criminal activity – because Kinsey's information would help them in their ethnic warfare with their enemies. This is the same reason they supported Planned Parenthood. Far from being Communists, the subversives in the foundations represented the exact opposite end of the political spectrum. They represented the plutocratic ruling class who wanted to subvert the democratic institutions of this country because they understood that political power in a democracy is a function of demographic strength – sheer numbers – and having embraced the contraceptive and the eugenics movement it spawned, they understood that they were on the losing side of that equation.

If the trustees of the Rockefeller Foundation had been unaware of what was happening in their own board meetings, that situation came to an end on October 2, 1951, when the foundation received a letter from the Honorable Mr. Cox asking them to open up their files for government inspection.[12] All of the board members who had warned that Kinsey's trading on their name was going to get them in trouble could now say "I told you so." The foundation which liked nothing so much as working behind the scenes was now blinking into the spotlight of a congressional hearing, and feeling a bit esposed. A little over two weeks later, on October 18, the foundation responded by saying that "no grant was ever made by the Rockefeller Foundation for Mr. Hughes or his work."[13] On October 31, Dean Rusk wrote to Cox, asking for time, explaining that the forty-year history of the Rockefeller Foundation involved total grants of more than $470 million and that reporting in any significant detail on how that money had been spent would require a serious accounting effort.

When the Rockefeller Foundation's board of trustees met on April 4, 1951, the official letter from Cox was still six months in the future, but the handwriting was on the wall, and the reaction against Kinsey was vehement. Virtually none of the new board members had given Kinsey their histories, and it was these people, led by John Foster Dulles, who led the attack. Eventually Alan Gregg prevailed, more by virtue of his age than anything else, and Kinsey's funding was passed by a narrow 9 to 7 margin, but Kinsey must have known that with a margin like that his days were numbered. In December 1951, shortly after the Cox Committee contacted the foundation, the ASA rendered its negative verdict on Kinsey's statistics, and Corner tried to salvage the situation by claiming that statistics were not all that significant a part of Kinsey's research, when in fact they were the heart of it. If the Kinsey Report were not an accurate picture of what average Americans did sexually, then it was worthless. The ASA, in other words, in spite of much foundation-induced qualification, had just announced that the Kinsey Report was so flawed it was worthless.

The directors of the Rockefeller Foundation, as dismayed as they had become with Kinsey, were not going to change their long-range strategy of using sex as a form of control simply because Kinsey's statistics were not accurate. Instead of repudiating his study, the Rockefeller Foundation shifted the focus of activities to the law, funding new organizations which would lobby for changes in the penal code based on findings which the foundation now knew were bogus. Beginning in 1950, the Rockefeller Foundation began granting funds to the American Law Institute to help promote its model penal code. Manfred S. Guttmacher, brother of Alan Guttmacher, who was to become president of Planned Parenthood, and so in a position to know what was going on from the inside, gave some indication that the Rockefellers' desire to restructure the country's laws, particularly those regarding sex offenses, had been part of their long-term strategy. "It was in 1950," Guttmacher wrote in his 1968 book, *The Role of Psychiatry and the Law*, that

> the American Law Institute began the monumental task of writing a model penal code. I am told that a quarter of century earlier the Institute had approached the Rockefeller Foundation for the funds needed to carry out this project, but at that time, Dr. Alan Gregg, a man of great wisdom, counseled the Foundation to wait, that the behavior sciences were on the threshold of development to the point at which they could be of great assistance. Apparently the Institute concluded that the time has arrived.[14]

The twenty-five-year hiatus would also explain Gregg's impatience with Yerkes's inability to persuade Watson to come up with the behaviorist tools that would allow them to modify the law. It would also explain their impatience with Yerkes for funding research on primates. The Rockefellers, as Beardsley Ruml had told Watson, were interested in results, and that meant strategies that would allow them to predict and control behavior as Watson had promised. With Kinsey's reports, the Rockefellers had the social engineering tool they needed. Once the public was made aware of Kinsey's work and impressed with its scientific plausibility, the Rockefeller Foundation could simply discard that tool and move on to the next phase of social engineering, which involved changing the law, especially the law as it concerned sexuality. This was so because, in Guttmacher's words, "the Model Penal Code holds that [sexual] matters [were] to be handled by spiritual overseers rather than by the police and the courts."[15] The scientists were to be the new "spiritual overseers," and the Rockefellers, since they controlled the purse strings, were to be the overseers' overseers.

In May of 1952 an article entitled "The Challenge of a Model Penal Code" appeared in the prestigious *Harvard Law Review*. Its author, Herbert Wechsler, was a professor at Columbia who had served as a confidential assistant to Franklin Roosevelt and then as an aide to Francis Biddle and the American judges at the Nuremberg War Crimes Tribunal. Wechsler confirms the same timetable for social engineering that Guttmacher mentioned in his book, explaining that "for almost 20 years, the American Law Institute's agenda" for a model penal code remained "unfinished business," until 1952, that is, when "the Rockefeller Foundation . . . granted funds which will permit the undertaking to proceed."[16] Wechsler then goes on to explain just what that agenda entails and how crucial Kinsey's sex histories were to its completion. Just as Kinsey had shown that science was superior to morals as a guide to life, now Kinsey's findings were going to show that science was superior to the law as the ultimate arbiter of human conduct. This was so because

> the law . . . employs unsound psychological premises such as "freedom of will" or the belief that punishment deters; that it is drawn in terms of a psychology that is both superficial and outmoded, using concepts like "deliberation," "passion," "will," "insanity," "intent"; then even when it takes the evidence of psychiatric experts, as on the issue of responsibility, it poses questions that a scientist can neither regard as meaningful or relevant nor answer on his scientific terms; and finally that though the law purports to be concerned with the control of specified behavior it rejects or does not fully use the aid that modern science can afford.[17]

By the time that Congress had got wind of what the Rockefellers had done in funding Kinsey, the Rockefellers were ready to abandon Kinsey and were already funding another instrument based on research they knew to be false and a man they were ready to cut loose as a loose cannon. On July 1, 1952, Dean Rusk succeeded Chester Barnard as president of the Rockefeller Foundation. Rusk, it seems, had deep reservations about Kinsey's sampling techniques. Rusk had also not been in on the early enthusiasm for Kinsey, nor had he given Kinsey his sexual history. Rusk was, therefore, free to come to the conclusion that Kinsey was expendable, especially in light of the unfavorable publicity that he had brought to the foundation.

On January 20, 1953, the Rockefeller Foundation, under Rusk's tutelage, issued "Officer Procedures for Avoiding Grants to Subversive Individuals," which stated, "It is the policy of the Rockefeller Foundation to make no grant, gift, loan contribution or expenditure, either directly or indirectly to any organization on the list of subversive and related organizations prepared by the Attorney General of the United States."[18] The statement was, of course, meaningless, and if it were meant to fend off the congressional investigation, it failed. During the summer of 1953, the House of Representatives passed a resolution creating a special committee to investigate tax-exempt foundations, with B. Carroll Reece, Republican of Tennessee, as its chairman.[19]

The victors always write history, and subsequent accounts of the Reece-Rockefeller battle prove this rule by impugning the motives of the committee as a way of claiming that there was really nothing to investigate in the first place. Wayne Hays, a Democrat on the committee and a figure who played a crucial role in subverting its ability to get to the truth and promote that truth to the American public, claimed that the whole thing was motivated by political ambition. "I talked to Mr. Reece," he stated later, "when the [Reece] committee was being formed and he told me that he believed that the foundations had conspired to prevent Senator Taft from being nominated for President, and they kept him from being Secretary of State."[20] In an article which evidently impressed the board of the Rockefeller Foundation,[21] Helen Hill Miller portrayed the Cox and Reece Commissions as the return of the America First crowd who wanted to steer the country back to isolationism. Miller never mentions Kinsey or the crimes which he had committed in the name of science. Instead she claims that Reece was upset by what he perceived as "propaganda for globalism, including international communism," and was acting as the front man for "those who wanted to get rid of the United Nations, those who wanted to get rid of Eisenhower and those who wanted to get rid of Robert Hutchins chancellor of the University of Chicago." In spite of support like this from virtually the entire fourth estate, everyone at the Rockefeller Foundation was "quite disturbed."[22]

On August 20, 1953, Kinsey's female volume appeared, and with its publication Kinsey reached the high point of his fame. On August 24, 1953, a flattering portrait of Kinsey, one which omitted the clear signs, visible in photographs of Kinsey at the time, that he was suffering the consequences of his outrageously decadent behavior, appeared on the cover of *Time* magazine along with an article which described what a dedicated scientist and upright family man he was. The reaction to the female volume, however, was not as favorable as the reaction to the male volume. Part of the reason was undoubtedly that Kinsey's homosexual animus against women came through in the book. Women, Kinsey felt, were essentially "undersexed moralists who served as willing agents of social control."[23] Bill Dellenback, Kinsey's photographer, felt that the female volume was typical of "the vicious approach to females" that homosexuals have "in their nature."[24] Kinsey's attitude toward child molestation was also beginning to cause concern. "If children were not culturally conditioned," Kinsey wrote, "it is doubtful if it would be disturbed by sexual approaches of the sort which had usually been involved in these histories."[25] Men and women, the great scientist concluded, were "badly mismatched."[26] Or so it seemed to someone of his homosexual proclivities. In fact, if Kinsey had had his way there never would have been a female volume. He would have much rather followed the male volume up with a book on homosexuality, a topic much closer to his heart. Within two weeks of the publication of the female volume, Kinsey had secured an agreement with the homosexual Mattachine Society to get histories from its members.

But by this point Kinsey's world was coming apart. Within months of his apotheosis on the cover of *Time* magazine, the Reece Committee, in March of 1954, made it clear that they intended to subpoena him to testify. The commission also made it clear that they planned to investigate Kinsey's financial backers, and that meant the Rockefellers, in an area where, according to the memoranda of their own board members, they were aware that they had been involved in criminal activity. On May 10, 1954, the Reece Committee began its hearings before Congress. With a message that was already all but incomprehensible to the general public – namely, that the Rockefellers were Communists – the committee was also plagued by a series of competing events which distracted attention from its deliberations. This list included the McCarthy hearings, which were going on at the same time, *Brown v. School Board of Topeka,* the Supreme Court desegregation decision, and the fall of Dien Bien Phu in French Indochina. Add to that a press that was universally hostile to what they had to say, and you had the makings of a media blackout on anything of significance, and that meant anything having to do with sexual subversion and sexual control of behavior. In spite of the ideological limitations the anti-Communist crusade placed on his deliberations, Reece was more subtle than Cox in his understanding of subversion, which, the committee felt,

> does not refer to outright revolution, but to a promotion of tendencies which lead, in their inevitable consequences, to the destruction of principles through perversion or alienation. Subversion, in modern society, is not a sudden, cataclysmic explosion, but a gradual undermining, a persistent chipping away at foundations upon which beliefs rest. . . . In the modern usage of the term, "subversion," it is no exaggeration to state that in the field of the social sciences many major projects which have been most prominently sponsored by foundations have been subversive.[27]

Carroll Reece was handicapped by his inability to explain who "they" were or what "they" believed, and hence had to rely on communism to fill in the gaps, even to the point of proposing seriously that communists from the Soviet Union had infiltrated the Rockefeller Foundation without their knowing it. That being said, Reece did come up with the right villains in this drama, even if he couldn't articulate their plans very well, and even if he couldn't convince either Congress or the public to do anything about it. He also understood that the sheer wealth they had generated was a problem. Reece would compare the foundations with the Knights Templar and speak favorably of the pope's suppression of that organization. He would also cite Justice Brandeis's verdict about the growth of their concentrated economic power, quoting Brandeis's claim that foundations were a "state within a state so powerful that the ordinary social and industrial forces existing are insufficient to cope with it." Because they had the wealth of a state and operated at the same time beyond the scope of public governance, foundations could act as "venture capital" for subversive ideas which would otherwise be subject to the police power of the state. Venture capital also puts a premium on social change. As a prime example, Reece cited Rockefellers support of Kinsey:

> The Rockefeller Foundations supported the National Research Council's Committee for research in problems of sex, with a total of $1,755,000 from 1931 to 1954. Of this sum, the activities conducted by Dr. Kinsey received some $414,000 from 1941 to 1949, as reported by The Rockefeller Foundation to the Reece Committee. This amount is microscopic compared with the total of $6,000,000,000 annually spent on philanthropy in the United States. But the impact of this comparatively small sum on one subject was quite out of proportion to the relative size of the two figures. One may approve or disapprove of Dr. Kinsey's efforts, and judge variously their impact upon our sex mores. But the Kinsey incident does show that comparatively small donations may have big repercussions in the realm of ideas.[28]

If big money were added to the burgeoning sciences of control that came into existence during the twentieth century, the possibility of "immense powers of thought control" emerged as a threat to the democratic institutions of this country. Again the Reece Committee pointed to Kinsey as the archetypal social engineer operating on tax-exempt money beyond the police powers of the state as an agent of social change, subverting morals as an instrument of control:

> Thus, if Dr. Kinsey concludes that girls would be happier in the long run if their marriages were preceded by considerable, and even unusual, sex experience, then, say these "social engineers," the moral and legal concepts which proscribe it should be abandoned. . . . Political control is thus to be left in the hands of the "elite," the "social engineers." What the people want is not necessarily good for them; they are not competent to decide. The *Führers* must decide it for them, so that we can have a scientifically based and intelligent society.[29]

Claiming that the Rockefeller Foundation "became interested in systematic support studies in sexual physiology and behavior" in 1931,[30] Reece warned his fellow citizens against a concentration of power, wealth and influence much greater than that which brought about the trust busting of the first decade of the same century. But perhaps because it was associated with sex, the efforts of people like Kinsey were seen as either trivial or benign, especially in comparison to an enemy like communism, which seemed much easier to bring into focus. Sex has that numbing effect to it, which is precisely why the West, from the time of people like Euripides, has found it necessary to erect a fence of regulation around it. Now, weakened by the corruption of morals that was the inevitable consequence of war, the nation seemed either titillated by the prospect of more sexual freedom or preoccupied by what seemed like bigger issues.

On May 19, Albert Hoyt Hobbs of the University of Pennsylvania testified before the Reece Committee. Jones dismisses Hobbs as "a right wing sociologist,"[31] whose testimony was made up of equal parts of invective and paranoia. The charge is more indicative of Jones's bias than Hobbs's testimony, which had some incisive things to say about the use of science as a way of destabilizing morals, something which Hobbs saw as the clear intention of Kinsey's work:

> Despite the patent limitations of the study and its persistent bias, its conclusions regarding sexual behavior were widely believed. They were presented to college classes; medical doctors cited them in lectures; psychiatrists applauded them; a radio program indicated that the findings were serving as a basis for revision of moral codes relating to sex; and an editorial in a college student newspaper admonished the college administration to make provision for sexual outlets for the students in accordance with the "scientific realities" as established by the book.[32]

Hobbs also zeroed in on the child molestation, a fact which had been completely ignored by the media when the male volume appeared in 1948:

> In the second volume it is stressed, for example, that we object to adult molesters of children primarily because we have become conditioned against such adult molesters of children, and that the children who are molested become emotionally upset, primarily because of the old-fashioned attitudes of their parents about such practices, and the parents (the implication is) are the ones who do the real damage by making a fuss about it if a child is molested. Because the molester, and here I quote from Kinsey, "may have contributed favorably to their later sociosexual development." That is, a molester of children may have actually, Kinsey contends, not only not harmed them, but may have contributed favorably to their later sociosexual development.[33]

Hobbs would later tell Judith Reisman that if the subsequent allegations about criminal activity had been brought out during the hearings, the course of history would have been changed. The fact that the truth did not come out was in large measure due to the efforts of Wayne Hays of Ohio. Hays was especially outraged by the allegations against the Kinsey Institute. Hays asked to see the Committee file on Kinsey, whereupon the material disappeared never to see the light of day. In 1954, before the Committee's funding had been approved Hays stated categorically to chief investigator Dodd that "*he would oppose any further appropriation to our Committee unless the Kinsey investigation were dropped (*his emphasis*).*"[34] Hays's opposition was so vehement "that he threatened to fight against the appropriation on the floor of the House."[35] Hays effectively shut down the Kinsey investigation, and the press, instead of criticizing him for that obstruction of the public's right to know, praised him as a "knight in shining armor."[36]

Hays had the power to "prevent an orderly hearing," and he used that power to its fullest extent, effectively sabotaging the Reece Committee hearings. There is no indication that Hays had given Kinsey his sexual history, but time would show that he had sexual skeletons in his own closet when Elizabeth Ray, a mistress he had kept on the public payroll, made the affair and certain portions of her anatomy public in an article which appeared in *Playboy* years later.[37]

In December of 1954 the Reece Committee issued its final report, and predictably the country's newspapers took Wayne Hays's side in the dispute. The *New York Times* denounced the report for its "isolationist and reactionary beliefs" without explaining the conflict of interest at the heart of their own coverage. If it became known that Kinsey was involved in criminal behavior when Arthur Hays Sulzberger was on the board of the Rockefeller Foundation which funded his activities, it would have been at the very least an embarrassment and perhaps, if public outrage were awakened, more than that. Writing years later, Carroll Quigley, chronicler of the WASP anglophile establishment and its aspirations wrote that

> It soon became clear that people of immense wealth would be unhappy if the [Reece] investigation went too far and that the "most respected" newspapers in the country, closely allied with these men of wealth, would not get excited enough about any revelations to make the publicity worthwhile, in terms of votes or campaign contributions.[38]

Sulzberger's seat on the Rockefeller Foundation made his interest in suppressing the truth about Kinsey more than lack of excitement, but the result was the same. The information involving the relationship between people of immense wealth and the sex researcher was suppressed and the foundation which was funding sex research as part of its covert campaign of subversion and ethnic warfare could breathe easier again. But not before they had taken some action on their own. On August 24, 1954, months before the Reece Committee would issue its report and years before the appearance of Wormser's book documenting the case against the foundations, the *New York Times* reported that "funds for Dr. Kinsey were dropped as of midsummer because his Institute for Sex Research did not request a renewal of support."

If so, this must have been news to Dr. Kinsey, who was bitterly upset about not only the threat of financial loss but even more upset by the loss of credibility which denial of Rockefeller money would mean. As a result, Kinsey's compulsive sexual behavior, which had never been particularly stable, took a turn toward the lethal. Kinsey was a compulsive masturbator, whose behavior rendered him impotent except when stimulated by activity that was progressively more violent and self-destructive. He was suffering at the time from orchitis, or inflammation and enlargement of the testicles, which results from either venereal disease or excessive masturbation or both.

Driven to more and more terrifying sexual practices in the source of ever more elusive orgasms and severely depressed by thought of being deprived of foundation support, Kinsey's behavior became so bizarre it became life threatening. In August 1954, at around the same time that the *New York Times* announced that Kinsey was being dropped by the Rockefeller Foundation, Kinsey tied a rope around his scrotum and after throwing the other end of the rope over an exposed pipe in the sexual torture chamber he had constructed to his own exact specifications in the soundproof room in the basement of Wylie Hall, and holding the end of the rope in his hand, he jumped off the chair and dangled from the pipe with the full weight of his body supported by his already severely distended genitalia. It was an act of perverse desperation, and it probably led to his death less than two years later.[39]

There may, however, have been a method to Kinsey's madness. His self-mutilation coincided with the climax of the Reece Committee hearings. When the Committee was ready to subpoena him in September, Kinsey was in the hospital recovering from some undisclosed malady. He was still recovering in October and, as a result, still unable to testify. Since Kinsey was also addicted to barbiturates and amphetamines, he had reason enough to be in the hospital, but the timing remains, with the benefit of hindsight, suspicious. Kinsey's health would rally – once the threat of congressional subpoena passed – and he would go on to make trips abroad, where without knowing the language he would become an instant expert on sexual behavior in whatever country he visited. Kinsey would also visit Aleister Crowley's Abbey of Thelema with Kenneth Anger, the homosexual filmmaker. Kinsey was obsessed with obtaining Crowley's diaries for the institute, giving some indication that he was interested in putting Crowley's brand of sexual magic to use, perhaps to revive funding for the institute. Kinsey's health, however, never recovered, something which is obvious in the pictures which were taken of him at the time.

If he tried to cast its spells, Crowley's magic failed to work for Kinsey. Rusk had abandoned Kinsey for good. On April 25, 1955, The American Law Institute, funded by the Rockefeller Foundation, released its first Model Penal Code draft on sex offenders (#4) modeled in large part after Kinsey's recommendations, which helped alter American sex-offender laws and penalties. Jones claims that Kinsey "had little effect on the sex offender codes" and then, as if catching himself in a statement clearly at odds with the truth, adds, "at least not during his lifetime."[40] That may be because the ALI issued its model penal code based on Kinsey's research a little over a year before he died, when Kinsey had served his purpose. Kinsey's posthumous effect on penal "reform" in the Rockefeller mode was, however, enormous.

On June 1, 1956, Kinsey suffered a heart attack. On August 25, he died, presumably from another heart attack and pneumonia, but the full details surrounding his death have never been made public, probably because of what they would have revealed about his sexual practices. As if uttering at the same time their own "*nunc dimittis*" with Kinsey in the subversion of the moral order, Yerkes and Gregg died in the same year. The foundation which had made their subversion possible, however, continued as corporations often do, with a life of its own and bigger plans for the future.

Part III, Chapter 8

Washington, D.C., 1957

Eventually all of those photographers in all of those cheap lofts in lower Manhattan taking pictures of women like Bettie Page would inevitably draw attention to themselves through the entrepreneurial efforts of people like Irving Klaw and, more importantly, a certain Mr. Roth, who was convicted by a jury of his peers in the District Court of the Southern district of New York on four counts of a twenty-six-count indictment accusing him of mailing obscene circulars and an obscene book in violation of the federal obscenity statute. When the case finally made its way to the Supreme Court, Mr. Justice Brennan, writing for the majority, declared that "the dispositive question is whether obscenity is utterance within the area of protected speech and press."[1] Then, answering his own question, Brennan wrote that the Court holds "that obscenity is not within the area of constitutionally protected speech or press."[2] Not content to leave well enough alone, however, the Court went on to opine that "sex and obscenity are not synonymous,"[3] offering by way of explanation the observation that "obscene material is material which deals with sex in a manner appealing to prurient interest."[4] In order to determine what is prurient and what is not, the Court proposed the following test: "whether to the average person, applying contemporary community standards, the dominant theme of the material taken as a whole appeals to prurient interest."[5] In keeping with the spirit of the age in matters sexual, the Supreme Court had taken something clear and enforceable and replaced it with something muddy and dangerous. By claiming the ability to distinguish between sex and obscenity, the court also placed itself in the business of viewing pornography on a regular basis. According to Leo Pfeffer, *Roth v. United States* meant "that the Court in every case in which it accepted an appeal, would have to read the particular book or magazine [or] to sit through a showing of the film."[6] For fifteen years thereafter, randy law clerks would gather in chambers of the Chief Justices and watch porn films, shouting "I know it when I see it," the famous quote of Justice Potter Stewart, at particularly outrageous passages.

Even worse than the muddied thought of the majority were the sexually *laissez-faire* views of Hugo Black and William O. Douglas, who in their minority opinion in *Roth* claimed that obscenity *was* protected by the First Amendment. To buttress his case, Douglas cited "two outstanding authorities on obscenity," Lockhart and McClure, who opined in their book *Litera-*

ture, the Law of Obscenity, and the Constitution, that "The danger of influencing a change in the current moral standards of the community, or of shocking or offending readers or of stimulating sex thoughts or desires apart from objective conduct, can never justify the losses to society that result from interference with literary freedom."[7] Douglas went on to say that "the test that suppresses a cheap tract today can suppress a literary gem tomorrow."[8] What Douglas didn't mention in his dissenting opinion is that Lockhart based his findings on the Kinsey reports. "The Kinsey studies," Mr. Lockhart wrote in the book cited by Justice Douglas, but in a passage not cited in *Roth*, "show the minor degree to which literature serves as a potent sexual stimulant. And the studies demonstrating that sex knowledge seldom results from reading indicates [*sic*] the relative unimportance of literature in sex thoughts as compared with other facts in society."[9]

Lockhart's fame increased when he became director in 1970 of the notorious President's Commission on Pornography, which concluded that pornography did not influence behavior, a notion which sparked a violent minority rejoinder by Morton Hill, S.J., when it appeared. The President's Commission came to this conclusion, at least in part, as a result of a trip they made to the Kinsey Institute in Bloomington, Indiana, where they were subjected, like many before them, to "the treatment."

Roth's essentially unworkable judicial "test" for obscenity opened the floodgates for both another fifteen years of rootless obscenity decisions as well as a whole spate of porn films which sought to evade obscenity convictions by including within them portions which bespoke redeeming social value so that the material "as a whole" would not be deemed obscene. *I Am Curious (Yellow)*, for example, a Swedish film which featured full nudity and simulated sex was given redeeming social value by making repeated reference to the life of Martin Luther King, although what that had to do with the film's Swedish protagonist was never made clear.

By 1957, the year *Roth* was handed down, the civil rights movement had become the liberal quintessence of "redeeming social value." Hence, it was not surprising that the enterprising Swedes would want to include it in one of their porn films to avoid prosecution. By 1957, the civil-rights movement, using the Negro as the paradigm of sexual liberation which it had inherited from the Harlem Renaissance of the '20s, was on its way to becoming the prime vehicle for moral destabilization in the country. The white churches in the South, particularly, were shown to lack moral credibility because of their implication in segregation, and this was the opening wedge in removing any form of behavior which foundation-funded social engineers found repugnant. That they found Christian sexual prohibitions repugnant goes without saying. If the civil-rights movement was the thin end of the wedge in overturning and de-validating morality, the sexual revolution was the thick end of the same wedge. What went in as concern for the Negro came out at repudiation of sexual morality.

Just as the foundations had no need of Communists to help them promote their subversive activity, this venture into social engineering wasn't a coup engineered against the Protestant churches; it was one pulled off by the churches themselves against their own traditions and beliefs. As Paul Spike said of his father, the minister Robert W. Spike, the man at the World Council of Churches, the pre-eminent Protestant association, responsible for promoting racial harmony, "[M]y father encourage[d] me to be a rebel. . . . He sees civil rights as only one part of a vast social, technological, sexual and moral revolution."[10] Spike the younger even theorizes that his father "probably wished, in certain ways, he himself had been" like him.[11] And what was that like? Spike the younger tells us that "my favorites are Beat writers" and that "I have a special shelf with my collection of their works. Kerouac, Ginsberg, Corso."[12] White culture as imbibed by Paul Spike from his father was secularized Protestantism. Its demise was engineered not so much by outsiders, as by its own ministers, who had ceased to believe in what the churches they represented professed to believe. This group of ministers included people like Spike and Paul Tillich, whose wife reported on their forays to Small's Paradise in Harlem, where the distinguished Protestant theologian and his wife watched multi-racial sex shows. For them, "blackness" meant not so much the overthrow of Christian morality, although it certainly meant that; it meant the moral certification of that overthrow in the name of social justice for the Negro. But as Paul Spike's memoir makes clear, modernity's creation of the Negro as a paradigm of sexual liberation paved the way for the acceptance of the civil rights movement among the avant garde. "My father," Paul Spike writes, "actually knew Ginsberg and Corso and some of the early 'Beats.'"[13] The elder Spike met them when he was minister of Judson Memorial Church from the late '40s to 1955. Spike's ministry to the bohemians in Greenwich Village seems to have been a two-way street. Instead of converting the bohemians to Christ, the minister went native and started espousing bohemian theology himself. At Judson, his son says, Robert W. Spike was transformed "from a conservative Baptist into a modern pioneer in the wilderness of post-war American society. . . . He became a rebel, on his way to becoming a revolutionary. He was one of the most radical ministers in the American church."[14] "He is," Paul says of his father, "as typical of the sixties as any man was." The younger Spike remembers the 1963 Washington Civil Rights March as "one of the great events of my life." He recalls his father saying that he "felt for the first time in my ministry that the church was where it belonged in the middle of the street. There was an eschatological feeling about the whole day."[15] "I hope you know you got a great daddy," Floyd McKissick, then head of CORE told the younger

Spike. "Your daddy is a great man. If it weren't for him, hardly none of these white folks would have marched today."[16]

But precisely which Negro were the Spikes marching to support? Their image of the Negro was transmitted, as Paul Spike maintains, through the lens of late '40s Greenwich Village. Robert got his ideas from the Beat crowd first-hand; Paul got his through the writings of Ginsberg, Kerouac, et al. Or even third-hand through the lyrics of Bob Dylan. ("All I listen to this spring is Dylan," says Spike of early 1965.) And Dylan? "It was Ginsberg and Kerouac who inspired me at first," he said.[17] By the time Kerouac became aware of who Bob Dylan was, he was too sick to be interested and dismissed him as just "another fucking folk singer."[18] (Thomas Merton, to explore the Bob Dylan vein a bit more, was much more favorably impressed with the folksinger from Hibbing, Minnesota. So much so that when Jacques Maritain, the famous French Thomist, came to Gethsemane to pay the famous monk a visit, Merton paid him the dubious honor of playing Dylan's *Highway 61 Revisited* album, much to Maritain's puzzlement if not annoyance. Mott says that Merton's attempt to portray Dylan as the American François Villon was not a great success.[19])

Kerouac's portrayal of the Negro in *On the Road* was almost as influential with the cultural revolutionaries of the 1960s as Harriet Beecher Stowe's portrayal of the Negro had been with the abolitionists a century earlier. This is even more remarkable considering the fact there are no Negro characters of any stature in the novel. The novel is simply about the adventures of Sal and Dean (Jack Kerouac and Neal Cassady respectively), and whatever Negroes appear, appear solely as a function of their needs. They are repositories of the values which Sal and Dean attempt to invest in them. At one point Dean admits that he hasn't the faintest idea of what is going on in the mind of a certain black he sees, but that ignorance makes the need to project all the more urgent. After nearly running over an aged Negro in a mule-drawn wagon on one of his high-speed transcontinental journeys, Neal opines philosophically that "I would give my last arm to know; to climb in there and find out just what he's poor-ass pondering about this year's turnip greens and ham."[20] In other words, Cassady doesn't know what the Negro has on his mind, or, to express it better, what the old Negro is actually thinking pales in comparison to what he can be made to represent. Cassady was a crucial transitional figure in the post-World War II cultural revolution in the United States. His persona was Kerouac's closest approximation of the white man who implemented "Negro" values. After becoming the prime Beatnik prototype with the publication of *On The Road* in 1957, Cassady became one of the seminal hippie personae by joining Ken Kesey for one more trip across the United States, this time in a psychedelically painted bus, from which he would emerge periodically juggling hammers and dispensing LSD. Tom

Wolfe memorialized the later Cassady in his book *The Electric Kool Aid Acid Test*.

In another passage in *On the Road*, Sal and Dean "ended up with a colored guy named Walter."[21] The three drunken men barge into Walter's bedroom in the middle of the night to find his wife in bed. Unlike Cassady's wives, or Kerouac's mother, Walter's wife has no objections to their behavior. "His wife," Kerouac writes, "was . . . about fifteen years older than Walter and the sweetest woman in the world. Then we had to plug in the extension over her bed, and she smiled and smiled. She never asked Walter where he'd been, what time it was, nothing. . . . Walter's wife smiled and smiled as we repeated the insane thing all over again. She never said a word."[22]

As with the old man in the mule-drawn wagon, the attraction of Walter's Negro wife lies precisely in the fact that she says nothing to dispute either Dean's behavior or the desires he wishes to project on her. Once they are out in the street, Dean has turned the woman into the epitome of the type of woman he is looking for, i.e., someone who will not object to his adolescent irresponsibility. "Now you see, man," Dean confides to Sal, "there's a real woman for you. Never a harsh word, never a complaint. . . ; her old man can come in any hour of the night with anybody and have talks in the kitchen and drink the beer and leave any old time. This is a man and that's his castle." he pointed up at the tenement."[23]

Kerouac, like Merton, sees the ghetto as full of sexual pathology, drugs and alcoholism, but unlike Merton, Kerouac likes it for precisely these reasons. The Negro provides lapsed Catholics like Kerouac and Cassady with a justification for their own sexual irresponsibility. That the fantasy of the endlessly sexually enabling Negro woman should remain unfulfilled and unfulfillable seems a foregone conclusion. It was put to the actual test, however, in Kerouac's novel *The Subterraneans*, which recounts the story of his affair with the Negro/American Indian Mardou Fox.

"By god," Kerouac says when he sees Fox perched on the fender of a car in front of the San Remo bar in Greenwich village, "I've got to get involved with that little woman" and then adds significantly "maybe too because she was Negro." Kerouac, however, would have done better to regard Negro women from afar. He did better with the black girl in the Denver twilight who thought he was Joe. After his sexual conquest of Mardou Fox, he writes: "I awake . . . and see beside me the Negro woman with parted lips sleeping, and little bits of white pillow stuffing in her black hair, feel almost revulsion, realize what a beast I am for feeling anything near it. . . so I feel like leaving at once to get 'back to my work.'"[24]

So interracial sex turns out to be less than the cosmic experience Kerouac anticipated. Interracial sex turns out to be pretty much like the intraracial variety, which is to say either licit or illicit depending on the marital state of the participants. On the far side of the cosmic experience that sex with the Negress promises to be, Kerouac finds the same old problems of love and commitment and family responsibility that had caused him so much trouble when he slept with white women. Kerouac had to learn the hard way that race does nothing to change the moral dynamics of sexual intercourse. Racial categories of black and white are no substitute for the more significant moral categories of licit and illicit. The latter variety of sexual activity led to feelings of guilt and revulsion, and race and the romance of the ghetto with its kicks and "blackness" did little to palliate those feelings the morning after.

Leo Percepied, the Kerouac persona in *The Subterraneans*, finds that after he has consummated the relationship, "the adolescent cocksman having made his conquest," he has this compulsion to run home to his mother. Kerouac finds himself in the painful situation of being attracted to a situation caused by family pathology which he can only replicate in his relationship with Mardou. Kerouac's compulsion to leave, his inability to persevere in the relationship to the point of some permanent commitment, only brings out the family pathology that Kerouac found so attractive in the first place. Only now he is exposed to it from Mardou's point of view. The ghetto as the locus of sexual irresponsibility is what both Kerouac and Cassady found attractive in the first place. But this sexual irresponsibility looks different when seen from the point of view of the woman and child who get abandoned, and since Mardou fits into both of those roles it is not surprising that she sees things differently. "Why do you have to rush off so fast, as though almost hysterical or worried?" she wonders. Whether she ever finds out is a question difficult to answer, given the fact that everything is strained through Percepied's distorting psyche. However, she does get annoyed enough to say at one point after Percepied announces that he is leaving: "I'm jealous that you have a home and a mother who irons your clothes and all that and I haven't."[25]

It seemed like a particularly unhip thing to say. Kerouac is interested in the Negro purely because of the sexual pathology he finds in the ghetto. Mardou Fox, on the other hand, is interested in having a mother who will iron her clothes. She is interested in domesticity. He consummates the relationship only to discover that the Negress who epitomized this liberation is interested in the home he abandoned or, more importantly, refused to replicate. He chose instead to live with his mother in the suburbs and have an affair with the black girl in the Village, who is jealous because she can't have the home that the beatnik refused to provide for her.

Kerouac wrote *The Subterraneans* in three nights on a teletype roll. Whenever the muse flagged, Kerouac sought to augment her absence with a steady supply of Benzedrine. As a result, the work has the drugged, manic quality of a speed freak going to confession, much stream-of-consciousness smoke but little fire of either art or insight. So when the nervous energy starts to wear down at the end of the short book, the best Percepied can do in assessing the relationship and the meaning of the race of his lover is to tell her:

> as part Negro somehow you are the first, the essential woman, and therefore the most, most originally most fully affectionate and maternal – "Eden's in Africa," I'd added one time – but now in my hurt hate turning the other way and so walking down Price with her every time I see a Mexican gal or Negress I say to myself, "hustlers," they're all the same, always trying to cheat and rob you – harking back to all relations in the past with them – Mardou sensing these waves of hostility from me and silent.[26]

Eden may be in Africa, but it is clear that this particular affair with this particular Negress is going to be another Paradise Lost. Percepied gets ugly in the accusations he makes, and it's not difficult to see a kind of racism arising that is simply the projected disgust of someone who failed to adhere to the moral law and then was incapable of placing the blame where it belonged. It is interesting to speculate whether this rebound from miscegenation contributed to the culture of racism in the South (Faulkner seems to think it did) but that is the scope of another book. As for Kerouac, the black Eden descended into one long, hung-over guilt trip, revolving around "the weight of my need to go home, my neurotic fears, hangovers, horrors." In the end, *The Subterraneans* is nothing more than what he finds most reprehensible about bohemia, namely, "the Talking Class trying to rationalize itself out I suppose out of a really base almost lecherous materialism." That or an especially graphic description of the effects of alcoholism on social interaction. In one of the many lucid moments that pop up out of the generally turgid, drug-crazed prose of the book, Kerouac ruefully admits that "now you threw away a little woman's love because you wanted another drink."[27]

It was not surprising that his interracial love affair should fail because by 1953 Kerouac had a string of broken relationships behind him already. In November of 1950, Kerouac met an attractive woman by the name of Joan Haverty and impulsively married her before the month was out. Joan worked at a department store and read novels for possible use as movie scripts while Jack wrote. He had just received a $1,000 advance for his novel *The Town and the Country* and was looking forward to a life in which all he would have to do was write. But things didn't end up the way he expected. In May of 1951, Robert Giroux rejected the manuscript that would eventually become *On the Road*, and in the same month Joan told him that she was pregnant. The shock of losing both his status as a writer and the financial support he was getting from his wife compounded by the fact that he was now going to have to become the family breadwinner and might even have to get a normal job to support the family was too much for Kerouac. In an action that would prove characteristic of his life, Kerouac moved out. Dennis McNally tells us that "the idea of eight-hour wage slavery in support of a child frightened Jack too much in his vulnerable state."[28] Rather than face the prospect of getting a job,

Kerouac contested the paternity. He, in McNally's words, "decided that it wasn't his child and ravingly denied paternity to his closest friends."[29] Janet Michele Kerouac was born on February 16, 1952. Kerouac contributed nothing to her support until she was ten years old. In fact, he never saw her until she was a teenager. In 1968, a sixteen-year-old hippie girl arrived in Lowell and went to the house of the only Kerouac in the phone book, Jack's cousin Herve, whose wife saw the unmistakable family resemblance, and brought her to visit with Jack.

There was no big scene of reconciliation. She was on her way to Mexico and all he could think to ask her was if she had been getting the $12 a week child support payments he had been sending her lately. It was too late for Kerouac to be a father in any meaningful sense of the word anyway. Within a little over a year, Kerouac would die of a ruptured vein in his esophagus at the age of 47. It was a classic alcoholic's death, and the visitation of his daughter, absorbed into the hippie movement which Kerouac's writings had helped spawn, was the crowning act in the flight from sexual responsibility which characterized his life.

Oikophobia, the fear of the household, had beoame the defining characteristic of the modern writer. Virtually all of the writers of the Harlem Renaissance (with the exception of Arna Bontemps) had what might be characterized as a morbid fear of paternity, if by paternity we also include the responsibility of raising the child after it has been fathered. This rejection of the family became the defining act of the modern writer. It was the matrix out of which virtually every aspect of modern ideology grew. By the late '40s, Kerouac had any number of literary models, both black and white, to chose from, including Carl Van Vechten, Max Eastman, Claude McKay, and Nancy Cunard. In each case, the defining act which launched their careers as literary subverters of moral norms was desertion, followed by divorce and the refusal to care for offspring. In each instance, the question of sexual responsibility got caught up in issues of race. Race became the cover for the rationalization of what was basically sexual dereliction.

The same was true of Kerouac. The dream of a "fellaheen" existence far from white ambitions and in close proximity to "the dusky knee of some mysterious sensual gal" simply did not work out when he was given his chance with the actual Negress Mardou Fox. Given the nexus of unrestrained appetite that Kerouac's life had become, his vision of the good life, "a pornographic hasheesh daydream in heaven," could only be fulfilled in a whorehouse, as it was in the climactic sequence of *On the Road*. By the end of his life, Kerouac's only consolation was that he had become brutally honest about the whole Beatnik phenomenon: "We didn't have a whole lot of heavy abstract thoughts. We were just a bunch of guys who were out trying to get laid."[30]

In *On The Road*, Neal/Dean tells Jack "we know time – how to slow it up and walk and dig and just old-fashioned spade kicks, what other kicks are there?"[31] "Spade Kicks" entailed the lapsed white Catholic's attempt to replicate ghetto pathology, complete with illicit sex, drugs, alcohol, and jazz playing in the background. Whites could have done this by themselves without mixing with other races; however, the racial background added a certain metaphysical element which was essential in anesthetizing their troubled conscience. At one point Jack/Sal tells Neal/Dean, whom he describes as a "Jesuit" and "ex-altar boy," that "You can't go all over the country having babies like that. Those poor little things'll grow up helpless."[32] Considerations like this, however were quickly forgotten, as Sal and Dean moved across the country from one ghetto to another (where illegitimacy seemed to have lost its stigma) on their way to Mexico, where drug consumption had lost its stigma as well. In *Lonesome Traveler* (the title is a telling description of Kerouac's spiritual state), Kerouac talks about "this fellaheen feeling about life, that timeless gaiety of people not involved in great cultural and civilizational issues – you can find it almost anywhere else, in Morocco, in Latin America entire, in Dakar, in Kurd land."[33]

In *On the Road*, Sal describes "driving across the world and into the places where we would finally learn ourselves among the Fellahin Indians of the world, the essential strain of the basic primitive, wailing humanity that stretches in a belt around the equatorial belly of the world."[34] Once Sal and Dean arrive in Mexico all the metaphysical issues get resolved into a few easy questions: "Hey, kid, you got ma-ree-wa-na?"[35] for starters, and how far to the whorehouse? as a follow up. Once inside, Sal describes "trying to break loose to get at a sixteen-year old colored girl who sat gloomily inspecting her navel through an opening in her short shirty dress across the hall."[36] But the colored girl proved to be unapproachable, and so he had to content himself with one of the Mexican women, who was not quite as valuable symbolically. That and listening to the background music of the sexual revolution, "the mambo beat is the conga beat from Congo, the river of Africa and the world; it's really the world's beat."[37] The whorehouse is the *terminus ad quem* of the novel. It symbolizes the aspirations of the main characters; it is, in fact, the end of the road: "this strange Arabian paradise we had finally found at the end of the hard, hard road." It offers sex without guilt because it is suffused with the ideology of solidarity with the world's oppressed peoples. It is sex disconnected from social awareness, from culture, from "civilizational issues." Given enough dope, sex, and loud music, the palliation of conscience almost works, but suddenly a sound intrudes from the real world. "Somewhere," Sal tells us, "I heard a baby wail in a sudden lull, remembering I was in Mexico after all and not in a pornographic hasheesh daydream in heaven."[38] The sound of a baby crying reminds Sal that sex has issue and consequences after all, and it forces our heroes back onto the road again. The only way to repress this truth is by hopping into the car, turning up the volume on the radio, and rolling another cigar-sized, opium-doused joint.

If this is heaven, then it is a lot like the Nigger Heaven Carl Van Vechten described twenty years earlier. The whorehouse at the end of the road in Kerouac's novel is Nigger Heaven Revisited. However, now the whites are not the voyeuristic spectators at the cabaret of Negro decadence. Now the whites have become characters in the novel itself, trying to become "Negro" by aping the sexual decadence they see. The goal is the same, flight from "white" values; the means is also the same, jazz-inspired decadence and the use of race relations as a palliative for the sexually troubled conscience. "All Mexico," Sal tells us in an example of projection equal to anything produced by Carl Van Vechten, "was one vast Bohemian camp."[39] Sal's trip to the third-world whorehouse has since become a common cultural phenomenon; German travel agencies now send whole plane-loads of horny Germans off to Thailand for cheaper thrills than are available on the *Reeperbahn* in Hamburg. It is a particularly crass form of Third World exploitation, but since it involves sexual license it is rarely portrayed as such. Kerouac provided one of the main rationales for this type of sexual tourism. But beyond that, his popularity was tied up with the fact that he portrayed the aspirations of the rising postwar generation. *On the Road* provides a glimpse of what America was to become over the next quarter century. The aspirations of bohemia became a mass phenomenon after the war. A cultural revolution would transform all of America's institutions. "White" values, which were primarily an enculturation of Protestant Christianity with reference specifically to the family and work, were replaced by "spade kicks," or a white man's attempt to replicate the pathological mores of the ghetto. The family home was replaced by the automobile, drugs, sexual liberation, loud music, and the notion of race as the holy cause whereby guilt-ridden whites could achieve authenticity.

Viking accepted *On the Road* for publication in mid-December of 1956. By mid-January the media were beginning to react. There was an interview in the *Village Voice*, followed by a February 1957 article in *Mademoiselle* which was little text and mostly pictures of the intriguing-looking Beats outside the City Lights Bookstore in San Francisco. Jack was annoyed by the picture because the cross he had been wearing outside his shirt had been airbrushed away. If Beat was going to make it into the mind of impressionable teenage girls, it would do so only after it had been sanitized of religious associations. By the fall of 1957, *On the Road* was on the bestseller list, sharing space with James Gould Cozzens's *By Love Possessed* and Grace Metallious's *Peyton Place*, and the idea of the "beatnik" (the term was coined by San Francisco columnist Herb Caen, who considered the Beats and Sputnik equally far out) was on its way to becoming a national phenomenon. For those who would never read Kerouac's novel, there were mass cultural phenomena which would convey a message based on the mass media's reading of what he was trying to say. Max Schulman's Dobie Gillis books were adapted for TV with the specific addition of the "beatnik" Maynard G. Krebs, whose prime characteristic in addition to a sparse goatee and a cut-off sweatshirt was an aversion to work. The movie *On the Road* was never made, although Mort Sahl expressed an interest. Kerouac would have preferred Marlon Brando in the lead role, but what he got instead was the sanitized TV series, *Route 66*, which seemed to be more of an extended advertisement for the Chevrolet Corvette than the quest for spade kicks. The series proposed automobile-powered *Wanderlust* purged of the sexual compulsion which made it a psychic imperative. *The Village Voice* lauded *On the Road* as "a rallying point for the elusive spirit of rebellion of these times."[40]

Perhaps no one expressed the metaphysics of this transformation better than Norman Mailer. In his essay "The White Negro," also published in 1957, Mailer cleared away much of the hype and obfuscation that had been created by the popular culture's rendering of Beat, by claiming that "the source of Hip is the Negro."[41] And lest the reader think that Mailer is referring to just any Negro, he goes on to make it clear that it is the sexual mores of the ghetto which he and his generation of hipsters find particularly attractive.

By the mid-fifties with the death of Stalin and the repudiation of his legacy by Khrushchev as well as the slowly accumulating evidence of the massive nature of his crimes, Communism had all but lost its hold on intellectuals in the West. However, the matrix which made Communism flourish, the rebellion against God and the moral order that was coming into its own with the first modern generation around the time of the outbreak of the First World War, was still there and in fact flourishing as it never had before. The itch for sexual revolution paved the way for the acceptance of Bolshevism among America's radicals in 1917, and that itch, if anything, was becoming more imperious. The longing for sexual liberation, which had been the prerogative of the few in the years before the First World War had become the obsession of the many in the period following the Second World War. And with the failure of Bolshevism to inspire the Left, the Left looked to the Negro as the paradigm of the newly-liberated man, in a liberation that was more sexual than economic. The ghetto Negro became influential through his music, but the main attraction was the breakdown of family life which characterized life in the ghetto. According to Norman Mailer,

> the presence of Hip as a working philosophy in the sub-worlds of American life is probably due to jazz, and its knifelike entrance into culture, its subtle but so penetrating influence on an avant-garde generation's . . . disbelief in the socially monolithic ideas of the single mate, the solid family and the respectable love life.[42]

As with Van Vechten and the proto-modern decadents who created the Harlem Renaissance in the '20s, the whites who created the beatnik mass phenomenon of the '50s were also attracted to the Negro race primarily because of the family pathology and the promise of sexual liberation and "spade kicks" which they found in the ghetto. Beat bespoke a rebellion against "white" civilization, which is to say against the Christian moral code, and most specifically Christian prohibition against sexual activity outside the confines of marriage. By the time the '50s arrived, the economic crisis of the '30s had been resolved, and the sexual pull of a society which abolished the moral law was emanating more strongly from the ghetto than it was from the Soviet Union. According to Mailer, who articulated the aspirations of his class,

> the Negro (all exceptions admitted) could rarely afford the sophisticated inhibitions of civilization, and so he kept for his survival the art of the primitive, he lived in the enormous present, he subsisted for his Saturday night kicks, relinquishing the pleasures of the mind for the more obligatory pleasures of the body, and in his music he gave voice to the character and quality of his existence, to his rage and the infinite variations of joy, lust, languor, growl, cramp, pinch, scream and despair of his orgasm. For jazz is orgasm, it is the music of orgasm, good and bad, and so it spoke across a nation, it had the communication of art . . . it spoke in no matter what laundered popular way of instantaneous existential states to which some whites could respond, it was indeed a communication by art because it said, "I feel this, and now you do too."[43]

Writing in 1957, Mailer effectively writes the Negro who aspires to lead a moral life in an intact family out of the race, presaging in an uncanny way how the NAACP would attempt to do the same thing thirty some years later to Clarence Thomas. The crux of the matter is culpability. According to Mailer, "the Negro *was forced* [my emphasis] into the position of exploring all those moral wildernesses of civilized life which the Square automatically condemns as delinquent or evil or immature or morbid or self-destructive or corrupt."[44] Since the Negro was forced to do what Mailer, et al., wanted to do of their own free wills, then he wasn't culpable. He was the victim of racism. However, in becoming a victim of social injustice, the Negro thereby calls into question the whole moral credibility of the social order which victimizes him. As a result of the moral discrediting of white society which came about as a result of segregation, the white imitator of ghetto sexual mores can feel free of guilt. He is only reacting to a corrupt society too. The White Negro stands on the sidelines and applauds as the Negro moves "in that other direction where all situations are equally valid." Mailer obviously finds some sort of vicarious consolation in the fact that "in the worst of perversion, promiscuity, pimpery, drug addiction, rape, razor-slash, bottle-break, what have you, the Negro discovered and elaborated a morality of the bottom."[45] The "hipster" was, "a new breed of adventurers, urban adventurers who drifted out at night looking for action with a black man's code to fit their facts. The hipster had absorbed the existential synapses of the Negro, and for practical purposes could be considered a white Negro."[46]

The real Negro does not interest people like Mailer. Mailer is only interested in someone who is willing to symbolize what he wants symbolized, namely, sexual liberation. Insofar as the Negro wants to lead a moral life, or raise a family or believe in God or thank the nuns who taught him in grade school, as Clarence Thomas did, or do any of the things Mailer rejects as "square," he is rendered invisible. This is accomplished with the help, of course, of Negroes who are willing to collaborate in their role as sexual revolutionaries.

The story of Eldridge Cleaver presents an interesting case in point. Cleaver went from being a convicted rapist to a literary phenomenon overnight on the strength of one book, *Soul on Ice*. Cleaver in the late '60s was the Negro *du jour* every bit as much as Langston Hughes was during the Harlem Renaissance and Claude McKay was during the Fourth Congress of the Third Communist International because he was willing to espouse sexual revolution and praise all the right people. Like the poor sharecropper in *Invisible Man*, Cleaver found himself lionized because of his sexual sins. Cleaver was a spokesman for his race precisely because he was a rapist and because he was willing to claim that "rape was an insurrectionary act." This was the sort of thing that Norman Mailer had been writing all along. Cleaver was promoted because he was willing to be used as cannon fodder in the frontal assault on sexual morality. "It delighted me," Cleaver wrote, telling the Left exactly what it wanted to hear, "that I was defying and trampling upon the white man's law, upon his system of values, and that I was defiling his woman."[47] It should come as no surprise after reading Mailer, et al., that this was precisely the sort of attitude they found delightful too. Calling sexual morality the "white man's law" had a not-so-subtle relativizing effect that made further transgressions a lot less hard on the conscience.

In his introduction to *Soul on Ice*, Maxwell Geismar refers to Cleaver as "one of the discoveries of the 1960s," "a black soul which has been 'colonized' . . . by an oppressive white society that projects its brief, narrow vision of life as eternal truth." However, the main attraction lies in Cleaver's "Laurentian sexual mysticism" and the fact that he "never misses the sexual core of every social (or racial) phenomenon."[48] Cleaver, for his part, is only too happy to reciprocate with compliments of his own. He is fulsome in his praise of all the right people, i.e., those involved in the cultural revolution which was helping to abolish Christian sexual mores. "I have been terribly impressed by the youth of America, black and white. . . . I have come to feel what must be love for the young people of America," said Cleaver who was in his early thirties at the time, "and I want to be part of the good and greatness that they want for all people." Cleaver also sees "beauty" in the "demonstrations all over the country, the FSM [Free Speech] movement, the teach-ins" and would "just love to be in Berkeley right now, to roll in that mud, frolic in that sty of funky revolution . . ." as a way of learning the intricacies of "the stymied upbeat brain of the New Left."[49]

Cleaver was to get his wish every bit as much as he would find out that what he wished for was not what he really wanted. As a result of the publication of *Soul on Ice*, he was made Minister of Information of the Black Panther Party and as a result catapulted into the center of left-wing politics just as the civil-rights movement with its commitment to nonviolence fell apart. In *Soul on Ice*, Cleaver proved that he could cite all the right passages from all the right people. Cleaver cited "Norman Mailer's 'The White Negro,' which seemed to me to be prophetic and penetrating in its understanding of the psychology involved in the accelerating confrontation of black and white in America." He also cited "the remarkable passage from Jack Kerouac's *On the Road*, in which Jack walked through Denver 'At lilac evening. . . wishing I were a Negro, feeling that the best the white world had offered was not enough ecstasy for me, not enough life, joy, kicks, darkness, music, not enough night.'" Cleaver saw Kerouac as one of the leaders of the cultural revolution that was to bring ghetto mores to the middle class. The Negro, with his association with the civil rights struggle, was the symbol which made this subversion of values palatable: "The non-beat disenchanted youth were attracted magnetically to the Negro revolution." The older generation, Cleaver tells us, are alarmed to "see these white youth taking the initiative, using techniques learned in the Negro struggle to attack problems in the general society." And the techniques they learned were the working vocabulary of the cultural revolution which was reaching its climax in 1968: "the long hair, the new dances, their love for Negro music, their use of marijuana, their mystical attitude toward sex – are all tools of their rebellion."[50] These are precisely the "spade kicks" advocated by Dean Moriarity in *On the Road*. The Negro was at his symbolic best when he provided both the vocabulary and the moral force behind the movement to overthrow the Christian God and his moral code.

As Cleaver was to learn, though, this was the only reason the liberals were interested in the Negro. If particular individuals were to wander off the reservation (or plantation), they would incur the wrath of the powers that had promoted them in the first place. It was a lesson Cleaver would have to learn the hard way. Writing in the late '70s, Cleaver claimed that his influence in the Black Panthers "came from two sources: my celebrity status as the best-selling author of *Soul on Ice* and my ghetto background which never choked at the sight or sound of a gun."[51] There was, of course, outside help as well. The Panthers allied themselves with the increasingly violence-prone SNCC, which, as an erstwhile civil-rights group, had access to "the generous money support of many liberals," without which "we could not have operated as long as we did." From there, the center of balance quickly shifted to support from the Communist Party and the Socialist Workers Party, which led to more disillusionment. "Marxists in America," Cleaver writes, were interested in supporting the programs of the Black Panther Party, but they also wanted something in return, to the point where Cleaver "began to sense that the Reds were opportunists for their own enhancement rather than activists in search of social justice for blacks."[52] The lack of help from the Communists along with the increasingly violent episodes that the Panthers were organizing and the threat of a new prison term eventually drove Cleaver into exile in Cuba and Algeria. His experiences with the "revolutionary" governments of these countries and the subsequent involvement of the Black Panther party in illegal activities as a way of raising money (in Algeria they forged passports, having been instructed on how to do this by the German Terrorist organization the *Rote Armee Faktion*, and fenced stolen cars) simply accelerated the downward spiral of his disillusionment with the cause of the Left as in any way a solution for the problems of the Negro.

In *Soul on Fire*, Cleaver gives a fairly detailed analysis of how ghetto pathology ended up in left-wing politics. He was raised by a father who was authoritarian but often absent from the home. As a result of that and the fact that the family moved to Los Angeles when Cleaver was a teenager, ghetto mores began to supplant parental authority. Cleaver found himself attracted to the Chicano gangs in East LA because "they had more freedom from family restraint than the black boys had, at a time when I was beginning to break away from the controls of my home." The bone of contention became the time which Eldridge had to be home each night. If Cleaver would arrive home late, his father would beat him, which confirmed him in his determination to rebel. One night Cleaver fought back effectively enough to intimidate his father. The victory proved to be Pyrrhic though. The father's authority already weakened by lack of economic opportunity wasn't able to withstand the attack from his own son. Cleaver resolved to kill his father with a knife if he ever threatened to beat him again, but the precautions were unnecessary. Instead of reasserting his authority, Cleaver's father simply abandoned the family. "He disappeared, went away," was Cleaver's way of describing his father's reaction to his own adolescent rebellion. "It was five years before I saw him again."

The disappearance of the father was the green light for the young Cleaver's involvement in ghetto pathology and the criminality which landed him in prison. Cleaver traces "my own personal fascination with Joseph Stalin" to the fact that Stalin too had an authoritarian father. However, left-wing politics came only later, after the decline in family life led to criminality and prison. It is not difficult to see how family pathology got Cleaver in prison and how his own experiences were not untypical for the black family of the 1940s and early '50s. The beleaguered black father had a respect threshold below which he would not go. Most of that respect was taken from him by the society at large. When the rest of it was denied by a rebellious family, he reached a point where he could or would take no more and simply left. The prime source of the challenge came from Cleaver's postwar-era peers, a group which was becoming more and more involved in the sort of behavior portrayed in *On the Road*. Cleaver was twelve years old when Kerouac started hitchhiking to Denver to link up with Neal Cassady. The "spade kicks" of the ghetto, sexual license, drugs, criminality, the mystique of the automobile, provided the challenge to parental authority and filled the vacuum that was created when the father left. By the time that the ghetto gangs supplanted the authority of the father, the decline into criminality was, if not predetermined, then at least predictable. That that criminality would turn into political activism is also understandable, given the cultural revolution that was going on at the time. As at the time of the French Revolution, the prison became the symbol of the illegitimacy of the established order. Just as the Marquis de Sade was freed from the Bastille to confirm the new order, so the Left would spring a like-thinking Negro to rule over the new order, or at least over the short life of the Black Panther Party.

But in a curious way, the family proved to be the undoing of ideology in Cleaver's life. Throughout his revolutionary period in Cuba, Algeria, and France, Cleaver remained loyal to the pre-eminently counterrevolutionary institution; he remained married to the same woman the whole time. In spite of his posturing in *Soul on Ice* about white women – "I'd jump over ten nigger bitches just to get to one white woman. . . . I love a white woman's dirty drawers."[53] – Cleaver married Kathleen Neal, who is black (albeit light-skinned) in 1967. From the point of view of left-wing politics, her race was less significant than the fact that Cleaver continued to stay married to her. Cleaver's obsession with white women was first of all a function of being a black male in prison in a world in which virtually all of the pinups of the time portrayed white women. *Playboy* did almost exclusively white women in its centerfolds. His use of the white woman as goddess was simply a way of attacking the white man's God, which is to say the God of Christianity. "He who worships the Virgin Mary," he wrote in *Soul on Ice*, "will lust for the beautiful, dumb blonde. And she who yearns to be rocked in the arms of Jesus will burn for the blue eyes and white arms of the All-American boy."[54] So attacking the white woman as the black rapist is simply a way of attacking the moral prohibitions of the "white man's god."

Much more relevant to his revolutionary point of view was the fact that Cleaver stayed married to the same woman for all those years, and beyond that that she bore him two children. Cleaver reckons the birth of his children as the turning point in his disillusionment with Marxist ideology. It spelled the end of his atheism and the end of his commitment to the cause of the Left as the only vehicle for Negro liberation.

> The most powerful, single breakthrough, in my Communist-held position, was the birth of my children. For me, each one was sort of a cosmic, spiritual event. A miracle . . . first, Maceo, and then my daughter. I didn't come out of the Marxist philosophy all at once. But this crack appeared like a breach in the wall – and the crack which never closed was the affirmation of life that gripped me at my children's birth and kept saying to me: here is a soul, here is a link in the chain of life. . . . And when that opening appeared, other questions followed and hastened the crumbling of the Communist intellectual empire.[55]

This passage provides an interesting counterpoint to the deconversions of virtually all of the prominent moderns, especially those who came to support the cause of the Negro, in that their deconversions were almost invariably associated with abandoning a spouse. Carl Van Vechten, Max Eastman, Claude McKay, Nancy Cunard, Jack Kerouac, all abandoned spouses and oftentimes children as the definitive act which launched them on their careers as sexually liberated moderns in general and advocates of negritude in particular. In the case of McKay and Eastman, the abandonment of wife and child was followed by an almost immediate departure for the Soviet Union and immersion in the political struggles of the early years of the Bolshevik Revolution.

Cleaver, by remaining married, committed the archetypal counterrevolutionary act, an act which was to undermine his whole commitment to left-wing politics. By following the exigencies of human sexuality through the commitment that perfects it to its fruition in children, Cleaver found that Marxist atheism no longer made sense. In both cases, belief followed behavior. The normal social order made no sense in light of sexual liberation put into practice, and failure to repent led inexorably to social activism that tried to mandate that behavior for the society at large. Similarly, revolutionary activism made little sense to Cleaver when viewed from the point of view of the father of a stable family. Character had come to supersede race as the prime criterion of value. After the birth of his children, Cleaver "learned that without inner control, a moral perspective, and a spiritual balance that flowed out of Christian love, justice, and caring, the Communist promises were to become the largest fraud of all."[56] Becoming a parent was a subversive act; it subverted the entire ideology of the Left which was based to a hitherto unsuspected degree on actualizing the tenets of sexual liberation in one's life. Without the engine of sexual liberation, the train of leftist ideology came to a halt. "My own experience as a parent," Cleaver writes about his conversion, "was basic enough philosophy to instruct me that there was a Supreme Being, with or without Karl Marx's endorsement. My convictions jelled so that I was willing to acknowledge that there was a God who had designed and ruled over this universe, much to the chagrin of my French revolutionary drinking friends."[57]

The reaction of the Left was swift and predictable. Cleaver was excommunicated from the Negro race. Cleaver relates a conversation with the white homosexual and cultural revolutionary Jean Genet, hero of Sartre's *Saint Genet* and author of the theater of the absurd classic, *The Blacks*. Cleaver made the mistake of saying "some positive things about France," which "absolutely pushed Genet's button." "'Not only are you a child,'" Genet said, trying to think up the worst insult he could imagine, "'you're white!'"[58]

Cleaver's former Black Power fellow travelers were of much the same opinion. Black Representative Ron Dellums, whom Michael Harrington describes as "in 1986 the only card-carrying member of the Democratic Socialists of America on Capitol Hill" and someone whose involvement in the civil rights struggle went back to family connections with the Brotherhood of Sleeping Car Porters, "concluded that there was no place for me in the United States." When Cleaver announced that he was returning to the United States to face trial, "Members of the Black Panther Party held a series of press conferences denouncing me as an FBI informer and a CIA agent, claiming that I had secretly testified before a session of a Senate Judiciary Committee. To top it off they asked the black people not to help me."

So much for racial solidarity. In the years during which Cleaver was in exile, the revolution had succeeded in this country. But it was not the revolution Cleaver had anticipated when he settled in Algeria. The revolution did not so much adopt the structures of communism, as much as the matrix out of which communism drew its sustenance. Instead of a replay of the Bolshevik Revolution of 1917, America found itself in the throes of a cultural revolution against God and the Christian moral order based on race and sex. The Negro was needed as a front for sexual liberation. Those Negroes who "confessed the name of Jesus Christ" were, as Eldridge Cleaver found out, advised to remain in France.

Cleaver discovered to his surprise that "my old friends were getting elected and gaining nice appointments. Friends were getting elected to Congress; another became lieutenant governor of California; some were now mayors of cities that were once in flames. Talk about a brave new world; it looked as if it was on its way." All this gave Cleaver some hope that things might be changing for the better. What he soon came to realize though was that things were improving only for Blacks of a certain persuasion. When Cleaver asked for their assistance in getting back into the country, he was told, "The black people in charge don't want to hear your name, Eldridge. There is no place for you, so why don't you just settle down and become a black Frenchman and enjoy all those French pastries."[59]

Cleaver remembers the advice as "like a sentence – another era of serving time." Only this time the jailers were former fellow-travelers who had succeeded at the cultural revolution while Cleaver was outside the country failing to bring about a political one. "What is this cultural revolution you're talking about," Mick Jagger asked William Burroughs in 1980. "Do you realize," said Burroughs speaking "as if to a backward child," "that thirty or forty years ago a four-letter word could not appear on a printed page? You're asking what cultural revolution? Holy shit, man, what d'you think we've been doing all these years."[60] Cleaver had missed the cultural revolution, but he succeeded in bringing about a spiritual one in his own life and as a result of his commitment to monogamy.

It was in 1959 or '60 while serving time in San Quentin that Cleaver read Thomas Merton's *The Seven Storey Mountain*. Cleaver was a Catholic at the time ("I chose the Catholic church because all the Negroes and Mexicans went there. The whites went to the Protestant chapel.") but appalled nonetheless at the prospect of the monastic life which he equated with a self-imposed prison sentence. Cleaver was "mystified by Merton," but "could not believe in his passionate defense of monkhood."[61] "Let me say it right out," Cleaver wrote expressing the judgment of the boys in San Quentin, "we thought Merton was some kind of nut."

Cleaver was, however, impressed "with Merton's description of New York's black ghetto – Harlem," specifically the passage "What has not been devoured in your dark furnace, Harlem, by marijuana, by gin, by insanity, hysteria, syphilis?" which he cited in *Soul on Ice*. If he was impressed, however, the impression was not deep enough to prevent Cleaver from becoming a Black Muslim, "chained in the bottom of the pit by the Devil," or prevent his subsequent slide into Marxism. He never explains why he went from being a Catholic to being a Muslim and a Marxist revolutionary, but if he had been keeping up with the writing of Thomas Merton he would have found little to keep him within the Catholic fold. In *Conjectures of a Guilty Bystander*, which appeared around the time Cleaver was writing *Soul on Ice*, Merton proposes nothing but the most standard liberal apologies for the civil-rights movement as his contribution to race relations. The specifically Catholic critique which at least adumbrated a moral dimension to the problems in Harlem as sketched out in *Seven Storey Mountain* had all but completely disappeared by the '60s, and in its place we had little more than an etiolated Catholicism which can do nothing but advocate what the liberals are perceived as doing much better. It was typical, in many ways, of the insecurity which seized the Catholic Church in the period immediately following the Second Vatican Council.

"No matter how we may criticize Europe and America," Merton says, "they are still in full strength, and in their liberal minority the hope of the future still lies."[62] Merton wrote this at about the same time that the "liberal minority" was busy attacking the Moynihan Report because of the connection it made between the ghetto and family stability. If Cleaver was looking for a reason to remain in the Catholic Church, it was clear he wasn't going to find it in a book like *Conjectures of a Guilty Bystander*, because all Merton could offer there were sentimental nostrums which ignored the moral dimensions of ghetto life he had adumbrated twenty years earlier. "There are things the Negro knows," Merton tells us in *Conjectures*, "that the white man can never know."[63] Just how Merton knows these things "the white men can never know," he never gets around to telling us. This sort of thing is either sentimental, or patronizing, or racist depending on how much charity one wants to expend in construing it. Merton is also not above discerning "this *secret heritage, this revelation of God*" [my emphasis] "in the singing of Mahalia Jackson as well as in some of the very great, obscure artists of jazz."[64]

It is Merton at his bathetic worst. Mailer was more acute in the "White Negro" when he called jazz "the music of orgasm, good and bad." This description is hardly great art either. It is the sort of cultural commentary that gives orgasm a bad name, but at least it does not attempt to see something mystical in what is essentially the cultural protocol of the disintegration of Negro family life in America. As a cultural commentator, Merton had become absorbed by the society he had fled twenty years before. It is a commentary on two things: the power of the popular culture of the times and the decline of Thomas Merton, and by extension the whole of Catholic social action. By the time the '60s arrived, even hermit monks were listening to Joan Baez and Bob Dylan and, what is worse, allowing their cultural categories to be formed by them. Thomas Merton wasn't any more capable of understanding what was going on in the civil rights movement than Joan Baez was, and that was because they were both listening to the same records and singing the same songs.

That music, mild by comparison to what would come later, would have its effect on Merton. Those who came to visit, a not insignificant number of people for a man who considered himself a hermit, soon learned to bring along a case of beer and a bottle of whiskey. Merton went drinking and then swimming with more than one female visitor. At one point he referred to the Goliards, whose ribald medieval poetry was put to music in the '30s by Carl Orff in his *Carmina Burana,* as "beat monks." Merton was on his way to becoming one himself.

In *Catholic Counter Culture in America 1933–62* James Terence Fisher refers to both Kerouac and Merton as "the last Catholic romantics." Merton became a "beat monk" under the influence of the emerging counterculture which took as its paradigm "spade kicks" and the ghetto's debilitating effect on family life and sexual morality. When, toward the end of his life, Merton founded the poetry magazine *Monk's Pond*, he was insistent on having Kerouac contribute to it. Unlike Merton, Kerouac seemed more and more drawn to the vocabulary of his childhood Catholicism as he approached the end of his life (they died within a year of each other). When one of his mistresses taught him to paint, Kerouac insisted on doing portrait after portrait of then Pope John XXIII. In a similarly religious vein, Kerouac always insisted that the term "Beat" came from "Beatitude."

In a TV interview conducted for CBS, a skeptical Mike Wallace asked: "You mean that the Beat people want to lose themselves?" To which Kerouac responded: "Yeah. You know, Jesus said to see the Kingdom of heaven you must lose yourself."[65] On another TV show, Kerouac said that every night he prayed to "my little brother, who died, and to my father, and to Buddha, to Jesus Christ and to the Virgin Mary. . . . I pray to those five people." If this was Catholicism, and in some sense it was, then it was a singularly syncretistic variety. Kerouac had stopped practicing the faith when he left for New York on his quest for "spade kicks" in the early '40s. By 1953, the sexual excess, the drinking and the drugs, and general dissipation were getting to him, and he felt the need of some spiritual alternative, some way out, but not one evidently that threatened the status of his vices. As a result, he turned to Buddhism. Fisher says that "Kerouac turned to Buddhism as justification for his fear of success and the world because there was no usable Catholic alternative."[66] However, it is easier to see in Kerouac's choice of Buddhism a sort of spiritual compromise. He wanted a spirituality without a morality to go along with it, or at least he didn't want the Catholic spiritual package with its prohibitions against lust and drunkenness. With Buddha as his guide Kerouac plunged into a regimen of complete isolation in the woods – as a forest ranger on a fire tower, to give just one example – followed by the loneliness which drove him back to bars and further drinking bouts in the city. If this was a spiritual regimen, it's difficult to discern what its opposite might be. But Buddhism as practiced by the Beats was anything but a rigorous endeavor, especially not in the moral realm. In fact, this proved to be its chief attraction. Describing the attraction that Buddhism held for William Burroughs, Ted Morgan claims that

> The attractive feature of Buddhism was that it had no gods, it was not a religion like Christianity or Islam or Judaism, there was no bearded authority figure threatening you with eternal damnation if you did not confess your sins, there was no powerful institutional church with its mosques and cathedrals and its army of priests. . . . Buddhism was flexible and formless enough and had enough different branches, to appeal to men as different as Jack Kerouac, Allen Ginsberg, Gary Snyder, and John Giorno.[67]

Buddhism also exerted a powerful appeal on Thomas Merton. Fisher attributes this to Merton's "gradual rejection of Catholic triumphalism. . . . Merton's turn to the East signaled a new era of personal force and maturity." A reading of *Conjectures* will, I think, lay to rest any doubts about Merton's "new era of personal force and maturity." All Merton can do is weakly second the liberals ("the hope of the future"!) from what he now perceived as the sidelines of life. Merton's attraction to Buddhism can be seen on one level at least as simply another manifestation of his absorption into beatnik culture. Merton had become a Beat monk. He was influenced by Kerouac every bit as much as Bob Dylan and David Bowie were. Because the soon-to-be dominant popular rock/drug/sex culture seemed so different from what he had come to see as mainstream America in the '30s and '40s, Merton was fooled into thinking it somehow different. Like Eldridge Cleaver, Thomas Merton failed to note the arrival of the cultural revolution.

At another point Fisher claims that "Merton's pursuit of Eastern wisdom freed him from his role as exemplar of selfless Catholic obedience,"[68] an assertion which gets closer to the heart of the matter. For Kerouac, Buddhism was an alcohol-sodden attempt to get back to the Catholic spirituality of his boyhood. For Merton, it was an attempt to move in the exact opposite direction on the part of someone who was reverting to bohemian type. In both cases, we witness a massive failure of Catholic culture to inform the categories of two of its most talented sons. In Merton, the situation had come full circle. The man who in 1941 had taken flowers to Harlem and had railed against the "dark furnace" which devoured its inhabitants with marijuana, gin and syphilis, ended his career by becoming a "White Negro" in search of "spade kicks." The man who began his apostolate to the Negro by bringing flowers to Friendship House ended it by falling under the spell of the junkies and alcoholics who were the front men for the sexual revolution which would transform this country into an extended ghetto of broken families and sexual license according to their notion of "spade kicks."

The disintegration of the Catholic Negro apostolate caused a double impoverishment. First of all, Catholic intellectuals lost their identity as Catholics in the cultural revolution which adopted the Negro as its paradigm of liberation. Kerouac and Merton were characteristic of the early and late phases of this development. Kerouac used the Negro image explicitly in a way that was adopted by the entire culture through the Beat movement. Merton, who had some sense of the moral dimension of the problem in the '40s, ended by being absorbed into the liberal desire to expunge the notion of sexual morality from the picture. The Negro suffered as well. In the flush of success from the civil-rights victories, the Negro leadership forgot that there was a moral dimension to the problem. As the Negro became the broker of moral legitimacy in the secular world, the root of ghetto pathology in family breakdown resulting from sexual immorality got lost in the sentimental portrayals of marches in the South.

By the mid-'60s, it would have been considered downright impious to suggest that Catholics might be able to make their own contribution to race relations apart from their participation in officially sanctioned civil rights marches and protests. In this regard, Thomas Merton was only symbolic of a whole generation of Catholic clergy in this country. The Rev. George H. Dunne, S.J., wrote about his impressions of a recent march in Montgomery,

Alabama. "The average Alabaman is convinced that the only people in the civil rights movement are queers, beatniks, and communists. The three girls with identical Joan Baez type melancholy hairdos, whom I saw padding the street in their bare feet after James Baldwin as the demonstration dispersed were not, I thought, helping to weaken this opinion."[69]

Neither was James Baldwin for that matter, who made no secret of his homosexuality. Whether Father Dunne knew this or not is uncertain. In this one instance, we needn't have feared for the virtue of the three Joan Baez look-alikes. Father Dunne, however, goes on to get the whole message coming out of the march exactly wrong. "The cause here," he opines in direct contradiction to what his senses have just made apparent, "was not the freedom to act like a beatnik . . . but the freedom of the Alabaman Negro to enjoy the full rights of American citizenship."[70] In the light of the evidence Father Dunne himself presents, it is unlikely that the young ladies had anything that abstract on their minds. Being a beatnik was a way to enjoy sexual liberation while at the same time believing that that activity was leading to increased voting rights. If the girls had been sleeping with white racists or stockbrokers, their consciences would have reacted differently.

Ellen Tarry, a black Catholic writer who arrived in Harlem when it was still in vogue in the late '20s, saw blacks seventy years later as "without a champion" and having been without one since the death of the Rev. John LaFarge, S.J., editor of *America*, founder of the Catholic Interracial Council Movement, and the man who invited Baroness de Hueck to found Friendship House in Harlem. "We have not had a leader since that time," Tarry said. Nor have they had a program since the mid-'60s. "The whole movement has been splintered, whether you are Catholic or Protestant, since the death of Martin Luther King," Tarry said. Tarry remembers the Moynihan Report, but never identified it as a "Catholic" initiative, much less as the initiative of someone who was also inspired by the same Father LaFarge who inspired her.

South Bend, Indiana, 1962

During the '50s, especially before *Roth v. United States* lamed obscenity prosecution, a curious double bind arose in relations between the American and Italian film industries and their respective cultures. Hollywood was bound by the production code, largely a Catholic enterprise which came into being during the early '30s. They could not portray nudity or profanity. In order to break the code, producers like Joseph E. Levine would bring over Italian films, by directors like Federico Fellini, made largely in Rome, the headquarters of the Catholic Church. One of Fellini's short films was part of a trilogy which provoked the *Burstyn* court case in New York in the early '50s, where the Catholics went to the barricades to defend the culture against what they saw as a deluge of degenerate films coming from Catholic Italy. Certain Italians, however, were equally upset by the effect that American films were having on Italy. One of the people most upset was Pope Pius XII, who had much to say on the role of television and film. But as Pius XII slowly slipped into his dotage during the '50s, others took up his cause. Alfredo Cardinal Ottaviani was so concerned about the effect of film that he created his own chain of movie theaters, to insure that only films that had no detrimental effect on morals would be shown.

Writing in 1950, at a time when Pius XII and Cardinal Ottaviani were preoccupied with the Communist menace, W. W. Charters talked about the effect that film had on children in dark theaters:

> Watching in the dark of the theater, the young child sits in the presence of reality when he observes the actors perform and the plot of the drama unfold. He sees the actions of people living in a real world – not of actors playing a make-believe role. His emotions are aroused in ways that have been described. He forgets his surroundings. He loses ordinary control of his feelings, his actions, and his thoughts. He identifies himself with the plot and loses himself in the picture. His "emotional condition may get such a strong grip that even his efforts to rid himself of it by reasoning with himself may prove of little avail." He is possessed by the drama.[1]

The quote comes not from an indignant Catholic prelate concerned about the manipulation of passion but from a collection of essays edited by Bernard Berelson, one of the prime psychological warriors of the '50s and eventually the head of John D. Rockefeller's Population Council. In many ways, Cardinal Ottaviani couldn't have framed the case against Hollywood better himself, and over the course of the '50s, as the threat of Communism waned, the threat from Hollywood grew in inverse proportion. Ottaviani became so concerned at the effect that Hollywood culture was having on Catholic life in Italy that he and Cardinal Tardini went to Pius XII's successor, Giuseppe Roncalli, during the very conclave which named him Pope John XXIII, and told him that he must convene an ecumenical council to deal with the sclerotic state of Church administration and the threat to the Church from the outside, a threat just over the horizon but no less palpable for that. Ottaviani was responsible for the writing of all of the preliminary documents of Vatican II, most of which were scrapped by the Council, which was looking for new ways of dealing with the problems facing the Church. The issue of methodology, however, should not distract us from the intention that drove the convoking of the council. Ottaviani and Tardini were convinced that the Church was not prepared to face the onslaught against morals and family life that was being orchestrated through the media by the United States, their ostensible partner in the anti-Communist crusade. In his document on "The Moral Order," dated January 15, 1962, Ottaviani criticizes the attempt

> to substitute the useful, the agreeable, the good of the race, the interests of a class, or the power of the state, as the criterion of morality. Thus, philosophical systems, literary fashions, and political doctrines have been created and propagated. These try to substitute for the Christian moral order the so-called morality of situation or individualistic morality, often condemned by Pius XII and finally condemned by a decree of the Holy Office in February of 1956. These also try to substitute the morality of independence (i.e. divorced from the Christian morality) for the idea of God, sanction and obligation.[2]

The reference to those who elevate "the interests of class" seems clear enough. However, as one reads further, it becomes clear that Ottaviani's preliminary document on the moral order is best seen as an attack on both sides of the Cold War, and before long the attacks on the Church's supposed ally in the anti-Communist crusade take precedence over the attacks on their putative common enemy. Ottaviani attacks those who create "so-called conflicts. . . between art and morality, or between freedom of expression and conscience,"[3] an oblique reference to the increasingly beleaguered situation of the Legion of Decency in its efforts to uphold moral standards in cinema in the face of Hollywood's determined efforts to bring nudity to the big screen. Ottaviani attacks finally all "errors which degrade human dignity under the false pretext of freeing man from all bonds that would restrict his nature in some way. The moral order has the task, not only of leading man to his true end, but of defending him against all doctrines and practices that would enslave him to the minds, modes and passions that are contrary to the dignity of his intellect."[4]

Enslaving the mind to passions which are contrary to the intellect was precisely the project that was being pursued by the psychological warriors throughout the '50s. The whole point of advertising was to have its messages elude the mind's rational control, to manipulate the customer into buying something he didn't need, or into buying something for reasons other than utility. Throughout the '50s the OSS alumni were putting their discoveries at the lucrative service of American corporations who were using them to co-erce consumers into making choices that were not in their own interest. "Since World War II," Simpson writes,

> the U.S. government's national security campaigns have usually over-lapped with the commercial ambitions of major advertisers and media companies, and with the aspiration of an enterprising stratum of university administrators and professors. Military, intelligence and propaganda agencies such as the Department of Defense and the Central Intelligence Agency helped bankroll substantially all of the post-W.W.II generation's research into techniques of persuasion, opinion measurement, interroga-tion, political and military mobilization, propagation of ideology and al-lied questions. The persuasion studies, in particular, provided much of the scientific underpinning for modern advertising and motivational tech-niques.[5]

As Ottaviani continues, the object of his ire becomes more apparent. After telling us that "the moral order defends the immutable principles of Christian modesty and chastity" he goes on to say,

> we know the energies spent at the present time by the world of fashion, movies and the press in order to shake the foundations of Christian moral-ity in this regard, as if the Sixth Commandment should be considered out-moded and free rein should be given to all passions, even those against nature. The council will have something to say concerning this subject. It will clarify and eventually condemn all the attempts to revive paganism and all the trends that in the abuse of psychoanalysis tend to justify even those things which are directly contrary to the moral order.[6]

Moscow was hardly known as a leader in the fashion world, nor was it known as a significant producer of movies. The attack here is against the West in general and Hollywood in particular. Ottaviani condemns "the mod-ern world" just about *in toto,* along with its emphasis on "technical progress, its modes of life, and its growing means of propaganda and publicity" in a way that would have prompted Paul Blanshard to say "I told you so," even at the ecumenical council which had the reputation of opening up the windows of the Church to the winds of Liberalism.

Propaganda and publicity, it should be remembered, were the stock in trade of the United States regime and of the CIA, which was ostensibly the Vatican's ally in the war against communism. But by the time of the Council in the early '60s, the alliance was over. And it was over primarily because it was becoming increasingly clear that the "propaganda and publicity" Ottaviani warned against were being used more effectively against Catholics than against Communists. There were signs on both sides – *Ostpolitik* on the part of the Vatican, and the contraceptive campaign on the part of the Rockefellers – that a new era was dawning, an era which reached its culmination in 1974 at the United Nations' sponsored Bucharest Conference on World Population, where the Vatican forged an alliance with Communist-bloc countries and the third world to block Rockefeller's attempt to institute Malthusian birth quotas throughout the world.

John D. Rockefeller III's interest in the Catholic Church reawakened in the early '60s for a number of reasons. To begin with, the Catholic Church was the only enemy to the Rockefeller eugenics campaign left standing. With the defection of the mainline Protestants on sexual issues, Catholics were the only obstacle to the policies Rockefeller wanted to implement throughout the world. JDR III was also intrigued by the news he was hearing about the impending Vatican Council. Rockefeller's biographers, Harr and Johnson, mention that "the papacy of John XXIII, who was elevated in 1958, seemed to promise a liberalizing of Roman Catholic doctrine." During the early '60s it had become virtually a foregone conclusion among liberal Catholics that the Church would change its teaching on birth control. If so, JDR III was willing to do whatever he could to help that process along.

But the attraction was mutual. At the same time the Rockefeller interests were looking for an opening whereby they could undermine the Catholic Church's opposition to eugenic sexuality, certain American Catholics were looking for more acceptance from the Protestant consensus, and that meant acceptance by the people who ran the foundations. René Wormser complained that Catholics were frozen out of social science research as a result of the conscious policy of the foundations. As of 1957, Wormser could claim,

> There are thirty million Catholics in this country, who maintain scores of universities and colleges. Their institutions do not figure among the favored of the foundation complex, nor are academicians connected with them likely to receive research grants from the complex. Perhaps there is a good reason for this discrimination. If so, I cannot guess what it might be. True, Catholic institutions were included among the institutional donees to which The Ford Foundation recently donated a huge aggregate of money, a step which deserved the most enthusiastic approval of the general public. But when it comes to special, individual grants, to find a Catholic institution as a donee is a rarity indeed.[7]

For some time during the late '50s Father Theodore Hesburgh, C.S.C., president of the University of Notre Dame, had been as concerned about this lack of support from the foundations as Wormser was. Father Hesburgh was willing to do whatever it took to get that support and, according to one source, went to the foundations, who told him that to qualify for money he would have to remove certain faculty members. Hesburgh proved amenable to the suggestion and as a result not only started to get grant money but also was appointed a trustee of the Rockefeller Foundation in 1961. He would later become its chairman during the years when the Rockefeller Foundation was heavily involved in abortion advocacy.

By the early '60s, it was clear that both Catholics like Hesburgh and the eugenic foundations felt that they had something to gain by collaborating. What Catholics like Hesburgh wanted was obvious. They wanted money, but they also wanted an entrée to the interlocking world of foundation respectability of the sort that had transformed Kinsey from an obsessive masturbator and voyeur into a great scientist. Grantsmanship, certain Catholics were learning, was in many respects an all-or-nothing proposition. Because the foundations were, in effect, a conspiracy of interlocking directorates serving a common ethnic interest, once a university got money from one, it was in the position of getting money from all of them, and as the '60s progressed and the government expanded its role in funding higher education, foundation acceptance meant access to government money as well. Finally, in the early '70s, that arrangement was codified into law when the Supreme Court decided in *Lemon v. Kurtzman* that it was unconstitutional to give government money to Catholic grade schools, but, as ratified in the *Tilton* decisions, acceptable to give it to Catholic universities. The main difference between the two schools was secularization. Catholic universities had secularized themselves, largely by alienating themselves from the Church, and Father Hesburgh was the architect of that secularization. What the foundations wanted was just as specific. They wanted the Catholic Church to drop its opposition to contraception, and people like John D. Rockefeller III felt that Father Hesburgh could play a crucial role in accomplishing that end.

On October 10, 1962, one day before the opening of the Second Vatican Council, Rockefeller's Population Council, "following discussions among leading Catholic authorities, representatives of Planned Parenthood, and the officers of the Population Council" granted $5,000 to the University of Notre Dame to host a "two-day meeting in December which would bring together representatives of different religious and other points of view to discuss problems of population growth, with particular interest in exploring areas of possible convergence in approaching these problems."[8]

The conference would actually not take place until early 1963, but the groundwork preparing for it took place throughout the summer of 1962. The initial impetus for the conference came not from Hesburgh but from a CBS documentary, "Birth Control and the Law," which aired on May 10, 1962. One of the participants was the Reverend John A. O'Brien, C.S.C., a Notre Dame theologian who had caught the eye of the pro-contraceptive crowd when an article of his entitled "Let's Take Birth Control Out of Politics" had appeared in the November 10, 1961, issue of *Look* magazine. The CBS documentary was widely denounced in the Catholic press as pro-contraceptive propaganda. Rev. John B. Sheehin criticized moderator Eric Severeid's fawning attitude toward Planned Parenthood and called the documentary "an extended commercial for that organization."

The Reverend John C. Knott, family-life director of the National Catholic Welfare Conference in Washington, claimed that "CBS gave evidence of having become a public relations medium for a particular philosophy of life with an oversimplified solution to human problems" and went on to wonder why CBS didn't allow Catholics equal time. Evidently he missed the contribution of Father O'Brien, or perhaps he didn't feel that Father O'Brien's suggestion that a group of Catholic and Protestant experts should get together to "try to iron out the problem" qualified as the Catholic position. Either way he was evidently not impressed with Father O'Brien's position.

Other people were, however. On July 6, 1962, Cass Canfield, Chairman of Planned Parenthood Foundation of America and a board member of the Population Council, wrote to Father O'Brien to tell him how he had been following his writings on birth control for a number of years and had been impressed with what O'Brien had to say on the recent CBS telecast. In the interest of fostering "dialogue" in this area among religious groups, Canfield invited O'Brien to take part in a "small discussion – primarily of Catholic, Protestant, and Jewish clergymen" at a New York hotel on the morning of October 25 "to discuss fertility regulation in the context of responsible parenthood and population growth." In closing, Canfield added a few "very general questions" which might be discussed at the meeting, such as "what is the general thinking from various viewpoints on the 'population problem'" and "what are the opportunities – among religious groups themselves, and between religious groups and the Planned Parenthood Federation – for cooperative thought and action on these vital matters."[9]

On July 24, Canfield received a response not from Father O'Brien, but from George Shuster, assistant to Father Hesburgh at Notre Dame, informing him that O'Brien's attendance at the Planned Parenthood conference was out of the question. "It is impossible, as matters stand now," Shuster wrote

> "for Catholic priests and laymen who follow directives (and this is the kind you doubtless want) to attend a meeting sponsored by Planned Parenthood. The time is not yet ripe for that. Those invited would have to secure permission from the New York Chancery Office to attend, and there would seem no possibility that the answer would be affirmative."
>
> Shuster's objections, upon closer inspection, revolved more around form than substance.[10]

Consequently, instead of the New York meeting, Shuster proposed holding virtually the same meeting at Notre Dame, implying that the name Notre Dame would somehow purge the meeting of disagreeable associations as well as helping Catholics eager to collaborate on birth control to evade the watchful eye of Cardinal Spellman:

> This arrangement would enable prominent Catholics to attend without difficulty, for any problem involving participation in a meeting sponsored by Planned Parenthood would have been removed. The University has arranged [for this] and is currently doing so in a series of meetings in various fields at which important problems are being discussed on a basis of parity between Catholics and others.[11]

In a letter to JDR III on July 31, Canfield can hardly contain himself, calling Shuster's response "the answer to a maiden's prayer." Canfield was no maiden, and he probably didn't pray much either, but an opening of some significance had finally been found with the Catholics, the last roadblock to universal acceptance of contraception. During the '50s the Population Council had had contact with a Jesuit from Baltimore by the name of William J. Gibbons, who requested funding for a "New York Professional Sodality" from the Population Council which would attempt to study the problem of overpopulation as essentially a moral problem. The Population Council was underwhelmed by Fr. Gibbons's proposal. Frederic Osborn in a memo to Dudley Kirk opined that "it is hard to see how there could be much serious exchange of ideas on such premises," especially since Father Gibbon was proposing that each meeting start with a pledge "to respect the right of each parent to participate in the creation of life." If this was what the Catholics had in mind, then the Population Council wasn't interested. What Shuster was proposing at Notre Dame was a whole new ball game, however, and Canfield urged JDR III to fund it claiming that it "should serve a very useful purpose."

Frank Notestein, who was in on the discussion, seemed to concur with Canfield and listed a number of potentially positive outcomes as resulting from it. To begin with the Population Council and the pro-contraception Protestants who were invited could exert pressure

> of the supportive sort on the liberal Catholics attending, to strengthen in the Church those elements which recognize a) the need for tolerance of non-Catholic views, b) the desirability for restraint on the part of Catholics seeking legal restrictions that prevent non-Catholics from following their own moral views, and c) the need for greater attention to parental responsibility in Catholic teaching.[12]

Beyond that, the conference would provide "an opportunity for the Catholics to educate non-Catholics in their position, particularly with a view to letting us see, in sophisticated form, the almost immutable constraints faced by the Church in certain parts of its position and the operations which are amenable to change."[13]

Notestein felt that it was unrealistic to feel that a conference of this sort could get the Church to change its teaching on birth control, but it could help

> to strengthen that element in the Church with which we have many common aspirations and a minimum of differences. [With this in mind,] it would be pointless to publish the results of the conference because that

would incur the wrath of episcopal authorities and harden the positions into two immutable fronts. The only influence the pro-contraceptive party can have is on those influential Catholics who attend the meeting.[14]

Notestein adds, "[I]t is also important, on these premises, that we select for attendance not representative Catholics but Catholics who represent the position nearest our own. This is the group whose influence we would be endeavoring to enlarge."[15] The Population Council would fund the Notre Dame meeting, in other words, on the condition that only "liberal" Catholics, i.e. those willing to work for a change in the Church's position on birth control, be invited. Notestein even suggests "leaving out people such as Father Zimmerman," evidently referring to the Rev. Anthony Zimmerman, S.V.D., a noted opponent of population control. In another letter to JDR III on August 2, Notestein reiterated his opposition to inviting "representative Catholics." The only people to be invited were Catholics "who represent the position nearest our own."

> Personally I would like to re-emphasize my opinion that an endeavor be made to have this group include only the liberal-minded Catholics. We will get simply nowhere if right-wing groups are involved. These conversations should be between the people on both sides who have minimum differences of opinion.[16]

Throughout the negotiations for the conference, there is no indication that either Shuster, who conducted the correspondence, or Hesburgh, whose approval is noted throughout, objected in any way to the Population Council's dictating to Notre Dame the type of Catholic Notre Dame was allowed to invite to its conference. Evidently Notestein's specification that only liberal Catholics should be invited was not construed as an offense against Hesburgh's principle of "true autonomy and academic freedom in the face of authority of whatever kind lay or clerical external to the academic community itself," the principle he enunciated in his Land o' Lakes statement in 1967 when he alienated the University of Notre Dame from the Catholic Church by placing it under a lay board of trustees. When it came to the demands of the Population Council, Hesburgh's truculence evaporated and was replaced by the most supine amenability. Notestein obviously feels that Father Hesburgh is precisely one of their kind of Catholic and nominates him as chairman of the conference in place of JDR III, whose connection with contraception and population control might prove too controversial. "My guess," Notestein wrote referring to Hesburgh, "is that he would be effective in blocking long-winded arguments in theology, which are useless once the positions are understood. No one is going to make converts at the theological level."

JDR III was evidently persuaded by Notestein's arguments. In a letter to Cass Canfield on August 6, JDR III characterized Shuster's proposal as "an encouraging next step in an important and sensitive area." He is also persuaded by Notestein's suggestion "that the individuals who might attend be selected from those who have liberal views; otherwise it would be difficult for the meetings to be very constructive."[17]

By early August the Notre Dame Conference was pretty much a done deal, at least in the higher echelons of the Population Council. By September 1962 the Population Council was dictating not only who was to be invited but what books were to be displayed and discussed (e.g., *A Citizen's Perspective on Population* by J. D. Rockefeller and *Does Overpopulation Mean Poverty?* by Joseph Jones) as well as the questions to be asked and without too much stretching of the imagination the answers to those questions as well. Hesburgh's abject acceptance of Rockefeller's terms gives some indication that academic freedom was essentially a pretext which would allow Notre Dame to get foundation money. In one of his memoirs, Hesburgh talked about defending American theologian John Courtney Murray against Cardinal Ottaviani. In many ways, the example was paradigmatic in Hesburgh's mind. Academic freedom meant protecting Catholics against the influence of Rome. It meant as well supine acceptance of whatever schemes the eugenic regime proposed whether it was the contraceptive or affirmative action, which Hesburgh supported in the Bakke case in the 1970s. In 1962, as the final plans were being made for the Notre Dame Conference, Hesburgh offered no objections to stipulations from the Population Council on who might attend their contraception conference. Hesburgh offered no objections to the fact that they dictated what materials were to be displayed, who was to be invited (and not invited), or what would be discussed. "Conferees," Canfield wrote in his memo 'Some Random Suggestions about the Notre Dame Conference,' "should discuss question of whether the adherents of any faith have a right to try and influence legislation, except as individuals expressing their own views."

It didn't take a genius to figure out the right answer to a question phrased in that tendentious manner. Catholics of the liberal sort were to proclaim publicly that their opposition to contraception was "personal" and that they wouldn't dream of imposing their views on others, and most certainly they would not try to influence legislation. The fact of the matter is that at this point Rockefeller did not feel he could get the Church to change its teaching on contraception; at a later date he would be of another opinion on the matter. He did feel though that the Population Council might persuade liberal Catholics to persuade their less enlightened co-religionists that they as Catholics had no business trying to influence legislation concerning contraception in the United States. Planned Parenthood had already targeted the Connecticut contraception statute for overturning, as a prelude, Leo Pfeffer would later say, for state-subsidized contraception aimed at primarily Negro welfare recipients. The main obstacle in the implementation of this design was the opposition of the Catholic Church.

Canfield kept hammering home the point that when it came to contraception, reasonable Catholics – i.e. the kind who wanted money from the Rockefellers – were supposed to keep their opinions to themselves. This was the purpose of the conference, and by accepting the Population Council's money on their terms, Hesburgh showed that he acquiesced in the arrangement. The conferees were to understand that if "a religious group, as such, should try and influence legislation, [that] would bring up the question of tolerance." The reason, according to Canfield, the Population Council was putting up the money was in the "hope that the liberal views of certain Catholics will gain greater currency within the Church and that practical considerations in connection with limiting population (as well as biological research, partly or wholly sponsored by Catholics) will lead them to become less and less restrictive as to methods."[18]

Fred Jaffe, associate director of information and education at Planned Parenthood, took part in the memo dialogue and came to pretty much the same conclusions. The conference should "focus on objectives rather than methods." This would pare the differences down to size and also, although he doesn't state this, make the Church seem unreasonable by its insistence that certain methods are illicit, whereas the Population Council could give the impression to being open to them all. Jaffe concluded by submitting his list of acceptable Catholics. These would include the already mentioned Father Gibbons, S.J., Father Joseph Gremillion of the National Catholic Welfare Conference, who would have a long association with Notre Dame, Father Hesburgh, and Father Walter Imbiorski of the Cana Conference in Chicago, who would eventually run off and get married and die without a Catholic funeral.

On October 29, Shuster again wrote to Canfield discussing publicity and indicating that he was involved in not a little duplicity in this regard. He requested that no advance publicity be given to the conference lest the wrong people get wind of it, including perhaps the local bishop. In the same letter, however, he indicates that in the hope of "indirect benefits" he has invited "one or two editors of key Catholic periodicals." This echoes pretty much what Shuster said to Canfield in August when he claimed that "we are walking upon relatively difficult terrain and a measure of caution, in the hope of better things to follow is indicated." Shuster was not so much interested in keeping the symposium secret as he was in managing the way the information on it came out. Publicity would only be harmful if the wrong people showed up beforehand. Notestein in a note written after the conference hopes that "there were no unfortunate leaks so far as publicity is concerned," and Shuster assures him that "there were no leaks, thank heavens."

"Hope of better things to follow" from Shuster and Hesburgh's point of view meant more money from more foundations for more conferences undermining the Church's position on contraception. On June 5, 1963, Shuster submitted a proposal asking for funding for virtually the same conference to the Ford Foundation. The conference was "to achieve a consensus which would first serve as a firm and clear basis for dialogue, and second point out areas for future study and discussion," which is pretty much what the first one had done. However, this time Shuster sweetens the pot by adding that "the objective is to prepare a final statement and distribute it widely." The statement would, it was understood, be Catholic academe calling for a change in the Church's teaching, something that would most probably not change the teaching but something which would prove embarrassing to the Church nonetheless, especially if it were promoted by the media. "I am not going to stress further the obvious importance of this effort," Shuster wrote to Oscar [Bud] Harkavy, head of the Ford Foundation, "The interest of *Cardinal Meyer* [Shuster's emphasis] – which is the only part of this letter which is at present confidential – suffices to indicate that these deliberations may find an echo far beyond the confines of the United States."[19]

The Rockefeller crowd got the proposal passed on to them directly from Harkavy (something which indicates just how close the interlock between the foundations was). Harkavy was in effect asking the people at the Population Council whether he should fund Notre Dame's grant or not, and the Population Council seemed less than enthused by the prospect of another conference much less a whole series of conferences. The Population Council had gone to bed with Notre Dame and in the morning decided that it didn't respect her anymore. Ford would eventually go on to sponsor a whole series of conferences during which the Catholics assembled at Notre Dame denounced in increasingly strident terms the Church's position opposing contraception. But the contempt in which the Population Council held Notre Dame is evident in the tone of their memos. Dudley Kirk after suggesting that they might "sponsor this and play it further by ear" goes on to wonder "whether to feel flattered or otherwise at being the only heretic proposed for inclusion in the first conference." Which prompts Marshall C. Balfour to add, "Hooray for the heretic: the cards are surely stacked against him! That is, unless, the way is being prepared for Pope Paul to change the rules of the game."[20]

The wing of the Catholic Church whose conferences were sponsored by Rockefeller money were clearly planning for such an eventuality. Since most of the players were both old and ostensibly celibate, there is no reason to believe that they were hoping to benefit directly from such a change. But a change in the Church's teaching would mean that they as Catholic academics would be acceptable to the foundation power brokers and an acceptable member of the American Protestant consensus, the WASP ethnos, as well. They would be considered Americans in full standing, which has always been the aspiration of a certain kind of Catholic in this country. With people like Father Hesburgh calling the shots for Catholics in the United States, the pope could unpack his bags for good this time. Changing the Church's teaching on contraception would furthermore show that Hesburgh and company had considerable clout among their co-religionists. If they could show that they had delivered the vote on contraception, they might be valuable for wringing other concessions from the Church further down the line – in case the Protestant consensus did a 180° turn on abortion, for example. Perhaps this is why people like Shuster and Hesburgh pursued the idea of the contraception conferences with such avidity throughout the mid-'60s.

Throughout the entire degrading process of applying for a grant which specified not only who Notre Dame could and could not invite, the books that were to be discussed as well as the questions and (by implication) answers that were to arise during the course of discussion, there is not one indication that Father Hesburgh thought that the academic freedom of Notre Dame was being compromised. His vigilance for academic freedom virtually ceased to exist when it came to the Rockefellers, who set much more stringent stipulations than any proposed by Cardinal Ottaviani or the Vatican. This policy of no enemies to the left was to have several far-reaching consequences. First of all, academic freedom was defined as *de facto* the right to proselytize for sexual liberation. This was true not only of Catholic universities but across the board. Political correctness is in the final analysis the use of academe to justify sexual engineering. Secondly, through Hesburgh's efforts, the Church lost control of Notre Dame and in the place of Catholicism liberalism was installed as the university's regnant ideology. Thirdly, sexual liberation would come home to roost at Notre Dame as the theology department was plagued by a series of sexual scandals throughout the period following the 1967 Land o' Lakes statement, its declaration of independence from Church control. In September 1987, Rev. Niels K. Rasmussen, O.P., head of the liturgy program at Notre Dame, was found shot to death in the basement of his home surrounded by homosexual pornography, the paraphernalia of sado-masochism, and automatic weapons. When Notre Dame tried to give Rasmussen a Christian burial – against the express wishes of his will-cum-suicide note – a bomb threat interrupted the services and emptied Sacred Heart Church on campus. Rasmussen's case is only the most spectacular instance of a series of sexual scandals which take place with such regularity that no one gets very upset about them anymore.[21] As a result, blackmail has become a common if unacknowledged form of intimidation influencing the governance of the university to the detriment of Catholic principle, turning the university into an instrument of the WASP ethnos to the detriment of Catholic interest both political and cultural.

Congressman Carroll Reece of Tennessee had become so alarmed at the power of tax-exempt foundations like Ford, Carnegie, and Rockefeller that he convened Congressional hearings on the role these foundations were playing in undermining the democratic institutions of the United States. By the mid-'50s it was clear that the CIA/Foundation/Anti-Catholic cabal was heavily involved in "black operations," i.e., operations against citizens of the United States, which clearly constituted illegal activity. The threat of communism had allowed this door to be opened, and now anyone who opposed the goals of the above group or threatened to expose their methods was fair game to be targeted. Congressman Reece had to learn this the hard way. But he was only an individual. In terms of groups that were going to be targeted, the next victim after black operations were tolerated against domestic communism was obvious. It was the Catholics, and the psychological warfare waged against the Church in the United States would be the battle over contraception, which reached its culmination in mid-'65 when the Supreme Court handed down its *Griswold v. Connecticut* decision and Senator Ernest Gruening of Alaska started holding hearings about overpopulation and how the government meant to solve this problem.

Congressman "Reece," Simpson writes,

> took as his theme that major US foundations – including the Rockefeller Foundation, the Ford Foundation, the Carnegie Corporation and the Social Science Research Council – were engaged in a campaign to promote socialism and "one World" government through funding social science studies Reece regarded as critical of the US and the "free enterprise" economic system. He singled out John Dewey, Samuel Stouffer, and Bernard Berelson , among others, as the purported ringleaders.[22]

Bernard Berelson was trained as a librarian but by the late '40s was considered an expert in public relations and the manipulation of public opinion. One year after the publication of Blanshard's book on Catholic power, Berelson co-edited *Public Opinion and Communication* with Morris Janowitz, one of the seminal works on communications theory, and a good indication of how the psychological warfare techniques refined during World War II were now going to be turned on the American public as a way of controlling them through the manipulation of the new media, i.e., radio and television. Berelson establishes the book's major premise in his introduction: "Growing secularization has meant that more and more areas of life are open to opinion rather than divine law and to communication rather revelation. Growing industrialization has not only extended literacy; in addition, it has provided the technical facilities for mass communication."[23]

The goal of secularization was the reduction of all of life's imperatives to "opinions," which is to say not the expression of moral absolutes or divine law. Once this "secularization" occurred, the people who controlled "opinions" controlled the country. Berelson is equally frank about where the new science of public opinion originated:

> Research in the field was accelerated during World War II by demands for studies on the effect of communications upon military personnel, adjustment to army life and attitudes toward military leaders, enemy propa-

ganda, and civilian morale. After the war this growing interest led to the
establishment of additional university centers for the study of public opinion and communication by the methods of social science. Together with
the continuing activities of industry and government, they now represent a
large scale research enterprise.[24]

Just how large scale would become clear before long. But before that
happened some significant changes had to be made to the realm of what was
communicable. In 1959 Berelson wrote that "the 'great ideas' that gave the
field of communications research so much vitality ten and twenty years ago
have to a substantial extent worn out. No new ideas of comparable magnitude have appeared to take their place. We are on a plateau."[25] The way off of
this plateau was clear enough if one read Berelson's 1950 book carefully,
particularly his claim that "there is a virtual pro-religious monopoly on communications available to large audiences in America today."[26] Religious belief meant ipso facto the opposite of opinion, and therefore ideas not subject
to the manipulation of the people who controlled the communications media.
What needed to be done then was move large areas of thought from the realm
of religion to the realm of opinion if any significant breakthroughs in political control through manipulation of the media were to take place. Sexual morality was the most important area of religious thinking that needed to be
moved into the realm of "opinion," where it would then be under the control
of psychological warriors like Berelson and those who paid his salary,
namely, the Rockefellers.

And this is precisely what happened. During the 1960s, at the same time
Hollywood was trying to break the production code and introduce nudity to
the big screen, Berelson was hard at work for John D. Rockefeller III running
opinion polls whose purpose was to change the attitude of the American public toward contraception. Of particular interest in this regard were the attitudes of Catholics, whose opinions Berelson manipulated through a series of
leading questions that were put to Catholics in the wake of Pope Paul VI's
appearance at the UN in 1964. Question number eight of the survey Berelson
was working on at the time asked: "The Roman Catholic Church does not approve many methods of birth control. Do you believe that the Church should
change its position on this matter?" It didn't take a brain surgeon to figure out
the right answer to this and other tendentious questions, whose purpose was
to insinuate the idea that the Church should change her teaching into the
mind of the population at large.

The Population Council was working behind the scenes in other areas as
well. Through the Notre Dame Conference, Notre Dame sociologist Donald
Barrett made contact with the Population Council, to whom he applied for a
grant. The Population Council, in another instance of the same interlock we
have already seen, then forwarded the application to the Ford Foundation
which granted Barrett $500,000 in the mid-'60s. The story becomes more

complicated when Barrett, with Hesburgh's help, got appointed to Pope Paul VI's birth control commission. Now someone who was receiving money from the foundation establishment at the very time it was trying to change American laws and Catholic teaching on contraception was voting on the commission Paul VI had established to decide whether the Church should change its position on the same topic. It was a flagrant case of conflict of interest, but no one seems to have noticed at the time. The same can be said of Pat and Patti Crowley, head of the Catholic Family Movement at the time. The Crowleys had also been appointed to the birth-control commission because of their connection to Notre Dame while at the same time getting money from the Rockefellers to undermine the Church's teaching on contraception. According to Robert McClory, their biographer, just as the Church was about to issue *Humanae Vitae*, "the Crowleys, *with a grant from the Rockefeller Foundation* [my emphasis], made plans for an international forum on the Christian Family in the World to be held in Italy during the summer of '68."[27]

Part III, Chapter 10

Washington, 1964

In November of 1964, around the time the secret conferences on contraception were being held at Notre Dame, Lyndon Johnson had just been swept by a landslide into the White House, and the nation, as it had been during the Great Awakening and periodically ever since, found itself in the midst of one more moral crusade, this one being known as the civil-rights movement. Like abolition, multiculturalism and the anti-smoking campaign of the 1990s, the civil-rights movement received the blessing of the WASP ethnos, and, largely through the instrumentality of foundation funding, especially the Ford Foundation, it was prosecuted with their interests in mind. This meant that it would have an inevitable sexual subtext, one that would become painfully apparent when it came to the sexual mores of the black family.

The conventional explanation of that movement was somewhat different. By 1964, the end of the Second World War was almost twenty years in the past, and there was a sense that the nation had acquired enough material and spiritual capital to move forward toward a solution to one of its most persistent problems, namely, the race issue, especially its economic dimensions. Four years earlier John F. Kennedy had been elected on a platform which seemed to capitalize in a vague way on this desire to do something. Michael Harrington had written *The Other America,* which brought attention to the people who had been left behind by the increasing wave of post-war prosperity. The largest and most easily identifiable segment of those left behind was the Negro, and their cause had maintained an increasingly commanding grip on the nation's attention over the previous ten years. Beginning with the *Brown v. Board of Education of Topeka* decision in 1954, the federal government had increasingly thrown its weight behind the struggle to dismantle the legacy of racial segregation which the South had erected after the Civil War. In 1963 President Kennedy was assassinated in a southern city, and in 1964 Lyndon Johnson, his successor, actualized the legacy of his predecessor by enacting the civil-rights bill that would bear that year's name.

During the summer of 1964, the civil-rights struggle captured the nation's attention in Atlantic City, when the Mississippi freedom delegation tried to unseat that state's delegates to the Democratic Convention. It was a significant sour note in what was otherwise a love fest celebrating the foregone conclusion that Lyndon Johnson was going to get the party's nomination and the presidency a few months later. If that note of discord seemed out of place in Atlantic City, it was a note that was to be heard with increasing frequency over the next four years, as the liberal sense of purpose that captured the nation with the rout of Barry Goldwater and his brand of conservatism turned increasingly sour. In the course of those four years, President Johnson would go from a man who was an avid supporter of the black cause to someone bitterly disappointed by it and its leaders, leaders he would come to feel were only interested in political posturing and handouts from the government. The liberal establishment, which in the early '60s included the civil-rights movement, was content to destroy its working relationship with the president in the name of opposition to the war, ideological purity, and racial separatism. Black leadership, decimated by the death of Martin Luther King, drifted into ever more self-defeating political posturing and an even more self-defeating espousal of various forms of leftism and violent revolution. During the Johnson administration, a revolution of sorts did take place, but it was cultural in nature and not the political revolution the Left expected. The people who began the decade by asking not what their country could do for them but what they could do for it ended the decade by calling for the government's overthrow, and when that failed focused their revolutionary zeal on their own lives looking for ways to eradicate any traces of the social order there.

In late 1964, racial politics and demagoguery were only synonymous in reference to white southern politicians. Blacks, by adhering to a strategy of non-violent resistance, were in firm possession of the moral high ground. The civil-rights movement was not then perceived as just another group interested in shaking down money from the federal government. It was not then perceived as something solely within the Negro's sphere of interest either. It was rather seen as the cutting edge of social reform in this country. The dark legacy of the past was finally going to be expunged as the sunlight of interracial cooperation spread across the land. Freedom was a concept taken from the days of slavery and applied not only to the descendants of the slaves but to those who looked upon this movement as a paradigm of social progress as well. The children of this century of failed utopian experiments, many of which were based on race, showed no inclination to being anything but slow learners in this regard. The grim experiences of twenty to thirty years before were swept away in the euphoria of the moment that was the '60s and the certitude that the South in this country was backward, an embarrassment, and just plain wrong.

Never before in recent memory was the conservatism which dominated American politics in the aftermath of Wilson's failed foreign policy looked upon with such disfavor. Just what was it that these Southerners wanted to conserve? If it was something other than ill-gotten privileges based on race, that something was not making it into the mainstream of American public opinion. Similarly, was it really possible to portray Barry Goldwater as a defender of the common good and social order? Was that possible with George Wallace? No, in 1964, conservatism was synonymous with reaction, and the prime reaction was against the noble southern Negro and his quest for political equality. That same sense of fairness that would be outraged thirty years later by affirmative action was outraged then by the flagrant attempt to deny the Negro his rights.

However, the general sense of liberal good will vis-à-vis the race issue at this time did little to hide the fact that the civil-rights movement had achieved pretty much what it set out to do by 1964, and, in terms of strategic initiatives, was running on empty. The legal structure of segregation had been dismantled. The civil-rights movement had trained its moral forces for a campaign in the South that had been largely won, not without sacrifices but won nonetheless over a remarkably short period. Now they were suddenly at a loss. Or stated less dramatically, they were at the very least at a crossroads. Should they concentrate their efforts on the strategies which had proven tried and true in the past? Should they agitate for the passage of more bills based on protests in the South? Or should they broaden the movement to include the status of the increasingly large numbers of Negroes in the large cities of the North, whose problems seemed particularly intractable and related to the fast disappearing Jim Crow laws of the South in a way that was not immediately apparent. Bayard Rustin, to give just one example, found jobs for 120 teenagers in Harlem after the Harlem riots of 1964. "A few weeks later," this report continues,

> only twelve of them were still working. One boy told Rustin he could make more playing pool than the $50 a week he had been earning; another could make more than his $60 salary by selling "pot"; another turned down a four-year basketball scholarship to a major university because he preferred to be a "pimp."[1]

Just how did anecdotes of this sort fit in with the image of the noble Negro of the South who seemed so Christian in his determination to be nonviolent in the face of enormous provocation that he put an entire nation to shame? It was a problem that not only blacks found perplexing.

During the fall of 1964 a Catholic undersecretary at the Department of Transportation in the Johnson Administration devoted his time to pondering the question of Negro poverty and the connection between that poverty and the family. Daniel Patrick Moynihan had arrived at the White House as a part of the previous administration's New Frontier and had stayed on into the Johnson Administration after Kennedy's assassination. His original theater of operations was the Department of Labor, and so as part of his study he began to examine that department's statistics on the correlation between unemployment rates and rates of marital disruption. Late in November of 1964, after Lyndon Johnson had been returned to the White House in a landslide of

public approval, Moynihan decided to write an internal government document on the Negro family, one that might provide a policy alternative to the
growing and increasingly unfocused demands of the civil-rights establishment. Moynihan felt that anti-segregation bills, no matter how effective they
were in assuring the moral high ground and funding for the civil-rights
movement, were not an adequate way to get at the heart of the problem. "I
woke up a couple of nights later," Moynihan recounted describing the aftermath of the Johnson landslide,

> at four o'clock in the morning and felt I had to write a paper about the Ne-
> gro family to explain to the fellows how there was a problem more diffi-
> cult than they know and also to explain some of the issues of
> unemployment and housing in terms that would be new enough and
> shocking enough that they would say, "Well, we can't let this sort of thing
> go on. We've got to do something about it."[2]

The opportunity to do something was unique. A significant constellation
of situations both domestic and foreign had created a major window of opportunity. According to Moynihan, in 1964 the nation had reached a moment
"that had never occurred before." It was a moment, Moynihan would later relate in a postmortem on the report in *Commentary*, which combined "a willingness to accept a considerable degree of social innovation" with "genuine
feeling for the problems of Negroes."

> The world was at peace. The president had enormous majorities in Con-
> gress. The success of the New Economics was by then manifest: the Bu-
> reau of the Budget was already forecasting a $45 billion increase in the
> level of federal revenues by 1970 – an increase, further, which doctrine or-
> dained had to be spent in order to accrue. No demonstrators were abroad,
> no confrontation between white power and black protest was building up
> anywhere. In this atmosphere of maximum reasonableness and calm, an
> atmosphere in which the President could without great risk do nothing,
> and which for that very reason provided an opportunity for history to be
> made, the President, seizing the opportunity, set in motion a major initia-
> tive.[3]

The initiative was based on Moynihan's research that fall. From December 1964 through March 1965 Moynihan and his staff put together the document that would eventually bear his name. During the course of the research
and planning involved in creating the document, Moynihan shared his ideas
with Press Secretary Bill Moyers, who relayed enthusiastic comments from
the President. Encouraged by the initial reaction, Moynihan eventually came
up with a thesis that would challenge some fundamental assumptions about
American political life. One of the most significant challenges was to the notion of American individualism. In the place of the dyadic structure of government and individual, Moynihan was proposing the intermediary structure
of the family as the prime criterion of social health among Negroes and the
prime locus of government activity in raising them to economic parity with

whites. The thesis at the center of the Moynihan Report had to do with family policy: "At the heart of the deterioration of the fabric of Negro society is the deterioration of the Negro family." The Moynihan Report proposed economic help for heads of black families. Family health, specifically increasing intactness and decreasing illegitimacy, was to become the government's criterion of social improvement. In February 1965, Moynihan told a conference on poverty that "the question of poverty is leading us to a major reassessment of the effect upon family structure of the way we do things in this country."

Initial reaction was positive. The president was reported as saying, "Pat, I think you've got it." In March of 1965, 100 copies were printed. Johnson had decided to make the ideas in the Moynihan Report, specifically the key claim that Negro poverty was related to "the deterioration of the Negro family" the cornerstone of his new civil-rights policy. The period of legislation, it was thought, was over. Race relations were to enter a new stage. In less than a year, a revolutionary change had taken place in social policy in the Johnson administration. Racial issues were subsumed into the larger question of poverty, and the family became the criterion for social health and the basis for social programs. A family policy was commonplace among European nations, but it had never existed in any coherent fashion in this country before. Now it was to be inaugurated as a way of solving the race problem that had plagued this country for the past 100 years.

In early June 1965, Johnson presented his new program to the civil-rights establishment in the form of a speech at Howard University, the traditionally Negro university in Washington, D.C. Before giving his speech, Johnson had it cleared with the major civil-rights leaders in the land. The reaction was overwhelmingly positive. According to Yancey and Rainwater, Martin Luther King, Roy Wilkins, and Whitney Young "expressed their enthusiasm and anticipated other civil rights leaders' pleasant surprise on hearing the speech." Robert Carter, general counsel for the NAACP, called it "an amazing comprehension of the debilitation that results from slum living."

"The family," Lyndon Johnson told the assembled civil-rights leaders in launching his new initiative,

> is the cornerstone of our society. More than any other force it shapes the attitudes, the hopes, the ambitions, and the values of the child. When the family collapses it is the children that are usually damaged. When it happens on a massive scale the community itself is crippled.
>
> So, unless we work to strengthen the family, to create conditions under which most parents will stay together – all the rest: schools and playgrounds, public assistance and private concern, will never be enough to cut completely the circle of despair and deprivation.[4]

In retrospect, it seems clear that Johnson looked on the family as a motherhood issue at just the time when motherhood and the family were on their way to becoming the most divisive issues in the nation. It seems just as clear that neither Johnson nor the Negro leadership were aware of this at the time. If the Johnson Administration had been looking for a revolution in American social policy, they could have chosen no paradigm so revolutionary as defining the family as the criterion for social health. Moynihan was correct in seeing the United States as virtually alone among the civilized nations in having no family policy, yet in proposing family as the criterion of social policy, no one seems to have anticipated the antipathy of the forces that were behind the civil-rights movement, or to what extent that movement had become a pawn of the Left. Moynihan saw it with hindsight in the postmortem he published in *Commentary*. "For the first half of the 1960s," he wrote,

> the liberal Left, for the most part white, very nearly dominated the Civil Rights Movement, most conspicuously of course in SNCC and CORE, but also in the older-line organizations. The relation was not unlike that of the Marxist Left to the trade unions of the 1930s. The mass of the movement in each instance was made up of rank-and-file persons, with, on the whole, quite conventional views and expectations. But surrounding the leaders was an echelon of intense, purposeful, powerful, and dedicated persons of a quite different character. And behind them was a community of sorts, in universities, in churches, in large cities, small businesses, and assorted journalistic enterprises that provided funds, ideas, support, followings: all those things that make for effective political action. There is no need to exaggerate its coherence in order to perceive that something like a community of opinion has existed here.[5]

Moynihan does not deny the strife in such a community, but claims nonetheless that this coalition could achieve "substantial accord" on issues that mattered to it. As it would turn out, the family meant a great deal to these people, but not in the way that Lyndon Johnson anticipated. Although no one seemed to notice it at the time, support for the family meant curtailment of the sexual revolution, which was just then spreading across the nation with the help of the foundations and universities and journalistic enterprises – in short, the "community of sorts" Moynihan failed to notice at the time. Moynihan in particular and the Johnson administration in general failed to see the connection between the Left-dominated civil-rights movement and the commitment to sexual liberation and eugenics which had always been close to the heart of the eugenic foundations that were funding the civil rights movement. In terms of the personalities driving the civil rights movement, it was Sanger and Rockefeller all over again, with latter day Claude McKays and Max Eastmans thrown in as well. In 1967 Moynihan could still refer in a naive way to the Left as the nation's "secular conscience," without seeing how that conscience was burdened by sins against sexual morality, and how that sort of conscience was particularly sensitive to government initiatives which sought to foster family stability. As Michael Harrington, a key player in the link-up between the Left and the civil-rights movement, said: "this was not at all a sour-faced, pietistic [endeavor] . . . . Everybody was out getting laid."[6]

This blindness vis-à-vis the Left's "secular conscience" was *a fortiori* the case in 1965. No one in the Johnson administration was prepared for the change of opinion which took place over the summer. Since the administration wasn't prepared, it could mount no defense against the force of opinion among the civil-rights elite as it turned against its new family policy. The conventional explanation of why prevailing liberal opinion changed usually has to do with the escalation of the war in Vietnam. The same liberal constituency that ran the civil-rights movement was becoming increasingly disenchanted with Johnson's foreign policy and began using the civil-rights movement as a platform from which they could denounce the war. The riot at Watts is also sometimes offered as an explanation, but that in itself is one of the main things that still needs to be explained. The civil-rights movement was faced with an increasingly paradoxical situation: the more legislative victories they achieved, the more restive the rank-and-file Negro became in northern cities. Some began to feel that the civil-rights movement was raising expectations that it could not fulfill. In the end, Martin Luther King was unable to contain the violence his final march had spawned in Memphis. The uprising in the northern ghetto was proving to be a particularly destructive counter-image to the saintly nonviolent Negro set upon by police dogs in the South. In the summer of 1965 when the Watts riots followed the passage of that year's landmark civil-rights bill by a matter of days, it was becoming increasingly clear that no one had a convincing explanation of why black violence followed so closely on the heels of such legislative victories.

Perhaps it was in just this spirit of perplexity that Press Secretary Bill Moyers gave a copy of the Moynihan Report to Washington columnists Evans and Novak. Or maybe Moyers gave Evans and Novak the Moynihan Report because he felt that the rioting in the cities of the North could best be explained by family pathology. At any rate, once their column describing it appeared, the scrutiny increased, and as that happened the Left increasingly made it known that they did not like what they saw.

Yancey and Rainwater in their analysis lead the reader to believe that the heart of the issue was a public-relations problem. The chief difficulty lay in the fact that the Moynihan Report was a document written originally for a small group of government officials and then publicized by journalists, who wanted to achieve maximal punch for their articles by emphasizing the most inflammatory aspects of the report. Yancey and Rainwater feel that the Evans and Novak article which appeared on August 18, 1965 with lurid quotes like "exposes the ugly truth about the big city Negro's plight" was "the most influential news story connecting the report." They also feel that it was the most damaging. It did the most damage by diverting the public's attention away from the report's proposal on unemployment to a criticism of "the breakdown of the Negro family." The implication is that a more successful public-relations job might have saved this initiative. The verdict is based on the perception that the real nature of the proposal was misunderstood, whereas a reading of the opposition shows that the opposite may have been true. The opposition mounted because the critics understood only too well the message of the report and the fact that it was based on sources the Left found uncongenial. In this regard, the critics of the report were more perceptive than its defenders. Yancey and Rainwater try to place the blame on the welfare establishment and their desire for increased budgets; however, a look at the forces opposing the Moynihan Report leads one to believe that opposition was wider and deeper than that. More was at stake here than the ability to increase one's departmental budget. The more one reads the sources of the document, the more one is impressed with hindsight at how antithetical they were to the values which pervaded the civil-rights movement and its liberal supporters.

One major source for the report, one conveniently overlooked when the charges were made that Moynihan was a white racist, was the writing of E. Franklin Frazier, the Negro sociologist from Howard University and classmate of Langston Hughes and Thurgood Marshall. Frazier claims that large segments of Negro family life were fatally weakened by a succession of slavery, Reconstruction, and the rootless life of the urban North. Frazier in many ways looked upon the last manifestation as the most devastating, but the common consequence of all of these historical forces was a weakened family and – the point that Yancey and Rainwater tried to minimize – moral turpitude. Frazier does not downplay the effects of slavery, segregation, and racism; however, he makes it clear that the pathology which got its start under those conditions is not likely to disappear as soon as those conditions go out of existence. The pathology may have come about under those systems, but it has taken on a life of its own.

In his study *The Negro Family in the United States*, Frazier claimed that "In the new environment [i.e., the slave states of the South] the Negro's sexual impulses . . . were liberated from group control and became subject only to the external control of the master and the wishes and attitudes of those with whom he formed unions. . . . When the sexual impulses of the males were no longer controlled by African customs and mores, they became subject only to the periodic urge of sexual hunger."[7]

In many ways Frazier seems to prefer slavery to the period immediately following because of the stability of the social order and the ties between slave and master. "When the yoke of slavery was lifted, the drifting masses were left without any restraint upon their vagrant impulses and wild desires. The old intimacy between master and slave, upon which the moral order under the slave regime had rested, was destroyed forever. . . . Promiscuous sexual relations and constant changing of spouses became the rule with the demoralized elements in the freed Negro population."[8]

The alternative to this social chaos was the traditional family which owned income-producing property, often a farm, and which was under the authority of a father. This particular family constellation was congruent with Negro prosperity both during and after the fall of slavery and the Reconstruction period. Emancipation, in this regard, had little effect on Negro prosperity. Those who had stable families and acquired property under slavery did well then and under reconstruction in spite of the enormous handicaps they faced at both times. The "well-organized family under the authority of the father" was able to make the transition from slavery to freedom in spite of the overwhelming odds against it. One hundred years later the country was to learn that those who lacked this starting point were unable to prosper or in many cases survive in the face of an overwhelming number of government programs and policies as much in its favor as the regime in the South had been to its detriment. "Following the collapse of the slave regime," Frazier wrote, "the families that had achieved a fair degree of organization during slavery made the transition without much disturbance to the routine of living. In these families, the authority of the father was firmly established, and the woman in the role of mother and wife fitted into the pattern of the patriarchal household. . . . The father became the chief, if not the sole breadwinner."[9]

Frazier's view, it should be clear by now, goes counter to both the glorification of freedom which lay at the heart of both the civil-rights movement of the '60s and movement for the abolition of slavery of a century before. The Negro patriarchal family was the prime criterion of Negro prosperity. In the struggle to keep that family together, the comparative freedoms of the North – freedom, for example, from the moral restraints imposed by rural churches – proved more detrimental to the Negro than the system of slavery imposed by the whites. Much of black culture in this century – Frazier cites the blues and jazz as an example – is an expression of the inability to weather the challenges which freedom placed before the Negro. In many ways, the situation described in the North was worse than that of the South because in "the northern city he had not only escaped from the traditional subordination to white overlords but had also cut himself loose from the moral support of relatives and neighbors. . . . Family desertion has been one of the inevitable consequences of the urbanization of the Negro population."[10]

Frazier is in many ways true to the pastoral tradition, which condemns city life in general; however, in doing so he misses the transvaluation of traditional values that was part and parcel of the culture of modern cities in America in the twentieth century. Modernity put a premium on rebellion against God and escape from the moral norm, and as this philosophy spread through the instruments of culture, it began to permeate urban centers throughout the north. Indeed, the attraction of the city was seen specifically in terms of escape from the tyranny of Christian sexual morality in its Protestant redaction as enculturated in the rural South and small-town Midwest. The Negro was not immune to this sort of seduction. It is portrayed vividly in a work like DuBose Heyward's *Porgy*, specifically in Sportin' Life's seduction of Bess. In the Gershwin musical version, Bess is told, "In Harlem we'll go struttin'/and there ain't nuttin' too good for you."

Frazier's vision is consonant with the other source of the Moynihan Report, namely, Catholic social teaching. "As the result of family disorganization," Frazier wrote in 1950, "a large proportion of Negro children and youth have not undergone the socialization which only the family can provide." He then goes on to describe the dislocation in the Black family in a way that is reminiscent of the writings of Pope Leo XIII:

> The disorganized families have failed to provide for their emotional needs and have not provided the discipline and habits which are necessary for personality development. . . . Since the widespread family disorganization among Negroes has resulted from the failure of the father to play the role in family life required by American society, the mitigation of this problem must await those changes in the Negro and American society which will enable the Negro father to play the role required of him.[11]

The role of the father which found emphasis in Frazier had special meaning for Moynihan as well, who had grown up in a broken family in Hell's Kitchen in New York City and had become a shoeshine boy at the age of thirteen. It was while working with black shoeshine boys on street corners that he first became aware of the similarities of between "the wild Irish slums" of the late nineteenth century and the Negro ghettos of the mid- to late twentieth.

Moynihan was raised without a father, but as a Catholic he became cognizant of Catholic social teaching on the family. He mentions the writings of the Jesuit John LaFarge during the '30s. LaFarge was associated with Friendship House and the Baroness de Hueck Doherty, the woman whose efforts in Harlem made such an impression on Thomas Merton. Moynihan's proposal grew out of Catholic initiatives like that, a fact soon noticed by his opponents in the culture wars of the '60s, which were in many ways the culmination of the eugenic anti-Catholic campaign which Blanshard publicized in the late '40s. Yancey and Rainwater are less specific but make the connection more emphatically: Moynihan's views, they wrote,

> were strongly influenced by Catholic welfare philosophy, which has emphasized the idea that family interests are the central objective of social welfare and of social policy in general. He had observed that most European nations and Canada had adopted family allowance programs to cope with difficulties of income maintenance at low-income levels.[12]

The connections between the Moynihan Report and Catholic social teaching are neither abstruse nor difficult to find. Writing in *Rerum Novarum*, the encyclical which inaugurated the entire modern tradition of Catholic social teaching, Pope Leo XIII states that "the right of ownership, which we have shown to be bestowed on individual persons by nature, must be assigned to man in his capacity as head of the family."[13] In the same paragraph, Pope Leo XIII goes on to say that "the family, like the State, is by the same token a society in the strictest sense of the term, and it is governed by its own proper authority, namely the father."

In keeping with the hierarchical nature of Catholic teaching, the authority of the father is subordinated to the authority of the moral law, which is just one manifestation of the will of God, the ultimate Father. All of these various orders find their congruence in the common good of a well-ordered state:

> It is vitally important to public as well as to private welfare that there be peace and good order; likewise, that the whole regime of family life be directed according to the ordinances of God and the principles of nature, that religion be observed and cultivated, that sound morals flourish in private and public life, that justice be kept sacred, and that no one be wronged with impunity by another, and that strong citizens grow up capable of supporting and, if necessary, of protecting the State.[14]

According to the principle of subsidiarity, the state was free to intervene in the affairs of the family only if the family had failed in some radical way. One example of such massive failure was "if the natural bonds of family life should be relaxed among the poor . . . the power and authority of the law, but of course within certain limits, manifestly ought to be employed." The Moynihan Report was proposing just this sort of intervention. Yet even in this instance, those government programs should have as their first and primary goal the reinstitution of the moral law: "First and foremost Christian morals must be re-established, without which even the weapons of prudence, which are considered especially effective, will be of no avail to secure well-being."[14] Anyone who was even remotely aware of Catholic social teaching could hardly be unaware that when the popes talked about strengthening the family, they were talking about the strengthening of the moral law. In *Quadragesimo Anno* Pius XI claimed that "all that We have taught about reconstructing and perfecting the social order will be of no avail without a reform of conduct."[15]

If the discussion of Yancey and Rainwater proves anything, it shows that in many ways the Left was more aware of this fact than Moynihan or his supporters, and they wanted no part of any "reform of conduct" that infringed on the ever-burgeoning forces of sexual liberation. In addition to regretting the lack of better public relations, Yancey and Rainwater try to distance themselves from the moral message that was at the heart of what Moynihan was proposing. In this instance, one has more sympathy for the liberal critics. At least they knew what was involved, and they fought against it in a way completely consistent with their ideology of personal freedom. Yancey and Rainwater, however, can only complain that

> In the public version of the report, it would have been well to reduce the

discussion of illegitimacy because of the inflammatory nature of the issue with its inevitable overtones of immorality. . . . Certainly in many of the newspaper accounts a sensitive reader will note veiled accusations of immorality. . . .[17]

In the aftermath of its failure, it became apparent that the Moynihan report's defenders seemed embarrassed to the point of apology by the moral implications the report itself raised. Perhaps because it did not count as good sociology, there was a shyness in dealing with the moral underpinnings of the report. Instead of dealing with the issue directly by saying, in effect, yes, social reform is impossible without a reform of conduct, Yancey and Rainwater pretended that one could have a program which calls for strengthening family life without mentioning the moral underpinnings of family life, namely sexual morality. "One has a right to expect," Yancey and Rainwater opine, "that intelligent social observers will deal with the problem by taking it out of a Puritan moral-immoral dialogue and placing it in the context of social causes and social costs."[18]

But of course this is precisely what the Left was unwilling to do. Instead of dealing with the issue of sexual morality openly, the report's defenders could only seek refuge in their status as social scientists. In attempting to defuse the "gut reaction" of the Left, the Johnson administration only exacerbated it, by not dealing forthrightly with the root cause. "Few social scientists," Yancey and Rainwater claim,

> would admit to a personal conscious view that having an illegitimate child is "immoral." But the reactions of a great many social scientists to the use Moynihan made of illegitimacy data would suggest that they are struggling with such a view within themselves which they project on the larger public. They seem to be saying, "It's not that I think there's anything wrong with having an illegitimate child, it's just that conventional people do and therefore we ought not to talk about this."[19]

The fears of liberals went deeper than that. What Moynihan was proposing attacked the root of what they believed in every bit as much as Catholic social teaching did. If social progress for the Negro meant proclaiming the necessity of personal morality, particularly in the sexual sphere, then that was a price too high to pay. The Negro could go back to his ghetto and stew in his own juices if racial justice meant something as radical as all that.

In his own postmortem, Moynihan cites an article by Marcus Raskin in *Ramparts*, attacking him and the notion that the government had any concern with the morality of its citizens. Likewise, Christopher Jencks traced the Moynihan Report to the conservative tradition, where "the guiding assumption is that social pathology is caused less by basic defects in the social system than by defects in particular individuals and groups which prevent adjusting to the system. . . . The prescription is therefore to change the deviants not the system."[20] Jencks, who was a fellow with the Institute of Policy

Studies in Washington at the time, and therefore in a position to know, claimed that "radicals have maintained . . . that involvement in such issues [i.e. those concerning the family] is a first step toward 1984. (This hostility . . . seems to derive largely from a fear that the government will try to impose sexual continence and fidelity – virtues which almost all critics think greatly over-rated.)"[21]

What the liberal Left saw in the Moynihan Report was an attempt to roll back their hard-won sexual freedoms. This particular attempt to strengthen the Negro family proposed a sexual morality that they had deliberately jettisoned en route to becoming part of the sexually enlightened Left. One of the main reasons they were interested in the Negro in the first place was because the Negro (or certain Negroes) exhibited such guilt-free, uninhibited sexual lives. The liberals were willing to choose the ghetto in 1965 because they had in effect been choosing the ghetto all along. Their interest in the Negro grew out of an interest in Negro jazz, and all that that stood for in imagery fostered by whites interested in overturning the social order. The liberals had basically the same point of view toward the Negro as the Ku Klux Klan but with the values completely inverted. For the liberal, the uninhibited lives of the lower class in touch with primitive (i.e., sexual) nature were superior to lives lived according to "white" (i.e., Christian) morals. Like the hero of Jack Kerouac's novel *On the Road*, the liberal walked the halls of Congress or the Ford Foundation "wishing I were a Negro," searching for "spade kicks." The Negro provided an alternative gospel, according to which family responsibility was to be eschewed in favor of "ecstasy, joy, kicks, darkness [and] music." Like the Ku Klux Klan, the Left was ready to write the moral Negro out of the race as an irrelevant aside. The "real" Negro, the one the disaffected whites wanted most to emulate, was the pimp and the stud. Negritude meant sexual license without guilt.

Freshly arrived in New York as a refugee from Nazi Germany, Paul Tillich, the liberal Protestant theologian, found himself in a similar situation. The *mise en scene* is related by his wife Hannah in a memoir that exposes the sexual roots of modernity with devastating clarity, so devastating in fact that Tillich's reputation as a theologian has yet to recover from the blow its publication dealt. Whenever they traveled or moved, the Tillichs were in the habit of first visiting the red light districts of their new surroundings. Hannah found whorehouses "a window into hidden truth." When they arrived in New York as refugees from Nazi Germany in the '30s, they were disappointed that New York didn't have a red-light district in the same way that, say, Amsterdam did, but then they found Harlem. "We found some sort of consolation in Harlem," she wrote.

> Somebody must have taken us to Small's Paradise, where one went up a
> steep staircase, watched by an old pockmarked Negro, whose muddy uni-

form with gold braid we feared a little. Later we would shake hands with him. Inside the dark, long room, we sat facing clouds that drifted behind an orchestra of Negroes, who played noisily and shrilly. It was as if we had entered a tropical forest with parrots screaming, dark faces peering out of the jungle, falsetto voices, and brilliant colors. A Negro danced with me, a Negress with Paulus.

We felt relaxed at Small's and returned there with our friends, grateful voyeurs, taking in the primeval charm of the hearty men and swaying women. We considered it an aesthetic show. We did not think at all in economic, political, or social terms.

Once we dared to go to a show in a basement where there were mostly Negroes. In the dancing space at the center of the room occasional performances were given. A nude Negress painted gold, having danced with a Negro twice her size, leaned her body against a post and masturbated with violent snakelike movements, while her former partner and another girl unmistakably performed the acts of intimate sex. It did not seem vulgar or fleshy. It was filled with the natural vivacity of these beautiful black people.

People at the seminary did not think our adventures such a good idea. They had misgivings about our dancing with Negroes. Later, others objected to our aesthetic attitude concerning Negroes. Paulus and I had talked about the black image from primeval times on, the dark people being considered the least aristocratic . . . in psychic circumstances, the black or dark one always the devil. . . the black soul against the white soul . . . black as a magic color expressing evil or dark, underground powers.[22]

In the eyes of the modern elite, the Negro had become the instrument for overturning of Christian values. That most Negroes themselves were Christians meant little to people like the Tillichs, little in relation to what they could be made to symbolize. And as for actual Negroes, there were plenty who were willing to collaborate with the arbiters of modernity in return for financial and other gains. In the mid-1920s, that alliance was known as the Harlem Renaissance. It was promoted chiefly by white decadents like Carl Van Vechten, whose novel *Nigger Heaven* found its climax in a young black writer attending a Black Mass. It was a touch which Hannah Tillich would have appreciated, but it offended the Negroes who were interested in the family life Van Vechten disdained. W. E. B. DuBois and others complained that the only Negroes who got through to the white publishing world were those who pandered to the modern whites' craving for decadence.

In a memoir written after Tillich's death, Rollo May described the influence Tillich had on his life as a result of meeting him in January of 1934 at Union Theological Seminary, which was not far from Harlem. "A wave of freedom swept over me," May said describing Tillich's influence on his personal development, " – freedom from all the futile arguments of undergraduate days." Most of these foolish arguments had to do with the existence of

God and His moral law. "I felt freed also from the nagging inner compulsion to believe," May continued, and then went on to describe some of the "futile arguments" which fell by the wayside under Tillich's tutelage:

> Paulus' statement took away my security, that childish belief to which, against all intellectual development, I apparently still clung. I knew that God for most people was the guarantor of the status quo; he protected them from fundamental upset, from moral anarchy. God guarded the sanctity of marriage, he was against crime, he protected property (especially if you belonged to one of the sects that sprang from Calvinism).
>
> The word "atheist" conjured up all the opposite things: a satanic person who is antimoral, who believes in free love, who is dishonest and would torture your grandmother, plus all the invective hurled at "atheistic communism" in our day. Infantile as were these vestigial remnants of my early imprinting, and outrageous to my reason as they still are, I cannot deny that they existed somewhere in my consciousness. It required not logic but living, and time, to mature beyond such superstitions. It also required living and time to absorb what Paulus was trying to say.[23]

In place of all that, according to May, Tillich promoted the idea that "the concept of god is continually changing; it is flexible, dynamic, always 'in process.' . . . [T]he phrase 'god above God' does express the eternal in a metaphor which does not crystallize into dogma."[24]

Obligingly enough, "god above God" doesn't ask much of us, certainly not much in the realm of sexual restraint. In this regard, He is remarkably like Paul Tillich himself, and this was his prime attraction to moderns like May, who wanted belief without restraints. May gives the following account of one of Tillich's sermons:

> Nothing is demanded of you – no idea of God, and no goodness in yourselves, not your being religious, not your being Christian, not your being wise, and not your being moral. But what is demanded is only your being open and willing to accept what is given to you, the new Being, the Being of love and justice and truth, as it is manifest in Him Whose yoke is easy and Whose burden is light.[25]

"The meaning of this statement quoted above," May goes onto tell us, is "that there is demanded of us no belief in a particular god, nor of being religious in a particular sense, nor being Christian, nor being moral. . . . My faith and hope is that this new religious outlook will be characterized not only by internationalism but by interracism and intersexism as well."[26]

At Union Theological Seminary, liberal race relations were well on their way to replacing Christianity as the orthodoxy of the 1940s and '50s. Tillich's influence is hard to minimize. Martin Luther King wrote his dissertation comparing Tillich and Henry Wiemann. Tillich was still alive in the '60s, but more importantly his influence had been institutionalized in institutions like the National Council of Churches, and it was precisely the National Council of Churches which led the opposition to the Moynihan Report.

Part III, Chapter 11

Washington, 1965; Rome, 1965

Emboldened by the sense that they now had a combination of state-of-the-art contraceptive devices at their disposal, John D. Rockefeller III and the Population Council began to press their advantage. Within days of Johnson's landslide victory in November of 1964, and right around the time Daniel Patrick Moynihan was mulling over the plight of the black family, Rockefeller and Bernard Berelson traveled to Washington seeking an audience with Lyndon Baines Johnson. What they got was a meeting with Dean Rusk, secretary of state under John F. Kennedy, and the Rockefeller operative who had pulled the plug on Kinsey when Kinsey's sex surveys became a matter of public embarrassment in the wake of the Reece hearings. Through Rusk's ministrations, a sentence was inserted into Johnson's January 4, 1965, State of the Union message, in which the president announced to the world that he would "seek new ways to use our knowledge to help deal with the explosion in world population and the growing scarcity in world resources." Rockefeller's biographers see the statement as "a decisive turning point" in changing the public's aversion to contraception and paving the way for the government's involvement in disseminating at first information about contraception and then the contraceptives themselves.

Griswold v. Connecticut, handed down in the early summer of 1965, was another crucial step in this process. Writing after the victory had been safely won, Leo Pfeffer was completely candid in explaining why a law prohibiting the sale of contraceptives which never got enforced had to be struck down. This was so "because their presence made it impossible for the state to encourage contraception, something it now increasingly deems necessary to do. The middle income and the affluent, married and unmarried, use contraceptives; the poor have babies. When the poor, often racial minorities, are on the welfare rolls, taxpaying Americans rebel and expect the state to do something about it. . . . The national government already established this policy as part of its program of aid to underdeveloped countries, but the States could hardly follow suit as long as their own laws forbade the practice."[1]

The liberals were, in effect, playing a double game here. They were using race to overturn the notion that the social order was somehow dependent on the moral order, and then they were using the loosened sexual morals as a way of prosecuting a eugenics campaign against the same blacks who had made that loosening possible in the first place. The South had condoned segregation, and they were all Christians; therefore, Christianity had been discredited as a force with anything to say about how this society should be structured. The mainline Protestant denominations were completely in agreement with this strategy even if it seemed on the surface to be to their detriment, because they were just as avid for sexual liberation. To the extent that the mainline Protestants capitulated on the sexual front, they sought to compensate by increasing their efforts for racial justice.

Part II of the double game had to do with eugenics. Once the social order had been weakened by the liberals using race as a cover for sexual liberation, contraceptives were prescribed as the cure for welfare, by cutting back on the number of blacks, i.e., welfare recipients, that were being born. The blacks, who were used as the pretext to change social mores, became the first victims of the change as they were targeted by the population controllers as the "beneficiaries" of expanded government services which were more often than not just a pretext for the legitimization of contraceptive eugenics. *Griswold v. Connecticut* was the major breakthrough in this regard. Now the government could push forward with its population-control programs without coming into conflict with state laws.

Perhaps emboldened by this string of stunning successes, JDR III decided to take his struggle for contraception a step further. He decided to confront the enemy in his own lair. With the help of Father Theodore Hesburgh, president of the University of Notre Dame and board member of the Rockefeller Foundation, JDR III arranged an audience with Pope Paul VI, who was mulling over the issue of birth control at the time and, it was hoped according to the Enlightenment view of history, might prove to be even more liberal than John XXIII, who was as different from his predecessor as day was from night. Hesburgh, who is described as "decidedly liberal in his own views on population although he would not go as far as JDR on some aspects."[2] was only too happy to oblige. After being briefed by a number of Jesuit professors from Georgetown university on "the complexities of the Catholic Church that curtailed the freedom of any Pope," Rockefeller met with Pope Paul VI for forty-five minutes in mid-July of 1965.

Years later in a letter to Henry Cabot Lodge, the man who arranged for the murder of Ngo Dinh Diem, the Catholic president of Vietnam, when Lodge was appointed U.S. emissary to the Vatican, Rockefeller described the meeting as "warm and friendly," but at the same time "not too meaningful or constructive in terms of the population question as I did not feel that I could push too hard and he obviously could not be entirely frank with me as to his own personal views when he had the major decision on birth control pending." The decision in question, as expressed in the papal document which would eventually come out under the name *Humanae Vitae* in 1968, must have been a bitter disappointment for Rockefeller. Five years after his meeting with the pope and two years after the appearance of *Humane Vitae*,

Rockefeller was still obsessed with the Church's opposition to birth control. So much so that he was willing to trade on his friendship with Lodge as a way of getting his point across to the same pope who had so pointedly ignored his views in the summer of '65. "The population question," JDR III wrote to Lodge, "is the most important subject which you would have to discuss with his Holiness, assuming that you have a close and informal relationship."[3] One gets the impression that Rockefeller never got over the fact that the pope never took him up on his offer to help co-write *Humane Vitae*. Rockefeller wrote to Lodge in 1970 explaining that "still today the Church could make a major contribution if it were willing to make a positive statement."

The Church's failure to make what Rockefeller considered a "positive" statement could hardly be ascribed to lack of zeal on the part of Mr. Rockefeller. Within minutes of his brief meeting with the pope in July of 1965, Rockefeller was reproaching himself out loud for not having expressed his case forcefully enough. In an attempt to calm him down, Msgr. Paul Marcinkus, later head of the Vatican bank, suggested that JDR write the pope a letter expressing any points which might not have been made during the meeting. A day later on July 16, 1965, JDR duly sent off his letter on "the importance of the population problem . . . and the role that the Church might assume in its solution."[4]

The incident read like a chapter out of an unpublished Henry James novel. The earnest Protestant American with his two newly invented contraceptives and a boundless faith that technology and progress will solve all of the world's ills confronts the head of the old world's seminal institution, an Italian gentleman by the name of Montini. "There is no problem more important facing mankind today," Mr. Rockefeller informed the pope earnestly. If the pope failed to heed Mr. Rockefeller's advice "we will face disaster of an unprecedented magnitude."[5]

. Mr. Rockefeller then went on to explain his invention to the pope, calling the IUD "a breakthrough of truly major proportions, making available a method which is safe, effective, inexpensive and feasible under the most difficult living conditions. Experience with its use to date indicates that it will prove highly acceptable to great masses of people everywhere."[6] The IUD was driven off the market in the United States within a matter of years as a result of product liability lawsuits. Those who claim that the Church missed a historic opportunity by issuing *Humanae Vitae* would do well to ponder the consequences for papal credibility, much less infallibility, if Paul VI had taken Mr. Rockefeller's advice and endorsed the IUD as a means of Catholic-approved birth control. When it came to giving advice, JDR was used to the undivided attention of religious leaders, who in general seemed to benefit financially in direct proportion to how avidly they implemented his agenda through the agencies of their denomination. The Quakers, whose idea of missionary work included installing IUDs in Mexican women, are a good example in point. It was perhaps the accommodating nature of the mainline Protestants which led JDR to dispense with niceties and get blunt with the pope and point out to His Holiness what might happen if the pope failed to see things JDR's way. "As I see it," Rockefeller wrote to the pope,

> if the Church does not supply this leadership, there will be two consequences: one, the present accelerating pace toward population stabilization will proceed, country by country, without over-all guidance or direction, particularly on the moral side: on the other, if I may speak perfectly frankly, the Church will be bypassed on an issue of fundamental importance to its people and to the well-being of all mankind. The flooding tide cannot be stopped or even slowed, but it can be guided. Because I believe so keenly in the importance of the role which your church has to play in our troubled world of today, I am deeply concerned to see a situation developing which in the long run, it seems to me, inevitably will be harmful to the Church's position around the world.[7]

One wonders what was going through the pope's mind as he read these lines. Was he supposed to feel a sense of gratitude at being saved, along with his Church, from being swept aside by the flooding tide of progress and history? Or was it something more like the Italian version of "If you're so damn rich, why aren't you smart?" Either way, history shows that the pope passed on JDR's suggestion. History shows just as conclusively that many liberal Catholics in the United States were much more willing to accommodate JDR's wishes than the pope was, especially if the institutions they ran might benefit from the largesse of Rockefeller funding or that of other foundations. Father Hesburgh, who arranged the meeting between Rockefeller and the pope, is a good case in point.

In his letter to the pope, Rockefeller wanted to know if it were possible "to shift the focus of this concern from the method itself to the uses to which the method will be put. Would it be feasible to state that the Church will leave to the discretion of the individual family its choice as to the method it will use to determine the number of its children provided the method is not harmful to the user and provided it does not interfere with the meaning and importance of sexual union in marriage?"[8] This, of course, was the position the Population Council took as the condition for sponsoring its conference on population at Notre Dame. Father Hesburgh had proved to be as amenable on this point as the pope would later prove intractable. Mr. Rockefeller's visit had other consequences as well. It convinced the pope that his main enemy lay now to the west and not to the east and brought about as a result the end of the anti-Communist crusade and the beginning of the Vatican's *Ostpolitik*. On June 26, 1966, less than a year after the pope's meeting with John D. Rockefeller III, Agostino Casaroli, the generally acknowledged architect of the Vatican's *Ostpolitik*, flew to Belgrade and signed an agreement normalizing relations between the Vatican and Yugoslavia.[9]

Since sex was simply an instrument – something like a knife – according to the Rockefeller view of things, "could not the full weight and prestige of the Church be brought to bear on prescribing the circumstances under which the chosen method will be used? . . . To express the above more concisely, what I am suggesting is that specific methods be regarded as merely instruments, like knives, whose use is morally good or bad depending on the intentions of those who employ them."[10] It was the sort of consequentialism which Father Charles Curran would advocate roughly two years later in a book published by the University of Notre Dame Press. The pope was, however, not buying. The Catholic Church did not buy the view implicitly in 1968 with the issuance of *Humanae Vitae*, and it still did not buy it twenty-five years later, this time explicitly, with the issuance of *Veritatis Splendor*. Of course, the Catholic universities and theologians bought into the Rockefeller view at around the same time that Father Hesburgh arranged Rockefeller's meeting with the pope. They made their break with the Church explicit when Hesburgh issued his Land o' Lakes statement in the summer of 1967.

Rockefeller went on to add that dissemination of contraceptives would diminish recourse to abortion, implying that he opposed the practice, when in fact he was already involved in funding abortion advocacy in the United States. What he was proposing as his contribution to the pope's birth-control encyclical would later come to be known as consequentialism, the notion that the good or evil of any action is ontologically free of its essence and solely determined by the intentions of the moral agent and the consequences which flowed from the act. This would become a prominent feature of Catholic dissent as the decade progressed. It would be the cornerstone of the position of Charles Curran, the man who would mount the most effective protest against *Humanae Vitae* in the United States, and it could be picked up at any number of conferences being sponsored by foundation money in the United States. JDR didn't succeed with the pope, but his arguments were heard with increasing frequency coming from the mouths of Catholic theology professors.

In October of 1965 the whole series of conferences on contraception at Notre Dame which began under the aegis of the Population Council in 1962 and whose continued funding was provided by the Ford Foundation, finally emerged from the secrecy under which they were held with the issuance of what George Shuster had promised Rockefeller three years earlier, namely, a statement by Catholic academics contesting the Church's position on birth control. In October 1965, Religious News Service announced the publication of a "remarkable statement on birth control prepared this Spring by thirty-seven American scholars, the very existence of which was not revealed" until seven months after it had been written. Catholic scholars, at least thirty-seven of them, were now on record in calling the Church's position on contraception "unconvincing." The statement had been delivered personally by

Rev. Theodore Hesburgh to the Rev. Henri De Riedmatten, secretary of the papal commission on birth control. The story broke in the Paris edition of the *New York Times*, in an article written by John Cogley which included the text Hesburgh carried to the birth-control commission as well.

Not surprisingly the Notre Dame statement, which was hammered out from March 17 to March 21, 1965, claimed that "the crisis of world population" was the main reason that the Church's teaching had become "unconvincing." The statement went on to list a number of propositions endorsed by the members of the conference, specifically:

- The members of the conference, respectful of the authority of the Church, are convinced that the norms established in the past are not definitive but remain open for further development. (Point # 2)
- The members of the conference do not find convincing the arguments from reason customarily adduced to support the conventional position. These arguments do not manifest an adequate appreciation of the findings of physiology, psychology, sociology, and demography, nor do they reveal a sufficient grasp of the complexity and the inherent value of sexuality in human life. (Point #3)
- The majority of the members were of the opinion that there is dependable evidence that contraception is not intrinsically immoral, and that therefore there are certain circumstances in which it may be permitted or indeed even recommended. (Point #5)
- The members were persuaded that in matters of public policy in a morally pluralistic society, Catholics while rendering witness to their beliefs need not for reasons of private morality oppose governmental programs of assistance in family limitation, provided that the consciences of all citizens are respected. (Point #7)

The last point was especially important. It was one of the suggestions laid down by the population Council as a condition for funding the 1962 Notre Dame Conference. Now, *mirabile dictu*, it appeared as if a group of "responsible" Catholic scholars had arrived at the same conclusion all by themselves, simply by pondering the exigencies of Catholic theology. With all of the crucial links in terms of funding and personnel tucked invisible behind the scenes, the fact that the same ideas kept cropping up in such seemingly unrelated places was simply ascribed to the fact that great minds always traveled in the same circles. As we shall see, the notion that Catholics should not oppose government funding of contraceptives would soon rear its head again before the summer of '65 was out.

The ideas which came out of the '65 conference were, of course, not the sole property of Rockefeller and the Population Council. By the summer of '65 a consensus was emerging which had a number of interested parties involved. One of the signers of the Notre Dame statement, for example, was

Notre Dame graduate and trustee, Thomas P. Carney. Carney was at the time of the conference vice-president in charge of research and development for C. D. Searle Company of Chicago, a major pharmaceutical house which was involved in marketing the birth-control pill at the time. When the deliberations of the Notre Dame conference on birth control became public, one person who was particularly outraged at Notre Dame's duplicity was a lawyer from Harrisburg, Pennsylvania by the name of William Bentley Ball. Ball was also legal counsel for the Pennsylvania Catholic Conference, and it was in this capacity that he wrote to Archibishop John Krol, head of the conference, and ordinary of the Archdiocese of Philadelphia. Claiming that the conference at Notre Dame "does not make my task any easier," Ball related the experience of a Catholic physician who attended the conference "and was sickened by what he heard" which "involved a unified attack on the position which Your Excellencies have taken, even to the point of referring to me in a prepared paper."[11]

"The conference," Ball continued, "was chaired by a Notre Dame graduate named Carney, who is vice president of Searle, perhaps the leading manufacturer of contraceptives in the USA."[12]

When it came to the discussion of birth control at Notre Dame, the field was hardly level, nor were the observers disinterested. In addition to academics eager for grants, pharmaceutical companies like Searle had representatives at the conference to insure a favorable outcome from their point of view. Notre Dame seems to have been happy with the collaboration as well. In 1967, Thomas Carney, who graduated from Notre Dame thirty years earlier with a degree in chemistry, was appointed to the board of trustees; in 1969 he was given an honorary degree; in May of 1971 he was awarded the Edward Frederick Sorin Award, the highest award granted by the Notre Dame Alumni Association.

The Catholic press for the most part took the belated announcement of the secret Notre Dame conference as if it were an encyclical from the pope. "For the first time in my reading experience at least," wrote Msgr. George W. Casey in *The Boston Pilot*, "a committee of responsible moral theologians and sociologists meeting under Catholic auspices have made a public declaration giving endorsement, however qualified, to contraception."[13] Msgr. Casey was much taken with the boldness of the Notre Dame statement even if it had been hammered out in secret seven months before. The fact that it was being publicized in the fall of '65 meant for him that a change was in the offing. The fact that people could say things like this and suffer no consequences meant that the teaching must be in doubt. In other words, the monsignor was reacting more to how the statement was propagated and how it was disseminated through the media and how the Church reacted to that dissemination than to the content of the document itself or the reasoning behind its assertions. The fact that the statement was signed by experts who claimed to be Catholic in effect took care of the problem of content, since most people would not presume to call themselves experts. The reaction to the Notre Dame statement was also a tribute to the loyalty which Catholics had toward institutions sponsored by the Church. In the minds of most people at the time, there was little difference between Notre Dame and the Church, a fact which the foundations sponsoring the conference used to maximal effect. The combination of residual trust in Catholic institutions along with a sense that the Church was changing as a result of the Council, along with the population explosion drumbeat that Rockefeller and others were orchestrating in the media, all contributed to the sense that some sort of glacial unstoppable movement was in progress, and that one's attitude toward contraception was some indication of whether one sailed with the tide or got swept away in the flood. "Signs are mounting," Msgr. Casey opined with specific reference to contraception, "that the reform and the renewal instituted by Pope John will be best remembered from what it does or doesn't do with regard to this agonizing problem."[14]

One indication that the efforts of Rockefeller and the Population Council were having their effect was the fact that the government was starting to get involved on their side of the issue. Johnson's endorsement of population control in the 1965 State of the Union message was followed six months later in June of 1965 with *Griswold v. Connecticut*. Then following *Griswold*, throughout the summer of 1965, Sen. Ernest Gruening of Alaska chaired a Senate committee which held hearings on what was coming to be termed the "population explosion." The hearings were orchestrated with two major effects in mind: first of all, the populace was to have the dangers of overpopulation impressed on it in the direst terms possible, and secondly, there was to be virtual unanimity among those addressing the Gruening committee. The fact that there were no dissenting voices was to give the impression that a consensus of the best and the brightest already existed on the issue and that the only thing left for the Senate to do was to put the recommendations of the population-control solons into action.

The predictions were nothing if not dire. The teeming masses were portrayed as an imminent disaster, something on the level of nuclear war. "Deluge" was a term frequently heard. Senator Gruening himself was of the opinion that "[I]f our population growth does not stabilize, we may reasonably assume that we will lose the freedoms, privileges, and good life we enjoy today."[15] Senator Joseph S. Clark of Pennsylvania, bringer of New Deal politics to Philadelphia, whose second wife was on the board of Planned Parenthood of Philadelphia, had become by the mid-'60s a tireless proselytizer for government-funded contraceptives. "In my opinion," said Senator Clark before the Gruening hearings, "with the exception of the problem of war and peace, this is the most critical matter which confronts our country today."[16] Robert C. Cook, president of the Population Reference Bureau, told the

Gruening hearings that "the point of demographic no return" was "not far in the future." For the uninitiated, the point of demographic no return was "that moment when mushrooming population growth makes disintegration and despair unavoidable." General William H. Draper, Jr. vice chairman of Planned Parenthood – World Population, told the committee that he conceived of population as a "bomb" which must be defused "so that mankind does not multiply itself into oblivion."

"Like cancer cells multiplying in the human body," Draper continued changing his metaphor but not the pathological condition it hoped to portray, "it will, unless slowed down, destroy our present day civilization just as surely as would a nuclear conflict."

Not surprisingly, given the attitude that Gruening was trying to foster, John D. Rockefeller III, chairman of the board of the Population Council, was called to testify as well. And just as unsurprisingly, JDR told the Senator from Alaska that "no problem is more urgently important to the well-being of mankind than the limitation of population growth. As a threat to our future, it is often compared with nuclear warfare."[17]

On the evening of August 10, Ball watched the NBC evening news with Huntley and Brinkley and listened to Stuart Udall, formerly of the Department of the Interior, and Alan Guttmacher of Planned Parenthood announce that the hearings were proceeding smoothly and that so far no opposition had surfaced. That, of course, was precisely the point of orchestrating the hearings so that only the pro-population-control side got heard. But Ball, who was responsible for representing the Church in the State of Pennsylvania was wondering if the people at the National Catholic Welfare Conference in Washington hadn't fallen asleep at the switch. Was it really true that the Catholics were planning to sit this one out? Ball wondered. A few phone calls indicated that this was precisely the case, and he was taking the time to register his alarm with Archbishop Krol. Ball had contacted William "Bud" Consedine, the legal counsel for the NCWC in Washington, only to find out that the NCWC was "staying out of this" because they felt, so Consedine said to Ball, that the bill wasn't going to pass anyway. Ball was dismayed at what he heard. With the summer drawing to a close, it looked as if the hearings would conclude with not one voice expressing any opposition, and not one representative of the Church allowed to testify, not so much because Gruening refused to permit such testimony but rather because the National Catholic Welfare Conference decided that it had nothing to say on the matter.

The more Ball probed for answers on this perplexing matter, the more alarmed he became. After his initial contact with Krol and after receiving permission to testify on behalf of Pennsylvania, Ball contacted Msgr. Francis Hurley, who attempted to discourage Ball from following through with his intention to testify. Speaking as a representative of the Pennsylvania Ordinaries, according to Hurley, would create friction in other states where wel-

fare departments had already instituted birth-control programs under the
anti-poverty program with the express consent of bishops in those areas.
Hurley felt that the position Ball was planning to take would be an embarrassment to those bishops.

As the date set for Ball's testimony neared, it became clear that Hurley's
objections were more than just procedural. The procedural maneuvering,
i.e., Hurley telling Ball that the NCWC wanted to pick its own time and place
to take a stand on birth control, was complicated by the fact that they claimed
to be waiting for "directives from Rome" on the matter. Behind both procedural objections there was the matter of substance. Hurley in particular and
the NCWC in general did not agree with Ball's confrontational attitude on
government involvement in contraception. The sticking point was again racial, or at least this was the excuse given for not opposing what was going on
at the Gruening hearings. Hurley wondered if it were right to kill the
anti-poverty program just because it included elements that promoted birth
control. Hurley, in other words, accepted the poverty programs at face value,
whereas Ball saw them as a front for expanding the power of the secular state
at the expense of the Church, and beyond that something inspired by the even
darker motivation of eugenic suppression of the Negro birth rate.

The impasse was never resolved. Ball continued to think of Hurley as an
intelligent dupe who was out of his depth because he wasn't trained in the
law. As a result, Ball felt that Hurley should not have been negotiating for the
Church. Because the impasse never got resolved, mistrust started to build on
both sides. Hurley and the NCWC put forward their own candidate as a
spokesman for the Church, a Jesuit at Georgetown by the name of Dexter
Hanley. Ball and Krol, for their part, began to feel that the NCWC was working to undermine their position.

On the eve of Ball's testimony as a spokesman for the Catholic bishops
before the Gruening hearings in August of 1965, Ball announced to Krol that
on August 12 the Economic Opportunity Act had been amended to include,
at Senator Clark's request, specific authorization for birth-control projects.
Ball used the rest of his letter to complain bitterly to Krol about how the
NCWC was handling (or failing to handle) the whole issue of government
funding for contraceptives, a policy whose blame he lays at the feet of Msgr.
Hurley point by point:

> 1) the NCWC never opposed the introduction of birth control into the
>   anti-poverty program.
> 2) Msgr. Hurley's personal position (which appears to be carried out in
>   NCWC policy) is that the Church should not oppose publicly financed
>   birth control.
> 3) he approves the enclosed family planning statement by Father Hanley
>   et al.
> 4) he expressly disapproved the view against family planning expressed
>   by me in *Commonweal.*

5) he thinks that I should not testify at the Gruening hearings upon behalf of any bishops, but solely as an individual.

6) the NCWC has taken no position at the Gruening hearings.[18]

During the time in which the NCWC did nothing, ostensibly while "awaiting further indications from Rome," the Gruening Commission spent the entire summer giving the impression that the case in favor of government-funded contraception was virtually unanimous. As the summer passed day by day, with no response from the Catholics, Ball can hardly contain his amazement.

"I cannot believe," Ball told Krol, "that after 50 years of preaching against birth control, the bishops of the USA have handed Planned Parenthood a total triumph. . . . Yet that is the fact. There is little point in protesting the use of state funds for birth control by the Pennsylvania Department of Health when national Catholic policy has sanctioned such use."[19]

Ball was scheduled to testify before the Gruening Commission on August 24, but it was clear that he felt demoralized from the lack of support coming from the NCWC in Washington.

"I am woefully tired of being a self-starter insofar as the NCWC is concerned," he told Krol. "The basic weakness, of course, lies in the fact that the horse seems to have gotten out of the barn already."[20]

On the eve of Ball's testimony before the Gruening committee, Krol wrote to Egidio Vagnozzi again complaining specifically this time about "Father Hanley, S.J." who had testified on August 9 before the family law section of the American Bar Association on "Problems of Public Policy Arising out of Tax-Supported Family Planning." As Krol had come to expect, Hanley's position, which was sympathetic to the idea of tax-supported family-planning programs, was widely publicized and was as a result widely regarded as the Catholic position on the issue. Krol went on to complain to Vagnozzi that this sort of misinformation was making dramatic inroads on the way Catholics viewed the issue. He cited a Gallup poll in 1953 which claimed that 53 percent of Catholics said that birth-control information should be available to anyone who wanted it. In January of 1965, 78 percent of Catholics polled expressed the same view. Similarly, 60 percent of Catholics felt that the Church would approve some method of birth control like the birth-control pill, and 81 percent believed that that approval would come within the next ten years.

Vagnozzi, for his part, can only respond by sharing "Your Excellency's concern about the attitude of some individuals with regards to the Holy Father's directive on birth-control discussions. Unfortunately, these persons or self-styled experts are succeeding in creating a false impression as to the Church's position on this subject. Frankly, I think that there should be more concern."[21]

"As you say," Vagnozzi concluded, "this is a serious problem."

It was clear from their correspondence, that both Krol and Vagnozzi felt that the misrepresentation of the position of the Church and the ban on discussion, which was, in effect, only being followed by those who adhered to Church teaching, was having serious repercussions among the faithful because of the malformation of public opinion by the pro-contraceptive media. This in turn was having serious ramifications in the realm of public policy. The only countermeasure which the Church was able to mount during an entire summer of contraceptive propaganda, Krol told Vagnozzi, would be Bill Ball's testimony, which was scheduled for the morning of August 24.

When Ball finally arrived at the subcommittee hearing room at the capitol on the morning of August 24, he was surprised to find that he was no longer to testify as scheduled. He had been replaced in the line-up by none than the Rev. Dexter Hanley, S.J. A look a Father Hanley's testimony gives some indication of why Gruening found his views more congenial than Ball's. Father Hanley began his testimony on a note that was Catholic enough. He claimed that "the only morally acceptable form of voluntary family regulation is through continence, either total or periodic. Any public program which will either directly or indirectly challenge these premises will meet opposition from Catholics." But after saying that, Hanley effectively took the teeth out of the Catholic position by claiming that it affected them alone and that in a pluralistic society the good Catholic would not seek to impose his will on society as a whole. Hanley's idea of "a practical and political accord" meant in effect the marginalization of the Catholic Church on the issue of birth control and the further secularization of culture with its concomitant decline in social order. Catholic opposition to contraception was portrayed as the moral analogue to their refusal to eat meat on Fridays. While "it would be ideal," Father Hanley opined, "if all citizens could share the same basic moral codes and convictions," the fact that they don't somehow means that the Catholics should withdraw their objections to anything which the secular state wants, but which the Church opposes. "Government," Hanley claimed, "is not the proper organ to decide the truth of conflicting views."

> Hence, while firmly maintaining my basic moral positions as a Catholic, I believe that I can support a government program which, in its legitimate concern about education, health and welfare in a rapidly expanding population, permits each citizen a fully free moral choice in matters of family planning and aids him in implementing this choice.[22]

Now it may be that Father Hanley hammered out his position in his room all by himself with nothing but an open copy of Denzinger before him, but the fact remains that there are remarkable similarities between his position and the position Mr. Rockefeller and the Population Council specified as the necessary condition for the grant he gave for the Notre Dame conference in 1962. The other fact which remains is that Hanley was invited to precisely these conferences, so in all likelihood he knew the "progressive" position on the matter of birth control, and he knew the position that would insure Catholics a welcome response from people like Rockefeller on the matter. It didn't take a genius to figure things like this out; in fact, it would take a moron not to figure them out, and Father Hanley was not a moron. Beyond that Hanley's position had the blessing of Msgr. Hurley and the bureaucrats at the NCWC, who were increasingly inclined to push their own agenda at the expense of the teaching of the Church and beyond that inclined to make policy behind the bishops' backs. The insertion of Hanley into the line-up at the Gruening hearings was just one indication of them pursuing their policies at the expense of their employers, the bishops.

Bill Ball did eventually get to testify on August 24, but as the last speaker of the day. As if that weren't bad enough, the fact that the Church's position was, in effect, represented as two different points of view – his and Hanley's – gave the impression that the Church was of two minds on the issue of government-sponsored birth control. In the face of an artificially orchestrated unanimity of opinion on the part of the secularists on the dangers of a population "bomb" which was about to go off momentarily, the Church's position seemed vacillating and unsure by comparison.

Of course, that was only the case if one ignored Ball's actual testimony, which was a powerful indictment of government-sponsored birth-control plans as both detrimental to the citizens' freedoms and covertly eugenical as well. Hamstrung by both the Vatican's prohibition on the one hand and an increasingly prohibitive notion of the separation of church and state proposed by the secularists on the other, Ball did a brilliant job of portraying government-sponsored birth control as a threat to civil freedoms. Ball's argument was based on two Supreme Court cases of recent memory. From *Griswold* he established the right to privacy and from the *Engel* and *Schempp* cases, he talked about the freedom from government coercion when religious issues were concerned. If the Supreme Court could argue that prayer or Bible reading being offered in school was intrinsically coercive to those who did not share the Judeo-Christian view and, therefore, an impermissible infringement on the separation of church and state, then a social worker probing his client's views on sexuality and procreation could hardly be construed as less invasive or less of a breach of that separation. This was true of anyone on welfare, according to Ball, but it was especially true of Catholics on welfare, or in any other capacity affected by a public entity.

According to Ball's testimony, "the main features of the bill pose serious dangers to civil liberty while offering no genuine prospect of relieving the problems of poverty, crowding and disease which they purport to solve."[23] Beyond that, birth-control programs were necessarily coercive, as that term was defined in the recent school prayer decisions. This was so because the main target group in birth-control programs had always been the poor.

Telling a person he is free to accept the proffered birth control is not ameliorated by adding that he is free to refuse. The very fact that the government,
which is the source of the person's livelihood, is offering the services means
that the government feels that the contraceptive is a good thing to offer, and
by extension that the welfare recipient would do well to accept. The exchange is by its nature coercive. For the Catholic, the state is intruding into a
sphere around which it just erected a very high wall of separation.

If the Court were sincere in its concern over the separation of church and
state, it doubtless would have accepted Ball's argument. With the benefit of
hindsight, however, it is difficult to see how the government was being sincere in the matter. The doctrine of privacy, invoked by Justice Douglas in
1965, seven years later was used to justify the decriminalization of abortion,
but it was not used to stop the government's ever-deepening involvement in
funding contraceptives. The lesson seems plain enough in retrospect. Privacy meant in effect the protection of sexual liberation against the threats
posed to it by organized religion. Eventually, the doctrine of privacy would
be invoked to protect two homosexuals caught *in flagrante dilectu* in an automobile parked on a street in Albany, New York. The doctrine of privacy in
this instance was used to strike down that state's law prohibiting sodomy. It
was just one more example of how the terms the secular state used to widen
the acceptance of sexual liberation could never be used at face value to
threaten the aforementioned expansion.

In this regard, one could fault Ball for naiveté, but that would invite undue cynicism, especially in light of the evidence of the time. In 1965 it was
not apparent that Justice Douglas was not sincere when he referred to marriage as something sacred and private in *Griswold*. Ball was simply using the
language available to him as a lawyer, in a country that ostensibly placed
great regard in the notion of rule by law.

Ball also mentioned the fact that in recent times both the courts and the
legislatures had simultaneously broadened the definition of social welfare
and narrowed the power of government over individuals. Common to both
features was a "concern for the weaker members of society . . . most recently
this concern has been more emphatically extended to the criminally accused,
the alien, the Negro and the poor." Gruening's bill was calling for something
which went contrary to both trends. "S. 1676," according to Ball, "is, plainly
and simply, a bill for the establishing of a domestic and international birth
control program and for the creating of permanent federal governmental organs for the carrying out of the same." Ball complained that not only would
such an entity be of its nature intrusive and coercive, he went on to say that
the onus of its intent would fall on the Negro.

"The note of racial eugenicism . . ," Ball continued, "is inescapable in the
proposal of S. 1676. . . . In this hour of the painful emergence of our Negro

brothers into the American society, surely this consideration should be weighed in the balance with the assumed but unproved benefits of S. 1676's birth control proposal." Ball concluded by saying the whole bill reflected the psychology of "the White Man's Burden" and should be rejected as a result.[24]

Ball's approach to the birth-control issue seems to have taken the secular establishment and its Catholic Amen Corner by surprise. John Cogley, who can safely be categorized as representing both bodies in his capacity as religion writer for the *New York Times*, was favorably impressed by Ball's testimony – at least at first. In an article which appeared two days after Ball's testimony, Cogley not only mentioned that Ball "heavily relied on decisions of the Supreme Court" in his presentation, he also gave the impression that the argument about the intrinsically coercive nature of government-funded birth control was persuasive. Ball's decision to fight fire with fire seemed to be bearing fruit, at least in the impression it made on Cogley at the *New York Times*, who seconded the notion that someone's rights were bound to be violated and that that someone would invariably be the "client." "The fact that the citizen," Cogley opined, "was in the position of 'client' of an all-powerful government put him in the danger of being 'susceptible to subtle pressure.'"[25] One gets the impression that Cogley was expecting a frontal attack on the morality of birth control conducted by Ball in the name of the bishops, and that when this did not occur he was caught a bit off balance.

Within a matter of days, however, Cogley changed his mind about Ball's testimony and went on the offensive by accusing Ball of making it under false pretenses. Since he couldn't very well go back on what he said about the content of Ball's presentation, Cogley decided instead to attack the auspices under which he spoke.[26] Cogley intimated that Ball was lying when he claimed that he had spoken on behalf of the American hierarchy. Cogley's article was full of innuendo and unnamed sources, but the intent was clear. Discredit the messenger by claiming that he did not represent the Catholic position

"At least one member of the administrative board of the National Catholic Welfare Conference," Cogley wrote without naming names, "the only body that can speak for the American bishops, had no knowledge that the statement was to be made with the conference's authorization."[27]

On the Sunday (August 29, 1965) immediately following Ball's testimony before the Gruening Hearings, Patrick Cardinal O'Boyle delivered a sermon on "Birth Control and Public Policy" at St. Matthew's Cathedral in Washington. The sermon got widespread coverage in the press, and its influence was felt in Washington. The Church in the person of Archbishop O'Boyle was taking a stand on the poverty program and the attempt by the government to deal with the plight of the poor in general and the Negro poor

in particular through eugenic means. The sermon was a clear attempt on
O'Boyle's part to draw a line in the sand, and the line had to do with the in-
sinuation of birth-control programs into the budget of the War on Poverty.

"In the United States," O'Boyle began, "progress in the field of racial
and social justice has been nothing short of phenomenal."[28] O'Boyle's sermon was intended to put Washington on notice that no matter how phenomenal, no matter how "holy" a cause the civil rights movement had become, the
Catholic Church was not going to tolerate it as a front for advancing public
acceptance of birth control.

Implicit in O'Boyle's challenge was a rebuke of the accommodationist
polices of the NCWC up until that time. "Committees of the Congress and
other public bodies," O'Boyle said, "hearing no official expression to the
contrary, have assumed that 'silence gives consent' and have initiated programs intruding on the private lives of citizens – programs in which, to put it
bluntly, the government has no business." In addition to breaking with the
policies of the NCWC, O'Boyle called into question the whole notion of a
"population explosion," conceding at the very most that "there may well be
at this moment areas of relative overpopulation in certain parts of this country – the so-called Negro ghettos of some of our northern cities, for example." Even if this were the case on a widespread basis, O'Boyle made it clear
that birth control, especially in programs sponsored by the government, was
not going to alleviate social problems.

A program of such dubious benefit is clearly outweighed by its negative
side, which involves a threat to the American family, specifically as a result
of "the gradual intrusion of government into the private lives of its citizens."
Taking his cue from Ball, O'Boyle cited Supreme Court cases to bolster his
arguments. Justice Brandeis's "right to be left alone" was given modern application in *Griswold v. Connecticut*: "Now," concluded O'Boyle, "if the
government is enjoined by this decision from forbidding the practice of birth
control, it logically follows that it is likewise forbidden to promote it."
O'Boyle then went on to attack the Gruening bill specifically, if not by name.

> In spite of these unmistakable constitutional roadblocks, a bill is now be-
> fore the Senate sub-committee on Foreign Aid expenditures that would
> formally and directly involve the federal government in birth prevention
> programs, including the dissemination of information and materials at
> public expense. . . . . In a number of cities, there have been attempts to link
> promotion of birth control with the new antipoverty program, on the the-
> ory that, as one senator put it, "the poor are more likely than any other
> group to have large families."[29]

"That," O'Boyle thundered from the pulpit, "is not the government's
business. The choice of how many children a couple should have is the sole,
personal responsibility of the spouses. It is not less their responsibility if they
happen to be poor."

The line in the sand was clear. The Church would support the civil rights movement's War on Poverty and the concomitant expansion of the welfare state only if that expansion remained within the bounds of the moral law. Once that line was crossed, the government could expect opposition from the Catholics. This, of course, is precisely what the secularists had feared all along. Rockefeller and his minions at the Population Council were only interested in Catholics who were willing to relegate their moral beliefs to the realm of personal predilection. This had been the *sine qua non* for funding the contraception conferences at Notre Dame, and it was the heart of Hanley's position in front of the American Bar Association and the Gruening hearings. It was also at the heart of the NCWC's strategy, which, Krol suspected, had gone out of its way to insinuate Hanley and his position into the Gruening hearing lineup in place of Bill Ball.

O'Boyle was, in effect, arguing for an honest interpretation of the separation of church and state, and on sexual matters this is precisely what the church would never get because, in virtually all important aspects, the separation of church and state was nothing more than a pretext for the establishment of the secular agenda as the law of the land, and sexual liberation as a front for eugenic control was, as time would show with increasing clarity, one of the secularists' non-negotiable demands.

"For a government agent," O'Boyle stated, "to inquire respecting details of their sexual life, or in any way to suggest to them practices respecting sex which may do violence to their religious beliefs, is a clear violation of the sacred right of privacy which the Supreme Court held to be inviolate."[30] O'Boyle was arguing, in other words, that it was inconsistent to ban prayer as a violation of religious beliefs but at the same time promote contraception. This was, of course, true, but it was also true that this self-contradiction lay at the heart of the secular agenda.

"In great issues of this kind," O'Boyle continued, "where opinion is sharply divided the first and most important consideration in searching for a solution is the preservation of the God-given right of conscience. Catholics, for example, have no right to impose their own moral code upon the rest of the country by civil legislation. By the same reasoning, they are obliged in conscience to oppose any regulation which would elevate to the status of public policy a philosophy or practice which violates rights of privacy or liberty of conscience. The citizen's freedom cuts both ways. . . . In situations, like this, involving serious moral issues in which people strive to form a right conscience, the role of government is clear – strict neutrality. . . . The moment the government presumes to 'give advice' in this delicate area, it opens the door to influencing the free decision of its citizens. And from influence it is only a short step to coercion."[31]

Unfortunately, Archbishop O'Boyle, like all the bishops, was fighting a war on two fronts on this issue. In addition to warning the government away from funding birth-control programs, he had to admonish the Catholics to adhere to the Church's position. "A Catholic," O'Boyle claimed turning his direction to the second front for a moment, "accepts voluntarily, by the very fact of his membership, the official teaching of the Church in matters of faith and morals. And, my dear good people, the Church's teaching with regard to contraception has been both clear and consistent."[32] As an indication that that teaching was not going to change, O'Boyle quotes the statement of Pope Paul VI that "we do not have a sufficient reason to regard the norms given by Pope Pius XII in this matter as surpassed and therefore not binding."

"If next week," O'Boyle asked in concluding his homily, "you were asked to sacrifice one of your children to ease the 'population explosion,' which one would you choose? . . . Surely in the glorious history of this great nation, we have found better guides to the Great Society than the four horsemen of artificial birth control, abortion, sterilization and euthanasia. . . . This is the philosophy of defeatism and despair."[33]

In a letter expressing satisfaction over the reception of his sermon, O'Boyle mentioned the outrage his mentioning the Great Society in a negative light caused. The light, of course, was only contingently negative. If the Johnson Administration continued on its current course, it would have to deal with the Church casting doubts on its moral *bona fides*. But O'Boyle nonetheless decided to take the criticism to heart and in future publications backed off any mention of the Great Society. The message was clear without it anyway.

Over the fall of '65 Ball, Krol, and O'Boyle collaborated on a policy designed to thwart the entrance of the United States government into the field of birth control. On October 29, Ball had a four and a half hour meeting with O'Boyle in Washington during which he laid out three possible responses to the birth-control issue. The first response was "peaceful coexistence," which Ball characterized as the position advocated by Msgr. Hurley and the NCWC. The arguments in favor of this policy were the ones the liberals found most congenial, namely, ecumenical cooperation, civil peace, and avoiding jeopardy to the antipoverty program. Pursuing this policy would cause minimal damage to the interest of the liberals in benefits from the welfare state because it in effect would remove the Catholic Church from the fight. Option number two was the policy of limited opposition advocated by Father Hanley. This policy would resist government birth-control programs unless provisions were made banning coercion, protecting privacy, and excluding abortion and sterilization. Ball was skeptical about both strategies, feeling that the birth-control movement was already gaining power to the point of being uncontrollable by any means and that government funding would make them so powerful that they would effectively be beyond any legal apparatus designed to control them. His objection to limited opposition policy was of the same sort. And he cited his experiences with Planned Parenthood as an indication that legal controls of the sort Hanley was urging, even if accepted on paper would prove worthless in practice. In applying for a $90,000 grant in Philadelphia under the Economic Opportunity Program, Planned Parenthood targeted the plan for a 100 percent Negro area in the north-central part of the city. In addition to that, the people staffing the program were not medically trained but had been trained to pursue Planned Parenthood's social program. According to the grant application, the "home visitors" trained by Planned Parenthood go to the houses of their "clients" to "note the conditions under which the family lives and [to] seek the information necessary for effective future programming." If grants were funded under those conditions, it seemed foolish, according to Ball's reasoning, to expect such programs to be neither intrusive nor coercive no matter what the safeguards.

As a result, Ball advocated a policy of "full opposition," but not without first adding a few caveats. Full opposition was going to be uphill work because birth control had become a billion-dollar industry which was willing to spend a considerable amount of time and money to create a mentality in favor of government funding for its services. Krol, who had serious doubts of his own about both the effectiveness and the loyalty of the NCWC staff, seemed undeterred by the grim picture Ball painted. Without hesitation, he opted for the strategy of full opposition. In a letter dated November 2, 1965, responding to Ball's description of his meeting with Archbishop O'Boyle, Krol agreed that "the policy of peaceful co-existence and even the policy of limited opposition would be a waste of time and effort, and implicitly conceding victory to our opponents. Full opposition is the only reasonable course left open."[34]

Within two weeks of Krol's decision, Ball was in Rome giving a confidential briefing to the general body of bishops there on the dangers of government-funded birth control and the best strategy in dealing with it. Perhaps because he could speak his mind without fear of reproach from the media, Ball sketched out a very cynical picture of the War on Poverty. The Economic Opportunity Act, the main funding vehicle for antipoverty programs had become, according to Ball, "a major artery for government birth control in the United States." This money was directed exclusively to the poor and would be used against them in ways both coercive and intrusive. Ball cited the $90,000 program proposed by Planned Parenthood for the North Philadelphia ghetto as an example.

When Ball returned from Rome he had not only the support of key bishops but the blessing of the Holy See as well. Dealing with Catholics in the Johnson Administration was to prove more difficult, though, than getting a blessing from Rome. On December 13, 1965, at 3:45 P.M., Ball met with Sargent Shriver, head of the Office of Economic Opportunity, to discuss the bishops' concerns. Ball got immediately to the point. There was, he said, strong support among the bishops for the antipoverty program but deep dissatisfaction over the use of the program to promote birth control. Ball then challenged the legal authority of the birth-control funding directly. There was, Ball said, no legal authority to use the program to fund birth control in terms of statutory interpretation and construction. Shriver, in other words, was acting illegally and had been acting so all along. Implicit in the statement was the threat that Ball acting on behalf of the bishops' might take the OEO to court if Shriver did not prove amenable to less contentious means of persuasion.

Shriver responded by dismissing the threat from the Church and making it clear that he felt he faced an even more potent threat from the Left. As a result he "could not venture to defer even for a moment the approval of pending applications." Shriver made it clear that the OEO would approve any birth-control project that had been recommended by a local antipoverty council. Because of the inaction of the NCWC at the program's inception, a precedent had been set, and Shriver could not now go back on that precedent without indicating that he had been acting illegally all along. Shriver continued by saying that he was anxious to "make a good record" by funding as many applications "of every sort possible" prior to the end of the year.

When asked by Ball whether he could hold off until February 1, Shriver replied in the negative, and then indicated that he was "under pressure" from Dr. Guttmacher of Planned Parenthood and others who wanted funding for projects which involved financing for abortion and sterilization. In addition to that, Shriver informed Ball that he was under pressure from Protestants and Other Americans United to defund any project sponsored by the Catholic Church. POAU felt that any involvement of the Church in welfare activity supported by the government was a violation of the separation of church and state. Shriver refused to accede to POAU's demands and tried throughout the interview with Ball to portray himself as a man who was trying to tread the reasonable middle ground on the issue. But it was just as evident that he was defining the middle in terms of the political forces being brought to bear on him at the time, and in the absence of a strong policy on the part of the NCWC he was being pushed considerably to the left of what the Catholic bishops found acceptable.

As a final attempt to sway Shriver, Ball brought up the fact that the Congress had refused to adopt the Clark birth-control amendment that September, and that this reflected Congress's intention to exclude birth control from the poverty program, but Shriver was not only unmoved, he also went on the offensive by warning Ball that the more the Church raised a fuss over the birth-control issue, the more unlikely it would be that her agencies would be included in poverty projects. On that not-so-veiled threat, the meeting ended.

Ball left the meeting convinced of two things: first of all, after talking to Shriver and his assistant, Ball was convinced that the authorization for birth control was lacking, and secondly, that Shriver and the OEO would continue to fund birth-control programs because reversing themselves on the matter would expose them to greater legal and political jeopardy than continuing would. As a result, Ball drew a number of conclusions. Most significantly, he concluded that further attempts at persuasion were pointless and that the bishops should look into the possibility of litigation as a way of making their point. Given the Congress's veto of the Clark amendment, this approach stood a good chance of success. Beyond that, Ball concluded that the bishops missed a golden opportunity in the beginning of 1964, but even with that as the case, they had no choice but to take a stand on the OEO birth-control programs because "if no resistance is offered to the OEO programs, Planned Parenthood should soon be 'in business' at public expense throughout the U.S.A." Once programs like that got rolling they would only increase in scope to include abortion, sterilization, and "birth rationing," the idea that everyone should be made sterile unless otherwise permitted by the government to have children. It was an idea that was making its way through the media through the efforts of people like William Shockley, who received the Nobel Prize for inventing the transistor and then promptly used that as a platform for increasingly strident calls for racial eugenics. As before, the Church was outgunned on just about every front, but Congress's reaction to Ball's testimony and O'Boyle's sermon gave reason for hope.

The hope proved to be short-lived. According to Ball, the bishops had a historic opportunity in the fall of 1965. But largely as a result of the footdragging of the NCWC legal staff, the winter months passed and the Church had "taken an historic non-step." By May of 1966, Ball felt that "many will look back with horror upon what can only be described as an historic default." Especially galling from Ball's point of view was the fact that the NCWC was fleeing from a very beatable opponent, from "a legion of kapok dragons," as he put it in a letter to Krol. If the Church were able to present the case that government birth control created a threat to the right of privacy, Ball felt that a large segment of public opinion might be won over. But Ball found himself more often than not engaged in a one-man campaign, while at the same time Father Charles Whelan, S.J., with the backing of the NCWC, was claiming that it was absurd to fear government's involvement in the birth-control issue. The Hanley-Whelan faction, Ball complained, was so fearful of "imposing Catholic morality" on others, that they were opening the door to abortion, sterilization, and racial eugenics – all in the name of making peace with the liberal social agenda. Disbelief is the characteristic emotion of Ball's increasingly exasperated correspondence with Krol. "This whole question of government birth control has become to me a thing like death," he writes. "You look at it and you can't believe it's so."

Part III, Chapter 12

Washington, D.C., November 1965

There was a sense in which the "beloved community" of black and white together took on concrete reality in the intimacy of the bedroom.
Sara Evans, *Personal Politics*

In his autobiography, Paul Blanshard criticized what he called Pope Paul's "bachelor psychosis." As a prime manifestation of that psychosis, Blanshard mentioned the pope's "dramatic appearance before the United Nations in 1965," and the fact that instead of promoting birth control as the solution to the world's problems, he suggested instead that the wealthier nations "must strive to multiply bread so that it suffices for the tables of mankind" rather than promote contraception, "in order to diminish the number of guests at the banquet of life." "The Pope," Blanshard continued, "even had the temerity to maintain his dogmatic position on birth control when he went to India."[1]

In November 1965, one week before the White House Conference that was part of the original plan proposed by Lyndon Johnson in his spring of 1965 speech at Howard University, and around the same time Bill Ball was urging Sargent Shriver to keep birth control out of the War on Poverty, a coalition of sixty representatives of New York churches and civil-rights organizations held their own pre-conference conference, demanding that the issue of "family stability" be struck from the agenda of the upcoming White House meeting. Leading the opposition were Benjamin Payton, a Negro sociologist and minister, and Robert W. Spike, executive director of the National Council of Churches's Commission on Religion and Race, Suddenly the civil-rights leaders who had been positively fulsome in praise of the Johnson initiative in the spring were undergoing a change of heart.

"My major criticism of the report," said Floyd McKissick, the new director of CORE, "is that it assumes that middle class American values are the correct ones for everyone in America." "Moynihan," McKissick continued, evidently unaware that Moynihan himself came from a broken family, "thinks everyone should have a family structure like his own. Moynihan also emphasizes the negative aspects of the Negroes and then seems to say that it's the individual's fault when it's the damn system that really needs changing."[2]

Clarence Mitchell, of the Washington office of the NAACP, objected to the report because it "implied that it was necessary for the improvement of the Negro community to come from within."[3] Among those who took part in the criticism at an Executive Office Building meeting on October 30 were Whitney Young, who approved of the proposal in the spring, and a young Washington, D.C., activist by the name of Marion Barry. Barry, who would achieve dubious fame of his own twenty-five years later, when as mayor of Washington, D.C., he would be arrested by federal agents for possession of crack cocaine, was on his way to carving a career as civil-rights leader and shaker down of federal funds. Given the evidence on his sex life that would come out during his trial, it is not surprising that Barry would object to aid to the Negro being tied to "family stability." If those criteria had ever been enforced, it is unlikely that Barry would have got a dime of federal money.

But with hindsight, it's hard to see how anyone would have got any money, if those criteria were applied rigorously to the people asking for the grants. Barry in this regard was the rule and not the exception. The civil-rights movement saw in the Moynihan Report a roll-back of its sexual freedoms. And, in short, it was afraid. They could not confront the problem honestly because to a large extent the problems under discussion were their own. In the end, the civil-rights movement decided to back away from any initiative that dealt with sexual morality and asked for government money instead. In addition to asking that the issue of family stability be struck from the agenda, they decided to ask the president for an "Economic Development Budget for Equal Rights in America" which would cost the country's taxpayers a mere $32 billion per year in 1965 dollars. This move confirmed Johnson in his belief that the only thing the civil-rights establishment could do was bitch and moan about white racism and then stick out their hands for government conscience money. In his 1967 postmortem on the Moynihan Report, Daniel Patrick Moynihan expressed a note of ambivalence about the civil-rights movement. He claimed that "the nation needs the liberal Left" as a "secular conscience," yet at the same time he faulted the liberals for destroying what was clearly a promising opportunity for this nation's underprivileged Negroes: "this was the point of unparalleled opportunity for the liberal community and it was exactly the point where that community collapsed."[4] Just why it collapsed Moynihan never explains; however, in retrospect, it had become clear that the civil-rights movement was deeply involved in the same sort of behavior that Moynihan was criticizing in ghetto blacks. The last thing the people like Martin Luther King, Jr., wanted to hear in 1965 was that there were social consequences to sexual misbehavior.

In his *Commentary* postmortem, Moynihan claimed that Robert W. Spike had played a "decisive" role in defeating the notion that Black progress was tied to family stability: "The reaction of the liberal Left to the issue of the Negro family was decisive (the Protestant reaction was clearly triggered by it). They would have none of it. No one was going to talk about their poor people that way."[5]

One year after the Moynihan Report had been defeated, Spike was found bludgeoned to death in a newly dedicated campus-ministry building in Columbus, Ohio. Spike, it turns out, was a homosexual and had been murdered by a man he had picked up while in town for the dedication ceremony. In a book which was published in 1965, Spike talked about the spiritual condition of the men of his generation and, by extension, himself. "Their sins rise up to haunt them," he writes.[6] "Not since the abolitionist period," he continues, "have the churches and their people become as conscious of their guilt and their need for action as in recent months."[7] In an article which appeared in February of the year he died, Spike talked about how the civil-rights movement arose in the '60s, composed of the "long-suffering Negro population" and "large numbers of guilt-stricken whites." At the heart of Spike's quarrel with the Moynihan Report lay his quarrel with "family stability." "It is no wonder," Spike writes, "that his report is so much resented by Negroes. Faulty generalizations about white and black families are never qualified by any reference to other norms of family stability than having a father in the house."[8] In retrospect, it is not difficult to see behind Spike's complaint his own "guilt-stricken" reaction to the double life he was leading as homosexual and head of a household. It is clear that he is getting his own sexual payoff from this "revolution in human freedom," which, he complains, first tells people that they are free and then keeps "pulling on the almost invisible wires that direct their motion."[9]

In *The Content of Our Character*, Shelby Steele gives a fairly conventional and unconvincing explanation of the concept of "white guilt." It is unconvincing for a number of reasons, but primarily because the evidence of the times indicates that there was a more conventional explanation of the same phenomenon. Ockham's razor, it seems, should apply in moral matters as well. With the help of people like Paul Tillich, Spike converted to the values of modernity, probably sometime in the late '40s when he became pastor of Judson Memorial Church in Greenwich Village and an associate of Jack Kerouac and Allen Ginsberg and the other founders of Beat. Spike had been living the double life of a homosexual pastor for some time, something which had led to a great deal of personal torment.

In a memoir published in 1973, Spike's son Paul reminisced about his father's tormented life and gives us interesting hints about the connection between social activism and the troubled conscience. Paul remembers his father telling him "that Baldwin and others had said to us for the first time, 'You are the man!' We felt a sense of personal guilt, of personal responsibility for the denial of full justice to Negro citizens, resulting in the deterioration of relationships between the races to the place it was in the spring of 1963."[10] The younger Spike criticizes white involvement in the 1963 March on Washington as "getting a contact high off black nightmares," but he never gets around to telling us why those who were so active in pursuing equal rights for the Negro were the ones who were most plagued by "white guilt." The elder Spike, however, makes clear that the civil-rights movement is just a part of a larger revolution of morals, one that presumably had its roots in the late '40s beat culture the then-young minister from Ohio encountered when he became pastor in Greenwich Village. "He sees," Paul says of his father, "civil rights as only one part of a vast social, technological, sexual and moral revolution."[11] "Working to free black Americans, he has become free. . . . The civil rights struggle gives the church a new chance to act in a 'Christian' way without that implying narrow-minded or prudish behavior. It may even be the last chance for the Protestant Church in America."[12] It is clear from the testimony of his son that the elder Spike saw the civil-rights movement as just one part of a general transformation: "the crusading minister of Judson has written many articles for national publications, worked hard in the civil rights and antiwar movements, and has been perhaps the key man in reforming the abortion law in New York state."[13]

The source of Spike the elder's guilt is much easier to explain than the conventional explanations of "white guilt," proffered by people like Shelby Steele:

> In the sixties . . . White guilt became so palpable you could see it on people. At the time, what it looked like to my eyes was a remarkable loss of authority. And what whites lost in authority, blacks gained. You cannot feel guilty toward anyone without giving away power to them. So, suddenly, this huge vulnerability opened up in whites and, as a black, you had the power to step right into it. In fact, black power all but demanded that you do so.[14]

Spike was a homosexual leading a double life as both a minister and a family man. He used the Negro as the front for his sexual dereliction, which is what the WASP ethnos had been doing ever since it bankrolled the Harlem Renaissance. That is reason enough for guilt feelings. But there is more to it than that. At the same time it was acting out its version of "spade kicks," the WASP ethnos was also using the War on Poverty as a covert eugenic attack on black fertility and subverting initiatives like the Moynihan Report, which attempted to strengthen the black family. All in all, Spike and the National Council of Churches were involved in behavior that should have troubled even the laxest conscience.

Modernity means sexual liberation. Sexual liberation creates guilt. The only way to deal with guilt among those who refuse to repent is the palliation that comes from social activism. Involvement in social movements like the civil-rights, abortion-rights, and gay-rights movements became a way of calming troubled consciences. The relation between the liberal Left and the civil-rights leadership was symbiotic. The guilt which accrued from carrying out the agenda of the Left, which invariably involved some form of sexual liberation, was anesthetized by involvement in fighting for the Negro's "freedoms," which invariably meant some form of eugenic sterilization to weaken black demographics and the political power which accrued from it. As Paul Spike said of his father, "Working to free black Americans, he himself became free." The right racial politics allowed him to justify the particular sexual vices he craved. His particular craving had to do with homosexuality. Fighting for freedom meant that his conscience was momentarily freed from the burdens that living a double life placed on it. Social activism on behalf of the Negro was the palliative which calmed the sexually burdened conscience of the liberal Left. The Moynihan Report stepped right into the middle of this complicated psychic equation and threatened to expose the sexual roots of Liberal adherence to the cause and the main leverage whereby blacks could extort concessions from their guilty white, sexually liberated collaborators. No amount of tact or public relations could disguise this fact from the Left. As a result, they united in opposition to the notion of family stability, and all but made inevitable the spread of family pathology among the Negro. The liberals chose to perpetuate the ghetto as a bulwark to preserve the sexual revolution.

Of course, the civil-rights leadership was not exempt from this dynamic either. They too were subject to the same moral laws, and as subsequent biography has shown, they too were as heavily involved in sexual liberation as the liberal Left. Bayard Rustin, like Spike, was a homosexual. Rustin, a close associate of A. Philip Randolph, president of the Brotherhood of Sleeping Car Porters and the most noted national black leader, was a former member of the Young Communist League and had been convicted in the early '60s of homosexual activity with two other men in a parked car. Blacks in this situation needed the high moral ground to calm their consciences every bit as much as the whites did. And as a result they were just as eager to defeat a proposal which necessitated a reform of conduct as the whites were. As the militants raged, less radical black leaders were unable to lead because they were compromised sexually, and they knew that the militants knew it.

The situation of Martin Luther King is a good case in point. In 1965 King flew to Miami for a Ford Foundation-funded Leadership Training Program for black ministers. King spent much of his time holed up in his hotel room, probably because of the controversy below. One of the speakers was Daniel Patrick Moynihan, whose report King had endorsed a few months earlier. Moynihan later described the meeting in a letter to a Ford Foundation executive as "an atmosphere of total hostility." It was, he wrote, "the first time I have ever found myself in an atmosphere so suffused with near madness. . . . The leadership of the meeting was in the hands of near-demented Black militants who consistently stated one untruth after another (about me, about the United States, about the President, about history, etc. etc.) without a single voice being raised in objection. King, Abernathy and Young sat there throughout, utterly unwilling (at least with me present) to say a word in support of non-violence, integration, or peaceableness."[15]

King, who supported the initiative that spring, could not support it now because he was too sexually compromised himself. As a result, the black leadership capitulated to the militants, and the civil-rights movement chose to perpetuate family pathology rather than relinquish sexual liberation. Garrow makes abundantly clear that King's reputation as a womanizer was common knowledge among the SCLC leadership and beyond. He cites an account as early as the '50s in *The Pittsburgh Courier*, a widely read national black newspaper, warning a "prominent minister in the Deep South, a man who has been making the headlines recently in his fight for civil rights," that he "had better watch his step." According to Garrow, "the paper announced detectives hired by white segregationists . . . were hoping 'to create a scandal by catching the preacher in a hotel room with a woman other than his wife, during one of his visits to a Northern city.'" As a result of his sexual involvement, King could not object to the vilification of Moynihan at the Miami ministers' meeting. When it came to sexual issues, the very issues the Moynihan Report raised, King was unable to lead. He was too badly compromised. The militants knew his weakness and exploited it to their own advantage.

On the issue of sexuality, King was a deeply divided man. On the one hand, when confronted, he would attempt to justify his behavior. When a friend raised the subject of what Garrow calls "his compulsive sexual athleticism," King answered, "I'm away from home 25 to 27 days a month. Fucking's a form of anxiety reduction."[16] However, publicly King would espouse the Christian view. "Sex," he said in one of his sermons at Ebenezer Baptist Church,

> is basically sacred when it is properly used and . . . marriage is man's greatest prerogative in the sense that it is through and in marriage that God gives man the opportunity to aid him in his creative activity. Therefore, sex must never be abused in the loose sense that it is abused in the modern world.[17]

The disparity between his private life and his public pronouncements would leave King wide open to charges of hypocrisy should the black militants choose to make such charges. J. Edgar Hoover was engaging in a similar form of blackmail from the other end of the political spectrum, a source of constant anxiety for King and his supporters. King could little afford to have the same sort of charges emanating from his own movement. So it is not surprising that he would remain silent.

More often than not King simply gave expression in his sermons to the conflicts between inclination and belief in his personal life rather than taking a stand for either the Christian or the sexual-liberationist options: "Because we are two selves, there is a civil war going on within all of us," he said at Ebenezer. "There is a schizophrenia . . . within all of us," he said in another sermon. "There are times that all of us know somehow that there is a Mr. Hyde and a Dr. Jekyll in us." However, "God does not judge us by the separate incidents or the separate mistakes that we make but by the total bent of our lives."[18]

It is no surprise that what has come to be known as the fundamental-option theory would seem attractive to King. It has an attraction to people who fail to get control of some bad habit, as well as those who feel compromised by the double lives they lead. In addition to adumbrating the conflict in his sermons, King was drawn to theories which seemed to rationalize his behavior. Garrow cites one source who points out that King "was eager to learn systems of thought about God which he could connect with to rationalize and fill out his own inclinations – inclinations shaped by his experiences." "When Schleiermacher stressed the primacy of experience over any external authority," King wrote to one of his former seminary professors, "he was sounding a note that continues to ring in my own experience."[19]

Garrow also notes that King's womanizing was a constant source of strain in his marriage and goes on to indicate that at the time of his death, King's marriage was in danger of ending in divorce. "Had the man lived," one staffer remembered, "the marriage wouldn't have survived, and everybody feels that way."[20] King was simultaneously headed in the two directions that the Moynihan Report highlighted with painful clarity. King, the public figure, was fighting against segregation in the South, but King the private figure was heading in the direction of the absent, sexually irresponsible father which Moynihan claimed was the root of social pathology in the ghettos of the North.

> Three relationships had flowered to the status of something more than occasional one-night stands, and for almost the past two years King had grown closer and closer to one of these women, whom he saw almost daily. The relationship, rather than his marriage, increasingly became the emotional centerpiece of King's life, but it did not eliminate the incidental couplings that were a commonplace of King's travels.[21]

As a result King felt increasingly torn and increasingly unable to take control of a movement that was heading toward violence and racial separatism. Moynihan remembers King toward the end of his life as "still wanting a bill." Both Stanley Levison and King's wife Coretta referred to King as "guilt-ridden." Chicago businessman and King associate in SCLC William A. Rutherford remembers SCLC as "a very rowdy place" and felt that "the movement altogether was a very raunchy exercise." Garrow relates that

> Rutherford's first shock stemmed from reports of an Atlanta group party that had featured both a hired prostitute as well as the unsuccessful ravishing of a seventeen-year-old SCLC secretary. Rutherford raised the subject

at an executive staff session, "and the meeting cracked up in laughter. . . ."
King was laughing too, a further reflection of SCLC's "very relaxed attitude toward sex" and the "genuine ribald humor" that predominated.[22]

Subsequent studies and memoirs of those involved in the civil-rights
movement have confirmed that the behavior King exhibited was typical of
the SCLC in particular and the Civil-rights movement in general. In *Personal Politics*, Sara Evans traces the birth of the feminist movement to the
sexual liberation practiced in the civil-rights movement, particularly during
the summer of 1964. According to Evans, "the sit-in movement and the freedom rides had an electrifying impact on northern liberal culture" with the result that "the children of northern liberals and radicals" joined the movement
"with passionate commitment."[23] Just how passionate the commitment was
comes out in the various accounts of white women Evans draws on. One
young woman described how

> a whole lot of things got shared around sexuality – like black men with
> white women – it wasn't just sex, it was also sharing ideas and fears, and
> emotional support. . . . My sexuality for myself was confirmed by black
> men for the first time ever in my life, see. In the white society I am too
> large. . . . So I had always had to work very hard to be attractive to white
> men. . . . Black men . . . assumed that I was a sexual person . . . and I
> needed that very badly.[24]

Both sides in this sexual equation, according to Evans, "were hungry for
sexual affirmation and appreciation."[25] So much so that in retrospect, Martin
Luther King's term "the beloved community" took on a whole new meaning:
"A generation steeped in ideas drawn from existential theology and philosophy translated the concept of 'beloved community' into a belief in the power
of transforming human relationships. . . . There was a sense in which the 'beloved community' of black and white together took on concrete reality in the
intimacy of the bedroom."[26] According to Evans, one male black leader described how white female volunteers "spent that summer, most of them, on
their backs, servicing not only the SNCC workers but anybody else who
came. . . . Where I was project director, we put white women out of the project within the first three weeks because they tried to screw themselves
across the city." "Guilt lurked in all directions," Evans claimed, "and behind
that guilt lay anger."[27] And behind the anger lay the rise of feminism, and
abortion rights, and homosexual activism, and affirmative action and a
whole culture of grievance fueled by sexual guilt and the various movements
which extort blackmail as a result of it.

The situation came to a head in the fall of 1964 following the voter regis-
tration drives of that summer. In November 1964 around the same time that
Daniel Patrick Moynihan woke up in the middle of the night with an idea for
the new direction of the civil-rights movement, Stokely Carmichael was re-
galing white admirers with his ideas on the position of women in the move-

ment at a SNCC staff retreat at Waveland, Mississippi. He was responding to a position paper (number 24) presented at the meeting: "SNCC Position Paper (Women in the Movement)"; the authors' names (Casey Hayden, pre-Jane Fonda wife of Tom, and Mary King, whose husband would later murder Allard Lowenstein, had written it in discussion with Mary Varela) had been "withheld by request." After a day of acrimonious discussion, Carmichael took a bunch of female admirers and a bottle of wine to a dock overlooking the Gulf of Mexico and after asking rhetorically about the position of women in the movement, answered by saying: "The only position for women in SNCC is prone."[28]

"Carmichael's barb," Evans recounts, "was for most who heard it a movement in-joke. It recalled the sexual activity of the summer before – all those young white women who supposedly had spent the summer 'on their backs.'"[29] Even though she disagrees with much of Evans's assessment, Mary King thought Carmichael's remark was funny at the time. "We all collapsed with hilarity," she wrote in her memoir.

Funny or not, the remark is often taken as the opening shot in the war between the sexes that has come to be known as the feminist movement. The women had learned their lesson well. They were in an even better position to extort concessions from sexual guilt than the blacks were. Evans had learned the lesson first hand. She reports on one conference, where "The politics of moralism reached new heights as the moralism of middle-class guilt clashed head on with the morality of righteous anger. . . . Each time the conference capitulated to black demands, the majority of whites applauded enthusiastically in apparent approval of their own denunciation."[30]

Mary King does her best not to drive a wedge between the politically correct coalition of feminist and black; however, the evidence in her book points to the sexual exploitation practiced in the civil-rights movement as the cause of feminism every bit as much as it does in Sara Evans's book. King feels that the interracial sexual relationships also led to black separatism because the black women in the civil-rights movement were having their boyfriends taken away from them by the accessibility of too many liberal white women of easy virtue.

> This complex dynamic created stress between the veteran black women and white women on the SNCC staff, because the black women could see the allure of the white women volunteers to black male staff. Such desire was unacceptable intellectually, but, psychologically, for some men, it was compelling. I have often wondered whether resistance to this pattern might not have contributed to the surge toward black nationalism that showed itself in SNCC after the November 1964 Waveland meeting. Black men, suddenly exposed to large numbers of white women volunteers – with many of the local men talking to a white woman for the first time in their lives as an equal – suddenly had the real or hypothetical opportunity to break an old taboo. Black women who were field secretaries

and project directors, working side by side with black male colleagues all day, found that after hours some of the latter sought the company of the white women volunteers.[31]

"Our lives," Mary King concludes, "defied conventional morality."[32] "'Freedom' and 'liberation,'" writes Sara Evans, "were absolutes – to be fought for and won." What neither lady can bring herself to see is the consequences of that "freedom" from the moral law, especially among the people who were supposed to be its beneficiaries. The primary victim of this project was the Negro himself. When Undersecretary Moynihan proposed the choice between a cure based on a reform of morals and further decay, the Left chose decay as a way of saving the sexual revolution. In the years since the civil-rights movement made that decision, illegitimacy among all blacks increased from 20 percent to over 70 percent. The situation which Moynihan described as an epidemic for blacks in 1965 has become the norm for American society as a whole, which now has an illegitimacy rate of 21 percent. The civil-rights leadership, deeply compromised sexually as well, acquiesced in that choice. Rather than give up their stake in the sexual revolution and the money which they got to orchestrate the eugenic engineering of their own people, they condemned the black underclass to a prolonged term in the ghetto by averting their eyes from their own sexual degradation and focusing the nation's attention instead on white racism as the *radix malorum*. Even the blacks who are the beneficiaries of the liberal conscience money that affirmative action has become seem enmired in the self-defeating and self-conferred image of themselves as helpless victims.

In the end, it turns out that the feminists were right after all. At least as far as the civil-rights movement was concerned, the political was personal. Both the black and the white leadership had too much invested in sexual liberation to take an honest look at the pathology of the ghetto and its cause in family breakdown. The white Left had always been interested in promoting the Negro as a paradigm of sexual liberation. It was in many respects their only interest in the Negro. Promoting Negro decadence as "primitive" and closer to nature was the best way to bring about the transvaluation of all values and the demise of the Christian ethos of the West.

Part III, Chapter 13

Los Angeles 1966

Prologue in Louisville, March 1966

Toward the end of March 1966, Thomas Merton was brought to St. Joseph Hospital in Louisville for a an operation to unfuse two of his vertebrae. While luxuriating during his recuperation in the ability to lie on his back without pain, Merton looked up six days after the operation, on the last day of March, to notice that a student nurse had come into his room. She was there, she told him, to give him a sponge bath. She was thirty years younger than he, and, in spite of the fact that she had been told to respect his privacy, she announced that she was familiar with his work. A conversation ensued, and continued throughout his stay in the hospital. By the time he left to go back to Gethsemane, the Trappist monastery fifty miles to the southeast, the world's most famous monk was in love.

If the idea of the ascetic author of *The Seven Storey Mountain* falling in love with a woman young enough to be his daughter seemed implausible, that was because much of what Merton wanted to tell about his youthful sexual indiscretions had been edited out of the book by the censors at Gethsemane. As Merton made clear in his diaries, he was being haunted by sexual ghosts at the time of his operation. By the time of his operation, Merton was also the author of *Conjectures of a Guilty Bystander*, which was also being serialized in *Life* magazine. If there were ever an indication of what had happened to American Catholics in the period after the war, the gap between Merton's two books gives some indication of what it was. Catholics had survived the anti-Catholic campaign of Paul Blanshard and his Ivy League supporters and had taken their place at the center of the national stage, only to be undone by their own success. Merton's access to the mainstream media would prove, when looked at with the gift of hindsight, to be a two-way street. If it meant that he had a large national audience, it also meant that the media had access to him – something of significant consequence for a man who chose to become a monk, leave the world behind and immure himself in a hermitage in the woods of rural Kentucky.

The steady stream of visitors that Merton entertained there gave some indication that his isolation was less than that of the desert Fathers. In addition to undergoing psychoanalysis at the hands Dr. Gregory Zillborg – something which precipitated a flood of psychoanalytic jargon into his writing –

Merton and his hermitage became a stopping-off point for spiritually inquisi-
tive celebrities of all sorts who wanted to spend time with the famous monk
and author. In the summer of 1959, Natasha Spender, wife of poet Stephen
Spender, "blew in with a girl from the Coast, Margot Dennis."[1] As had become his custom by then, Merton took his guests and some food and drink to
one of the nearby ponds, where Margot, "transformed into a Naiad-like creature, smiling a primitive smile through hanging wet hair," went swimming,
evidently without a bathing suit. In terms of asceticism, Merton was no Simon Stylites; he wasn't even keeping pace with his Trappist brothers, even
though the hermitage he inhabited alone was supposedly an indication that
he had gone beyond them. Eventually the laxity would catch up with Merton
in his infatuation with the student nurse he referred to in his diaries as M.

On May 5, Merton had his friends James McLaughlin and Nicanor Parra
drive him to the Louisville airport, where

> M. and I had a little while alone and went off by ourselves and found a
> quiet corner, sat on the grass out of sight and loved each other to ecstasy. It
> was beautiful, awesomely so, to love so much and to be loved, and to be
> able to say it all completely without fear and without observation (not that
> we sexually consummated it).[2]

The entry gives some indication that sexual consummation was on Merton's mind. On May 7, at a picnic at a nearby lake celebrating the annual running of the Kentucky Derby, Merton's behavior with M. caused discomfort
to everyone in attendance. The relationship reached its consummation on
May 19, the feast of the Ascension, when a nurse friend dropped M. off near
the monastery and the two of them found a secluded place in the woods
around the Vineyard Knobs where they ate ham and herring, drank wine,
read love poems and "mostly made love and love and love for five hours."
Merton later wrote in his journal that through the encounter his

> sexuality has been made real and decent again after years of rather frantic
> suppression (for though I thought I had it all truly controlled, this was an
> illusion). I feel less sick, I feel human, I am grateful for her love which is
> so totally mine. All the beauty of it comes from this, that we are not just
> playing, we belong totally to each other's love (except for the vow that
> prevents the last complete surrender).[3]

By June, Merton's behavior was so out of control that it had come to the
attention of his Trappist superiors. One of the monks had overheard a telephone conversation between Merton and M. and had reported him to Dom
James Fox, Merton's abbot. Fox was understanding but demanded a "complete break." And Merton, like many religious at the time, was faced with the
unenviable prospect of either repudiating his religious vows or cutting himself off from the woman he loved.

During the summer of 1966, at the end of the Second Vatican Council
and the beginning of the sexual revolution, the world seemed alive to new

sexual possibilities, especially for Catholic nuns and priests, many of whom confidently expected that the Catholic Church's discipline on celibacy was about to be lifted. Joining them in a chorus of mute anticipation were the Catholic laity, who were just as confident in their expectation that the ban on artificial birth control would be lifted soon as well. Pope Paul VI had appointed a layman-staffed advisory board, and it was assumed – correctly, it turns out – that they would vote to overturn the Church's long-standing ban on contraception, a ban which had been reaffirmed as recently as thirty years before in Pius XI's encyclical *Casti Canubii*. Because of Pope John XXIII, President John F. Kennedy, and the Vatican Council, Catholics had become the focus of so much media attention, they failed to see distortions in the mirror which the media, dominated by alumni of the OSS and other psychological warfare operations, held up to their collective face. They failed to understand how seriously malformed their opinions were becoming at the hands of people like Xavier Rhynne and Michael Novak and other media enthusiasts who felt to a man that the long reign of anti-Catholic bigotry in the United States had come to an end and that all the Church needed to do to create its own happy ending was join hands with the liberal Zeitgeist, as reported in places like *Time* and the *New Yorker*, drop a few medieval sexual prohibitions, and walk off into the sunset.

During the summer of 1966, right around the time that Merton was grappling with the competing claims which his religious vows and the young student nurse were making on him, the Immaculate Heart nuns of Los Angeles invited a New York psychiatrist to their retreat house in Montecito to conduct an encounter workshop. The nuns liked the workshops so much that a year later they invited a psychologist by the name of Carl Rogers and his associates to begin something they called the Education Innovation Project with the entire order and all of the schools it ran for the archdiocese of Los Angeles.

Rogers had become famous in 1961 with the publication of his book *On Becoming a Person*. He along with Abraham Maslow, whose book *Toward a Psychology of Being* came out one year later in 1962, had become the two leading proponents of what came to be known as humanistic or third-force psychology. The third force referred to a therapy that was based on both Freud and Watson but was more "client centered." In Rogerian therapy, the client solved his own problems with minimal interference from his therapist guide, who gave little more than non-committal answers as a way of guiding the patient to truths that the client knew but chose not to see. Another name for this therapy was nondirective counseling, A creation of the early 1940s, it had been proposed, according to Rogers's assistant W. R. Coulson "as a humane replacement for behaviorism in the laboratory and Freudian psychoanalysis in the clinic."[4]

In 1965 Carl Rogers began circulating a paper entitled "The Process of the Basic Encounter Group" to some religious orders in the Los Angeles area. One group which found his ideas intriguing was the Sisters of the Immaculate Heart of Mary. This should not be surprising because the California-based IHM nuns had already established the reputation of being "innovative." In the early '60s, Sister Aloyse, the order's superior, had brought in the Dutch psychologist-priest Adrian van Kaam for retreat exercises during which "all community rules were suspended."[5] The results of this sort of innovation were predictable. After allowing the psychologists in, the nuns became aware of "how dictatorial superiors were and in turn how dependent, submissive and helpless nuns were when it came to working with the outside world."[6] By the spring of 1965, James Francis Cardinal McIntyre, archbishop of the archdiocese of Los Angeles, had become upset at the large number of Immaculate Heart nuns who had asked to be dispensed from their vows. Large, as time would show, was a relative term in this respect. Soon the number of nuns asking to be laicized would turn into a flood, and the sensitivity training which Carl Rogers would unleash on the order under the auspices of the Education Innovation Project would play a major role in their leaving. By the time the experiment was over, the order would cease to exist, leaving subsequent generations to puzzle over an incident which had become a classic instance of renewal gone wrong in the aftermath of Vatican II.

With the benefit of hindsight, anyone who read Rogers's paper should have been aware of this possibility from the beginning. In a version of that paper which appeared in the July 1969 issue of *Psychology Today*, entitled "Community: The Group Comes of Age," Rogers explained that

> In mixed intensive workshops positive and warm, loving feelings frequently develop between members of the encounter group and, naturally enough, these feelings sometimes occur between men and women. Inevitably, some of these feelings have a sexual component and this can be a matter of great concern to the participants and . . . a profound threat to their spouses.

Or to their religious vows, Rogers might have added.

Right around the time that Rogers was circulating "Involvement in the Basic Encounter," a draft of a paper published two years later as "The Process of the Basic Encounter Group" among the Immaculate Heart nuns in 1965, the Vatican Council came to a close. A close reading of the pertinent documents would show they reaffirmed Catholic tradition. But at that time close readings had been eschewed in favor of readings in keeping with the spirit of Vatican II, which seemed eager to second whatever the secular *Zeitgeist* was proposing at the time. On September 2, 1966, Pope Paul VI implemented the earlier conciliar decree on religious life, *Perfectae Caritatis*, by issuing a *Motu Proprio* in which he urged all religious "to examine and renew their way of life and towards that end to engage in wide-ranging experimentation." The pope added the following caveat: "provided that the purpose, nature and character of the institute are safeguarded." In keeping with the spirit of the times, the caveat was all but universally ignored. In fact, those most eager to experiment were those also most likely to ignore it. The IHM sisters were among the first to respond, and within six weeks, the pontiff's letter had been circulated among the 560 members of the community. A number of commissions were appointed to study carefully all aspects of their religious commitment.

Religious orders like the Immaculate Heart Nuns, already bigger than they had ever been in the history of their existence, now seemed on the verge of even greater accomplishments as they renewed themselves by getting rid of outmoded forms of dress and behavior. Now the same baby boom which their schools had educated was providing nuns to staff the order. A generation of demographic increase was beginning to pay off. One member of that generation who had decided to become an Immaculate Heart nun was Jean Cordova. Cordova graduated from high school in the spring of 1966, and on a sunny September 6, 1966 she and four of her nine brothers and sisters drove up to the novitiate in Santa Barbara where she was to begin her life as a nun.

On January 1, 1967, Jean Cordova was called into the mother's superior's office and told that she and her fellow novices were being sent to live in the "real world," which in this instance meant a building surrounded by chainlink fence and barbed wire in downtown Los Angeles near skid row, where Cordova would lie awake at night watching the pulsing red light on top of Los Angeles city hall and wonder what had happened to her and the convent she had chosen in lieu of this "real world." Cordova arrived at the novitiate expecting something different from what she eventually got. Her bitterness at what amounted to bait and switch tactics (even if perpetrated inadvertently) was still palpable twenty years later.

> They promised me monastic robes, glorious Latin liturgy, the protection of the three sacred vows, the peace of saints in a quiet cell, the sisterhood of a holy family. But I entered religious life the year John XXIII [*sic*] was taking it apart: 1966. The fathers of the Holy Roman Catholic and Apostolic Church were sitting at the Vatican Council destroying in the name of CHANGE, my dreams. Delete Latin ritual. Dump the habit. Damn holy obedience. Send nuns and priests out into the REAL world. If I had wanted the real world, I'd have stayed in it.[7]

As part of her entry into the real world, Cordova was enrolled at Immaculate Heart College, the flagship school of the order, where she was subjected to the Education Innovation Project first-hand through sensitivity training and second-hand through the teachers who had also taken the sensitivity training. Perhaps no one epitomized the new nun better than "famous people like Sister Corita [Kent]" an artist nun who was famous for her graffiti-inspired paintings which illustrated passages from the Bible like the Beatitudes in updated language, i.e., "Happy the poor in spirit," instead of the more traditional term "Blessed." Cordova remembers one art course in which she and other nuns were required to run across the tops of desks while dabbing paint onto canvases. She remembers being told that in doing this she and the other nuns were "expressing ourselves." She also remembers taking a course with Sister Richard, "a great brain in philosophy," who "tied the sacrament of baptism in with the order of the cosmos."[8]

Similarly, nothing epitomized the new spirituality better than sensitivity training. One of Sister Richard's colleagues in the English department wrote that as a result of the sensitivity training she had received as part of the Education Innovation Project, she had redesigned all of her courses. "My classroom behavior," she wrote, "is radically different now. I have been able to confess anxiety to my classes and consequently feel more comfortable in the classroom than ever before. I invited the girls to call me by my first name, and after a couple of weeks they are doing so. This allows for a lot of free exchange. I am not giving grades and I am not even giving exams. They are writing their own questions, the ones that are meaningful to them. Then they are discussing them."

In their enthusiasm for Rogers's encounter groups, the older sisters seem to have missed the fact that students like Jean Cordova found the whole experience more troubling than exhilarating. "A lot of times," wrote one of Cordova's fellow students, "I've heard that faculty felt they were being forced . . . to say things they didn't want to say; I myself feel very uncomfortable about being shut in with people who break down and say things I feel I shouldn't have heard. I think it creates a kind of embarrassment, which would seem to be a hindrance in relationships rather than a help. Still I do feel that I've gained a lot of insight into other peoples' behavior." Another student was even more troubled. "I felt at a loss today in that encounter group: very naked, as though everyone knows too much about me."[9]

Before long, many of the nuns started to feel naked as well, mainly because as a result of the loosening of controls in the order in the name of California-style openness, they were taking off their clothes and having sex with other nuns. Instead of doing a close reading of Rogers's paper on groups, especially the passage about how encounter groups often led to "feelings which have a sexual component" and acting according to procedures consonant with the vow of chastity, the Immaculate Heart nuns, in the name of openness and innovation, decided that they had to learn the same lesson about human passion in the expensive school of experience. In the name of openness, religious asceticism vanished from convent life. Cordova stopped going to Mass at 6:30 in the morning because nuns weren't "required" to go to Mass anymore. As religious practice evaporated from their lives, the nuns turned to each other for support. Particular friendships flourished, and in the atmosphere of the times, some of these friendships inevitably turned sexual.

This, of course, meant that life in the convent became both mean-spirited and chaotic. During the spring of 1967, Cordova noticed that many of the nuns weren't going to Mass anymore. This meant the beginning of

> lots of particular friendships, a whole sub-culture of in-group and out-group, who they were and how they did it and how you could just lie your way out of anything. To a lonely postulant in a miserable friendless world, it was an absurd outrage. I fell out of love with Jesus and the IHMs, who betrayed and mocked my innocence. . . . I was sinking in the quag-mire of broken dreams. . . . All I have ever wanted to be was a nun. Now I was, and it was hell.[10]

Jean Cordova found that she couldn't talk to her parents about the changes, probably because her parents were as bewildered by the unprece-dented sequence of events as she was. "Mom was a sheltered, upper class convent raised Irish Catholic from Queens, Long Island, who probably first read about birth control in the *LA Times* between her ninth and tenth kid." In the bewildering atmosphere of the up-dated chaotic convent, where the IHM nuns were told to be open to their feelings in the encounter groups they were attending, Cordova found solace in sexual contact with one of the other nuns. Both embittered and sexualized by her experience in the convent, Cordova converted to lesbian activism with the same fervor which she offered to the pre-conciliar Church.

> I harnessed my anger into love for gays as an oppressed people. My bitter-ness demands the straight world to move over and accept our rights. I have learned that my anger takes me where others are afraid to go and that out-rage is good in the eyes of whatever Higher Power gives us righteous, if misguided, anger to protect us.[11]

Other IHM nuns had similar experiences. Sister Mary Benjamin, like Jean Cordova, was driven to the IHM novitiate by her large Catholic family, who piled out of the station wagon "like a baseball team" when they arrived there in 1962. Like Jean Cordova, Sister Mary Benjamin was enrolled as a student at Immaculate Heart College, where four years later, during the sum-mer of 1966, she was "introduced to sensitivity training, the order's first ven-ture into the human potential movement."[12] In her encounter group, Sister Mary met Eva, "a heavy, dark-skinned woman with deep brown eyes and black hair." Given the spirit of the times, the alchemy of this relationship was just as predictable as that which seduced Jean Cordova: "The order no longer prohibited particular friendships," Sister Mary recounted matter of factly, "so the contact turned sexual."[13] Sister Mary sought council from a priest, but apparently he had been infected by the spirit of the times as well and "re-fused to pass judgment on my actions. He said it was up to me to decide if they were right or wrong. He opened a door, and I walked through, realizing I was on my own." When Sister Mary told Eva that she was "worried that I had a terrible crush on her," Eva responded by saying, "Great! Enjoy it!"[14]

Sister Mary's relationship with Eva turned out to be less than enjoyable, however. After the friendship became sexualized, a painful breakup ensued, which in turn precipitated a break with the Catholic Church. Sister Mary, like most lesbians, was then cast adrift on a sea of transient relationships, and one relationship which proved just as transient was her relationship with the Catholic Church. "In loving Eva," she wrote, "I was growing in a direction at odds with convent goals of obedience and service to the Church. I began to make decisions, not out of guilt, but according to the voice of my intuition and the wisdom of my body. I began to see the Church more objectively. It was run by men, not God. My allegiance to the Church was no longer fate but choice."[15]

Actually, if Sister Mary had been reading Wilhelm Reich, she would have realized that once she started acting on her illicit sexual impulses, her break with the Church was more fate than choice. Once she began acting out her lesbian impulses, her break with the Church was inevitable. Because she was subsequently dragooned into feminism, Sister Mary simply lacked the intellectual categories to understand what had happened to her. Everything was now a question of "liberation" from oppression, and since the culture she embraced had hundreds of years of experience in portraying convent life as a form of oppression, it is not surprising that she would see matters that way too. If there were sinister forces at work in precipitating Sister Mary's departure from the convent and the Catholic faith, the lesbianism which replaced her Catholicism as the religious center of her life precluded any clear understanding of them. The categories of lesbian politics took control of her mind and precluded any other explanation of what had happened to her.

Like Jean Cordova, Jean O'Leary entered the convent in 1966. Like Jean Cordova, she was immediately plunged into the regimen of the "renewed" religious order, which meant "we were together constantly, talking endlessly and intensely in sensitivity and encounter groups about love and hope and philosophy."[16] As with the two previous examples, all this "intensely emotional talk" about "great thinkers and modern psychology" inevitably led to sexual feelings, which inevitably led to sexual activity, which inevitably led to a religious crisis when it became apparent that the nuns were acting in ways which were incompatible with the vows they had taken. At this point, the nuns had to make a choice, either to conform their lives to their principles or their principles to their lives. For those who persisted in their sexual activity, the result was a foregone conclusion. As Reich had predicted in the *Mass Psychology of Fascism*, illicit sexual activity has loss of faith as one of its inevitable sequelae. Like Sister Mary, Jean O'Leary turned to a priest for guidance, but as in the previous instance, the priest was himself a psychologist who had been brought into the order to facilitate the very encounter groups which were the catalyst for the sexual activity which was causing the problem. Unsurprisingly, no spiritual help was forthcoming from this corner, and

Jean O'Leary began another affair, this time with the novice mistress, before eventually drifting out of the community and into political lesbianism as its surrogate.

At around the same time that Jean O'Leary was acting out her sexual impulses, Abe Maslow, one of the creators of the psychology which enabled her and other nuns to act on their newly discovered sexual impulses, was having second thoughts about the whole encounter-group phenomenon. "I've been in continuous conflict," he wrote in his diary, "for a long time over this, over Esalen-type, orgiastic, Dionysian type education." Maslow had not always had conflicts of this sort. Writing in the *Journal of Psychology* in 1949, Maslow said confidently that "I can report empirically the healthiest persons in our culture . . . are most (not least) pagan, most (not least) instinctive, most (not least) accepting of their animal nature."

Three years before Carl Rogers's paper on encounter groups circulated among the nuns in Los Angeles, on April 17, 1962, Abraham Maslow gave a lecture to a group of nuns at Sacred Heart, a Catholic women's college in Massachusetts. Maslow noted in a diary entry of the same date that the talk had been very "successful," but he found that very fact troubling. "They shouldn't applaud me," he wrote, "they should attack. If they were fully aware of what I was doing, they would [attack]."[17]

Just why the nuns should have attacked him becomes evident from a reading of other journal entries written around the same time. Maslow was aware that encounter groups were toxic for Catholics in general and especially toxic for Catholic religious. Anyone who promoted encounter groups among Catholics was promoting ipso facto their demise as Catholics, even if he did so in the name of liberation and with that as his intent. For the liberal Jew or Protestant, the nun was the textbook case of someone in need of "liberation" and in the context of Catholic religious life and the vows upon which it was based, liberation could only mean annihilation. On February 25, 1967, Maslow wrote in his diary, "Maybe morons need rules, dogmas, ceremonies, etc." He then made a note to order a book entitled *Life among the Lowbrows* for the Brandeis library. He may have ordered it because the author of that book noted in it that "feebleminded clients behaved much better and felt better being Catholic and following all the rules." Since the nuns weren't feebleminded, this meant that bringing "self-actualization" to the nuns meant destroying their commitment to their vows and the Catholic Church. Perhaps this is why Maslow felt they shouldn't have applauded his talk in 1962. Maslow, who had spent time at the National Training Laboratories' headquarters in Bethel, Maine, where encounter groups, with the help of subsidies from the Office of Naval Research, had been created, knew that they were funded as a form of psychological warfare, and he had an inkling of the effect they would have on nuns, but it was up to his colleague Carl Rogers to do the actual experiment.

"I guess what I'm trying to say here," Maslow wrote in his journal in 1965, the same year that Carl Rogers began circulating his paper on the psychology of small-group encounters among the IHM nuns and around the same time that the nuns started to leave the convent, "is that these interpersonal therapeutic growth-fostering relationships of all kinds which rest on intimacy, on honesty, on self-disclosure, on becoming sensitively aware of one's self – and thereby of responsibility for feeding back one's impression of others, etc. – *that these are profoundly revolutionary devices*, in the strict sense of the word – that is, of shifting the whole direction of a society in a more preferred direction. As a matter of fact, it might be revolutionary in another sense if something like this were done very widely. I think the whole culture would change within a decade and everything in it."[18]

What was true for the culture was *a fortiori* true of religious orders in the Catholic Church. The whole culture did change, as a matter of fact, after implementation of encounter groups became widespread, but nowhere was the change as dramatic as in the Catholic Church, where it literally destroyed the orders which tried to experiment with it. After making contact with their inner selves, the nuns all wanted to leave their orders and have sex, although not always in that order. "A sign of this potency," Rogers's assistant W. R. Coulson wrote some thirty years later, "was the conversions that followed Rogers's workshops. A Catholic priest took part in a five-day workshop in the 1960s, then left the priesthood to study psychology with Rogers, who had been his group facilitator. It happened repeatedly. Of the workshop that converted him, the priest wrote that he began somewhat skeptically, but "by Wednesday. . . something new and intriguing and intoxicating as well as frightening has become real all around me . . . . [It] seemed like a beautiful birth to a new existence. . . . I had not known how unaware I was of my deepest feelings nor how valuable they might be to other people . . . . Never in my life before that group experience had I experienced 'me' so intensely."[19]

The priest may not have noticed it, but both Maslow and Rogers were involved in the sexual engineering of behavior. Catholic religious, who were expected to lead ascetic lives while at the same time being told that love was the reason for their asceticism, were now experiencing the "love" they had always talked about in previously abstract and rarefied terms, and they were for the most part unhinged by the experience. The effectiveness of the encounter group was based on the deliberate violation of the sexual inhibitions which made everyday life possible. When the inhibitions dropped, the emotion which flooded in to fill the vacuum seemed a lot like the love which Christians were supposed to practice on their neighbors, when in point of fact it was more akin to unfettered libido, which could now be used by the facilitator as the energy which brought about the social engineering they desired. Maslow was never shy in proposing sexual activity as a form of social engineering. In a passage which appeared in his book *Eupsychian Management* (but was subsequently deleted by the editors who reissued it in 1998 as *Maslow on Management*), Maslow said:

> it always struck me as a very wise kind of thing that the lower-class Negroes did, as reported in one study, in Cleveland, Ohio. Among those Negroes the sexual life began at puberty. It was the custom for an older brother to get a friend in his own age grade to break in his little sister sexually when she came of a suitable age. And the same thing was done on the girl's side. A girl who had a younger brother coming into puberty would seek among her own girl friends for one who would take on the job of initiating the young boy into sex in a nice way. This seems extremely sensible and wise and could also serve highly therapeutic purposes in various other ways as well. I remember talking with Alfred Adler about this in a kind of joking way, but then we both got quite serious about it, and Adler thought that this sexual therapy at various ages was certainly a very fine thing. As we both played with the thought we envisaged a kind of social worker in both sexes, who was very well trained for this sort of thing, sexually but primarily as a psychotherapist in giving therapy literally on the couch, that is for mixing in the beautiful and gentle sexual initiation with all the goals of psychotherapy.[20]

Maslow's use of the Negro as a paradigm of sexual liberation was part of a long tradition of race-based sexual engineering which surfaced in the 1920s with the Harlem Renaissance and reached its culmination the civil-rights movement of the '60s. So was his idea of the psychotherapist "giving therapy literally on the couch." Both tactics would be waged against Catholics in the *Kulturkampf* of the 1960s as a way of changing their outmoded attitudes and moving them in a direction more congenial to the progressive facilitators.

By the late '60s, which is to say, shortly before his death, Maslow was confronted not with the theory of encounter groups and third-force humanistic psychology, but with its ever-increasing and more widespread practice, and what he saw appalled him. The reverence for learning which he associated with Jews had all but dried up at Brandeis, where he was teaching and could measure the effect of his theories on students first-hand.

> One trouble with liberals, humanists, psychology 3 [humanistic psychology], McGregor, Esalen, Rogers, et al. is in their giving up of evil, or at least their total confusion about it. As if there were no sons of bitches or paranoids or psychopaths or true believes in the world to crap things up, even in a Utopian environment. My class has lost the traditional Jewish respect for knowledge, learning and teachers. I don't want it.[21]

By 1967, Maslow was referring to the self-actualization which encounter groups were supposed to bring about as "S. A. stuff," which had become in turn, just part of the "Esalen-Dionysian" enterprise. One year before his death, he could now detect in all of these activities the odor of "insanity and death."[22]

The misgivings expressed by the creators of humanistic psychology were not shared by their more enthusiastic epigones, who were more bent on "giving therapy literally on the couch," especially among the nuns, than in expressing their misgivings about the consequences for higher things which flowed from this sort of behavior. In *Hollywood Priest*, his memoir of his years as a TV producer and Paulist Priest, Rev. Elwood "Bud" Kieser describes meeting a nun he identifies only as "Genevieve" at the IHM retreat house in Santa Barbara in 1964.[23] (Kieser's story has uncanny similarities with the story of James F. T. Bugental, one of Rogers's followers who had a practice in Los Angeles and ended up marrying former IHM nun Elizabeth Keebler.)[24] During the fall of 1965, Kieser was in Rome covering the end of the Vatican Council. When he returned at the end of the year, he realized that he had fallen deeply in love with Sister "Genevieve," who announced when they met again at the retreat house that she was going to begin psychotherapy. Kieser was taken aback by the announcement, but claims that he "admired her courage in facing the situation and trying to do something about it." Kieser never gets around to explaining just what "the situation" was or why it required treatment in 1966, but a large part of the reason was the encounter groups the nuns were involved in. According to the tenets of encounter psychology, you had to be crazy to repress your libido. Since all nuns repressed their libidos, they were all *ipso facto* crazy and therefore candidates for therapy, although only the bravest had the guts to descend into their unconscious to prove the point.

Not surprisingly, Genevieve found therapy painful. As a result, she turned to Father Kieser for guidance, wondering whether she should continue because she was not sure she could trust her therapist. Kieser, who had read a book the therapist had written, assured her that she could trust Harry, the pseudonym Kieser applied to the therapist. It was advice that Kieser would live to regret. To begin with, the prime result of Genevieve's therapy was convincing her that her decision to enter the convent had been based on "repression rather than the sublimation of her sexual drives." And now, in the midst of the sexual revolution of the '60s, when Genevieve was in her late thirties, "those mechanisms of repression seemed to be coming apart."[25]

Just why those mechanisms were coming apart becomes apparent when Kieser describes the type of therapy to which Sister Genevieve was being subjected:

> Very early in her therapy, her therapist – let's call him Harry – had suggested a degree of sex play to help her with her repressions. Almost all therapists would today consider this a serious breach of professional ethics. But in the 1960s such procedures were not uncommon. She went along. When she told me, I was furious. She decided to stop. But she was vulnerable. So was he. Once started this kind of thing is difficult to keep in check. It became a problem that plagued her therapy.[26]

By the summer of 1967, the problem became so serious that Harry arranged another therapist for "Genevieve." But by the fall, they started seeing each other outside therapy, and the sexual relationship only intensified, something which "Genevieve" shared with Father Kieser, who was now consumed with both "pure masculine jealousy" and justifiable indignation at a flagrant abuse of the doctor-patient relationship.

Harry the Therapist was, of course, married to another woman at the time, a woman whom he would eventually abandon to marry Sister Genevieve. Father Kieser, for his part however, has a difficult time deciding whether his feelings are motivated by moral outrage or by simple jealousy. He is so upset that he contemplates killing Harry the Therapist, but for all that, he never really understands what is happening, even though he mentions the fact that the sexual revolution of the '60s might have something to do with it:

> We were both caught up in the cultural revolution that characterized American society and the Catholic Church during the 1960s. The consensus that characterized both society and Church was beginning to come undone. On every side authority, creed, and institutions were being challenged. Dogmas were suspect, certainties rejected, absolutes called into question, values rigorously scrutinized, and rules routinely broken. The sexual revolution was in full swing, and its initial message seemed to be: If it feels good, go with it.[27]

Kieser was not only caught up in the cultural revolution of the 1960s, he was witnessing the engine which drove it first-hand, and yet he remained blind to what was right in front of his eyes. Wilhelm Reich could have explained it to him. Adultery and religious vows don't mix. People involved in both have to choose eventually one or the other. Since sex of this sort is highly addictive, the choice often goes against the vows religious made to serve the Church. Sex was the best way of "liberating" nuns from their convents. As Leo Pfeffer would say in 1976, the cultural revolution of the '60s was a battle between the Enlightenment (as espoused by liberal Protestants and Jews) and the Catholic Church. Sex was simply the most effective weapon the Enlightenment would bring to bear in this battle. Reich had explicated the use of sex as a way of destroying religious faith, especially among the clergy, in his magnum opus of sexual politics, *The Mass Psychology of Fascism*, which was undergoing a revival around the same time that Kieser was puzzling over Sister Genevieve's behavior. But Kieser hadn't read Reich, and even if he had he was probably incapable of understanding it. The reason is simple enough. Kieser had so adopted the psychological categories of his oppressors, he couldn't understand what was happening right in front of his eyes to Sister Genevieve and her order. Because of his closeness to Sister Genevieve, Kieser in fact became the chief enabler of her demise as a nun, something which he perceived dimly – "I felt somehow responsible. If

I had decided differently, would she be deciding differently?"[28] – but only after it was too late.

Kieser tried valiantly to understand what was going on, but failed each time, thwarted by the categories the culture had given him. Who could argue with liberation after all? Even if it meant the repudiation of vows. In each instance, Kieser's attempt to understand what was happening to his nun friend was thwarted by the categories of the plumbing psychology which allowed him to get her in trouble in the first place. "Were her faith difficulties connected to her sexual ones?"[29] Kieser wonders, making a wild stab and hitting the bull's eye at the same time. But even when he comes up with the correct answer, he can't pursue it because of the psychological categories he has imbibed from California culture. "I do not know, but I know that when you repress any one facet of your humanity, you do violence to every other facet. Sexual repression not only inhibits your ability to relate to someone of the opposite sex. It also inhibits your ability to relate to God."[30] So in order to remedy her inability to relate to God, should Sister Genevieve engage in sexual activity with her therapist because that breaks down repression? Kieser seems incapable of doing anything other than pouring more gasoline on the fire. In order to get a better grip on what was going on, Father Kieser decided to attend "one of the marathon therapy sessions then in vogue" which Sister Genevieve had been attending. The encounter lasted twenty-two hours, but by the end of it, Kieser still couldn't understand the connection between encounter groups and Sister Genevieve's loss of faith and subsequent sexual bondage. In fact, not only did Kieser not see the encounter as part of the problem, he came away from it "exhilarated." Kieser himself had been sucked into the mechanism that was destroying the IHM order, and he wasn't even aware of what happened to him. "Her therapy continued to be painful," continued the ever-clueless Father Kieser. "Sometimes it seemed that she was caught in a whirlpool that was sucking her down and down into extinction."[31]

At Thanksgiving of 1967, Genevieve informed Father Kieser that Harry the Therapist had left his wife and was filing for divorce. Sister Genevieve was now living with her therapist until the divorce became final, whereupon they planned to marry. One more IHM nun was headed out the door, and encounter-group therapy was what enabled her to leave. Kieser described himself as shattered by the revelation "because this marked her definitive breach with the Church and seemingly with those values – love, fidelity, self-sacrifice, respect for the rights of others, honesty – that the church had nurtured in us, and which I had always thought we had in common." Genevieve didn't seem too happy either, admitting to Kieser that "she would feel guilt for what she was doing to his wife for the rest of her life."[32]

The flagship of the Immaculate Heart order, Immaculate Heart College, was located right in the middle of the therapy and psychology which would find in California the best exemplar of the lifestyle it promoted. Los Angeles was, more or less, halfway between Esalen in Big Sur just south of San Francisco and the Mexican border, and it was just north of La Jolla, where Carl Rogers was located at the Western Behavioral Sciences Institute. It was also in the immediate vicinity of a number of therapists, some of whom were associates of Rogers, who would play a major role in the Education Innovation Project. According to W. R. Coulson, Rogers's assistant in the EIP, "the Team from WBSI was on the Immaculate Heart campus to teach and exemplify what would soon begin to be called their 'quiet revolution' in education." According to Coulson, "WBSI wasn't the only alien presence. Other consultants arrived, having heard that the nuns were ripe for psychological experimentation."[33]

If the implication of "psychological experimentation" sounds sinister, it should be added that the nuns were eager to become guinea pigs. The nuns had reached the pinnacle of their power as an organization at the same time that Catholics were enjoying the unprecedented political acceptance of which the election of John F. Kennedy to the White House was the most obvious example. The Immaculate Heart order had 560 nuns at an early point in the project and ran a system of 60 schools. Like nuns across the United States, which numbered 186,000 at the time, the Immaculate Heart Order had reached the apogee of its size and influence in the twenty years since the end of World War II.

Since both the Immaculate Heart Nuns and Carl Rogers reached the height of their influence at around the same time and around the same place, it was inevitable that they would come into contact. Born in 1902, the same year as Paul Blanshard, Rogers, like Blanshard, was drawn early in life to the ministry, but also like Blanshard, he abandoned the ministry – after two years at Union Theological Seminary – in lieu of studies at Columbia University. Unlike Blanshard, Rogers did not study with Dewey directly, but he imbibed his spirit from Dewey's disciples, one of whom, William H. Kilpatrick, ran his classes on the philosophy of education in ways similar to later encounter groups. For both men, science at Columbia University (for Blanshard, sociology; for Rogers, psychology) became the vehicle which would achieve what the liberal Protestant pulpit promised but could not deliver. During the 1930s, Rogers was working as a guidance counselor in Rochester, New York, when, almost by accident, he discovered a technique which would help neurotics move forward with their lives. Leading them by subtly manipulative questioning to the issues that had stalled them. Rogers called his key insight "the clarifying response." "The main aim of the counselor," he wrote in his 1942 book, *Counseling and Psychotherapy: Newer Concepts in Practice*:

is to assist the client to drop any defensiveness, any feeling that attitudes should not be brought into the open, any concerns that the counselor may criticize or suggest or order. If this aim can be accomplished then the client is freed to look at the situation in its reality without having to justify or protect himself.[34]

In 1965 Rogers wrote that his first involvement with encounter groups was "an intensive post-doctoral workshop in psychotherapy in 1950." In *Carl Rogers on Encounter Groups*, he moved the date back to when the encounter group was first conceived in the aftermath of World War II. During the years 1946 and '47, Rogers and his associates at the Counseling Center of the University of Chicago were involved in training counselors for the Veterans Administration, when he was asked to come up with a psychological-training mechanism which would help these counselors reintegrate soldiers returning from the war into civilian life. Rogers soon discovered that intensive group experiences were more effective in changing behavior than cognitive training. Rogers goes on to say that the Chicago group did nothing to expand this approach. Even granting that, however, it is clear that other people were pursuing the same ideas at the same time and that gradually over a period of twenty years, all of these elements came together in the encounter group of the 1960s.

By 1966, when Carl Rogers began experimenting with the Immaculate Heart nuns and the effect that encounter groups had on them, the encounter group or sensitivity training or the T-group had been in existence for about twenty years and had been modified by those who made use of it. Rogers describes the mix as "Lewinian thinking and Gestalt psychology on the one hand, and client-centered therapy on the other."[35] Rogers's "clarifying response" had become one of the standard tools for encounter groups. According to Rogers, Sensitivity Training was:

> relatively unstructured, providing a climate of maximum freedom for personal expression, exploration of feelings and interpersonal communication. Emphasis is upon the interactions among the group members, in an atmosphere which encourages each to drop his defenses and his façades and thus enables him to relate directly and openly to other members of the group – the basic encounter.[36]

By the 1960s, Rogers was using encounter "therapy" not on neurotics, as in the '30s in Rochester, and not on returning GIs, whose disorientation at civilian life may have resembled neurosis, but on "normal" people. In fact, in terms of their orientation toward other people and the altruism of their motivation, the IHM nuns were clearly above normal. That being the case, the desire to have a client "drop his defenses" takes on meaning that at the very least needs clarification or at worst begins to sound slightly sinister, in the same sense that Maslow mentioned its revolutionary capacities in regard to the nuns he met a few years earlier. The value judgments Rogers makes – mask vs. real person, etc., – become more questionable, the more normal his "clients" become. If the criterion in dealing with "clients" is not health, what are we to make of the value judgments scattered throughout the following passage?

> [I]t becomes increasingly evident that what they have first presented are façades, masks. Only cautiously do the real feelings and real persons emerge. The contrast between the outer shell and the inner person becomes more and more apparent as the hours go by. Little by little, a sense of genuine communication builds up, and the person who has been thoroughly walled off from others comes out with some small segment of his actual feelings.[37]

Were the Immaculate Heart nuns "real persons"? Or were they hiding behind "façades"? How was Carl Rogers supposed to decide, since the nuns were not suffering from mental illness? The only sense in which these questions have therapeutic value is if the person is suffering from some sort of mental disorder. If that is not the case, then the vocabulary all points in the direction of social engineering. Carl Rogers may very well have thought that the nuns were mentally ill simply by the fact that they were nuns, but in this instance, therapy has clearly entered the realm of politics (or religion). Rogers is involved, in this instance, not in trying to heal them but to change them into something he feels is better than a nun. Even if he decides to change them into "better" nuns, he can only act on that premise in light of what he considers good and bad politically and not psychologically, since the nuns were not ill, nor was Rogers claiming that they were. All of the value judgments in Rogers's description of encounter groups need a context before they can be properly understood. If the client is neurotic, the context is health. If the clients are healthy – which was presumably the case with the IHM nuns – the context is politics, and what goes by the name of therapy is really social engineering, no matter how "nondirective" the therapist/facilitator claims to be. Rogers's own testimony makes it clear that he saw encounter groups in precisely this political light, which is another way of saying that he saw them as social engineering and not therapy.

By 1968, which is to say two years into the Education Innovation Project, Rogers and Coulson got the sense that something was wrong. By that point in the program over three hundred nuns had asked to be laicized, and the order had been split into two mutually antagonistic groups who were fighting over the order's financial assets. The progressive faction was also waging a publicity campaign against Cardinal McIntyre. The only way in which the project could be looked upon as a success was by adopting the public-relations jargon that was currently being used to describe the war in Vietnam. Like the U.S. troops over there, Rogers had to destroy the order in order to save it. The only way the Education Innovation Project could be termed a success is if its intent was to destroy the order in the first place.

Eventually, Coulson would go on to apologize publicly for his efforts. and become a vocal opponent of the very thing he promoted in the '60s. Instead of apologizing, however, Rogers got defensive. By the time he wrote his book on encounter groups in 1969–70, Rogers would claim his enemies were all right-wing nuts. The incongruity of the non-directive Dr. Rogers attacking his political opponents so intemperately gives some indication that there was a political agenda at work in the encounter groups from the very beginning. But if that were the case, it was an agenda that was all but invisible to the untrained eye. In this Rogers was a typical example of the English ideology, which claimed, like Newton, that it "framed no hypotheses" and then worked out an intricate system of control behind that façade. "Putting it in my own words," Rogers wrote, "encounter groups lead to more personal independence, fewer hidden feelings, more willingness to innovate, more opposition to institutional rigidities."[38] Just how Rogers is to say an institution is rigid, in the absence of medical criteria, never gets explained. What does come out in the subsequent discussion is a clear profile of his political enemies, who at the time he was working with the IHM nuns were accusing him of "brainwashing." "All types of intensive group experience," he opines, "have come under the most virulent attack from right-wing and reactionary groups. It is, to them, a form of 'brainwashing' and 'thought control.'"[39]

Turning the tables on his critics, Rogers accused them of orchestrating a right-wing takeover of the country, showing that his "therapy" had a political component after all. It seems that Dr. Rogers framed some hypotheses after all, and they had a very distinct political tinge to them:

> Currently, the possibility of a takeover by the extreme right seems more likely in this country than a takeover by the extreme left. But the encounter group movement would be led out of existence in either case, because rigid control, not freedom, would be the central element. One cannot imagine an encounter group in present-day Russia or even Czechoslovakia, though there is ample evidence that many individuals in those countries yearn for just the kind of freedom of expression it encourages. . . . If there is a dictatorial takeover in this country – and it becomes frighteningly clearer that it might happen here – then the whole trend toward the intensive group experience would be one of the first developments to be crushed and obliterated.[40]

Rogers then gives some indication that his political categories were formed in the immediate aftermath of World War II by claiming that his right-wing adversaries were examples of the "authoritarian personality," which Theodor Wiesengrund Adorno had described in a book which had been funded by CIA money right around the same time that Paul Blanshard's book came out, and could be seen as another indication of the desire among the thinkers who had been funded by foundations to link Catholicism and fascism. According to Rogers:

> James Harmon, in a carefully documented study, concludes that there is ample evidence that the right wing has a large proportion of authoritarian personalities. They tend to believe that man is by nature, basically evil. Surrounded as all of us are by the bigness of impersonal forces which seem beyond our power to control, they look for "the enemy," so that they can hate him. At different times in history "the enemy' has been the witch, the demon, the Communist (remember Joe McCarthy?), and now sex education, sensitivity training, "nonreligious humanism," and other current demons.[41]

As a way of countering the suspicions of his critics that sensitivity training was some conspiracy to brainwash the unsuspecting masses, Rogers claims that the movement just grew like Topsy:

> One factor which makes the rapidity of the spread even more remarkable is its complete and unorganized spontaneity. Contrary to the shrill voices of the right wing (whom I will mention below), this has not been a "conspiracy." Quite the contrary. No group or organization has been pushing the development of encounter groups. . . . There has been no financing of such a spread, either from foundations or governments.[42]

Rogers is not being honest here. First of all he knew that, although the IHM nuns contributed something toward funding of the Education Innovation Project, it was being paid for in part by the Merrill Foundation and the Mary Reynolds Babcock Foundation, which was based on the R.J. Reynolds tobacco fortune. Rogers in addition must have known that he had veteran psychological warriors on his staff because the EIP team cited his credentials in the proposals they wrote up to obtain funding for an early version of the project. Rogers's associate in the IHM Education Innovation Project, Jack Gibb, wrote on the grant proposal that while attending the University of Chicago in 1949, he had "developed an intensive program of laboratory and field research into the nature and determiners of defense levels in small groups. This research was supported by the Office of Naval Research between 1953 and 1962." It was the Office of Naval Research, along with the notorious Carnegie Foundation, which funded the original National Training Laboratories project from 1947 to 1950. Not only had encounter groups, contrary to what Rogers said, been subsidized by both government and foundations, they had been subsidized by them specifically as a form of psychological warfare.

Encounter groups, as Rogers himself indicates by his oblique reference to Kurt Lewin in describing the sources of sensitivity training, were a creation of the CIA's psychological warfare campaign. Like Wilhelm Reich, Kurt Lewin was a German Jew who left Germany in 1933 when Hitler came to power. Like Rogers, Lewin had been influenced by both Freud and Watson. According to Kleiner, Lewin "believed with the Freudians that subconscious echoes of past traumas drive our deepest feelings, and he also believed with the behaviorists, that people could be programmed to respond predictably to stimuli."[43] Unlike both Watson and Freud, Lewin felt that "many other forces could affect a person's ability to decide."[44] Unlike both Freud and Watson, Lewin felt that a number of forces, a whole "forcefield," in fact, composed of "the person's marriage and family relationships, fears and hopes, neuroses and physical health, work situation and network of friends"[45] controlled the decisions he made.

Perhaps because of all the psychic forces which got brought to bear on an individual, Lewin felt that social groups were the most effective means to influence behavior. In the '40s, he and his assistant Ron Lippitt set out to prove this by experimenting on YMCA groups in Iowa City. Once the war broke out, isolated social scientists like Lewin and Lippitt were gradually drawn into the orbit of research on psychological warfare. "The war," according to Kleiner, "was generally an immense catalyst for social science in America (and England), because it pulled university researchers from their isolated posts. They worked together on real-world problems such as keeping up military morale, developing psychological warfare techniques, and studying foreign cultures."[46] Also drawn into the psychological warfare orbit was Lewin's assistant Ken Benne, who, like Blanshard, had studied under John Dewey at Columbia. Gradually, a consensus emerged among the psychological warriors that, in Kleiner's words, "social change had to be managed *intelligently* – not through force, manipulation, or greedy exploitation."[47] Encounter groups were simply the most effective instrument science had yet devised to manage social change through the manipulation of peer pressure. How that instrument got used would depend on the social priorities of the class of people who had invented it, and after the successful conclusion of World War II, those people shifted their concerns from fascism to the "Catholic problem," most specifically the demographic threat which Catholic sexual teaching posed to continued WASP hegemony in the United States.

The second main source of Encounter Groups was Gestalt Therapy, a creation of Fritz Perls and Paul Goodman which was just as antithetical to Catholic sexual morality as the psychological warfare of the WASP elite. Gestalt Therapy was based to a large extent on the psychological ideas of Wilhelm Reich, who saw unfettered sexual activity as the best way to wean people away from their belief in God. Perls was resident guru at Esalen, a few hours' drive north of Los Angeles, by the time Carl Rogers became involved with the Immaculate Heart nuns. His techniques were well known throughout California, spread by contact through Perls at Esalen and by Reich's student Alexander Lowen, whose Bioenergetics were based on the Reichian idea of breaking down a person's "body armor" and thereby helping him with the battle against sexual repression and its transcendent counterpart, belief in God. Michael Weber in his book *Psychotechniken: Die*

Neuen Verführer sees the rise of encounter-group techniques in German seminary training as a Trojan Horse whose purpose was the deliberate destruction of religious vocation, the weakening of both the Protestant and Catholic Churches in Germany, and the subsequent triumph of the secular point of view. Weber also traces the rise of this attack on German religious life to the National Training Laboratories. "In September 1963," according to Weber, "in Schliersee in Oberbayern, 30 German teachers were subjected to a three-week long workshop run by the National Training Laboratories. The purpose of the T-group was to 'influence' their authoritarian teaching style."[48] Weber also thinks that the Immaculate Heart nuns' Education Innovation Project was part of the same campaign to lame religious life. Thirty years later the T-group had become an essential part of German religious training. Weber sees the heart of encounter as a form of sexual manipulation. "Sexuality," he writes, "plays a crucial role in the group-dynamic-based continuing education of priests, a program which involves the sexualization of the person who gets trained."[49] Sexualization, according to Reich was "the mortal foe of religion." That means that "only through the destruction of sexual repression and the alienation of the child from its relationship with his parents" can political liberation of the sort that Reich believed in succeed. This is *a fortiori* the case for religious, and Weber sees in the massive spread of encounter groups in seminary training the introduction into religious orders of a strategy whose purpose is truly Reichian, namely, sexualization as a prelude to annihilation.

In spite of Rogers's protest to the contrary, Kleiner shows that encounter groups were associated not only with psychological warfare but with brainwashing. "As it happened," Kleiner wrote,

> there was an expert on brainwashing within the NTL community, a young psychologist named Edgar Schein, who came to McGregor's department at MIT in the late 1950s, had gone to Inchon at the end of the Korean War to help repatriate American prisoners of war. Schein learned from his research in Korea that the Chinese social control had taken place without drugs, hypnosis, Pavlovian conditioning or even torture; all that was used was peer pressure. Just as in a T-Group, the Communists had put the POWs in a cultural island, cut them off from all contact with outsiders, and surrounded them with friendly Chinese "big brothers" (who had been promised a reward for reforming their Western cellmates.)[50]

Schein promptly applied what he learned in Korea to the development of encounter groups for the benefit of the NTL. Schein saw few similarities between POW camps and civilian life in America, until, that is, he looked more closely at the most influential management training centers in the United States, places like GE's Crotonville and IBM's Sands Point. Since the constraints of corporate life constituted an effective form of the milieu control essential to making encounter techniques work, Schein thought T-groups would work in the corporate world. Schein didn't mention it, but a related conclusion was even more obvious. Convents created even more "milieu control" than big corporations, and so were the ideal setting for brainwashing via encounter groups.

Eventually Robert Blake, another NTL alumnus, would put Schein's theory into practice when he held the first corporate sensitivity training session at the Bayway refinery of Standard Oil of New Jersey, then known as Esso. Blake had spent a year and a half at Tavistock, which was the British psychological warfare operation. Tavistock staged encounters on a much more extensive basis than what was being offered at the National Training Laboratories in Bethel, Maine. Unlike its American counterparts, Tavistock was more interested in control than "peak experiences." Perhaps because of this orientation, Blake, in Kleiner's words, realized that in all T-groups, "no matter how nondirective the facilitator tried to be, he or she was still subtly dictatorial, even more dictatorial (because of its subtlety) than the harshest CEO, because all of that control was hidden."[51] The links between Eric Trist of Tavistock, Douglas McGregor of MIT, Kurt Lewin, the founder of NTL, and Robert Blake give some idea of how closely connected the psychological warriors were with each other and with the creation of encounter groups and how intimately encounter groups were linked with the interests of the Anglophile intelligence establishment which created it.

On November 28, 1953, Dr. Frank Olson, a U.S. Army scientist, was found dead on the sidewalk outside the Statler Hotel in New York City. A few days later, his death was ruled a suicide. Twenty-two years later, the Rockefeller Commission, set up by President Ford to look into the CIA's illegal domestic intelligence operations, announced that Olson had been the subject of a CIA experiment, during which he was administered a dose of LSD. The Rockefeller Commission claimed that Olson jumped out of the hotel window in the midst of an LSD-induced psychosis, but Olson's son Eric thinks he was murdered because he was appalled by the human experimentation that was going on and prepared to blow the whistle on it. "The use of hallucinogens, hypnosis, electroshock and other procedures in an attempt to control the way people behave was," according to Eric Olson, "the CIA's equivalent of the Manhattan [atom bomb] Project."[52] According to the authors, who are British,

> The long-term aim of these experiments with mind-altering drugs is thought by those who have studied the MK-Ultra programme to have been to ensure the dominance of Anglo-American civilization in what eugenicists call the "war of all against all – the key to evolutionary success." Brainwashing would be used not only to defeat the enemy but to ensure the compliance and loyalty of one's own population.[53]

The link between encounter groups and the Anglophile intelligence establishment also gives some indication of how the techniques of psychological warfare would get used after the war. Christopher Simpson in his book *The Science of Coercion*, lists the Office of Naval Research as one of the major conduits of government money into academe for the funding of psychological warfare.[54] He goes on to call the people interested in psychological warfare a "reference group" rather than a "conspiracy," but the distinction is largely semantic. At the heart of psychological warfare studies was a group of men, largely alumni of the wartime OSS and Ivy League secret societies like Skull and Bones at Yale who had migrated into the mainstream media and the large foundations. This group shared the concerns of the anglophile elite about the "Catholic problem," as articulated by Paul Blanshard, and were in a position to do something about it. John T. McGreevy has shown convincingly that Paul Blanshard, in spite of his reputation elsewhere as an anti-Catholic bigot, enjoyed the all-but-universal support of this influential class of people at the heart of the WASP ruling-class elite. John Dewey praised Blanshard's "exemplary scholarship, good judgment and tact."[55] In a symposium sponsored by the American Unitarian Association convention on May 25, 1950, McGeorge Bundy, the quintessential establishment figure of the '50s and '60s, praised Blanshard's book as "a very useful thing."[56]

The same people who were concerned about the "Catholic problem" were also heavily involved in communications theory, which included things like encounter groups, which was in turn a front for psychological warfare. "The evidence thus far shows," according to Simpson,

> a very substantial fraction of the funding for academic U.S. research into social psychology and into many aspects of mass communication behavior during the first fifteen years of the cold war was directly controlled or strongly influenced by a small group of men who had enthusiastically supported elite psychological operations as an instrument of foreign *and domestic* policy since World War II. They exercised power through a series of interlocking committees and commissions that linked the world of mainstream academe with that of the U.S. military and intelligence communities. Their networks were for the most part closed to outsiders; their records and decision-making processes were often classified; and in some instances the very existence of the coordinating bodies was a state secret [my emphasis].[57]

The connection between the people concerned about the "Catholic problem" and the people involved in psychological warfare becomes all but inescapable when we learn that the two most important sources for funding for psychological warfare during the cold-war years were the Russell Sage Foundation and the Rockefeller Foundation. The Russell Sage Foundation was the publisher of Kurt Back's book on encounter groups, *Beyond Words*. The head of the social science division of the Rockefeller Foundation was Leland DeVinney, who co-authored the American Soldier Series with Samuel Stouffer, a well-known psychological warrior. In addition to using its own money to promote psychological warfare, the Rockefeller Foundation was a conduit for CIA money, channeling at least $1 million in CIA funds to Hadley Cantril's Institute for International Social Research. "Nelson Rockefeller," according to Simpson, "was himself among the most prominent promoters of psychological operations, serving as Eisenhower's principal adviser and strategist on the subject during 1954–55."[58]

Once again the Rockefeller family becomes the crucial nexus in understanding not only the identity of the class (or ethnic group) which was instrumental in the creation of psychological warfare but why it was created and against whom it would be used. The Rockefeller family, perhaps more than any other wealthy family in America, assumed the leadership of the WASP class in this country. The Rockefellers' concerns became their concerns and vice versa. According to Thomas Mahl,

> These were the people sociologist C. Wright Mills later identified in his book *The Power Elite* (1956). The United States, wrote Mills, was controlled not by the mass of its citizens as described by democratic theory, but by a wealthy Anglo-Saxon Protestant elite from Ivy League schools. In a flurry of caustic reviews, critics, often Cold War liberals, heatedly denied that there was such an elite.[59]

When William Stephenson, the British secret agent known as Intrepid, was sent to the United States to set up the British Security Coordination, the intelligence operation that was created to bring America into the war on the side of England, he did so knowing that he had the tacit if not overt support of a very influential class of people. It was this ethnic group which supported Planned Parenthood and psychological warfare, and since this class looked to the Rockefeller family for leadership it was natural that Stephenson should turn to the Rockefellers for support and that they would respond generously. Stephenson's concerns were the Rockefellers' concerns, and the Rockefellers' concerns were the concerns of the country's ruling elite. Hence, it should come as no surprise where Stephenson established his American headquarters. Shortly after arriving in the United States,

> Stephenson took over the thirty-eighth floor of the International Building in Rockefeller Center, which the Rockefellers, anxious to help, let for a penny rent. This was a convenient address. Several British agencies promoting intervention were also housed here. The British Press Service was located on the forty-fourth floor. The British intelligence front group Fight for Freedom located its operations on the twenty-second floor in the same building, also rent-free.[60]

With the Rockefellers providing tacit leadership, the WASP ethnic ruling class was concerned, as Arthur W. Packard had said, about "differential fertility," which is why they supported the eugenics movement and its propaganda arm, Planned Parenthood. Concern about differential fertility was just another way of saying concern about Catholics, since Catholics at this time did not use contraception, and the Catholic Church at this time, backed by the big city political machines and spokesmen like Msgr. John Ryan, was the most formidable opponent to the decriminalization of contraception. Concern about eugenics, in other words, meant concern about "the Catholic problem." Once the war against fascism was won, the WASP establishment turned its attention to its main demographic and political domestic opponent, namely the Catholic Church. If the WASP establishment which was instrumental in the creation and prosecution of psychological warfare was locked in a knock-down drag-out political struggle with the Catholic Church over sexual and demographic issues, then it would stand to reason that they would use the former technique as a way of solving what they perceived as the latter problem. This meant dealing with Catholic education, which was the Church's most effective antidote to the "socialization" offered by the John Dewey-inspired public schools. That concern was manifested in a series of Supreme Court decisions beginning with *Everson* decision in the late '40s and culminating the Lemon decisions in the early '70s.

Paul Blanshard, it should be remembered, had some very pointed things to say about Catholic nuns and their relationship to Catholic education in his book *American Freedom and Catholic Power*. In thinking about Catholic education, the most important thing to keep in mind, according to Blanshard, is

> the fact that the economic structure of Catholic schools is threatened with collapse by the growth of modern liberalism among young Catholic women. The Catholic school system is essentially an enterprise of nuns who work without salaries. If the supply of nuns should be cut off, the system would rapidly disintegrate.[61]

The key to destroying the Catholic school system and thereby crippling the influence of the Catholic Church in American politics was to make sure that young Catholic women were "reared in the free and hearty atmosphere of modern America,"[62] which meant of course public schools and exposure to the sexual liberation that lay at the heart of Blanshard's conversion from a minister to a liberal activist. The key was to promote "emancipation" among young Catholic women because "if the present attitude of emancipated Catholic young women continues, the hierarchy may ultimately be forced by economic pressure to turn over a large part of its private-school system to democratic public control."[63]

In July of 1967, the forty-three nuns who had been elected to represent the various chapters of the Immaculate Heart order met at Montecito, where they authorized large-scale experimentation, citing as its justification the *motu proprio* which Paul VI had issued less than a year earlier. One month later, they issued a statement saying that as of June 1968, "no Sister of the Immaculate will be assigned to a teaching position who does not have certification."[64] On October 16, 1967, fresh from a trip to Rome where she had conferred with Cardinal Suenens of Belgium, Sister Anita Caspary met with

Cardinal McIntyre and presented him with the order's resolutions. Cardinal McIntyre construed the statement on teacher certification as an ultimatum which imposed on him an arbitrary and mandatory deadline. Instead of capitulating to their pressure, McIntyre told Caspary that he would consider another date but if the nuns insisted on their condition, they were "perfectly free to withdraw from the archdiocese."[65] When Sister Anita said she would resubmit the proposed changes in the order to another vote, McIntyre made it clear that he had no intention of having a religious order in his diocese "that did not have and practice a rule of life more rigid than that proposed."[66]

At this point the story appeared in the *New York Times*, which informed its readers that the IHM order would soon implement "liberal changes" in its rule. Caspary was quoted in a newspaper article which appeared on the same day she met with the cardinal as saying that "Sister Corita is the perfect example of what could be done in our Order."[67] Caspary went on to say that "we have many other sisters like her, and we hope to have even more diversity and freedom."[68] McIntyre, in other words, was learning about the nuns' intentions at the same time the readers of the *New York Times* were, a fact that caused relations between the cardinal and the nuns to go from bad to worse.

The *New York Times* article marked the beginning of the publicity campaign which the IHM nuns were to wage against the cardinal and Rome for the next two years. In it McIntyre was universally cast as the villain, while the nuns, whose order was undergoing psychological warfare which they themselves were at least in part funding, were portrayed just as universally as enlightened and progressive. Since the media were dominated by the same group which had promoted psychological warfare and Paul Blanshard's anti-Catholic campaign, the nuns were now being egged on in their confrontation with the cardinal archbishop of Los Angeles by people who saw the destruction of the order as a sign of progress. *The New York Times*'s religion writer, John Cogley, who would soon defect from the Catholic faith, wrote articles which epitomized the flavor of an Enlightenment morality play, which characterized most press accounts. The IHM nuns, according to his account, were "a liberal light shining in the ultra-conservative darkness of the Los Angeles archdiocese," and McIntyre's attempts to prevent the order from engaging in its own self-destruction were portrayed as "being as foolish as trying to hold back the dawn."[69]

Thus fortified by the *New York Times*, and perhaps emboldened to a new openness by the encounter groups she had been attending, Sister Anita continued to pour out her soul to sympathetic reporters, who urged the order on toward self-destruction in the name of renewal. Shortly after appearing in the *New York Times*, Sister Anita granted an interview to John Dart of the *Los Angeles Times*, calling her row with the cardinal a "major breakthrough" for Roman Catholic nuns in America. She said the "renewal will be more profound than any thus far announced for any American religious society of Catholic women."[70] While noting that "all the new measures are experimental in nature," she saw "little reason to suppose that those innovations which prove beneficial will not then be made permanent."[71] As for religious garb, Caspary said that no style would be adopted as normative, "but sisters engaged in varying occupations may wear varying habits suitable for their work."[72] Noting that the Immaculate Heart Sisters have in mind nothing less than a profound redirection of their communal lifestyle, *Commonweal* labeled their proposals "landmarks."

On October 23, 1967, Sister Anita informed McIntyre that the IHM leadership had "unanimously reaffirmed by secret ballot the content of the total document."[73] Caspary then went on to inform his eminence that the new rule which the IHM nuns had just adopted was "deeply Christian and expressive of the kind of religious life in the community to which we are committed."[74] McIntyre may have thought the nuns were committed, or he may have thought they ought to be committed, but his eminence was not impressed with the rule of life they were proposing, informing Sister Anita that he was not going to allow "our convents to become hotels or boarding houses for women."[75] Caspary, as a result, had to return to the IHM nuns and inform them that the Cardinal's reaction was "negative." It was at this point that the nuns first started talking about being "fired," a claim which quickly got picked up by the press. On November 15, the *National Catholic Reporter,* announced on page one: "McIntyre to oust 200 updating nuns" when in fact McIntyre had told them that they were free to withdraw if they could not accept the conditions which he established for work in the archdiocese. Joining the fray on the side of the nuns, Andrew Greeley, who had visited the nuns at Immaculate Heart College in 1965 and was evidently taken with the order's lifestyle, announced that the rules they had submitted to McIntyre were "sensible and balanced, and represent[ed] the path all religious are going to have to follow if they are to survive."[76]

Father Kieser soon found himself caught up in the battle as well. McIntyre's rejection of the proposed updated rule for the IHM order, fanned by sympathetic media attention, had precipitated a massive rebellion on the part of clergy in the archdiocese. Kieser had had the advantage of seeing first-hand the effects which both therapy and encounter groups were having on nuns like his friend "Genevieve," and yet was incapable of seeing what was going on as an assault against the order. Blinded by the categories which he adopted so uncritically from the media, Kieser joined the war against repression by becoming a member of what he termed "the underground church": "We brought in progressive speakers from other parts of the country, tried to embarrass the Cardinal into allowing a priests' senate, did everything we could to shore up the beleaguered Immaculate Hearts, and celebrated underground Masses."[77] Evidently learning nothing from what happened to "Genevieve," Elwood Kieser checked in for a stay at Esalen to get in touch with his underground self. By then Gestalt guru Fritz Perls was nearing the end of his stay at Esalen. In 1970 he moved to Canada where he founded his own Gestalt Kibbutz on Lake Cowichan. After undergoing a serious operation, Perls grew tired of the intravenous needles in his arm and started to remove them. When a nurse entered the room and told him to leave them alone and lie down, Perls replied "Shut up, you aren't going to tell me what to do," whereupon he got up out of the bed and promptly fell over dead. Perls's favored method for diagnosing sexual repression during his last days at Esalen was to place his tongue into the mouth of his clients, both male and female, for an extended session of French kissing. If he found an attractive young woman who seemed to be suffering from this malady, he would invite her to remove her clothes and join him in one of Esalen's hot springs.

Father Kieser doesn't tell us whether Perls diagnosed him for sexual repression; he also doesn't tell us how his stay at Esalen concluded. He mentions only that after he left Esalen, he

> took sensitivity training at Carl Rogers's Institute of the Person [*sic*; Kieser actually took the training at WBSI] in La Jolla. The communication in these sessions was sometimes deep and honest, and these groups frequently became close. At the end of each day, we would gather in the backyard of the Catholic chaplain's house at the university for the Eucharist. These Masses were intense and full of feeling. But the emotional highs could not last.[78]

By January of 1968, the archdiocese of Los Angeles was preparing for the departure of the IHM nuns from the school system. On January 8, Sister Anita attempted to draw the children's parents into the battle by stating her case in a letter which was sent to all of the pastors of parishes staffed by IHM nuns. When the Apostolic Delegate to the United States asked Caspary to refrain from discussing the matter publicly, Sister Anita responded by going on a lecture tour. That was followed by a letter-writing campaign which induced twenty-nine Jesuits to sign an open letter on their behalf. That in turn inspired an equal number of Jesuits from the same province to announce that they did not side with the IHM nuns. As a result of their efforts at communicating their case to the public, the IHM sisters, according to Msgr. Patrick Roche, had "succeeded in creating an atmosphere of confusion and unhappiness which baffles understanding."[79]

On February 21, 1968, acting with unprecedented alacrity for a Roman curial office, the Sacred Congregation for Religious handed down its decision, announcing that the nuns had to adopt a uniform habit, that they had to attend Mass every day, that the point of their education efforts was "to labor for the salvation of souls" and – cruelest cut of all – that they had to submit to the authority of the local bishop in this and other disputes. The reaction was swift in coming. On March 9, 1968, the *Pasadena Independent Star* announced that 525 of the 600 [*sic*] IHM nuns were planning to resign and form "a loose confederation of religious women." The nuns tried to mount another publicity campaign to get Rome to change its decision, but the petition drive upon which it was based fizzled, failing to get the 5,000 signatures they hoped for. A separate petition garnered the signatures of 194 prominent American churchmen, including Harvey Cox, author of *The Secular City* and Arthur Lichtenberger, presiding Bishop of the Episcopal Church in the United States and presumably someone who had the best interests of the Catholic Church at heart when he signed.[80] The net result of the squabbling was that the nuns who did not leave broke into two opposed camps, "neither of which was open to compromise with the other."[81] Eventually a legal settlement was reached, one which favored the liberal camp, which got most of the community property.

On July 29, 1968, just as the furor over the Immaculate Heart nuns was dying down, the Vatican issued *Humanae Vitae*, its encyclical reaffirming the Catholic Church's traditional ban on contraception, and a new furor arose, orchestrated by Father Charles Curran, a moral theologian at Catholic University in Washington, D.C., which made the nuns' story look like a tempest in a teapot by comparison. John D. Rockefeller III's attempt to change the Catholic Church's teaching on contraception had failed. His attempt to create an internal front in the Church, however, had succeeded. As a result of Rockefeller's efforts at Notre Dame, *Humanae Vitae* opened up an internal division within the Catholic Church which would last into the next millennium. Orchestrating a media campaign that both followed and dwarfed the one launched by the Immaculate Heart nuns, Charles Curran succeeded in persuading a majority of Catholics in the United States that *Humanae Vitae* did not constitute infallible Church teaching and that American Catholics could in good conscience use contraception. The liberal clergy collaborated with the Rockefellers in arriving at a solution to "the Catholic problem" based on widespread acceptance of contraception among Catholic married couples. Contraception became, as a result, the solution to the "Catholic problem" in two ways: First of all, it drove down the Catholic birthrate, which had been troubling Paul Blanshard and those who supported him since the end of World War II. Once Catholics adopted the contraceptive practices of the WASP ruling class, they were no longer a demographic threat. Secondly, the contraceptive divided Catholics into two groups: liberals who accepted it and conservatives who did not, and with this division Catholics lost the political clout they wielded in the days of Msgr. John Ryan.

During the summer of 1968, at some time between the time when the turmoil over the nuns was dying down and the turmoil over *Humanae Vitae* was just beginning, W. R. Coulson was team-teaching a graduate course with Carl Rogers when he noticed that Rogers stopped what he was doing and broke down and cried in front of the class. What brought the tears to Rogers's eyes was the impending break-up of his daughter Natalie's marriage to Lawrence H. Fuchs, a professor of politics at Brandeis University. The full story wouldn't come out until 1980 when Natalie, taking back her maiden name, told the story of her "liberation" from her marriage and family in a memoir entitled *Emerging Woman*. Natalie had decided to take courses with her husband's colleague, Abraham Maslow, in 1958, the same man who had written that the most authentic people were the most instinctive in 1949 but by 1968 was having second thoughts over "Esalen-type, orgiastic, Dionysian type education." Apparently Natalie Fuchs latched onto the former Maslow and not the latter, for in her memoir she would describe not only leaving her family and husband, but also her sexual affairs with numerous men, including impromptu debates with their enraged wives, as well as her discovery of masturbation, as well as a long account of taking LSD under the guidance of Lois Bateson at Esalen. Lois was the wife of Gregory Bateson, former husband of Margaret Mead, and like his ex-wife a major player in the field of psychological warfare.

"The encouragement of Abe Maslow helped me gain courage to become a student,"[82] Natalie wrote in her memoir, and now Carl Rogers was faced with inescapable evidence of the sort of behavior his psychological techniques were creating. Encounter groups were beginning to give evidence that they were a lot like nuclear fission, which is to say a mixed blessing at best and something potentially toxic to anyone who came in close proximity to them at worst. Like Wilhelm Reich unsheathing a plug of radium at Rangeley in Maine, Carl Rogers was beginning to see the toxic contamination that encounters were wreaking on those exposed to their effects. Harold Lyon was an East Coast associate of Rogers's assistant in the late 1960s and early '70s, and after attending an encounter group with him in New York City, Lyon began to take their message to heart. In 1977 Lyon wrote a book in which he attempted to document the effect of encounter on his spiritual life:

> I have grown to the place where I now have what might be called "a religion of the self." I believe that most of the answers are within myself and that learning to tap the love and beauty and strength within myself is really a worshipping of the inner self. In essence, I believe in God. God is within each of us. We are all God. . . . I now meditate to the god within my own inner self, and each time I meditate, I discover new resources of boundless love and beauty within myself.[83]

Shortly after becoming God, Lyon, who was a federal education official at the time and the author of *Learning to Feel, Feeling to Learn: Humanistic Education for the Whole Man*, was arrested for sexual offenses and soon thereafter got written up in a book on "sex addiction." After his arrest made the front page of the *Washington Post*[84] Lyon lost his government job and went to jail, where he underwent a second conversion during which he decided that he wasn't a god after all and converted instead to Christianity. Now Lyon will not allow his psychology books in his house, fearing that they will contaminate someone else and cause still more damage.

James Kavanaugh enjoyed a brief moment of fame during the mid-'60s after writing an ephemeral best-seller called *A Modern Priest Looks at His Outdated Church*, in which he pleaded for, among other things, Catholic acceptance of contraception. Shortly after his book came out Kavanaugh stopped being a modern priest, leaving the priesthood and becoming a psychotherapist. Shortly thereafter, he stopped being a therapist as well when his license was suspended after he was charged with sexually molesting his patients.[85] In 1970, thirteen of Rogers's students and followers founded the (in retrospect, aptly named) Center for Feeling Therapy and after a short while were planning to export it to Europe when a scandal intervened causing all thirteen founding members to appear before the California board of medical inquiry to face charges that some of them had engaged in the sexual molestation of their patients, forcing those who became pregnant to abort their children.[86]

There may have been other reasons for Carl Rogers's tears. At around the same time he learned of the collapse of his daughter's marriage, he also learned that sensitivity training courses were now becoming mandatory at universities across the country. The political takeover he fantasized had arrived, and it was being perpetrated not by the right-wing nuts Rogers had warned his readers about but by the touchy-feely left, using an instrument he himself had developed. That chain of events had convinced Rogers, in Coulson's words, that "compulsory sensitivity training would simply be wrong," but he could no more stop that chain of events than he could put his daughter's marriage back together. The encounter groups which he had been so instrumental in creating, had taken on a life of their own, and now in the hands of therapists less scrupulous than he, they were causing a good deal of psychic damage.

"My understanding," Rogers said, "had always been that people could choose this course or not, as they wished. To think that you are required to take this course and the encounter groups that go with it offends me very, very deeply, . . . right now, I'm involved in one of the major fights of my professional life to try to obtain freedom, real freedom, for a group that I happen to like. And that's why I was so weepy and upset when I was speaking about the value of freedom last week. And if you think that was some kind of act, that I was talking passionately about freedom and at the same time compelling you people to be here – you don't know me. Nobody is going to be in this course because they are compelled to be."[87]

Today, unfortunately, compulsory sensitivity training is common in academe and industry, as well as in government and church work, in spite of Rogers's objections. As long as Rogers remained in control of the encounter, it remained within certain bounds of propriety, but Rogers could not be in charge of all encounters, nor could he prevent his less scrupulous colleagues from exploiting them for their own ends. All that Rogers could say, according to Coulson, is "Well, I don't do that." To which his colleagues would say, "Well, of course you don't do that, because you grew up in a an earlier era, but we do and it's marvelous. You have set us free to be ourselves."

Rogers felt this way because he knew that the encounter was an intrinsically manipulative exercise. Since Rogers was familiar with the origins of the encounter group, he knew it got its start as part of the post-World War II psychological warfare project. He knew as well that associates like Jack Gibb had training in this area, and he knew that the situation could easily be exploited by people less scrupulous than he. The encounter group, he wrote in his book on that topic,

> may all too easily fall more and more into the hands of the exploiters, those who have come onto the group scene primarily for their own personal benefit, financial or psychological. The faddists, the cultists, the nudists, the manipulators, those whose needs are for power or recognition, may come to dominate the encounter group horizon. In this case I feel it is headed for disaster. It will gradually be seen by the public for what it would then be: a somewhat fraudulent game operation not primarily for growth, health and constructive change, but for the benefit of its leaders.[88]

Rogers knew that T-groups were intrinsically manipulative because the group members were telling him this themselves:

> In a recent workshop, when one man started to express the concern he felt about an impasse he was experiencing with his wife, another member stopped him, saying essentially, "Are you sure you want to go on with this, or are you being seduced by the group into going further than you want to go? How do you know the group can be trusted? How will you feel about it when you go home and tell your wife what you have revealed, or when you decide to keep it from her? It just isn't safe to go further." It seemed quite clear that in his warning this second member was also expressing his own fear of revealing himself, and his lack of trust in the group.[89]

Carl Rogers clearly felt that the group could be trusted, but his belief was based more on "faith" of some sort than on an empirical judgment he had arrived at after a careful examination of the facts. Rogers, like his intellectual forebear Ralph Waldo Emerson, was an ex-Congregationalist in whom the concept of original sin had simply evaporated. That was his religion and, once he stopped counseling people who were demonstrably ill, that was the regimen he imposed under the guise of indirection upon the people with more traditional Augustinian views who ended up in his encounter groups. Arnold Green had raised the whole idea of encounter groups as a form of social control in an article entitled "Social Values and Psychotherapy" which had appeared in the *Journal of Personality* in 1946. "Rogers claims," Green wrote, "that the therapist must possess no moralistic or judgmental goals whatsoever. Yet it is interesting that in every single case he describes as successful the client always attaches himself to goals that would meet the hearty approval of any Methodist minister."[90]

Rogers was stung by the criticism and responded directly in his book *Client-Centered Therapy*, which appeared five years later. "Neither in practice nor in theory can we go along with the comment by Green that client-centered counseling is simply a subtle way of getting across to the client the cues which indicate approval of cultural values. His hypothesis could be partially maintained in some of the early client-centered cases, but it does not appear to be supported at all in the present handling by experienced counselors. As client-centered therapy has developed, it becomes more and more clear that it cannot be explained on such a basis."[91]

Rogers made the same point in a 1962 debate with B. F. Skinner, who claimed that therapy, no matter how non-directive it claimed to be, was still "operant conditioning." Just how subtly manipulative Rogers can be comes across in this account of the forty-four-year-old woman "who has been dominated all her life by her mother."[92] Since the woman is "too terrified to tell her mother of spending an evening with a male friend (George) whom she loves,"[93] Rogers sets out to liberate her from her mother, in probably the same subtle fashion in which he set out to liberate the nuns from their convent by reinforcing all of the choices which favor eliminating either responsibility or family bonds in favor of those values which promote "independence." When the woman finally shunts her mother, who is in her late seventies at the time, off to an apartment to live by herself, Rogers applauds her actions using terms which bespeak the values he wants to promote: "She has at last cut the umbilical cord and managed to say (not without some difficulty I am sure), 'I am a separate person from you.' She is now truly celebrating her Independence Day, her Fourth of July."[94] If this passage isn't an example of providing "cues which indicate approval of cultural values," then what is it?

If abandoning her mother also means abandoning the moral order in sexual matters, then this is a price which Carl Rogers clearly thinks she ought to pay. Did the encounter group, Rogers wonders, "change her attitudes, toward man-woman relationships, moving her away from orthodox morality? Did it make her emotionally unstable? Without any doubt, the answer to all of these questions is a resounding yes! It proved terribly unsettling; it caused deep unhappiness and depression; it changed her relationship with her mother in such a way as to drive her mother into hysterics; it brought wild fluctuations in her emotional reactions; it caused her to be more acceptant of her loving feelings toward a married man."[95]

If it did all those things, Rogers still thinks it was a small price to pay if it enabled her to divest herself of another shackle, in this case, her aged mother. And what does freedom look like? It looks a lot like rootless consumerism. The woman now lives alone, leading "her independent life in her apartment," where she has "been furnishing it, enjoy collecting art . . . and . . . beginning to do a little creative cooking and a small bit of entertaining."[96] Even if he was unaware of what he was doing, Rogers was acting as an agent of socialization for the rootless suburbanites of consumer culture, who felt that consumption was more important than family ties. Even Kurt Back, who is positively disposed toward encounter groups, sees them as based on a value system which fosters rootlessness and consumption over family ties and self-restraint. According to Back, the areas where encounter groups flourished most were

> the new suburbs and the West, especially California . . . pointing up the direct connection between mobility and sensitivity training. Encounter groups have become a respectable "lonely hearts club" for newcomers or those without roots in a community. The new norms of immediacy and letting oneself go to a strong emotional experience are conducive to rapid integration into a new setting as well as departure without emotional damage.[97]

Rogers was hardly being non-directive when he persuaded the forty-four-year-old woman to get rid of her mother and have an affair with a married man; he was subtly manipulating her by manipulating her passions. His therapy was based on a whole set of cultural values, ones which coincided hand-in-glove with the consumer culture of the times, but which were at the same time a set of values whose existence he could never admit to himself. Rogers's values were based not on long-term relationships and moral commitment but rather "possibilities for the rapid development of closeness between and among persons, a closeness which is not artificial, but is real and deep, and which will be well suited to our increasing mobility of living. Temporary relationships will be able to achieve the richness and meaning which heretofore have been associated only with lifelong attachments."[98] Encounter groups provided a way for suburbanites to attain instant intimacy. If they became sexually involved, if their marriages broke up, if the whole family disintegrated into rootless individuals passing aimlessly through each others lives – as it had in the case of Natalie Rogers and her lesbian daughter Frances – it was a small price to pay in exchange for peak moments in the encounter group.

In a system like this, sexual fidelity is not a prime value. Again, Rogers never tells us that he is denigrating the moral order; we pick it up by osmosis from the subtle cues he throws into the conversation, as when he mentions the film *Rachel, Rachel* and praises Rachel for being

> willing to accept her sexual feelings and give herself to a young man whom she has unquestionably idealized. The love affair is not what one

would call a success and she is deserted by her boyfriend, but nonetheless she has learned that it is only by taking a risk that she can genuinely encounter another human being. This learning stays with her and strengthens her as a person to move out into the unknown world.[99]

Rogers never used words like "good" and "bad," but his therapy, like all actions, is predicated on his understanding of those terms. Non-directive therapy was successful in evading the defenses neurotics erected to defend themselves against the truth about themselves they both wanted and didn't want to know. It was, therefore, *a fortiori* even more effective in insinuating a form of social engineering and domination into what claimed to be therapy for the healthy.

Carl Rogers never really admitted that the experiment with the IHM nuns ended in failure. This fact admits of two explanations: 1) that he couldn't admit the fact to himself, or 2) that he thought the project was a success. The second possibility is more sinister than the first, and brings up the possibility that Rogers thought he was doing the nuns a favor by liberating them from their "narrow convent rooms." The second possibility also brings up a related question. Was Rogers using the encounter group as a form of psychological warfare against the Catholic Church? W. R. Coulson, who worked with Rogers, is still wrestling with the issue with the benefit of over thirty years of hindsight. In a 1994 interview in *Latin Mass* magazine, Coulson claimed that he, Rogers, "was probably anti-Catholic; at the time I didn't recognize it because I probably was too. We had a bias against hierarchy." In an even more recent interview with the author, he said that because Rogers had so many Catholics working for him, he was "prudent about saying anything about Catholicism." Finally, Coulson settled on a third possibility. "On the other hand, he didn't have to say anything. If he could draw Catholics into the process, the result was inevitable. That was more congruent with what he believed." The evidence was there for Rogers to see, and he cited it in his books. Encounter groups fostered "individual independence, openness, and integrity" and as a result are "not conducive to unquestioning institutional loyalty." As an example of the effect encounter groups have had, Rogers tells the reader that "priests and nuns, ministers and professors, have left their orders and churches and universities because of the courage gained in such groups, deciding to work for change outside the institution rather than within it."[100]

Far from being apologetic about encounter groups causing nuns and priests to lose their vocations, Rogers sees this outcome as unabashedly positive, and in portraying it as such, he gives some insight into his own religious orientation, and how he would bring about the demise of the Immaculate Heart order and think he was doing a good thing. As the above passage indicates, the key to understanding Rogers's intentions in the Immaculate Heart affair is understanding his religious views, since in the absence of criteria like health Rogers could only apply his personal religious and moral views as the direction which his therapy should take, no matter how subtly he directed the conversation and disguised his intentions.

Rogers, a Congregationalist who went to Union Theological Seminary for two years, then dropped out and fell under John Dewey's spell at Columbia Teachers' College, was always reluctant to talk about religion and especially reluctant to talk about his own religious beliefs. In an article which appeared in 1985, Rogers quotes with approval a workshop participant who said of her encounter group, "I found it to be a profound spiritual experience. I felt the oneness of spirit in the community. We breathed together, felt together, even spoke for one another. I felt the power of the 'life-force' that infuses each of us – whatever that is."[101] Whatever it was, it prompted Rogers to a momentary reflection on the transcendent. "I am compelled to believe that I," he wrote, "like many others, have underestimated the importance of this mystical, spiritual dimension."

Noticing Rogers's penchant to describe religion in a way that invariably made it antithetical to organizational structure and hierarchy, Thomas C. Oden described the human potential movement as a new form of eighteenth-century Pietism in his 1972 book, *Intensive Group Experience: The New Pietism*. Common to both encounter groups and Pietism was a belief that religion was not something associated with any organization. Rather, it was a new form of consciousness which enables a "direct transcendental experience of God" through a carefully orchestrated emotional experience involving the religious group – either the Quaker meeting with its absence of liturgy and dependence on spontaneous assertion at the behest of the Holy Spirit or the Methodist revival with its excess of emotion. In each instance, the true power for a change in the social order must stem from the individual. Once this movement spreads it often takes on the form of reform political movements, as was the case with Abolitionism in New England. Either way, in both Pietism and encounter groups, experience always has priority over authority. The only authority which is recognized is the one which works by stealth under the cover of the movement of the spirit, either of the Holy Spirit or the spirit of the individual. The prime concern is to bring about a transformation of consciousness which in turn will bring about a transformation of the culture at large resulting from the erotic and mystical experiences that individuals have during their encounter. Taking his cue from Oden, Michael Weber noticed similarities between sensitivity training and the pietist version of public confession. "The Father Confessor," according to Weber, "because of Luther's concept of the priesthood of all believers, can now be a woman or a brother; it is the group which hears and heals, which protects and which accepts. Now the penitent has been rescued from the darkness of the confessional and the cold virtuosity of private spiritual training."[102]

Weber's description of democratized confession brings up the connection between Pietism and Illuminism, a connection others have noticed as well. Agethen notes that it was "above all in the Protestant states of Northern Germany" where both Pietism and Illuminism spread most rapidly, and that the spread of both led to widespread acceptance of the ideas of the Enlightenment. Common to both Illuminism and Pietism was an inclination to involvement in psychologisitc self-analysis and a sophistication of psychological understanding as it applied to things like repentance for sin and willingness to confess, which were in their turn based on examination of conscience and self-observation.[103] All of these manifestations were absorbed via the religious practices of eighteenth-century religious sects like the Quakers into the psychic repertoire of sensitivity training.

The same sort of techniques were still in use among the Quakers as late as the 1950s. Morton Kaplan tells the story of teaching at Haverford College, a Quaker school outside Philadelphia, during the 1953–54 academic year, when it was discovered that one of the students was prejudiced against Negroes. Teams of teachers and students, according to Kaplan, held sessions with him over a period of a year until he affirmed that he was no longer prejudiced. The Quakers may have termed it "gentle persuasion," but Kaplan saw in it a form of brainwashing and an early version of the orchestration of small-group peer pressure which would find its ultimate expression in sensitivity training. "They could not understand," Kaplan said of the Quakers, "that I thought it better for the young man to keep his prejudices than that he be subjected to such coercive brainwashing."[104]

One of the most sinister of all foundations, the Josiah Macy, Jr., Foundation, traces its penchant for funding psychological warfare and things like the birth-control pill to "the Quaker traditions of simplicity, sincerity and devotion to the service of mankind" as manifested in the life of its founder Kate Macy Ladd. Similarly, Kleiner finds it unsurprising that sensitivity training has religious undertones, considering the family backgrounds of the psychological warriors who created it. Douglas McGregor's father, for instance,

> had been a midwestern reverend; he came out of the great American Protestant liberal tradition, the tradition of Quaker meetings, community barn raisings, and Ralph Waldo Emerson. Perhaps it was not coincidence that so many other NTLers – including Lee Bradford, Ken Benne, Ron Lippitt, and the eminent T-group advocate Carl Rogers – had similar backgrounds. . . . Traditional religious pietism added an element of both force (in the sense of moral legitimacy) and direction to the social engineering that had been programmed into encounter groups from the beginning, something that was not lost on experts on brainwashing like Edgar Schein, who was "well aware that certain exercises, tasks set up by the facilitator, can practically force the group to more of a here-and-now communication or more of a feelings level.[105]

Since the confessional elements in T-groups meant they were a form of Illuminism, that also meant that they were a form of social control, but because T-groups were refracted through the lens of American Pietism, those who made use of the techniques could absolve themselves of any sinister intent, which is what seems to have happened in the case of Carl Rogers. Rogers was simply liberating nuns from their convents where they were slaves to the whore of Babylon. Luther got his wife this way, so why should Americans raised in that tradition see it as reprehensible? T-groups democratized Illuminism. They were also a typical expression of the English ideology, which eschewed overt force and preferred Masonic style secret organizations which could engineer consensus from behind the scenes.

In his role as the non-directive group leader always claiming that he had nothing to force on his unwitting clients, Carl Rogers was a classic expression of the English ideology and the religious movements which epitomized it and the secret societies which implemented it. Like Newton, Rogers framed no hypotheses. What claimed to be non-directive and client centered was in reality, however, an Illuminist technique that accomplished psychic control through a subtle manipulation of the passions. (In the epigones who emulated Rogers, the manipulation was not so subtle.) In proposing encounter groups as simultaneously a form of both exoteric liberation and esoteric control, Rogers was proposing something completely compatible with both his religious tradition and his ethnic heritage, and in bringing it to bear on a willing if unsuspecting group of California nuns, he was using this technique in a way that was compatible with the interests of the ethnic group to which he belonged, an ethnic group which was then engaged in a cultural civil war that was being waged against the Catholic Church.

Rogers was even more reluctant to talk about his ethnicity than he was to talk about his spirituality, but Natalie Rogers, in her inimitable way, fills in some of the gaps here.

"I grew up," she writes in *Emerging Woman*,

> adamantly agnostic, pragmatic, a skeptic about anything religious or spiritual, with a down-to-earth orientation. I scorned notions of god, of life after death. I dismissed the possibility of psychic phenomena and denied that dreams might be an important part of life. In college the only spiritual philosophy I ever accepted was Emerson's view of the Over-Soul.[106]

In describing the moral code according to which her parents raised her, Natalie says that she "grew up in an era where many of us were given the following messages: 'Girls stay virgin until married'" but also "birth control and family planning are the right and duty of responsible couples."[107] At another point, Natalie praises her mother as "an outspoken leader for the right of women to choose whether and when they will get pregnant."[108] At another point, Natalie Rogers criticizes her mother for not going far enough in educating her away from moral prejudice in matters sexual: "Although she was a progressive on the political scene – giving her time to the Margaret Sanger/Planned Parenthood movement – I didn't find her views of my behavior very liberal. . . . Between age forty and sixty you missed an opportunity to become more fully you – more independent in your art work or fully effective with Planned Parenthood."[109]

Taken as a whole, Natalie's comments show that members of her family were typical examples of the progressive WASP, their ethnic group, which had adopted the use of the contraceptive, and then as a result of that got drawn into eugenic warfare against those groups which didn't use contraception, most notably blacks and Catholics. Support for Planned Parenthood meant for Natalie's parents' generation support for the eugenic crusade that characterized the WASP ethnics' concern about differential fertility. Having adopted the use of the contraceptive as part of their moral code, they were too ethnically provincial to see that it contradicted the rest of their sexual morality. The only coherence this world view had was ethnic. As a result, the Rogers family joined in the great WASP ethnic project, the eugenics movement as prosecuted by Planned Parenthood as it turned into the anti-Catholic crusade of the post -war period. W. R. Coulson never remembers discussing his large family with Rogers, but his wife remembers getting a matchbook with Planned Parenthood's address on it after the birth of their seventh child. His wife also clearly remembers Helen Rogers giving a donation of $10,000 to Planned Parenthood.

Because of his support of Planned Parenthood, Carl Rogers was engaged in ethnic conflict with the Catholics who were his clients in therapy. That he didn't advertise the fact was due in equal measure to his personality and his ethnicity, neither of which was comfortable with overt or antagonistic declarations of clear intent. "A facilitator," Rogers wrote in his book on encounter groups, "is less effective when he pushes a group, manipulates it, makes rules for it, tries to direct it toward his own unspoken goals."[110] In a videotaped interview Rogers told Warren Bennis in 1976 that

> Nobody knows where I'm going until I've gone so far they can't stop me. . . . And really in large measure, that's the way I've gone through life. Nobody (Rogers laughs) knows where I'm going until I've gone so far they can't stop me, that's one thing . . . and also I don't like to be interfered with on the way. . . . It's a strange word to apply because it seems contradictory, but I'm in a way sort of stealthy."[111]

In the same interview Rogers said that he got the idea of indirection from his parents, something which he gave a revolutionary twist: "One of the fascinating things about my parents' control was that it was so subtle that it did not seem oppressive. I was a good boy, but that seemed to be the way I should be. It didn't seem as though I had to be this way against my will."

Bennis: "Yeah, that's neat. Marx said the sign of a truly oppressed person is when they don' t know they're oppressed.

Rogers: "There's a lot of truth to that.[112]

Rogers here evidently forgot that moral behavior is natural because, in scriptural terms, it is written on the heart. By the time he was being interviewed, Rogers had completely internalized the Watsonian view that man had no nature. As a result everything was conditioning, and every conditioning technique was potentially brainwashing. What Rogers knew that Watson didn't was how to be subtle, how to be (to use his word) "stealthy." Because his influence was always indirect, Carl Rogers was virtually irresistible. Not too long after a speech he gave in 1969 at Sonoma State listing the qualities of the man of the future, one of Rogers's colleagues referred to him as a "quiet revolutionary," and Rogers applied the term to himself thereafter until his death.

Natalie seems to have tried to learn the same lesson from her father without as much success. "My father, Carl Rogers," she wrote in her memoir, "has always been the earth from which my philosophical roots have been nourished. He values the integrity of each individual not only in his words but in his way of living. He has never dominated, controlled, or tried to push me. I have felt accepted and appreciated even when we disagree."[113]

No one is ever coerced in Rogerian therapy. Or, better put, no one is ever aware that he is coerced in Rogerian therapy. This subtle system of control based on the manipulation of passion was, however, full of unintended consequences for the ethnic group which used it to wage cultural war on their opponents. One of the unintended consequences was the generational decline of those who made use of it. That decline began with the sexual liberation of Carl and Helen, though that is certainly not how they saw it, when they became involved in the use of the contraceptive. That fateful step led to divorce, adultery, masturbation, drug use, compulsive promiscuity in their daughter Natalie's generation, and it led to lesbianism in the next generation in Frances Fuchs, her daughter, who is now active in lesbian politics in California.

The WASP elite chose contraception and psychological warfare as a way of defeating the Catholics and maintaining their hegemony over the culture that was slipping out of their grasp, but in the final analysis their strategy backfired because in the end it was their own children who adopted the tenets of sexual liberation even more avidly than the sexually repressed Catholic priests and nuns, and in adopting the tenets of sexual liberation, they put themselves out of existence. In the end, the sexual revolution was just another word for the anti-Catholic campaign, and Carl Rogers, the modern pietist, tried to destroy them by liberating them, or he tried to liberate them by destroying what made them Catholic.

"Never in my life before that group experience," one Catholic priest wrote,

> had I experienced "me" so intensely. And then to have that "me" so con-

firmed and loved by the group, who by this time were sensitive and reacting to my phoniness, was like receiving a gift I could never have hoped
for, because until then I never dreamed that it could exist.

. . . I was in the seminary at that time and have since been ordained a
priest. But within my vocation as a priest there have been profound
changes both inside me and outside me. Inside, I began to grow from a boy
to a man. Outside I became much freer in relation to authority and human
respect. Inside me I was so much more present to myself and therefore to
others that my work as a counselor and a therapist shot up one hundred per
cent in its effectiveness.

Anyway I began to become. . . . I have so much more hope in the future
of man. Because if we can touch one another as persons the way it can
happen in an encounter, then "redemption" begins to happen for all of us,
and we emerge from a death-like existence of loneliness and diminution to
a possibility of fully-aliveness. I can really say "yes" to mankind, because
I have discovered in a deeply personal way, in a way which I can deeply
feel as well as think, that each person in the world is an abundant reservoir
of life and love that only needs to be tapped to be made available for
self-nourishment and for the refreshment of others.[114]

Other priests were not so sanguine. Weber tells the story of a seminarian
in Germany who was exposed to sensitivity training and as a result "feeling
like a tool without a will of my own in the hands of the group leader. In each
group exercise, I wanted to win his attention and recognition. I couldn't pray
anymore and I also suffered from psychosomatic disturbances."[115]

On December 10, 1968, Thomas Merton had just finished the morning
lecture at a conference he was attending in Bangkok, Thailand, when he announced to his audience, "I think I am going to disappear." Merton had resolved the sexual crisis that was threatening his vocation to the priesthood by
pulling back from his affair with M., partially at least because he feared that
he would become "enslaved to the need for her body." He felt in part as well
that the "objective fact of my vows is more than a juridical obligation. It has
deep personal and spiritual roots. I cannot be true to myself if I am not true to
so deep a commitment."[116] After making his cryptic announcement to the attendees at the conference in Bangkok, Merton went up to his hotel room
where he inadvertently pulled a defective fan on top of himself in the bathtub
and died of heart failure and burns caused by electric shock.

At around the same time, Sister Mary Benjamin, IHM, decided that she
was going to leave the Immaculate Heart nuns. In discussing her decision,
she never mentions the effect that her sexual practices might have had on her
decision. All she can mention is the images that her sexual practices had created in her mind, turning the convent's walls into a "prison."

"The fear that drew me there for protection had lost its power. The convent could do nothing now but hold me back. My spirit was starving for the
life I had surrendered as a child. It was time to catch up. I felt like a long distance runner about to run the first mile of her marathon."[117]

For the first lap in her spiritual marathon, Sister Mary flew to New York in 1970 with a suitcase of second-hand clothes. While there she became sexually involved with a guy named Larry, who sucked his thumb in his sleep. She also had sex with a number of other people from whom she contracted sexual parasites. Then, tiring of her boyfriend she moved off into a series of even more transient lesbian relationships, until, finally, at the prompting of political and spiritual forces she was never able to understand, she "proclaimed [her]self a dyke." At that point, she went off in search of the lesbian equivalent of the community she had abandoned when she left the Immaculate Heart nuns. By the mid-'80s she was living alone again, oftentimes in a tent in the woods, where she claimed to be communing with spirits.

Ann Campbell's life followed much the same trajectory after she left the convent in 1971. Ann had her first sexual experience in 1969 when she was 30 years old. The results could have been predicted by Wilhelm Reich:

> Gradually I backed away from Mass and the sacraments. By then there was so much flexibility in scheduling that no one noticed. I would sometimes go to confession and allude to my transgressions; at times I went guiltily to Communion and asked God to forgive me. This went on for two and a half incredible years.[118]

When she finally left the convent in 1971, Campbell "claimed that my convictions on social justice, racial equality, peace and intellectual freedom were the reasons," something which she finds less persuasive fifteen years after the fact than she did at the time. The real reason for leaving the convent was sexual: "I had finally acknowledged that my love for this woman was inconsistent with my vows. And since I judged this love to be incompatible with God's plan, I was prepared to pay the price in guilt and inner misery until I could extricate myself. My theology of freedom had deserted me."[119]

Unable to find comfort in either religion or the rejection of religion, Campbell tried to drown her anguish in alcohol, but all the alcohol succeeded in doing was give her the "sensation that I had lost control over my own life's direction."[120] Eventually, "drinking to blot out feelings became a nightly ritual" as the isolation which her "liberation" from convent life and family ties brought about became intolerable. When ex-nuns like Ann Campbell really needed counseling, there was no one there to do the counseling. And in retrospect, what could people like Carl Rogers have offered her? She was already liberated; she was already free of sexual repression. What more did Illuminist counseling have to offer, once the victim had adopted the categories which were to bring about her happiness? By 1970 the Immaculate Heart nuns were gone from the scene. The operation was a success; the patient died.

At around the same time that the IHM order fell apart, Harry the Therapist and Genevieve the ex-nun got married, after Harry's divorce came through. At around the same time, after his stay at Esalen and Rogers's Center for the Person in La Jolla, Father Kieser decided to undergo therapy at the hands of a therapist whose "general orientation was existential and Jungian, both of which I found simpatico."[121] Father Kieser's therapist

> made no attempt to interpret what I was seeing through the prism of his own set of dogmatic categories (as far as I know he had none). Nor did he ever suggest a course of action beyond the process of therapy itself. His job was to help me to discover the truth. It was my job, with the freedom of the newly discovered truth he gave me, to make the decisions.[122]

Like Father Kieser, the overwhelming majority of American Catholics never knew what hit them. They lost a cultural war that they didn't even know was being waged against them. Because the Catholics lost that cultural war, the victors in that struggle would use the same techniques – psychological warfare, feminism, population control, pornography, encounter groups – to subject larger segments of American life and larger segments of the world to their control. Sensitivity training would be introduced to the public schools over the next thirty years, where it would be presented under various guises – as "character education," "drug education," and "sex education" under brand names like DARE, Deciding, Tribes, Valuing Values, Choices and Decisions, the Michigan Model, Magic Circle, Me-ology, Quest, Here's looking at you, Values and Choices, Project Charlie, DECIDE, etc. Assaulted by this form of "social engineering at its worst," American students would be "regimented into shock-troops of a new politically correct millennium."[123]

Part III, Chapter 14

New York, 1969

By the late '60s Jack Kerouac was famous as the founder of a movement which he felt had become increasingly alien to what he believed. Whenever he would tell people like Mike Wallace that "beat" was short for beatific, an incredulous or embarrassed silence would ensue and the subject would get changed. During the fall of 1968, Kerouac was invited to pontificate on the then-emerging hippie movement by William F. Buckley, the conservative icon, on his TV show *Firing Line*. "The hippies," Kerouac opined while sipping scotch from a coffee mug, were "apparently some kind of Dionysian movement." Moving effortlessly if incoherently from defending the hippies as "good kids," Kerouac launched into an attack on fellow beatnik, Lawrence Ferlinghetti for perverting what Kerouac saw as essentially Catholic and beatific into "the beat mutiny, the beat insurrection, words I never use, being a Catholic." Kerouac was becoming increasingly alienated from the movement he had been used to launch. His piety may have increased but his drinking increased along with it, making the piety seem incongruent at best and ludicrous at worst. Before long the drinking would take its toll. On October 20, 1969, Jack Kerouac began hemorrhaging at his Florida home from varicose veins in the esophagus, the result of years of heavy drinking. In the middle of the night, his mother took him to St. Anthony's Hospital, where he died the classic alcoholic's death at 5:30 AM on October 21, 1969.

Just before appearing on *Firing Line*, on the way up to the studio in the elevator, Kerouac spoke briefly with Ed Sanders, one of founding members of a New York band known as the Fugs, who wanted to tell Kerouac how much his writing and life had inspired him. Kerouac's response was short and to the point. "Get the fuck off my back, kid," he said. At around the same time that Kerouac made his last TV appearance, another member of the Fugs by the name of Tuli Kupferberg met a Yugoslavian filmmaker by the name of Dusan Makavejev. Makavejev was in New York because he had just got a grant from the Ford Foundation. After meeting Kupferberg and his friends, Makavejev got an idea for a film, a documentary of the sort that would have "redeeming social value," which is to say a film with lots of naked women engaging in sexual activity. It would be a film on Wilhelm Reich, because New York was the center of the cultural world just then, and in the center of the world Wilhelm Reich was making a comeback. Reich had died in prison in Lewisburg, Pennsylvania, in 1959 after being convicted of selling orgone boxes to the FDA. He died convinced that President Eisenhower was sending Air Force planes to watch over him and still hoping that he would get a grant for his work on orgone energy from the "Rockerfellows." The Reich who came back from the dead ten years later was a reincarnation not of the man who sold orgone boxes and supported President Eisenhower. The Reich who came back from the dead was the man who did sex-pol work in Berlin in 1930.

By the time Reich had been re-discovered by the New Left in 1969, he had been dead for ten years, but that fact was irrelevant, because the Reich the cultural revolutionaries were interested in promoting had stopped writing in 1933 anyway. On January 4, 1971, Christopher Lehmann-Haupt wrote a review of the new Farrar Straus edition of *The Mass Psychology of Fascism*, which announced in effect that the Reich revival had begun in earnest. "Wilhelm Reich," Lehmann-Haupt proclaimed, "the Austrian sexologist and inventor of the so-called orgone energy accumulator, has made a comeback." Reich, according to the review, was the father of youth culture, the sexual revolution, and the feminist movement. Kate Millett's book *Sexual Politics* was written under his influence. Beyond that, Reich was better at reconciling Freud and Marx than Marcuse, especially by expounding his "credo that sexual man was man liberated from his need for authority, religion, and marriage." Reich, in other words, "makes considerable sense," at least to someone sympathetic to the goal of sexual liberation. Lehmann-Haupt was, in fact, so enamored of Reich's vision of sexual liberation he was even willing to take a second look at his theory of orgone energy. "Perhaps it's time to reconsider all of Wilhelm Reich," he concluded.

Four months later, on April 18, 1971, the *New York Times* returned to Reich, this time devoting a feature-length article in their Sunday magazine to his thought. In "Wilhelm Reich: The Psychiatrist as Revolutionary," David Elkind described how student communards in Berlin pelted the police with soft-bound copies of Reich's *The Mass Psychology of Fascism*. (Was it compassion or frugality that kept them from using hardbound copies?) Reich "was being resurrected everywhere in Europe as a hero/saint to students demanding social reform," and "many American young people" were "now discovering that Reich is very much their kind of Revolutionary too." This was the case because his message was more appealing to the American Left, who felt that they could bring down the state by sexual license without the sublimation urged by Freud or the political revolution urged by Marx.

Over the summer of 1971, Dusan Makavejev released the film he had begun while in the United States on a grant from the Ford Foundation called *WR: Mysteries of the Organism*. Like *I am Curious (Yellow)* it juxtaposed pornography with political harangue, thereby assuring the viewer that it had redeeming social merit and would escape obscenity prosecution. The film also showed footage of Tuli Kupferberg stalking people on the streets of

New York City wearing an army helmet and carrying a toy M-16. The political message was unmistakable. The New Left was going to repudiate both Stalin and U. S. Imperialism in a mystical convergence based on shared indulgence in sexual appetite. It was, like, make love, not war, or some more prolix version of the same thing, all traceable, according to Makavejev, to Reich's influence. "He was a kind of prophet of a new time," Makavejev told *Film Quarterly* in their Winter 1971 issue. "He started the sex-pol movement in Germany; in 1930 they had about 30,000 members and organized lectures all over Germany. Reich's ideal was that the Communist Party should organize youth around dance halls, not to get young people to dull political lectures – to find young people where they are."[1] Which meant, of course, encouraging masturbation. "Sex-economic clinical experience teaches us," Reich wrote in '30s,

> that those who never had the courage to masturbate have the most unfavorable prognosis. Sexual feelings have been suppressed (perhaps even for a while successfully), the sexual apparatus has not been used, and then when authoritarian society finally permits gratification, the apparatus fails; it has become "rusty."[2]

The American revolutionaries were now busy making sure that their "apparatus" didn't become "rusty," by finally summoning, if not the will to bring down the state, then certainly "the courage to masturbate." Makavejev devoted a good deal of his film to the work of Betty Dodson, "the well-known drawer of erotic drawings and painter of erotic paintings," whose specialty was teaching women how to masturbate because it made women feel, "you know . . . very liberated."[3] To give some sense of historical continuity under Reich's influence, the dates "Berlin, May 1, 1931 . . . Belgrade, May 1, 1971" flash on the screen and then Betty Dodson comes on and talks about how a woman who was in "this women's lib group together, it's a consciousness raising group . . . really had no masturbatory experience or background! She was in her early thirties . . . she didn't masturbate, she was totally dependent on . . . a man, a partner to make orgasm, which is a lousy posture to be . . . and she started to practice masturbation and she was amazed at . . . at some of the things that happened to her and her orgasm became much more intense."[4]

In case his readers hadn't seen the film, David Elkind made the same point in his *New York Times* article. "Reich noted," he tells us, "that whenever the patient reported that he had masturbated with complete satisfaction that his symptoms lessened. Reich proceeded to analyze the patient's guilt over masturbation. When this chronic guilt was alleviated and the patient could masturbate regularly with complete gratification, his symptoms subsided to the extent that he could work and socialize to a degree not possible for him before."[5] The film, of course, devoted its sexual footage to showing the well-endowed Milena having sex with soldiers and then declaiming

Reichian mumbo-jumbo like: "Body tissue deprived of life energy turns cancerous. Cancer is the hysteria of cells condemned to death. Cancer and fascism are closely related."[6] Footage of masturbation, it turns out, is not as stimulating as real sexual activity.

With Makavejev's film, the Reich boom reached its high-water mark. The techniques of manipulation that Reich's character analysis enabled continued to be refined in places like Esalen by people like Fritz Perls and would get applied in unlikely places like seminaries for religious. Perls learned about Reich through Paul Goodman and together they created what came to be known as Gestalt Therapy, which was Reich's theories, especially those involving "body armor" in action. Michael Weber argues that Reich's theories via Perls's Gestalt Therapy eventually became a covert form of social control that wrought serious damage in religious orders in Germany, just as Reich said they would. They also made equally destructive inroads in American corporate and academic life, where ice-breaking exercises like blind milling became part of the repertoire of psychic manipulation. "Liberation from repression" had become a powerful tool for social control, both in small groups and in the mass media.

Elizabeth Wurtzel never mentions Reich in *Bitch*, her '90s memoir, but she mentions feminism, which was, as Kate Millett's book made clear, exoteric Reichianism. The Consciousness-raising sessions of the '70s were, as Makavejev said, direct descendants of Reich's sex-pol work in the '30s. Wurtzel does, however, talk extensively about using sex as a form of social control, something which she calls, in her inimitable way, "pussy power."[7] "Delilah," she tells us, "had the right idea. . . . Delilah embodies the failure of this male prerogative when it comes to regulating human emotions."[8] Samson and Delilah "offer the first example," according to Wurtzel," of what we now call sexual politics. Samson is unbeatable militarily, a discovery the Philistines make to their chagrin, but through his infatuation with Delilah he becomes "enslaved to his dick"[9] and, as a result, easily defeated. Sex is a form of political control; this is the lesson that Israel learned from Samson's demise, and indeed they learned it throughout the Bible, usually the hard way, which is to say, by being punished by military defeat after falling into idolatry, which was an excuse for illicit sexual activity.

Wurtzel is onto something here. Or is she? No sooner does she praise Delilah as "a precursor to all strong, modern, willful women . : . women who do just what they want," the kind of woman, in other words, which Wurtzel aspires to be, than she is full of ambivalence about the object of her praise. Wurtzel admires women who use sex as a weapon, and she especially admires the character Madonna plays in *Body of Evidence* because "she kills with her pussy," but at the same time she is full of misgivings when she tries to apply this lesson to her own life. Once again, the issue comes down to the relationship between power and control, between reason and appetite. Do those who capitulate to their desires control them, or are they controlled by them?

"I am completely free," Miss Wurtzel tells us,

> and as far as my life goes, I have all the power. In fact, I have turned thirty in an era when for the first time in history a woman can feel as unencumbered and unbound as I do. And yet, for all the power I command in not being some man's dependent appendage, I generally walk around through life feeling pretty powerless.[10]

As with most feminists, Wurtzel has difficulty reading her own texts. Delilah, as in our own day when her spiritual descendants write stroke books for chicks, is an agent of the priests of Dagon. Delilah doesn't control the power she wields any more than Wurtzel does. The power controls her. Hence Wurtzel's sense of powerlessness even after the liberation from repression occurs, or, better said, especially after the liberation from oppression occurs. The only power Wurtzel retains unequivocally is the power to mess up her own life, a power which she has evidently exercised repeatedly. "When I have a man in front of me," she tells us, "even one I really like, one who is quite literally putty in my hands and whatever else, I feel the incredible urge to use the power he has given me to ruin his life."[11]

And her own, one might add, because the only way one finds fulfillment in life is by sharing it with someone else, by, in effect, giving that life over to someone else and having the other person do the same thing. That mutual giving is the essence of sexuality. Masturbation is the most basic violation of that truth. Using masturbation (or any other form of sexual vice) as "liberation from repression" is like using suicide as the antidote to murder. No one else can kill you because you killed yourself. In triumphing over repression, you have defeated yourself by enslaving yourself in the name of liberation.

Wurtzel is not alone in learning this truth the hard way. Reich learned the same lesson in slightly more complicated fashion. On January 5, 1951, Reich unsheathed a gram of radium in his laboratory at Organon in Rangeley, Maine, thereby contaminating the entire area and exposing everyone there to radiation sickness. He thought that orgone energy would counteract the effect of nuclear energy, but it turned out that the opposite was true. In the final analysis though, his "Oranur" experiments were nowhere near as toxic as his sexual experimentation. In both instances, he tried to control one of the primal forces of nature and in both instances the forces ended up controlling him.

By the late '70s, the Reich boom was over, looking at the dawn of the Reagan Era a little bit like the leisure suit gathering dust at the back of the closet. The left might say, and indeed it has said, that Reagan was the tyrannical reaction to the excesses of the sexual revolution, but they still seem incapable of accepting the rationale, adumbrated in Plato, which would explain the change.

The real reaction, however, wasn't political. It was cultural and inchoate. Sex led to horror. *Alien* was the sequel to *Deep Throat*. By 1979, no one thought oral sex was fun anymore. The ladies testifying at the Meese Commission made that point unmistakably clear. Katie Roiphe remembers the same era, feeling the "general atmosphere of anxiety and apprehension" even though "there was no biological threat to which we could attach our vague premonitions of disaster, no herpes, no AIDS."[12] The diseases were in retrospect the least horrific of the sequelae flowing from the "liberation from repression" that was the sexual revolution. The real source of horror was the release of appetite from rational control and what that did to otherwise normal human beings. In seeking "liberation from repression," the culture discovered that the punishment fit the crime in an uncanny way; in fact, the punishment was the crime. Liberation was slavery at best; more often than not, it was death too. "I remember," Katie Roiphe wrote in her memoir of the time, *Last Night in Paradise,*

> taking a bright yellow paperback of *Looking for Mr. Goodbar* from my parents' bookshelf and reading it more than once; I remember being haunted by the image of this naked woman bleeding to death on her bed. I remember also the image of her sitting in the bar, sipping her white wine, pretending to read a book, and waiting to pick up a strange man, an image strangely shadowed by my knowledge of what was going to happen to her. Her death seemed somehow natural for an act of random violence. It also seemed to hold some implications about my own life, about the men, bars, wine, and strangers in my future, that I only dimly understood. I wouldn't have been able to explain the danger I felt, curled up on my parents' chintz couch reading the cheap paperback, but I felt it nonetheless.[13]

Along with *Alien*, *Looking for Mr. Goodbar*, which was made into a film in 1978, was one of the seminal events of the late '70s, when sex turned into horror on a pan-cultural basis. Roiphe might have understood the trajectory better if she had read Plato's *Republic*, but a school system which promotes masturbation is not going to waste its time undermining its efforts to enslave its students by teaching Plato. Eric Voegelin, who has read Plato, thinks that his description of

> the transition from the democratic to the despotic soul may well be considered the masterpiece of Platonic psychology. In the democratic state of the soul, all appetites are on the same footing and compete with another for satisfaction. . . . This state of amiable, and perhaps aesthetic, rottenness, however, exhausts itself, and now the last abyss of depravity opens. For beyond the ordinary luxuriance of desires lie the ultimate lusts which "stir in a soul in its dreams" but ordinarily kept down by the controls of wisdom and law. In dreams, the beast goes on its rampage of murder, incest and perversions.[14]

The trajectory is, nonetheless, clear. The democratic soul, which frees itself from all restraint in pursuit of sexual gratification, is followed by the tyrannical soul, which brings horror and perversion, which etymologically means denial of the truth. "The decomposition of the well-ordered soul," according to Voegelin, "leads, not to disorder or confusion, but to a perverted order. It seems that Plato was acutely aware of the spirituality of evil and of the fascination emanating from a tyrannical order."[15]

The tyrant is addiction in a metaphorical sense – in other words, passions which demand to be satisfied and command the rational being who should control them to do their bidding – but the tyrant can also be construed in a very literal sense as the man who rules over the people who are corrupted by their passions, through the agency of those very passions. The man who is controlled by his appetite is also controlled by the man who controls his appetite for him. In general we think of the age of tyranny as short-lived, and we think of the tyrants that way too. Robespierre, Hitler, Stalin all presided over the despotic reaction to democracy run amok. Stalin's reign, however, could hardly be considered brief in human terms. And with him, we begin to discern a more disconcerting possibility. What if someone were smart enough to maintain the perverted order indefinitely?

The first principle to be recognized is that "sexual life is not a private affair," Reich tells us. "The sexual restructuring of man, for the establishment of the capacity for full sexual pleasure, cannot be left to individual initiative but is a cardinal problem of all social existence. . . . The whole population must acquire the secure feeling that the revolutionary leadership is doing everything it can to guarantee sexual pleasure, without reservation, without any ifs and buts."[16]

The real question, the one posed by Aldous Huxley, is whether the regime in which "normality is redefined as perversion and perversion as normality" will get clever enough to refine the techniques of servitude to become so pleasurable that no one notices the horror any more or has the will to object.

Part III, Chapter 15

Notre Dame, Indiana, 1970

In June 1970, the Reverend Theodore M. Hesburgh, C.S.C., president of the University of Notre Dame, received the American Association of University Professors's Alexander Meiklejohn Award for his "outstanding contribution to the cause of academic freedom." Hesburgh was the first Catholic ever to receive the award, and the AAUP went out of its way to explain that this fact was not some fortuitous afterthought in its deliberations. Hesburgh was being rewarded for defending the integrity of the Catholic university against the predations of the Catholic Church. Hesburgh received the award because he believed, as he had stated in the Land o' Lakes statement three years before, that a "Catholic university must have true autonomy and academic freedom in face of authority of whatever kind, lay or clerical, external to the academic community itself." Lest there be any doubt about which authority might prove most threatening at Notre Dame, the AAUP cited Notre Dame's stance in the wake of *Humanae Vitae*, the 1968 encyclical of Pope Paul VI which labeled contraception immoral. Hesburgh was praised because "external ecclesiastical controls at some other Catholic universities have not been permitted at Notre Dame."

The sentiments were edifying if one shared the ideological view which spawned them, but they were deceptive as well. Hesburgh after all did claim to be defending the Catholic university against "authority of whatever kind," but in practice – and the AAUP award makes this clear – the main defense was against the meddling of the Catholic Church, specifically the curia in Rome. Hesburgh makes this fairly explicit in his autobiography, *God, Country, and Notre Dame,* where he dedicates an entire chapter to the topic of academic freedom. "In 1954," he writes, "we had a classic confrontation over the issue of academic freedom, with Notre Dame on one side and the Vatican on the other." In this confrontation, Father Hesburgh sided with the liberal American Jesuit John Courtney Murray against every liberal Catholic's favorite villain since the time of Vatican II, Alfredo Cardinal Ottaviani. In this Enlightenment morality play, the forces of American light and progress triumph over the forces of Italian darkness and dogma. It was a bit like a Henry James plot as told by a less refined mind.

Reading Hesburgh's autobiography, one comes quickly to the conclusion that this American-progressive-versus-Roman-authoritarian paradigm was not only representative; it was normative; it was exhaustive. "Authority of any kind" was Hesburgh's way of saying the Vatican. As long as he could define the struggle in those terms he would look good to everyone but people in the curia. Certainly he was looking good to the people at the AAUP in 1970. But casting the conflict in those terms tells in effect only half the story. Rome was hardly the most serious threat to academic freedom at the time. Curious by its absence from Hesburgh's largely self-serving account of himself as a defender of academic freedom is any mention of the role which foundations played at Notre Dame at the time. One gets the impression that the only people who threatened academic freedom were aging clerics like Cardinal Ottaviani or that the progressive types who staffed places like the Ford, Rockefeller, and Carnegie foundations at the time were completely disinterested when it came to how their money was to be spent.

In many respects, Notre Dame's attitude toward academic freedom was a one-way street. It blocked traffic from Rome as a way of expediting commerce with New York and Washington, homes of the foundations and the Supreme Court respectively. Hesburgh's position looks plausible as a defense of academic freedom only when he gets to present the evidence. Notre Dame's attitude toward the showing of Martin Scorcese's film *The Last Temptation of Christ* on campus in 1989 is a good indication of this double standard in action. When a number of people, professors and students alike, claimed that the film was blasphemous and that a Catholic university had no business exposing undergraduates to scenes of Jesus Christ and Mary Magdalen having sexual intercourse, Hesburgh's successor, Rev. Edward Malloy, C.S.C. wrote to the effect, "The movie, *The Last Temptation of Christ*, is but one of a wide range of films to be shown on campus this year. I am confident that those who choose to view it will have plenty of opportunity for discussion and analysis, including from a Christian perspective." The message is clear: some people might consider this sort of thing disrespectful of the person of Jesus Christ, but academic freedom prevails at Notre Dame, even when it involves highly offensive portrayals of Christ's non-existent sex life. The undergraduates at Notre Dame duly absorbed the message that they were to be scrupulously tolerant when it came to matters venereal, even if they involved aspersions cast on their Lord and Savior. "So what Jesus did in his private life is totally up to Him," one sophomore opined at the time.

Twenty-five years earlier, however, when Notre Dame was run by the man destined to receive the Meiklejohn Academic Freedom Award, the university had a different attitude toward films and censorship. In December 1964, the University of Notre Dame, with President Theodore M. Hesburgh co-signing as a plaintiff, filed suit in New York Supreme Court seeking to enjoin Twentieth-Century Fox from releasing *John Goldfarb, Please Come Home*, a film starring Shirley MacLaine which revolves around the complications which arise when a rich Arab purchases the Notre Dame football team. Hesburgh claimed that the film was guilty of "knowingly exploiting for private benefit the high prestige and good name of the University without consent and over its objections." Father Hesburgh went on to claim that distribution of the film would "cause irreparable damage" to Notre Dame.

If Notre Dame's willingness to haul people into court is any indication of what it holds sacred, then it is clear that the person of Jesus Christ finishes a distant second to Notre Dame's football team. It is also clear that academic freedom at Notre Dame suffered from the same double standard in its application. When it came to "authority of whatever kind . . . external to the university itself" there were no enemies to the left. The only threat came from the Vatican.

On September 30, 1970, three months after Father Hesburgh received his award for defending academic freedom, the Commission on Obscenity and Pornography founded by HR 2525 three years earlier issued its report to the press. What would eventually come to be known as the Lockhart Commission had been called into existence three years earlier, largely over concern about the flood of obscene material which the *Roth* decision had unleashed nine years before.

On April 20, 1967, hearings were held in Washington on HR 2525, a bill creating a commission to be known as the Commission on Obscenity and Pornography. Representative Dominick V. Daniels of New Jersey, who presided over the meeting, decried "the inexorable flow of noxious, hard-core pornography [that] continues to fill our newsstands, pour unsolicited into our homes and threatens to contaminate young and impressionable minds." One of the main purposes of the commission was "to study the effect of obscenity and pornography upon the public – and particularly minors – and its relationship to crime and other anti-social behavior." Members of Congress had been feeling heat from their constituents, especially about obscene materials coming unsolicited through the mails as the '60s were plunging toward a chaotic close. Previously agreed-upon taboos were being broken regularly in underground newspapers and on the stage. In the *Roth* case, the Supreme Court stated that obscenity was not speech protected by the First Amendment; however, the justices established a formula for ascertaining obscenity that was to prove virtually impossible to apply: "whether to the average person, applying contemporary community standards, the dominant theme of the material taken as a whole appeals to prurient interests." Later the court further weakened its own formula by saying that the community in question was the entire country and not some definable geographical entity like a county or congressional district. The result of the Supreme Court's uncertain trumpet was a veritable flood of obscene material being let loose through the mails, and the virtual occupation of whole sections of certain cities by the forces of vice for a profit. The burden of dealing with the first wave of the assault fell upon the shoulders of the politicians.[1]

"I suspect," testified Senator Karl Mundt of South Dakota, "that half of my mail comes from mothers who are frantic because mail pours into their home and there is no way to stop it. I have the feeling that those who raise the plaintive cry of censorship, do it for purposes other than to guarantee constitutional rights. I hope you disregard those arguments. It is the false shield placed in front of people who refused to come out and argue for filth on its merits. . . . They try to hide behind those noble arguments as they go down in the mire and continue to try to enhance and increase juvenile delinquency in this country."[2]

The crucial issue, then as now, was the effects of pornography upon those for whom it is not intended. Mundt refers to those who "say this has no appeal to normal people, and abnormal people have a perfect right to get through the mail what they want. But they send it to the normal children of normal families all over this country, without any request from these families to change normal human beings into abnormal people."

It was clear that no one was going to come out and testify for the benefits of pornography – not yet anyway – but the job of controlling it was made more difficult by the hesitations of both liberals and conservatives. Lawrence Speiser, director of the Washington office of the American Civil Liberties Union, called for scientific studies "to determine if there is a causal relationship between the reading and the viewing of noxious printed or pictured material and the commission of crimes or other antisocial acts." Up until the point when it became clear that Congress was going to establish the commission no matter what the ACLU thought, the ACLU opposed the very idea of a commission at all. Bowing to the inevitable, Speiser sought to direct it along a path congenial to ACLU interests – a tactic that was to prove much more successful – by demanding that they follow "scientific" criteria: "While scientific study is needed," Speiser opined, "anything less than that is to be feared."[3] Just what "scientific" meant would become clear when the entire Lockhart Commission showed up at the Kinsey Institute for instruction in matters sexual.

The bankruptcy of contemporary conservatism was made readily apparent in the testimony of columnist James J. Kilpatrick, then editor of the *Richmond News Leader* and author of a nationally syndicated column in the *Washington Evening Star.* "Put on my choice between dirt and censorship, I would opt for the dirt," Kilpatrick told the committee. "The dirt, at least, can be seen, and I can avoid it, or sweep it up or paint over it or accept it as one of the smelly irritants of a free society. But you cannot always see censorship in action; you may know of its silent exercise. Those of us who believe in a free society, and all of us are committed to it, ought to believe in a society that is free for ideas that are offensive to us."[4] Kilpatrick eventually came down for laws against obscenity, but they were so qualified by moral and intellectual agnosticism as to be all but worthless suggestions. Conservatism at this point in the country's history meant libertarianism, which meant basically hands off what was considered private behavior. It would take another decade and a half of bitter experience before people would realize that pornography is anything but private behavior. It was first of all big business, and secondly a prime source of antisocial activity.

Having gone to school at the Kinsey Institute, the commission found that "there are no great fortunes to be made in stag film production."[5] Pornography was a $500 million dollar industry then and by the time the Meese Commission decided to undo the damage the Lockhart Commission had wrought, it grossed around $8 billion a year. In addition, the Lockhart Commission concluded that "patterns of sexual behavior were found to be very stable and not altered substantially by exposure to erotica" and that "exposure to erotica had no impact upon moral character." Based on its analysis of sex crimes in Denmark, the Lockhart Commission concluded that "the increased availability of explicit sexual materials has been accompanied by a decrease in the incidence of sexual crime." In conclusion, the Lockhart Commission decided that there was "no evidence to date that exposure to explicit sexual materials plays a significant role in the causation of delinquent or criminal behavior among youth or adults. The commission cannot conclude that exposure to erotic materials is a factor in the causation of sex crime or sex delinquency."[6] What began as a mandate from Congress to curtail pornography ended up as a soap box from which the porn industry proclaimed libertarian clichés and anti-family propaganda. Pornography was, in fact, good for you. "The use of pictorial depiction of explicit sexual activity with discussion," the commission opined, "provides not only information but also a reduction of inhibition and embarrassment in talking about sex." Citizen action groups, however, "can seriously interfere with the availability of legitimate materials in a community by generating an overly repressive atmosphere and by using harassment in seeking to implement their goals."[7]

As a result of their "investigation" the Lockhart Commission recommended "the repeal of existing federal legislation which prohibits or interferes with consensual distribution of 'obscene' [their quotes] materials to adults." Two members of the commission, Otto N. Larsen and Marvin E. Wolfgang, recommended that no restrictions be placed on the circulation of obscene materials to juveniles. "There is no substantial evidence," they wrote in their minority report, "that exposure to juveniles is necessarily harmful. There may even be beneficial effects."[8]

The most vehement reaction to the report's conclusions came from within the commission itself. Rev. Morton A. Hill and Winfrey C. Link issued a minority report blasting the majority document as "a Magna Carta for the pornographers."[9] They accused the report of being "slanted and biased in favor of protecting the business of pornography, which the commission was mandated by the Congress to regulate." Hill and Link then went on to show that commission chairman William B. Lockhart, appointed by then-President Johnson in direct contradiction to the guidelines established by Congress, and the general counsel appointed by Lockhart, Paul Bender, had long been members of the ACLU and had used the $2 million appropriated for the commission by Congress to guarantee that the findings of the commission would coincide with ACLU policy on pornography.[10] This meant completely ignoring evidence from law enforcement officials and manipulating whatever scientific evidence was then available in order to come up with a no-harm conclusion. Running his own parallel investigation at his own expense, Hill came up with enough evidence on the harm of pornography to make his minority report the only really convincing document in the entire report. (Eventually it was the Hill-Link minority findings which were accepted by Congress and not the majority report, but by the time the report had made the news, the damage had already been done.) Unlike the majority report, the minority report allowed the testimony of law-enforcement officials. Herbert W. Case, a former inspector for the Detroit Police Department said, "There has not been a sex murder in the history of our department in which the killer was not an avid reader of lewd magazines." Detective Lieutenant Austin B. Duke of the St. Louis County Police Department reported, "I have never picked up a juvenile sex offender who didn't have this stuff with him, in his car or in his house."[11]

The Hill-Link findings were far from just anecdotal. Even without the "benefit" of fifteen years' inundation of hard-core pornography – the legacy of the Lockhart Commission – there was ample evidence that pornography did in fact cause deviant behavior. The Propper study, paid for by the commission itself, revealed "among younger age boys a very high relationship between (a) the age at which they saw a picture of sexual intercourse and (b) the age at which they first engaged personally in sexual intercourse.... Propper, in his study of 476 reformatory inmates . . . noted again and again a relationship between high exposure to pornography and 'sexually promiscuous' and deviant behavior at very early ages, as well as affiliation with groups high in criminal activity and sex deviancy."[12]

Citing a study by Davis and Braucht, Hill found that exposure to pornography was "the strongest predictor of sexual deviance among the early age of exposure subjects. . . . In general then, exposure to pornography in the early age subgroup was related to a variety of precocious heterosexual and deviant sexual behaviors."[13]

The Mosher and Katz study, also sponsored by the commission, "clearly support[s] the proposition that aggression against women increases when that aggression is instrumental to securing sexual stimulation (through seeing pornography)."[14] The Goldstein study, also financed by the commission, found that rapists were the group reporting the highest "excitation to masturbation" rates by pornography in the adult (80 percent) as well as teen (90 percent) years. Considering the crime they were imprisoned for, this suggests that pornography (with accompanying masturbation) did not serve adequately as a catharsis, prevent a sex crime, or 'keep them off the streets.'" Eighty percent of the rapists reported "wishing to try the act that they had witnessed or seen demonstrated in the pornography exposed to them." When asked if they in fact did follow through with such sexual activity immediately or shortly thereafter 30 percent of the rapists said "yes."[15]

Hill and Link then took the commission to task for the studies that it did accept, especially the notorious Kutchinsky study which purported to show that sex crimes decreased in Denmark after the legalization of pornography. "The fact is," Hill and Link write in the minority report:

> that in a society such as modern Copenhagen where premarital sex and illegitimacy bear no social stigma; where hardcore pornography is sold at every corner kiosk and at the "porno" or "sex shops" that dot the city, where live sex shows are legally conducted and exploited in the daily newspapers; where prostitutes block the sidewalks and wave from apartment windows, in such a society I am amazed that any sex crimes are reported. . . . The only reason for a 31 percent statistical decrease in sex crimes is the fact that what was previously considered a crime is now ignored or legal.[16]

Subsequent research into the effects of pornography has confirmed the findings of the Hill-Link minority report and have at the same time completely discredited the catharsis theory that was the foundation of the majority report. Exposure to pornography does not result in satiation, as the majority report claimed. It may result in satiation to a particular picture or film, but at the same time the viewer in becoming satiated simply requires a more bizarre form of stimulation to achieve the excitement he previously received with relatively "normal" pornography. In addition exposure to pornography creates in the viewer a fundamentally distorted view of sexuality that can lead to assaults on women. In their article "Massive Exposure to Pornography," published in 1984, Zillman and Bryant find that "massive exposure to pornography fosters a general trivialization of rape. It can only be speculated that this effect results from the characteristic portrayal of women in pornography as socially nondiscriminating, as hysterically euphoric in response to just about any and every sexual or pseudo-sexual stimulation, and as eager to accommodate any and every sexual request. Such a portrayal, it seems, convinces even women of the hyperpromiscuous nature of women."[17]

Part III, Chapter 16

Hialeah, Florida, 1972

In the early afternoon of October 28, 1972, when the Reich revival was in full bloom, the police dispatcher in Hialeah, Florida, got a call from a man named Harry, who claimed that his wife had become violent and needed to be subdued. When the police officer arrived on the scene he found the once famous pin-up model Bettie Page in front of the house beating her husband Harry with her fists and bellowing curses at him. After Officer Fitzpatrick led Bettie away to the back of the police car, he returned to the house to get a statement from Harry. When he returned to the car, he found Bettie in the back seat with her dress pulled up and her pants pulled down, masturbating with a hanger the officer had left in the car. His verdict was that the suspect was "out of her mind, completely berserk."[1]

Bettie was found unfit to stand trial and committed to a mental institution. Seven years later she was out on the streets again, this time living in California, when her neighbor saw her emerge from the bushes wielding an eight-inch-long serrated bread knife, which Bettie began to plunge repeatedly into the woman's body. When the woman's husband came to her aid, Bettie began stabbing him as well. Bettie had spent her adult life arousing the passions of others; now after a life of promiscuous relations with various men, she discovered that those same passions had taken on a life of their own and were now telling her what to do. "Desire doubled is love," the fifth-century B.C. sophist Prodicus had written, and "Love doubled is madness." In the expensive school of experience, the moderns were rediscovering what the ancients had known all along. "Excessive passion," according to Bruce S. Thornton's reading of that tradition, "is fundamentally a form of insanity, a destruction of the rational mind's control over the body, a suspension of reason's power that allows the soul to be overwhelmed by the chaos of the natural appetites and emotions."[2]

Bettie led a dissolute life beginning with her eighteenth year. While in high school she was one of the top students in her class and planned at the time to become a teacher. By the mid-'50s, when she was approaching forty, she had descended into psychosis. She had become incapable of finishing any of the many Bible courses she enrolled in and was a threat to the life and well-being of those around her. Foster gives all of the usual Freudian explanations, including the most plausible – the one, by the way, which Freud rejected as the seduction theory – namely, that she had been molested by her father as a child. No one should minimize the trauma associated with events like that, but by the same token, the trauma in this instance took on psychic importance the further away in time it receded, which is a good indication that it functioned as a screen memory for something more closely associated to the present, namely, her sexual behavior as an adult.

If the particulars of modesty are culturally relative, the consequences of lust are not. The first consequence of promiscuity, according to the order of being, is the dissolution of the self. The self is constituted by its relationships; the trauma of a father transgressing those boundaries might have been healed by an understanding husband in a permanent monogamous relationship, but that was not Bettie's fate. The easy money from the photo sessions must have made easy relationships seem equally inconsequential, but at a certain point psychic reality caught up with Bettie, and when it did the passions the self aroused at will began to assert their hegemony over a self that was no longer in a position to control them.

In 1957 Bettie simply dropped out of the New York pin-up scene and moved to Florida, where she became involved with a man thirteen years her junior. They eventually got married, but as with her other marriages, this one didn't last either, and with each failed relationship, we can see that the glue that held her personality together was becoming more elastic and less retentive. It was at this point in her life that Bettie got religion, as many women do. If she had been living in Corinth during the time St. Paul was writing to the formerly dissolute citizens of that city, she would have been told to keep her head covered and her mouth shut during religious services. Bettie never had any children; by the time she was approaching forty she must have realized that she never would have any and started to devote her spare time to raising plants by way of compensation. "She meticulously watered and cared for the plants," Foster tells us, "as if they were the children she never had."[3]

The religion Bettie eventually got had little to do with the morality traditionally associated with Christianity. Bettie was still good looking enough to pick up a man at a dance, which is what she did in Miami, when she met a divorced telephone lineman by the name of Harry Lear. She was still interested in marriage, which is what happened once again, but she was incapable of remaining married because her craziness keep intruding into the relationship until it finally destroyed it. In spite of studying theology at a number of Bible institutes, Bettie came to believe that there were seven gods, and she knew this because she would have extended conversations with them while locked in the bathroom. It was after an especially long conference in the home of an aging widow in California that Bettie rushed out of the bathroom with a serrated bread knife in her hand and proceeded to stab her neighbor repeatedly, almost killing her in the process.

Bettie was forty-nine years old at the time, and the policeman concluded that she was mentally ill, a judgment with which the court which committed her to a mental institutions concurred. But what is a mental illness? Psychiatrists of the Thomas Szasz school compare the term "mental illness" to saying that God has appendicitis. The mind cannot be ill because it is not a physical entity. In a Freudian age, the term has come to mean exculpation, and the "triumph of the therapeutic," to use the Philip Rieff's term. But what does mental illness mean? In addition to meaning the loss of behavior in conformity to the canons of what society calls civil, this state of mind means the inability of the self to integrate experiences and desires in a coherent pattern of behavior. If a healthy person is one whose self has hegemony over his desires, a mentally "ill" person is someone where the opposite is the case. By the time Bettie was forty-nine years old, her desires – whether concupiscible or irascible – had hegemony over her self. Bettie simply did what the voices, i.e., her out-of-control passions, told her to do. Rather than admit that promiscuity leads to this state unerringly, the culture which promotes sexual license chose instead to say that the monster they had created to satisfy their illicit desires was crazy and leave it at that. Bettie was found not guilty by reason of insanity and committed to a mental hospital. She was described as "mentally ill" when a better diagnosis might have been that her self had simply collapsed under the assault of her desires, to the point where the desires and not the self had taken charge of her behavior.

The culture which had turned her into an icon would rather not admit this fact because by admitting that it would be admitting culpability in her demise. Instead we find as the only explanation a radical discontinuity to the point of incoherence – she slept with all these guys; she went nuts – all smoothed over by the psychic numbing which fifty years of pornography created in those who consumed it. Bettie, we are told by the way, liked horror movies, but her biographer understands the connection between sex and horror every bit as little as Bettie herself, a lady who was doomed to live the trajectory she never learned to understand.

The consequences of extrapolating this sort of behavior to the culture at large have occurred to others as well. Philip Cushman writing in the May 1990 issue of *American Psychologist* describes the historical trajectory that usually gets denominated "liberation" by the sexual Whigs as "the emergence of the empty self." Unlike the Victorian self which is defined by relationships made possible by adherence to the moral law,

> the current self is constructed as empty, and as a result the state controls its population not by restricting the impulses of its citizens, as in Victorian times, but by creating and manipulating their wish to be soothed, organized, and made cohesive by momentarily filling them up. The products of the social sciences, and of psychology in particular, have often worked to the advantage of the state by helping to construct selves that are the means of control.

Cushman goes on to say that the configuration of the self which has emerged since the end of World War II is "empty in part because of the loss of family, community and tradition. It is a self that seeks the experience of being continually filled up by consuming goods, calories, experiences, politicians, romantic partners, and empathic therapists in an attempt to combat the growing alienation and fragmentation of its era."

The cultural paradigm of numbed decadence which Richard Weaver feared in *Ideas Have Consequences* has, in other words, become the cultural norm. The sexual engineers have created a world in which sexual excess led to madness with increasing regularity, but because the instruments of culture approved of this transformation by calling it "liberation," it was only rarely described in any accurate fashion. The numbness which resulted from the widespread dissemination of transgressive imagery of the sort that started with the photos of Bettie Page was turning people into sexual monsters.

Shortly before Bettie Page was apprehended by the Hialeah police, a young woman by the name of Linda Boreman was lying on a chaise lounge outside her parents house not far away in Fort Lauderdale, Florida, recuperating from a car accident when a high school friend from New Jersey drove up from Miami and introduced her to a man by the name of Chuck Traynor. Traynor was six years older than Boreman, and she found him slightly attractive. More than slightly attractive was his car, a burgundy Jaguar XKE, not the kind of car the people she usually dated usually drove. Traynor was unusual in other ways, although Boreman did not know that at the time.

Boreman had been raised in Yonkers by her policeman father and a mother who had sent her to Catholic schools, where she aspired first to be a nun and then to get married and raise a family. In Traynor, Boreman saw a way of escaping from under parental domination. It was a bit like jumping from the frying pan into the fire. Nothing happened on the first few dates. Then the seduction began in earnest. Traynor persuaded Boreman to have sex, and each time she agreed to his demands the ante got raised, and each time the sexual demands became more perverse and bizarre, the bondage increased. Traynor's sexual demands were a technique for extinguishing the self that had moral objections. Once that was out of the way, the sexual partner was turned into a sexual object, and the sexual object was turned into a sexual slave.

As part of his regimen of control, Traynor would regularly hypnotize Boreman and then get her to do things she would not otherwise have done under post-hypnotic suggestion. Claiming that it would help her to stop smoking, Traynor used hypnosis to eliminate Boreman's gag reflex and then taught her the fellatio technique that would make her famous as Linda Lovelace in *Deep Throat*, the top grossing porno film of all time. That, however, was in the future. In between naiveté and porno stardom, Traynor turned Boreman into a prostitute and used all of the instruments of control on her that pimps know to keep women in line. The result was that Boreman became, in her own words, a "robot,"[4] in many ways the fulfillment of the prophecy of the Marquis de Sade that "woman is a machine for voluptuousness." After a session which Traynor arranged with five men in a motel room in Florida, Boreman would claim, "I felt as though my self had been taken away from me. I was not a person anymore. I was a robot, a vegetable, a wind-up toy, a fucking and sucking doll. I had become someone else's thing."[5]

The use of sex as a form of domination would only deepen the longer she remained with Traynor, who eventually took her to New York, where the lofts of New York City that Bettie Page had known had taken a decided turn in the direction of degradation. It was while in New York City that Traynor arranged to the filming of Boreman having sex with a dog. The results were predictable. With each new degradation, Boreman slipped more completely under Traynor's control. That was, in effect, the main purpose of the degradation, to keep her docile and feeling, as she put it later, "totally defeated."[6]

After the episode with the dog, Boreman was taken to a party where her fellatio technique came to the attention of a porno film maker by the name of Gerry Damiano, who came up with the idea of doing a big-budget 35mm film based on Boreman's specialty. Six months later, Boreman, now under the name of Linda Lovelace, awoke to find that the world considered her not a prisoner in the white slavery business, but a star. By 1972 pornography had become respectable. It had become in the words of the New York Times, "chic," so chic in fact that the New York Times news staff spent their lunch hour viewing the film.[7] Joining the reporters from the Times in enjoying viewing Boreman being sexually assaulted were "Johnny Carson, Mike Nichols, Sandy Dennis, Ben Gazzara and Jack Nicholson, as well as some French UN diplomats who insisted on paying with traveler's checks."[8] All of these folks felt, according to the Times, that "there is no harm or shame in indulging their curiosity – and perhaps even their frankly prurient interest – by going to see Deep Throat."[9]

The courts evidently disagreed, for on December 18, 1972, the film house which showed Deep Throat went on trial, bringing forth all of the usual suspects – in this instance Kinsey protégé John Money of Johns Hopkins – willing to testify to the film's redeeming social value. The judge, however, remained unimpressed, announcing that "this is one throat that deserves to be cut," when he handed down the guilty verdict on March 7, 1973, levying a $2 million fine. Pondering the significance of it all, William Pechter, writing in Commentary could only opine that it indicated that "we want pornography . We want it, but we don't want to admit to wanting it, and so we want it cloaked in art or in some other socially respectable disguise."[10]

Part III, Chapter 17

Washington, D.C., 1974

In January 1974, when Linda Lovelace was still filling seats at the Adult New World theater in New York City, John D. Rockefeller III was getting ready to attend the world population conference in Bucharest with the deep sense of self-satisfaction that comes to the few people in the course of human history who have changed the world by their own efforts. Instead of being celebrated for his efforts, Rockefeller was in for an unpleasant surprise when the Vatican, the Soviet Bloc, and the Third World teamed up to reject his proposals. Bringing the Vatican and the Communists together on an issue was no small accomplishment, and John D. Rockefeller III had done it virtually single-handedly. But having become accustomed to molding public opinion to suit his desires, Rockefeller was not going to be deterred from setting birth quotas throughout the world just because the world didn't want them. Instead, he turned to the United States government, confident that it would accomplish by stealth what he had failed to do by persuasion.

On April 24, 1974, Henry A. Kissinger inaugurated that new era of subjugation abroad by sending to the secretary of defense, the secretary of agriculture, the director of the Central Intelligence Agency, the deputy secretary of state, and the administrator of the Agency for International Development, with a copy to the chairman of the Joint Chiefs of Staff, a memorandum titled "Implications of Worldwide Population Growth for U.S. Security and Overseas Interests." That study came to be known subsequently as National Security Study Memorandum 200 or NSSM 200. That memo stated: "The President has directed a study of the impact of world population growth on U.S. security and overseas interests. The study should look forward at least until the year 2000, and use several alternative reasonable projections of population growth."

The immediate occasion for NSSM 200 was the defeat the United States plan for establishing birth quotas for the world had just suffered at the United Nations-sponsored population conference in Bucharest. There the Holy See along with Communist and Third World countries, led by Algeria, denounced the United States and the West for practicing what they called "contraceptive imperialism." John D. Rockefeller III seems to have taken the rebuff personally and spent the last few years of his life engaged in soul-searching about the population-control enterprise, but by then his ideology had become the cornerstone of this country's foreign policy and beyond his power to revoke. NSSM 200 was reaffirmed as the cornerstone of the United States population policies on November 26, 1975, in a separate memo, National Security Decision Memorandum 314 (NSDM 314), which endorsed both the policy recommendations in the study and those additional points proposed by Kissinger. It was signed by Brent Scowcroft, and, in spite of being declassified in the late '80s, is still in force.

Rockefeller had changed the world in the nick of time too. The Bucharest conference took place just months before population bombers like Paul Ehrlich had predicted that world-wide famine would begin as the result of overpopulation. In addition to books like Paul Ehrlich's *Population Bomb* and the less famous but even more dire book by the Paddocks, *Famine 1975*, then president of the World Bank, Robert S. McNamara, stepped to the podium at Notre Dame before the graduating class of 1969 and announced in the direst terms that "the usual date predicted for the beginning of the local famines is 1975–1980."[1] In making this statement, McNamara was simply following the lead of people like Paul Ehrlich, who wrote in the *Population Bomb*: "I have yet to meet anyone familiar with the situation who thinks India will be self-sufficient by 1971, if ever."[2] By September 1977, which is to say two years after famine was supposed to have devastated India, the Indian grain reserve stood at about 22 million tons, and India began to be faced with the problem of how to store the stocks "that overflowed warehouses and caused mounting storage costs" so that they would not be "ruined by rain or eaten by predators."[3]

By the mid-'70s India began exporting food, but not before they had their own experience of population control at the hands of people like Robert McNamara, who announced to the Notre Dame graduates in 1969 that "the food-population collision will duly occur. The attempts to prevent it, or meliorate it, will be too feeble. Famine will take charge in many countries. It may become, by the end of the period, endemic famine. There will be suffering and desperation on a scale as yet unknown."[4]

There was suffering in India all right, but it wasn't caused by lack of food. It was caused rather by people like Robert McNamara. As his solution to the problem of "overpopulation," Mr. McNamara announced that "family planning is going to have to be undertaken on a humane but massive scale." Well, Mr. McNamara got it half right in India: family-planning programs there were certainly massive, but they were hardly humane. The record of mass sterilizations done without consent or knowledge to hapless peasants who received a transistor radio in exchange for not having children and then perhaps died of an infection is one of the darkest chapters of the eugenic movement, which is hardly this century's noblest social movement to begin with. Between mid-1975 when Indira Gandhi declared the "population emergency" and when it ended in 1977 with the fall of the Gandhi government, 6.5 million men were given vasectomies, mostly against their will, and a total of 1,774 men died as a result of the operations.[5] During the height of this mayhem, McNamara flew to India to cheer on the ministry of health and family planning in November 1976, praising the Indian government for its "political will and determination" in attempting to solve what he continued to refer to as the population problem.

According to Kissinger's memo, motivation is a key component to the United States population-control program. Key congressional supporters need to be stroked "to reinforce the positive attitudes of those in Congress who presently support U.S. activity in the population field and to enlist their support in persuading others."[6] Another key aspect is the role of multilateral institutions like the UN, whose involvement as a conduit of U.S. aid money forestalls accusations of "contraceptive imperialism." The study notes, for example, that of the thirteen countries targeted for contraceptive intervention (India, Bangladesh, Pakistan, Nigeria, Mexico, Indonesia, Brazil, the Philippines, Thailand, Egypt, Turkey, Ethiopia and Colombia), some have already become "receptive to assistance" for population activities. In other high-priority countries, however – India and Egypt, for example – "U.S. assistance is limited by the nature of political or diplomatic relations or – in Nigeria, Ethiopia, Mexico, and Brazil – by the lack of strong government interest in population reduction programs.[7] In such cases, external technical and financial assistance, if desired by the countries, would have to come from other donors and/or from private and international organizations (many of which receive contributions from AID)."[8] The document states that the "[U.S. Department of] State and AID played an important role in establishing the United Nations Fund for Population Activities (UNFPA) to spearhead a multilateral effort in population as a complement to the bilateral actions of AID and other donor countries."[9] It notes repeatedly the need for the indirect approach to population control in the developing world, and advises, for instance: "There is also the danger that some LDC leaders will see developed country pressures for family planning as a form of economic or racial imperialism; this could well create a serious backlash."[10] It acknowledges that the use of multilaterals to achieve U.S. population objectives would require that additional amounts of money be provided to those institutions until such time as population assistance becomes accepted by Less Developed Country leaders. But the use of multilateral agencies to achieve the U.S. foreign policy objectives serves an additional purpose: "It is vital that the effort to develop and strengthen a commitment on the part of the LDC leaders not be seen by them as an industrialized country policy to keep their strength down or to reserve resources for use by the 'rich' countries. Development of such a perception could create a serious backlash adverse to the cause of population stability."[11] The last sentence gives away the purpose of population control, namely, the effort on the part of the industrialized countries with low birthrates to hold onto world hegemony by nullifying the demographic advantage of countries where the birth-rate is high.

At its core, the population offensive launched by the neo-Malthusian regime which took power in this country in the '60s had two flaws: first, it was fundamentally dishonest. It was imperialism disguised as humanitarianism, with the UN and the World Bank acting as front groups. And secondly, the population control offensive only worked where it didn't need to work at all. In other words, it accelerated the demographic decline in the developed world that was the source of neo-Malthusian concern about differential fertility in the first place. Population control had no effect in Africa because the Africans hadn't reached the demographic transition, the stage of affluence which must be reached before children are seen as a liability. In the affluent north where those nations had reached the demographic transition, propaganda for contraception simply made a bad demographic situation worse. The reason population control didn't work in Africa is simple. There is virtually no discretionary income in Malawi; you can't send women to law school in Burkino Faso. Your wife can't get a job teaching part-time in Kenya or working at K-Mart in Liberia. Not only is there no "excess" income in those places, there is no excess population in those places either; in fact, virtually every sub-Saharan country is underpopulated, and underpopulation is the primary cause of famine and poverty there. The most effective instruments in driving birth rates down – affluence, modernization, feminism, education, etc. – don't apply in impoverished countries. If the industrialized nations had been honest about providing development, they might have driven birth rates down, but since the purpose of population control was depriving those countries of the economic and political leverage which was based on population increase, the contraceptive campaigns failed across the board. The people in poor countries in Africa simply had nothing to lose, and in a situation like that children were the only tangible assets a couple had, and certainly their only guarantee of support in old age. As a result, the population controllers achieved, in the words of one of their famous memos, little more than "the smell of burning rubber." They had little else to show for their efforts as places like Africa continued to pullulate because the foundations could find no leverage in making them want to stop having children, which they still see as a benefit. There are, of course, the coercive loans floated by the World Bank, but in the absences of a certain level of prosperity, they don't work either.

In his book *Nature Against Us*, Peter J. Donaldson cites a memo by population controller John Sullivan entitled "The Smell of Rubber Burning." The memo in question referred to a request for a grant of $50,000 from the Nepal mission to monitor the burning of condoms whose shelf life had expired and which had, therefore, to be destroyed.[12] "In Asia," writes

Donaldson, who, it should be remembered, is a defender of population control programs and worked for them himself,

> where 75 percent of all AID-purchased contraceptives were sent, the problem was too many – not too few – contraceptives. In addition to the smell of burning rubber in Nepal, the AID mission in Bangladesh requested a moratorium on deliveries of oral contraceptives. The mission in the Philippines canceled a $6 million loan, in part because it had discovered at least three year's worth of contraceptives in storage. . . . Pakistan had the same problem, as unused supplies exceeded their shelf lives.[13]

Within a few years of the installation of NSSM 200 as the cornerstone of United States foreign policy – as early, in fact, as the late '70s – the efficacy of AID's programs were being questioned by the population controllers themselves. In fact, as Donaldson himself indicates, the entire population control profession was afflicted with a sense of crisis when his book came out in 1990. The old supply-side solutions popularized by Reimert Ravenholt and his successor at AID during the Reagan years, Peter McPherson, simply did not work and resulted in nothing more in most cases than, as John Sullivan wrote, the "smell of burning rubber." Donaldson cites a picture of an AID worker shoveling condoms and pills out of a helicopter as a satire on the program sent to its director as a way of helping him to reorient his priorities, but it had little effect on its intended recipient, perhaps because it had too much truth for comfort in it. As the population controllers came to the conclusion that the Third World wasn't much interested in "family planning," they turned increasingly to coercive programs of the sort tried in India and still in place in China. The 1994 UN Conference on Population and Development in Cairo was in many ways an admission of the failure of both "family planning" of the sort parodied by the man shoveling condoms out of a helicopter and "population control" of the nasty coercive sort that got practiced across Asia. In place of both failed alternatives with their stupid heavy-handedness, their waste of money, and their inherently coercive nature, the UN operatives in Cairo attempted to substitute feminism, "women's health," and "development" as alternative justifications for driving down the birthrates of developing countries.

Reading the oftentimes discouraged reports of the population controllers, one comes quickly to the conclusion that there are essentially two different sorts of community in this world when it comes to birth control. When a country reaches a certain state of affluence or modernization (or both taken together), the couple decides to limit the number of children it has because it sees children as economically disadvantageous. This turning point is known in population-control circles as the demographic transition. Once a country reaches it, family limitation happens all by itself; before it gets reached, which is to say, before a country gets that affluent, no amount of condoms or pills will bring it about, which is currently the state of affairs in Africa, much to the consternation of demographers who fear African fertility. Donaldson argues that far less affluence is necessary than was previously thought to usher in the demographic transition, but he does not dispute its existence.

Following the Supreme Court's *Roe v. Wade* decision in 1973, there was a certain amount of disingenuousness in playing abortion off against contraception, as there was in the Reagan/Bush administrations, which got to portray as a right-to-life victory ever-increasing budgets to limit the fertility of the Third World. With victories like this, the poor needed no defeats. The results of this cynical political maneuvering was a self-perpetuating system in which the anti-abortion forces perpetuated population control in the name of fighting abortion. "Pro-life," conservative Newt Gingrich personally intervened during the summer following the Republican Revolution of 1994 when the House zeroed out funding for Title X and restored the funding for population control. Donaldson cites the case of James Buckley, conservative architect of the Mexico City policy, who nonetheless in 1982 as undersecretary of state for security assistance, Science and Technology "served as point man in the fight to save the AID population budget from cuts threatened by the Office of Management and Budget."[14] The Information Project for Africa reports that in Colombia "the early population program became hopelessly mired in criticism coming from all sides." That is until Planned Parenthood

> invented the abortion debate [and] the carefully-planned diversion paid off. Abortion quickly became the topic of contention, and opponents of the birth control campaign ceased talking in terms of the de-population program. In comparison to this phantom "abortion problem," the American-donated rubbers seemed the lesser of two evils. And at last, the planners of the "global family" were able to introduce a variety of contraceptives that weren't contraceptives at all – such abortifacient drugs and devices as the IUD, certain oral contraceptives, hormonal implants, and injectables. . . . So useful was this distraction that by the early 1980s, a Planned Parenthood spokesperson was able to proclaim a major victory, saying that religious leaders in Colombia had "prudently" dropped their opposition to everything but abortion.[15]

All of this points out the futility of using the devil to drive out Beelzebub. Those who claim that the funding of contraception will reduce the number of abortions are either disingenuous or misinformed. But the debate over foreign aid and its involvement in population control is useful, even if depressing, because it gives us the best introduction into the real meaning of the so-called "sexual revolution." Chesterton used to define birth control as "no birth and no control." In this he was half right; contraception means no birth, and it means no self-control, but the absence of self-control in matters sexual invariably means the presence of instruments of political control which fill the moral vacuum created by immoral action.

To put the horse before the cart, to put things, in other words, in their proper order, the sexual revolution was the domestic version of the same adventure in political engineering that got imposed on the rest of the world under the name of population control. At first glance, it seems as if we are dealing with two different things: one imposed on others from without, one embraced willingly by the victims themselves in the name of "liberation," but those distinctions are really not the crucial distinctions. A better description of the dichotomy might be between rhetoric and reality. Population-control programs are always portrayed as something helpful in public statements, but invariably they are proposed as debilitating to the countries on the receiving end in classified documents. Bridging the gap between rhetoric and reality are books like Donald Warwick's *Bitter Pills*, in which the author announces that "although the guiding objective of national policy was to reduce Kenya's birth rate, the publicly announced rationale for family planning was the spacing of births for improved health."[16] This leads us to the first hermeneutical rule in understanding the true meaning of population control: health is always a code word for weakening the country demographically.

This truth leads us to other more basic truths: for example, the truth that population is an asset to a country and not a liability, a fact which emerges when one reads military assessments of population. In a series of memoranda issued by the National Security Council in the mid-'70s, the NSC discussed the probable consequences of decreasing population growth in the United States and increasing population growth in the Third World. The most basic fact is that:

> The United States and its Western allies are declining as a percentage of world population. Whereas 6 percent of the world's people resided in the United States in 1950, the U.S. accounted for only 5 percent of the world's people in 1988, and its population is expected to be no more than 4 percent of the world total by the year 2010.[17]

The results of this demographic decline in terms of ability to field an army and wage a war are clear: "[d]eclining fertility rates will make it increasingly difficult for the United States and its North Atlantic Treaty Organization (NATO) allies and the Soviet Union and its Warsaw Pact allies alike to maintain military forces at current levels."[18]

> That demographic fact, in effect, defused the East/West confrontation and may have contributed to its ultimate resolution following the collapse of the Soviet empire. However, unlike the former Soviet Union and other Warsaw Pact nations, the nations of the southern hemisphere have birth rates much higher that those of the West, leading to a North/South confrontation that will succeed the Cold War as the major arena of military concern for people like the folks at the National Security Council. The same analysis that saw a demographic stand-off in East/West relations projected that "exceptionally high fertility rates" in the developing world "could lead to expanded military establishments in affected countries as a

productive alternative to unemployment," and that developing nations "may have a built-in momentum to capitalize on unused manpower for purposes of both internal and external security."[19]

The same NSC document also examined the effects of declining population in the West, projecting that the increasing ratio of elderly people to working-age people would reduce the proportion of productive workers while, at the same time, increase the need for social services, thus reducing available revenues to the military. Moreover, it said, the "aging" of the society "implies a reduction in productivity and the possibility of economic stagnation," and could also mean "less overall money exists because the productive population base has shrunk."[20]

Decline in fertility and birth rate, in other words, means a decline in national power and military might. If this is true for the United States military, it is true for other countries as well. So U.S. "aid" in helping other countries lower their birth rates is really an attempt by the United States to weaken them militarily, as the NSC document and other recently declassified documents make perfectly clear.

The drop in the quantity of people also means a change in quality as well. The NSC memo indicates that the population within the United States, too, is changing, "as the proportion of blacks, Hispanics, and Asians increases."[21] The report questions whether the U.S. armed forces will be able to recruit the "quality" of personnel needed for the high-tech wars of the future: "One of the most important questions facing the U.S. military in the years ahead under all-volunteer conditions will be not whether it can recruit the required quantity of manpower but whether it can entice the required quantity with the required qualities to join," it states.[22] "Aptitude requirements in certain high-tech jobs currently would disqualify as many as 70 percent of the male population and almost 90 percent of all otherwise eligible women." "As the population continues to shrink," the NSC memo continues, "competition to fill vacancies undoubtedly will intensify between the military, colleges, and civilian employers. As this competition intensifies, recruiting costs seem likely to escalate, and pay levels will have to be increased to keep pace with the civilian job market. Pumped-up pay or bonuses for enlistment and reenlistment, when combined with other defense expenditures, could seriously squeeze the federal budget."[23]

A bad demographic situation for the United States is even worse for the nations of Europe, where birth rates have fallen even further below replacement level. The increasing manpower shortage among NATO countries will bring about "increased tension over conventional burden sharing . . . even a heightened possibility that the alliance's forward defense posture will unravel."[24]

But as Darwin and his followers recognized, the real danger of a declining birth rate arrives when it is matched by another population which is increasing, the fate of the North vis-à-vis the South, which threatens to displace its affluent neighbors by replacing them over the course of a few generations. Africa, because it is the fastest-growing region in the world, is a cause of special concern. "Between 1988 and 2010," the NSC study reveals, "Africa's population will more than double to 1.2 billion, about 16.6 percent of the global total. Between 1985–2030 the total increase will be 1.1 billion. Nigeria, with an estimated 103 million people in 1988, is expected to double in size by 2009, triple by 2024, and quadruple by 2035, adding 312 million people to the world's population in 50 years. By 2035 Nigeria is expected to surpass both the United States and the Soviet Union to become the third largest country in the world."[25]

In other words, the point which the UN and U.S. population controllers never got around to telling Third World women is that population growth is an asset after all, and not a liability as the population controllers portray it, and the increase in population in Africa and the decrease in the United States has the U.S. military worried. By listening to the concerns of the military we can understand a few basic truths about population. To begin with, it is in U.S. national interest and not in the interest of the countries on the receiving end of population aid to promote population-control programs. The U.S. does this as a way of preserving America's power in the absence of an expanding birth rate. This leads us to a series of corollary truths. First of all, population is the economic precondition for wealth and the military precondition for power. Even high-tech armies need a large population to support the industries which produce high-tech weapons. The expansion of the West which began with Columbus's discovery of the New World was accompanied by an unprecedented demographic expansion, without which that colonial expansion would not have been possible. Technological development played a role in the dominance of the West, but, as Julian Simon has explained, technological development is not something which happens independently of population growth. The demographic constant in all of this is people producing wealth by providing for their families. The more people at hand, *ceteris paribus,* the more wealth that gets produced. Simon argues that "in the long run additional people actually cause food to be less scarce and less expensive, and cause consumption to increase."[26]

> How and why did total output and productivity per worker and per acre increase so fast? Supply increased so fast because of agricultural knowledge gained from research and development induced by the increased demand, together with the increased ability of farmers to get their produce to market on improved transportation systems.[27]

Population control is full of myths; however, the myths are intended primarily for public consumption. The truths are reserved for classified military documents. So in addition to the truth that people produce wealth and so create, as a result, a world of "non-finite" resources (to use Simon's term), another truth emerged over the course of the twentieth century as well: the well-off at a certain point stopped having large families.

In 1944 King George VI of England established the Royal Commission on Population to examine the problem of national fertility decline and its implications for the British Commonwealth. The first fact that it established was the British had stopped having large families. Everything else, every other demographic consequence, flowed from that fact.

> The widespread practice of birth control is undoubted, and our survey of the causes suggests that, although the extent and efficiency of its practice may vary, no changes in the social environment are likely to lead men and women to abandon this means of control over their circumstances. This fundamental – and momentous – adjustment to modern life has to be accepted as the starting point for consideration of the probable future trend of population.[28]

The Royal Population Commission came as well to the conclusion that the problem was not unique to England, but it was unique to the affluent West:

> The modern fall in the size of the family towards and often below replacement levels, is a phenomenon common to most of the peoples of Western civilisation, and virtually confined to them. While their rate of increase has been drastically reduced in consequence during the present century, that of some Oriental peoples has undergone a marked acceleration, as the result of a rapid fall in mortality coupled with the continuance of high birth rates.[29]

It reminds one of another Englishman, writing another sort of work at about the same time. In J. R. R. Tolkien's trilogy *Lord of the Rings*, the ring fellowship notices that many of the houses of Minas Tirith are vacant. Worse still is the attitude of Denethor, who is charged with defending the city but has secretly given into despair, believing that "the West has failed." The Royal Population Commission deals with "imponderable considerations" of the moral sort as best they can:

> There is much to be said for the view that a failure of a society to reproduce itself indicates something wrong in its attitude to life which is likely to involve other forms of decadence. The cult of childlessness and the vogue of the one-child family were symptoms of something profoundly unsatisfactory in the Zeitgeist of the inter-war period, which it may not be fanciful to connect with the sophistications and complacencies which contributed to the catastrophe of the second world war.[30]

The Royal Commission traced the degeneration of English society to one root: the "main cause, and very probably the only cause, of this fall was the spread of deliberate family limitation."[30] Based on a specific attitude to life, the decline in family size was class-specific as well, proceeding "fastest among the higher occupational categories" and "considerably slower among Roman Catholics than in the rest of the population."[32]

This disparity in fertility linked to income and education led the commission to raise the specter of differential fertility, which haunted the eugenics movement before the war:

> Of the social groups, those with the highest incomes, and among individual parents within each social group, the better educated and the more intelligent, have smaller families on the average than others. We are not in a position to evaluate the expert evidence submitted to us to the effect that there is inherent in this differential birth rate a tendency towards lowering the average level of intelligence of the nation, but there is here an issue of the first importance which needs to be thoroughly studied.[33]

The ideology of population control is simply a combination of fact #1: people produce economic wealth and military power, and fact #2: the affluent have smaller families. The English upper classes converted to Darwinism at the same time that they stopped having large families. As a result, they began to be concerned about something they referred to as "differential fertility," which meant that while the "best people" (i. e., people of their class) limited the size of their families, the rest of the world, especially the pullulating races of the Southern Hemisphere, did not. As good Darwinians they realized that the population with the higher fertility rate would eventually replace the population with lower fertility rate. Out of that fearful realization the idea of population control was born.

In its initial years, the eugenics movement called for, in Margaret Sanger's words, "a nation of thoroughbreds" as well as "more children from the fit, fewer from the unfit," Sanger and her backers, of course, were supposed to determine the criteria of fitness along racial and class lines. The big parting of the waters for the eugenics movement came as a result of the excesses of one of its most fervent disciples, namely, Adolf Hitler. Hitler did for eugenics what the politician named by Churchill did for sodomy – he gave it a bad name. And with the rise of the United States as the world's dominant power after World War II, the country whose regime would rely heavily on advertising and public relations did what comes natural to such people: they changed the name of the Birth Control League to Planned Parenthood and set about to achieve the same goals as the eugenics movement but by different means.

The major changes in the eugenics movement, changes which took place after World War II, did not have to do with the ends the eugenicists wanted to achieve but rather the means they chose to attain them. The same people were still concerned with differential fertility, but after the war, with the rise of mass-communications media like TV and the influence tax-exempt foundations had over research and the universities, it became clear, at least in affluent countries, that the best way to achieve eugenic goals was by psychological manipulation based on the capture of the means of communication. Get the people to do it to themselves. Portray demographic control as liberation. Portray an attempt to lower birth rates as concern for "health." These ideas would reach their culmination in the sexual revolution of the '60s.

The period from the end of WWII to the 1960s saw a long unsuccessful struggle on the part of the forces of moral restraint to stem the tide of Illuminist politics, which can be defined as the ability to manipulate people through their vices. The Second Vatican Council was, in this respect, a major cultural counter-offensive on the part of the Catholic Church, but one which got quickly co-opted by the very instruments of culture it sought to tame. During the '60s, the neo-Malthusians, a loose group of wealthy individuals and foundations with an Anglo-American point of view, gradually came to dominate the public consciousness through a series of well-financed and well-orchestrated publicity campaigns, the foremost of which was the overpopulation scare, which became the subject of congressional hearings in 1965 and thereafter was adopted as the cornerstone of foreign policy by the U. S. government.

The milestones of this revolutionary movement are available from any history of birth control: the Draper Commission of 1959, followed by its rejection by President Eisenhower at the urging of the nation's Catholic bishops; this was followed by Lyndon Johnson mentioning the dangers of overpopulation in his 1965 State of the Union address. What no one could have known at the time is that Johnson did it at the express urging of John D. Rockefeller III and Bernard Berelson who traveled to Washington during the fall of 1964 to a meeting for this express purpose. Johnson's announcement was followed in the Spring of '65 by *Griswold v. Connecticut*, the Supreme Court decision which declared the ban on contraceptive sales unconstitutional. Leo Pfeffer was to say later that the Court decriminalized contraception because the government wanted to get into the contraception business itself and could not very well dispense something illegal. *Griswold* was in turn followed for the next few years by the Gruening hearings, described by Phyllis Piotrow as the one most significant event in the contraceptive revolution. During the course of the hearings, which were chaired by Sen. Ernest Gruening of Alaska, a friend of Margaret Sanger, one "expert" after another appeared before Congress urging the government's involvement in the promotion and distribution of contraceptives. By the end of the 1960s, the United States was involved in the promotion of contraception both domestically and abroad. From a nationalistic perspective, this involved a political self-contradiction because what weakened foreign nations also weakened America. But the contradiction is best explained by adding that those who proposed neo-Malthusian policies did not hold the good of the nation as their highest good. If population were a good thing both economically and militarily, as just about every classified document concedes, why were the neo-Malthusians – Draper, Rockefeller, et al. – interested in promoting birth control domestically?

In order to answer that question, we have to define their position a bit more precisely. Hitler's position in this regard was more consistent. He supported abortion for non-Aryan peoples and opposed it for the Aryans. Hitler was a German nationalist and a racist, where race was the *conditio sine qua non* of citizenship. Unlike the more classical exponents of demographic politics, the neo-Malthusians were not acting in the national interest. They were acting in what they perceived as class interest (coinciding largely with an Anglo-American racial identification). This class was transnational and benefited from business dealings across the world. Beyond that, and perhaps most importantly, the neo-Malthusians were also engaged in a revolutionary struggle at home. Their first task was to take over the United States government, and then use that government as the instrument of their policy abroad. In this regard, the promotion of birth control at home was not in the best interests of the United States because it accelerated the demographic weaknesses already in existence in the neo-Malthusian classes, but it did make sense as a counter-attack against domestic enemies. And since the neo-Malthusians defined as the enemy anyone on the other side of the differential-fertility equation, promotion of birth control at home would strengthen their hand in their revolutionary struggle to change the default settings of the culture to something more congenial to their goals.

The major domestic opponent to the neo-Malthusian revolutionaries was, of course, the Catholic Church. The first birth-control offensive was a domestic campaign aimed at Catholics and blacks because those groups had the highest fertility rates. Population control got practiced at home before it got exported. The sexual revolution of the '60s was, in effect, a demographic attack on Catholics that was so successful that within a period of ten years it effectively neutralized the only effective domestic opposition to the eugenics regime. One need only look around to see how effective the assault on the Catholic position opposing population control was. In many ways it was a disinformation campaign of unprecedented strategic genius. The Catholics were the main force driving the post-WWII baby boom. As the National Security Council could have predicted, with demographic growth came both economic power and political power. In 1960, the first Catholic president in the history of a very anti-Catholic country was elected president. The demographic handwriting was on the wall. The United States was on its way to becoming a Catholic country. At least this is what the neo-Malthusians, versed in, if not obsessed with, demographics, must have thought. And then the contraceptive put an end to all that by ending the baby boom demographically and dividing the Catholic opposition intellectually. The blacks lost the demographic wars of the '60s too in a much more dramatic fashion. As a result of contraceptive-oriented "poverty" programs the black family was all but destroyed. Illegitimacy went from 20 percent to 70 percent. Black leadership was held hostage first to the foundations, like Ford, which funded the civil rights movement and then to the federal government. By the mid- '70s, the neo-Malthusians had effectively taken over the government and were then free to implement their eugenics theories as government policy. Population control, after serving as the vehicle for subjugating enemies at home, became the instrument for the same sort of subjugation abroad.

In the meantime, the same neo-Malthusian campaign applied domestically continued to drive the birth rate down and increase the differential fertility which drove the campaign in the first place. Ironically, if the neo-Malthusians had really concentrated on raising the standard of living in the Third World (what they claimed to be doing), they might have brought about the decline in fertility they desired, but for people who claimed to have the big picture in view, they proved to be remarkably shortsighted.

The results of the neo-Malthusian revolution of the '60s have, as a result, been unmitigated disaster. Domestically it led to the destruction of the black family, the undermining of democratic institutions, and the establishment of sexual liberation as means of political control, a control that few seem to recognize and virtually no one knows how to end. In terms of foreign policy it proved to be a disaster in a different way, especially to our "friends," i.e., anyone who allowed USAID a free rein in his country. By the mid-'80s, Indira Gandhi, Anwar Sadat, the Shah of Iran, and Ferdinand Marcos were all either out of work or dead, killed, or expelled by their own people rebelling against the imposition of population control. What they had in common was a supine acceptance of American population control measures, adopted to the detriment of their own people, who reacted in predictably violent ways.

Indira Gandhi was assassinated by her own bodyguard in 1984. Three years earlier, the same fate had befallen Anwar Sadat, who, according to one biographer, "boasted that David and Nelson Rockefeller, the magnates of the Chase Manhattan Bank, as well as Robert McNamara, the president of the World Bank, were his personal friends, and therefore he could make use of his private connections in the world to produce a turnabout in the economy." Sadat was aware of the fate of the Shah, also a friend of the Rockefellers, whose wife, like the wife of Ferdinand Marcos, had taken control of Iran's population-control program. Sadat's fate was more like Gandhi's than the Shah's. On October 6, 1981, Sadat was assassinated by a young artillery officer, who hoped to usher into being in Egypt the same Islamic era which had dawned in Iran two years earlier.

According to Fred Schieck, Manila director of the U. S. Agency for International Development (AID) in the 1980s, Imelda Marcos took "direct, personal, and public interest in" population-control programs in the Philippines, administering $70 million worth of pills, condoms and IUDs to fellow Filipinos.[34] But by the end, even she began to realize that the AID intervention in her country was going to prove as personally disastrous to her as it had to other condom pushers. By mid-1985, a year before the Marcos government fell, Imelda was telling Schieck that she would continue collaborating behind the scenes but had to withdraw her public support because it had become so unpopular. Two years later AID operatives were complaining that the Aquino government was "kowtowing to the Church," which was their way of saying that it was not implementing the same policies which had led to the fall of the Marcos regime.[35]

Coercion never works over the long run, certainly not in an area as intimate as having children, and running roughshod over clients always seems to bring on a backlash. But beyond that, the neo-Malthusians seem to have created the very scenario they feared the most, a fact noted by Alfred Sauvy, who warned that Malthusian propaganda and fears of "over-population" would affect most the very people who were most reluctant to have children. "The fear of seeing others multiply," he wrote

> thus leads to a diminishing vitality, to a recrudescence of Malthusian attitudes in populations already sapped by demographic aging. At the same time, the populations that elicited those fears remain unaffected. . . . The usual perils of preachers who address only the already-converted are therefore compounded by the risk of reducing their very numbers from one generation to the next. Thus the spread in levels of fertility between countries, regions, and social classes, and so on is further extended, even though the goal was to narrow the gaps.[36]

Which may be just another way of saying that the meek will inherit the earth.

Part III, Chapter 18

Philadelphia, 1976

In October 1976, as part of that city's celebration of the bicentennial of the Declaration of Independence, a law professor by the name of Leo Pfeffer arrived in Philadelphia to give a paper at the Society for the Scientific Study of Religion called "Issues that Divide: The Triumph of Secular Humanism." The sexual revolution was now over in America, and it was over because it succeeded beyond the wildest dreams of its most perfervid supporters. During the fifteen years prior to Pfeffer's talk, America had quite simply revised its culture to eliminate laws which conflicted with sexual libertinism. If America were a computer, one could say that the default settings had been changed. At the beginning of the seventh decade of the twentieth century, the culture of the country was based on a pan-Protestant reading of Christianity whose assumptions favored, in imperfect form albeit, a rough approximation of the moral law. By the end of the decade, the default settings had been changed in favor of a culture that was individualistic, rationalistic, and hedonistic, especially in matters sexual. It was not just that people's behavior had changed; those changes had been inscribed in the both the culture and the constitution, or at least how it was interpreted, in the rules that governed people's lives, and Leo Pfeffer was one of the main agents of that change.

At the time of his talk in Philadelphia, Leo Pfeffer was professor of constitutional law and chairman of the Department of Political Science at Long Island University in Brooklyn, New York. The credentials seemed hardly distinguished. In a profession where prestige exists in inverse proportion to the amount of time an academic spends in the classroom, Professor Pfeffer had what seemed to be a distinctly unglamorous joint appointment in an undistinguished state school. A look at the awards he had garnered in the years before the talk, however, gives a better indication of his accomplishments and the changes he himself was instrumental in bringing about. Born in Hungary on Christmas Day in 1910, Pfeffer arrived in the United States at the age of two, was naturalized a citizen in 1917, and married in 1937. At the time of his speech in Philadelphia in 1976, Pfeffer had received awards from Americans [formerly Protestants and Other Americans] United for the Separation of Church and State, the Minnesota Jewish Community Council, the New York Unitarian Universalist Church, the Brooklyn Civil Liberties Union, the Horace Mann League, the Unitarian-Universalist Association, the American

Jewish Congress and the Committee for Public Education and Religious Liberty.

At the time of his talk he was Special Counsel to the American Jewish Congress, as well as counsel for the Religious Coalition for Abortion Rights, and a member of the advisory committee on the National Project for Film and the Humanities. In the years following his talk he would receive an award from the American Jewish Congress in 1980 and the Humanist of the Year Award in 1988. Pfeffer's bio reads like a road map of the revolutionary changes that had swept through American society over the previous twenty years. If Pfeffer had come to talk about the "triumph of secular humanism," he was well-qualified. He had been intimately involved in virtually all of the battles that had brought about that triumph. Beginning with the *Schempp* decision in the early '60s and ending with the *Lemon* decision in 1970, Pfeffer was the architect of the legal strategy which removed the last vestiges of Protestant culture from the public schools and denied government funding to Catholic schools. If his listeners wanted a description of how the triumph came about, it was clear that Pfeffer could give a first-hand account.

With the candor of a victor who had nothing more to fear from his opponents, Pfeffer was never vague about who it was he was fighting all these years. For Pfeffer, the enemy was, quite simply, the Catholic Church. In a memoir which appeared a year before his talk in Philadelphia (published with mordant irony in the liberal Catholic magazine *Commonweal*), Pfeffer went to some length to explain his animus against the Catholic Church. "I did not like it," Pfeffer wrote

> because it was monolithic and authoritarian and big and frighteningly powerful. I was repelled by the idea that any human being could claim infallibility in any area, much less in the universe of faith and morals, and repelled even more by the arrogance of condemning to eternal damnation those who did not believe it.[1]

The Church which Pfeffer grew up hating (if that is not too strong a word) was the Church he got to know as a Jewish immigrant in New York City. During the time Pfeffer was growing up and getting started in the legal profession, the Catholic Church was, in his opinion, "one if not the single most powerful political force in the nation." It was a time, when, to use his own words, "Pius XI and Pius XII reigned over the Catholic world and Cardinal Spellman ruled in the United States. It was the pre-John XXIII-Vatican II era, and it was during this period that my feelings towards the Catholic Church were formed."[2]

In the *Commonweal* memoir, Pfeffer refers to his daughter's threat when she didn't get her way to "marry a Catholic army officer from Alabama," because that particular configuration of Catholicism, the military, and the South embodied all that Pfeffer did not like about America. At another point

Pfeffer talked about the impression Catholic schools made on him as a young man:

> I often saw children lined up in separate classes as they marched in. All the children were white; each group was monosexual; all the boys wore dark blue trousers and white shirts, all the girls dark blue jumpers and white blouses; all the teachers were white and wore the same nuns' habits.[3]

Once Pfeffer gets started, the reasons for his animus against the Catholic Church start to pour forth in an increasingly frank as well as an increasingly hostile litany of offenses against the liberal *Weltanschauung*. Pfeffer did not like the fact that the Church opposed the Equal Rights Amendment; he is annoyed that "among the children outside the parochial school on the way to my office there are only a sprinkling of black faces"; he does not like the fact that the Vatican still defends papal infallibility and *Humanae Vitae*, the 1968 encyclical banning the use of contraceptives; he even opposes the practice of having first confession before first communion. ("I know it's none of my business," he adds as if realizing that his animus is getting out of control even by his own standards, "but you asked didn't you?")[4] Pfeffer disliked the Church because of its size and because of its unity and because of its internal coherence and because of its universality, all of which contributed to its political power. He disliked it as well because it was, in his words, "monolithic," because with "monolithity," he tells us, "goes authoritarianism."[5]

Pfeffer had nothing against religion per se; he only opposed "monolithic," "authoritarian" religions, i.e., religions with enough clout to have a say in how the culture got organized. But even that is misstating the case somewhat. As James Hitchcock noted, neither Pfeffer nor the liberal media objected in 1973 when the Supreme Court established as the law of the land a policy on abortion virtually identical with the position of the United Methodist Church; nor did the fact that the author of the opinion was himself a Methodist cause them much concern.[6] The reason is simple enough. The media and their backers by and large agreed wholeheartedly with the decision. When it comes to the separation of church and state, some religions are more equal than others, and some are clearly more threatening than others as well, and in Pfeffer's view Catholicism stood alone in this regard.

If the Catholic Church had been willing to declare contraception and abortion the eighth and ninth sacraments respectively, it seems doubtful that people like Leo Pfeffer would have been upset by her authoritarianism. The fact remains, however, that she wasn't and therein lies the real reason for the animus of the liberals. During the entire post-World War II period in the United States, the Catholic Church opposed the main article of faith of secular humanism, namely, sexual liberation. Beginning with the creation of the Legion of Decency in 1933 and culminating in the opposition to *Roe v. Wade* forty years later, the Catholic Church had consistently picked up the banner of sexual morality which the mainstream Protestant denominations had let fall. The one great thaw in the liberal animus toward the Church came in the early '60s during the Second Vatican Council, when it looked as if the Church might reach a *modus vivendi* with modernity by legitimating the use of contraceptives. That dream was laid to rest in 1968 when Pope Paul VI slammed the door shut on the *conditio sine qua non* of cooperation with the liberal regime. When the news of *Humanae Vitae* hit the streets, the Liberals broke off relations and turned instead to a combination of open hostility and fomenting rebellion within the ranks. The lull in the fighting in the sexual revolutionaries' ongoing *Kulturkampf* with the Church ended abruptly in 1968. Thereafter, the hostilities were out in the open again.

Pfeffer's animus toward the Church never really changed, but it did abate somewhat, primarily because the Church's influence in society had diminished and because the confusion in its own ranks increased – in no small measure because of Pfeffer's activities. "What do I think about the Church today?" Pfeffer asked rhetorically in the mid '70s, "In short, I still do not like it, but I do not like it less than I did not like it during that period, and the reason is that, while it is still what it was before, it is considerably less so, if you can make out what I mean."[7]

We can without too much difficulty make out what Pfeffer means. The only good Church was a confused Church. The more it approached the divided, tentative, and contradictory condition of Jewish and Protestant denominations, the more Pfeffer liked it. If the Church was less powerful in 1976 than it had been under Pope Pius XII and Cardinal Spellman, Leo Pfeffer was in no small way responsible for that diminution of power and influence. Unlike the *Kulturkampf* waged by Bismarck in Germany during the 1870s, the one waged by people like Pfeffer and the Rockefellers in America during the 1960s proffered the carrot of government funding, publishing contracts, foundation money, and *pro bono* legal services more readily than the stick of government regulation. As a result, the cultural revolutionaries in America in the 1960s found a fifth column within the Church willing to aid and abet their plans. By subsidizing an obviously schismatic group like the Old Catholics, Bismarck guaranteed Catholic solidarity. There was no Prussian Charles Curran, no Prussian Theodore Hesburgh. The story of the cultural revolution in America in 1960s is the story of the Catholic Church at war on two fronts. There was the enemy outside the gates, people like Pfeffer and the Rockefellers, and there were the collaborators within, who were often taking the money of the cultural revolutionaries to undermine the Church's position. Pfeffer, it should be remembered, published the memoir of his campaign against the church in a Catholic magazine. He also included in the same article a group of Catholics he found congenial to his cause. "I voted for John Kennedy in 1960," Pfeffer tells the *Commonweal* readership, and then goes on to give a list of liberal Catholics he could also conceive of voting for in the future. They would include "Robert Drinan, Justice William Brennan, Eugene McCarthy, Senator Phillip and/or Jane Hart, Dorothy Day, Theodore Hesburgh, and almost any member of the editorial board of *Commonweal*, although," he adds with a wry touch, "I would not necessarily want my daughter to marry them."[8]

Before we are very far into Pfeffer's account of how he won the cultural revolution it becomes apparent that the major area of contestation was sexuality. Pfeffer fought on the side of the Protestants to decriminalize the contraceptive, and he fought on the side of his fellow Jews to free Hollywood from the Catholic-inspired production code. As one sign of Cardinal Spellman's inordinate influence over American culture, Pfeffer mentions the fact that the Roberto Rosellini film *The Miracle* was declared blasphemous in the state of New York in the early '50s. In 1952 the New York State blasphemy law was struck down by the Supreme Court in the case of *Joseph Burstyn, Inc.* v. *Wilson*.

The other area of cultural revolution delineated by Pfeffer had to do with whose idea of the family would dominate in the culture. The major issue in the '60s was contraception, but that was soon replaced by abortion in the '70s. In the early '60s, to give some indication of the magnitude of the change which took place, it was illegal in many places in the United States to sell contraceptives. By the end of that decade the government was not only not prohibiting the sale of contraceptives, it was distributing them itself. The two instances are not only indications of the situation before and after the revolution, they are causally related as well. The law had to go because the revolutionaries wanted government to get into the contraceptive business. According to Pfeffer,

> the anti-contraception laws had to be removed from the books because their presence made it impossible for the state to encourage contraception, something it now increasingly deems necessary to do. The middle income and the affluent, married and unmarried, use contraceptives; the poor have babies. When the poor, often racial minorities, are on the welfare rolls, taxpaying Americans rebel and expect the state to do something about it.
>
> Why did it take a more activist approach to anti-contraception laws? The answer may lie in the fact that the justices recognized the need to get the laws off the books to enable the States to take affirmative action toward encouraging and assisting birth control, or at the very least not to prevent private groups from doing so; but they also realized that as a matter of political reality the States were not going to repeal the laws, as the twice-unsuccessful effort in Connecticut evidenced.[9]

In addition to describing the areas of contestation in America's *Kulturkampf*, Pfeffer also describes his understanding of just who the contending parties are. Again, the dividing line is essentially sexual. On the one had there were the Catholics, who

hope for an America in which, if not all will be Catholics, all will adhere to
Catholic values: no divorce, no contraception, no abortion, no obscene
books or pictures, no homosexuality, everybody worshipping God in his
own way, government solicitous of and helpful to religion, and children
and adults equally obedient to their parents and lawful authority.[10]

Arrayed on the other side of the front lines of the cultural war are "liberal
Protestants, liberal Jews, and deists [i.e., secular humanists]," who

seek a different America: one in which individuals enjoy maximum freedom of thought and expression, contraception is used and encouraged to
control population and avoid the birth of babies that are unwanted or cannot adequately be cared for, women's right to control their own bodies is
recognized and respected, the sexual practices of adults, whether of the
same or of different sexes, are of no concern to anyone but themselves,
governmental institutions avoid manifestations of religiosity, public
schools are free of sectarianism, and citizens are not forced to fight in a
war they deem immoral or in any war.[11]

During the same month that Leo Pfeffer gave his triumph of secular humanism speech announcing the Enlightenment's victory over the Catholic
Church, the Catholic Church, as if to prove to the world that it had been
beaten, announced a celebration of the American bicentennial that went by
the name of Call to Action. If Charles Curran's protest against *Humanae
Vitae* was the '60s equivalent of the fall of the Bastille, then Call to Action
became the Catholic equivalent of the tennis court oaths. The actions culminating in the Call to Action conference began two years before the conference took place in Detroit from October 20 to 24, 1976. The bishops were
interested in participating in a celebration of the nation's bicentennial, but
the nation was not in much of a mood for celebration. Watergate, the impeachment of President Nixon, and the ongoing, never-ending war in Vietnam occupied the nation's mind for the two years leading up to the
bicentennial. While this sort of fare filled the evening news and occupied the
nation, perhaps by way of indirection, the cultural revolution which had begun in the mid-'60s was busy consolidating its gains in less visible ways.

By the early '60s, Eddie Bernays's program for "invisible government"
through control of the instruments of culture had become part of the common
intellectual patrimony of a number of Jewish organizations, who put the information to use in a campaign to remove prayer from public schools. Later
the same tools were used by Hollywood in its war on the Production Code
and the Legion of Decency in their battle over who was to control the film industry. The crucial issue at the dawn of the '60s was nudity on the screen.
Hollywood was feeling financially threatened by TV on the one hand which
was stealing its family audience and the new skin magazines, like *Playboy*,
which got founded in the wake of the Kinsey reports and the perfection of
glossy color photography and were testing the borders of pornography in

wake of the *Roth* decision of the Supreme Court. In many ways, it was the Weimar Republic's battle over *Kulturbolschewismus* all over again, except that this time there was no effective conservative resistance. The Catholics tried in their way to play this role but were hindered by Jewish dominance in the media of communication and division in their own ranks following the Second Vatican Council. Leo Pfeffer knew that the Catholics were out-gunned and tried to explain that fact as tactfully as possible. "American Jewry," he wrote, "partly too because many Jews, far more proportionately than the other faiths, are commercially and professionally involved in the cinema and publishing, has been overwhelmingly antipathetic to the crusade for morality and censorship in the arts and literature" which by mid-century had been taken over by Irish Catholics.[12] Because the mainline Protestant de-nominations had abdicated their role as moral arbiters in matters sexual by the '60s and the Evangelicals were not yet a significant political force, the battle over the Hollywood Production Code came down to an essentially Jewish-Catholic struggle, a fact noted by Pfeffer in his speech on the triumph of secular humanism: "After World War I, Irish-oriented American Catholi-cism began taking over leadership in anti-obscenity militancy. . . . Catholic organizations such as the National Office for Decent Literature and the National Legion of Decency . . . became the nation's most militant and effec-tive defender of morals and censorship."[13]

After a number of unsuccessful attempts with vehicles like Billy Wilder's *Kiss Me, Stupid*, released in 1964, Hollywood finally succeeded in breaking the code in 1965 with the release of the Eli Landau film *The Pawn-broker*. During the course of the film a woman playing a black prostitute opened her blouse and exposed her breasts to the camera, breaking as a re-sult, Section Seven, Subsection Two, of the Motion Picture Production code and one of Hollywood's last remaining taboos. I have told the story of the breaking of the code elsewhere, primarily from the perspective of the Legion of Decency which saw *The Pawnbroker* not as the harbinger of serious cine-matic art but rather something that in the Legion's Msgr. Thomas Little's words, would "open the flood gates to a host of unscrupulous operators to make a quick buck."[14] The next seven years of cinema were to prove Msgr. Little and the Legion right as a trickle of bare breasts eventually became a flood of on screen nudity, culminating in 1973 with the release of *Deep Throat* and the *Devil in Miss Jones*, two porno epics which made it into the list of the industry's ten top grossing films for that year.

The summer of '65 saw as a result two great victories for the forces of "liberation," which were immediately transmuted into instruments of social control. The film industry was now able to use nudity to draw people into its theaters, and the government could now use the contraceptive as a solution to social problems. The first led to the exponential growth of the pornography industry, which redefined the universe of sexual expectations in a way that would prove devastating to women; the second eventuated in the destruction of the concept of the family wage and the emigration of women from the home into the workforce, where over a thirty-year period the male as provider would be replaced by both husband and wife earning what the husband alone earned before. Behind both examples of "liberation" loomed the specter of control, a fact which was true in a broader sense as well, because the result of both "liberalizations" was a sexually destabilized society, where more and more people succumbed half-unwittingly to the financial exploitation of their passions, and became as a result, sexual and financial helots. Reason, as the classical tradition pointed out, provides the only point of stability in any social order. The more people that the Enlightenment could persuade to exchange a life based on reason for a life based on passion, the more people the "invisible rulers" could control through the Illuminist science of advertising and its adjuncts. Of course, part of the fallout from any sexual liberation is social chaos based primarily on family disruption, and so once again, in the wake of the '60s' cultural revolution, horror began to make its appearance as a significant popular genre.

This is so for the reasons we have already mentioned, but also because the control of the human person that "population control" allows is far more intimate and, therefore, far more complete than any previous form of political domination. Michel Schooyans makes the point that even "Marx's proletariat still had their children as their only riches. . . . On the other hand, the contemporary problem forces the individual into the most precarious situation, since it deprives him of all control over *his own concrete future*, over a real future for his offspring: a kind of *alienation* heretofore unknown."[15]

The result of "birth control" is not only more radical than the slavery of classical antiquity, but the means to that end are different as well. Instead of forcing people to act for the ends of those in power, the "invisible rulers" now induce the ruled to do so by getting them to act according to the rulers unspoken sexual guidelines, because in controlling the agency responsible for the transmission of life, the controllers control human life at its source and, therefore, most crucial point. "This kind of domination," according to Schooyans,

> is at once more cunning, more pernicious and more fatal in its effects. It is not at all new, but it has grown in an unprecedented way because of two decisive factors. On the one hand, it has benefited from the use of the most sophisticated techniques of propaganda and indoctrination. On the other hand, its effectiveness is assured by the media's guarantee of publicity. . . . For contemporary totalitarianism the question is no longer one of exercising physical coercion; henceforth it is a matter of destroying the Ego in what is most profoundly personal in me. This is why contemporary totalitarianism has intellectual life as its target. It pummels the masses, but the intellectuals it reeducates by filtering, directing and dealing in informa-

tion. It inculcates a portable ideology, for ideology can encroach upon intelligence and disarm its critical ability, imprisoning it in a "gulag of the spirit." Bit by bit, intellectuals are ensnared by manipulators of knowledge who are in the pay of the party, the race, the army, the powerful. Science is fostered to the degree that it delivers new technologies that can be integrated into a global strategy for domination.[16]

As always, the instrument of control is passion: "Man, under the guise of being liberated and excited by the possibility of maximizing individual pleasure, disregards the stakes and consequences of sexuality."[17] By taking control of pleasure at its source in sexuality, the neo-Illuminists simultaneously take control of human life, which has the same source, and as an added bonus, the controllers also dominate the human conscience, by manipulating its guilt as a way of defending the actions that enslaved the person in the first place. Liberal politics becomes then first the incitation to sexual vice, then the colonization of the procreative powers that are indissoluably associated with sexuality, and finally the political mobilization of the guilt which flows from the misuse of procreative power in an all-encompassing system that gives new meaning to the term totalitarian. Schooyans is one of the few people who sees the full ramifications of this biocratic revolution:

> We are at the dawn of a total war beyond the limits of anything we have known, and the horizon is already aflame with it. The present war is truly total in the sense that, by means of power over life, it aims at control over human beings in what is most inalienable; their existence, their personal capacity for making judgments, and decisions, and their responsibility before their conscience. The present war simultaneously involves each of these aspects as the stakes, the means and the goal.[18]

This is what *Kulturkampf* meant in America in the 1960s, and this was why Leo Pfeffer came to Philadelphia in 1976 on the 200th anniversary of the Declaration of Independence to claim victory in the cultural wars and proclaim the triumph of secular humanism. Divide and conquer was the strategy which the Enlightenment under the direction of people like Leo Pfeffer used against the Catholics, and the social order of the republic was the first casualty of this campaign.

Once it began on October 20, the Catholic bishops attending the Call to Action conference in Cobo Hall in Detroit soon became aware that they were no longer in control of their own celebration. The Call to Action conference in 1976 was in many ways the sign that the Catholic fifth column which the Rockefellers had subsidized at Notre Dame had come out in the open and wanted to run the Church according to its own lights.

"U.S. Catholics have spoken," wrote Mark Winiarski in the *National Catholic Reporter*, the newspaper that represented the interests of the fifth column clerics most faithfully. The idea of a "democratic" consultation was used to disguise the special pleading of the clerical dissenters, who wanted in effect the best of both worlds: the resources of the Catholic Church and sexual liberation. So the *Reporter*'s slant on the first Call to Action conference was that "Catholics" had spoken. The people of God had spoken and, *mirabile dictu*, they wanted the same things the sexual Enlightenment wanted, namely, "ordination of women, married priests, remarried divorced Catholics spared excommunication, determination of conscience on birth control, a national arbitration board to control the bishops, [and] civil rights for gays."[19]

In other words, the agenda of Call to Action was indistinguishable from that of Leo Pfeffer and the Rockefellers, and the purpose of their efforts was to weaken the revolutionaries' main enemy, the Catholic Church. In addition thereto, those assembled in the name of the Church in Detroit in 1976 demanded that "The NCCB and Catholic publishers should expunge all sexist language and imagery from official church publications after January 1978."[20] Beyond that, they demanded that "The NCCB and every diocese should undertake affirmative action programs." Under "Personhood," the conference affirmed, among other things that Communion should be given in the hand in keeping with the dignity of the human person, that the Church should endorse the ERA as well as its political opposite pole, namely. a constitutional amendment to protect fetal life. And, last but not least, under the heading "Humankind," they demanded that "Third World peoples should be invited to this country to raise the consciousness of our people."[21]

The people of the Third World were undoubtedly honored by the invitation, but before long, as the proposals became longer and more politically charged, many observers began to wonder just how representative this body was of American Catholics at large, and if it was not, just whose interests, then, were these delegates representing? As even the unfailingly sympathetic Thomas Stahel wrote for *America*, "Who were the people who passed all these proposals?"[22]

Many bishops were equally curious. As if to provide an answer, John Cardinal Krol, archbishop of Philadelphia, was overheard saying that the meeting had been taken over by "rebels."[23] Bishop Kenneth Povish of Lansing, Michigan, compared the gathering to the 1972 Democratic convention which nominated Sen. George McGovern." "I remember my father," Bishop Povish said, "a Democratic voter all his life, asking afterwards, 'who was representing me at the (expletive deleted) convention.'"[24] Even the normally sympathetic Archbishop Joseph Bernardin disavowed the results of the conference, "the result was haste and a determination to formulate recommendations on complex matters without adequate reflection, discussion and consideration of different points of view."[25] Beyond that, "special interest groups advocating particular causes seemed to play a disproportionate role." Then, in typical fashion, Bernardin disavowed his disavowal two days later, issuing a statement to NC News Service saying he "did not repudiate" the conference.[26]

The strategy behind the sexual mobilization of the Catholic clergy could be deduced in equal measure from Wilhelm Reich and Martin Luther. The example of sixteenth-century Germany and the Lutheran revolt was apropos. Luther spent much of his time writing to various priests and clerics urging them to marry and thereby break the solemn vows they had made. His motives in urging marriage on apostate nuns and priests were clear. Once that spiritual transaction had been accomplished, the apostate priest was firmly in the Lutheran camp, a fact that Luther exploited for its maximal political effect. Libido culminating in broken vows was the engine that pulled the Reformation train. It was a uniquely effective way of organizing ex-clergy in opposition to the Church. Once they had made two contradictory sets of solemn vows, there was no way out. The marriage vows were, of course, invalid; however in the natural order of things, especially after children arrived, they seemed every bit as compelling. "Within me," one unhappy priest who succumbed to the trap wrote to a brother who was still a monk, "a constant conflict rages. I often resolve to mend my course, but when I get home and wife and children come to meet me, my love for them asserts itself more mightily than my love for God, and to overcome myself becomes impossible for me."[27]

The genius of this revolutionary plan lay in its use of sexual passion as a means of social control. By breaking their vow of chastity, religious became committed to sexual liberation, to the social program of the cultural revolution, and, as a result, to changing the Catholic Church from within. The sexualized religious became a permanent revolutionary cadre determined to make the Church conform its laws to their behavior, and since the cultural revolutionaries controlled the religious by manipulating their passions, this meant that the Church would have to conform its teaching to their program for total social control.

In May of 1974, right around the time the American Bishops and their assistants were making the initial plans for the 1976 bicentennial celebration that would be known as Call to Action, Father John Krejci, a priest on leave of absence from his diocese in Nebraska, completed his doctorate in sociology at the University of Notre Dame, having written his dissertation on "Leadership and Change in Two Mexican Villages."

Beginning in the mid-'60s, the University of Notre Dame, where Krejci received his doctorate, was a crucial part of two very different worlds. Dissent was as yet an unknown phenomenon and would not come out in the open until the summer of 1968 when Charles Curran organized the protest against *Humanae Vitae*. One year earlier, in the wake of Curran's successful tenure battle at Catholic University, Father Hesburgh engineered his Land o' Lakes statement, whereby he and a number of other presidents of Catholic universities, effectively alienated a large amount of Church property, namely those colleges and universities, from Church control. But no one seemed to know that was the effective meaning of Land o' Lakes at the time.

As a result, religious orders continued to send their nuns, priests, and brothers to an institution that was no longer a Church institution and had in fact shifted its allegiance to the major foundations of this country in a bid to get first their money and then federal funding, the sequel to foundation money as the government got more and more into the education business. During the summers of the late '60s, literally thousands of nuns as well as other religious would converge on the campus of the University of Notre Dame ostensibly to continue their education but also to imbibe the *Zeitgeist* in an especially undiluted form. Notre Dame was heavily into sexual liberation for a number of reasons. To begin with, there was the effect the pill was having on the culture at large, and then there was the effect the pill was having on Notre Dame in particular. Donald Barrett was a professor of sociology at Notre Dame at the time. He was aon the papal birth control commission as well. So much was publicly known at the time. Not so public was the fact that he had been a participant at the Rockefeller conferences and as a result had applied to the Population Council for a grant to study contraceptive use. He eventually received around half a million dollars from the Ford Foundation while still deliberating on the papal birth-control commission over the liceity of contraception.[28] In any other venue, this would have been known as conflict of interest. In the Catholic Church in America, it was known as independent thinking and newfound maturity. William D'Antonio, head of the sociology department during the late '60s, was becoming well known as a result of his name appearing on Planned Parenthood ads condemning the pope.

One of the thousands of nuns who came to Notre Dame during the '60s was a lady by the name of Jean Gettelfinger. Like Father Krejci, she came to get her graduate degree in sociology. Unlike him, she never finished. Instead of getting a degree, she got a husband, and that husband was Father John Krejci. Jean Gettelfinger was one of the many nuns who left their narrow convent rooms in the '60s with the university, specifically the Catholic University which was supposed to be contributing to their formation, as the enabling device for leaving. One observer of the Notre Dame scene during the '60s said that this phenomenon was not uncommon; nor, we might add, was it particularly hard to understand. The general sense among religious that things were changing received powerful reinforcement at Notre Dame, primarily because the Notre Dame faculty and administration were one of the prime engines of change.

Add to that the fact that we are not talking about abstract forces of history but rather something as intimate as libido and its mobilization as part of the cultural revolution, and we can get some sense of the ferment at Notre Dame during the late '60s. Nuns and priests could be seen strolling hand in hand around the lakes. There was much talk of a "third way," somewhere between marriage and celibacy, partaking of the best aspects of both, no doubt. The impossible dream of a married clergy, of contraceptive sex, and most of the other ideas that make up the Call to Action agenda, got hatched like a new bacillus in the hothouse atmosphere of the Notre Dame summer school and similar academic institutes across the country, and since the growth of this impossible idea was congenial to the cultural revolutionaries' goals it was fostered by their institutions.

So at some point Father Krejci and Sister Gettelfinger left the religious life and got married. Theirs was not an isolated incident. Unlike the Krejcis, many priests and nuns became intimate and did not leave to get married. This group, combined with those that did leave, gradually coalesced into a group that began to lobby in an increasingly insistent way for change in the Church's discipline regarding both sexuality and the religious life, and more often than not both taken together.

It's not hard to see the attractions both had separately. As religious in the most affluent country the world has ever known, priests and nuns got to live the vow of poverty in what was at best a deeply attenuated, symbolic form. Some indication of the rigor of religious life at Notre Dame can be seen in the fact that many married couples with families came there for vacations during the summer to swim in the lakes and play golf. A rigorous life teaching school for nine months followed by the Sybaris of the Notre Dame summer school must have been quite a change. That change coupled with the fact that everything else was changing must have made this group of religious think that anything was possible. And if the inevitable was going to happen anyway, why not act on it in advance. Then when the Church didn't change, disappointment turned to anger, and anger to a determination to force the change that should have happened but never did. It must have seemed so tantalizingly close back then – the best of both worlds! The life of a religious free of material cares plus the sexual fulfillment of the married state. It was, as the Germans say, a chance to slaughter the cow and milk it too.

By the time John Krejci received his Ph.D., which was also the time when the first consultations for the 1976 Call to Action conference began, this philosophy of the "third way," which is another way of saying dissent, which is another way of describing the beachhead the cultural revolution had made in the Catholic Church, had made deep inroads among the nation's religious, and the vector of transmission was largely the Church's educational system, specifically, its system of higher and ongoing education, the summer programs at Notre Dame transposed across the country. From a demographic point of view, Call to Action had a very specific profile: it was essentially an organization of clerics, ex-clerics and people who make a living working for the Church, men and women who had adopted the sexual values, and oftentimes mores, of the dominant culture while working for the Church. Notre

Dame had a crucial role to play in the formation of this group during the decade from the mid-'60s to the time of the actual Call to Action conference in October of 1976.

In January 1977, three months after the Call to Action conference in Detroit and Leo Pfeffer's declaration of victory in the culture wars in Philadelphia, the Rockefeller Foundation announced that it had appointed as its new chairman the Rev. Theodore M. Hesburgh. Hesburgh's decision to accept the chairmanship of the Rockefeller Foundation on January 14, 1977, unleashed a storm of indignation on the part of pro-life activists across the country in general and Catholic pro-lifers in particular. Stung by the criticism, Hesburgh responded in the Notre Dame student newspaper by claiming that his critics were misinformed about Rockefeller's stand on abortion. "The foundation has nothing to do with abortion," opined Hesburgh, "In fact you'll never find the word 'abortion' in the report." Father Hesburgh concluded that his critics should know the facts before they made inflammatory statements.

In an article published in the same student newspaper on April 20, 1977, Professor Charles E. Rice of the Notre Dame Law School proved beyond the shadow of a doubt that the word 'abortion' did in fact rear its ugly head in the report of the Rockefeller Foundation. The foundation report for 1975 lists a grant to the American Civil Liberties Union Foundation for $5,000 "for distribution to American obstetricians/gynecologists of the educational brochure, *The Abortion Controversy – A Doctor's Guide to the Law*." Planned Parenthood Federation of America received $900,000 from the Rockefeller Foundation in the second quarter of 1974 for its "Centers for Family Planning Program Development."[29]

Rice goes on to cite one instance of Rockefeller-funded support for abortion after another:

> The February 1977 issue of the Rockefeller-subsidized publication, *Abortion Research Notes*, announced the formation in September 1976 of the National Abortion Council as a successor organization to the Association for the Study of Abortion, another group supported by the Rockefeller Foundation. The National Abortion Council was formed "with the primary aim of fostering the accessibility of quality abortion services." The Rockefeller-supported *Abortion Research Notes* announced that it had participated in the organizational meeting of NAC and was "pleased to present the NAC Statement of Principles," the tenor of which is exemplified by the statements, "It is essential that abortion be readily available at reasonable fees," and "Parental and spousal consent should not be required."[30]

Rice also cites Rockefeller Foundation support for the Population Law Center, formerly the James Madison Constitutional Law Institute, which "has played," according to Rice, "a crucial role in changing American law to permit abortion." In the last half of 1974, the Rockefeller Foundation made a grant of $50,000 to the Institute for its "program in population law." Rice cites a similar grant made in 1972 and sees it as particularly significant because "during 1972 the James Madison Constitutional Law Institute handled the entire appeal for the abortion side in *Roe v. Wade,* and in the companion case of *Doe v. Bolton* it filed the principal pro-abortion brief and wrote the legal arguments related to the medical aspect of the case."[31] All of this led Rice to conclude that "in a realistic sense the Center is the legal spearhead of the abortion movement."

Father Hesburgh was a member of the board of directors of the Rockefeller Foundation during this entire period. It is, therefore, difficult to understand just exactly what he means when he says that "the foundation has nothing to do with abortion." When Hesburgh was asked for a clarification after the appearance of the Rice article by the National Catholic News Service, he declined further comment.

On July 10, 1978, John D. Rockefeller died in an automobile accident. He was 72 years old at the time. Six months later, on January 26, 1979, John's brother Nelson died under mysterious circumstances involving his secretary.

Twenty years after the original Call to Action celebration, on March 6, 1996, Bishop Fabian Bruskewitz of Lincoln, Nebraska, received a letter on Call to Action Nebraska stationery announcing the formation of Call to Action Nebraska, "an affiliate of the national Call to Action organization." It was this letter that was the proximate cause of Bishop Bruskewitz's by-now famous action. One co-signer of the letter was a John Krejci, a professor of sociology at Wesleyan University in Lincoln. It was this letter and the pending twentieth anniversary celebration of the first Call to Action Conference in Detroit which led Bruskewitz to excommunicate Call to Action and a number of other groups in the Lincoln diocese. On April 11, 1996 Call to Action representative James McShane met with the bishop to argue his case. By his own admission, he didn't get very far. When McShane complained about the severity of the punishment, Bishop Bruskewitz brushed his concerns aside by claiming that its "force could easily be lifted with obedience and repentance."[32]

Part III, Chapter 19
Evansville, Indiana, 1981

When Tom Schiro awoke on the morning of February, 4, 1981, he knew that something was wrong. Schiro had been working since November as a temporary employee of Tri-State Repair, helping to renovate the company's building at 1201 E. Tennessee Street in Evansville, Indiana. He had been living at Rescue House, a half-way house for prisoners ever since he had been taken off Vandenburgh County's work-release program. Schiro had been arrested for rape but never convicted, even though he had been convicted of other crimes. Somehow his arrest record got lost in the shuffle when he had been released and assigned to the half-way house in Evansville. He had been accused of raping a seventeen-year-old girl from Mt. Carmel, Indiana, in 1978, but the charges had been dropped. Rescue House director Ken Hood was to say later that if he had known that Schiro was a sex offender he never would have allowed him into his program. But in September of 1980, nobody seemed to know even though by his own reckoning Schiro had committed nineteen or twenty rapes by then.

Schiro was also an alcoholic and a drug addict, and his efforts at rehabilitation during late 1980 and early 1981 were focused on getting these two addictions under control. He was attending AA meetings and seemed to be making progress in that area. Unfortunately, he had another addiction for which no program yet existed. Schiro was addicted to pornography as well. According to Mary Lee, whom he met in May of 1979 and with whom he lived until June of 1980 when he went to jail, Schiro was never without pornography. She felt, in fact, that he couldn't live without it, no more than he could live without masturbating, which he did on the average of ten or twelve times a day. In fact, over the years a certain pattern of behavior had evolved in Schiro of which the drugs and the pornography were integral parts. "It seemed," Mary Lee said, "that whenever he started looking at the books he had to get high." And whenever he looked at the books and got high, he, in Lee's words, "went out at night." Schiro had been a voyeur since the age of twelve. He had a peeping route in the way that others his age had paper routes. He would find certain residences, usually basement apartments, and ascertain the sleeping habits of the people who lived there. Then he would stand outside their windows and masturbate as he watched them sleep or make love. It was only a matter of time before he was climbing through the windows to rape the women inside according to the fantasies he had generated from the various pornographic magazines he owned.

Schiro returned from jail in the fall of 1980 dried out, but soon his old habits returned. He felt that having a job entitled him to the things he enjoyed, and so the pornography gradually began to make its return. And with the pornography came the whole train of pornography-related behavior – pornography, then the pot, then the booze, and then masturbation; then he would go out at night. At first he would go out only once a month, but his habit built up gradually. "Everything was just like being on a slide," Mary Lee said, "You know it was real fast. It was from once a month to once a week to twice a week and then by November it was every night."[1]

Schiro's behavior was a function of pornography. Pornography got him drinking, and once he was drunk and his inhibitions were lowered he felt compelled to act out the fantasies he had seen in the X-rated book stores. When Schiro and Mary Lee moved to Evansville, his behavior got worse. He began to beat her, at one point knocking her two front teeth out. By the late fall of 1980 he was all but out of control. When Lee was at work Schiro would take her two-year-old son Willie to the Evansville mall and use him as a prop for panhandling, saying that he needed the money to feed his child. He would then take the money and spend it at adult bookstores. Sometimes he would spend $20 on one session at what he called the "quarter movies." These were the peep shows at the adult bookstores. For a quarter Schiro could see two or three minutes of a 15 minute film loop. The contents of the quarter movies were generally the most hard core of all the offerings at the adult book stores. When Mary Lee once asked Schiro where he had got the idea for a particularly bizarre form of sexual behavior, he answered by saying that he had learned it from these film strips.

In early December Schiro told his employer at Tri-State Repair, Robert Wheeler, that he had seen one of the women living at the house across the street come out to get the mail clad only in a pajama top and panties. The scene was the type of thing that Schiro never forgot. Over the next two months the image sank into his pornography-saturated psyche and emerged later as a fantasy that demanded action. He had made up his mind that he was going to rape the woman who lived across the street from where he worked. By February 4 the fantasy had become irresistible. According to the testimony of Mary Lee, Schiro said that when he woke up he just knew that something was wrong. He said the feeling got stronger and stronger, that he became afraid that something bad was going to happen.

Schiro spent the day of February 4, 1981, slowly being drawn into his own pornography-inspired obsessions. He was being inexorably transformed into an actor in his own quarter movie. Throughout the day on the job Schiro intoxicated himself by inhaling an industrial solvent. After leaving work at 2:30 in the afternoon, he went to a local tavern where he stole a pint of whiskey. He then took the whiskey to an X-rated book store and consumed it as he initiated his ritual of perusing first the magazines and then working his way back; to the harder-core quarter movies. Dr. Frank Osanka, a psychologist who specializes in child abuse and pornography, testified at Schiro's trial that the quarter movies were in general more sado-masochistic, more rape-oriented, and more violent than the generic movies at adult bookstores. As Schiro became more intoxicated, his behavior became correspondingly more belligerent. At one point he ran out of quarters and went for change, exposing himself to the cashier. The woman attendant gave him his change, and he went back and purchased some more movie time. The next time he ran out of quarters, he returned to the cashier still exposed but this time was belligerent about it. This time the woman threw him out. At this point he began making his way toward a house at 1210 Tennessee Street to keep his appointment with the woman who had gone out to get the mail in her pajama top and panties.

He never found her. He found her roommate instead. Laura Jane Luebbehusen had put on a robe for the evening. She was having a mixed drink and watching television, planning to take a bath and then go to bed. She had moved to Evansville from Ferdinand, Indiana, a small town fifty some miles off to the northeast. She worked as a truck driver for Charles Chips. She was a lesbian and living with the younger, prettier woman Schiro had seen from his work place. Her name was Darlene Hooper. She worked as a hostess at the Executive Inn in Evansville. She had been married and, in fact, was to spend the night of February 4 with her ex-husband. There is evidence that the lesbian relationship between Hooper and Luebbehusen was threatening to break up. In a note found in the trash can after the murder, Luebbehusen wrote to Hooper: "Honey, I do love you and don't want to leave either. So what we have to do is quit fighting. I love you, Laura."[2]

At 9:30 PM Schiro knocked on the door of 1210 E. Tennessee. "My car broke down," he said to Luebbehusen. "Can I use your phone? I want to call my dad."

"Sure," said Laura Jane, and she let him into the house.

Had Mary Lee had the benefit of reading the Lockhart Commission Report, she would have known that "exposure to erotica had no impact upon moral character"[3] and that "the increased availability of explicit sexual materials [in Denmark, at least] has been accompanied by a decrease in the incidence of sexual crime."[4] She also might have learned that "available research indicates that sex offenders have had less adolescent experience with erotica than other adults." In sum, she would have learned that "empirical research designed to clarify the question has found no evidence to date that exposure to explicit sexual materials plays a significant role in the causation of delinquent or criminal behavior among youth or adults."[5]

Since Mary Lee did not have the benefit of reading the Lockhart Commission Report, she ended up doing empirical research of her own and this entailed getting beaten repeatedly and having her two front teeth knocked out as Schiro's behavior degenerated into the savagery that pornography generated passions create. Her testimony contains first hand observation of how pornography inspires behavior by arousing the passions to the point where they are no longer under rational control. Mary Lee observed "the same pattern," which began with the "[pornographic film] loops," followed by liquor and dope and then deviant sexual behavior. Once the pattern got established, it was impossible to predict Schiro's behavior. "Like if we would be talking, having a conversation or watching TV or something, all of a sudden he would be really angry, like I said something that he didn't like or I don't know but just boom and he was mad." It was at unpredictable moments like that that Mary got her two front teeth knocked out. At another point Schiro gave her bruised ribs and a black eye. At another point he bit her and then chased her down the street. "It was horrible," she recounted to the court. "It was like he was possessed. . . . It was almost an inhuman laugh and he kept saying, 'you can't get away from me.'"[6]

In his more lucid moments, Schiro seemed aware that he had become the thrall of his own disordered passions. During one of his assaults on Mary Lee, he would repeat to her, "you are making me do this. I don't want to do this, but I can't stop, and you are making me do this."[7]

Lee's testimony gives a graphic account of the bondage that pornography creates in its victims.

"He knew that people said it was wrong and he knew that someone who was normal didn't do these things and he didn't want to do them. He just couldn't stop though. Something would get inside of him and there he would go. He had no control over it though because he hated doing it. He would cry and say, 'why do I do these things? Help me stop. What can I do to quit this. I don't want to do this anymore.' He wanted to be like the guy next door, you know, with the car in the garage and the dog. I hate the things that he had done but I can't say I hate Tom because I know that he is sick. He couldn't stop doing the things he did."

The same pattern repeated itself in the encounter with Laura Jane. After gaining entrance to the house by lying about his car, Schiro persuaded her to have consensual intercourse. Then after waking, he became enraged at her for no apparent reason and began beating her over the head with first a bottle and then an iron, Laura Jane continued to struggle until Schiro strangled her. Then he dragged her into the living room of the house and sodomized her corpse. While doing this he was, according to Lee's testimony, "crying the whole time and saying, 'God, please stop me. Don't let me do this. Please help me. God, I just can't quit.'"[8]

Schiro's trial received some attention at the time of the Meese hearings on pornography in the mid-'80s. In general, however, the testimony of those whose addiction to pornography led to murder and other crimes was generally suppressed by the media which sought to portray masturbation to pornography as not only harmless but also as an expression of freedom. Something similar happened to the testimony of mass-murderer Ted Bundy, who told Dr. James Dobson hours before Bundy was executed that pornography led him to do what he did. The editor of the Evansville newspaper told me after handing me a copy of Schiro's autobiography that pornography had no effect on behavior, even though Schiro and his girlfriend said the exact opposite. This suppression of the truth continues for a number of reasons. First of all, because the publishing industry is now heavily involved in pornography, and it is not in their interest to explain to the public that they are in the business of enslaving people. Secondly, the great myth of the enlightenment is "liberation." If it could be shown that the sexual liberation brings about bondage, then those who use the term to their advantage would be powerless to control behavior. Finally, no one wants to admit that passions can get out of control because it contradicts the central Promethean myth of the Enlightenment. Just as Ben Franklin harnessed electricity for mankind's benefit, so the sexual revolutionaries have liberated sexual energy from the moral law for the same end. To say that "liberated" passions were imperious masters who enslaved those who unleashed them would be to deny the most sacred tenet of the Enlightenment thinker. Therefore, evidence which supports that proposition is suppressed.

Thirteen hours after Schiro arrived at the door, Darlene Hooper discovered Laura Jane's battered body just inside the front door of their house on the living room floor. Rigor mortis had set in. The body's face and hair were covered with blood. A blood-stained pair of jeans was lying a few feet away. A ski jacket and insulated undershirt were pulled up around the neck of the victim, who had been raped while alive, beaten over the head with a whiskey bottle and an iron and then strangled. The body had also been raped and sodomized after death. Given Schiro's state of mind and given the internal logic of pornography, it was only a matter of time until somebody got killed. Death runs like a leitmotif through all pornographic practice. Necrophilia is only the logical extension of the tendencies already there. There are those who get killed by asphyxiating themselves while masturbating; there are those who murder their victims, particularly children, because they are afraid of getting caught; there are those who accidentally kill their victims in the process of some bondage routines, and there are those like Schiro, who, according to psychologist Frank Osanka, "saw just enough of the simulated sex and murder situations that he just had to try it himself."[9]

"After several times in my interview with him," Osanka continued, "I finally concluded that he knew he was going to kill this woman when he went in there, and so I just said to him, 'Did you intend to kill her?' and [he said]

'Yes.' He was fairly consistent on that. And when I asked why, he would say that he had never done that before."[10]

Thomas Schiro's behavior could be predicted from the type of pornography he had internalized. His life paralleled the trajectory which pornography had traveled since his birth in 1961. Sometime during 1967, the same year the Lockhart Commission on obscenity and pornography was formed, six-year-old Tom Schiro discovered some films owned by his father. One of them was called *Bedtime;* it was a World War II-vintage pornography film. Accounts on how Schiro became acquainted with the film vary. Schiro claims his father showed it to him. The father claims that Schiro discovered it on his own. One thing is certain; once Schiro saw the film, he never forgot it. It never lost its fascination for him. In fact, when he moved in with Mary Lee fourteen years later he insisted on showing it to her. She remembers it as an old film that "was broken into a million pieces. I think he said it came from World War II . . . but he said he had been looking at it for years." According to Osanka, "*Bedtime* is a film that depicts a man and a woman in bed in various acts of sexual involvement. The significant point of the film is that the camera keeps coming back to the woman's face.

"The woman's face consistently is one in which she is looking as if she is feeling uncomfortable, and she is looking as if she is in pain, and she is looking as if this is a disagreeable experience and at the same time her body is reacting in enthusiastic fashion. The fact that the camera kept going back and forth between the genital contact and her face gives the impression that her body was so enthusiastic in the sexual contacts but her face was distorted or angry or in pain so you get the impression that she's enjoying pain from the sex."[11] It was a lesson in sex education that young Schiro never forgot. When pressed on the issue of the woman's face, Osanka conceded that she could be conveying distaste or even boredom as much as pain. The point is that the six-year-old Schiro was confronted with material he had no way of understanding. There was nothing in his experience that could act as a check on his conclusions. There was no one to interpret this film as a sordid simulacrum of the real meaning of human sexuality. The film became the explicator of sex for Schiro. This lesson was only confirmed later on as Schiro became exposed to progressively more violent and perverted examples of pornography. The stimulus was so powerful it caused Schiro to act in a certain way, causing life to imitate art. Once Schiro internalized the film as his first most powerful lesson in sex education, his behavior became a self-fulfilling prophecy. Sex meant violation and pain, but Schiro concluded that the victim enjoyed the experience nonetheless. Schiro's experience once he began to act out his fantasies only confirmed him in his pornography-nurtured view of sex.

According to Osanka,

> what has occurred with Tom happens in many pedophiliacs, that is the individuals who habitually abuse children, that is that he had a psycho-

sex-drive, halting as a result of premature unguided exposure to erotica before he was physically or psychologically ready to integrate that into his personality. Much of his subsequent sexual behavior, sexual aggression is repetitive of the film. For example, peeping here is not a great deal of difference between peeping in windows, which are a screen, and masturbating and watching a film and masturbating.[12]

Schiro's life provides a textbook-like illustration of the trajectory that pornography addiction takes in an individual's life. Schiro's life became a quest for erotic materials, from nudist-type picture magazines of the type one would find in drug stores to sneaking into X-rated drive-in theaters, where he could watch the sado-masochistic movies and snuff movies, in which people are portrayed as being killed through sexual assault. According to testimony to Osanka, Schiro enjoyed these movies immensely, taking particular pleasure in the pain he could see on the victims' faces. Schiro came of age when the stream of pornography in this country was increasing to a flood-tide. It was his misfortune to be swept away by it and the misfortune of his victims to be swept away with him.

Schiro saw his first hard-core sado-masochist film at the age of eleven. As with *Bedtime* he could retain the details of what he saw years afterward. He recounted to Osanka at least ten years later scenes of extreme violence, women being raped and knifed, men being flagellated. It was obvious to Osanka that he enjoyed recalling these particular scenes. "They are important to him," the psychologist told the court during Schiro's trial, "because of the disorder he is suffering. He is overpowered by this need for orgasmic release, which he had conditioned and developed over a period of years, and the only release is through more and more bizarre forms of masturbation. For example, in relating the number of rapes and the specifics of the rapes he would say that very often by the time he broke into a home he would not have an erection, and so he would have to lie on the floor and use his picture books in order to be able to get an erection in order to be able to go into the next room to start the ritual of hovering over the body of the victim in order to ejaculate in the face of the victim. The whole practice of ejaculating on the victim is a recurring theme in pornography today. He very specifically likes those parts of the films when he watches the peep shows." Schiro was by no means only indebted to hard-core material as his educator in depravity. He claimed that he learned the technique for breaking into homes to commit rapes from the made-for-television movie called *Cry Rape*.

The crucial fact of Schiro's life was that pornography influences behavior. It functions as an aid to masturbation. Even more significant though is the fact that when these pornographic images got incorporated into Schiro's masturbatory fantasies, they demanded to be acted out. Acting out is the only way that the addict can find the stimulation he needs to complete his act of masturbation. According to Osanka, "most people who look at pornography over any extended period masturbate in conjunction with the material. People don't masturbate to train magazines or baseball magazines, but they do to pornography magazines. What happens is that the masturbation coupled with the visual image places the individual in the situation to the point where in some people it goes past fantasy to the point where people really believe that they can achieve those types of things and there's an increased desire for acting them out. Since he started so early, all sexuality is masturbation to Schiro. With the women he'd rape he'd have a hard time unless he was masturbating."[13]

Edward Donnerstein, an authority on pornography and sexual aggression, testified at Schiro's trial that "there is a direct link between exposure to certain types of pornography, particularly images that are aggressive in nature – in fact images which Mr. Schiro was exposed to very, very early and found very sexually stimulating – and increases in calloused attitudes about rape, increases in the belief that women desire and enjoy being raped and increases in a willingness, in fact, to say one would commit rape and also increases in aggressive behavior against women. . . . Mr. Schiro believes in fact the victim finds these types of aggressive acts very pleasurable."[14]

According to Donnerstein, Schiro "viewed pornography which showed rapes of women, pornography which showed sadistic acts against women and against men and pornography which is showing masochistic very aggressive types of acts, and he consistently said in interviews that he finds those very, very sexually arousing, so sexually arousing, particularly in the instances where he was drinking, that he literally wanted to, if he could, rip the page out and rape the woman or have intercourse with the woman on the page, but since he couldn't he would seek out an unwilling victim."[15]

In spite of its flaws and the fact that the Congress which brought the commission into being rejected its findings, the Lockhart Commission report was widely disseminated throughout the liberal media establishment as "proof" that pornography was harmless. The recommendation that existing laws be repealed, along with the fact that prosecution of obscenity cases virtually ceased, created the impression in the public mind that the obscenity laws had *in fact* been repealed. Clive Barnes epitomizing the liberal reaction to the commission in the very act of promoting its results could conclude that "women are the underprivileged sex when it comes to erotica and that this underprivilege derives from male supremacy."[16] The conclusion was that more smut would make America a better place.

It wasn't long before evidence to the contrary started showing up. In 1973, the stag film went public with the widespread dissemination of the X-rated film *Deep Throat*. The film's main character, Linda Lovelace, became an overnight celebrity in articles in the liberal press that tried to bring respectability to a woman performing deviant acts on the wide screen. Nora Ephron wrote an article in which she quoted Lovelace as saying, "I totally enjoyed myself making the movie. I don't have any inhibitions about sex. I just hope everybody who goes to see the film loses some of their inhibitions."[17] Lovelace, after escaping from her pimp cum manager, later described her descent into what used to be called white slavery in less flattering terms.

Throughout the '70s, it was becoming increasingly apparent that giving free rein to sex meant that sex would quickly devolve into something else. By the '70s sado-masochism had become so prevalent that it was used as a part of an advertising campaign to sell records for the Rolling Stones. "I'm Black and Blue from the Rolling Stones, and I love it," said a lady on a billboard in Hollywood with ropes around her arms and bruises on her thighs. It was becoming increasingly clear that sex was not stopping at just sex. In 1976 the movie *Snuff* was released, which purported to show a woman being murdered and then dismembered on the screen for the sexual delectation of the viewing audience. The film caused the first large-scale, media-approved reaction to pornography since the Lockhart Commission told the world that America would be a better place with more pornography. Feminists across the country protested the movie. In San Francisco in 1978 feminists organized a Take Back the Night March through San Francisco's pornography district. In New York in 1979 biweekly tours of 42nd Street were being offered by an organization known as Women Against Pornography. Andrea Dworkin and Catherine A. Mackinnon attempted to have ordinances passed in Indianapolis and Minneapolis which would make pornography illegal because it violated women's rights.

By the mid-1980s, however, it was clear that pornography was an issue that split the feminist movement. A large number of feminists, mostly lesbian, saw nothing wrong with pornography because they used it themselves. Mackinnon found herself attacked in the pages of *off our backs,* a lesbian monthly. Commenting on an article on pornography by Alice Henry which appeared in the November 1984 issue of *off our backs,* Sharon Page of Chicago applauds the author and the journal "for breaking the silence in showing that radical feminists are *not,* after all, monolithic followers of the Mackinnon/Dworkin antiporn analysis and strategy. . . . Porn/erotica *can* play a progressive role in showing women taking pleasure apart from the married/reproductive context – if we reclaim it to do so." It was the beginning of a strategy which the publishing industry would adopt in the 1990s as a way of defusing feminist protest against pornography.

Andrea Dworkin, who seems to have become deranged by reading too much pornography, was typical of the feminist overreaction which condemned not only pornography but sexual intercourse as well as something quintessentially male. Males, according to Dworkin, were ipso facto a pathological phenomenon. Pornography was simply the most visible symptom of the disease, in the way that the sore is an indication of herpes. Maleness was the universal *radix malorum.* "Terror," Dworkin writes in *Pornography: Women Possessing Men,* "*is* the outstanding theme and consequence of male history and male culture. . . . Terror issues forth from the male, illuminates his essential nature and his basic purpose." According to Dworkin, there was virtually no difference between rape and marriage. "Marriage as an institution developed from rape as a practice. Rape, originally defined as abduction, became marriage by capture. Marriage meant the taking was to extend in time, to be not only use of, but lifelong possession of, or ownership." As with most feminist analysis, Dworkin's views preclude the need for explanation. Schiro, one could say, was a rapist because he was a male. Pornography just allowed his maleness free expression. Men exploited women sexually because they were men. Exploitation exists because men exist, and so on.

The belief that sexual perversion and exploitation and pornography were all a function of maleness is, however, becoming less tenable in the face of the evidence. First of all, feminists, especially lesbians, are increasingly frequent users of pornography. One need only read the book ads for Lambda Press and Naiad Press to find this out. Naiad Press, in fact, had no qualms about selling the rights to a number of the stories in its best-seller *Lesbian Nuns* to the unabashedly pornographic *Forum* magazine, which was owned by *Penthouse,* one of the big three of one-handed magazines. A new lesbian journal, *On Our Backs,* makes use of standard, undoctored sado-masochistic material. As a result, and as has already happened in the heterosexual and male homosexual demimonde, life is beginning to imitate art. Gloria Kaufman, a South Bend feminist, writing in the May 1985 issue of *off our backs,* explained how she sent two young recruits to the feminist movement to the Michigan Womyn's [*sic*] Music Festival for what she "supposed would be an edifying experience." Unfortunately the recruits stumbled upon the festival's sado-masochism workshop, where they saw "a group of women in leather standing over another woman on the ground, lacerations and blood all over her body, and blood all over the ground."[18]

Kaufman then finds herself confronted with what seems like a contradiction in the feminist movement. "How is it," she asks, "that we disapprove of men's cutting up women, but we tolerate women's cutting up of women?"[19] Kaufman takes pride in the pluralism of feminism. She has heard the arguments of the S/M crowd but remains unconvinced. "S/M people," she opines, "will tell you that the bleeding is superficial and controlled. That is not reassuring."[20] Kaufman's greatest fear though is that the S/M crowd will give lesbianism a bad name. "Since the practitioners of S/M are lesbians," she argues with a logic difficult to refute, "it validates homophobia in the minds of some non-lesbian feminists. . . . Homophobia based upon irrational fear is difficult but possible to combat. Homophobia based upon knowledge of real-life sadism is exceedingly difficult perhaps impossible to eradicate."[21] The facts, in other words, are the best argument in support of homophobia.

Lest her lesbian readership conclude that she has gone too far in the direction of intolerance, Kaufman makes it clear that she is only opposed to the *public* display of womyn lacerating other womyn. "Let it be clear that I am calling into question no one's expression of sexuality in the privacy of her home."

The belief that deviant sexual behavior of the sort portrayed in pornographic films and practiced at the Michigan Womyn's [*sic*] Music Festival can remain within limits and thereby insure that no one will get hurt has been the cornerstone for the liberal apologia for the dissemination of pornography. Tom Schiro grew up against this background of ever-deepening decadence, went from being a masturbator to a voyeur to a rapist to a murderer in following one clearly defined trajectory that anyone who was familiar with the themes pornography portrayed over the past ten years should have been able to predict.

If one considers how he ended up, Schiro's early years are remarkable for their absence of pathology. Schiro was adopted at the age of five days. His foster parents did not divorce, nor was Schiro the victim of child abuse of either the physical or sexual variety. In fact the opposite seemed to be the case. If anything Schiro was spoiled as a child. "Ever since I can remember," he wrote in a thirty-nine-page autobiography after he was arrested, "Mommy and Daddy have given me everything I wanted. I always got what I wanted. My birthday is two days before Christmas so I'd get double the presents. I got fourteen bikes in thirteen years." When Schiro didn't want to do something, he didn't do it. If he didn't want to go to school, he would pretend that he was sick. "The nurse used to try to tell me I wasn't sick, but I'd start crying cause I knew mommy would come and get me. And she did."[22]

Much has been written contributing to the mystification of rape, most of it by feminists. It is, according to them, the expression of the male reign of terror over females. In her much-cited book *Against Our Will,* feminist Susan Brownmiller makes out of rape a cosmic principle:

> Man's discovery that his genitalia could serve as a weapon to generate fear must rank as one of the most important discoveries of prehistoric times, along with the use of fire and the first crude stone axe. From prehistoric times to the present, I believe rape has played a critical function. It is nothing more or less than a conscious process of intimidation by which *all* men keep *all* women in a state of fear.[23]

When one examines the actual life of an actual rapist, the explanations seem less cosmic and seem to have more to do with human passion left to grow wild under the unnatural stimulation of pernicious influences like pornography and drugs. When Mary Lee described Schiro's sexual practices to the court, she gave some insight into how a deranged sexuality, of the sort described in and fostered by pornography, could lead in itself to rape. "He would just get on and pump away," Lee said of their love life, "until he was finished and then get off. I would try to say 'no,' but he never took 'no' for an answer." A rapist, in other words, is someone who never takes 'no' for an answer. Tom Schiro was propelled through life by pornography-incited fantasies which became more and more bizarre and more imperious as time went on. His addictions to drugs and alcohol simply made him more likely to act out the scenarios he spent so much time viewing. And once he acted out one scenario the craving was set in motion to act out another more bizarre one further down the road.

"I remember going to book stores," he wrote, describing one of his earliest memories, "and looking at girly books or photography books and hopeing [*sic*] they'd have naked pictures in them. I started peeping in windows. It was exciteing [*sic*]. . . . I started smoking pot in 7th grade. I always cried a lot, especially about not having friends."[24]

Schiro received little moral guidance from his father. After being caught peeping and being picked up by his father at the police station, Schiro remembers his father saying, "If you want something to screw, why didn't you ask me. We'd get you a hooker or something rather than peeping in windows." In spite of the embarrassment he caused his family, Schiro was once again not punished. "I don't think I got put on restriction or nothing," Schiro added. Psychologist Frank Osanka felt that Schiro got caught up in bad habits which involve a necessary progression from one phase to the other.

> Getting access to girlie magazines that are readily available [led to] seeing in the girlie magazines ads for other kinds of material and then to seeking those out. In the past that meant as a youngster sneaking in to X-rated drive-ins or, as Schiro did, to somehow team up with another adult who had these kinds of materials and getting sexually involved with them, as Schiro did, to eventually getting into the adult bookstores. There's a progression of severity, an increase in bizarreness of material which I think is dangerous, but today it's not even necessary to go through all those steps. Today there is such widely available triple X-rated material at video rental stores that are not adult book stores; these are family movie rentals that have the section that sells the X-rated movies. And many of those movies have many of the more violent themes that were only available in adult bookstores.[25]

When asked what the most significant change in pornography was since the [Lockhart] Report of the Commission on Obscenity and Pornography, Father Morton Hill, S.J. cited the expansion of pornography into other media, most notably the home videocassette business.

Given the type of practices one becomes accustomed to watching in pornography and the habit of masturbation that invariably accompanies such viewing, it should come as no surprise that the addict sees no magic line separating what the liberals would call private behavior from rape. Schiro took to rape as the natural extension of his already perverted sex life. He had learned not to take "no" for an answer. He couldn't say "no" to himself; why should he take that answer from other people?

"It was in April of 77 that we moved [to Indiana]," he wrote in his autobiography. "Then I started main-lineing [*sic*] cocaine. I started peeping in windows again in Princeton. I didn't have a real friend. Everybody thought I was a fool & had a big mouth. When I try to pay people a complement [*sic*] it would always come out a [*sic*] insult.

"I don't know how many girls I screwed in Princeton [Indiana]. Maybe 8. I don't know where the idea of rape came in, but it excited me. One night I went over to Mt. Carmel & peeped in windows to look for a naked girl to rape. I found her. Before this I'd always go around in my car & [masturbate]. I'd stop girls along the road & ask them for directions some place. It was like a compulsion. I couldn't stop myself. I did it so many times. It was an everyday thing. It excited me." Schiro then describes the mixed feelings he got from exposing himself. "It was so exciting. I don't know how I felt. I know I was out of my mind. I was always scared of getting caught but I couldn't stop.

"I was scared. I remember after each time I did these things I said to myself, my God what have I done? I couldn't stop myself."[26]

According to the catharsis theory propounded by the Lockhart Commission, Schiro should have been content to look at his pornographic films and books and masturbate in private. It didn't work out that way, and the proponents of pornography have yet to come up with an explanation of why. The answer transcends the categories even of good psychologists because it has to do with the nature of sexuality itself, which is intrinsically other-directed. If it is not directed toward a spouse and put at the service of life, it will be directed toward people who have been turned into objects, and then it will head toward death. The Reverend Richard Roach, S.J., a moral theologian at Marquette University, sees sex as an either/or situation. Denial of its God-ordained purpose leads inevitably to the depravity which has been so adequately documented in recent years.

> When sex is moved from the authentic conjugal expression, you really introduce sado-masochism because the very physical structure of sex gives a dominant and penetrating figure and submissive and penetrated figure – no matter how active the woman is – and that very physical structure is potentially sadomasochistic. Sex can be used as put down. All of that element is redeemed in authentic conjugal love and that's why authentic conjugal love is in the long run the only sex that is consoling. And that other element remains in all illicit sex in varying degrees. Now in homosexuality it is immediately present in a very large degree even at the very early romantic stage of homosexuality because one has to artificially or wrongly submit to the other or do things that are disgusting for this pleasure, even if it's traded back and forth, so there's a mega-potency for sado-masochism. The very anatomical and psychological structure of sex is

potentially that at all times and is redeemed only by the honest to God structure of conjugal love for which it was made.

As Schiro became more deeply immersed in pornography, his behavior became more and more overtly sadistic. He beat up his girlfriend Mary Lee a number of times in the months leading up to the murder. He would repeatedly drown and then revive Lee's son Willie in their bathtub. Schiro also developed a relationship with a manikin in an Evansville department store window. He would tell her his problems, and at one point became very upset when her wig was changed. He even asked the manikin for permission to marry Mary Lee. In retrospect psychologist Osanka feels that this behavior along with his instructions to Lee that she should not move during sex indicated an increasing attraction to necrophilia. Schiro at one point indicated an interest in working at a funeral home so that he could have sexual relations with dead bodies. Sex with the dead was the one thing that Schiro hadn't tried, and the idea of it became an obsession with him, so much so that, according to Osanka, he knew he was going to kill his next victim. The one thing that remained constant in Schiro's slide toward the ultimate violation was his constant use of pornography. It was the gas that fueled his obsession.

"When I met Mary," he wrote, "after the first month of living together I use [sic] to get my girly books and look at them while we screwed. I'd make believe I was screwing the girls in the book. It was exciting. Mary would like to watch my face. I don't think she really liked me doing it. Girly books excite me so much. I've always looked at them. I can remember when I get horney from looking at girly books & watching girly shows I'd wanna go rape somebody. Everytime I'd [masturbate] I'd be thinking of rape and the women I had raped remembering how exciting it was, the pain on there [sic] faces. The thrill, the excitement."[27]

The connection between illicit sex and death is the last thing the propagandists for sexual revolution would admit, but it's been there all along. Tom Schiro had to find out the hard way. The tragic linkage of male homosexual activity to suicide is well known. While exact numbers are hard to come by, the rate of suicide among the homosexually active seems to be twenty or more times higher than in the general population. As abortion has shown, a sex-saturated culture quickly becomes one obsessively concerned with death. The only way Schiro could satisfy his increasingly bizarre and imperious sexual desires was through closer and closer approximations until finally it was death alone that would satisfy him, and one young woman's life was the price he was willing to pay for sexual satisfaction. Schiro has been on death row in the Indiana State Penitentiary at Michigan City since 1982. He continues to masturbate ten to twelve times a day, now to mental images of the dead body of the woman he murdered. His life is one never-ending cycle of tumescence and remorse lived out, appropriately enough, on death row.

Part III, Chapter 20

Washington, D.C., 1983

In May 1983 Judith Reisman, then a recent Ph.D. in communications who was on the faculty doing research at the University of Haifa in Israel, was guest on a talk show hosted by right-wing pundit and former Nixon aide Pat Buchanan. During the course of the discussion Reisman indicated that the sexualized portrayal of children in magazines like *Playboy* was leading to an epidemic of copy-cat child abuse by juveniles and adults. One of the listeners who found her claims intriguing was Alfred Regnery (son of the conservative publisher Henry Regnery) who had just been appointed head of the United States Department of Justice's Office of Juvenile Justice and Delinquency Prevention. The OJJDP had a budget to subsidize research, and since Regnery had no desire to give out grants to what he considered the same old left-wing network which had received them in the past, Reisman seemed like just the person to give impetus to the Reagan shakeup of Washington politics. Reisman met with Regnery and other Justice Department officials on May 24, and they assured her that they were interested in funding research which could establish a "causal relationship between sexualization and violence involving children in mainstream pornography" but told her that she should locate a university to administer the grant. When she mentioned this to Jack Martin, the owner of a Texas publishing house who was interested in her work, Martin responded by saying that he was a friend of Richard Berendzen, then president of American University. Martin felt that Berendzen would be interested in the project.

It was a feeling which turned out to be true. In early June 1983, Martin arranged a meeting between Reisman and Dr. Robert Norris, vice provost of the university, who indicated that the university was "quite enthusiastic" about what they considered an important project, which also not coincidentally had the prospect of important government funding attached to it as well. Norris concluded by informing Reisman that she could count on being appointed to a full research professorship, with free tuition for her children, once the funding had been approved. Backing up what Norris had conveyed verbally, the university notified Reisman, in a letter dated August 31, 1983, that she had just been appointed full research professor. Then, after a period during which everything fell in place in a manner that approached the miraculous, things started to go wrong. Because she was a neophyte in the particularly vicious political struggles which characterized the area where government money and academic ambition intersect, Reisman wasn't aware of what was going on until it was too late.

Reisman had been born Judith Ann Gelernter in 1935 in Newark to a family of German/Russian Jewish communists of the sort that might have attended one of Alexandra Kollontai's lectures when she arrived in New York during World War I. Unlike Kollontai, the Gelernter family, who were involved in the seafood business, drew a clear line between left-wing politics and sexual liberation. Reisman remembers a mother who welcomed her home every day after school and a father who loved her mother and a family who arranged impromptu musicals around the family's piano, where they listened to her Aunt Mary, who had rejected an offer to sing with the Metropolitan Opera, sing Yiddish and American folk songs. The musical culture of the Gelernter family eventually rubbed off on Judith, who went on to become a vocalist and producer of music segments for educational television (PBS), the Milwaukee Public Museum, the Cleveland Museum of Art, and Captain Kangaroo, a popular children's program in the '50s and '60s.

The family idyll continued into Reisman's own family and only ended in 1966 when her then ten-year-old daughter Jennie as well as other neighborhood children were sexually molested by a thirteen-year-old neighbor boy who had been sexualized by repeated exposure to his father's collection of *Playboy* magazines. Seeking support or at least an explanation for what had happened, she spoke to an aunt who told her that children were "sexual from birth." When a classmate from Berkeley told her the same thing, she began to wonder who the source of the idea was. It was then that Judith Reisman made her first contact with the work of Alfred Kinsey. It wouldn't be her last.

On July 23, 1981, Reisman delivered a paper entitled "The Scientist as a Contributing Agent to Child Sexual Abuse: A Preliminary Study," in which she brought up, for the first time in the thirty-two years since it had been published, the material on child sexuality in Tables 30–34 of the Kinsey male volume and wondered how this data could have been obtained without involvement in criminal activity. Before giving her report, Reisman had written to male volume co-author Paul Gebhard to ask about the data in Tables 30–34. Gebhard wrote back saying that the data had been obtained from parents, school teachers, and some male homosexuals, including "some of Kinsey's men" who had used "manual and oral techniques" to catalogue the number of orgasms they said they could stimulate in infants and children.[1] Virtually the entire sex industry-sex research establishment worldwide was in attendance at the meeting in Jerusalem, but the reaction to the talk was silence, stunned or sullen or otherwise, until a Swedish reporter wondered out loud why the assembled experts had nothing to say.

The silence was understandable. Just about everyone in attendance had cited Kinsey as their mentor, and some even knew about the criminal activity involved in Kinsey's research. They all knew that Kinsey's research was the basis of their "science," which is to say, the legitimizing basis for everything they did. Kinsey was the foundation of that house of cards. If what he had done could be discredited, it threatened the sexual empire which had been built since his death and upon which they all depended for a livelihood. Later when word got out that Reisman had government money to pursue her thesis and show a link between Kinsey's exploitation of child "sexuality" and *Playboy, Penthouse,* and *Hustler*'s exploitation of the same thing, stunned silence turned to determined, if behind the scenes, action. According to Reisman, "the Kinsey Institute had secretly threatened American University with a lawsuit if I was allowed to carry out my study."[2] Reisman discovered this and other facts when she deposed June Reinisch, then head of the Kinsey Institutes, when she attempted to sue the Kinsey Institute for defamation.

Unaware that any movement against her was afoot, Reisman began to notice problems with the actual disbursement of the grant shortly after it had been awarded. On August 22, 1983, Pamela Swain, Director of Research and Program Development at OJJDP, wrote to Regnery informing him that the Reisman project was no more than a limited survey of research literature, which could be accomplished by OJJDP for approximately $40,000 to $60,000. From July until December of 1983, Robert Heck, Reisman's OJJDP program manager, told her on several occasions that he was encountering unusual administrative delays. In order to expedite the implementation of the grant, Heck deleted all references to *Playboy, Penthouse,* and *Hustler* and any indication that those magazines might contribute to either sexual abuse of children or delinquency, in spite of the fact that it was part of her original mandate to examine them. Then on December 22, 1983, Reisman was told Congress had approved the grant to explore "The Role of Pornography and Media Violence in Family Violence, Sexual Abuse and Exploitation and Juvenile Delinquency" for the amount of $798,531.

With the grant finally approved, Reisman met with AU's director of Contracts Administration, Stanley Matelski, on December 27, 1983, only to learn that AU was now having second thoughts about being the sponsoring institution. "We don't know if we want to go ahead on this grant," Matelski told Reisman. "We're not sure we want to sign it." When questioned about the abrupt change in attitude from the enthusiastic reception her idea got in June, Matelski said that columnist Jack Anderson had called AU and was investigating the grant and apparently intended to do an negative article on the project. As a result, Dr. Anita Gottlieb, head of the AU public-relations department and a one-time associate of Anderson, recommended that AU drop the grant because the university did not want unfavorable publicity. Commenting on the expected adverse publicity, Matelski indicated that an individual "higher" in the University was in agreement with the recommendation to drop the grant.

At around this time, Gordon Raley, staff director for Congressman Ike

Andrews (NC) became involved in the story when he called AU and said that the Reisman project was "illegal." James Wootton, OJJDP Deputy Administrator, would later say that Judith Reisman was simply a pawn in a war waged by people who were out to get Al Regnery because of his conservative views, but the vehemence and the magnitude of the attack indicated more was at stake than the job of one political appointee. At stake was the credibility of the sex education and pornography industry because all of them were based on Kinsey, and now Kinsey was under attack.

The method of attack was to portray Reisman's grant as a waste of taxpayers' money, something that would discredit her project to the conservative audience which would otherwise be favorably disposed to what Reisman had to say about the effects of pornography. On February 6, Jack Anderson made good on his threat and wrote an article, which appeared in the *Washington Post* and was syndicated nationally, calling the Reisman project, "another scheme that stinks of Voodoo science." On February 20, 1984, *USA Today* ran an article based on a January 19 interview with Raley, who said, "I have never seen a grant as bad as this, nor an application more irresponsibly prepared." Given the billions of dollars the government had already poured into every form of pork barrel research imaginable, the vehemence of Raley's statement went beyond mere hyperbole. Something big was clearly at stake here, and it wasn't the fiscally insignificant sum of $800,000.

The grant was finally approved for disbursal on February 10, but Reisman's troubles were far from over. Encouraged by the attacks in the media, Raley scheduled judicial subcommittee oversight hearings on the OJJDP and Reisman's grant for April 11, 1984. Once American University received the money, Reisman began to experience the same sort of delays from their grants department whenever she attempted to obtain the administrative support necessary for the project. Her efforts to talk to President Berendzen were rebuffed when Dean Frank Turaj informed her on May 16 that all communication with the president would have to go through him. At around the same time, Myra Sadker, the woman who had signed the letter appointing Reisman full research professor, resigned and was replaced by the new dean, David Sansbury, who announced on his initial visit to Reisman's office that he felt that the results of her research might be used to stifle First Amendment freedoms.

At this point, the one-handed magazines got openly involved in the fight. In July 1984, *Playboy* ran a feature attacking Reisman –" Fat Grants and Sleazy Politics: Reagan's Porn Paranoia" – in its August issue, calling Reisman's project a "Big Brother censorship program." One month later, Larry Flynt, then in jail fighting an obscenity charge, penned a similarly derogatory piece in *Hustler*. Newspapers like the *Atlanta Journal* and *USA Today* did similar pieces, as did *The Monitor*, the publication of the American Psychological Association.

Shortly after the *Playboy* article appeared, Senators Arlen Specter (R, PA), Howard Metzenbaum (D, OH) and Edward Kennedy (D, MA) held Senate hearings on the grant, which involved questioning not only Reisman but also Richard Berendzen, and Dean Frank Turaj of AU, as well as Alfred Regnery, James Wootton, Robert Heck, and Pamela Swain of OJJDP. Reisman's staff, already under pressure to meet their deadline, were frightened and harassed, and she was threatened with dire consequences unless she appeared before the oversight committee immediately. During these hearings, Specter would ask leading questions of the following sort: "Do you have any intention of abandoning the project as a result of these proceedings?" He also demanded to see child pornography, and when Reisman handed him a "Chester the Molester" cartoon, Specter, ignoring the title, claimed there was no molestation in the cartoon, even though the same cartoon was used to help convict its creator, Dwaine Tinsley, of incestuous abuse of his daughter several years later.

According to Susan Trento, "no one would help Reisman prepare for the hearings." As a result Reisman went into the hearings, unaware of what their true purpose was, which according to Trento, was that the politicians were posturing for the press. Which press she doesn't say, nor does she say who the press represented in this struggle. Later after Reisman learned that Howard Metzenbaum had been interviewed in *Penthouse*, she felt he should have acknowledged this conflict of interest and recused himself.

AU President Berendzen begrudgingly defended Reisman on academic freedom grounds before the subcommittee hearings, but back at AU actions were being taken to gut the project, or at least to restructure it radically. As soon as AU signed the grant the AU Institutional Review Board demanded that Reisman not examine or refer to Kinsey's work in anything she did with her grant money. On September 10, Myra Sadker and Frank Turaj met with Reisman and presented her with a new organizational chart for the project, one which now put Sadker in overall control of the program. Sadker was now also named "Research Director" and "First Author" of the project design. Reisman refused and threatened to sue. On October 9, AU Provost Milton Greenberg met with Reisman to inform her that the university was now only proceeding with the grant reluctantly. He also made clear that he felt there was no proof that what was portrayed in the pages of *Playboy*, *Penthouse*, and *Hustler* had any effect on behavior. "All your colleagues," Greenberg told Reisman, read these magazines, so "no one will listen to you, no matter what you find."

Following the attacks in *Playboy* and *Hustler*, Reisman's grant was reduced to $200,000, but even this didn't satisfy its critics. On December 10, 1984, Gordon Raley was quoted as saying in a UPI article that "the scope of this project should have been reduced a year ago, and it should have been reduced to zero." Shortly after leaving his position as Subcommittee Staff Director in 1985, Raley wrote an especially critical article attacking Reisman, entitled "Reisman's $734,000 Thrill." The article appeared in *Penthouse,* in its November 1986 issue, along with the type of graphics Reisman was criticizing.

In the meantime, the same unfavorable press, including a front-page article which appeared on May 3, 1985, in the *Washington Post*, continued unabated. Under the cloak of fiscal accountability, the press was calling for what amounted to prior censorship of the research, and failing to get the grant canceled, they did their best to discredit the results before the research had been completed. At first glance, the reaction seemed out of all proportion to the stimulus, but then it became known that the Reagan Administration was about to promote a major antipornography initiative of its own, and the attack on Reisman could be seen as a preemptive strike on something bigger just over the horizon. The purpose of the media attack was to trivialize any concern with pornography as a waste of the taxpayers' money. On May 13, Raley was quoted in *Time* magazine as saying, "We don't need a study to determine that child pornography is bad. We could use some assistance in doing something about it."[3] What Raley neglected to say is that Reisman was involved in documenting the use of children in the big three one-handed magazines – *Playboy, Penthouse*, and *Hustler* – and it was doubtful that Raley wanted any help attacking them, especially since one of his articles had appeared in *Penthouse*. Then the reason for all of this defensiveness became apparent.

On May 20, 1985, newly appointed Attorney General Edwin Meese called a press conference at the Department of Justice in Washington, D.C., to announce the members of the Attorney General's Commission on Pornography. The new commission was called into being a year before when President Reagan signed into law the Child Protection Act of 1984. According to Meese, "the president made this request in response to the many complaints about pornography that have been registered throughout the nation. The purpose of the commission is to reassess the impact of pornography on society over the past fifteen years, especially its increased violence and the spread of pornography to other media, the video recorder, the telephone, and even the computer." Among its objectives, the Meese Commission was to "determine the nature, extent, and impact on society of pornography in the United States, and to make specific recommendations to the Attorney General concerning more effective ways in which the spread of pornography could be contained, consistent with constitutional guarantees." Among other things the scope of the commission included "a review of the available empirical and scientific evidence on the relationship between exposure to pornographic materials and antisocial behavior, and on the impact of the creation and dissemination of both adult and child pornography upon children." Since that seemed to be a reference to Reisman's project, all of the commotion over one grant suddenly became clear. The sexual dulling that goes with pornography had progressed by 1985 to the point where the only thing the average citizen got upset about anymore was child pornography. Hence, if there were to be any curtailment of the spread of porn, it would have to be based on the indignation which the exploitation of children caused. The commission was to terminate one year from the date of the first commission meeting. That was held in Chicago on July 24 and 25, 1985.

Ten days after Attorney General Meese announced the formation of his pornography commission, AU Provost Greenberg called Reisman into his office to tell her that under no circumstances would she be allowed to work on her grant beyond the November 30, 1985 cut-off date. Reisman was also notified that her Xerox equipment would be removed by November 27. On October 29, Reisman was informed that she had to get the grant done two weeks sooner than the deadline Greenberg had given her in May.

In the end Reisman completed a draft grant report on schedule in late 1985 in spite of the fact that AU changed the deadline on her, reducing the amount of time she had still further (and despite the friction and problems among her staff due to both external and internal harassment). She was forced out of AU immediately upon delivery of the report; however, the draft remained at AU for clerical "editing" before it was mailed to the project peer group for comments, corrections, and additions. Instead of editing Reisman's document, AU took nine months to rewrite her report. The gutted AU version with the peers' confused criticisms was then forwarded to the Justice Department, where Verne Spiers, the new OJJDP administrator, lost no time in announcing that the study they had commissioned was rejected due to multiple serious flaws. Regaining access to her report for nine weeks, Reisman began the painstaking task of reading and correcting the 1,600 page report, putting back in what AU had taken out.

It would have been an impossible task for a lone researcher to accomplish but Reverend Jerry Falwell heard of her situation and flew Reisman and her papers to Lynchburg, where he gave her access to secretaries and a graphic artist. Since AU locked Reisman out of her computer disks and her data files, over the next nine weeks, by diligently checking her original hard copy against AU's gutted and altered version, all of the data were re-entered, re-checked and the document re-created. Although Reisman had salvaged AU's promise that all of her materials would be delivered to the Attorney General's commission on pornography no later than January 31, 1986, the materials were never delivered.

In January 1986 shortly after Reisman was forced out of her position at American University, Sanford Ungar, a journalist who had worked for public radio, was appointed dean of the AU school of communication. Ungar did not have a degree in communications, which made his appointment as dean seem somewhat odd to Reisman when she heard about it. But eventually the reason for his appointment became clear when Ungar emerged that summer as a spokesman for Americans for Constitutional Freedom, the front group which the Media Coalition – i.e., the masturbation industry – had set up to fight the Meese Commission. Reisman claims that the appointment was part of a deal by which wealthy prospective donors would give money to the AU school of communications. In the summer of '86, Ungar would appear on the McNeill-Lehrer news program representing Americans for Constitutional Freedom, which he described as "businesses and individuals who are concerned about some of the aftermath of the Justice Department's Pornography Commission . . . people who are worried about this sort of hysteria – the current frenzy over pornography and the attempt to start intimidating people to remove perfectly lawful materials from stores, libraries, classrooms."[4]

Right around the time Ungar was appointed dean at AU, on January 21, 1986, Linda Boreman testified before the Meese Commission in New York. During her testimony, she described being kicked and beaten during the filming of *Deep Throat* in Miami as well as being held in bondage by Chuck Traynor as a prostitute. Perhaps sensing just how devastating Boreman's testimony would be, the masturbation industry organized a pre-emptive strike a week before. On January 16, 1986, Betty Friedan and other *prominenti*, organized a press conference that eventually got released as a pamphlet entitled: *The Meese Commission Exposed: Proceedings of a National Coalition Against Censorship*. In attendance, in addition to Ms. Friedan were Kurt Vonnegut, Colleen Dewhurst, who eventually became head of the National Endowment for the Arts, and Harriet Pilpel of the ACLU, who made a career of defending Alfred Kinsey long after the man was in his grave, threatening to sue Pat Buchanan for a column he had written about Reisman's expose of the deceased sexologist. Friedan, who made a career out of portraying herself as sensitive to the needs of women, not only ignored the testimony of women like Linda Boreman, who were tortured for the nation's sexual titillation, but actually blamed them as traitors to their sex by collaborating with the Reagan administration in general and Attorney General Meese in particular. In fact, Friedan, ignoring the testimony of women who were both degraded and physically injured as a result of pornography-inspired sexual experimentation, outdid herself by claiming that "suppressing pornography is extremely dangerous to women."[5]

Just why that was so, she never got around to explaining. Not that Ms. Friedan likes pornography – "I find a lot of it. . . very boring," she opined – "but I recognize the right of others who choose to be titillated in that way" – even, evidently, for the trajectory of pornography by this time had made it clear – if the torture and death of women were necessary to gratify that wish. "You know," Ms Friedan continued, "some pornography certainly does degrade wom.ean. It also degrades men and it degrades sex. The pornography that pushes violence is particularly deplorable. But the forces that want to suppress pornography are not in favor of suppressing guns."[6]

The *non sequitur* about guns notwithstanding, what the Meese Commission and the unfortunate ladies who testified there had learned the hard way was that pornography generated an inherently unstable psychic trajectory that began with illicit sex, frequently ended in torture, and sometimes ended in death. Friedan said in her statement that "the ultimate obscenity in America was murderous violence" without the slightest indication that by 1986 the evidence about the source of murderous violence in libido emancipated from morals was all a matter of public record, the very record which Friedan's testimony hoped to suppress. "The pimp," one escapee from white slavery told the Meese Commission,

> made pornography of all of us. He also made tape recordings of us having sex with him and recordings of our screams and pleading when he gave us brutal beatings. It was not unusual for him to threaten us with death. He would later use these recordings to humiliate us by playing them for his friends in our presence, for his own sexual arousal and to terrorize us and other women he brought home.[7]

By 1985, all of the brutality and personal tragedy associated with twenty years of sexual liberation and almost thirty years of liberalized obscenity laws had begun to flow into the public consciousness, and once it became apparent that pornography was not a victimless crime, people were willing to act on what they had learned. On April 10, 1986, the president of Southland Corporation, owner of 4,500 7-Eleven stores nationwide announced that it would no longer sell *Playboy*, *Penthouse,* or *Forum* magazines in its stores. The letter also made it clear that Southland was basing its decision in part on "Judith Reisman's report before the Commission's hearing on Child Pornography." Reisman's testimony on "Images of Children, Crime and Violence in *Playboy, Penthouse and Hustler*," had been given to the Commission on November 12, 1985, two weeks before she had been driven out of her offices at AU. Southland's announcement caused such a public furor that other major drug and convenience stores as well as many "mom and pop" stores followed suit, announcing that they too were no longer going to offer the *Playboy* and other one-handed magazines for sale in their stores.

Four days after the announcement, Reisman was called into Jennifer Murphy's office and told that the university was very concerned about the 7-Eleven letter. AU had been editing Reisman's report since November without her input, and Murphy was concerned about how the information might be used. It was clear now that both Reisman and the Meese Commission were considered a major threat to the masturbation industry's profits. As a result, the industry decided that press conferences with Betty Friedan were not going to do the trick. What they needed was a much more concerted effort. The Media Coalition needed help in staging an across-the-board assault on the Meese Commission, one that would involve front groups which could take on the mainstream media and divert attention from Reisman's findings and all of the horror stories people like Linda Boreman were telling. The new strategy involved direct contact with the decision makers and was designed to influence them with "friendly" persuasion.

On May 16, 1986, Playboy Enterprises filed suit in federal court against Attorney General Meese and members of the attorney general's commission on pornography. In July 1986, an article by Sanford Ungar attacking Meese appeared in the July issue of *Esquire*. In it Ungar characterized Meese as a small-town Rotarian who was out of his depth in Washington politics. Worse still Ungar implied that Meese wanted to be accepted by the very people who held him and his ideals in contempt. After leaving public radio, Ungar worked as head of the public-relations division of Gray and Co., a Washington lobbying agency. Both Meese and his wife Ursula were close personal friends with President Berendzen of AU; both Meese and Berendzen were friends with Bob Gray, president of the already mentioned Washington public relations firm, and it was to Gray and Co. that the masturbation industry turned in its hour of need.

The counter-offensive was swift in coming. On May 30, 1986, Alfred Regnery resigned as head of the OJJDP. On June 5, 1986, less than two months after Southland Corporation announced that 7-Eleven would no longer be selling one-handed magazines in its stores, Steve Johnson of Gray and Co. wrote a letter to John M. Harrington, Executive Vice President of the Council for Periodical Distributors Associations, thanking him for their meeting a week before. In that meeting, attended also by Gray and Co. associates Frank Mankiewicz and Ray Argyle, Johnson and Harrington discussed the problems, both potential and actual, which the Meese Commission, which was scheduled to release its report in less than a month, posed to the publishing industry as well as strategies, both long and short-term, to discredit the commission. The publishing industry had formed an ad-hoc committee called the Media Coalition to combat the Meese Commission's efforts. Membership in the Media Coalition read like the who's who of the publishing industry and included: the American Booksellers Association, the Association of American Publishers, the Council of Periodical Distributors, the International Periodical Distributors Association, and the National Coalition of College Stores, which meant that some of them had a direct financial interest in the sale of pornography, a fact which came up in the Johnson letter, when he said that the financial interests of the Media Coalition would have to be disguised by transferring the attention of the public to First Amendment issues. That this was not going to be easy or cheap became clear when Johnson began discussing the cost of the project and arrived at a figure of $75,000 a month as his initial estimate. Moreover, Gray was apparently only one of several PR firms hired to help the Media Coalition.

Working with ACLU lawyer Michael Bamberger, this same group along with the Freedom to Read Foundation, the ACLU, the Association of American University Presses, the NYCLU, and St. Martin's Press, which later published Wendy McElroy's apologia for porn, *XXX*, had filed an *amicus curiae* brief in 1981 in favor of the defendant in the Paul Ira Ferber child-pornography case. The same group of organizations, again under the leadership of the ACLU's Mr. Bamberger, sued the city of Indianapolis after it passed an ordinance designed by Catherine Mackinnon which recognized pornography as sex discrimination.

Johnson makes clear in his memo, however, that the effectiveness of the Media Coalition, was limited by the perception that all they were really interested in defending were their own financial interests. "Creation of . . . a broad, issue-oriented group and selection of a national spokesperson," according to Johnson, "would help dispel the notion that opponents of the Commission's work are only interested in protecting their own financial interests or are somehow 'pro-pornography.'" As a result, Johnson suggested that the Media Coalition select "a national spokesperson not directly involved in publishing" because that "would help opinion leaders, policy makers and the general public understand that the issue here is not pornography but rather First Amendment freedoms."

The group under this impartial "spokesperson" "would include academicians, civil libertarians, religious leaders, civic and community leaders, politicians, business and foundation executives, authors and editors, columnists, commentators and entertainers. This new group might be called "Americans for the Right to Read" or "The First Amendment Coalition." William Buckley later wrote that Gray and Co. had called him about the pornography issue, giving some indication that the plan was put into effect. Eventually, the Media Coalition settled on the name "Americans for Constitutional Freedom," an organization which Susan Trento describes as "one of those covert activities that Gray and Company were so good at setting up – dummy front organizations."[8]

The Gray and Co. plan, according to Johnson, would focus on the following strategy: first and foremost it would deny that pornography is "in any way a cause of violent or criminal behavior," which was of course the gist of what women were saying when they testified before the Meese Commission. The wave of women's stroke books (to be discussed in detail later) which appeared in the '90s were a development of this same theme, funded by the same industry which was paying Gray and Co. $75,000 a month to discredit the Reisman and the Meese Commission. During the '90s, instead of claiming that porn does no harm through the medium of a public relations firm, the industry was paying women to write books in which they claimed that porn helped them to become sexually autonomous by freeing them from dependence on men for their orgasms. Secondly, the Gray and Co. campaign against the Meese Commission would claim that pornography "diverts our attention from real economic and social problems," and finally it would claim that the whole Meese Commission was "orchestrated by a group of religious extremists whose tactics and goals are clearly not representative of mainstream public opinion."

In addition to the public-relations campaign under the direction of Frank Mankiewicz, Johnson also proposed in his letter an attempt to influence legislators directly through Gray and Co.'s chief lobbyist, Gary Hymel, who served as "former top aide to House Speaker Thomas P. (Tip) O'Neill" and could, therefore, promise "knowledge of and access to the legislative and administrative decision-making process." In a final flourish that is either fatuous or brutally cynical, Johnson assures Harrington that Gray and Co.'s lobbying staff is "accustomed to working with our Public Relations staff in orchestrating national grass-roots campaigns on behalf of our clients."

The purpose of the campaign was to generate the illusion of widespread, "grass-roots" support, when in fact Johnson himself admitted in his letter that "the [Meese] Commission's findings and recommendations will likely find widespread public acceptance." In a society which claimed to be democratic, it was essential to cloak the financial interests of those who profited from exploiting sexuality behind a façade of "grass-roots" support. Mendacity was essential to manipulation of this sort; without it, the manipulation would not work.

The memo was a good indication of how the political system worked in the United States, but beyond that it was also an indication of how commercialized lust functioned in that system. The essence of a republic is devotion to the common good. The essence of empire is power, the power not of the people, but of one faction over another. Just as the republic needs virtue in order to function, the empire runs on lust. Empire is politically organized appetite. Each faction strives to use the power of the state to gratify its own desires. As politicians succumb one by one to the lure of money to ensure their election and re-election, the order of the state becomes determined by those who pay the highest price for it. Those with the most money control appetite. So to insure that they stay in power, they promote unfettered appetite, feeling that the ultimate outcome of what are essentially financial transactions will be in their favor. Wilhelm Reich felt that only socialism could lead to sexual freedom, and that unfettered sexual freedom would lead to socialism. It turns out that he was wrong. Capitalism was much better at exploiting sexual appetite, and the political system it created is much better at turning unfettered appetite into a form of political control via economic exploitation. In the 1990s, unfettered appetite meant charging a price for what used to be free. It meant the reduction of all aspects of life to a form of consumerism. It meant promoting bondage, both spiritual and economic, in the name of freedom. Ultimately, the followers of the Enlightenment believed what Augustine said when he claimed in the *City of God* that a man had as many masters as he had vices, but not in the way that Augustine said it. The Enlightenment simply reversed the values while espousing essentially the same concept. The Enlightenment promoted vice among its victims as a way of becoming both their economic and political masters. Plato was right; freedom of this sort did lead to slavery. Sexual liberation was a form of political control.

At the same time that the PR campaign was getting started, the purges continued at OJJDP. By June 16, James Wootton was gone, forced to resign and, shortly thereafter, subjected to an FBI investigation to intimidate him further. Wootton was replaced by Pamela Swain, who had leaked her memo criticizing Reisman's study to the press in August of 1983, shortly after the project had been approved. The campaign to discredit the commission reached its culmination in July of 1986 when the Meese Commission issued its report, and Attorney General Meese, at the urging of Bob Gray, distanced himself from the very report which bore his name. "The former California prosecutor," according to Trento, "renowned for his toughness, actually agreed to stand up in public and say that *Playboy* and *Penthouse* were not obscene. He said he had read *Playboy* in his youth."[9] "As soon as he was made to see the folly of it, he very quickly disengaged himself," is how one Gray and Co. executive put it. "It made Meese a laughing stock," he added. In spite of their efforts, or perhaps because of them, Gray and Co. went on to receive grants from the Justice Department to promote some of the department's other programs. The Meese report relegated Reisman's research to a three-line footnote. The Meese report could not find one mainstream publisher for its final report until a cook book publisher reprinted the findings to make them accessible to the public.

On or about November 10, 1986, Pamela Swain admitted to Judith Reisman that although AU had held and altered her work for nine months, OJJDP was going to release her gutted report in three days. Reisman was given three days to deliver her corrected original report to OJJDP. Pamela Swain had indicated in response to a phone call from Dr. Reisman, that the report would have to be released to the public and press by OJJDP ten days after its receipt under Freedom of Information requirements. This was, of course, untrue. On November 13, 1986, Reisman delivered four corrected copies of the 1,600 page report to OJJDP Administrators Verne Spiers and Pamela Swain. The reports came complete with five full peer approval reviews and letters. Instead of being pleased that their money was not wasted, however, within twenty-four hours (avoiding Freedom of Information rulings), Mr. Spiers had turned over the four copies to AU for disposal. Only the uncorrected copies would be released to the public by OJJDP, and it was on the basis of these versions that it was roundly condemned by the press. On October 29, 1991, the next OJJDP Administrator, Robert Sweet Jr., described Reisman's research as "a sound study, producing high quality data in a complex and difficult area conducted in a scientifically acceptable fashion."[10]

In early November, the Justice Department tried to reach a settlement in the *Playboy* suit by offering to issue a statement claiming *Playboy* had never been found obscene. The statement was essentially meaningless. Obscenity, which had always been under the police powers of the state and had never been protected speech under the First Amendment, had been conflated in *Roth* and subsequent decisions with pornography and as a result had lost its meaning as a legal term. Following *Roth*, the state could prosecute cases of hard-core pornography, which was only one class of obscenity, but even these prosecutions would cease once the Clinton administration took office. *Playboy*, however, sought additional concessions. Shortly after the DOJ made its settlement offer, Meese publicly stated that he had read *Playboy* and *Penthouse* as a young man and that he didn't regard them as obscene. Four months after the attempt to settle the case, in March 1987, Meese told a crowd in Philadelphia, "In my opinion there has not been any court that has held *Playboy* or *Penthouse* to be within the Supreme Court definition of obscenity. And I don't feel that those are the kinds of things that should be subject to prosecution under the law." Meese here was clearly referring to the revised view of obscenity which had been introduced into the law with the *Roth* decision and not the traditional definition, found in *Regina v. Hicklin*, which claimed that "the test of obscenity is this, whether the tendency of the matter charged as obscenity is to deprave and corrupt those whose minds are open to such immoral influences and into whose hands a publication of this sort may fall."[11] The conservatives had adopted the premises of the cultural revolutionaries. That coupled with the peer pressure Washington could exert when its base of power was threatened caused Meese to repudiate the report which bore his own name.

On November 19, 1986, Howard Kurtz of *The Washington Post* announced that "Serious Flaws Shelve $734,000 Study." A few days later, in a *Chronicle of Higher Education* article, George A. Comstock, professor of public communications at Syracuse University, someone who had been called in to evaluate the project as an outside expert, said AU had tampered with the Reisman report, omitting key findings that Reisman had included in a draft. Comstock said that American University "wasn't really committed at all to seeing this completed." The *Chronicle* concluded that "bad publicity [had] made the university uncomfortable."

If so, the university was in for a good deal more discomfort in the immediate future. In May of 1990 AU President Berendzen was arrested for making a series of "30 to 40" obscene phone calls to a thirty-three-year-old local woman who had responded to an ad Berendzen had placed in a local paper offering child care. During the course of his conversations with the woman, Berendzen not only discussed "in gross detail" having sex with children, "but also offered children to me and my husband as sex slaves."[12] Berendzen also discussed in graphic detail "his extensive collection of videotaped child pornography."[13] On May 23, 1990, Berendzen pleaded guilty to two counts of making obscene phone calls in Fairfax County District Court. As part of his rehabilitation, Berendzen checked into the Sexual Disorders Clinic at Johns Hopkins Hospital, home of Dr. John W. Money, the man who testified in 1973 that viewing a film like *Deep Throat*, "could have a 'cleansing action' on people's sex lives."[14] In spite of his conviction, Berendzen received a million dollar settlement from AU and remained on as a professor.

Part III, Chapter 21

Washington, D.C., 1992

The counterattack from the publishing industry didn't derail the Meese Commission, Meese's own disavowal to the contrary. In fact, all of the recommendations of the Meese Commission were eventually written into law. Alan Sears, who served on the Meese Commission, also helped draft the legislation which flowed from the commission's work. The prime recommendation was a federal task force to prosecute obscenity charges. This task force caused a major rollback of porn during the late '80s and early '90s. City after city was successful in shutting down X-rated bookstores. The Southland Corporation pulled *Playboy, Penthouse,* and *Hustler* from its Seven-11 stores, which caused circulation to plummet. Florida, according to Sears, was on its way to becoming a porn-free state – except for one county, whose District Attorney inexplicably refused to prosecute obscenity cases. That county was Dade County, and the name of the DA was Janet Reno, and she became Attorney General when William Jefferson Clinton took office in 1992. That event signaled the end of the federal task force to prosecute pornography. The Clinton administration, in spite of promises to the contrary during the first campaign, sent a clear message to the industry that they could expand with impunity. Which is precisely what they did.

Freed from the threat of federal prosecution, the masturbation industry launched a pan-cultural offensive whose goal was the mainstreaming of pornography. That offensive included *Boogie Nights* and *The People vs. Larry Flynt,* both of which were propaganda films for the masturbation industry. The latter film took the Gray and Co. admonition about the first amendment to heart, by beginning as a T & A film and ending as a courtroom melodrama in which the Larry Flynt character tells the audience that no one's rights are safe unless he is free to sell one-handed magazines.

Boogie Nights was the story, after a fashion, of John Holmes, a porn star who was involved in murder for drugs and then died of AIDS. *Boogie Nights* is absolutely true to life, except that in the film Holmes doesn't murder anyone and doesn't die of AIDS. The film is also R-rated, which means it doesn't show any real pornography either. At the end of the film, the Holmes character is welcomed back to the porn-producing "family," which, in spite of all the drugs they do, is much nicer than Holmes's biological family. None of the reviews in this country seemed to get the simple point made in the German press that "the success of *Boogie Nights* makes the other film capital on the other side of the Hollywood hills [i.e., where 90 percent of the pornography gets produced] suitable for polite company."[1] The fact that something this obvious can only be stated in a German magazine shows how deeply one part of the industry interlocks with the other, and how the production of pornography or the defense thereof pervades the entire communications industry. "It's only a matter of time," said Marianne Wellershof in *Spiegel*, "before porno films are once again shown in first run theaters."[2]

First-run movies and the boom in women's memoirs make up just two facets of a cultural offensive to make porn respectable again after the damage it received in the late '80s at the hands of the feminists like Mackinnon and Dworkin and the Meese Commission. The universities have joined forces too, coming up with a spate of conferences which lend academic respectability to pornography. Annie Sprinkle, the performance artist, got to show clips from her pornographic videos at a conference entitled "Exposed" at the University of California at Santa Cruz. She shared the bill with Elizabeth Birch, head of a national homosexual organization called the Human Rights Campaign. Giving some indication that sexual deviants were one of his key constituencies, President Clinton appeared at an HRC fund-raiser and on the cover of their magazine. Taken together Sprinkle and Birch showed how sex worked as a form of political control. Sprinkle showed pornography to the audience, and Birch talked about how she and her organization punished anyone in the 1994 Congress who voted for the Defense of the Family Act. The regime, as exemplified by its state-subsidized universities, first incites its citizens to sexual activity and then punishes them with the threat of exposure – hence, the conference title? – if they fail to go along with the political mobilization of vice.

Capitalizing on its location in the middle of the "other film industry on the other side of the Hollywood hills," the University of California at Northridge held the First Annual World Pornography Conference in early August 1998. That conference featured live sex performances in the various conference rooms made available to conferees by the hotel. The "Revolting Behavior" Conference held at SUNY New Paltz in late 1997 gained much media attention, partially at least because one of the SUNY system's board of trustees called for the resignation of the president of the New Paltz campus after the conference was held. By the second term of the Clinton Administration, pornography was well on its way to being a fixture at university campuses. In the March 29, 1999 issue of the *New Yorker*, James Atlas summed up the trend by saying that "the pedagogic enshrinement of porn is by now an established fact."[3] As one of its leading practitioners, Atlas mentions Linda Williams, the keynote speaker at the Northridge Pornography conference, whose book *Hard Core, Power, Pleasure, and the Frenzy of the Visible*, he calls "an erudite and closely argued assessment of porn films."[4] "For Linda Williams," Atlas opines, "porn in the academy emerges naturally out of the academy's preoccupation with politics." What Atlas, of course, does not tell us is how porn functions as a form a political control, primarily because he is blinded by all of the establishment clichés about it being a form of liberation. Like most of the industry-sponsored speech which has appeared since the Meese Commission issued its report, Atlas and Williams go out of their way to indicate that women not only like pornography but are now heavily involved in producing it as well. Atlas even goes so far to say that "women have begun to control the means of production of porn."[5]

As if to foster that illusion, the same publishing industry which turned to Gray and Co. for help in undermining the Meese Commission in the '80s brought out a series of women's memoirs in the '90s, all of which indicated that women were avid consumers of pornography and used it as an aid to masturbation. In an article entitled "Women Behaving Badly," which appeared in the February 1997 issue of *Vanity Fair*, Michael Schnayerson described "a new wave of female memoirists, mostly young and attractive, [who] are mining intimate details of their sex lives, alcoholism, mental illness and even adult incest." This sort of literary exhibitionism has made them the "toasts of the publishing world." Schnayerson goes on to say that the scribbling ladies of the 1990s are "using the memoir in a way men haven't had to: as a form of liberation."

The article goes on to indicate that the veracity of these memoirs is dubious at best, a fact which Schnayerson underscores by mentioning that "many of the new memoirists are primarily novelists," including Kathryn Harrison, whose memoir about her incestuous relationship with her father turns out to be remarkably similar to a novel she wrote on the same theme a few years back. Schnayerson notes that a "profile of the author in *Publishers Weekly* noted that other critics suspected the novel was a memoir in disguise" but can't quite bring himself to the obvious conclusion, namely, that her memoir is probably just a novel in disguise. He concludes his analysis of the latest literary trend by opining that "today's readers clearly want storytellers who feel as naked and alone as they do." As if to prove Schnayerson right, Elizabeth Wurtzel tastefully exposes one airbrushed breast on the cover of her memoir *Bitch: In Praise of Difficult Women*, while giving prospective readers the finger.

The literary descendants of the Belle of Amherst, or her less talented sisters which Hawthorne complained about as a "mob of scribbling women" who wrote for publications like *Godey's Lady's Book*, were now writing memoirs with titles like *Talk Dirty to Me* and *Bitch*. Carol Avedon wrote *Nudes, Prudes and Attitudes: Pornography and Censorship* in 1994. One year later she collaborated with Alison Assiter on *Bad Girls and Dirty Pictures: The Challenge to Reclaim Feminism*. In 1995, St. Martin's Press brought out Wendy McElroy's *XXX: A Woman's Right to Pornography*. And one year later Nadine Stroessen, the head of the ACLU, had her book *De-*

fending Pornography: Free Speech, Sex and the Fight for Women's Rights
published by Scribners.

No matter what the title, the message is always the same – chicks like
pornography, pornography is liberating, masturbation is the logical expression of feminism, masturbation means sexual autonomy, and so on and so
forth. Lisa Palac, who billed herself as the queen of cyberporn in her book
The Edge of the Bed, tried out a new angle by talking about pornography as
delivered by computers, but after a while even she was forced to admit that
the cyber angle was just another way, like the Playboy Philosophy of years
gone by, of justifying looking at dirty pictures. In publishing Ms. Palac's
memoir, the masturbation industry also celebrated one of its most significant
technological advances. It was accomplished during the lull in obscenity
prosecutions which the Clinton administration brought about, namely, the
rise of the Internet as a delivery device for pornography. Congress attempted
to deal with this new situation by passing the spectacularly misnamed Communications Decency Act, which purported to regulate porn on the Internet
but in fact ended up protecting purveyors of porn from liability, something a
mother whose son was molested found out when she tried to sue America
Online, the server which sponsored the chat room which enabled the molestation. "Cybersex," Ms. Palac writes, "has led to an increased cultural acceptance of masturbation as bona fide sex, not a sex substitute. Cybersex
sanctioned mutual masturbation as something healthy and fun that could be
practiced by people who were not even in the same room. Digital technology
transformed the idea that masturbation is something you do when you're a
lonely loser who can't get laid into something that's hip, safe, and cyber."[6]

When one member of the Meese Commission wondered why the
pornographers didn't produce material for women, the pornographers just
laughed. They didn't because there was no market for such a thing. Many
"lonely losers" were involved in the consumption of pornography, but they
were all male. Palac's book may be an attempt to open up that market to
women, but it is most probably written for the "lonely losers" who do use the
stuff and find women talking about it as a turn-on or a salve for a conscience
burdened with guilt which arises from exploiting women. With this end in
mind, Palac goes on to assure her readers that she is a "better person"

> because of – not in spite of – all the sex I've been exposed to. The sexual
> images and ideas thrown at me by rock and roll, porn, television, Holly-
> wood movies and cyberspace have ultimately left me feeling more liber-
> ated than oppressed, more enlightened than frightened. . . . Once I figured
> out how to use porn and come – how to look at an erotic image and use my
> sexual imagination to turn desire into a self-generated orgasm – my life
> was irrevocably and positively changed. . . . For the first time in my life, I
> felt sexually autonomous.[7]

In other words, the lonely losers should feel good about themselves because a hip, good-looking, smart (she knows how to use a computer) cyber-savvy chick like Lisa Palac masturbates just like them, and she feels so good about herself that she has written a book to share her good fortune with them. In spite of its pretensions, Palac's book ends up being little more than an extended infomercial for the pornography industry, which until the arrival of the Clinton administration and the Internet, had fallen on hard times. Palac tells us that she was "the perfect candidate for cybersex" because "I wasn't getting laid, I liked to masturbate and I could type."[8]

What then does it mean when mobs of scribbling women spill ink by the barrel extolling one-handed sex? Palac tries to exploit the technological angle in her book. "In virtual life," she tells us, "we can disengage from our bodies and all that travels with them: vanity, insecurity, sexual chemistry."[9] But when all is said and done, it's still masturbation she's promoting, with all the odium associated with that act. Evidently the only way to make it appealing to its essentially male clientele is by claiming that women do it too and love it and even write books about how great it is. Asking the ladies who write stroke books for chicks what they mean is like asking a galley slave how the Battle of Salamis is going. According to the wisdom of the West, lust darkens the mind, and in these memoirs we find empirical verification of that fact. In order to understand why it is important that women write books like these, one has to go *ad fontes,* to a text like *The Bacchae* of Euripides, who understood in an inchoate but prescient way what happened to the city when the women left their looms and went off to dance naked on the mountainside. If the men had done something like that, the idea would have been worthy of treatment by Aristophanes and not Euripides. It would have been a comic excuse for derisive laughter. But, as Pentheus found out when Dionysos appealed to his own prurient interest in the matter, it is not a laughing matter when the women do it. Rather it is a threat to the social order; it threatens the very foundations of the state. Once we understand that we begin to understand some things of import. Not why women write books like this – there have always been whores who are willing to sell sex for a price – but rather why the publishing industry wants to promote the idea that chicks like masturbating to pornography and why the regime tolerates the pornography they promote. As Euripides understood, he who controls the sexual mores of women controls the state. The *agon* of wills at the beginning of the play between Pentheus and Dionysos concerns precisely this issue. Whoever controls sexual behavior controls the state. And he who controls the mores of women controls sexual behavior. That is the first lesson of sexual politics. He who understands that law understands why pornography and sex education and abortion and the government funding of contraceptives are all non-negotiable conditions for the current regime. Without them, they could not rule.

The current wave of female stroke books is the logical outcome of feminism, which was how the mandarins behind the cultural revolution of the '60s got the women of this country to leave their looms and dance naked on the mountainside. We're talking about the restructuring of society that comes about when the women leave their looms. We're talking about the media-driven war on nature that seeks to prevent women from returning to their looms once they recognize that their Bacchic liberation has led to little more than dismembered children, broken homes, and, to cite the words of Agave when the intoxication wore off, "horror, suffering and grief." The mob of wanking women is generally inept when it comes to seeing much less explaining the big picture. However, some of them have a flash of insight every now and then by adverting to someone who does understand, someone like Wilhelm Reich. "Sexually awakened women," Reich wrote in the *Mass Psychology of Fascism,* which appeared in translation in this country in 1949 and became a book with a significant following during the '70s, "affirmed and recognized as such, would mean the complete collapse of authoritarian ideology."[10] Modernity, here as always, is nothing more than the truths of antiquity stood on their head. What Euripides intended as a warning, people like Reich and Nietzsche turned into exhortation. Reich played a crucial, if largely posthumous role in this restructuring. He was the philosopher of "sexual revolution" (his term) and the explicator of how sexual deviance could be put to political use. *Die Sexualität im Kulturkampf* was the original title of the book by Reich which eventually got translated as *The Sexual Revolution.* The change in title is instructive. A book on the role sexuality played in cultural warfare got changed into something that was supposed to portray a broad-based grass-roots revolution, akin in genus to the American Revolution, the act which created this country. It was, of course, nothing of the sort.

Sallie Tisdale's *Talk Dirty to Me* is an expanded version of an article which appeared in the February 1992 issue of *Harper's.* It purports to expound "an intimate philosophy of sex" but, like Palac's book, is another stroke book for chicks – this time without computers. "There is a wonderful and awful moment for each of us," Tisdale rhapsodizes,

> when we practice masturbation as a conscious act – when we know what to do and why we want to do it, and make plans. Though I'd been chastised for my unconscious masturbation when quite young, it was not a sin until I planned and carried it out consciously. And ever afterward, masturbation has been accompanied by a strange, potent mix of emotions: desire, guilt, excitement, shame, fantasy, and, especially, the fear of getting caught. The fear of letting anyone else know I know.[11]

Tisdale goes on to extol the writings of Betty Dodson, who in 1974 wrote a book entitled – you will be expecting this – *Liberating Masturbation,* which Tisdale describes as a "cheerful, unashamed paean to getting off in the privacy of your own room."[12] What begins as a hymn of praise to liberation quickly degenerates into plain old consumerism of the sort these people find repugnant when advertisers attempt to induce them to buy floor-wax but not when they use it to induce them to buy vibrators. "And vibrators," Tisdale tells us lapsing into the same no-muss, no-fuss jargon, "make female orgasm as quick, easy, reproducible, and simple as any male orgasm, ever. They are machines of revolution."[13]

   To begin with, it is not self-evident that women desire orgasms that are "quick, easy [and] reproducible" as opposed to, say, those which are an expression of love and life, but the one thing the mob of wanking women never seems to question is the tenets of consumerism, and how market forces became the vehicle for sexual revolution. This is why their prose so often sounds as if it has been confected after watching ads on day-time television. Tisdale may not have a clue that the meaning of sexuality is its mutuality – none of the wanking women do, or if they do they won't say so – but she knows big business when she sees it. Thus, in spite of herself, Tisdale does give us a fairly accurate picture of what the "machines of revolution" have wrought. Sexual liberation means simply transposing the matter of sex from the arena of love and family to the field of commerce, where someone can make a profit off it. Whores have always been familiar with this transaction. "Simply as a well-established, multimillion-dollar business it has to be taken seriously," Tisdale writes, giving some indication that she might not take sex seriously otherwise.[14] "Pornography is an expression of that conservative icon, the free market."[15] And if women want to be taken seriously they have to market themselves according to free market principles. In other words, they have to start patronizing X-rated bookstores.

   "The only way porn will expand," Tisdale tells us, "is by women entering its walls and pressing outward, to make more space. I know I break a rule when I enter the adult store, whether my entrance is simply startling or genuinely unwelcome. . . . . And I know that if more women simply walked into this store, this world, that particular man's vision of women would begin to change."[16]

   The message is clear. Women will change the world by becoming sexual consumers. "Porn needs to change, improve," she says at another point, "and it's women who will do that improving, and not by ignoring it."[17] Tisdale all but tells her readers to frequent pornographic bookstores – all in the name of liberation, of course – but it also turns out that this kind of liberation is a financial windfall for the industry, and the industry in this era of mergers includes film studios, TV, mass-circulation magazines, and New York publishing houses of the sort that publish Tisdale's book as well. In terms of genre, the sexual memoir fits most readily into the category of paid political announcement.

   The story doesn't stop there, however. Wanking women like Tisdale aspire to give us the big picture, which is to say the political meaning as well as the economic meaning of liberated sex, or how the latter fits in with the former. Pornography is good because it "uproots traditional female roles of passivity, creates emotional confusion, stimulates introspection, and presents a world without the nuclear family. . . . It represents sex *as* Revolution."[18]

Revolution, in this instance, means that industry-subsidized hacks like Tisdale and Palac are going to lead other females out of "bondage" to the moral law. Sexual liberation once again turns out to be a form of control. Once again freedom means consumerism; freedom means conforming one's behavior to the financial interests of the masturbation industry, which includes the firm that published Tisdale's book. Masturbation also happens to be good for business because its message is "to give up resistance to appetite."[19] With that last phrase, Ms. Tisdale opens the bag and the cat starts to crawl out. What Ms. Tisdale fails to tell us is that masturbation creates a world of docile consumers whose pleasures lead to ever-increasing addiction and isolation, which is to say, a simultaneous and ever-increasing dependence on pornography and the fantasies it generates. In the name of liberation, the consumer of pornography becomes progressively more isolated from all other human contact, including those with the opposite sex which normally lead to marriage and offspring and ultimately the creation of communities which enable the citizen a measure of independence and support. All of that is abolished by the sexualization of culture which pornography and masturbation promotes. In this sense, masturbation and pornography are clearly forms of social control. In a world where sex leads to neither marriage nor kinship, it can only lead to isolation, addiction and death. The controllers of consumer culture promote the stimulation of appetites whose satisfaction comes only through the channels which the pornographer controls for a fee. The man who becomes addicted to his vice learns to love his vice while simultaneously hating himself. The same people who have enslaved him spend their time and money persuading him – through books like the ones we are discussing – that he has reached the furthermost pinnacle of liberation when in reality he has succumbed to self-imposed bondage. This is the purpose of rationalizations like the Playboy Philosophy of days gone by; it is also the purpose of stroke books like *Talk Dirty to Me*. The promotion of masturbation is simply another way of foreclosing both life and love in the interest of financial gain, foreclosing, in other words, any horizontal connection with a spouse of the same age as well as any vertical connection with future generations. Masturbation is, in other words, the ultimate form of solipsism and, as a result, the ultimate form of control. Masturbation closes off intimacy to everything but one channel, the one controlled by the pornographer, where the masturbator can satisfy any fantasy as long as he has his credit card handy.

Unlike the sexual liberation of years gone by – the '60s variety, for example, which promoted fornication and adultery in the name of things like free love and open marriage – state-of-the-art sexual liberation of the '90s means one thing and just about one thing only, namely, masturbation to pornography. The reason for this is, upon reflection, simple enough. Masturbation to pornography is more profitable than the other two options; it is more financially lucrative than any other sexual option, including prostitution, to which it is obviously related both etymologically and otherwise. In an age in which the technological reproduction of images becomes ever more realistic, and an age in which these images can be delivered electronically into the home of everyone who has a computer and in the future to everyone who has a TV, the possibilities for financial exploitation are too lucrative to ignore. And with financial exploitation goes political control. Financial exploitation is the nose of that camel. Perhaps this is why Tisdale is so insistent on making masturbation synonymous with sex. For her, in fact, all sex is essentially masturbatory. "In this sense," she writes, "all sex is masturbation – the other person's body is an object by which we have intense but wholly internal pleasure, and our orgasm is a self-created and unshared universe. . . . This may be the best explanation for why the orgasms of masturbation can be more powerful and feel more physically whole than those shared. They are simply safer."[20]

Again we have the no-muss, no-fuss approach that equates sex with ready-made cake mixes. Along the way, sexual autonomy is defined in terms indistinguishable from sexual isolation and bondage, and the only thing that makes the justification half-way plausible is the clichés of Madison Avenue and the ACLU. As with abortion, which is portrayed as safer than child birth, pornography is portrayed as safer than marriage. Missing from the equation is the violence it is and the violence it causes in those who become addicted to it. "As for using pornography as a 'blueprint' for violence," Tisdale tells us, "not only are such images hard to find, I think this belief supposes far more concentration on the part of impulsively violent people than reality should warrant. And how many murders have been inspired by religion?"[21]

This brings us to the other purpose of the stroke books for ladies, namely, their role in attacking the Meese Commission on Pornography and the feminists who collaborated with it. The same rules apply here as elsewhere. If you want to undermine the position of the Catholic Church, the best way to do it is to create a front group, something like Catholics for Free Choice, an entity funded by pharmaceutical houses which make contraceptives. If you want to undermine the idea that pornography victimizes women, you need a woman to convey that message. All of that testimony of women like Linda Boreman at the Meese Commission hearings was being erased from the cultural record by the memoirs of the wanking women. "By 1985," Palac writes,

> the Meese Commission recommended greater restrictions of sexually explicit material based on the unconfirmed theory that pornography causes harm. Beginning in the mid-1980s, and continuing well into the 1990s,

Andrea Dworkin and Catharine Mackinnon proposed anti-porn ordinances in Minneapolis, Indianapolis and Cambridge, Massachusetts, that
would allow women to sue for damages for the harm caused by pornography. All three were ultimately voted down, but were a big success at stir-
ring up fear. Censorship continues to be promoted as a necessary defense
against the monsters who lurk somewhere out there.[22]

Was Chuck Traynor a monster? Rather than answer this question honestly, Palac omits any real account of the suffering of women like Linda
Boreman and the numerous women who testified before the Meese Commission about how they were injured by boyfriends trying to imitate what they
saw on the screen. Rather than tell the truth about the people who have been
hurt by porn, Palac tries to tie the Meese Commission to the "repressive"
'50s instead:

Who really wants to go back to, say, the 1950s when blacks had to ride in
the back of the bus, when Senator Joe McCarthy destroyed people's lives
in his hunt for suspected Communists, when people chose to die rather
than talk about their depression, come out of the closet, deal with their alcoholism or any number of sensitive issues because those realities just
didn't fit into the precious picture of the All-American family? I know I
don't.[23]

Nor does the industry which publishes Ms. Palac's memoirs, and this is
true for one simple reason. The Meese Commission did considerable damage
to the pornography industry in this country. All of the stroke-book ladies
mention Dworkin and Mackinnon, who in many ways became victims of
their own ideological excesses but along the way created a whole new front
for combating pornography, one which rose out of the ideological bosom of
the Left, and so for a while left the industry without an effective response. In
addition to the feminist attack on pornography, activists from the other end
of the political spectrum were increasingly successful in organizing boycotts
of convenience stores which resulted in ever dwindling sales of *Playboy,
Penthouse* and *Hustler* as the '80s progressed.

Wilhelm Reich saw the connection between sexual revolution and revolutionary politics more clearly than most people, and certainly more clearly
than the chicks who quote him in their stroke books. Sallie Tisdale has read
Reich. Like the average grad student, she is smart enough to figure out what
he has to say but not smart enough to understand the big picture, which is to
say, the implication of Reich's philosophy for women and the culture which
promotes the project of "liberation from repression."

Tisdale's connection to Reich was more intimate than most. Since she
was born the same year he died in prison, she didn't get a chance to sleep
with him. But she got a chance at the next best thing; at the age of sixteen, she
attended a Reichian summer camp where she underwent Reichian therapy.
Tisdale doesn't go into details, but the camp sounds like the sort of thing that

would lead to child-molestation charges if the statute of limitations hadn't run out: "Even now, twenty years later," she writes,

> if I meet one or the other of the people with whom I did therapy, I need only say the word "group" to explain a feeling. Reichian therapy was hard, rough-edged, potent, and dangerous; it was physically painful and sometimes emotionally devastating. The powerful, almost obsessed therapists who led us through the physical and psychological exercises designed to break down our muscular and emotional armor may have done me a fair bit of harm as well as good. But they were the first and only adults in my young life to talk to me as a sexual creature, to acknowledge not only that I was sexual but that I suffered from sexuality – that sex was important, legitimate, and real. To Reich "the body alone spoke truth." My Reichian therapists were the first people in my life to speak truth about my body to me.[24]

Just what truths, Tisdale never gets around to telling. But the details are in a way unimportant. Sallie Tisdale was changed by Reich, during the heyday of the Reich revival in the United States, into the person she is today. That in effect is the whole story – beginning, middle, and end – but the story still needs to be explicated. Reich, who was known for pleading the cause of adolescent sexuality, including masturbation, created a therapy that sexualized children, but beyond that he created the ideology whereby those sexualized children could be put to political use, which is precisely what happened to Sallie Tisdale, although she really doesn't understand what happened to her. That philosophy was the political core of the sexual revolution of the '60s and its political ramifications are still being refined today by people who may or may not be smarter than Tisdale but are still working out the political implications of the same principles. Reich, in other words, was the man who understood how to make political use of sex. By the 1990s Reich's sex-pol ideology was part of the conventional wisdom of the left and implemented by the Clinton administration as a form of control.

Within days of taking office, President Clinton, in addition to promoting homosexuals in the military, removed most of the anti-abortion conditions attached to United States-funded population-control programs, regulations established by the Reagan administration and spelled out in its address to the UN-sponsored conference in Mexico in 1984. The Clinton Administration also advocated lifting the ban on direct U.S. funding of abortion in foreign countries. Then, as if to insure that actions did not speak louder than words, in April 1993 White House spokesman Dee Dee Myers assured the press that the Clinton Administration considered abortion "part of the overall approach to population control."[25]

A little over a month later, on May 11, the State Department's undersecretary for global affairs, Timothy Wirth, gave a speech in which he chastised governments which chose not to go along with the Clinton Administration's world-wide abortion advocacy as "hid[ing] behind the defense of sovereignty." "Difficult as it is," he continued, leaving no ambiguity about where the Clinton Administration stood on the issue, "we must also discuss thoroughly the issue of abortion . . . . Our position is to support reproductive choice, including access to safe abortion."[26]

In January 1994, Wirth reiterated the same position and emphasized that "reproductive choice" included abortion. He went on to give some indication of the "reproductive choices" the world's women were going to have by stating that the goal of the Clinton Administration was that "comprehensive family planning must be available to every woman in the world by the year 2000."

On March 16, 1994, in preparation for the United Nations conference on population and development to be held in Cairo in September, the State Department sent an "action cable" to all overseas diplomatic and consular posts requesting "senior level diplomatic interventions" in support of U.S. priorities for the Cairo conference. Among "the priority issues for the U.S." were "assuring . . . access to safe abortion." The cable went on to inform U.S. diplomats throughout the world that "the United States believes that access to safe, legal and voluntary abortion is a fundamental right of all women." It also went on to add that "the current text is inadequate as it only addresses abortion in cases of rape or incest. . . . The United States delegation [to the Cairo conference] will also be working for stronger language on the importance of access to abortion services."[27]

In April 1994, at the PrepComm III meeting in New York, the wrangling over the pro-abortion passages in the document reached an impasse in spite of the bullying tactics of Dr. Fred Sai and the jeering of the NGOs in attendance. The meeting broke up with the disputed passages left unresolved in brackets and the final formulation to be hammered out in September in Cairo. One Vatican delegate remembered the meeting in New York as "confrontational," primarily because of "highly offensive remarks from chairman Fred Sai against the Holy See."[28]

"Whenever the Holy See spoke, [Sai] would make ironic or sarcastic remarks. He would express irritation that the Holy See was speaking," behavior the delegate considered "completely in conflict with all the ethics of an impartial chairman."[29]

On April 5, 1994, Pope John Paul II made known his opposition to the direction the Cairo conference was taking by sending a letter to President Clinton in which he claimed there was "reason to fear that [the draft of the final document] could cause a moral decline resulting in a serious setback for humanity, one in which man himself would be the first victim." "The idea of sexuality underlying this text," the pope continued, "is totally individualistic, to such an extent that marriage now appears as something outmoded." In reading the document, the pope was left with "the troubling impression of something being imposed: namely a lifestyle typical of certain fringes within developed societies, societies which are materially rich and secularized. Are countries more sensitive to the values of nature, morality and religion going to accept such a vision of man and society without protest?"[30]

The Clinton Administration's heavy-handed promotion of abortion was destined to bear fruit in unanticipated ways. To begin with, no one in the Clinton Administration seems to have reckoned with the vehemence of the pope's protest. When Clinton himself met with the pope in early June 1994 as part of his trip to Europe to commemorate D-Day, he announced that significant progress had been made in resolving their differences, only to be confronted by the Vatican afterwards saying that no such thing had happened. In the polite world of diplomatic protocol, such forthrightness in contradicting the statements of an important visitor was unprecedented.[31]

The net result of this mendacity on the part of the Clinton Administration was simply to heighten the sense of confrontation looming over the meeting. Vatican vs. Clinton Administration stories began cropping up with regularity throughout the summer of 1994. On the eve of the Cairo conference, the press director of the Holy See, Joaquin Navarro-Valls weighed in with his own contribution in the *Wall Street Journal*, claiming that:

> The Holy Father is not merely defending a sort of Catholic view about life and family. He is in fact pointing to the key issue on which future humanity must make a choice. This issue of human life and population undergirds all others. A false step here leads to a general disorder of civilization itself. A small error in the beginning leads to a large error in the end, as Aristotle said. This error is precisely what is at issue.

By their overreaching, by their pandering to the most extreme elements of the feminist movement, the Clinton Administration had single-handedly revived the image of the ugly American, this time bent on supervising the bedrooms of the world telling the world just how many children it was allowed to have. Beyond that, they effectively promoted the pope into the world's foremost defender of the moral order, not just among Catholics but among believers in general, including Islam, and among the smaller, more defenseless nations of the Third World who could reject the ministrations of the Clinton Administration and its UN fellow travelers only at their financial peril. Beyond that, the Clinton Administration probably did more to create goodwill among Muslims and Christians than anyone in the past twelve hundred years. All in all, it was a series of impressive accomplishments by anyone's reckoning.

In a fashion that has become typical of this administration, the Clinton White House realized its mistake too late and then tried to lie its way out of its predicament, only making matters worse. Overreaching followed by retreat and prevarication have become the hallmark of the Clinton Administration, and in this regard Cairo was no exception. On August 25, 1994, virtually on the eve of the conference, Vice-president Al Gore convened a press conference at the National Press Club during which he assured the gathered reporters that the Clinton Administration "has not sought, does not seek and will not seek to establish any international right to an abortion," calling claims to the contrary "outrageous allegations."[32]

It was a bold move on the part of the Clinton Administration, especially considering the amount of pro-abortion advocacy that was already part of the public record, but it called forth an equally bold countermove on the part of the Vatican. If Gore's speech was supposed to be construed as an irenic gesture on the part of the Clinton Administration, the gesture failed dramatically. Within a matter of days, the Vatican countered with what the *New York Times* termed "an unusual personal attack today on Vice president Al Gore, accusing him of misrepresenting the gathering's intentions on abortion."[33]

"The draft population document," said Vatican press secretary Joaquin Navarro-Valls, "which has the United States as its principal sponsor, contradicts in reality Mr. Gore's statement."[34]

In addition to being the first time that the Vatican identified the Clinton Administration as the source of the document's proabortion policies, it was also the first time that the Vatican, as the *Times* put it, "publicly attacked a high American official by name."[35] It was the second time in one summer that the Vatican, breaking with diplomatic protocol had named names, and in both instances it had, in effect, called both the president and vice-president of the most powerful nation on earth liars.

It was no wonder, then, that the press found this meeting intriguing. The backpedaling on Gore's part was also a sign that the Clinton Administration realized it had been caught overreaching once again. Elected by fewer votes than Michael Dukakis had received in 1988, Clinton had developed a habit of staking out grandiose programs without counting the cost, then retreating when there was any sign of significant opposition, then claiming that they had got what they wanted all along after the battle had been lost. Gore's Cairo statement came sandwiched between the failure of the first crime bill and the admission that the administration's health care bill, which was also a stealth abortion campaign, had failed as well.

In an article which President Clinton would claim influenced his views on population in the time preceding the Cairo conference, Robert Kaplan talked about the spread of anarchy in places like West Africa, tracing the pathology, predictably, to overpopulation. "West Africa," Kaplan writes,

> is becoming the symbol of world-wide demographic, environmental and societal stress, in which criminal anarchy emerges as the real "strategic" danger. Disease, overpopulation, unprovoked crime, scarcity of resources, refugee migrations, the increasing erosion of nation-states and international borders, and the empowerment of private armies, security firms and international drug cartels are now most tellingly demonstrated through a West African prism. West Africa provides an appropriate introduction to the issues, often extremely unpleasant to discuss, that will soon confront our civilization.[36]

As with the "Pope bans birth control; millions starve" ads, an air of *non-sequitur* hovers over Kaplan's thinking. Just what is the cause of this anarchy? Is it overpopulation? Or is it simply the breakdown of moral order? By the end of the article, Kaplan testifies against his own thesis by describing an overcrowded Muslim "slum" in Turkey where Islam is the rule of life and the family is intact and he, as a result, feels perfectly safe: "Slum quarters in Abidjan," he writes,

> terrify and repel the outsider. In Turkey it is the opposite. The closer I got to Golden Mountain [a shanty town in Ankara] the better it looked, and the safer I felt. I had $1,500 worth of Turkish lira in one pocket and $1,000 in traveler's checks in the other, yet I felt no fear. Golden Mountain was a real neighborhood. The inside of one house told the story: the architectural bedlam of cinder blocks and sheet metal and cardboard walls was deceiving. Inside was a home – order, that is, bespeaking dignity. I saw a working refrigerator, a television, a wall cabinet with a few books and lots of family pictures, a few plants by a window and a stove. Though the streets became rivers of mud when it rains, the floors inside this house were spotless.[37]

Just what, then, one is tempted to ask after reading the above passage, is the difference between the slums in Abidjan and those in Ankara? Is it population density? Evidently not. The difference begins with the intactness of the family, which is ultimately traceable to conformity to the moral law. Just what contribution will the introduction of condoms make to this picture? The same that they and other contraceptives have made in the black family in America, namely, the disruption of the moral order, the breakdown of the family, the rise of anarchy. Why is Liberia any different from Chicago in this regard? And if the slums of Ankara are different – and according to Kaplan's own testimony, they are – then the cause of the difference lies not in the quantity of the population but in its quality. The difference, in other words, is traceable to how these people behave, not their numbers. The moral order, as mediated by the Koran, creates order in a way that condoms do not. To the extent that the foreign policy of the United States (and now the United Nations as well) is based on the dissemination of contraceptives at the expense of real development, to that extent they will spread the very anarchy they hope to contain.

Morality is reason in the practical order. Anything which undermines morality undermines reason, and without reason man is no better than the animals which, Malthus discovered, procreate themselves into extinction unless checked by nature. Man without morals is in precisely the same situation as the bacteria in the bucket, which became the paradigm of Malthus's geometric population growth, a view which he himself rejected solely because it failed to take into account man's reason and his ability to calculate future consequences.

Kaplan, unable to understand his own texts, concludes by rehashing the same old, now discredited Neo-Malthusian scare stories. Yet, Malthus, in spite of the ideology which takes his name, changed his views on population when he came to understand the role that reason plays in human procreation. "The preventative check," he wrote to Benjamin Franklin, "is peculiar to man, and arises from that distinctive superiority in his reasoning faculties, which enables him to calculate distant consequences."

Julian Simon was quick to draw the obvious consequences from Malthus' second thoughts:

> If people are to control their fertility in response to the conditions facing them, they must be capable of rational, self-conscious forethought that affects the course of sexual passion – the kind of planning capability that animals apparently do not possess. Therefore we must briefly ponder the extent to which reason and reasoning have guided the reproductive behavior of individual persons in various societies at different periods in their histories. To put the matter bluntly, we must inquire into the notion – often held by the well-educated – that uneducated people in poor countries tend to breed without foresight or conscious control. For most couples in most parts of the world, marriage precedes child-bearing. . . . It is therefore relevant to a judgment about the amount of reasoning involved in "breeding" that marriages are contracted, in most "primitive" and poor societies, only after a great deal of careful thought, especially with reference to the economic effects of the marriage. How a marriage match is made in rural Ireland shows the importance of such calculations.[38]

"There is clear evidence," Simon concludes, "that poor people's sexual behavior is sensibly responsive to objective circumstances."[39] If, one hastens to add, their reason is not blinded by passion. Perhaps this is why the Margaret Sangers of the world were so avid to place totalitarian controls on the world's sexual behavior. They were extrapolating from their own experience. Since they have failed so spectacularly at the project of self-control, they assume that no one can succeed. Perhaps this explains President Clinton's interest in population control as a substitute for self-control.

In promoting contraception, however, the population controllers brought about the fulfillment of the very thing they fear. For in promoting contraception, they undermined the moral order, and in undermining the moral order, they subverted reason, and in subverting reason, they removed the only check not only on the destructive passions but on man's ability to make rational plans about how many children he should have.

The Liberal Regime loves to substitute technique for morals, a penchant which has led to one catastrophe after another in this century. The Liberal Regime loves to play both arsonist and fire department, and the UN Cairo conference was no exception to this rule. By spreading contraceptives, they undermined the moral order and brought about the very anarchy they feared. However, the regime itself is so blinded by its own unruly passions that the only thing it can propose as the world's fire department is pouring gasoline its own burning house.

By the time he arrived in the White House for his second term in office, William Jefferson Clinton had become the paradigm of Enlightenment man. Unable to control his own desires, he devoted his life to controlling others by manipulating theirs and dragging them into the same bondage he understood first-hand. Just how all of this would be used politically became evident when President Clinton became enmeshed in the Monica Lewinsky affair, a textbook case of how sex could be mobilized to political advantage by the people who controlled the instruments of communication. The story began with the president of the United States groping someone who had come to his office to ask for a political favor. Linda Tripp, a career civil servant who first started working at the White House during the Bush administration, gradually got pulled into the net of deceit that Clinton had spun around himself trying to maintain his hold on power. Tripp saw a woman come out of Clinton's office in disarray and later said that the woman had had a sexual encounter with the president, for which statement she was promptly denounced as a liar. She vowed not to be caught in the same trap twice, and started tape recording her conversations. As the investigation in the Paula Jones sexual harassment case crept closer and closer, Tripp realized that she was in the classic bind always faced by underlings in immoral regimes. If Tripp lied, as the administration had, and as it was pressuring its employees to do, she could be charged with perjury; however, if she told the truth, she would probably lose her job and might be subject to other forms of retaliation if Clinton remained in office. (She would eventually be prosecuted for illegally taping a phone conversation.) It was a no-win situation, and it was in many ways a paradigm for the meaning the Clinton Administration had for the entire country: Go along with the lie or be punished.

And so, trying to wriggle her way out of the dilemma, Tripp started to tape her conversations with Monica Lewinsky, the young lady she met when both women got transferred from the White House to the Pentagon. Lewinsky was in many ways the culture's paradigm of the ideal [young] woman. She had no problem lying; she had no problem engaging in perverse sexual activity, as long as it fostered her career, although there was that edge of disgust on the tapes and the residual contempt for the man, old enough to be her father, who would encourage this type of exploitative behavior. Lewinsky was also the paradigmatic feminist because she was willing to trade first sex and then complicity in a scheme to suppress the truth as a stepping stone to some job for which she was unqualified. She didn't get the job Vernon Jordan tried to arrange for her at American Express because she couldn't pass a rudimentary English test. The feminists, perhaps horrified at the face staring back at them in the mirror, headed for the tall grass, where most of them had been hiding ever since the Paula Jones case started moving through the courts. When one intrepid reporter finally caught up with former Congresswoman Patricia Schroeder at her sinecure at Princeton University, the lady who excoriated Clarence Thomas for sexual harassment during his nomination to the Supreme Court, opined lamely that there were only so many hours in the day, as her explanation for the absence of feminist support for Paula Jones.

The real answer was simpler: people who looked as if they lived in a trailer park shouldn't expect support from feminists, especially when the defendant in the case had done more to promote abortion than any president in history. The façade of sexual solidarity, it turns out, was just that. The pretext that feminists spoke for women really meant that certain women were willing to function as the ladies' auxiliary for the ruling class and its interests and quite willing in the end to offer up less important women on the altar of that sacrifice. Shortly after Monica Lewinsky became a political liability, the same crowd that frothed at the mouth during the Clarence Thomas hearings about women's rights and sexual harassment were now calling Miss Lewinsky, from behind the veil of anonymity, "a little nutty and a little slutty." As in the case of abortion – and *l'affaire Lewinsky* coincided uncannily with the twenty-fifth anniversary of *Roe v. Wade* – the lesson was all too obvious for those with eyes to see: the lusts of the powerful were more important than the lives of weak. Monica Lewinsky was just a twenty-four-year-old late-term fetus thrown onto the garbage heap of sexual convenience, as the feminists looked the other way once again, because her case did not fit into their agenda.

The talking-class feminists found that Clinton put them in an especially uncomfortable position. Columnist Ellen Goodman struggled valiantly with the fact that her favorite politician was engaged in behavior that would be grounds for lynching if perpetrated by someone at the other end of the political spectrum, and came up with the notion that Americans had become more "morally sophisticated" since the Clarence Thomas hearings. What she meant to say was that they had stopped trying to believe that there should be some congruity between a person's public and private life. Molly Ivins, another feminist columnist, not particularly inclined to all this ambivalence and agonizing about feminist lack of principle, had a simpler point to make. "I, for one," she wrote in her column, "do not think that the president's sex life has squat to do with his job." If the big question mark when it came to Bill Clinton was not his intelligence, but his honesty; the exact opposite was the case with Molly Ivins. Between the two of them, between a stultified talking class and the mendacious politicians who exploited them for their own ends, the sexual revolution had created a major problem for the country which had embraced sexual liberation. The moral problem at the heart of sexual revolution had created a major political crisis.

Clinton was clearly at the heart of a crisis of his own making. His only consolation was that he was not alone. Most of the talking class had been corrupted by the same sexual revolution which had corrupted him over the past thirty years. In this respect, he could count on the decadence of those whose job it was to report or comment on his behavior. The best column in this regard was written by Patricia Smith of the *Boston Globe*, who gave, perhaps inadvertently, some indication of how the talking class behaved on its off hours. Shortly after her column appeared, Smith had to resign because as a reporter, it seemed, she simply made up her stories, something she hints at in her column, when she writes: "We all have secrets. The media will have a field day if I'm ever nominated for the Supreme Court. There's the unfortunate 'sniff this' episode; the pompom squad tryout fiasco; the fact that I have indeed inhaled – rather deeply – and I wouldn't be afraid to admit it. . . . And who hasn't , at some time or another in their sexual history, found themselves sharing sweat and sleeping quarters with a no-no? Who hasn't slept with the wrong one at the right time, the right one at the wrong time, or the absolutely wrong one at the definitely wrong time? And for heaven's sake, who hasn't engaged in a hasty two-minute encounter in a stalled elevator in the Sears Tower?"[40]

The lesson here is clear. The talking class had adopted sexual liberation as its moral code. What they probably didn't understand at the time is that once they adopted it as their code of behavior, they condemned themselves to promote that behavior in others even more influential than themselves, lest in condemning it, they leave themselves open to blackmail or charges of hypocrisy. Those who have had sex in stalled elevators are like the proverbial people in glass houses. This sort of behavior also cuts the nerve of indignation. People who engage in it don't write columns calling for the impeachment of presidents who engage in the same kind of immoral behavior. That is why it is in the interest of the ruling class to promote sexual liberation as a way of consolidating its power. The people who engage in this type of behavior are besotted and stultified and unable to object to any violation of the law, moral or positive, because they themselves are unindicted co-conspirators in the same scheme.

This same form of blackmail extends to the public at large. *Demos*, as usual, never really understood the full political ramifications of the sexual issues involved in *l'affaire Lewinsky*. He was persuaded to think that in condoning the illicit sexual behavior of the president, he was allowing himself the same sort of freedom from moral constraint, when in fact the exact opposite was the case. President Clinton could act like poor white trash because he was part of the ruling class and one of the illusions they loved to create is that they are just like the rest of us. This, of course, is not true. They are not like the rest of us because they are rich and/or powerful, and so when they urge *Demos* to break the moral law in the interest of some specious liberation they are really bringing about his enslavement.

Why? Because the moral law is the only thing that protects the poor. Because *Demos* is neither rich nor powerful. The only protection he has against the predations of the rich and the powerful is the law, which is to say the moral law and the positive one based on it. If he liberates himself from the moral law, he creates a society in which desire is the only measure of right and wrong. But a world like this, no matter what *Demos* thinks, is not democratic because in the absence of moral order, the desires of the rich and powerful will always triumph over the desires of the weak and the poor. The lesson of *Roe v. Wade* is quite simple: The desires of the powerful are more important than the life of the weak. The same applies to the political world at large. A world liberated from morals is a world in which the rich get to do whatever they want.

So *Demos* got it wrong because he failed to understand that a world without morals is a radically two-tiered universe, power and wealth being the main distinction between these two groups. *Demos* is seduced into supporting sexual liberation with the promise that he can now do whatever he wants. This is followed by a momentary sense of intoxication, which is followed by a period of acting out his fantasies, which is followed by another more sobering thought: If I can do anything I want to them, *Demos* suddenly realizes, then they can do anything they want to me. In that thought, we begin to understand why horror is always the natural consequence of sexual liberation.

The general anarchy which sexual liberation brings about is a function of power. In the absence of morals, the rich will get away with murder because their desires are more powerful, and power in this context becomes the only measure of right and wrong. Either might makes right, or we are all bound by the terms of a moral order which is not of our making. There is no third alternative. If *Demos* abandons the moral order, he is *ipso facto* guaranteeing his subjugation because *Demos* is *ipso facto* neither rich nor powerful, simply by the fact that he is *Demos*. This is how sexual liberation functions as a form of political control, a principle which was demonstrated in graphic detail during the second Clinton Administration.

Demos, after watching television all these years, thinks that he belongs to the same class as the people who rule over him. He thinks he has the same prerogatives. But that is not the case. A world in which the ruler is rewarded for lying is a world in which his subjects can be punished for telling the truth. This is the lesson which Linda Tripp had to learn the hard way. The only protection the poor will ever have on this earth is the moral law, enculturated as part of the positive law. The only way a nation can guarantee rights is in light of that moral order, and any nation which subverts that moral order can only propose force, which is the rule of the rich and the powerful, as its substitute. In *Troilus and Cressida*, Agamemnon talks about a world without "degree," which is to say a world without order – moral, political or musical. In this world, "the rude son should strike his father dead," because right and wrong have been replaced by force:

> Force should be right, or rather, right and wrong
> Between whose endless jar justice resides,
> Should lose their names and so should justice too.
> Then everything includes itself in power,
> Power into will, will into appetite,
> And appetite, a universal wolf,
> So doubly seconded with will and power,
> Must make perforce a universal prey,
> And last eat up himself.

If right and wrong lose their names, force is all that is left, and in a world run by force, the rich will be rewarded for their vices every bit as conscientiously as the poor will be punished for their virtues. The lesson of the Clinton presidency and the O. J. Simpson trial and *Roe v. Wade* and the sexual revolution which brought this regime to power in the '60s is very simple: the rich and the powerful can get away with murder. *Demos* goes along because his besotted mind is too darkened to understand that sexual liberation is a form of political control.

President Clinton was impeached for perjury by the House of Representatives in December 1998. In the months leading up to the impeachment Clinton used all the power at his disposal to mobilize the forces of sexual license as a way of remaining in office. Clinton's policy, ever since the moment he took office when he struck down abortion restrictions and opened the way for homosexuals in the military, was the sexual revolution. He supported the sexual revolution for obvious personal reasons, but he also supported it because it was in his political interest to do so. He, more than any other president in this nation's history, understood how sexual license could be used to political advantage. Deriving a good deal of his financial backing from Hollywood, he knew that a nation that spent billions a year on pornography would not be able to respond with indignation, much less outrage, when the president of the United States was implicated in his own X-rated performance in the Oval Office. Clinton courted the homosexuals assiduously and was the first president ever to speak before a group of homosexuals, in this instance the Human Rights Campaign. Clinton rose to power supporting this ideology, and he was not about to abandon it when the Lewinsky affair broke.

On September 10, *Salon Magazine*, a journal which was to become an organ of the Clinton administration during the impeachment proceedings, announced "the so-called Doomsday scenario" as one of the options the same Clinton Administration was considering to retain its hold on power.

This "scenario" was "the dreaded Armageddon in which the personal pecca-
dilloes of everyone – Republican, Democrat, journalist – are exposed if
Clinton's infidelities are dragged into the open." A few days later, *Salon*
obligingly put the "Doomsday scenario" into effect by reporting on an affair
which Henry Hyde, chairman of the judiciary committee then considering
impeachment, had had thirty years earlier. "Everyone," said Henry Jaffe of
Salon, "will be punished. It will be a total meltdown."

Once Clinton refused to resign, the press was forced to support him as
the guarantor of their sexual vices. It was during the Lewinsky scandal that
Toni Morrison referred to Clinton as the nation's first black president, implying that all blacks were sexual degenerates. At around the same time, Alan
Dershowitz of the Harvard Law School announced that those who believed
in sexual liberation had to support Clinton; otherwise, they faced the prospect of a right-wing coup. Gradually, as the charges against Clinton grew, a
subtle change of heart swept through the talking class. Maureen Dowd, who
would later go on to win the Pulitzer Prize following her *volte face* on
Clinton, was a good case in point. Dowd lambasted Clinton as a selfish jerk
week after week. In a letter to his supporters, Dr. James Dobson even cited
one of Dowd's columns as evidence of a hostile press. Then, suddenly, when
the Starr report came out and the evidence against Clinton became inescapable, Dowd changed her mind and began attacking the special prosecutor instead of the president. It was as if this dog had suddenly run to the end of its
leash and got jerked back to reality. Why? Perhaps because by this point it
became clear that bigger issues were at stake. By not resigning from office,
Clinton turned the Lewinsky affair into a referendum on the sexual revolution. Now that he was not going to go quietly and take the rap, it was time to
close ranks and defend what Clinton said he stood for. Within hours of the release of the Starr Report, Dowd was attacking the prosecutor as vehemently
as she once attacked the president. Clinton had saved himself by wrapping
his political fortunes in the mantle of sexual liberation. A vote against
Clinton was now a vote against the '60s, and all that that decade stood for in
the minds of the liberated intelligentsia. Maureen Dowd said so herself: "The
avenging, evangelical prosecutor never seems to give a thought to how his
relentless chase is driving the nation. He seems determined not only to overthrow the President, but to overturn the '60s and restore the black-and-white
moral code that existed before the decade of sex, drugs and draft evasion."[41]

Anthony Lewis said much the same thing. The independent prosecutor,
according to Lewis, would "bring about a fundamental change in the political direction of this country, effectively changing the results of our last two
elections. It would be a *coup d'état*."[42] The attack on Clinton would have
"enormous consequences for our politics." Lewis then went on to list the
consequences, all of which had to do with the sexual revolution:

Abortion would be targeted for a range of new restrictions, including even a constitutional amendment to outlaw it. And concern with sexual matters would not be likely to stop there. There would be legislation to limit U.S. help for population control efforts around the world. Federal regulations to give equal treatment to homosexuals would be another target. The law forbidding grants to "indecent" art could be expanded to other fields.[43]

Hollywood, next to the black population Clinton's most avid support group, was not backing away from supporting Clinton any more than the fourth estate. At a fund-raiser in Hollywood, Marshall Herskovitz, a Democrat who was producer of the television series "thirtysomething" claimed that "the [Lewinsky] scandal is really a referendum on sexual morality in the country."[44] By the time the vote on Clinton went to the United States Senate in early 1999, the molders of public opinion were so committed to the worship of Dionysos that they were willing to junk the rule of law in order to preserve it. Which is precisely what the Senate did. In early 1999, the Senate refused to convict President Clinton of high crimes and misdemeanors, and in casting that vote the Senate made clear that thirty years of sexual liberation had done its work. The populace had been corrupted by three decades of sexual license, and that meant that the people who had been corrupted chose President Clinton as the guarantor of their illicit sexual desires even if this meant repudiating the rule of law and accepting political bondage as the price they were willing to pay for sexual liberation. In making that decision, the Senate brought the American experiment in ordered liberty to a close. The nation's founding fathers had always warned that the American constitution could not function, to use John Adams' words, "in the absence of a moral people." The Clinton crisis had proven just that. The remedies proposed by the Constitution for "high crimes and misdemeanors" simply could not be applied in the face of overwhelming evidence of the president's guilt because the president had portrayed himself as the guarantor of the nation's sexual vices, and the Senate which had been conditioned by thirty years of sexual decadence, believing him, chose not to apply those remedies. With that refusal, the rule of law upon which Americans had always prided themselves was replaced by the worship of Dionysos as the nation's established religion. The fourth estate heaved a huge sigh of relief when it happened, but that is because they were blinded by their own vices from seeing the full implication of the Senate's decision not to act. Those who had gone before them had seen the implications, but even if they, like Lazarus, had come back from the dead, there is no indication that the nation's leaders would have listened to their warnings. "Society," Edmund Burke had written 200 years before the American senate reached its verdict,

> cannot exist, unless a controlling power upon will and appetite be placed somewhere; and the less of it there is within, the more there must be without. It is ordained in the eternal constitution of things, that men of intemperate minds cannot be free. Their passions forge their fetters.[45]

Notes

Introduction
1. John Heidenry, *What Wild Ecstasy: The Rise and Fall of the Sexual Revolution* (New York: Simon & Schuster, 1997), p. 12.
2. Ibid., p. 405.
3. Saint Augustine, *City of God* (New York: Doubleday, 1958), p. 40.
4. Marquis de Sade, *Justine, Philosophy in the Bedroom, & Other Writings*, compiled and translated by Richard Seaver and Austryn Wainhouse (New York: Grove Press, 1965), p. 315.
5. Ibid.

Part I, Chapter 1: Ingolstadt, 1776
1. Richard van Duelmen, *Der Geheimbund der Illuminaten* (Stuttgart: Frommann-Holzbooog, 1975), p. 25.
2. A. Barruel, *Memoirs Illustrating the History of Jacobinism* (Fraser, Mich.: Real View Books, 1995), p. 648.
3. Van Duelman, pp. 71–72.
4. Baron d'Holbach, *The System of Nature or the Laws of the Moral and Physical World* (New York: Burt Franklin, 1970), p. iii.
5. Manfred Agethen, *Geheimbund und Utopie: Illuminaten, Freimaurer und deutsche Spaetaufklaerung: Mit einem Geleitwort von Eberhard Schmitt* (München: R. Oldenbourg Verlag, 1984), p. 106.
6. D'Holbach, p. 11.
7. Ibid., p. 15.
8. Van Duelman, p. 112.
9. Ibid., p. 127.
10. Agethen, p. 192.
11. Van Duelmen, p. 92.
12. Ibid., p. 122.
13. Ibid., p. 95

Part I, Chapter 2: Paris, 1787
1. Francine du Plessix Gray, *At Home with the Marquis de Sade* (New York: Simon & Schuster, 1998), p. 316.
2. Maurice Lever, *Sade: A Biography* (New York: Farrar, Strauss, Giroux, 1993), p. 343.
3. Ibid., p. 340.
4. Marquis de Sade, *Justine, Philosophy in the Bedroom, & Other Writings*, compiled and translated by Richard Seaver and Austryn Wainhouse (New York: Grove Press, 1965), p. 544.
5. Ibid., p. 603.

6. Sallie Tisdale, *Talk Dirty to Me: An Intimate Philosophy of Sex* (New York: Anchor Books, 1994), p. 281.
7. Sade, p. 201.
8. Aldous Huxley, *Ends and Means: An Inquiry into the Nature of Ideals and into the Methods Employed for Their Realization* (New York & London: Harper & Brothers Publishers, 1937), p. 314.
9. Gray, p. 170.
10. Ibid., p. 148.
11. Sade, p. 605.
12. Ibid., p. 608.
13. Huxley, p. 315.
14. D'Holbach, p. 15.
15. Lever, p. 351.
16. Ibid., p. 421
17. Gray, p. 316.
18. Lever, p. 382.
19. Ibid., p. 387.
20. Ibid., p. 415.
21. Ibid., p. 397.
22. Ibid., p. 402.
23. Ibid., p. 430.
24. Ibid., p. 430.

Part I, Chapter 3: London, 1790
1. William Godwin, *Enquiry concerning Political Justice*, Isaac Kramnick ed., (New York: Hammondsworth Penguin, 1985), p. 11
2. Ibid., p. 14.
3. Mary Wollstonecraft, *A Vindication of the Rights of Men with a Vindication of the Rights of Woman and Hints*, edited by Sylvana Tomaselli (Cambridge: Cambridge University Press, 1995), p. 28.
4. Mary Wollstonecraft, *Collected Letters of Mary Wollstonecraft*, edited by Ralph M. Wardle (Ithaca, N.Y.: Cornell University Press, 1979), p. 36.
5. Ibid., p. 33.
6. William St. Clair, *The Godwins and the Shelleys: The Biography of a Family* (New York: W.W. Norton & Co., 1989), p. 44.
7. William Godwin, *Memoirs of Mary Wollstonecraft* (New York: Greenberg Publisher, 1927), p. 184.
8. Wollstonecraft, *Letters*, p. 38.
9. William Godwin, *Memoirs of the Author of a Vindication of the Rights of Woman* (New York: Garland Publishing, Inc. 1974), p. 100.
10. Claire Tomalin, *The Life and Death of Mary Wollstonecraft* (New York: Harcourt , Brace, Jovanovich, 1974), pp. 119–20.

Part I, Chapter 4: Paris, 1792
1. Wollstonecraft, *Letters*, p. 225.
2. Ibid.
3. St. Clair, p. 81.
4. Godwin, *Political Justice*, pp. 7–8.
5. Ibid., p. 12.
6. Lever, p. 440.
7. Godwin, *Memoirs*, p. 103.

8. Claire Tomalin, *The Life and Death of Mary Wollstonecraft* (New York: Harcourt Brace Jovanovich, 1974), p. 123.
9. Wollstonecraft, *Letters*, p. 40.
10. Godwin, Memoirs, p. 116.
11. Lever, p. 448.
12. Wollstonecraft, *Letters*, p. 236.
13. Ibid.
14. St. Clair, p. 105.
15. Tomalin, p. 185.
16. Ibid., p. 185.
17. Ibid., p. 189.
18. Wollstonecraft, *Letters*, p. 263.
19. Ibid., p. 273.
20. Ibid., p. 289.
21. Ibid., p. 291.
22. Ibid., p. 321.
23. Ibid., p. 321.
24. Ibid., p. 322.
25. Lever, p. 476.
26. Sade, p. 315.
27. Ibid., p. 316.
28. Ibid., p. 316.
29. Ibid., p. 317.
30. Bernard Berelson and Morris Janowitz, eds., *Public Opinion and Communication* (Glencoe, Ill.: The Free Press, 1950), p. 4.
31. Ibid.
32. E. Michael Jones, *Monsters from the Id* (Dallas: Spence, 2000).
33. Wollstonecraft, Letters, p. 47.

Part I, Chapter 5: London, 1797
1. A. Barruel, *Memoirs Illustrating the History of Jacobinism* (Fraser, Mich.: Real View Books, 1995), p. xix.
2. Daniel Pipes, *Conspiracy: How the Paranoid Style Flourishes and Where it Comes From* (New York: The Free Press, 1997), p. 74.
3. Barruel, p. 209.
4. Ibid.
5. Lever, p. 497.
6. Ibid., p. 503.
7. Ibid., p. 529.
8. Ibid., p. 530.
9. Ibid., p. 525.
10. Ibid.
11. Ibid.
12. Ibid., p. 556.

Part I, Chapter 6: London, 1812
1. St. Claire, p. 315.
2. Ibid., p. 321.
3. Ibid., p. 194.
4. Richard Holmes, Shelley: *The Pursuit*, pp. 44–45.
5. Holmes, p. 46.

6. Barruel, p. 13.
7. Ibid., p. 17.
8. Holmes, p. 47.
9. Ibid., p. 52.
10. Barruel, p. 463.
11. Ibid.
12. Holmes, p. 103.
13. Ibid.. p. 122.
14. Ibid., p. 126.
15. Ibid., p. 209.
16. Geoffrey Matthews, ed., *The Poems of Shelley* (London: Longman, 1989), p. 311, Line 18 ff.
17. Ibid. p. 322, line 64 ff.
18. Ibid., p. 339, Lines 193 ff.
19. Ibid., p. 391n.
20. Ibid., p. 354. Lines 62 ff.
21. Ibid., p. 354, lines 76–86.
22. Ibid., p. 360.
23. Sade, p. 605.
24. Matthews, p. 368.
25. Ibid., p. 370.
26. Ibid., pp. 372–73.
27. Ibid. p. 409.
28. Ibid.
29. Ibid., p. 415.
30. Ibid., pp. 416–17.
31. St. Clair, p. 366.
32. Barruel, p. 209.
33. Ibid., p. 74.
34. Ibid., p. 56.
35. Ibid., pp. 833–34.
36. Ibid., p. 820.
37. Lester G. Crocker, *Nature and Culture: Ethical Thought in the French Enlightenment* (Baltimore: The Johns Hopkins Press, 1963), p. 328.
38. Barruel, p. 115.
39. Ibid., p. 400.
40. Ibid., p. 401.
41. Ibid.
42. Ibid., p. 418.
43. Friedrich Nietzsche, *Werke in Drei Bänden* (München: Carl Hanser Verlag, 1954), vol. 1, pp. 56–57, my translation.
44. Barruel, p. 773.
45. Ibid., p. 419.
46. Ibid., p. 449.
47. Ibid.
48. Ibid., p. 454.
49. Ibid., p. 623.
50. Ibid.
51. Emily W. Sunstein, *Mary Shelley: Romance and Reality* (Boston: Little, Brown, & Co, 1989), p. 343.
52. Sunstein, p. 370.

53. St. Clair, p. 467.

Part I, Chapter 7: Paris, 1821
1. Boris Sokoloff, *The "Mad" Philosopher Auguste Comte* (Westport, Conn.: Greenwood Press, Publishers, 1961), p. 77.
2. Sokoloff, pp. 147–48.
3. Dietrich E. Franz, *Saint-Simon, Fourier, Owen: Sozialutopien des 19. Jahrhunderts* (Cologne: Pahl-Rugenstein, 1988), p. 73.
4. I have dealt with this development elsewhere, cf. *Dionysos Rising: The Birth of the Cultural Revolution out of the Spirit of Music* (San Francisco: Ignatius, 1994).
5. Richard Noll, *The Aryan Christ: The Secret Life of Carl Jung* (New York: Random House, 1997), p. 71.

Part II, Chapter 1: Paris, 1885
1. James Billington, *Fire in the Minds of Men* (New York: Basic Books, 1980), p. 99.
2. Nesta Webster, *World Revolution: The Plot against Civilization* (Boston: Small, Maynar Company, 1921), p. 307.
3. Johannes Rogalla von Biberstein, *Die These von Verschwoerung 1776–1945: Philosophen, Freimaurer, Juden, Liberale und Sozialisten als Verschwoerer gegen die Sozialordnung* (Frankfurt/M: Peter Lang, 1976), p. 160.
4. Biberstein, p. 194.
5. Ibid.
6. Biberstein, p. 195.
' 7. Pope Leo XIII, *Humanum Genus: Encyclical Letter of His Holiness Pope Leo XII on Freemasonry* (Rockford, Ill.: Tan Books and Publishers, Inc., 1978), # 10, p. 7.
8. Humanum Genus, #20, pp. 11–12.
9. Ibid., p. 11.

Part II, Chapter 2: Chicago, September 1900
1. Kerry W. Buckley, *Mechanical Man: John Broadus Watson and the Beginnings of Behaviorism* (New York: The Guilford Press, 1989), p. 29
2. Ibid., p. 31.
3. Ibid., p. 178.
4. David Cohen, *J. B. Watson: The Founder of Behaviourism* (Boston and London: Routledge & Kegan Paul, 1979), p. 135.
5. Buckley, p. 93.
6. Ibid., p. 85.
7. Ibid., p. 45.
8. Ibid., p. 74.
9. Ibid., p. 73.
10. Ibid., p. 120.
11. Ibid., p. 121.
12. Ibid.
13. J.B. Watson, *Behaviourism* (New York: W. W. Norton company, 1930), p. 11.
14. Ibid., p. 269.
15. Ibid., p. 22.
16. Ibid., p. 26.
17. Ibid., p. 302.
18. Ibid. p. 26.
19. Buckley p. 84.
20. James H. Jones, *Alfred C. Kinsey: A Public/Private Life* (New York: W. W. Norton & Company, 1997), pp. 419–20.

21. Ibid., p. 419.

Part II, Chapter 3: Bremen, 1909
1. C.G. Jung, *Memories, Dreams, Reflections* (New York: Vintage, 1961), p. 10.
2. Ibid.
3. E. Michael Jones, *Degenerate Moderns: Modernity as Rationalized Sexual Misbehavior* (San Francisco: Ignatius Press, 1993), pp. 153 ff.
4. Richard Noll, *Aryan Christ*, p. 91.
5. Ibid.
6. Peter Swales, "Freud, Filthy Lucre, and Undue Influence," *Review of Existential Psychology and Psychiatry*, 23 (1997), p. 115.
7. Phyllis Grosskurth, *The Secret Ring: Freud's Inner Circle and the Politics of Psychoanalysis* (New York: Addison-Wesley Publishing Company, Inc., 1991), p. 47.
8. L. J. Rather, "Disraeli, Freud, and Jewish Conspiracy Theories," *Journal of the History of Ideas* (1986), p. 117.
9. Grosskurth, p. 47.
10. Sigmund Freud, *The Psychopathology of Everyday Life* (New York: W.W. Norton and Co., 1965), p. 9.
11. Rather, p. 119.
12. Freud, *Psychopathology*, pp. 9–10.
13. Ibid., p. 14.
14. Nietzsche, *Werke*, Vol. I, pp. 56–57, my translation.
15. E. Fuller Torrey, M.D., *Freudian Fraud: The Malignant Effect of Freud's Theory on American Thought and Culture* (San Francisco: HarperCollins Publishers, 1992), p.6.
16. Jeffrey Moussaieff Masson, ed., *The Complete Letters of Sigmund Freud to Wilhelm Fliess (1887–1904)* (Cambridge, Mass.: Harvard University Press, 1985), p. 371.
17. Ibid.
18. J. M. Roberts, *The Mythology of Secret Societies*, p. 197.
19. Roberts, p. 193.
20. Barruel, p. 600.
21. Ibid., p. 419.
22. Ibid., p. 401.
23. Ibid., p. 402.
24. Manfred Agethen, *Geheimbund und Utopie: Illuminaten, Freimaurer und deutsche Spaetaufklaerung* (München: R. Oldenbourg Verlag, 1984), p. 210, my translation.
25. Ibid., p. 211.
26. Ibid., p. 189.
27. Barruel, p. 404.
28. Agethen, p. 210.
29. Ibid., p. 205n.
30. Ibid., p. 212.
31. Ibid.
32. Barruel, p. 405.
33. Ibid., p. 432.
34. Richard Webster, *Why Freud Was Wrong: Sin, Science, And Psychoanalysis* (New York: Basic Books, 1995), p. 336.

Part II, Chapter 4: Greenwich Village, 1913
1. E. Fuller Torrey, M.D., *Freudian Fraud: The Malignant Effect of Freud's Theory on American Thought and Culture* (New York: HarperCollins Publishers, 1992), p. 23.
2. Ibid., p. 24.
3. Ibid., p. 25.

4. Ibid.
5. Ibid., p. 28.
6. Ibid., p. 29.
7. Larry Tye, *The Father of Spin: Edward L. Bernays and the Birth of Public Relations* (New York: Crown Publishers, 1998), p. 6.
8. Ibid., p. 7.
9. Ibid., p. 8.
10. Ibid.
11. Ibid., p. 9.
12. Ibid., p. 97.
13. Ibid., p. 107.
14. Ibid., p. 197.
15. Edward L. Bernays, *Propaganda* (New York: H. Liveright, 1928), p. 97.

Part II, Chapter 5: Zürich, 1914
1. Noll, p. 200.
2. Swales, p. 119.
3. Ibid., p. 129.
4. Lavinia Edmunds, "His Master's Choice," *Johns Hopkins Magazine* (April 1988), p. 45.
5. Ibid. p. 42.
6. Ibid.
7. Ibid. p. 45.
8. Swales, p. 131.
9. Torrey, p. 18.
10. Ibid., p. 29.

Part II, Chapter 6: New York, 1914
1. Ellen Chesler, *Woman of Valor: Margaret Sanger and the Birth Control Movement in America* (New York: Simon & Schuster, 1992), p. 86.
2. Ibid., p. 91.
3. Ibid.
4. Ibid.
5. Ibid., p. 457.
6. Ibid., p. 104.
7. Ibid., p. 133.
8. Ibid., p. 136.
9. Ibid., p. 97.
10. Ibid., p. 136.
11. Tye, p. 253.
12. Chesler, p. 193.
13. Ibid., p. 191.

Part II, Chapter 7: Baltimore, 1916
1. Watson, *Behaviourism*, p. 41.
2. Buckley, p. 99.
3. Ibid., p. 97.
4. Ibid., p. 100.
5. Ibid., p. 97.
6. Walter Lippmann, *Public Opinion* (New York; Collier-Macmillan Limited, 1922), pp. 57–58.
7. Buckley, p. 99.

8. Ibid., p. 111.
9. Ibid., p. 82.
10. Ibid., p. 84.

Part II, Chapter 8: Paterson, New Jersey, 1916
1. Alexandra Kollontai, *The Autobiography of a Sexually Emancipated Communist Woman* (New York: Herder and Herder, 1971), p. 7.
2. Barbara Evans Clements, *Bolshevik Feminist: The Life of Aleksandra Kollontai* (Bloomington: Indiana University Press, 1979), p. 252.
3. Kollontai, *Autobiography*, pp. 10–11.
4. Clements, p. 53.
5. Ibid., p. 58.
6. Cathy Porter, *Alexandra Kollontai: The Lonely Struggle of the Woman Who Defied Lenin* (New York: Dial Press, 1980), p. 51.
7. Clements, p. 51.
8. Ibid.
9. Ibid.
10. Porter, p. 71.
11. Clements, p. 19.
12. Kollontai, *Autobiography*, pp. 11–12.
13. Clements, p. 16.
14. Ibid.
15. Porter, p. 64.
16. Clements, p. 59.
17. Kollontai, *Autobiography*, p. 6.
18. Alexandra Kollontai, *A Great Love*, trans. and intro. by Cathy Porter (New York: W.W. Norton &Co, 1980), p. 75.
19. Ibid., p. 76.
20. Ibid., p. 92.
21. Ibid., p. 128.
22. Ibid.
23. Ibid., p.109.
24. Ibid., p. 122.
25. Ibid.
26. Ibid.
27. Ibid., p. 124.
28. Ibid., p. 133.
29. Clements, p. 68.
30. Kollontai, *Autobiography*, p. 22.
31. Ibid., p. 73.
32. Clements, p. 118.
33. Porter, p. 297.
34. Clements, p. 134.
35. Ibid. p. 135.
36. Porter, p. 295.
37. Clements, p. 135.
38. Ibid.
39. Kollontai, *Autobiography*, p. 114.
40. Ibid., p. 79.
41. Ibid., p. 89.

42. Ibid., p. 40.
43. Farnsworth, p. 145.
44. Ibid., p. 151.
45. Ibid., p. 147.
46. Ibid., p. 155.
47. Clements, p. 172.
48. Ibid., p. 165.
49. Porter, p. 359.

Part II, Chapter 9: New York, 1917
1. Max Eastman, *Enjoyment of Living* (New York: Harper & Brothers Publishers, 1948), p. 586.
2. Ibid.
3. Ibid.
4. Ibid., p. 360.
5. Ibid., p. 393.
6. Ibid., p. 363.
7. Ibid., p. 362.
8. Ibid., p. 380.
9. Ibid., p. 381.
10. Ibid.

Part II, Chapter 10: Versailles, 1919
1. Tye, p. 19.
2. Edward L. Bernays, *Crystallizing Public Opinion* (New York: Liveright Publishing Corporation, 1923), p. 101.
3. Ibid., p. 102.
4. Ibid., p. 121.
5. Christopher Simpson, *Science of Coercion: Communication Research and Psychological Warfare 1945–1960* (New York: Oxford University Press, 1994), p. 15.
6. Tye, p. 98.
7. Edward L. Bernays, *Propaganda* (New York: Horace Liveright, 1928), p. 31.
8. Simpson, p. 18.
9. Tye, p. 95.
10. Bernays, *Crystallizing*, p. 150.

Part II, Chapter 11: Baltimore, 1919
1. John B. Watson, *Psychological Care of Infant and Child* (New York W.W. Norton & Company, Inc.: 1928), p. 14.
2. Buckley, p. 73.
3. Ibid., p. 124.
4. David Cohen, *J. B. Watson: The Founder of Behaviourism* (Boston and London: Routledge & Kegan Paul, 1979), p. 250.
5. Cohen, p. 258.
6. Buckley, p. 115.
7. Ibid., p. 118.
8. Cohen, p. 251.

Part II, Chapter 12: Berlin, 1919
1. David Bordwell, *The Films of Carl-Theodore Dreyer* (Berkeley: University of California Press, 1981), p. 217.

2. Charlotte Wolff, *Magnus Hirschfeld: A Portrait of a Pioneer in Sexology* (London & New York: Quartet, 1986), p. 70.

3. Christopher Isherwood, *Christopher and His Kind 1929–1930* (New York: Farrar, Straus, Giroux, 1976), p. 34.

4. Wolff, p. 193.

5. Magnus Hirschfeld, *Von einst bis jetzt: Geschichte einer homosexuellen Bewegug 1897–1922* (Berlin: Verlag Rosa Winkel, 1986), p. 211.

6. Wolff, p. 196.

7. Isherwood, pp. 26–27.

8. Joseph Nicolosi, *Reparative Therapy of Male Homosexuality* (Northvale, N.J.: Jason Aronson, 1991), p. 103.

9. Wolff, p. 432.

10. Scott Lively, Kevin Abrams, *The Pink Swastika: Homosexuality in the Nazi Party* (Keizer, Ore.: Founders Publishing Corp. 1995).

11. Erwin J. Haeberle, "Swastika, Pink Triangle and Yellow Star – the Destruction of Sexlogy and the Persecution of Homosexuals in Nazi Germany," *The Journal of Sex Research* 17, no 3, p. 271.

12. Ibid.

13. Ibid., p. 273.

14. Ibid., p. 280.

15. Lively, p. 96.

16. Ibid.

Part II, Chapter 13: New York, 1921

1. Daniel Pope, *The Making of Modern Advertising* (New York: Basic Books, Inc, 1983), p. 183.

2. Ibid., p. 258.

3. Ibid., p. 14.

4. Ibid., p. 76.

5. Ibid., p. 282.

6. Buckley, p. 133.

Part II, Chapter 14: New York, 1922

1. Claude McKay, *A Long Way from Home* (New York: Arno Press and The New York Times, 1969), p. 148.

2. Ibid., pp. 149–50.

3. Wayne Cooper, *Claude McKay: Rebel Sojourner in the Harlem Renaissance, a Biography* (Baton Rouge, La.: Louisiana State University, 1987), p. 9.

4. Ibid.

5. Ibid., p. 10.

6. Ibid., p. 14.

7. Ibid., p. 15.

8. Ibid., p. 28.

9. Ibid., p. 30.

10. Ibid., p. 65.

11. Ibid. p. 68.

12. Ibid. p. 69.

13. Ibid., p. 70.

14. Ibid., p. 73.

15. Ibid., p. 73.

16. Ibid., p. 75.

17. Ibid.
18. Claude McKay, *Home to Harlem* (Boston: Northeastern University Press, 1987), p. 274.
19. Ibid., p. 263.
20. Cooper, p. 258.
21. McKay, *Home*, p. 265.
22. Ibid., p. 272.
23. Cooper, p. 31.
24. McKay, *Home*, p. 300.
25. Ibid.
26. Ibid., p. 301.
27. McKay, *A Long Way*, p. 150.
28. Cooper, p. 169.
29. Ibid., p. 138.
30. McKay, *A Long Way*, p. 29.
31. Eastman, *The Enjoyment of Living*, p. 419.
32. Eastman, *Love and Revolution*, p. 247.
33. Claude McKay, Correspondence at the James Weldon Johnson collection at the Beineke Library at Yale University, July 25, 1919.
34. Cooper, p. 101.
35. Eastman, *The Enjoyment of Living*, p. 438.
36. Eastman, *Love and Revolution*, p. 325.
37. Ibid. p. 338.
38. Ibid., p. 340.
39. Ibid., p. 341.

Part II, Chapter 15: Moscow, 1922

1. Cooper, p. 172.
2. McKay, *A Long Way from Home*, p. 168.
3. Ibid., pp. 170–71.
4. Cooper, p. 187.
5. McKay, *A Long Way from Home*, p. 230.
6. Ibid., p. 231.
7. Ibid.
8. Ibid., p. 234.
9. Cooper, p. 192.
10. McKay, *A Long Way from Home*, p. 231.
11. E. Michael Jones, *Degenerate Moderns* (San Francisco: Ignatius, 1993), p. 153 ff. (The guilt-ridden minister in the crucial middle scaffold scene in Hawthorne's *The Scarlet Letter* simultaneously reveals and conceals his sin, by exposing his breast in the town square under the cover of darkness.)
12. McKay, *A Long Way from Home*, p. 229.
13. Ibid., pp. 233–34.
14. Ibid., p. 244.
15. Ibid., p. 245.
16. Claude McKay, *Banjo: A Story without a Plot* (New York: Harcourt Brace Jovanovich, Inc. 1929), p. 130.
17. Ibid.
18. Cooper, p. 245.
19. McKay, *Banjo*, p. 136.
20. Ibid., p. 292.
21. Ibid., p. 293.

22. Ibid., p. 163.
23. Ibid., p. 268.
24. Ibid., p. 320.
25. Ibid., p. 290.
26. Langston Hughes, *The Big Sea: An Autobiography* (New York: Hill and Wang, 1940), p. 19.

Part II, Chapter 16: Moscow, 1922
 1. Farnsworth, pp. 355–56.
 2. Clements, p. 233.
 3. Ibid.
 4. Ibid., p. 222.
 5. Farnsworth, p. 358.
 6. Ibid., p. 360.
 7. Porter, p. 446.
 8. Ibid.
 9. Ibid., p. 446..
10. Ibid., p. 448.
11. Clements, p. 446.
12. Porter, p. 445.
13. Ibid., p. 447.
14. Clements, p. 236.
15. Farnsworth, p. 342.
16. Ibid., p. 347.
17. Kollontai, *Autobiography*, pp. 47–48.
18. Ibid., p. xii.
19. Porter, p. 413.
20. Clements, p. 252.

Part II, Chapter 17: Moscow, 1926
 1. Adolf Hitler, *Mein Kampf* (München: Zentralverlag der NSDAP, F. Eher, Nachf., 1941), p. 751 (my translation).
 2. Wolff, p. 234.
 3. Ibid. p. 244.
 4. Isherwood, p. 17.
 5. Ibid., p. 16.
 6. Ibid. p. 17.
 7. Ibid., p. 12.
 8. Ibid., p. 10.
 9. Ibid., p. 11.
10. Nicolosi, p. 207.
11. Ibid. p. 164.
12. Ibid., p. 213.
13. Isherwood, p. 12.
14. Ibid., p. 5.
15. Nicolosi, p. 157.
16. Ibid., p. 24.
17. Ibid. p. 163.

Part II, Chapter 18: Vienna, 1927
 1. Myron Sharaf, *Fury on Earth: A Biography of Wilhelm Reich* (New York: St. Martin's Press, 1983), p. 56.

2. Ibid., p. 119.
3. Ibid., p. 120.
4. Ibid., p. 149.
5. Ibid., p. 151.
6. Ibid., p. 89.
7. Ibid., p. 129.

Part II, Chapter 19: New York, 1929

1. Tye, p. 33.
2. Ibid., p. 30.
3. Ibid., p. 33.
4. Ibid., p. 31.
5. Ibid., p. 23.
6. Ibid., p. 28.
7. Buckley, p. 139.
8. Tye, p. 42.
9. Edward L. Bernays, *Propaganda* (New York: Horace Liveright, 1928), pp. 9–10.
10. Ibid.
11. Ibid., p. 12.

Part II, Chapter 20: Berlin, 1929

1. Sharaf, p. 193.
2. Ibid.
3. Wilhelm Reich, *The Mass Psychology of Fascism* (New York: Farrar, Straus & Giroux, 1970), p. 154.
4. Sharaf, p. 193.
5. Wilhelm Reich, *The Sexual Revolution: Toward a Self-Regulating Character Structure* (New York: Farrar, Strauss and Giroux, 1974), p. 220.
6. Reich, *Mass Psychology*, p. 154.
7. Ibid., p. 155.
8. Ibid., p. 170.
9. Ibid., p. 182.
10. Ibid., p. 178.
11. Ibid., p. 182.
12. Ibid., p. 183.
13. Ibid., p. 187.
14. Lisa Palac, *The Edge of the Bed: How Dirty Pictures Changed my Life* (New York: Little, Brown and Company, 1998), p. 7.
15. Ibid., p. 15.
16. Ibid., pp. 14–15.
17. Sharaf, p. 61.
18. Ibid., p. 123.
19. Joseph McCarroll, "Transgressive Imagery," talk given to the Verein Psychologishen Menschenkenntnisse, Zürich.
20. Ibid.
21. Reich, *The Sexual Revolution*, p. 202.
22. Reich, *Mass Psychology*, p. 188.

Part II, Chapter 21: Berlin, 1930

1. Joachim C. Fest, *Hitler: Eine Biographie* (Frankfurt: Propylaen, 1975), p. 131.

Part II, Chapter 22: Moscow, 1930

1. Reich, *The Sexual Revolution*, p.175.
2. Ibid., p. 269.
3. Ibid., p. 207.
4. Ibid., pp. 193–94.
5. Ibid., p. 197.
6. Ibid., p. xviii.
7. Ibid., p. 185.
8. Ibid., p. 162.
9. Ibid., p. 181.
10. Ibid., p. 186.
11. Ibid., p. 186.
12. Ibid., p. 253.
13. Reich, *Mass Psychology*, p. 151.
14. Ibid., p. 150.
15. Ibid., p. 151.
16. Reich, *The Sexual Revolution*, p. 267.

Part II, Chapter 23: Washington, 1930

1. Rockefeller Archives, Office of the Messrs. Rockefeller, Medical Interests Birth Control Organizations – General 1930–39, III 2K Box 1 letter from Eleanor Dwight Jones, president of American Birth Control League to Lawrence B. Dunham, director of the Bureau of Social Hygiene 11/5/30.
2. Ibid.
3. Ibid.
4. John A. Ryan, *Social Doctrine in Action: A Personal History* (New York and London: Harper Brothers, 1941), p. 267.
5. Ibid. p. 5.
6. Ibid., p. 267.
7. Population by John Ryan, *The Catholic Encyclopedia* (New York: the Universal Knowledge Foundation, 1911).
8. Chesler, p. 327.
9. Elasah Drogin, *Margaret Sanger: Father of Modern Society* (Coarsegold, Cal.: CUL Publications, 1979), p. 96.
10. Ibid.
11. Paul R. Ehrlich, *The Population Bomb* (New York: Ballantine books, 1968), p.1.
12. Rockefeller Archives, III 2K Box 1 Office of the Messrs. Rockefeller, Medical Interests Birth Control Organizations – General 1930–39, JDR III to Jr. 3/17/34.
13. Rockefeller Archives, Office of the Messrs. Rockefeller, Medical Interests Birth Control Organizations – General 1930–39, Packard to JDR III 6/9/37III 2K Box 1.
14. Ibid.
15. Rockefeller Archives, Office of the Messrs. Rockefeller, Medical Interests Birth Control Organizations –General 1930–39, Mrs. Richmond Page to A. W. Packard 9/21/37, III 2K Box 1.
16. Ibid.
17. Ibid.
18. Rockefeller Archives, III 2K Medical Interests, Planned Parenthood Box 4 139.22.
19. Ibid.

20. Rockefeller Archives, III 2K Medical Interests, Planned Parenthood Box 4 139.22, memo from Arthur W. Packard 6/29/43.
21. Rockefeller Archives, Medical Interests Folder, Planned Parenthood Federation of America 1947–49 folder 139.22, memo to JDR Jr. from Arthur W. Packard in re: Planned Parenthood, 3/13/47.

Part II, Chapter 24: New York, 1934
1. Cooper, p. 291.
2. McKay, *Banjo*, p. 250.
3. Claude McKay, "Right Turn to Catholicism," unpublished ms., McKay mss, Lily Library, Indiana University , Bloomington, Indiana.
4. Ibid., pp. 19–20.
5. Ibid., p. 18.
6. McKay, correspondence, the James Weldon Johnson collection at the Beineke Library at Yale University, letter June 7, 1944 Max Eastman. to Claude McKay.
7. McKay, *A Long Way from Home* (New York: Arno Press and The New York Times, 1969), p. 224.
8. Arnold Rampersad, *The Life of Langston Hughes* (New York: Oxford University Press, 1986).
9. McKay, "Right Turn to Catholicism."
10. McKay, correspondence, the James Weldon Johnson collection at the Beineke Library at Yale University, letter October 16, 1944 Claude McKay to Max Eastman.
11. Ibid.
12. McKay, "Right Turn to Catholicism."
13. McKay, *Home to Harlem* (Boston: Northeastern University Press, 1987), p. 99.
14. Rockefeller Archives, III 2K Medical Interests Planned Parenthood Box 4 139.22, Memo December 26, 1944 from Arthur W. Packard.
15. Ibid.
16. Ibid.
17. Rockefeller Archives, Medical Interests Folder, Planned Parenthood Federation of America 1947–49 folder 139.22, memo to JDR Jr. from Arthur W. Packard in re: Planned Parenthood, 3/13/47.

Part II, Chapter 25: New York, 1932
1. Buckley, p. 153.
2. Ibid.
3. John B. Watson, *Psychological Care of Infant and Child* (New York W.W. Norton & Company, Inc.: 1928), p. 4.
4. Ibid., p. 12.
5. Ibid., pp. 12–13.
6. Ibid., pp. 81–82.
7. Ibid., p. 85.
8. Ibid.
9. Buckley, p. 143.
10. Watson, *Care*, pp. 41–42.
11. David Cohen, *J. B. Watson: The Founder of Behaviourism* (Boston and London: Routledge & Kegan Paul, 1979), p. 260.
12. Ibid., p. 265.
13. Ibid.
14. Aldous Huxley, *Brave New World* (New York: Modern Library, 1946), p. x.
15. James H. Jones, *Alfred Kinsey: A Public/Private Life* (New York: Norton, 1997), p. 422.
16. Tye, p. 111.

17. Christopher Simpson, *Science of Coercion: Communication Research and Psychological Warfare, 1945–1960* (New York: Oxford University Press, 1994), p. 23.
18. Ibid.
19. Ibid.
20. Jones, p. 423.
21. Ibid.
22. Ibid.
23. Ibid., p. 424.

Part III, Chapter 1: New York, 1940

1. Thomas E. Mahl, *Desperate Deception* (Washington: Brassey's, 1998), p. 6.
2. Michael Hunt, *Ideology and Foreign Policy* (New Haven and London: Yale University Press, 1987)
3. Ibid., p. 137.
4. Ibid., p. 134.
5. Mahl, p. 16.
6. Carroll Quigley, *Tragedy and Hope: A History of the World in Our Time* (New York: Macmillan, 1966)
7. Mahl, p. 37.
8. Jones, p. 472.
9. Ibid., p. 525.
10. Ibid., p. 532.
11. Ibid., p. 531.
12. E. M. Jones, *Degenerate Moderns*, p. 92.

Part III, Chapter 2: New York, 1941

1. Thomas Merton, *The Seven Storey Mountain* (New York: Harcourt, Brace, and Company, 1948), p. 146.
2. Ibid., p. 147.
3. Richard Crossman, ed., *The God that Failed* (Salem, N.H.: Ayer Company, 1949), p. 241.
4. Ibid.
5. Crossman, p. 238.
6. Merton, *Seven Storey Mountain*, p. 161.
7. Ibid., p. 163.
8. Ibid., p. 345.
9. Ibid.
10. Ibid., p. 346.
11. Ibid., p. 348.
12. Ibid., p. 157.
13. Dennis McNally, *Desolate Angel* (New York: Random House, 1979).
14. Thomas Merton, *Conjectures of a Guilty Bystander* (Garden City, N.Y.: Image Doubleday, 1968).
15. McKay, *Banjo*, p. 14.
16. Wardell Pomeroy, *Dr. Kinsey and the Institute for Sex Research* (New York: Harper and Row, 1972).
17. Jack Kerouac, *On the Road* (New York: Viking, 1957), p. 131.
18. McNally, p. 233.
19. Ted Morgan, *Literary Outlaw: The Life and Times of William S. Burroughs* (New York: Henry Holt and Co., 1988).
20. Abraham Maslow and James M. Sakoda, "Volunteer Error in the Kinsey Study," *The Journal of Abnormal and Social Psychology* 47, no. 2 (April 1952), p. 26.

21. Judith A. Reisman and Edward W. Eichel, Kinsey, *Sex and Fraud: The Indoctrination of a People* (Lafayette, La.: Huntington House, 1990), p. 221.
22. Ibid.
23. Pomeroy,
24. Ibid., p. 222.
25. Ibid.
26. Max Eastman, *Love and Revolution*, p. 100.
27. Norman Mailer, *Advertisements for Myself* (New York: G. P. Putnam's Sons, 1959).
28. Mailer, p. 363.

Part III, Chapter 3: Bloomington, Indiana, 1942

 1. Jones, p. 433.
 2. Ibid., p. 440.
 3. Ibid., p. 433.
 4. Ibid., p. 437.
 5. Ibid., p. 422.
 6. Ibid., p. 463.
 7. Ibid., p. 479.
 8. Ibid., p. 457.
 9. Ibid., p. 458.
10. Ibid., p. 643.
11. Ibid., p. 515.
12. cf. Esther Dyson, "The net is a great medium for conspiracy, while television is best for propaganda," *Release* 2.0, p. 49.
13. Jones, p. 438.
14. Ibid., p. 440.
15. Rockefeller Archives, RG.1.1 Series 200 Box 40, Folder 457.
16. Ibid.
17. Tim Tate, *Secret History: Kinsey's Pedophiles* (Yorkshire TV: Channel 4, 10/8/98).
18. Jones p. 508.
19. Ibid., p. 512.
20. Ibid. p. 513.
21. Ibid., p. 490.
22. Ibid., p. 491.
23. Ibid., p. 510.
24. Ibid.
25. Ibid.
26. Ibid., p. 518.
27. Judith Reisman, *Kinsey: Crimes and Consequences* (Arlington, Va.: Institute for Media Education, 1998), p. 84.
28. Ibid.
29. Samuel Steward, "Remembering Dr. Kinsey: Sexual Scientist and Investigator," *The Advocate* (November 13, 1980), p. 21.
30. Tate.

Part III, Chapter 4: New York, 1947

 1. Jones, p. 463.
 2. Ibid., p. 547.
 3. Ibid., p. 566.
 4. Reisman, p. 191.
 5. Ibid., p. 91.

Part III, Chapter 5: New York, 1947

1. Rockefeller Archives, III 2K Medical Interests Planned Parenthood Box 4 139.22.
2. Ibid.
3. Nancy Cunard, ed., *Negro: an Anthology*, edited and abridged (New York: Frederick Ungar Co., 1970), p. xxxi.
4. Harold Cruse, *The Crisis of the Negro Intellectual* (New York: William Morrow & Co., 1967), p. 15.
5. Michael Harrington, *The Long Distance Runner: An Autobiography* (New York: Henry Holt and Co., 1988),
6. Norman Mailer, *Advertisements for Myself* (New York: G.P. Putnam's Sons, 1959), p. 325.
7. Ibid., p. 340.
8. Ibid.
9. Kerouac, *On the Road*, p. 180.
10. Ibid.
11. Ibid.
12. Norman Podhoretz, "The Know-Nothing Bohemians," *Partisan Review* (Spring, 1958), cited in McNally, p. 350.
13. Cyprian Davis, *The History of Black Catholics in the United States* (New York: Crossroad, 1990), p. 259.
14. Max Eastman, *The Enjoyment of Living*, p. 476.

Part III, Chapter 6: Dartmouth, 1947

1. Paul Blanshard, *Personal and Controversial: An Autobiography* (Boston: Beacon Press, 1973) published under the auspices of the Unitarian Universalist Association, p. 189.
2. Ibid.
3. Ibid., p. 191.
4. Ibid., p. 209.
5. Ibid.
6. John McGreevy, "Thinking on One's Own: Catholicism in the American Intellectual Imagination 1928–1960," *The Journal of American History* (June 1997), p. 121.
7. Blanshard, *Personal*, p. 250.
8. Ibid., p. 6.
9. Ibid., p. 24.
10. Ibid., p. 115.
11. Ibid., p. 32.
12. Ibid., p. 113.
13. Ibid.
14. Ibid., p. 114.
15. Ibid.
16. Ibid., p. 282.
17. Ibid., p. 223.
18. Ibid.
19. Ibid.
20. Ibid., p. 224.
21. Ibid.
22. Ibid., p. 226.
23. Ibid., p. 51.
24. Ibid., p. 95.
25. Ibid., p. 99.
26. Ibid.

27. Ibid., p. 100.
28. Ibid., p. 208.
29. Ibid., p. 135.
30. Simpson, pp. 28–29.
31. Ibid., p. 22.
32. McGreevy, p. 113.
33. Paul Blanshard, *American Freedom and Catholic Power*, p. 6.
34. Ibid., p. 284.
35. Ibid., p. 284, p. 286.
36. McGreevy, p. 97.
37. Blanshard, *Personal*, p. 222.
38. McGreevy, p. 126.

Part III, Chapter 7: Bloomington, Indiana, 1950
1. Jones, p. 632.
2. Ibid., p. 633.
3. Ibid.
4. Reisman, p. 84.
5. Richard Weaver, *Ideas Have Consequences* (Chicago: The University of Chicago Press, 1948), p. 10.
6. Richard Foster, *The Real Bettie Page: The Truth about the Queen of the Pinups* (Secaucus, N.J.: Birch Lane Press, 1997), p. 164.
7. Rockefeller Archives, R.G 3.2 Series 900, box 14 Folder 85.
8. Ibid.
9. René A. Wormser, *Foundations: Their Power and Influence* (New York: The Devin-Adair Company, 1958), p. 174.
10. Wormser, p. 47.
11. Ibid.
12. Rockefeller Archives, Ibid.
13. Ibid., Ibid.
14. Riesman, p. 190.
15. Ibid.
16. Ibid., p. 192.
17. Ibid. p. 193.
18. Rockefeller Archives, Ibid.
19. Jones, p. 722.
20. Rockefeller Archives, Ibid.
21. Rockefeller Archives, Ibid., ("Investigating the Foundations," *The Reporter*, [November 24, 1953]),
22. Jones, p. 723.
23. Ibid., p. 677.
24. Ibid., p. 678.
25. Ibid., p. 689.
26. Ibid., p. 693.
27. Wormser, p. 184, p. 186.
28. Ibid., p. 32.
29. Ibid., pp. 94–95.
30. Ibid., p. 100n.
31. Jones, p. 734.
32. Wormser, p. 101.
33. Ibid.
34. Ibid., p. 351.

35. Ibid.
36. Ibid., p. 355.
37. Riesman, pp. 264–65.
38. Ibid., p. 260.
39. Jones, p. 738.
40. Ibid., p. 753.

Part III, Chapter 8: Washington, D.C., 1957
1. William W. Van Alstyne, *First Amendment: Cases and Materials* (Westbury, N.Y.: The Foundation Press, 1991), p. 679.
2. Ibid.
3. Ibid. p. 681.
4. Ibid.
5. Ibid.
6. Leo Pfeffer, *God, Caesar, and the Constitution* (Boston: Beacon Press, 1975), p. 311.
7. Van Alstyne, p. 691.
8. Ibid., p. 692.
9. Reisman, p. 241.
10. Paul Spike, *Photographs of My Father* (New York: Alfred A. Knopf, 1973), p. 63.
11. Ibid.
12. Ibid., p. 10.
13. Ibid.
14. Ibid., p. 32.
15. Ibid., p. 25.
16. Ibid., p. 27.
17. McNally, *Desolate Angel*, p. 307.
18. McNally, p.308.
19. Michael Mott, *The Seven Mountains of Thomas Merton* (Boston: Houghton Mifflin, 1984), p. 461.
20. Jack Kerouac, *On the Road* (New York: Viking, 1957), p. 113.
21. Ibid., p. 203.
22. Ibid.
23. Ibid., p. 203.
24. Jack Kerouac, *The Subterraneans* (New York: Grove Press, 1958), p. 17.
25. Ibid., p. 39.
26. Ibid., p. 94.
27. Ibid., p. 105.
28. McNally, p. 135.
29. Ibid.
30. Ibid., p. 330.
31. Kerouac, *On the Road*, p. 252.
32. Ibid., p. 253.
33. Jack Kerouac, *Lonesome Traveler* (New York: McGraw-Hill, 1960), p. 22.
34. Jack Kerouac, *On the Road*, p. 280.
35. Ibid.
36. Ibid., p. 288.
37. Ibid., p. 287.
38. Ibid., p. 291.
39. Ibid., p. 302.
40. McNally, p. 241.
41. Mailer, *Advertisements for Myself*, p. 340.
42. Ibid.

43. Ibid.
44. Ibid., p. 348.
45. Ibid.
46. Ibid., p. 341.
47. Eldridge Cleaver, *Soul on Ice* (New York: Ramparts Books, 1968), p. 14.
48. Ibid., p. xv.
49. Ibid., p. 16.
50. Ibid., p. 75.
51. Eldridge Cleaver, *Soul on Fire* (Waco: Word Books, 1976), p. 90.
52. Cleaver, *Soul on Fire*, p. 111.
53. Cleaver, *Soul on Ice*, p. 159.
54. Ibid., p. 161.
55. Cleaver, *Soul on Fire*, p. 135.
56. Ibid.,. 97.
57. Ibid., p. 208.
58. Ibid., p. 196.
59. Ibid., p. 210.
60. Morgan, p. 557.
61. Cleaver, *Soul on Ice*, p. 33.
62. Thomas Merton, *Conjectures of a Guilty Bystander* (Garden City, N.Y.: Doubleday Image, 1968), p. 74.
63. Ibid., p. 112.
64. Ibid.
65. McNally, p. 246.
66. James Terence Fisher, *Catholic Counter Culture in America 1933–62* (Chapel Hill: University of North Carolina Press, 1989), p. 229.
67. Morgan, p. 487.
68. Fisher, pp. 205 ff.
69. *America* (April 8, 1965), p. 660.
70. Ibid.

Part III, Chapter 9: South Bend, Indiana, 1962

1. *Public Opinion and Communication,* ed. by Bernard Berelson and Morris Janowitz (Glencoe, Ill.: The Free Press, 1950), p. 403.
2. *Preparatory Reports Second Vatican Council*, trans. by Aram Berard, S.J. (Philadelphia, The Westminster Press, 1965), p. 51.
3. Ibid.
4. Ibid.
5. Simpson, *Coercion*, pp. 3–4.
6. *Preparatory Reports*, p. 51.
7. Wormser, p. 235.
8. Theodore Hesburgh folder in the Population Council Files at the Rockefeller Archives, POP Council files, Box 49, Folder 73.
9. Ibid.
10. Ibid.
11. Ibid.
12. Ibid.
13. Ibid.
14. Ibid.
15. Ibid.
16. Ibid.
17. Ibid.

18. Ibid.
19. Ibid.
20. Ibid.
21. E. Michael Jones, "Requiem for a Liturgist," *Fidelity* (January 1988).
22. Simpson, *Coercion*, p. 102.
23. Berleson, p. ix.
24. Ibid.
25. Simpson, *Coercion*, p. 89.
26. Berleson, p. 457.
27. Robert McClory, *Turning Point: The Inside Story of the Papal Birth Control Commission, and How Humanae Vitae Changed the Life of Patty Crowley and the Future of the Church* (New York: Crossroad, 1995), p. 162.

Part III, Chapter 10: Washington, D.C., 1964
1. Lee Rainwater and William L. Yancey, *The Moynihan Report and the Politics of Controversy* (Cambridge, Mass.: The MIT Press, 1967), p. 12.
2. Ibid., p. 25.
3. Daniel Patrick Moynihan, "The Moynihan Report," *Commentary*, (February 1967), p. 31.
4. Ibid.
5. Ibid.
6. David J. Garrow, *Bearing the Cross: Martin Luther King, Jr. and the Southern Christian Leadership Conference* (New York: William Morrow & Co., 1986), p. 375.
7. E. Franklin Frazier, *The Negro Family in the United States* (Chicago and London: The University of Chicago Press, 1939, 1966), p. 19.
8. Ibid., p. 78.
9. Ibid., p. 130.
10. Ibid., p. 249.
11. Ibid, p. 100.
12. Rainwater and Yancey, p. 20.
13. *Rerum Novarum*, #20.
14. *Rerum Novarum*, #53
15. *Rerum Novarum*, #82
16. *Rerum Novarum*, #97.
17. Rainwater and Yancey, p. 162.
18. Ibid.
19. Ibid.
20. Christopher Jencks, *New York Review of Books* (October 14, 1965), in Rainwater and Yancey, p. 444.
21. Ibid.
22. Hannah Tillich, *From Time to Time* (New York: Stein and Day, 1973), pp. 176-7.
23. Rollo May, Paulus: *Reminiscences of a Friendship* (New York: Harper and Row, 1973), p. 88–89.
24. Ibid.
25. Ibid., p. 98.
26. Ibid., p. 99.

Part III, Chapter 11: Washington, D.C.; Rome, 1965
1. Pfeffer, *God, Caesar*, p. 96.
2. Harr and Johnson, *Rockefeller Century*, p. 169.
3. Rockefeller Archive Center, Special Collections RAC Population Council Register, Index RM. JDR III to Henry Cabot Lodge Jr. 8/13/70.

4. Rockefeller Archives, JDR III to Pope Paul VI 7/16/65
5. Ibid.
6. Ibid.
7. Ibid.
8. Ibid.
9. Hansjakob Stehle, *Die Ostpolitk des Vatikans* (Munich: Piper, 1975), p. 359.
10. JDR III to Pope Paul VI, 7/16/65.
11. The following material was taken from the Krol Papers at the archives of the Archdiocese of Philadelphia, Box 21, birth control folders, William Bentley Ball letter to Krol, 6/30/66.
12. Ibid.
13. Rt. Rev. George W. Casey, "Birth Control Is Waiting in the Wings," *The Boston Pilot* (October 9, 1965).
14. Ibid.
15. William B. Ball , "Population control: Civil and constitutional Concerns," *Journal of Religion and Public Affairs* (1967), p. 13.
16. Ibid.
17. Ibid., p. 14.
18. Krol Archives, birth control folders, Ball to Krol and Wright August 16, 1965.
19. Ibid.
20. Krol Archives, Box 29, folder 2, Ball to Krol, August, 1965.
21. Ibid. Vagnozzi to Krol, 8/26/65.
22. Krol Archives, birth control folders, statement by Rev. Dexter L. Hanley, S.J. before Gruening committee, Tuesday, August 24, 1965.
23. Krol Archives, birth control folders, statement of William B. Ball, August 24, 1965.
24. Krol Archives, Box 29, Folder 2, statement of William B. Ball before Gruening committee, August 24, 1965.
25. John Cogley, "Bishops' Unanimity on Birth control Bill in doubt," *New York Times* (August 30, 1965).
26. Ibid.
27. Ibid.
28. Krol Archive, birth control folders, "Birth control and Public Policy," sermon by Most Rev. Patrick A. O'Boyle, St. Matthew's Cathedral, Sunday, August 29, 1965.
29. Ibid.
30. Ibid.
31. Ibid.
32. Ibid.
33. Ibid.
34. Krol Archives, Box 29, folder 2, Krol to Ball 11/2/65.

Part III, Chapter 12: Washington, D.C., November 1965
1. Paul Blanshard, *Personal and Controversial: An Autobiography* (Boston: Beacon Press, 1973), p. 261.
2. Rainwater and Yancey, p. 200.
3. Ibid.
4. Moynihan, *Commentary*, (February, 1967), p. 31.
5. Ibid.
6. Robert W. Spike, *The Freedom Revolution and the Churches* (New York: Association Press, 1965).
7. Ibid.
8. Robert W. Spike, "Fissures in the Civil Rights Movement," *Christianity and Crisis* (February 21, 1966), pp. 18–21.

9. Ibid.
10. Paul Spike, *Photographs of my Father* (New York: Alfred A Knopf, 1973), p. 62.
11. Ibid., p. 63.
12. Ibid., p. 83.
13. Ibid.
14. Shelby Steele, *The Content of our Character* (New York: St. Martin's Press, 1990), p. 78.
15. Garrow, pp. 598–99.
16. Ibid., p. 375.
17. Ibid., p. 376.
18. Ibid., p. 587.
19. Ibid., pp. 638–39, n. 39.
20. Ibid., p. 617.
21. Ibid., p. 375.
22. Ibid., p. 586.
23. Sara Evans, *Personal Politics* (New York: Alfred A. Knopf, 1979), p. 60.
24. Ibid., p. 78.
25. Ibid., p. 79.
26. Ibid.
27. Ibid., p. 82.
28. Mary King, *Freedom Song: A Personal Story of the 1960s Civil Rights Movement* (New York: William Morrow and Co., 1987), p. 452.
29. Evans, p. 88.
30. Ibid.
31. Mary King, pp. 464–65.
32. Ibid., p. 465.

Part III, Chapter 13: Los Angeles, 1966

1. Michael W. Higgins, *Heretic Blood: The Spiritual Geography of Thomas Merton* (Toronto: Stoddart Publishing Company, 1998), p. 209.
2. Ibid., p. 218.
3. Ibid., p. 221.
4. Conversation with W.R. Coulson, 6/99.
5. Msgr. Francis J. Weber, *His Eminence of Los Angeles: James Francis Cardinal McIntyre* (Vol. II) (Mission Hills, Calif.: Saint Francis Historical Society, 1997), p. 419.
6. Ibid.
7. Rosemary Curb and Nancy Manahan, eds. *Lesbian Nuns: Breaking Silence* (Tallahassee, Fla.: Naiad Press, 1985), p. 3.
8. Ibid., p. 11.
9. Ibid.
10. Ibid., p. 13.
11. Ibid., p. 14.
12. Ibid., p. 183.
13. Ibid., p. 187.
14. Ibid.
15. Ibid., p. 188.
16. Ibid., p. 233.
17. Abraham Maslow, *Journals*, p. 157.
18. Ibid., pp. 166–68, my emphasis.
19. Carl Rogers, *Carl Rogers on Encounter Groups* (New York: Harper & Row, 1970), p. 75.

20. Maslow, *Journals*, p. 951.
21. Ibid., p. 1089.
22. Ibid, May 17, 1969.
23. Elwood Kieser, *Hollywood Priest: A Spiritual Struggle* (New York: Doubleday 1991), p. 158.
24. James F. T. Bugental, *Intimate Journeys: Stories from Life-Changing Therapy* (San Francisco: Jossey-Bass Publishers, 1990).
25. Kieser, p. 160.
26. Ibid., p. 169.
27. Ibid., p. 160.
28. Ibid., p. 170.
29. Ibid., p. 161.
30. Ibid.
31. Ibid., p. 162.
32. Ibid., p. 169.
33. W. R. Coulson, "Good-bye, Mary Edith," unpublished ms of talk presented to the 27th Mile HI Congress, Catholic Archdiocese of Denver, Denver, Colorado, 2/16/96.
34. W. R. Coulson, "The Role of Psychology in Current Educational Reform," unpublished ms. of talk given to Empire State Taskforce for Excellence in Educational Methods, New Paltz, New York, 12/13/97.
35. Carl Rogers, *Carl Rogers on Encounter Groups*, p. 4.
36. W. R. Coulson, "Rejoinder," *Measure*, p. 8.
37. Rogers, *Carl Rogers on Encounter Groups*, p. 8
38. Ibid., p. 12.
39. Ibid., p. 11.
40. Ibid., pp. 159–60.
41. Ibid., p. 12.
42. Ibid., p. 10.
43. Art Kleiner, *The Age of Heretics: Heroes, Outlaws and the Forerunners of Corporate Change* (New York: Currency Doubleday, 1996), p. 31.
44. Ibid.
45. Ibid.
46. Ibid.
47. Ibid., p. 33.
48. Michael Weber, *Psychotechniken – die neuen Verfuehrer: Gruppendynamki – die programmierte Zerstoerung von Kirch und Kultur* (Stein am Rhein/Schweiz: Christiana, 1997), p. 36, my translation.
49. Ibid., p. 135.
50. Kleiner, pp. 48–49.
51. Ibid., p. 53.
52. Kevin Dowlings and Philip Knightley, "The Spy Who Came Back from the Grave," *Night and Day: The Mail on Sunday Review*, August 23, 1998, p. 11.
53. Ibid., p. 13.
54. Simpson, *Coercion*, pp. 53 ff.
55. John T. McGreevy, "Thinking on One's Own: Catholicism in the American Intellectual Imagination, 1928–1960," *Journal of American History* (June 1997), p. 97.
56. Ibid.
57. Simpson, *Coercion*, p. 61.
58. Ibid.
59. Thomas Mahl, *Desperate Deception* (Washington, D.C.: Brassey's, 1998), p. 5.
60. Ibid., p. 6.
61. Blanshard, *American Freedom*, p. 287.

62. Ibid.
63. Ibid.
64. Francis J. Weber, p. 422.
65. Ibid.
66. Ibid.
67. Ibid., p. 432.
68. Ibid.
69. Ibid., p. 425.
70. Ibid., p. 423.
71. Ibid.
72. Ibid.
73. Ibid., p. 424.
74. Ibid.
75. Ibid.
76. Ibid., p. 425.
77. Kieser, . p. 177.
78. Ibid., p. 183.
79. Francis J. Weber, p. 427.
80. Ibid., p. 434.
81. Ibid.
82. Natalie Rogers, *Emerging Woman: A Decade of Midlife Transitions (*Point Reyes, Calif.: Personal Press, 1980), p. 21.
83. W. R. Coulson, "The Role of Psychology in Current Educational Reform," Paper delivered to the Empire State Taskforce for Excellence in Educational Methods, New Paltz, New York, December 13, 1997.
84. *Washington Post* (November 15, 1981), p. 1
85. Michael Weber, p. 88.
86. Ibid.
87. W. R. Coulson, "Rejoinder," *Measure* (August/September 1995), p. 9.
88. Rogers, *Carl Rogers on Encounter Groups*, p. 158.
89. Ibid., p. 17.
90. Green, pp. 211–12.
91. Carl Rogers, *Client Centered Therapy* (Boston: Houghton Mifflin, 1951), p. 49.
92. Rogers, *Carl Rogers on Encounter Groups*, p. 91.
93. Ibid.
94. Ibid., p. 99.
95. Ibid., p. 101.
96. Ibid., p. 103.
97. Kurt W. Back, *Beyond Words: The Story of Sensitivity Training and the Encounter Movement* (New York: The Russell Sage Foundation, 1972), p. 33.
98. Back p. 35.
99. Rogers, *Carl Rogers on Encounter Groups,* p. 113.
100. Ibid., pp. 72–73.
101. Rogers, "Reaction to Gunnison's Article on the Similarities Between Erikson and Rogers," *Journal of Counseling and Development* (May 1985).
102. Michael Weber, pp. 54–55, my translation.
103. Agethen, pp. 204–6.
104. Morton A. Kaplan, "Letters," *Measure* (August/September 1995), p. 3.
105. Kleiner, pp. 47–48.
106. Natalie Rogers, p. 148.
107. Ibid., p. 103.
108. Ibid., p. 171.

109. Ibid., p. 177.
110. Rogers, *Carl Rogers on Encounter Groups*, p. 66.
111. W. R. Coulson, "Rejoinder," *Measure*, August/September 1995, p. 12.
112. Ibid.
113. Natalie Rogers, p. 199.
114. Rogers, *Carl Rogers on Encounter Groups*, pp. 76–77.
115. Michael Weber, p. 123.
116. Higgins, p. 227.
117. Curb and Manahan, p. 188.
118. Ibid., p. 247.
119. Ibid., p. 246.
120. Ibid., p. 248.
121. Kieser, p. 187.
122. Ibid., p. 189.
123. W. R. Coulson, "Rejoinder," *Measure*, August/September 1995, p. 5.

Part III, Chapter 14: New York, 1969
1. "Fight Power with Spontaneity and Humor: An interview with Dusan Makavejev," *Film Quarterly* (Winter 1971), p. 3.
2. Reich, *The Sexual Revolution*, p. 109.
3. Dusan Makavejev, *WR: Mysteries of the Organism: A Cinematic Testament to the Life and Teachings of Wilhelm Reich* (New York: Avon Books, 1972), p. 57.
4. Ibid., p. 70.
5. David Elkind, "Wilhelm Reich: The Psychiatrist as Revolutionary," *New York Times Magazine* (April 18, 1971), p. 25.
6. Makavejev, p. 31.
7. Elizabeth Wurtzel, *Bitch: In Praise of Difficult Women* (New York: Doubleday, 1998), p. 48.
8. Ibid., pp. 46–47.
9. Ibid., p. 48.
10. Ibid., p. 89.
11. Ibid., pp. 89–90.
12. Katie Roiphe, *Last Night in Paradise: Sex and Morals at the World's End* (New York: Random House, 1998), p. 11.
13. Ibid., p. 127
14. Eric Voegelin, *Order and History, Volume Three: Plato and Aristotle* (Baton Rouge: Louisiana State University Press, 1957), p. 126.
15. Ibid., p. 127.
16. Reich, *Sexual Revolution*, p. 278.

Part III, Chapter 15: Notre Dame, Indiana, 1970
1. HR 2525, A Bill creating a Commission to be known as the Commission on Obscenity and Pornography. Hearings held in Washington, DC, April 20–24, 1967, Rep. Dominick V. Daniels, chairman.
2. HR 2525, p. 3.
3. Ibid.
4. HR 2525, p. 23.
5. The Report of the Commission on Obscenity and Pornography, Special Introduction by Clive Barnes (New York: Random House, 1970), p.22.
6. Ibid., p. 32.
7. Ibid., p.3.

8. Ibid., p. 446.
9. Ibid., p. 457.
10. Ibid., p. 458.
11. Ibid., p. 637.
12. Ibid., p. 465.
13. Report, pp. 466–67.
14. Ibid., p. 469.
15. Ibid., p. 469.
16. Ibid., p. 618.
17. "Effects of Massive Exposure to Pornography," by Dolf Zillman and Jennings Bryant in *Pornography and Sexual Aggression*, ed. Neil Malamuth, Edward Donnerstein (Orlando, FL: Academic Press, 1984), p. 134.

Part III, Chapter 16: Hialeah, Florida, 1972
1. Foster p. 118.
2. Bruce Thornton, *Eros: The Myth of Ancient Greek Sexuality* (Boulder, Colo.: Westview Press, 1997), p. 17.
3. Foster, p. 119.
4. Linda Lovelace, *Ordeal* (New York: Berkley Books, 1981), p. 50.
5. Ibid.
6. Ibid., p. 113.
7. Ralph Blumenthal, *NYT Magazine* (January 21, 1973), pp. 28 ff.
8. Ibid.
9. Ibid.
10. William Pechter, "Deep Tango," *Commentary* 56 (1973), pp. 64–66.

Part III, Chapter 17: Washington, D.C., 1974
1. Robert S. McNamara, *The McNamara Years at the World Bank: Major Policy Addressed of Robert S. McNamara 1968–1981* (Baltimore, Md.: Johns Hopkins University Press, 1981), p. 47.
2. Julian Simon, *The Ultimate Resource* (Princeton, N.J.: Princeton University Press, 1981), p. 64.
3. Ibid.
4. Ibid., p. 47.
5. *Excessive Force: Power, Politics and Population Control* (Washington, D.C.: Information Project for Africa, 1995), p. 187.
6. NSSM 200, p. 117. This document is available on the World Wide Web at http://www.africa2000.com
7. Ibid., p. 15.
8. Ibid., pp. 127–28.
9. Ibid., p. 121.
10. Ibid., p. 106.
11. Ibid., p. 114.
12. Peter J. Donaldson, *Nature Against Us: The United States and the World Population Crisis 1965–1980* (Chapel Hill: University of North Carolina Press, 1990), p. 85.
13. Ibid., pp. 85–86.
14. Ibid., p. 17.
15. Conversation with Elizabeth Liagin Sobo.
16. Donald Warwick, *Bitter Pills: Population Policies and their Implementation in Eight Developing Countries* (Cambridge: Cambridge University Press, 1982), p. 13.
17. *Population and National Security: A Review of U.S. National Security Policy 1970–1988* (Washington, D.C..: Information Project For Africa, 1991).

18. Ibid.
19. Ibid.
20. Ibid.
21. Ibid.
22. Ibid.
23. cf. http://www.africa2000.com, specifically the National Security Council Under Secretaries Committee Population Task Force First Progress Report, 1976.
24. Ibid.
25. *Population and National Security: A Review of U.S. National Security Policy 1970–1988* (Washington, D.C..: Information Project For Africa, 1991).
26. Julian Simon, *The Ultimate Resource* (Princeton, NJ: Princeton University Press, 1981), p. 69.
27. Ibid., p. 71.
28. Royal Commission on Population Report Presented to Parliament by Command of his Majesty, June 1949. London: His Majesty's Stationery Office, Cmd. 7695, pp. 43–44.
29. Ibid., p. 134.
30. Ibid., p. 136.
31. Ibid., p. 219.
32. Ibid.
33. Ibid., p. 227.
34. Katherine Ellison, *Imelda: Steel Butterfly of the Philippines* (New York, McGraw-Hill, 1988), p. 138.
35. Ibid.
36. *Excessive Force*, p. 207.

Part III, Chapter 18: Philadelphia, 1976

1. Leo Pfeffer, "The 'Catholic' Catholic Problem," *Commonweal* (August 1975), pp. 302–5.
2. Ibid., p. 304.
3. Ibid., p. 303.
4. Ibid., p. 304.
5. Ibid., p. 303.
6. James Hitchcock, *Years of Crisis* (San Francisco: Ignatius, 1985), p. 197.
7. Pfeffer, *Commonweal*, p. 304.
8. Ibid., p. 303.
9. Leo Pfeffer. *God, Caesar, and the Constitution* (Boston: Beacon Press, 1975), p. 97.
10. Ibid., p. 20.
11. Ibid., pp. 20–21.
12. Leo Pfeffer, "Issues that Divide: The Triumph of Secular Humanism," *Journal of Church and State* 19 (Spring 1977), p. 211.
13. Ibid.
14. E. Michael Jones, *John Cardinal Krol and the Cultural Revolution* (South Bend, Ind.: Fidelity Press, 1995), chapter 6.
15. Michel Schooyans, *Power over Life Leads to Domination of Mankind*, translated by Rev. John H. Miller, CSC, STD (St. Louis, Mo.: Central Bureau, Catholic Central Verein of America, 1996), p. 36.
16. Ibid., pp. 55–56.
17. Ibid., p. 56.
18. Ibid., p. 59.
19. Mark Winiarski, "Detroit: 1,300 vote hopes raise fears," *National Catholic Reporter* 13, no. 3, p. 1.
20. Ibid.

21. Ibid.
22. Thomas Stahel, "More Action than they Called for," *America* (November 6, 1976), pp. 292–96.
23. Winiarski, *NCR*, p. 1.
24. "Bishops across the Nation Give Wide Response to 'Call to Action' Assembly," an OSV roundup, *Our Sunday Visitor* (November 14, 1976).
25. Thomas C. Fox, "Made in Detroit," *Commonweal* (November 19, 1976), p. 747.
26. Winiarski, *NCR*, p. 1.
27. Heinrich Denifle, *Luther and Lutherdom* (Somerset, Oh.: Torch Press, 1917), p. 3.
28. Rockefeller Archives, Population Council, Box 49, Oscar Harkavy, Director of Ford Foundation to Dudley Kirk, Demographic director, The Population Council (December 18, 1964).
29. Charles E. Rice, *Observer* (April 20, 1977).
30. Ibid.
32. Ibid.
32. James McShane, Memo (April 11, 1996).

Part III, Chapter 19: Evansville, Indiana, 1981

1. Record of the Proceedings in the Supreme Court of Indiana, Thomas N. Schiro vs. State of Indiana, Testimony of Mary T. Lee, 1457.
2. Ibid., 563.
3. Report on the Commission on Obscenity and Pornography, p. 31.
4. Ibid.
5. Ibid.
6. Record, 1457.
7. Ibid.
8. Ibid., 1429.
9. Interview with Frank Osanka, August 1985.
10. Ibid.
11. Ibid.
12. Ibid.
13. Ibid.
14. Record, 1576.
15. Ibid.
16. Report of the Commission on Obscenity and Pornography, p. 3.
17. Nora Ephron, *Crazy Salad* (New York: Borzoi, 1975), p. 66.
18. *off our backs* (May 1985), p. 27.
19. Ibid.
20. Ibid.
21. Ibid.
22. Schiro, autobiography.
23. Susan Brownmiller, *Against Our Will: Men, Women, and Rape* (New York: Simon and Schuster, 1975), her emphasis.
24. Schiro, autobiography.
25. Osanka, interview.
26. Schiro, autobiography.
27. Ibid..

Part III, Chapter 20: Washington, D.C., 1983

1. Reisman, *Kinsey: Crimes and Consequences*, p. xx.
2. Ibid., p. xxi.
3. *Time*, "High priced ogling" (May 13, 1985).

4. *Reisman v. Thornburgh*, 175.
5. *The Meese Commission Exposed: Proceedings of a National Coalition Against Censorship* by Arlene F. Carmen , Colleen Dewhurst, Lisa Duggan, Betty Friedan, Richard Green , Leanne Katz, Max Lillienstein, Barry Lynn, Ann Welbourne-Moglia, Donal Mosher, Eve Paul, Harriet Pilpel, Anthony Schulte, Kurt Vonnegut, Public Information Briefing on the Attorney General's Commission on Pornography (January 16, 1986), p. 42.
6. Ibid.
7. *Attorney General's Commission on Pornography: Final Report* (Washington, D.C.: U.S. Department of Justice, July 1986), p. 810.
8. Susan Trento, *The Powerhouse: Robert Keith Gray and the Selling of Access and Influence in Washington* (New York: St. Martin's, 1994), p. 198.
9. Ibid.
10. The Reisman report is currently cited on the Department of Justice Webpage: http://www.ncjrs.og/database.htm.
11. David Lowenthal, *No Liberty for License: The Forgotten Logic of the First Amendment* (Dallas: Spence Publishing Company, 1997), p. 97.
12. *Time*, May 7, 1990.
13. *People*, May 14, 1990.
14. Paul L. Montgomery, "Johns Hopkins Professor Lauds 'throat' as a 'cleansing film,'" *New York Times* (January 3, 1973).

Part III, Chapter 21: Washington, D.C., 1992

1. Marianne Wellershoff, "Ein Star von 30 Zentimetern," *Spiegel* (January 23, 1998), p. 236.
2. Ibid. (my translation).
3. James Atlas, "The Loose Canon: Why Higher Learning Has Embraced Pornography," *New Yorker* (March 29, 1999), p. 60.
4. Ibid., p. 60.
5. Ibid., p. 64.
6. Lisa Palac, *The Edge of the Bed: How Dirty Pictures Changed My Life* (New York: Little, Brown and Company, 1998), p. 110.
7. Ibid., p. 35.
8. Ibid., p. 102.
9. Ibid., p. 110.
10. Reich, *Mass Psychology*, p. 105.
11. Sallie Tisdale, *Talk Dirty to Me: An Intimate Philosophy of Sex* (New York: Anchor Books, , 1994), p. 21.
12. Ibid., p. 37.
13. Ibid., p. 116.
14. Ibid., p. 123.
15. Ibid.
16. Ibid., p. 148.
17. Ibid., p. 155.
18. Ibid., p. 159.
19. Ibid., p. 221.
20. Ibid., p. 281.
21. Ibid., p. 135.
22. Palac, p. 148.
23. Ibid., p. 156.
24. Tisdale, p. 288.

25. "Clinton Socio-sexual Agenda Spurs Religious Backlash," *Human Events* (September 16, 1994), p. 1.
26. Ibid.
27. Ibid.
28. Conversation with delegate, 9/94.
29. Ibid.
30. *Wall Street Journal*, August 15, 1994.
31. Alan Cowell, "Vatican Says gore is Misrepresenting Population Talks," *New York Times* (September 1, 1994), p. 1
32. *Human Events*, (September 16, 1994), p. 1
33. Cowell, p. 1.
34. Ibid., p. A9.
35. Ibid., p. 1.
36. Robert Kaplan, "The Coming Anarchy," *The Atlantic Monthly* (February 1994).
37. Ibid.
38. Julian Simon, *The Ultimate Resource* (Princeton, N.J.: Princeton University Press, 1981), p. 177.
39. Ibid., p. 179.
40. Patricia Smith, "What Happens When the Spin Outweighs Sin?" *South Bend Tribune* (February 4, 1998), p. A5.
41. Maureen Dowd, "Power of Attorney," *New York Times* (September 20, 1998).
42. Anthony Lewis, "Christian Right Determined to Bring Clinton Down," *South Bend Tribunes* (October 11, 1998), p. A5.
43. Ibid.
44. "Hollywood still adores Clinton," New York Times News Service, *South Bend Tribune* (September 28, 1998).
45. Reisman, p. vi.

Bibliography

Agethen, Manfred. *Geheimbund und Utopie: Illuminaten, Freimaurer und deutsche Spaetaufklaerung* (München: R. Oldenbourg Verlag 1984).

Attorney General's Commission on Pornography: Final Report (Washington, D.C: U.S. Department of Justice, 1986).

Back, Kurt W. *Beyond Words: The Story of Sensitivity Training and the Encounter Movement* (New York: The Russell Sage Foundation, 1972).

Baker, Houston A., Jr. *Modernism and the Harlem Renaissance* (Chicago: The University of Chicago Press, 1987).

Baldwin, James. *Nobody Knows My Name: More Notes of a Native Son* (New York: The Dial Press, 1961).

Becker, Joseph M., S.J. *The Re-Formed Jesuits: A History of Changes in Jesuit Formation During the Decade 1965–75* (San Francisco: Ignatius, 1992).

Biberstein, Johannes Rogalla von. *Die These von der Verschwoerung 1776–1945.* (Frankfurt/M.: Herbert Lang Bern, Peter Lang, 1976).

_____. *Black Theology: A Documentary History, 1966–1979.* Edited by Gayraud S. Wilmore and James H. Cone. (New York: Orbis Books, 1979).

Blanshard, Paul. *American Freedom and Catholic Power* (Boston: Beacon Press, 1950).

_____. *Personal and Controversial: An Autobiography* (Boston: Beacon Press, 1973).

Bugental, James F. T. *Intimate Journeys: Stories from Life-Changing Therapy* (San Francisco: Jossey-Bass Publishers, 1990).

_____. *The Search for Existential Identity* (San Francisco: Jossey-Bass, 1976).

Cassady, Carolyn. *Off the Road: My Years with Cassady, Kerouac, and Ginsberg* (New York: William Morrow and Co. Inc., 1990).

Chisholm, Anne. *Nancy Cunard: A Biography* (New York: Alfred A. Knopf, 1979).

Cleaver, Eldridge. *Soul on Fire* (Waco, Texas: Word Books, 1978).

————. *Soul on Ice* (New York: Ramparts books, McGraw Hill, 1968).

Clements, Barbara Evans. *Bolshevik Feminist: The Life of Alexandra Kollontai* (Bloomington: Indiana University Press, 1979).

Collier, Peter, and David Horowitz. *The Rockefellers: An American Dynasty* (New York: Holt, Reinhart and Winston, 1976).

Comte, Auguste. *System of Positive Polity* (New York: Burt Franklin, 1968).

Cooper, Wayne F. *Claude McKay: Rebel Sojourner in the Harlem Renaissance, A Biography* (Baton Rouge: Louisiana State University Press, 1987).

Cruse, Harold. *The Crisis of the Negro Intellectual* (New York: William Morrow & Co., 1967).

Cunard, Nancy, ed. *Negro: an Anthology*, edited and abridged (New York: Frederick Ungar Publishing Co., 1970).

Curb, Rosemary, and Nancy Manahan, eds., *Lesbian Nuns: Breaking Silence* (Talllahassee, Fla: Naiad Press, inc., 1985).

Davies, Hunter. *William Wordsworth: A Biography* (New York: Atheneum, 1980).

Davis, Cyprian. *The History of Black Catholics in the United States* (New York: Crossroad, 1990).

Dowling, Kevin, and Phillip Knightley. "The Spy Who Came back from the Grave: A Murder Mystery the CIA Couldn't Bury," *Night and Day* (August 23, 1998), p. 111.

Du Bois, W. E. Burghardt. *The Souls of Black Folk: Essays and Sketches* (Chicago: A. C. McClurg & Co. 1903).

Duelman, Richard van. *Der Geheimbund der Illuminaten* (Stuttgart: Frommann-Holzbooog, 1975).

Dunne, George, S.J. "This Was Montgomery," *America* (May 8, 1965), pp. 660–64.

Eastman, Max. *Enjoyment of Living* (New York and London: Harper & Brothers Publishers, 1948).

Eastman, Max. *Love and Revolution* (New York: Random House, 1964).

Ellison, Ralph. *Invisible Man* (New York: Random House, 1982).

Engels, Friedrich. *Der Ursprung der Familie, des Privateigenthums und des Staats* (Stuttgart: Verlag von J. H. W. Diek, 1894).

Evans, Sara. *Personal Politics* (New York: Alfred A. Knopf, 1979).

Farnsworth, Beatrice. *Alexandra Kollentai: Socialism, Feminism and the Bolshevik Revolution* (Stanford, Cal.: Stanford University Press, 1980).

Foster, Richard. *The Real Bettie Page: The Truth about the Queen of the Pinups.* (Seacaucus, N.J.: Birch Lane Press, 1997).

Franz, Dietrich-E. *Saint-Simon, Fourier, Owen: Sozialutopien des 19. Jahrhunderts* (Cologne: Pahl-Rugenstein, 1988).

Frazier, E. Franklin. *The Negro Family in the United States* (Chicago and London: The University of Chicago Press,1966; original ed. 1939).

Garrow, David J. *Bearing the Cross: Martin Luther King, Jr. and the Southern Christian Leadership Conference* (New York: William Morrow and Co., Inc., 1986).

Gray, Francine du Plessix. *At Home with the Marquis de Sade: A Life* (New York: Simon & Schuster, 1998).

Godwin, William. *Memoirs of the Author of A Vindication of the Rights of Women* (New York: Garland Publishing, Inc., 1974).

_____. *Memoirs of Mary Wollstonecraft*, ed. W. Clark Durant (New York: Greenberg Publisher, 1927).

Gouhier, Henri. *La Jeuness D'Auguste Comte et la Formation du Positivisme* (Paris: Librairie Philosophique J. Vrin, 1933).

Harr, John Ensor, and Peter J. Johnson. *The Rockefeller Conscience: An American Family in Public and in Private* (New York: Charles Scribners' Sons, 1991).

_____. *The Rockefeller Century* (New York: Charles Scribners' Sons, 1988).

Harrington, Michael. *Fragments of the Century* (New York: Saturday Review Press, 1973).

_____. *The Long Distance Runner: An Autobiography.* (New York: Henry Holt and Co., 1988).

Hemenway, Robert. *Zora Neale Hurston: A Literary Biography* (Urbana, Chicago and London: University of Illinois Press, 1978).

Hesburgh, Theodore M. *God, Country, Notre Dame* (New York: Doubleday, 1990).

Heidenry, John. *What Wild Ecstasy: The Rise and Fall of the Sexual Revolution* (New York: Simon & Shuster, 1997).

Heyward, DuBose. *Porgy* (New York: Grosset & Dunlap, 1925).

Higgins, Michael W. *Heretic Blood* (Toronto: Stoddart, 1998).

Holmes, Richard. *Shelley the Pursuit* (New York: E. P. Dutton & Co. 1975).

Huggins, Nathan Irvin. *Harlem Renaissance* (New York: Oxford University Press, 1971).

Hughes, Langston. *The Big Sea: An Autobiography* (New York: Hill and Wang, 1940).

Jaki, Stanley. *The Road of Science and the Ways to God* (Chicago: University of Chicago Press, 1978).

_____. *The Origin of Science and the Science of its Origin* (South Bend, Ind.: Regnery/Gateway, Inc., 1978).

Jones, E. Michael. *Dionysos Rising: The Birth of Cultural Revolution Out of the Spirit of Music* (San Francisco: Ignatius Press, 1994).

_____. *John Cardinal Krol and the Sexual Revolution* (South Bend, Ind.: Fidelity Press, 1995).

Jones, James. *Alfred C. Kinsey: A Public/Private Life* (New York: W.W. Norton & Co., 1997).

Jones, Leroi. *Dutchman and The Slave* (New York: William Morrow Company, 1964).

Jung, C. G. *Memories, Dreams, and Reflections*, recorded and edited by Aniela Jaffe, translated from the German by Richard and Clara Winston (New York: Random House, 1989).

Kavanaugh, James. *A Modern Priest Looks at His Outdated Church* (New York: Trident Press, 1967).

Kellner, Bruce. *Carl Van Vechten and the Irreverent Decades* (Norman: University of Oklahoma Press, 1968).

Kerouac, Jack. *Lonesome Traveller* (New York: McGraw Hill, 1960).

_____. *On the Road* (New York: Viking, 1957).

_____. *The Subterraneans* (New York: Grove Press, 1958).

Kieser, Elwood E. *Hollywood Priest: A Spiritual Struggle* (New York: Doubleday, 1991).

King, Martin Luther, Jr. "A Comparison of the Conceptions of God in the Thinking of Paul Tillich and Henry Nelson Wieman." Boston University, Ph.D. Dissertation, 1955.

King, Mary. *Freedom Song* (New York: William Morrow and Co., 1987).

Kinsey, Alfred C. et al. *Sexual Behavior in the Human Female* (Philadelphia: W. B. Saunders Company, 1953).

Kleiner, Art. *The Age of Heretics: Heroes, Outlaws and the Forerunners of Corporate Change* (New York: Currency Doubleday, 1996).

Kollontai, Alexandra. *A Great Love* (New York: W. W. Norton & Co., 1981).

_____. *The Autobiography of a Sexually Emancipated Communist Woman* (New York: Herder and Herder, 1971).

Lever, Maurice, *Sade: A Biography*, translated by Arthur Goldhammer (New York: Farrar, Straus and Giroux, 1993).

Lovelace, Linda. *Ordeal* (New York: Berkley Books, 1980).

Lowenthal, David. *No Liberty for License: The Forgotten Logic of the First Amendment* (Dallas: Spence Publishing Company, 1997).

Mahl, Thomas E. *Desperate Deception* (Washington: Brassey's, 1998).

McGreevy, John T. "Thinking on One's Own: Catholicism in the American Intellectual Imagination 1928–1960," *The Journal of American History* (June 1997), pp. 97–131.

McKay, Claude. *A Long Way from Home* (New York: Arno Press and *The New York Times*, 1969).

_____. *Banjo: A Novel* (New York: Harcourt, Brace, Jovanovich, 1929).

_____. Correspondence at the James Weldon Johnson collection at the Beineke Library at Yale. McKay Mss. Lily Library, Indiana University, Bloomington, Indiana.

_____. *Home to Harlem* (Boston: Northeastern University Press, 1987).

_____. *The Negroes in America* (Port Washington, N.Y.: Kennikat Press, 1979).

McNally, Dennis. *Desolate Angel: Jack Kerouac, the Beat Generation, and America* (New York: Random House, 1979).

Mailer, Norman. *Advertisements for Myself* (New York: G.P. Putnam's Sons, 1959).

May, Rollo. *Paulus: Reminiscences of a Friendship* (New York: Harper and Row, 1973).

Merton, Thomas. *The Seven Storey Mountain* (New York: Harcourt, Brace and Company, 1948).

Morgan, Ted. *Literary Outlaw: The Life and Times of William S. Burroughs* (New York: Henry Holt and Company, 1988).

Mott, Michael. *The Seven Mountains of Thomas Merton* (Boston: Houghton Mifflin Co., 1984).

Moynihan, Daniel Patrick. *Family and Nation* (New York: Harcourt, Brace, Jovanovich, 1986).

_____. *On Understanding Poverty* (New York: Basic books, 1968).

Nisbet, Robert A. *The Sociological Tradition* (New York: Basic Books, 1966).

Oden, Thomas C. *The Intensive Group Experience: The New Pietism* (Philadelphia: The Westminster Press, 1972).

Pomeroy, Wardell. *Dr. Kinsey and the Institute for Sex Research* (New York: Harper and Row, 1972).

Porter, Cathy. *Alexandra Kollontai: The Lonely Struggle of the Woman Who Defied Lenin* (New York: Dial Press, 1980).

Powell, Nicolas. *Fuseli: The Nightmare* (New York: Viking Press, 1972).

Rainwater, Lee, and William L. Yancey. *The Moynihan Report and the Politics of Controversy* (Cambridge, Mass.: The MIT Press, 1967).

Rampersad, Arnold. *The Life of Langston Hughes* (New York: Oxford University Press, 1986).

Reynolds, Patrick, and Tom Shachtman. *The Gilded Leaf: Triumph, Tragedy and Tobacco* (Boston: Little Brown, 1989).

Riesman, Judith A. *Kinsey: Crimes & Consequences* (Arlington, Va.: The Institute for Media Education, no date).

Rogers, Carl. *Carl Rogers on Encounter Groups* (New York: Harper & Row, 1970).

_____. *Client Centered Therapy* (Boston: Houghton Mifflin, 1951).

Rogers, Natalie. *Emerging Woman, A Decade of Midlife Transitions* (Point Reyes, Cal.: Personal Press, 1980).

Sade, Marquis de. *Justine, Philosophy in the Bedroom and Other Writings* (New York: Grove Press, 1965).

St. Clair, William. *The Godwins and the Shelleys: The Biography of a Family* (New York: W.W. Norton & Co. 1989).

Saint-Simon, Claude-Henri. *The Political Thought of Saint-Simon* (New York: Oxford University Press, 1976).

Simpson, Christopher. *Science of Coercion: Communication Research and Psychological Warfare 1945–1960* (New York: Oxford University Press, 1994).

Siskind, Aaaron. *Harlem Photographs 1932–40* (Washington, DC: Smithsonian/National Museum of American Art, 1990).

Sokoloff, Boris. *The "Mad" Philosopher Auguste Comte* (Westport, Conn.: Greenwood Press Publishers, 1961).

Sowell, Thomas. *Race and Economics* (New York: David McKay Co. Inc., 1975).

Spike, Paul. *Photographs of My Father* (New York: Alfred A. Knopf, 1973).

Spike, Robert W. *The Freedom Revolution and the Churches* (New York: Association Press, 1965).

_____. "Fissures in the Civil Rights Movement," *Christianity and Crisis* (February 21, 1966), pp. 18–21.

Steele, Shelby. *The Content of Our Character*. (New York: St. Martin's Press, 1990).

Sunstein, Emily W. *Mary Shelley: Romance and Reality* (Boston: Little Brown and Co., 1989).

Tarry, Ellen. *The Third Door: The Autobiography of an American Negro Woman* (Westport, Conn.: Negro Universities Press, 1971).

Tate, Tim. "Secret History: Kinsey's Pedophiles" (Yorkshire TV: Channel 4, 10/8/98).

Tilly, Charles. *The Vendee* (Cambridge, Mass.: Harvard University Press, 1964).

Thornton, Bruce S. *Eros: The Myth of Ancient Greek Sexuality* (Boulder, Colo.: Westview Press, 1997).

Thurman, Wallace. *Infants of the Spring* (New York: The Macaulay Company, 1932).

Tillich, Hannah. *From Time to Time* (New York: Stein and Day, 1973).

Tomalin, Claire. *The Life and Death of Mary Wollstonecraft* (New York: Harcourt, Brace, Jovanovich, 1974).

Tye, Larry. *The Father of Spin: Edward L. Bernays and the Birth of Public Relations* (New York: Crown Publishers, 1998).

Van Vechten, Carl. *The Blind Bow-Boy* (New York, Alfred A. Knopf, 1923).

_____. *Nigger Heaven* (New York: Harper Colophon Books, 1926, 1971).

Walker, Margaret. *Richard Wright: Demonic Genius* (New York: Warner Books, 1988).

Wardle, Ralph M., ed. *Collected Letters of Mary Wollstonecraft* (Ithaca, N.Y.: Cornell University Press, 1979).

Weber, Msgr. Francis J. *His Eminence of Los Angeles: James Francis Cardinal McIntyre* Vol. 2 (Mission Hills, Cal.: Saint Francis Historical Society, 1997).

Weber, Michael. *Psychotechniken: die neuen Verfuerhrer* (Stein am Rhein: Christiana Verlag, 1997).

Williams, Linda. *Hard Core: Power Pleasure and the 'Frenzy of the Visible'* (Berkeley: University of California Press, 1989).

Wilson, W. Daniel. *Geheimraete gegen Geheimbuende: Ein Unbekanntes Kapitel der klassisch-romantischen Geschichte Weimars* (Stuttgart: J.B. Metzlersche Verlagsbuchhandlung, 1991).

Wollstonecraft, Mary. *A Vindication of the Rights of Men with A Vindication of the Rights of Women and Hints* (Cambridge: Cambridge University Press, 1995).

Index